The Hodges Harbrace Handbook

with MLA Update and Plagiarism Guide

Cheryl Glenn | Loretta Gray

CENGAGE
Learning·

Australia • Brazil • Japan • Korea • Mexico • Singapore • Spain • United Kingdom • United States

CENGAGE
Learning™

The Hodges Harbrace Handbook with MLA
Update and Plagiarism Guide

Cheryl Glenn | Loretta Gray

Executive Editors:
Maureen Staudt
Michael Stranz
Project Development Manager:
Linda deStefano
Senior Marketing Coordinators:
Sara Mercurio

Senior Production / Manufacturing Manager:
Donna M. Brown
PreMedia Services Supervisor:
Joel Brennecke
Rights & Permissions Specialist:
Kalina Hintz
Todd Osborne

Cover Image:

Getty Images*

* Unless otherwise noted, all cover images used
by Custom Solutions, a part of Cengage
Learning, have been supplied courtesy of Getty
Images with the exception of the Earthview
cover image, which has been supplied by the
National Aeronautics and Space Administration
(NASA).

ISBN-13: 978-1-4240-7928-5

ISBN-10: 1-4240-7928-4

Cengage Learning
5191 Natorp Boulevard
Mason, Ohio 45040
USA

Cengage Learning is a leading provider of customized learning solutions with
office locations around the globe, including Singapore, the United Kingdom,
Australia, Mexico, Brazil, and Japan. Locate your local office at:
international.cengage.com/region

Cengage Learning products are represented in Canada by Nelson Education, Ltd.

For your lifelong learning solutions, visit custom.cengage.com

Visit our corporate website at cengage.com

Printed in the United States of America

Brief Contents

For

THE HODGES HARBRACE HANDBOOK
Includes 2009 MLA Update

Understanding Plagiarism: A Student Guide to Writing Your Own Work

Contents

M PART II   MECHANICS

P   PART III   PUNCTUATION

PART IV   SPELLING AND DICTION

W PART VI   WRITING

R PART VII RESEARCH AND DOCUMENTATION

Preface

Welcome! This seventeenth edition of *The Hodges Harbrace Handbook* builds on two important innovations made to the previous edition. We have focused even more closely on the rhetorical demands of writing in a digital age; we provide students with guidance for completing assignments—delivered online or on paper—that require clear writing as well as effective graphics and images. Many students appear in our classrooms already fluent in the uses of technology, ready to learn about the rhetorical situation and the ways it can help them make decisions about choosing the most effective words and visuals and arranging those in the best way to achieve their purpose.

The History

The book you have in your hands has the richest—and longest—history of any handbook in the United States. First published in 1941 by University of Tennessee English professor John C. Hodges, the handbook was initially a direct result of Hodges's own classroom experience and his federally funded research, an analysis of twenty thousand student papers. Sixteen English professors of rhetoric from various regions of the United States marked those thousands of papers, after which Hodges worked with a cadre of graduate students to create a taxonomy of writing issues (from punctuation and grammar to style and usage) that would organize the first writing manual for American college students and teachers. This taxonomy, developed nearly seventy years ago, still underpins the overall design and organization of nearly every handbook on the market today. No other handbook or handbook author has yet devised a better means for providing students and teachers with easy access to the information they need.

Hodges's original *Harbrace Handbook of English* eventually evolved into *The Hodges Harbrace Handbook*, Seventeenth Edition, which continues the tradition of up-to-date reliability and practicality. Like John Hodges, we have used our classroom experience and our research to respond to the needs of teachers and students. In our classrooms, we have kept track of the questions students ask and the problems they have with their writing, and we have noted the specific issues that pose difficulties, both for them as they write and for us as we teach. We have revised this handbook accordingly, taking special care to respond to students' concerns (including concerns about the use of technology and about writing in the disciplines). We have also moved far beyond our individual classrooms, collaborating on a nationwide study that examines what exactly students consider to be the rewards and challenges of college-level writing. Preliminary results of that study influenced many of the decisions we made in producing this handbook—a handbook dedicated to providing both teachers and students with the ease of reference and attention to detail that have made the Harbrace handbooks the standard of reliability.

New to This Edition

■ **Chapter 36, "Online Writing,"** helps students assess the rhetorical situation in the online environment, whether they are participating in electronic messaging or a discussion forum or composing documents for online presentation. This extensively revised chapter explains the value of netiquette, visual elements that fulfill a rhetorical purpose, and hyperlinks that enhance online documents. Most important is the focus on composing effective, well-designed Web documents.

■ **New Student Papers** This edition features full-length student papers on wide-ranging topics, from learning a foreign language to changing forms of business communication. The following chapters have new student papers: 34, "Revising and Editing Essays," 35, "Writing Arguments," and 43, "Writing in Business." We have also added new research papers to the chapters devoted to style guides. A research paper on whether genetically modified crops will benefit developing countries follows MLA guidelines (chapter 40); a co-authored sociology paper on trends in tattooing is written and formatted according to APA standards (chapter 41).

Revised for This Edition
Attention to the rhetorical situation continues to invigorate all the writing and research chapters and most of the grammar chapters, whether the chapters are thoroughly redesigned or completely new. Several chapters have been extensively revised in light of contemporary composition pedagogy, while maintaining those features of traditional rhetorical theory that are still widely respected.

■ **Chapter 8, "Document Design,"** introduces students to the design principles underpinning the effective use of visuals in many kinds of documents. The principles of alignment, proximity, contrast, and repetition can support students in their selection and arrangement of visuals, helping them make their visual and verbal texts work together to reach their audience and fulfill their purpose.

■ **Chapter 27, "Consistency,"** encourages students to use a consistent tone, point of view, and time frame. By examining sample paragraphs, students learn to edit their essays with an eye for shifts in expression that may distract their readers. Students practice locating unnecessary shifts and revising sentences to fit the overall context of their essays.

■ **Chapter 43, "Writing in Business"** has been expanded to include a discussion of using PowerPoint for oral presentations, which includes example slides, as well as a new business report on communication in the workplace.

■ In this edition, we continue our thorough coverage of the guidelines from the **style manuals for academic writing** published by the Modern Language Association (MLA) and the American Psychological Association (APA). (*The Hodges Harbrace Handbook* itself follows *The Chicago Manual of Style*, which is the style guide used by most publishers.) Each documentation chapter opens with general guidelines that help students understand the patterns inherent in the particular documentation system. By studying these patterns, students become more efficient and accurate at creating bibiliographies. All the documentation chapters have easy-to-follow, color-coded examples of each type of citation (for a book, an article, and an online source), displaying the major components and their exact arrangement. In addition, tip boxes remind students of all the steps they need to follow as they compose their bibliographies.

■ *The Hodges Harbace Handbook*, Seventeenth Edition, includes a completely revised chapter on MLA documentation, based on the 2009 publication of the *MLA Handbook for Writers of Research Papers*, Seventh Edition. All MLA-style student papers in this updated version have been revised to reflect the changes to the style guide.

■ **Chapters 1 through 7,** the grammar chapters, have been revised to make concepts more accessible for those students with little background in writing in English. The exercises in these chapters continue to give students practice in areas they frequently find difficult.

Other Features

■ **Instructive visuals** are featured in most chapters. For instance, in chapter 35, "Writing Arguments," cartoons illustrate several rhetorical fallacies. In the research and documentation chapters, annotated visuals, such as screen shots of databases and Web sites, help students learn how to locate in these kinds of sources the information they need for their bibliographies. Most of the student-generated papers in this handbook include some kind of visual—photograph, table, or figure. In the process of referring to the visuals in this book, students will come to understand the specific ways these features communicate meaning to an audience, meaning that supplements and enhances the information conveyed by words.

■ **Thinking Rhetorically** boxes prompt students to consider the impact on their purpose and target audience of the choices they make in grammar, style, and punctuation. Many of the boxes present situations in which a writer has multiple options or in which a conventional rule may be broken, creating opportunities for students to determine which choice is the most effective one in terms of purpose and audience. These possibilities move students away from thinking that one rule fits all toward gauging the rhetorical effect of the sentence-level decisions they make.

■ **Multilingual Writers** boxes identify common areas of confusion for English language learners, whether English is their first or second (or third) language. In addition, these boxes address concerns that may arise for all students as they draft, revise, and edit their work.

- **Checklists** in most chapters provide tips for accomplishing a task (e.g., finding a research question) or prompts that remind students of the steps they need to follow in order to complete a project (e.g., designing an online document).

- **Tech Savvy** boxes help students use their word processors to produce documents for a variety of courses. The boxes cover topics ranging from the creation of dashes to the insertion of tables and graphs to advice for attaching files to e-mail messages.

Supplements
Technology Supplements

InSite™ for Writing and Research   This all-in-one online writing and research tool includes electronic peer review, an originality checker, an assignment library, help with common errors, and access to InfoTrac® College Edition. InSite makes course management practically automatic. Visit **http://insite .wadsworth.com**

InfoTrac® College Edition   Students can do in-depth research right from their desktop or laptop computer or catch up on the latest news online—using four months of access to InfoTrac College Edition. They can search this virtual university library's more than 18 million reliable, full-length articles from five thousand academic and popular periodicals (including the *New York Times, Newsweek, Science, Forbes,* and *USA Today*) and retrieve results almost instantly. They can also use InfoMarks—stable URLs that can be linked to articles, journals, and searches to save time when doing research—and access the InfoWrite online resource center for guides to writing research papers, grammar help, critical thinking guidelines, and much more.

Turnitin®   This online plagiarism-prevention program promotes fairness in the classroom by helping students learn to cite sources correctly and allowing instructors to check for originality before reading and grading papers. Turnitin checks student papers against billions of pages of Internet content, millions of published works, and millions of other student papers and generates a comprehensive originality report within seconds.

English21   The largest compilation of online resources ever organized for composition and literature courses, English21 is a complete online support system that weaves robust, self-paced instruction with interactive assignments. English21 engages students as they become better-prepared and successful writers and supports them through every step of the writing process, from assignment to final draft. English21 includes carefully crafted multimedia assignments; a collection of essays that amounts to a full-sized thematic reader; a full interactive handbook including hundreds of animations, exercises, and activities; a complete research guide with animated tutorials and a link to Gale's InfoTrac database; and a rich multimedia library with hand-selected images, audio clips, video clips, stories, poems, and plays. Access to Personal Tutor, an online environment with one-on-one tutoring and on-demand help from experienced tutors, is included with English21. To learn more, visit **http://academic.cengage.com/english21**.

English21 Plus   Access to English21 Plus is available for a nominal fee when packaged with new copies of the text. English21 Plus includes all of the features mentioned above as well as access to Wadsworth's InSite for Writing and Research™. InSite features an electronic peer review system, an originality checker, a rich assignment library, and electronic grade marking. To learn more, visit **http://academic.cengage .com/english21**.

The Hodges Harbrace e-book   A completely interactive experience, the e-book version of *The Hodges Harbrace Handbook* presents the entire handbook online, with integrated links that give students access to a wide variety of resources with the click of a mouse. The integrated **College Workbook** covers grammar, punctuation, usage, style, and writing. A variety of exercises with clear examples and explanations supplement the exercises found in the handbook. The Answer Key to the workbook is found in the Instructor's Resource Manual on the companion Web site for the handbook.

The Hodges Harbrace Handbook Web Site   The free companion Web site provides links, sample syllabi, quizzes and tests, and interactive exercises on the fundamentals of writing, including grammar, mechanics, and punctuation. A student paper library includes sample papers with accompanying editing and revising activities. The companion Website also offers the following components in printable format.

■ The **Diagnostic Test Package** allows comprehensive evaluation of students' writing skills through pre- and post-tests covering a variety of concepts in grammar, mechanics, usage, and spelling. The Diagnostic Test Package includes practice versions of the TAKS and CLAST tests as well as general diagnostic tests and writing prompts for essays—all designed to help instructors evaluate students' skill level.

■ The **Instructor's Resource Manual** gives instructors maximum flexibility in planning and customizing a course. Available on the instructor's companion Web site as well as on the PowerLecture CD-ROM, its pedagogically rich materials are organized into two main sections. "Part One: Questions for Teachers" raises a variety of pedagogical questions (and gives possible solutions) for you to consider when teaching your course with this handbook; "Part Two: Sample Syllabi and

Activities" offers sample syllabi with possible assignments for a semester-long course and for a quarter-long course. Additionally, this section contains sample in-class collaborative learning activities, technology-oriented activities, and critical thinking and writing activities. The Instructor's Resource Manual also includes the following supplementary materials: (1) an ESL insert aimed at helping mainstream instructors teach writing effectively to their ESL students, (2) an insert on disability issues as they relate to teaching first-year composition, (3) the Answer Key for the exercises in the handbook, and (4) the Answer Key for the online workbook.

CengageNOW™ for Writing   Students can boost their writing skills with CengageNOW, a Web-based, multimedia, writing assessment and learning program. This study system helps students understand what they know, as well as identify what they don't know, and helps them build study strategies to fill in the gaps and master the crucial rudimentary concepts of writing. Using a variety of technologies to accommodate many learning styles, CengageNOW covers all aspects of writing. Its interactive learning tools, such as Diagnostic Quizzes, Personalized Study Plans, and Multimedia Tutorials, will help students master the fundamentals of writing and build their confidence as they become more effective writers.

PowerLecture   A course preparation tool on CD-ROM, Power-Lecture includes The Hodges Harbrace PowerPoints, the Diagnostic Test Package, and the Instructor's Resource Manual. The PowerPoint component of PowerLecture is a set of slides designed to help instructors guide their students through the features, content, and organization of *The Hodges Harbrace Handbook*. These slides, which have been carefully created to help students get the most out of their handbook, illustrate the major features that will aid students in grasping important concepts.

Toolbox   Harness the power of the Internet and bring your course to life with Toolbox, a course management program. You can use its wealth of interactive resources along with those on the handbook's companion Web site to supplement the classroom experience and ensure that students have the resources they need to succeed in today's business world. You can even use this effective resource as an integrated solution for distance learning or a Web-enhanced course.

Printed Supplements

Instructor's Correction Chart   To make marking your students' papers easier, you can prop up on your desk this oversized, laminated chart, which lists all of the sections of the handbook and shows the editing symbols correlated to them.

Dictionaries   The following dictionaries are available for a nominal price when bundled with the handbook: *The Merriam-Webster Dictionary*, Second Edition; *Merriam-Webster's Collegiate® Dictionary*, Eleventh Edition; *Merriam-Webster Pocket Thesaurus*; and *Heinle's Newbury House Dictionary of American English with Integrated Thesaurus*. The latter was created especially for ESL students.

Acknowledgments

We would like to thank our colleagues who reviewed this handbook throughout the course of development. Their astute comments, frank responses, and thoughtful suggestions helped shape what is the final version—until the next edition. We thank them for taking the time out of their already busy schedules to help us.

Handbook Reviewers

Mary Adams, Steven Brehe, and Joyce Stavick, North Georgia College and State University; Jesse Airaudi, Baylor University;

Cathryn Amdahl, Harrisburg Area Community College; Karen Cajka, East Tennessee State University; Mechel Camp, Jackson State Community College; Joyce Cottonham, Southern University-Shreveport; Nancy Cox, Arkansas Tech University; Christopher Ervin, University of South Dakota; Maryanne Garbowsky, County College of Morris; Kim Gunter, University of North Carolina, Pembroke; David James, Houston Community College; Joseph Jones, University of Memphis; Bryan Moore, Arkansas State University; David Murdock, Gadsden State Community College; Robert Spirko, University of Tennesee, Knoxville; Eula Thompson, Jefferson State Community College; Linda Weeks, Dyersburg State Community College; Stephen Whited, Piedmont College; and Marla Wiley, Hinds Community College.

Focus Group Participants

Pat Belanoff, SUNY, Stony Brook; Laura Carroll, Abilene Christian University; Elyse Fields, Red Rocks Community College; Lynee Gaillet, Georgia State University; Patricia Jenkins, University of Alaska, Anchorage; Maureen Jonason, Concordia University; Rachel Robinson, Middle Tennessee State University; Michelle Sidler, Auburn University; and Christa Teston, Kent State University.

The seventeenth edition of this handbook took shape through extensive conversations and correspondence between the authors as well as with a number of members of the Cengage Learning/Wadsworth editorial staff. For their collective ideas, enthusiasm, support, and wise counsel, we remain grateful. In particular, we thank Publisher Lyn Uhl, Acquisitions Editor Kate Derrick, and Marketing Manager Jennifer Zourdos, whose unwavering enthusiasm and encouragment supported us through many months of work. Lianne Ames, Senior Production Project Manager, helped to bring this huge project to completion, and Jane Hoover carried out the copyediting with style and care. Anne Carter gave the book its clear and aesthetically pleasing interior design and cover. Without the help and support of these imaginative people, we simply could not have produced *The Hodges Harbrace Handbook*.

But it is Michell Phifer, Senior Development Editor Extraordinaire as well as friend—to whom we owe a special thanks. A scrupulously careful editor—and our constant intellectual companion—Michell successfully helped us balance our writing and research deadlines with our other professional commitments (teaching, for instance!). She regularly prodded us to think critically about each chapter, about our choice of images or textual examples, and especially about the project as an intellectual whole. Michell has been on our team for three editions, guiding our collaboration until the very last minute, when the presses rolled.

The successful completion of our work would not have been possible without the research assistance of Rebecca Wilson Lundin, Michelle Smith, and Brandy Scalise, all from The Pennsylvania State University. Consummate professionals, they helped us envision and frame chapter 36, "Online Writing," chapter 8, "Document Design," and chapter 43, "Writing in Business," providing more good information than we could possibly use. We want to thank Heather Jensen, Faith Haney, Richard Petraglia, Anna Seitz, Marianna Suslin, Rachel L. Pinter, Sarah M. Cronin, Kaitlyn Andrews-Rice, and Joe Delaney, whose academic writing samples bring this handbook to life. We want to mention the excellent proofreading help we received from undergraduate interns Sierra Stovall, Daniel Thomas Leayman, and Emilie Sunnergren. And we're also grateful for the help of the many colleagues and students whose conversations about writing enriched our understanding of composition pedagogy.

Finally, we are grateful to our friends and families. Although our faces toward the screen meant our backs toward you, you were never far from our thoughts. After all, without you, our work would be neither possible nor worthwhile.

To all of you reading this preface and using or considering using this handbook for the first time, know that we are grateful to you too. In fact, if you have advice for how we might improve the next edition or if we can help you in any way, write us c/o Cengage Learning, English Editorial Department, 20 Channel Center Street, Boston, MA 02210.

Cheryl Glenn
Loretta Gray
April 2009

G

"Sorry, but I'm going to have to issue you a summons for reckless grammar and driving without an apostrophe."

1 Sentence Essentials

When you think of the word *grammar*, you might also think of the word *rule*—a regulation that you must obey. But *rule* has another meaning: "a description of what is true in most cases." A grammar rule, then, describes how language is commonly or conventionally used. However, what is appropriate in one rhetorical situation (chapter 31) may not be appropriate in another. Thus, to know which rules to follow, you must first determine your intended audience, overall purpose, and specific context. Once you establish your rhetorical situation, you will be ready to consider the options the English language provides—an extensive selection of words and word arrangements will be at your disposal. By also learning basic grammar terms and concepts, you will better understand how to choose among the options available to you.

This chapter will help you

- identify the parts of speech (1a),
- recognize the essential parts of a sentence (1b),
- identify complements (1c),
- recognize basic sentence patterns (1d),
- recognize phrases (1e),
- recognize clauses (1f),
- recognize conjunctions and conjunctive adverbs (1g), and
- identify sentence forms and functions (1h and 1i).

1a   Parts of speech

When you look up a word in the dictionary, you will often find it followed by one or more of these labels: *adj., adv., conj., interj., n., prep., pron.,* and *v.* (or *vb.*). These are the abbreviations for the traditional eight parts of speech: *adjective, adverb, conjunction, interjection, noun, preposition, pronoun,* and *verb.* The definition of a word depends on which of these labels it has. When labeled as a noun, the word *turn* has several meanings, one of which is "curve" (*We were surprised by the turn in the road*). When *turn* is labeled as a verb, one of its possible meanings is "to change color" (*The leaves have turned*). By learning the parts of speech, not only will you be able to use a dictionary effectively, you will also be able to understand advice on punctuation and writing style.

(1) Verbs usually express action or being.

Thousands of verbs are **action verbs.** Just think of everything you do in one day: wake, eat, drink, wash, walk, drive, study, work, laugh, smile, talk, and so on. In contrast, only a few verbs express being or experiencing. These verbs are called **linking verbs** and include *be, seem,* and *become* and the sensory verbs *look, taste, smell, feel,* and *sound.* Both action verbs and linking verbs are frequently accompanied by other verbs that add shades of meaning, such as information about time (*will* study this afternoon), ability (*can* study), or obligation (*must* study). These verbs are called **auxiliary verbs** or **helping verbs.** See chapter 7 for more details about verbs.

The dictionary (base) form of most action verbs fits into this frame sentence:

We should _____ (it). [With some verbs, *it* is not used.]

The dictionary (base) form of most linking verbs fits into this frame sentence:

It should _____ good (terrible, fine).

THINKING RHETORICALLY

VERBS

Decide which of the following sentences evokes a clearer image.

The team captain **was** absolutely ecstatic.

Grinning broadly, the team captain **shot** both her arms into the air.

You probably chose the sentence with the action verb *shot* rather than the sentence with *was*. Most writers avoid using the verb *be* in any of its forms (*am, is, are, was, were,* or *been*) when their rhetorical situation calls for vibrant imagery. Instead, they use vivid action verbs.

(2) Nouns usually name people, places, things, and ideas.

Nouns fall into two main categories. **Proper nouns** are specific names. You can identify them easily because they are capitalized: *Bill Gates, Redmond, Microsoft Corporation.* **Common nouns** refer to any member of a class or category: *person, city, company.* There are three types of common nouns.

- **Count nouns** refer to people, places, things, and ideas that can be counted. They have singular and plural forms: *boy, boys; park, parks; car, cars; concept, concepts.*
- **Noncount nouns** refer to things or ideas that cannot be counted: *furniture, information.*
- **Collective nouns** are nouns that can be either singular or plural, depending on the context: *The **committee** published its report* [singular]. *The **committee** disagree about their duties* [plural]. (See **6a(7)**.)

Experience the Beauty of the Cayman Islands

Relax and watch the beautiful sunset at the infamous "My Bar"

Put on a "Mask and Fins" and see the island's Real Treasures

Nestle yourself in cozy, spacious Oceanview Rooms

Savor the spice of East & West Indian flavors at the SeaHarvest Restaurant

SUNSET HOUSE
www.sunsethouse.com

(800) 854-4767

Writers of travel brochures often choose action verbs to create images of fun-filled vacations.
(Courtesy of Sunset House.)

Most nouns fit into this frame sentence:

(The) _____ is (are) important

(unimportant, interesting, uninteresting).

THINKING RHETORICALLY

NOUNS

Nouns like *entertainment* and *nutrition* refer to concepts. They are called **abstract nouns**. In contrast, nouns like *guitar* and *apple* refer to things perceivable by the senses. They are called **concrete nouns**. When your rhetorical situation calls for the use of abstractions, balance them with tangible details conveyed through concrete nouns. For example, if you use the abstract nouns *impressionism* and *cubism* in an art history paper, also include concrete nouns that will enable readers to see the colors, shapes, and brushstrokes of the paintings you are discussing.

(3) Pronouns function as nouns.

Most pronouns (*it, he, she, they,* and many others) replace nouns that have already been mentioned. These nouns are called **antecedents** (6b). Sometimes an antecedent is a single noun.

<u>Dan</u> thinks **he** will have the report done by Friday.

An antecedent may also be a noun and the words modifying it.

My parents bought <u>the cheap, decrepit house</u> because they
thought **it** had charm.

A pronoun and its antecedent may be found either in the same sentence or in separate, though usually adjacent, sentences.

<u>The students</u> collaborated on a research project last year. **They** even presented their findings at a national conference.

The pronouns in the preceding examples are called **personal pronouns.** However, there are other types of pronouns as well. For a detailed discussion of pronouns, see chapter **5.**

THINKING RHETORICALLY

PRONOUNS

Why is the following passage somewhat unclear?

> The study found that students succeed when they have clear directions, consistent and focused feedback, and access to help. This led administrators to create a tutoring center at our university.

The problem is that the pronoun *This* at the beginning of the second sentence could refer to all of the information provided by the study or just to the single finding that students need access to help. If you discover that one of your pronouns lacks a clear antecedent, replace the pronoun with more specific words.

The results of this study led administrators to create a tutoring center at our university.

(4) Adjectives modify nouns or pronouns.

Adjectives most commonly modify nouns: *spicy* food, *cold* day, *special* price. Sometimes they modify pronouns: *blue* ones, anyone *thin.* Adjectives usually answer one of these questions: Which one? What kind of . . . ? How many? What color or size or shape (and so on)? Although adjectives usually precede the nouns they modify, they occasionally follow them: *enough* time, time *enough.* Adjectives may also follow linking verbs such as *be, seem,* and *become*:

The <u>moon</u> is **full** tonight.   <u>He</u> seems **shy.**

When an adjective follows a linking verb, it modifies the subject of the sentence (**1c(3)**).

Most adjectives fit into one of these frame sentences:

He told us about a/an _____ idea (person, place).

The idea (person, place) is very _____.

Articles are a subclass of adjectives because, like adjectives, they are used before nouns. There are three articles: *a, an,* and *the.* The article *a* is used before a consonant sound (**a** yard, **a** university, **a** VIP); *an* is used before a vowel sound (**an** apple, **an** hour, **an** NFL team).

MULTILINGUAL WRITERS

ARTICLE USAGE

English has two types of articles: indefinite and definite. The **indefinite articles** *a* and *an* indicate that a singular noun is used in a general way. For example, *a planet* refers to any planet, not to a specific planet. Indefinite articles are often used in the following contexts:

- Upon first mention of a noun. Use an indefinite article when you introduce a singular noun for the first time.

  Pluto is **a** dwarf <u>planet</u>.

- After the introductory word *there.* Use an indefinite article when you introduce a topic that includes a singular noun.

  There has been **a** <u>controversy</u> over the classification of Pluto.

- In definitions. When you are defining a word, use an indefinite article.

  A <u>planet</u> is a celestial body orbiting a star such as our sun.

- If a noun is plural or if it does not have a plural form, then no article is needed.

Planets orbit a star.   **Astrology** is the study of celestial bodies.

The **definite article,** *the,* is used before a noun that has already been introduced or when a reference is obvious. *The* often appears in the following contexts:

- For subsequent mention of a noun. Once a noun has been introduced, use the definite article to refer to it a second time.

  Scientists distinguish between planets and <u>dwarf planets</u>. Three of **the** <u>dwarf planets</u> in our solar system are Ceres, Pluto, and Eris.

- Subsequent mention does not always include exact repetition of a noun. However, the noun chosen must be close in meaning to a word already introduced.

  Scientists were not sure how to <u>classify</u> celestial bodies. **The** <u>classification</u> of Pluto proved to be particularly controversial.

- When indicating something unique. A noun may be considered unique if everyone in the audience will know what it refers to. Common examples are *moon, universe, solar system, sun, earth,* and *sky.*

  The <u>moon</u> is full tonight.

(5) Adverbs modify verbs, adjectives, and other adverbs.

Adverbs most frequently modify verbs. They provide information about time, manner, place, and frequency, thus answering one of these questions: When? How? Where? How often?

The conference <u>starts</u> **tomorrow.** [time]

I **rapidly** calculated the cost. [manner]

We met **here.** [place]

They **often** work late on Thursdays. [frequency]

Adverbs that modify verbs can often move from one position in a sentence to another.

Yesterday the team traveled to St. Louis.

The team traveled to St. Louis **yesterday.**

He **carefully** removed the radio collar.

He removed the radio collar **carefully.**

Most adverbs that modify verbs fit into this frame sentence:

They _____ moved (danced, walked) across the room.

Adverbs also modify adjectives and other adverbs by intensifying or otherwise qualifying the meanings of those words.

I was **extremely** curious. [modifying an adjective]

He was **unusually** generous. [modifying an adjective]

The changes occurred **quite** rapidly. [modifying an adverb]

The team played **surprisingly** well. [modifying an adverb]

For more information on adverbs, see **4a.**

THINKING RHETORICALLY

ADVERBS

What do the adverbs add to the following sentences?

The scientist **delicately** places the slide under the microscope.

"You're late," he whispered **vehemently**.

She is **wistfully** hopeful.

Adverbs can help you portray an action, indicate how someone is speaking, and add detail to a description.

(6) Prepositions set up relationships between words.

A **preposition** is a word that combines with a noun and any of its modifiers to provide additional detail—often answering one of these questions: Where? When?

We walked **through** our old neighborhood. [answers the question *Where?*]

We left **in** the early afternoon. [answers the question *When?*]

A preposition may also combine with a pronoun.

We walked **through** it.

Common one-word prepositions are *on, in, at, to, for, over,* and *under.* Common **phrasal prepositions** (prepositions consisting of more than one word) are *except for, because of, instead of,* and *according to.* For a list of prepositions and information on prepositional phrases, see **1e(4)**.

(7) Conjunctions are connectors.

Conjunctions fall into three categories: coordinating, correlative, and subordinating. A **coordinating conjunction**

connects similar words or groups of words; that is, it generally links a noun to a noun, an adjective to an adjective, a phrase to a phrase, and so on.

He played <u>football</u> **and** <u>basketball</u>. [connecting nouns]

The game was <u>dangerous</u> **yet** <u>appealing</u>. [connecting adjectives]

There are seven coordinating conjunctions. Use the made-up word *fanboys* to help you remember them.

F	A	N	B	O	Y	S
for	and	nor	but	or	yet	so

A **correlative conjunction** (or **correlative**) consists of two parts. The most common correlatives are *both . . . and, either . . . or, neither . . . nor,* and *not only . . . but also.*

The defeat left me feeling **both** <u>sad</u> **and** <u>angry</u>. [connecting adjectives]

Either <u>Pedro</u> **or** <u>Sue</u> will introduce the speaker. [connecting nouns]

For more information on coordinating and correlative conjunctions, see **1g(1)** and **1g(2)**.

A **subordinating conjunction** introduces a dependent clause (**1f(2)**) and indicates its relation to an independent clause (**1f(1)**).

The river rises **when** <u>the snow melts</u>.

Common subordinating conjunctions are *because, although, when,* and *if.* For a longer list of subordinating conjunctions, see **1g(3)**.

(8) Interjections are expressions of emotion.

Interjections most commonly indicate surprise, dread, resignation, or some other emotion. They may also be expressions used to get someone's attention. Interjections that come before a sentence end in a period or an exclamation point.

Oh. Now I understand.

Wow! Your design is astounding.

Interjections that begin or interrupt a sentence are set off by commas.

Hey, what are you doing?

The solution, **alas,** was not as simple as I had hoped it would be.

Exercise 1

Identify the part of speech for each word in the sentences below.

1. Lee and I hiked to Lake Ann.
2. The hike to the lake was short but quite challenging.
3. Oh, were we hot and dirty!
4. We found the perfect campsite near a spring.
5. After we unpacked, we swam slowly across the lake.

1b Subjects and predicates

A sentence consists of two parts:

> SUBJECT + PREDICATE

The **subject** is generally someone or something that either performs an action or is described. The **predicate** expresses the action initiated by the subject or gives information about the subject.

The <u>landlord</u> + <u>renovated</u> the apartment.
[The subject performs an action; the predicate expresses the action.]

<u>They</u> + <u>had sounded</u> reasonable.
[The subject is described; the predicate gives information about the subject.]

The central components of the subject and the predicate are often called the **simple subject** (the main noun or pronoun) and the **simple predicate** (the main verb and any auxiliary verbs). They are underlined in the examples above.

Compound subjects and **compound predicates** include a connecting word (conjunction) such as *and, or,* or *but.*

<u>The Republicans</u> **and** <u>the Democrats</u> are debating this issue. [compound subject]

The candidate <u>stated his views on abortion</u> **but** <u>did not discuss stem-cell research</u>. [compound predicate]

THINKING RHETORICALLY

SUBJECTS AND PREDICATES

Generally, sentences have the pattern subject + predicate. However, writers often vary this pattern to provide cohesion, emphasis, or both.

He + elbowed his way into the lobby and paused.
[subject + predicate]

From a far corner of the lobby came + shrieks of laughter.
[predicate + subject]

These two sentences are cohesive because the information in the predicate that begins the second sentence is linked to information in the first sentence. The reversed pattern in the second sentence, predicate + subject, also places emphasis on the subject (*shrieks of laughter*).

(1) Subjects are usually pronouns, nouns, or nouns with modifiers.

Notice that a pronoun, a noun, or a noun with modifiers can serve as the subject of the following sentence:

He
Lucas ⎤ organized the film festival.
My best friend ⎦

To identify the subject of a sentence, find the verb and then use it in a question beginning with *who* or *what,* as shown in the following examples.

Jennifer works at a clinic.

Verb: **works**

Who works? **Jennifer** (not the clinic) **works.**

Subject: **Jennifer**

Meat contains cholesterol.

Verb: **contains**

What contains? **Meat** (not cholesterol) **contains.**

Subject: **Meat**

Some sentences begin with an **expletive**—*there* or *it.* Such a word occurs in the subject position, forcing the true subject to follow the verb.

exp v s
There were **no exercise machines**.

A subject following the expletive *it* is often an entire clause. (See also **1f.**)

exp v s
It is essential **that children learn about nutrition at an early age**.

MULTILINGUAL WRITERS

Beginning a Sentence with *There*

In sentences beginning with the expletive *there,* the verb comes before the subject. The verb *are* is often hard to hear, so be careful that you do not omit it.

There_∧ many good books on nutrition.

(inserted above: are)

(2) The key word in the predicate is always a verb.

A verb may be a single word, or it may consist of a main verb accompanied by one or more auxiliary verbs. The most common auxiliaries are *be (am, is, are, was, were, been), have (has, had),* and *do (does, did).* Others, including *can, may,* and *might,* are called **modal auxiliaries.**

They **work** as volunteers. [single-word verb]

They **have been working** as volunteers. [verb with two auxiliaries]

They **might work** as volunteers. [verb with modal auxiliary]

Occasionally an adverb intervenes between the auxiliary and the main verb.

They **have** <u>always</u> **worked** as volunteers.

Exercise 2

Identify the subject and the predicate in each sentence, noting any compound subjects or compound predicates. Then, identify all main verbs and auxiliary verbs.

1. Magicians are in our oceans.
2. They are octopuses.

3. Octopuses can become invisible.
4. They just change color.
5. They can also change their shape.
6. These shape-changers look frightening.
7. Octopuses can release poisons and produce spectacles of color.
8. The blue-ringed octopus can give an unsuspecting diver an unpleasant surprise.
9. Researchers consider the poison of the blue-ringed octopus one of the deadliest in the world.
10. Octopuses and their relatives have been living on the earth for millions of years.

1c Complements

Complements are parts of the predicate required by the verb to make a sentence complete. For example, the sentence *The chair of the committee presented* is incomplete without the complement *his plans*. There are four different complements: direct objects, indirect objects, subject complements, and object complements. A complement is generally a pronoun, a noun, or a noun with modifiers.

The chair of the committee introduced—

her. [pronoun]

Sylvia Holbrook. [noun]

the new <u>member</u>. [noun with modifiers]

(1) A direct object follows an action verb.

The **direct object** either receives the action of the verb or shows the result of the action.

I. M. Pei designed **the East Building of the National Gallery.**

Steve McQueen invented **the bucket seat** in 1960.

Compound direct objects include a connecting word, usually *and.*

Thomas Edison patented **the phonograph <u>and</u> the microphone.**

To identify a direct object, first find the subject and the verb; then use them in a question ending with *what* or *whom.*

Marie Curie discovered radium.	They hired a new engineer.
Subject and verb: **Marie Curie discovered**	Subject and verb: **They hired**
Marie Curie discovered *what?* **radium**	They hired *whom?* **a new engineer**
Direct object: **radium**	Direct object: **a new engineer**

A direct object may be a clause (**1f**).

Researchers found **that patients responded favorably to the new medication.**

(2) Indirect objects usually identify to whom or for whom an action is performed.

Indirect objects typically name the person(s) receiving or benefiting from the action indicated by the verb. Verbs that often take indirect objects include *bring, buy, give, lend, offer, sell, send,* and *write.*

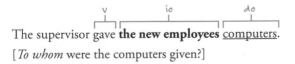

The supervisor gave **the new employees** computers.

[*To whom* were the computers given?]

$$\overset{v}{\overbrace{}} \overset{io}{\overbrace{}} \overset{do}{\overbrace{}}$$

She wrote **them** <u>recommendation letters.</u>

[*For whom* were the recommendation letters written?]

Like subjects and direct objects, indirect objects can be compound.

She offered **Elena and Octavio** <u>a generous benefits package.</u>

(3) A subject complement renames, classifies, or describes the subject.

The **subject complement** follows a linking verb (**1a(1)**). The most common linking verb is *be* (*am, is, are, was, were, been*). Other linking verbs are *become, seem,* and *appear* and the sensory verbs *feel, look, smell, sound,* and *taste.* A subject complement can be a pronoun, a noun, or a noun with modifiers; however, it can also be an adjective (**1a(4)**). The adjective may be accompanied by a word that softens or intensifies its meaning (such as *somewhat, very,* or *quite*).

The winner was —

you. [pronoun]

Harry Solano. [noun]

the person with the highest score.
[noun with modifiers]

ecstatic. [adjective]

(4) An object complement renames, classifies, or describes the direct object.

The object complement helps complete the meaning of a verb such as *call, elect, make, name,* or *paint.* Like the subject complement, the object complement can be either a noun or an adjective, along with any modifiers.

Reporters called the rookie **the best <u>player</u>.** [noun with modifiers]

The strike left the fans **somewhat <u>disappointed</u>.** [adjective with modifier]

Exercise 3

In the sentences in exercise 2, identify all direct objects, indirect objects, subject complements, and object complements.

1d   Basic sentence patterns

The six basic sentence patterns presented in the following box are based on three verb types: intransitive, transitive, and linking. Notice that *trans* in the words *transitive* and *intransitive* means "over or across." Thus, the action of a **transitive verb** carries across to an object, but the action of an **intransitive verb** does not. An intransitive verb has no complement, although it is often followed by an adverb (pattern 1). A transitive verb is followed by a direct object (pattern 2), by both a direct and an indirect object (pattern 3), or by a direct object and an object complement (pattern 4). A linking verb (such as *be, seem, sound,* and *taste*) is followed by a subject complement (pattern 5) or a phrase that includes a preposition (pattern 6).

BASIC SENTENCE PATTERNS

Pattern 1 SUBJECT + INTRANSITIVE VERB

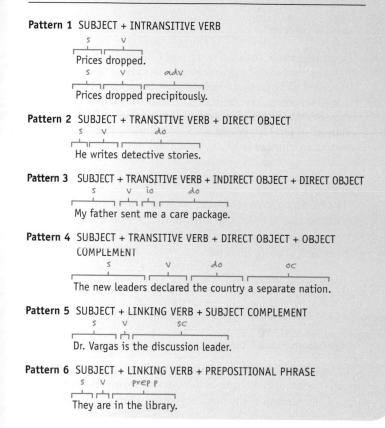

Prices dropped.

Prices dropped precipitously.

Pattern 2 SUBJECT + TRANSITIVE VERB + DIRECT OBJECT

He writes detective stories.

Pattern 3 SUBJECT + TRANSITIVE VERB + INDIRECT OBJECT + DIRECT OBJECT

My father sent me a care package.

Pattern 4 SUBJECT + TRANSITIVE VERB + DIRECT OBJECT + OBJECT
COMPLEMENT

The new leaders declared the country a separate nation.

Pattern 5 SUBJECT + LINKING VERB + SUBJECT COMPLEMENT

Dr. Vargas is the discussion leader.

Pattern 6 SUBJECT + LINKING VERB + PREPOSITIONAL PHRASE

They are in the library.

MULTILINGUAL WRITERS

WORD ORDER

Some languages, such as French and Cantonese, have sentence patterns similar to English sentence patterns. These languages are called **SVO (subject-verb-object) languages**, even though not all sentences have objects. The patterns for other languages vary. **SOV (subject-object-verb) languages** and **VSO (verb-subject-object) languages** are also common. Keep the SVO pattern in mind to help you write English sentences.

When declarative sentences, or statements, are turned into questions, the subject and the auxiliary verb are usually inverted; that is, the auxiliary verb is moved to the beginning of the sentence, before the subject.

Statement: A Chinese skater (has) won a gold medal.

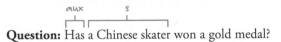

Question: Has a Chinese skater won a gold medal?

Often, a question word such as *what* or *why* opens an interrogative sentence. As long as the question word is *not* the subject of the sentence, the auxiliary verb precedes the subject.

Question: What has a Chinese skater won? [*What* is the object of *has won*.]

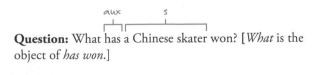

COMPARE: Who has won a gold medal? [*Who* is the subject of the sentence.]

If a statement does not include an auxiliary verb or a form of the linking verb *be,* then a form of *do* is added to form the corresponding question. Once again, the auxiliary verb is placed in front of the subject.

Statement: A Chinese skater won a gold medal.

aux   s

Question: Did a Chinese skater win a gold medal?

As you study sentences more closely, you will find patterns other than the six presented in this section. For example, another pattern requires mention of a destination or location. The sentence *I put the documents* is incomplete without a phrase such as *on your desk.* Other sentences have phrases that are not essential but do add pertinent information. These phrases can sometimes be moved. For example, the phrase *on Friday* can be placed either at the beginning or at the end of the following sentence.

I finished my assignment **on Friday.**

On Friday, I finished my assignment.

To learn how to write effective sentences by varying their structure, see chapter **30.**

MULTILINGUAL WRITERS

INVERTING THE SUBJECT AND THE VERB IN QUESTIONS

English is one of a few languages in which the subject and the verb are inverted in questions. Most languages rely on intonation to indicate that a question is being asked, without a change in word order. (English speakers occasionally use uninverted questions to ask for clarification or to indicate surprise.) In languages other than English, a frequently occurring option for making a statement into a question is to add a particle, such as the Japanese *ka.*

THINKING RHETORICALLY

SENTENCE PATTERNS

If you want to emphasize a contrast or intensify a feeling, alter the sentence pattern by placing the direct object at the beginning of the sentence. A comma is sometimes used after the direct object in such sentences.

They loved the queen. They despised **the king**.

They loved the queen. **The king**, they despised.

Exercise 4

1. Identify the basic pattern of each sentence in exercise 2.
2. Write a question corresponding to each of the sentences. Put a check mark next to those questions in which the subject and the verb are inverted.

1e   Phrases

A **phrase** is a sequence of grammatically related words without a subject, a predicate, or both. A phrase is categorized according to the most important word in it. This section introduces noun phrases, verb phrases, verbal phrases, and prepositional phrases as well as appositives and absolute constructions.

(1) A noun phrase consists of a main noun and its modifiers.
Noun phrases serve as subjects (**1b**) and complements (**1c**). They can also be objects of prepositions such as *in, of, on, at,* and *to*. (See **1e(4)** for a longer list of prepositions.)

The heavy frost killed **many fruit trees.** [subject and direct object]

My cousin is **an organic farmer.** [subject and subject complement]

His farm is in **eastern Oregon.** [subject and object of the preposition *in*]

THINKING RHETORICALLY

NOUN PHRASES

In the preceding example sentences, the adjectives *heavy, organic,* and *eastern* add specificity. For example, the noun phrase *an organic farmer* tells the reader more than *farmer* alone would. By composing noun phrases carefully, you will make your sentences more precise.

Much of Greenland lies within the Arctic Circle. ~~The area~~ is [This large island]
owned by Denmark. Its [native] name is Kalaallit Nunaat.

[*The area* could refer to either Greenland or the area within the Arctic Circle. *This large island* clearly refers to Greenland. *Its native name* is more precise than just *Its name.*]

MULTILINGUAL WRITERS

NUMBER AGREEMENT IN NOUN PHRASES

Some words must agree in number with the nouns they precede. The words *a, an, this,* and *that* are used before singular nouns; *some, few, these, those,* and *many* are used before plural nouns:

an/that opportunity [singular noun]
some/few/those opportunities [plural noun]

(Continued on page 26)

(Continued from page 25)

The words *less* and *much* precede nouns representing abstract concepts or masses that cannot be counted (noncount nouns) (**1a(2)**):

less freedom, **much** water [noncount nouns]

(2) A verb phrase includes a main verb and its auxiliary verbs.
A verb is essential to the predicate of a sentence (**1b**). It generally expresses action or a state of being. Besides a main verb, a verb phrase includes one or more **auxiliary verbs**, sometimes called *helping verbs,* such as *be, have, do, will,* and *should.*

The flight **arrived.** [main verb]

The passengers **have deplaned.** [auxiliary verb + main verb]

For a comprehensive discussion of verbs, see chapter **7**.

(3) Verbal phrases are used as nouns or modifiers.
A **verbal phrase** differs from a verb phrase (**1e(2)**) in that the verb form in a verbal phrase serves as a noun or a modifier rather than as a verb.

He <u>was</u> **reading** the story aloud. [*Reading* is part of the verb phrase *was reading.*]

Reading is fundamental to academic success. [*Reading* serves as a noun. COMPARE: **It** is fundamental to academic success.]

The student **reading** aloud is an education major. [*Reading aloud* modifies *the student.*]

Because of their origin as verbs, verbals in phrases often have their own objects (**1c**) and modifiers (chapter **4**).

He decided **to read** the story aloud. [The object of the verbal *to read* is *the story. Aloud* is a modifier.]

Verbal phrases are divided into three types: gerund phrases, participial phrases, and infinitive phrases.

Central to a **gerund phrase** is the *-ing* verb form (see 7a(1)). A gerund phrase serves as a noun, usually functioning as the subject (1b) or object (1c) in a sentence.

Writing a bestseller was her only goal. [subject]

My neighbor enjoys **writing** about distant places. [object]

Because gerund phrases act as nouns, pronouns can replace them.

That was her only goal.

My neighbor enjoys **it.**

THINKING RHETORICALLY

GERUNDS

What is the difference between the following sentences?

They bundle products together, which often results in higher consumer costs.

Bundling products together often results in higher consumer costs.

In the first sentence, the actor, *they,* is the focus. In the second sentence, the action of the gerund phrase, *bundling products together,* is the focus. As you revise, ask yourself whether you want to emphasize actors or actions.

Participial phrases include either a present participle (*-ing* form) or a past participle (*-ed* form for regular verbs or another form for irregular verbs). (See 7a for more information on verb forms.)

> **Planning** her questions carefully, she was able to hold fast-paced and engaging interviews. [present participle]

> **Known** for her interviewing skills, she was asked to host her own radio program. [past participle]

Participial phrases function as modifiers (4a(2)). They may appear at the beginning, in the middle, or at the end of a sentence.

> **Fearing** a drought, all the farmers in the area used less irrigation water.

> All the farmers in the area, **recognizing** the signs of drought, used less irrigation water.

> Farmers used less irrigation water, **hoping** to save water for later in the season.

The commas setting off the participial phrases in the preceding examples signal that the phrases are not essential for readers to understand who is using less irrigation water. Instead, the phrases add descriptive details or reasons to the sentence. Sometimes, however, a participial phrase provides necessary information that specifies who or what is being discussed. This type of participial phrase, an **essential phrase**, is *not* set off by commas.

> The reporter **providing the most accurate account of the war** was once a soldier.
> [The participial phrase distinguishes this reporter from others.]

For more advice on using punctuation with phrases containing verbals, see 12b(2) and 12d(1).

A present participle (*-ing* form) cannot function alone as the main verb in a sentence. It must be accompanied by a form of *be* (*am, is, are, was,* or *were*).

They _∧ **thinking** about the future.
      ^are^

THINKING RHETORICALLY

PARTICIPIAL PHRASES

If some of your sentences sound monotonous or choppy, try combining them by using participial phrases.

The ecstatic fans crowded along the city streets. They were celebrating their team's first state championship.

REVISED

Crowded along the city streets, the ecstatic fans celebrated their team's first state championship.

OR

Celebrating their team's first state championship, the ecstatic fans crowded along the city streets.

Infinitive phrases serve as nouns (**1a(2)**) or as modifiers (chapter **4**). The form of the infinitive is distinct—the infinitive marker *to* followed by the base form of the verb.

The company intends **to hire twenty new employees.** [noun]

We discussed his plan **to use a new packing process.** [modifier of the noun *plan*]

To attract customers, the company changed its advertising strategy. [modifier of the verb *changed*]

BEYOND THE RULE

SPLIT INFINITIVES

Some instructors advise against putting words between the infinitive
marker *to* and the base form of the verb.

Be sure to ~~carefully~~ consider the evidence. ^carefully^

This is good advice to remember if the intervening words create a
cumbersome sentence.

^Under the circumstances, the^
The jury was unable to~~, under the circumstances,~~ convict the
defendant.

However, most writers today recognize that a single word splitting
an infinitive can provide emphasis.

He did not expect to actually publish his work.

MULTILINGUAL WRITERS

VERBS FOLLOWED BY GERUNDS AND/OR INFINITIVES

Some verbs in English can be followed by a gerund, some can
be followed by an infinitive, and some can be followed by either.

Verbs Followed by a Gerund

admit   consider   dislike   finish
avoid   deny   enjoy   suggest

Example: She **enjoys playing** the piano.

Verbs Followed by an Infinitive

agree   decide   deserve   hope   need   plan   promise   seem

Example: She **promised to play** the piano for us.

Verbs Followed by a Pronoun, Noun, or Noun Phrase and an Infinitive

| advise | invite | persuade | teach |
| encourage | order | require | |

Example: Her father **taught** her **to play** the piano.

When an infinitive follows the verb *make* or *have* and a pronoun, noun, or noun phrase, the marker *to* is omitted.

Example: The teacher **had** the student **repeat** the song.

The marker *to* is optional when it follows the verb *help* and a pronoun, noun, or noun phrase.

Example: He **helped** her **(to) learn** the song.

Verbs Followed by Either a Gerund or an Infinitive

begin   continue   like   prefer   remember   stop   try

Examples: She **likes to play** the piano. She **likes playing** the piano.

Although either a gerund phrase or an infinitive phrase can follow these verbs, the resulting sentences may differ in meaning.

We **stopped discussing** the plan. [The discussion has ended.]

We **stopped to discuss** the plan. [The discussion has not yet started.]

Specialized dictionaries provide information on the use of gerunds and infinitives with verbs (see **19e(1)** for a list of recommendations).

(4) Prepositional phrases are used as modifiers.

Prepositional phrases provide information about time, place, cause, manner, and so on. They can also answer one of these questions: Which one? What kind of . . . ?

> **With great feeling,** Martin Luther King expressed his dream **of freedom.**
>
> [*With great feeling* describes the way the speech was delivered, and *of freedom* specifies the kind of dream.]

> King delivered his most famous speech **at a demonstration in Washington, DC.**
>
> [Both *at a demonstration* and *in Washington, DC* provide information about place.]

A **prepositional phrase** consists of a **preposition** (a word such as *at, of,* or *in*) and a pronoun, noun, or noun phrase (called the **object of the preposition**). A prepositional phrase modifies another element in the sentence.

> Everyone **in class** went to the play. [modifier of the pronoun *everyone*]

> The actors **in it** [the play] were all students. [modifier of the noun *actors*]

> Some students met the professor **after the play.** [modifier of the verb *met*]

A prepositional phrase sometimes consists of a preposition and an entire clause (**1f**).

> They will give the award **to whoever produces the best design.**

BEYOND THE RULE

ENDING A SENTENCE WITH A PREPOSITION

A grammar rule that has caused much controversy over the years is the one that advises against ending a sentence with a preposition. Most professional writers now follow this rule only when they adopt a formal tone. If their rhetorical situation calls for an informal tone, they will not hesitate to place a preposition at the end of a sentence.

He found friends **on** whom he could depend. [formal]
He found friends he could depend **on.** [informal]

SOME COMMON PREPOSITIONS

about	behind	except	of	through
above	beside	for	on	to
after	between	from	out	toward
around	by	in	over	under
as	despite	into	past	until
at	down	like	regarding	up
before	during	near	since	with

Phrasal prepositions consist of more than one word.

Except for the last day, it was a wonderful trip.

The postponement was **due to** inclement weather.

PHRASAL PREPOSITIONS

according to	due to	in spite of
apart from	except for	instead of
as for	in addition to	out of
because of	in case of	with regard to
by means of	in front of	with respect to

MULTILINGUAL WRITERS

PREPOSITIONS IN IDIOMATIC COMBINATIONS

Some verbs, adjectives, and nouns combine with prepositions to form idiomatic combinations (**20c**).

Verb + Preposition	Adjective + Preposition	Noun + Preposition
apply to	fond of	interest in
rely on	similar to	dependence on
trust in	different from	fondness for

(5) An appositive can expand the meaning of a noun or a noun phrase.

An **appositive** is most often a noun or a noun phrase that refers to the same person, place, thing, or idea as a preceding noun or noun phrase but in different words. The alternate wording provides extra details that make the reference clear. By using an occasional appositive, you can add both clarity and variety to your writing.

When an appositive provides essential information, no commas are used.

Cormac McCarthy's novel *The Road* won a Pulitzer Prize.
[The appositive specifies which of McCarthy's novels won the award.]

When an appositive phrase provides details that are not essential, commas set it off.

The Road, **a novel by Cormac McCarthy,** won a Pulitzer Prize. [The appositive provides extra details about the book.]

For more information on punctuating nonessential appositives, see **12d(2)**.

(6) Absolute phrases provide descriptive details or express causes or conditions.

An **absolute phrase** is usually a noun phrase modified by a participial phrase (**1e(3)**) or a prepositional phrase (**1e(4)**).

> She left town at dawn, <u>**all her belongings**</u> **packed into a Volkswagen Beetle.**

> <u>**Her guitar**</u> **in the front seat,** she pulled away from the curb.

The preceding absolute phrases provide details; the following absolute phrase expresses cause.

> **More vaccine having arrived,** the staff scheduled its distribution.

Be sure to use commas to set off absolute phrases.

Exercise 5

Label the underlined phrases in the following sentences as noun phrases, verb phrases, prepositional phrases, or verbal phrases. For verbal phrases, specify the type: gerund, participial, or infinitive. When a long phrase includes a short phrase, identify just the long phrase. Finally, identify any appositive phrases or absolute phrases in the sentences.

1. <u>The Smithsonian</u> is <u>the largest museum complex in the world</u>.
2. <u>Dedicated to the collection and diffusion of knowledge</u>, the Smithsonian comprises <u>over a dozen museums</u>.

3. People come <u>from every state</u> <u>to visit the museums</u>.
4. Scientists and scholars <u>visiting a Smithsonian museum</u> <u>can use its outstanding facilities</u>.
5. <u>Receiving a Smithsonian fellowship</u> is <u>the dream</u> <u>of many students</u>.
6. The Smithsonian owes <u>its existence</u> <u>to James Smithson</u>, <u>a scientist from Great Britain</u>.
7. Without ever <u>having visited the United States</u>, Smithson included this country <u>in his last will and testament</u>.
8. <u>His bequest firmly rooted in the Enlightenment ideals of democracy and education</u>, James Smithson left the citizens <u>of the United States</u> <u>an unsurpassable legacy</u>.

1f   Clauses

(1) An independent clause can stand alone as a complete sentence.

A **clause** is a group of related words that contains a subject and a predicate. An **independent clause,** sometimes called a *main clause,* has the same grammatical structure as a simple sentence: both contain a subject and a predicate (see **1b**).

$$\underbrace{\text{The students}}_{\text{s}} \underbrace{\text{earned high grades.}}_{\text{pred}}$$

Other clauses can be added to independent clauses to form longer, more detailed sentences.

(2) A dependent clause is connected to an independent clause.

A **dependent clause** also has a subject and a predicate (**1b**). However, it cannot stand alone as a complete sentence because of the word introducing it—usually a relative pronoun or a subordinating conjunction.

The athlete **who placed first** grew up in Argentina. [relative pronoun]

She received the gold medal **because she performed flawlessly.** [subordinating conjunction]

If it is not connected to an independent clause, a dependent clause is considered a sentence fragment (2c).

(a) Dependent clauses can be used as subjects or objects.

Dependent clauses that serve as subjects (1b) or objects (1c) are called **noun clauses** (or **nominal clauses**). They are introduced by *if, that,* or a *wh-* word such as *why, what,* or *when.* Notice the similarity in usage between noun phrases and noun clauses.

Noun phrases	Noun clauses
The testimony may not be true. [subject]	**What the witness said** may not be true. [subject]
We do not understand **their motives.** [direct object]	We do not understand **why they did it.** [direct object]
Send the money to **a charity.** [object of the preposition *to*]	Send the money to **whoever needs it most.** [object of the preposition *to* (1e(4))]

When no misunderstanding would result, the word *that* can be omitted from the beginning of a clause.

The scientist said **she was moving to Australia.** [*that* omitted]

However, *that* should always be retained when there are two noun clauses.

The scientist said **that she was moving to Australia** and **that her research team was planning to accompany her.** [*that* retained in both noun clauses]

(b) Dependent clauses can be used as modifiers.

Two types of dependent clauses—adjectival (relative) clauses and adverbial clauses—serve as modifiers. An **adjectival clause,** or **relative clause,** follows a pronoun, noun, or noun phrase and answers one of these questions: Which one? What kind of . . . ? Such clauses, which nearly always follow the words they modify, usually begin with a **relative pronoun** (*who, whom, that, which,* or *whose*) but sometimes start with a **relative adverb** (*when, where,* or *why*). Notice the similarity in usage between adjectives and adjectival clauses.

Adjectives	**Adjectival clauses**
Nobody likes **malicious** gossip. [answers the question *What kind of gossip?*]	Nobody likes news reports **that pry into someone's private life.** [answers the question *What kind of news reports?*]
Some **diligent** students begin their research early. [answers the question *Which students?*]	Students **who have good study habits** begin their research early. [answers the question *Which students?*]
The **public** remarks were troubling. [answers the question *Which remarks?*]	The remarks **that were made public** were troubling. [answers the question *Which remarks?*]

An **essential (restrictive) adjectival clause** contains information necessary to specify a noun reference. Such a clause is *not* set off by commas. The essential adjectival clause in the following sentence is needed for the reader to know which state carries a great deal of influence in a presidential election.

The state **that casts the most electoral votes** greatly influences the outcome of a presidential election.

A **nonessential (nonrestrictive) adjectival clause** provides extra details that, even though they may be interesting, are not needed for the purpose of identifying the preceding noun. An adjectival clause following a proper noun (**1a(2)**) is almost always nonessential. A nonessential adjectival clause should be set off by commas.

California, **which has fifty-five electoral votes,** greatly influences the outcome of any presidential election.

Many writers use *that* to begin essential clauses and *which* to begin nonessential clauses. You should follow this convention if you are required to use American Psychological Association (APA) or Modern Language Association (MLA) guidelines (although MLA acknowledges that some writers use *which* instead of *that* in essential clauses).

THINKING RHETORICALLY

ADJECTIVAL CLAUSES

If you find that your sentences tend to be short, try using adjectival clauses to combine them into longer sentences.

Dub is a car magazine. It appeals to drivers with hip-hop attitudes.

Dub is a car magazine **that appeals to drivers with hip-hop attitudes.**

A Hovercraft can go where many vehicles cannot. It is practically amphibious.

A Hovercraft, **which can go where many vehicles cannot,** is practically amphibious.

A relative pronoun can be omitted as long as the meaning of the sentence is still clear.

Mother Teresa was someone **the whole world admired.** [*Whom,* the direct object of the clause, has been omitted: the whole world admired *whom.*]

She was someone **who cared more about serving than being served.** [*Who* cannot be omitted because it is the subject of the clause.]

The relative pronoun is not omitted when the clause is set off by commas (that is, when it is a nonessential clause).

Mother Teresa, **whom the whole world admired,** cared more about serving than being served.

An **adverbial clause** usually answers one of the following questions: Where? When? Why? How? How frequently? In what manner? Adverbial clauses are introduced by subordinating conjunctions such as *because, although,* and *when.* (For a list of subordinating conjunctions, see page 43.) Notice the similarity in usage between adverbs and adverbial clauses.

Adverbs	**Adverbial clauses**
Occasionally, the company hires new writers. [answers the question *How frequently does the company hire new writers?*]	**When the need arises,** the company hires new writers. [answers the question *How frequently does the company hire new writers?*]
She acted **selfishly.** [answers the question *How did she act?*]	She acted **as though she cared only about herself.** [answers the question *How did she act?*]

Adverbial clauses can appear at various points in a sentence. Use commas to set off an adverbial clause placed at the beginning or in the middle of a sentence.

Because they disagreed, the researchers made little progress.

The researchers, **because they disagreed,** made little progress.

If you place an adverbial clause at the end of a sentence, you will usually not need a comma.

The researchers made little progress **because they disagreed.**

If, however, an adverbial clause at the end of a sentence contains an extra detail—the type of clause you would want a reader to pause before if he or she were reading it aloud—use a comma to set it off.

I slept soundly that night, **even though a storm raged outside.**

THINKING RHETORICALLY

ADVERBIAL CLAUSES

In an adverbial clause that refers to time or establishes a fact, both the subject and any form of the verb *be* can be omitted. Using such **elliptical clauses** will make your writing more concise.

While fishing, he saw a rare owl.
[COMPARE: **While he was fishing,** he saw a rare owl.]

Though tired, they continued to study for the exam.
[COMPARE: **Though they were tired,** they continued to study for the exam.]

Be sure that the omitted subject of an elliptical clause is the same as the subject of the independent clause. Otherwise, revise either the adverbial clause or the main clause.

While ᴵ ʷᵃˢ reviewing your report, a few questions occurred to me.

OR

While reviewing your report, ᴵ ᵗʰᵒᵘᵍʰᵗ ᵒᶠ a few questions ~~occurred to me~~.

For more information on the use of elliptical constructions, see **21c**.

1g　Conjunctions and conjunctive adverbs

(1) Coordinating conjunctions join words, phrases, or clauses.
In the following examples, note that coordinating conjunctions (1a(7)) link grammatical elements that are alike. Each conjunction, though, has a specific meaning.

> tired **yet** excited [*Yet* joins two words and signals contrast.]

> in the boat **or** on the pier [*Or* joins two phrases and marks them as alternatives.]

> We did not share a language, **but** somehow we communicated. [*But* joins two independent clauses and signals contrast.]

When a coordinating conjunction joins two independent clauses, as in the last example, it should be preceded by a comma. A coordinating conjunction may also link independent clauses that stand alone as sentences.

> The momentum in the direction of globalization seems too powerful to buck, the economic logic unmatchable. **But** in a region where jobs are draining away, and where an ethic of self-reliance remains a dim, vestigial, but honored memory, it seems at least an outside possibility.
> —BILL McKIBBEN, "Small World"

(2) Correlative conjunctions are two-part conjunctions.
Correlative conjunctions (1a(7)) join words, phrases, or clauses. However, they do not join sentences.

> **either** you **or** I [*Either . . . or* joins two words and marks them as alternatives.]

> **neither** on Friday **nor** on Saturday [*Neither . . . nor* joins two phrases and marks them both as false or impossible.]

Not only did they run ten miles, **but** they **also** swam twenty laps. [*Not only . . . but also* joins two independent clauses and signals addition.]

Generally, a correlative conjunction links similar structures. The following sentence has been revised because the correlative conjunction was linking a phrase to a clause.

did he save
Not only ∧ ~~saving~~ the lives of the accident victims, **but** he **also** prevented many spinal injuries.

(3) Subordinating conjunctions introduce dependent clauses.

A subordinating conjunction introduces a dependent clause (**1f(2)**). It also carries a specific meaning; for example, it may indicate cause, concession, condition, or purpose.

She studied Spanish **because** she wanted to work in Costa Rica.
[*Because* signals a cause.]

Unless the project receives more funding, the research will stop.
[*Unless* signals a condition.]

SUBORDINATING CONJUNCTIONS

after	how	than
although	if	though
as if	in case	unless
as though	in that	until
because	insofar as	when, whenever
before	once	where, wherever
even if	since	whether
even though	so that	while

The word *that* can be omitted from the subordinating conjunction *so that* if the meaning remains clear.

I left ten minutes early **so** I would not be late. [*That* has been omitted.]

However, when *that* is omitted, the remaining *so* can be easily confused with the coordinating conjunction *so*.

I had some extra time, **so** I went to the music store.

Because sentences with subordinating conjunctions are punctuated differently from sentences with coordinating conjunctions (**1a(7)**), be careful to distinguish between them. If *so* stands for "so that," it is a subordinating conjunction. If *so* means "thus," it is a coordinating conjunction.

(4) Conjunctive adverbs link independent clauses.

Conjunctive adverbs—such as *however, nevertheless, then,* and *therefore*—link independent clauses (**1f(1)**). These adverbs, sometimes called **adverbial conjunctions,** signal relationships such as cause, condition, and contrast.

CONJUNCTIVE ADVERBS

also	however	moreover	still
consequently	indeed	nevertheless	then
finally	instead	next	therefore
furthermore	likewise	nonetheless	thus
hence	meanwhile	otherwise	

Any conjunctive adverb can be used at the beginning of an independent clause. Some may also appear in the middle or at the end of a clause. *However* indicates contrast in the following sentences:

My mother and father hold many of the same values;
however, they favor opposing political candidates.

My mother and father seldom argue about politics in front of
their children; in front of a televised football game, **however,**
they bicker incessantly.

My mother and father have differing political views; they
rarely argue, **however.**

Because an independent clause can stand alone as a sentence,
the clause after the semicolon in each of the previous sentences
can also be written as a separate sentence.

My mother and father hold many of the same values.
However, they favor opposing political candidates.

My mother and father seldom argue about politics in front of
their children. In front of a televised football game, however, they
bicker incessantly.

My mother and father have differing political views. They
rarely argue, however.

For more information on the use of conjunctive adverbs and
related transition words, see **3c(5)**. For guidelines on punctuating linked independent clauses, see **12a** and **14a**.

Exercise 6

1. Identify the dependent clauses in the following paragraph.
2. Identify the underlined words as coordinating conjunctions,
   correlative conjunctions, subordinating conjunctions, or
   conjunctive adverbs.

   [1]<u>If</u> you live by the sword, you might die by the sword.
   [2]<u>However</u>, <u>if</u> you make your living by swallowing swords, you

will not necessarily die by swallowing swords. [3]At least, this is the conclusion Brian Witcombe and Dan Meyer reached <u>after</u> they surveyed forty-six professional sword swallowers. [4](Brian Witcombe is a radiologist, <u>and</u> Dan Meyer is a famous sword swallower.) [5]Some of those surveyed mentioned <u>that</u> they had experienced <u>either</u> "sword throats" <u>or</u> chest pains, <u>and</u> others who let their swords drop to their stomachs described perforation of their innards, <u>but</u> the researchers could find no listing of a sword-swallowing mortality in the medical studies they reviewed. [6]The researchers did not inquire into the reasons for swallowing swords in the first place.

1h Sentence forms

You can identify the form of a sentence by noting the number of clauses it contains and the type of each clause.

(1) A simple sentence consists of a single independent clause.

ONE INDEPENDENT CLAUSE

A **simple sentence** is equivalent to one independent clause; thus, it must have a subject and a predicate.

$$\overset{s}{\underbrace{\text{The lawyer}}} \overset{pred}{\underbrace{\text{presented her final argument.}}}$$

However, you can expand a simple sentence by adding one or more verbal phrases (**1e(3)**) or prepositional phrases (**1e(4)**).

Encouraged by the apparent sympathy of the jury, the lawyer presented her final argument. [The verbal phrase adds detail.]

The lawyer presented her final argument **in less than an hour.**
[The prepositional phrase adds information about time.]

(2) A compound sentence consists of at least two independent clauses but no dependent clauses.

INDEPENDENT CLAUSE + INDEPENDENT CLAUSE

The independent clauses of a compound sentence are most commonly linked by a coordinating conjunction. However, punctuation may sometimes serve the same purpose (**14a**).

The Democrats proposed a new budget, but the Republicans opposed it.
[The coordinating conjunction *but* links two independent clauses and signals contrast.]

The Democrats proposed a new budget; the Republicans opposed it.
[The semicolon serves the same purpose as the coordinating conjunction.]

(3) A complex sentence consists of one independent clause and at least one dependent clause.

INDEPENDENT CLAUSE + DEPENDENT CLAUSE

A dependent clause in a complex sentence can be a noun clause, an adjectival clause, or an adverbial clause (**1f(2)**).

Because he was known for architectural ornamentation, no one predicted **that the house <u>he designed for himself</u> would be so plain.** [This sentence has three dependent clauses. *Because he was known for architectural ornamentation* is an adverbial clause. *That the house he designed for himself would be so plain* is a noun clause, and *he designed for himself* is an adjectival clause within the noun clause. The relative pronoun *that* has been omitted from the beginning of the embedded adjectival clause.]

(4) A compound-complex sentence consists of at least two independent clauses and at least one dependent clause.

> INDEPENDENT CLAUSE + INDEPENDENT CLAUSE + DEPENDENT CLAUSE

The combination of a compound sentence and a complex sentence is called a **compound-complex sentence.**

Conflict is essential to good storytelling, **so** fiction writers often create a character **who faces a major challenge.** [The coordinating conjunction *so* joins the two independent clauses; the relative pronoun *who* introduces the dependent clause.]

THINKING RHETORICALLY

SENTENCE FORMS

If one of your paragraphs has as many simple sentences as the one below, try combining some of your ideas into compound, complex, or compound-complex sentences. As you do, you might need to add extra detail as well.

I rode the school bus every day. I didn't like to, though. The bus smelled bad. And it was always packed. The worst part was the bumpy ride. Riding the bus was like riding in a worn-out sneaker.

REVISED

As a kid, I rode the school bus every day, but I didn't like to. I hated the smell, the crowd, and the bumpy ride itself. Every seat was filled, and many of the kids took their shoes off for the long ride home on roads so bumpy you couldn't even read a comic book. Riding that bus was like riding inside a worn-out sneaker.

Exercise 7

Identify each sentence in the paragraph in exercise 6 as simple, compound, complex, or compound-complex.

Exercise 8

Vary the sentence forms in the following paragraph. Add details as needed.

We arrived at the afternoon concert late. We couldn't find any seats. It was hot, so we stood in the shade. We finally found seats under an umbrella. The shade didn't help, though. We could feel our brains melting. The music was cool, but we weren't.

1i   Sentence functions

Sentences serve a number of functions. Writers commonly state facts or report information with **declarative sentences.** They give instructions with **imperative sentences.** They use questions, or **interrogative sentences**, to elicit information or to introduce topics. And they express emotion with **exclamatory sentences.**

Declarative	The runners from Kenya won the race.
Imperative	Compare their times with the record.
Interrogative	What were their times?
Exclamatory	The runners from Kenya won the race! Check their times! What an incredible race that was!

Taking note of end punctuation can help you identify the function of a sentence. Generally, a period indicates the end of a declarative sentence or an imperative sentence, and a question mark ends an interrogative sentence. An exclamation point indicates that a sentence is exclamatory. To distinguish between an imperative sentence and a declarative sentence, look for a subject (1b). If you cannot find one, the sentence is imperative. Because an imperative is directed to another person or persons, the subject *you* is implied:

Look over there.
[COMPARE: You look over there.]

Advertisers often use imperatives to attract the reader's attention. (Courtesy of United Airlines.)

THINKING RHETORICALLY

QUESTIONS

One type of interrogative sentence, the **rhetorical question**, is not a true question, because an answer is not expected. Instead, like a declarative sentence, it is used to state an opinion. However, a positive rhetorical question can correspond to a negative assertion, and vice versa.

Rhetorical questions	**Equivalent statements**
Should we allow our rights to be taken away?	We should not allow our rights to be taken away.
Isn't it time to make a difference?	It's time to make a difference.

Because they are more emphatic than declarative sentences, rhetorical questions focus the reader's attention on major points.

Exercise 9

Identify each sentence type.

1. I did not look at the weather forecast.
2. Did you see me slosh through the puddles?
3. Next time remind me to bring an umbrella.
4. What a terrible day that was!

TECH SAVVY

Using a Grammar Checker

Most word-processing programs have features that help writers identify grammar errors as well as problems with usage and style, but these grammar checkers have significant limitations. A grammar checker will usually identify

- fused sentences, sometimes called run-on sentences (chapter 3),
- wordy or overly long sentences (chapters 21 and 24), and
- missing apostrophes in contractions (15a).

However, a grammar checker can easily miss

- sentence fragments (chapter 2),
- dangling or misplaced modifiers (chapter 25),
- problems with pronoun-antecedent agreement (6b),
- errors in subject-verb agreement (6a), and
- misused or missing commas (chapter 12).

Because these omissions can weaken your credibility as a writer, you should never rely solely on a grammar checker to find them. Furthermore, grammar checkers can mark as wrong words or phrases that you have chosen deliberately to suit your rhetorical situation (chapter 31).

Used carefully, a grammar checker can be a helpful tool, but keep the following advice in mind:

- Use a grammar checker only in addition to your own editing and proofreading.
- Always evaluate any sentences flagged by a grammar checker to determine whether there is, in fact, a problem.
- Adjust the settings on your grammar checker to look for specific types of errors. If you are using Microsoft Word, select Tools; then select either Spelling and Grammar or Options to customize your settings.
- Carefully review the revisions proposed by a grammar checker before accepting them. Sometimes the proposed revisions create new errors.

2 Sentence Fragments

As its name suggests, a **sentence fragment** is only a piece of a sentence; it is not complete. This chapter can help you

- recognize sentence fragments (**2a**) and
- revise fragments resulting from incorrectly punctuated phrases and dependent clauses (**2b** and **2c**).

2a Recognizing sentence fragments

A complete sentence consists of a subject and a predicate (**1b**), but a fragment is missing one or both of these parts. Sentence fragments are easy to recognize when they are not surrounded by other sentences.

The placement of a patient into a sleeplike state.

This fragment makes the reader wonder what *the placement of a patient into a sleeplike state* does or is. In other words, this fragment lacks a verb—the essential part of a predicate. When placed next to another sentence, however, this fragment is more difficult to recognize.

Alternative medical treatment may include hypnosis. **The placement of a patient into a sleeplike state.**

A fragment such as this one can often simply be attached to the sentence preceding it by adding appropriate punctuation.

> Alternative medical treatment may include hypnosis—**the placement of a patient into a sleeplike state.**

Another type of fragment has the essential components of a sentence but begins with a word that marks it as a dependent clause (**1f(2)**). Compare the complete sentence with the fragment.

> The depth of the trance for each person varies. [complete sentence]
>
> Although the depth of the trance for each person varies. [fragment]

The fragment makes more sense when attached to an independent clause (**1f(1)**).

> Most people can be hypnotized easily, **although the depth of the trance for each person varies.**

Note that imperative sentences (**1i**) are not considered fragments. In these sentences, the subject, *you,* is not stated explicitly. Rather, it is implied.

> Find out as much as you can about alternative treatments. [COMPARE: You find out as much as you can about alternative treatments.]

FOUR METHODS FOR IDENTIFYING FRAGMENTS

If you have trouble recognizing fragments, try one or more of these methods:

1. Read each paragraph backwards, sentence by sentence. When you read your sentences out of order, you may more readily note the incompleteness of a fragment.

2. Locate the essential parts of each sentence. First, find the main verb and any accompanying auxiliary verbs. Remember that verbals cannot function as main verbs (**7a**). After you find the main verb, identify the subject (**1b**). Finally, check to see that the sentence does not begin with a relative pronoun (**1f(2)**) or a subordinating conjunction (**1g(3)**).

   Test sentence 1: The inventor of the Frisbee.

   Test: Main verb? *None.*

   [Because there is no verb, this test sentence is a fragment.]

   Test sentence 2: Walter Frederick Morrison invented the Frisbee.

   Test: Main verb? *Invented.*

   Subject? *Walter Frederick Morrison.*

   Relative pronoun or subordinating conjunction? *None.*

   [The test sentence is complete: it contains a subject and a verb and does not begin with a relative pronoun or a subordinating conjunction.]

3. Put any sentence you think might be a fragment into this frame sentence:

   They do not understand the idea that _____ .

   Only a full sentence will make sense in this frame sentence. If a test sentence, other than an imperative, does not fit into the frame sentence, it is a fragment.

(Continued on page 56)

(Continued from page 55)

Test sentence 3: Because it can be played almost anywhere.

Test: They do not understand the idea that *because it can be played almost anywhere.*

[The frame sentence does not make sense, so the test sentence is a fragment.]

Test sentence 4: Ultimate Frisbee is a popular sport because it can be played almost anywhere.

Test: They do not understand the idea that *Ultimate Frisbee is a popular sport because it can be played almost anywhere.*

[The frame sentence makes sense, so the test sentence is complete.]

4. Rewrite any sentence you think might be a fragment as a question that can be answered with *yes* or *no*. Only complete sentences can be rewritten this way.

   Test sentence 5: That combines aspects of soccer, football, and basketball.

   Test: *Is that combines aspects of soccer, football, and basketball?*

   [The question does not make sense, so the test sentence is a fragment.]

   Test sentence 6: Ultimate Frisbee is a game that combines aspects of soccer, football, and basketball.

   Test: *Is Ultimate Frisbee a game that combines aspects of soccer, football, and basketball?*

   [The question makes sense, so the test sentence is complete.]

Exercise 1

Identify the sentence fragments in the following paragraph. Be prepared to explain how you identified each fragment. Revise the fragments by attaching them to related sentences or by recasting them as complete sentences.

¹The name *Calder* often brings to mind huge mobiles. ²Hanging from the ceilings of art museums. ³Well known for these playfully balanced arrangements of abstract or organic forms, Alexander Calder (1898–1976) was actually a versatile sculptor. ⁴His work ranging from jewelry to outdoor sculptures. ⁵Yet Calder did not begin his career as an artist. ⁶Instead, he studied mechanical engineering. ⁷Even though he came from a family of sculptors. ⁸Four years after he earned his degree, he enrolled in an art school. ⁹Moving to Paris shortly thereafter. ¹⁰Calder first earned worldwide recognition for wire sculptures. ¹¹In the 1930s, he started to experiment with motion. ¹²Eventually developing the mobiles he is best known for today.

2b Phrases as sentence fragments

A phrase (**1e**) may be mistakenly written as a sentence fragment. You can revise such a fragment by attaching it to a related sentence, usually the one preceding it. If you are unsure of the correct punctuation to use with phrases, see **12b** and **12d**.

Verbal phrase as a fragment

Early humans valued color. *, creating* **~~Creating~~ permanent colors with natural pigments.**

Prepositional phrase as a fragment

For years, the Scottish have dyed sweaters with soot. *, originally* **~~Originally~~ from the chimneys of peat-burning stoves.**

Compound predicate as a fragment

Arctic foxes turn white when it snows. ~~And~~ *and* thus conceal themselves from prey.

Appositive phrase as a fragment

During the Renaissance, one of the most highly valued pigments was ultramarine. ~~An~~ *—an* extract from lapis lazuli.

Appositive list as a fragment

To derive dyes, we have always experimented with what we find in nature. ~~Shells,~~ *: shells,* roots, insects, flowers.

Absolute phrase as a fragment

The deciduous trees of New England are known for their brilliant autumn color. ~~Sugar~~ *, sugar* maples dazzling tourists with their orange and red leaves.

Instead of attaching a fragment to the preceding sentence, you can recast the fragment as a complete sentence. This method of revision elevates the importance of the information conveyed in the fragment.

Fragment	Humans painted themselves for a variety of purposes. **To attract a mate, to hide themselves from game or predators, or to signal aggression.**
Revision	Humans used color for a variety of purposes. For example, they painted themselves to attract a mate, to hide themselves from game or predators, or to signal aggression.

Exercise 2

Revise each fragment by attaching it to a related sentence or by recasting it as a complete sentence.

1. A brilliant twenty-three-year-old Englishman. Isaac Newton was the first person to study color.
2. By passing a beam of sunlight through a prism. Newton showed that white light comprised all the visible colors of the spectrum.
3. White light passed through the prism. And separated into the colors of the rainbow.
4. Rainbows are arcs of color. Caused by water droplets in the air.
5. Sometimes rainbows contain all the spectrum colors. Red, orange, yellow, green, blue, indigo, and violet.
6. Particles of spray in waterfalls can act as prisms. Producing a variety of colors.
7. Our brains easily fooled. We sometimes see more colors than are actually present.

2c Dependent clauses as sentence fragments

A dependent clause punctuated as a complete sentence is a fragment. To revise such a fragment, attach it to a related sentence, usually the sentence preceding it.

The iceberg was no surprise. ~~Because~~ because the *Titanic*'s wireless operators had received reports of ice in the area.

More than two thousand people were aboard the *Titanic*. ~~Which~~ , which was the largest ocean liner in 1912.

Two other methods can be used to revise these types of fragments. You can recast the fragment as a complete sentence by removing the subordinating conjunction or relative pronoun and supplying any missing elements. This method of revision draws attention to the information originally conveyed in the fragment. Compare the following revisions with the ones above:

> The iceberg was no surprise. The *Titanic*'s wireless operators had received reports of ice in the area.

> More than two thousand people were aboard the *Titanic*. In 1912, this ocean liner was the world's largest.

You can also reduce a clausal fragment to a phrase (1e) and then attach it to a related sentence.

> More than two thousand people were aboard the *Titanic*, the largest ocean liner in 1912. [fragment reduced to an appositive phrase]

If you are unsure of the punctuation to use with phrases or dependent clauses, see chapter **12**.

THINKING RHETORICALLY

FRAGMENTS

When used judiciously, fragments—like short sentences—emphasize ideas, add surprise, or enhance the rhythm of a paragraph. Fragments are not appropriate for all types of writing, however. They are generally permitted only when the rhetorical situation allows the use of a casual tone.

May. When the earth's Northern Hemisphere awakens from winter's sleep and all of nature bristles with the energies of new life. My work has kept me indoors for months now. I'm not sure I'll ever get used to it.
—KEN CAREY, *Flat Rock Journal: A Day in the Ozark Mountains*

BEYOND THE RULE

ABBREVIATED SENTENCES

You encounter sentence fragments every day—in conversations, in e-mail messages, and even in some instructional materials. In conversation, someone might ask you, "Going anywhere tonight?" And you might respond, "Maybe." To end an e-mail message, you might write, "See you later." When preparing a meal, you have probably read instructions similar to these: "Just heat and serve." "Cook to golden brown." The writers of such instructions expect you to know what is to be heated or browned. These kinds of fragments, in which words that can be understood from the context are omitted, are called **abbreviated sentences**.

Exercise 3

Revise each fragment by attaching it to a related sentence or by recasting it as a full sentence.

1. The ship was christened *Titanic*. Which means "of great size."
2. The shipbuilders thought the *Titanic* was unsinkable. Because it had sixteen watertight compartments.
3. The ship sank in less than three hours. Even though the damage caused by the iceberg was not massive.
4. The extent of the damage to the ship's hull was unknown. Until researchers started examining the wreckage in the late 1990s.
5. In 1987, a controversial French expedition recovered dishes, jewelry, and other artifacts from the *Titanic*. Which were later displayed in France and Germany.

Exercise 4

Follow the guidelines in this chapter to locate and revise the fragments in the following paragraph. If you find it necessary, make other improvements as well. Be prepared to explain your revisions.

¹Folklore from around the world contains references to wild men in the woods. ²Such as the Greek saytrs, the Russian *leshiy,* and the Yetis of the Himalayas. ³In North America, many people, including normally skeptical citizens and scientists, are fascinated by stories of Sasquatch. ⁴A name originating in the Salish word *saskehavas.* ⁵Another name commonly used is Big Foot. ⁶An allusion to the size of the footprints reportedly belonging to a giant apelike creature. ⁷That smells bad. ⁸Most sightings of Sasquatch occur in the Pacific Northwest. ⁹From northern California to central Alaska. ¹⁰Although reports have come from almost every state. ¹¹During the settlement of the United States, stories of hairy ape-men were told by Native Americans. ¹²And later on by trappers. ¹³Teddy Roosevelt recorded one such story.

3

Comma Splices and Fused Sentences

Comma splices and fused sentences are sentence-level mistakes resulting from incorrect or missing punctuation. Both are punctuated as one sentence when they should be punctuated as two sentences (or two independent clauses). By revising comma splices and fused sentences, you indicate sentence boundaries and thus make your writing easier to read. This chapter will help you

- review the rules for punctuating independent clauses (**3a**),
- recognize comma splices and fused sentences (**3b**), and
- learn ways to revise them (**3c** and **3d**).

A **comma splice,** or **comma fault,** refers to the incorrect use of a comma between two independent clauses (**14a**).

Most stockholders favored the merger,ᴧthe management did not.
                                  but

Because a comma is a weak mark of punctuation, it is not conventionally used to join independent clauses. For this purpose, you should use a connecting word, a stronger mark of punctuation, or both.

A **fused sentence** consists of two independent clauses run together without any punctuation at all. This type of sentence is sometimes called a **run-on sentence.**

The first section of the proposal was approvedᴧthe budget will
                                          ; however,
have to be resubmitted.

To revise a fused sentence, include appropriate punctuation and any necessary connecting words.

3a   Punctuating independent clauses

In case you are unfamiliar with or unsure about the conventions for punctuating independent clauses, here is a short review.

A comma and a coordinating conjunction can join two independent clauses (**12a**). The coordinating conjunction indicates the relationship between the two clauses. For example, *and* signals addition, whereas *but* and *yet* signal contrast. The comma precedes the conjunction.

INDEPENDENT CLAUSE**, and** INDEPENDENT CLAUSE

The new store opened this morning**, and** the owners greeted everyone at the door.

A semicolon can join two independent clauses that are closely related. A semicolon generally signals addition or contrast.

INDEPENDENT CLAUSE**;** INDEPENDENT CLAUSE

One of the owners comes from this area**;** the other grew up in Cuba.

A semicolon may also precede an independent clause that begins with a conjunctive adverb such as *however* or *nevertheless*. Notice that a comma follows this type of connecting word.

The store will be open late on Fridays and Saturdays**; however,** it will be closed all day on Sundays.

PUNCTUATION IN SENTENCES CONTAINING CONJUNCTIVE ADVERBS

A comma used to set off a conjunctive adverb is sometimes omitted when there is no risk of misreading.

> The sea was unusually hot; **thus** the coral turned white.
> [No misreading is possible, so the comma can be omitted.]
>
> He was so nervous that his stomach was churning; **however,** he answered the question calmly and accurately.
> [The comma is needed. Without it, *however* might be interpreted as meaning "in whatever way" rather than "in contrast." COMPARE: However he answered the question, he would offend someone.]

A colon can join two independent clauses. The second clause usually explains or elaborates the first.

INDEPENDENT CLAUSE: INDEPENDENT CLAUSE

The owners have extended a special offer: anyone who makes a purchase during the opening will receive a 10 percent discount.

If you are following MLA guidelines, capitalize the first word of a clause following a colon when the clause expresses a rule or principle (**17d**).

A period separates clauses into distinct sentences.

INDEPENDENT CLAUSE. INDEPENDENT CLAUSE

The store is located on the corner of Pine Street and First Avenue. It was formerly an insurance office.

Occasionally, commas are used between independent clauses, but only when the clauses are short, parallel in form, and unified in meaning.

They came, they shopped, they left.

For more information on punctuating sentences, see chapters **12**, **14**, and **17**.

3b Recognizing comma splices and fused sentences

If you have trouble recognizing comma splices or fused sentences, try one of the following methods.

TWO METHODS FOR IDENTIFYING COMMA SPLICES AND FUSED SENTENCES

---

1. Locate a sentence that may be problematic. Put it into this frame sentence:

    They do not understand the idea that _____.

    Only complete sentences make sense when placed in the frame sentence. If just part of a test sentence fits, you have probably located a comma splice or a fused sentence.

    Test sentence 1: Plasma is the fourth state of matter.

    Test: They do not understand the idea that *plasma is the fourth state of matter.*
    [The test sentence makes sense in the frame sentence. No revision is necessary.]

    Test sentence 2: Plasma is the fourth state of matter, some scientists believe that 99 percent of the universe is made of it.

    Test: They do not understand the idea that *plasma is the fourth state of matter, some scientists believe that 99 percent of the universe is made of it.*

[The frame sentence does not make sense because there are two sentences completing it, rather than one. The test sentence contains a comma splice and thus should be revised.]

Revision: Plasma is the fourth state of matter. Some scientists believe that 99 percent of the universe is made of it.

2. Try to rewrite a possibly incorrect sentence as a question that can be answered with *yes* or *no*. If just part of the sentence makes sense, you have likely found a comma splice or a fused sentence.

Test sentence 3: Plasma is used for a number of purposes.

Test: *Is plasma used for a number of purposes?*
[The question makes sense. No revision is necessary.]

Test sentence 4: Plasma is used for a number of purposes it may even power rockets someday.

Test: *Is plasma used for a number of purposes it may even power rockets someday?*

[The question does not make sense because only one part of the test sentence has been made into a question. The test sentence is a fused sentence and thus should be revised.]

Revision: Plasma is used for a number of purposes. It may even power rockets someday.

You can also find comma splices and fused sentences by re-membering that they commonly occur in certain circumstances.

- With transitional words and phrases such as *however, therefore,* and *for example* (see also 3c(5))

  Comma splice: The director is not able to meet with you this week, however, next week she will have time on Monday and Tuesday.

  [Notice that a semicolon replaces the comma.]

- When an explanation or an example is given in the second sentence

  Fused sentence: The cultural center has a new collection of spear points, ~~many~~ of them were donated by a retired anthropologist.

  . Many (correction above "points, many")

- When a positive clause follows a negative clause, or vice versa

  Comma splice: A World Cup victory is not just an everyday sporting event, ~~it~~ is a national celebration.

  . It (correction above "event, it")

- When the subject of the second clause is a pronoun whose antecedent is in the preceding clause

  Fused sentence: Lake Baikal is located in southern Russia, ~~it~~ is 394 miles long.

  . It (correction above "Russia, it")

3c   Revising comma splices and fused sentences

If you find comma splices or fused sentences in your writing, try one of the following methods to revise them.

(1) Use a comma and a coordinating conjunction to link clauses.

By linking clauses with a comma and a coordinating conjunction (such as *and* or *but*), you signal the relationship between the clauses (addition or contrast, for example).

Fused sentence: Joseph completed the first experiment, *and* he will complete the other by Friday.

Comma splice: Some diplomats applauded the treaty, *but* others opposed it vehemently.

(2) Use a semicolon or a colon to link clauses or a period to separate them.

When you link independent clauses with a semicolon, you signal their connection indirectly. There are no explicit conjunctions to use as cues. The semicolon usually indicates addition or contrast. When you link clauses with a colon, the second clause serves as an explanation or an elaboration of the first. A period indicates that each clause is a complete sentence, distinct from surrounding sentences.

> **Comma splice**: Our division's reports are posted on our Web page, hard copies are available by request.

> **Revision 1**: Our division's reports are posted on our Web page; hard copies are available by request.

> **Revision 2**: Our division's reports are posted on our Web page. Hard copies are available by request.

> **Fused sentence:** His choice was difficult, he would either lose his job or betray his ethical principles.

(3) Rewrite one clause as a phrase or as a dependent clause.

A dependent clause (**1f(2)**) includes a subordinating conjunction such as *although* or *because,* which indicates how the dependent and independent clauses are related (in a cause-and-effect relationship, for example). A prepositional phrase (**1e(4)**) includes a preposition such as *in, on, because of,* or *in spite of* that may also signal relationships directly. Verbal, appositive, and absolute phrases (**1e(3)**, **1e(5)**, and **1e(6)**) suggest relationships less directly because they do not include connecting words.

> **Comma splice**: The wind had blown down trees and power lines, the whole city was without electricity for several hours.

> **Revision 1: Because the wind had blown down power lines,** the whole city was without electricity for several hours. [dependent clause]

Revision 2: **Because of the downed power lines,** the whole city was without electricity for several hours. [prepositional phrase]

Revision 3: **The wind having blown down power lines,** the whole city was without electricity for several hours. [absolute phrase]

(4) Integrate one clause into the other.

When you integrate clauses, you will generally retain the important details but omit or change some words.

Fused sentence: The proposal covers all but one point it does not describe how the project will be assessed.

Revision: The proposal covers all the points except assessment procedures.

Exercise 1

Connect each pair of sentences in two of the following ways: (a) join them with a semicolon or colon, (b) join them with a coordinating conjunction, (c) reduce one sentence to a phrase or a dependent clause (see 1g(3) for a list of subordinating conjunctions), or (d) integrate one clause into the other.

1. Our national parks offer a variety of settings. They attract millions of visitors every year.
2. The Grand Teton National Park includes a sixteen-peak mountain range. It offers extensive hiking trails and wildlife-viewing opportunities.
3. Yellowstone National Park is generally full of tourists. The geysers and cliffs are worth the visit.
4. Hikers especially enjoy their vacations at Yellowstone National Park. The park consists of two million acres of backcountry perfect for hiking.
5. Vacationers enchanted by cascading water should visit Yosemite National Park. The waterfalls at Yosemite reach heights of more than two thousand feet.

(5) Use transitional words or phrases to link independent clauses.

Another way to revise comma splices and fused sentences is to ~~use tra~~nsitional words and phrases such as *however, on the contrary,* ~~and in~~ *the meantime.* (For more examples, see the list on page 44.) ~~You ca~~n use these words and phrases to begin new sentences.

Fused sentence: Sexual harassment is not just an issue for

women $\wedge$ men can be sexually harassed too.
. After all,

You can also use them to join two clauses into one sentence.

Comma splice: The word *status* refers to relative position

within a group $\wedge$ it is often used to indicate only positions of
; however,

prestige.

If you have questions about punctuating sentences with transitional words and phrases, see **1g(4)** and **14a**.

As you edit fused sentences and comma splices, you will refine the connections between your sentences and thereby help your readers follow your train of thought. The following checklist will help you find and fix comma splices and fused sentences.

CHECKLIST for Comma Splices and Fused Sentences

1. Common Sites for Comma Splices or Fused Sentences

- With transitional words such as *however* and *therefore*
- When an explanation or an example occurs in the second clause
- When a positive clause follows a negative clause, or vice versa
- When the subject of the second clause is a pronoun whose antecedent is in the first clause

(Continued on page 72)

(Continued from page 71)

2. How to Fix Comma Splices and Fused Sentences

- Link the clauses with a comma and a coordinating conjunction.
- Link the clauses, using a semicolon or a colon.
- Separate the clauses by punctuating each as a sentence.
- Make one clause dependent.
- Reduce one clause to a phrase.
- Rewrite the sentence, integrating one clause into the other.

Exercise 2

Connect each pair of sentences by including a transitional word or phrase and any necessary punctuation.

1. The average human brain weighs about three pounds. The average brain of a sperm whale weighs seventeen pounds.
2. The body of a brain cell can move. Most brain cells stay put, extending axons outward.
3. The brain needs water to function properly. Dehydration commonly leads to lethargy and hinders learning.
4. Researchers studying brain hemispheres have found that many professional musicians process music in their left hemisphere. The notion that musicians and artists depend on the right side of their brain is considered outmoded.
5. Discoveries in neuroscience have yielded many benefits. Researchers have developed medication for schizophrenia and Tourette's syndrome.

3d Divided quotations

When you divide quotations with attributive tags such as *he said* or *she asked* (chapter **16** and **39d**), be sure to use a period between independent clauses.

Comma splice: "Beauty brings copies of itself into being,"

states Elaine Scarry, "it makes us draw it, take photographs of
      . "It
       ∧

it, or describe it to other people."

[Both parts of the quotation are complete sentences, so the attributive tag is attached to the first, and the sentence is punctuated with a period. The second sentence stands by itself.]

A comma separates two parts of a single quoted sentence.

"Musing takes place in a kind of meadowlands of the imagination," writes Rebecca Solnit, "a part of the imagination that has not yet been plowed, developed, or put to any immediately practical use."
[Because the quotation is a single sentence, a comma is used.]

Exercise 3

Revise each comma splice or fused sentence in the following paragraph. Some sentences may not need revision.

¹In the introduction to his book of true stories, *I Thought My Father Was God,* Paul Auster describes how he was able to collect these accounts of real and sometimes raw experience. ²In October 1999, Auster, in collaboration with National Public Radio, began the *National Story Project,* during an interview on the radio program *Weekend All Things Considered,* he invited listeners to send in their stories about unusual events—"true stories that sounded like fiction." ³In just one year, over four thousand stories were submitted Auster read every one of them. ⁴"Of the four thousand stories I have read, most have been compelling enough to hold me until the last word," Auster affirms, "most have been written with simple, straightforward conviction, and most have done honor to the people who sent them in." ⁵Some of the stories Auster collected can now be read in his anthology choosing stories for the collection was difficult, though. ⁶"For every story about a dream or an animal or a missing object," explains Auster, "there were dozens of others that were submitted, dozens of others that could have been chosen."

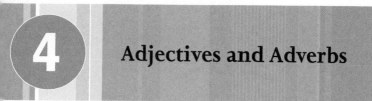

4 Adjectives and Adverbs

Modifiers are words, phrases, or clauses that modify; that is, they qualify or limit the meaning of other words. For example, if you were to describe a sandwich as "humdrum," as "lacking sufficient mustard," or as something "that might have tasted good two days ago," you would be using a word, a phrase, or a clause to modify *sandwich*. When used effectively, modifiers enliven writing with details and enhance its coherence.

This chapter will help you

- recognize modifiers (4a),
- use conventional comparative and superlative forms (4b),
- place modifiers effectively (4c), and
- revise double negatives (4d).

4a Recognizing modifiers

The most common modifiers are adjectives and adverbs. **Adjectives** modify nouns and pronouns (1a(4)); **adverbs** modify verbs, adjectives, and other adverbs (1a(5)). You can distinguish an adjective from an adverb, then, by determining what type of word is modified.

Adjective	**Adverb**
She looked **curious.** [modifies pronoun]	She looked at me **curiously.** [modifies verb]

Adjectives	Adverbs
productive meeting [modifies noun]	**highly** productive meeting [modifies adjective]
a **quick** lunch [modifies noun]	**very** quickly [modifies adverb]

In addition, consider the form of the modifier. Many adjectives end with one of these suffixes: *-able, -al, -ful, -ic, -ish, -less,* or *-y.*

accept**able**　rent**al**　event**ful**　angel**ic**　sheep**ish**　effort**less**　sleep**y**

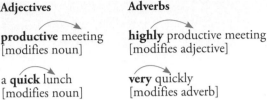

THINKING RHETORICALLY

ADJECTIVES

When your rhetorical situation calls for vivid images or emotional intensity, choose appropriate adjectives to convey these qualities. That is, instead of describing a movie you did not like with the overused adjective *boring*, you could say that it was *tedious* or *mind-numbing*. When you sense that you might be using a lackluster adjective, search for an alternative in a thesaurus. If any of the words listed there are unfamiliar, be sure to look them up in a dictionary so that you use them correctly.

Present and past participles (7a(5)) can also be used as adjectives.

a **determining** factor	a **determined** effort
[present participle]	[past participle]

Be sure to include the complete *-ed* ending of a past participle.

　　　　　　enclosed
Please see the ⌃enclose documents for more details.

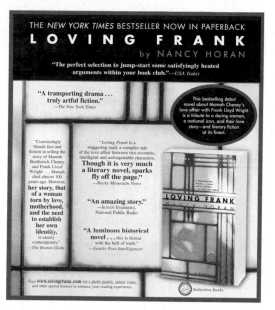

Book ads often include descriptive adjectives.

MULTILINGUAL WRITERS

USING PARTICIPLES AS ADJECTIVES

Both present participles and past participles are used as adjectives; however, they cannot be used interchangeably. For example, when you want to indicate an emotion, use a present participle with a noun referring to someone or something that is the cause of the emotion. In the phrase *the exciting tennis match,* the tennis match is the cause of the excitement. Use the past participle with a noun referring to someone who experiences an emotion. In the phrase *the excited crowd,* the crowd is experiencing the excitement.

(Continued on page 78)

(Continued from page 77)

Here is a list of commonly confused participles:

annoying, annoyed	frustrating, frustrated
boring, bored	interesting, interested
confusing, confused	surprising, surprised
embarrassing, embarrassed	tiring, tired

The easiest type of adverb to identify is the adverb of manner (**1a(5)**). It is formed by adding -*ly* to an adjective.

careful**ly**   unpleasant**ly**   silent**ly**

If the adjective ends in -*y*, the -*y* is changed to -*i* before -*ly* is added.

eas**y** [adjective]   eas**ily** [adverb]

If the adjective ends in -*le*, the -*e* is dropped and just *y* is added.

simp**le** [adjective]   simp**ly** [adverb]

However, not all words ending in -*ly* are adverbs. Certain adjectives related to nouns also end in -*ly* (*friend, friendly; hour, hourly*). In addition, not all adverbs end in -*ly*. Adverbs that indicate time or place (*today, tomorrow, here,* and *there*) do not have the -*ly* ending. Neither does the negator *not*. A few words—for example, *fast* and *well*—can function as either adjectives or adverbs.

They like **fast** cars. [adjective]

They ran **fast** enough to catch the bus. [adverb]

(1) Nouns can be modifiers.

Adjectives and adverbs are the most common modifiers, but nouns (**1a(2)**) can also be modifiers (***movie*** *critic,* ***reference*** *manual*).

MULTILINGUAL WRITERS

NOUN MODIFIERS

In noun combinations, the first noun is the modifier. Different orders produce different meanings.

A *company phone* is a phone that belongs to a company.

A *phone company* is a company that sells phones or provides phone service.

(2) Phrases and clauses can be modifiers.

Participial phrases, prepositional phrases, and some infinitive phrases are modifiers (**1e(3)** and **1e(4)**).

Growing in popularity every year, mountain bikes now dominate the market. [participial phrase]

Mountain bikes first became popular **in the 1980s.** [prepositional phrase]

Some people use mountain bikes **to commute to work.** [infinitive phrase]

Adjectival (relative) clauses and adverbial clauses are both modifiers (see **1f(2)**).

BMX bicycles have frames **that are relatively small.** [adjectival clause]

Although mountain bikes are designed for off-road use, many people use them on city streets. [adverbial clause]

Exercise 1

Underline the modifiers in the following paragraph.

[1]Although it seems unbelievable, there once was a race of little people. [2]The first skeleton of *Homo floresiensis* was found in September 2003 on an island near Bali. [3]Archaeologists working in the area excavated the skeleton from a limestone cave. [4]Some believe that this species of human is a version of *Homo erectus*, who arrived on the island and became small to adapt to its conditions.

(3) Adjectives and adverbs are sometimes confused.

An adjective used after a sensory linking verb (*look, smell, taste, sound,* or *feel*) modifies the subject of the sentence (**1b**). A common error is to use an adverb after this type of linking verb.

I felt ̶b̶a̶d̶l̶y̶ _bad_ about missing the rally. [The adjective *bad* modifies *I*.]

However, when *look, smell, taste, sound,* or *feel* is used as an action verb (**1a(1)**), it can be modified by an adverb.

She looked **angrily** at the referee. [The adverb *angrily* modifies *looked*.]

BUT She looked **angry.** [The adjective *angry* modifies *she*.]

The words *good* and *well* are easy to confuse. In academic rhetorical situations, *good* is considered an adjective and so is not used with action verbs.

The whole team played ̶g̶o̶o̶d̶ _well_.

Another frequent error is the dropping of *-ly* endings from adverbs. Although you may not hear the ending when you speak, be sure to include it when you write.

They bought only ~~local~~ grown vegetables.
(locally)

Exercise 2

Revise the following sentences to use adjectives and adverbs considered conventional in academic writing.

1. My brother said he was real nervous.
2. He did not think he could drive good enough to pass the driver's test.
3. I told him that to pass he would have to drive just reasonable well.
4. He looked calmly as he got into the tester's car.
5. As I knew he would, my brother passed his test easy.

4b Comparatives and superlatives

Many adjectives and adverbs change form to show degrees of quality, quantity, time, distance, manner, and so on. The **positive form** of an adjective or adverb is the word you would look for in a dictionary: *hard, urgent, deserving*. The **comparative form,** which either ends in *-er* or is preceded by *more* or *less*, compares two elements: *I worked **harder** than I ever had before.* The **superlative form,** which either ends in *-est* or is preceded by *most* or *least*, compares three or more elements: *Jeff is the **hardest** worker I have ever met.*

Positive	Comparative	Superlative
hard	harder	hardest
urgent	more/less urgent	most/least urgent
deserving	more/less deserving	most/least deserving

The following guidelines can help you decide when to add the suffix *-er* or *-est* and when to use *more/less* or *most/least*.

GUIDELINES FOR FORMING COMPARATIVES AND SUPERLATIVES

- One-syllable words generally take the ending *-er* or *-est*: *fast, faster, fastest*.

- Two-syllable words ending in a consonant and *-y* also generally take the ending *-er* or *-est*, with the *y* changed to an *i*: *noisy, noisier, noisiest*.

- Two-syllable adjectives ending in *-ct, -nt,* or *-st* are preceded by *more/less* or *most/least*: *less exact, least exact; more recent, most recent; more honest, most honest*. Two-syllable adjectives with suffixes such as *-ous, -ish, -ful, -ing,* and *-ed* are also preceded by *more/less* or *most/least*: *more/most famous, more/most squeamish, less/least careful, more/most lasting, less/least depressed*.

- Two-syllable adjectives ending in *-er, -ow,* or *-some* take either *-er/-est* or a preceding qualifier: *narrower, more narrow, less narrow, narrowest, most narrow, least narrow*.

- Words of three or more syllables are preceded by *more/less* or *most/least*: *less/least fortunate, more/most elegantly*.

- Some modifiers have irregular comparative and superlative forms:

little, less, least	*bad/badly, worse, worst*
good/well, better, best	*far, further/farther, furthest/farthest*

(See the Glossary of Usage.)

(1) Effective comparisons are complete and logical.

When you use the comparative form of an adjective or an adverb, be sure to indicate what two elements you are comparing. The revision of the following sentence makes it clear that a diesel engine and a gas engine are being compared.

A diesel engine is **heavier**~~than a gas engine~~.

Occasionally, the second element in a comparison is implied. The word *paper* does not have to be included after *second* in the sentence below. The reader can infer that the grade on the second paper was better than the grade on the first paper.

She wrote **two** papers; the instructor gave her a **better** grade on the second.

A comparison should also be logical. The following example illogically compares *population* and *Wabasha*.

The **population** of Winona is larger than **Wabasha**.

You can revise this type of faulty comparison in three ways:

- Repeat the word that refers to what is being compared.

  The **population** of Winona is larger than the **population** of Wabasha.

- Use a pronoun that corresponds to the first element in the comparison.

  The **population** of Winona is larger than **that** of Wabasha.

- Use possessive forms.

  Winona's population is larger than **Wabasha's**.

(2) A double comparative or superlative is redundant.

Use either an ending (*-er* or *-est*) or a preceding qualifier (*more* or *most*), not both, to form a comparative or superlative.

The first bridge is **more narrower** than the second.

The ~~most~~ **narrowest** bridge is in the northern part of the state.

Comparative and superlative forms of adjectives or adverbs that generally have absolute meanings, as in *a more perfect society, the most unique campus* (see the **Glossary of Usage**), and *less completely exhausted,* are rarely used in academic writing.

Exercise 3

Provide the correct comparative or superlative form of each modifier within parentheses.

1. Amphibians can be divided into three groups. Frogs and toads are in the (common) group.
2. Because they do not have to maintain a specific body temperature, amphibians eat (frequently) than mammals do.
3. Reptiles may look like amphibians, but their skin is (dry).
4. During the Devonian period, the (close) ancestors of amphibians were fish with fins that looked like legs.
5. In general, amphibians have (few) bones in their skeletons than other animals with backbones have.
6. Color markings on amphibians vary, though the back of an amphibian is usually (dark) than its belly.

4c   Double negatives

The term **double negative** refers to the use of two negative words—often modifiers—to express a single negation. Unless you are portraying dialogue, revise any double negatives you find in your writing.

He did**n't** keep any ~~no~~ records.

OR

He ~~didn't keep~~ **no** records.
_{kept}

Because *hardly, barely,* and *scarcely* denote severely limited or negative conditions, using *not* or *nothing* with any of these modifiers creates a double negative. The following example shows how a sentence containing a double negative can be revised:

I could**n't** **hardly** quit in the middle of the job.

OR

I could**n't** ~~hardly~~ quit in the middle of the job.

MULTILINGUAL WRITERS

NEGATION IN OTHER LANGUAGES

The use of two negative words in one sentence is common in languages such as Spanish:

*Yo **no** compré **nada**.* ["I didn't buy anything."]

If your native language allows this type of negation, be especially careful to check for and revise any double negatives you find in your English essays.

5   Pronouns and Case

When you use pronouns effectively, you add clarity and coherence to your writing. However, if you do not provide the words, phrases, or clauses that make the pronoun reference clear, you might unintentionally cause confusion. This chapter will help you

- recognize various types of pronouns (**5a**) and
- use appropriate pronouns (**5b**).

5a   Recognizing pronouns

A **pronoun** is commonly defined as a word used in place of a noun that has already been mentioned.

John said **he** would guide the trip.

A pronoun may also substitute for a group of words acting as a noun (see **1f(2)**).

The participant with the most experience said **he** would guide the trip.

Most pronouns refer to nouns, but some modify nouns.

This man is our guide.

The following sections introduce several types of pronouns: personal pronouns, reflexive/intensive pronouns, relative pronouns, interrogative pronouns, demonstrative pronouns, and indefinite pronouns.

(1) Personal pronouns are identified according to person, number, and case.

To understand the uses of personal pronouns, you must first be able to recognize person, number, and case. **Person** indicates whether a pronoun refers to the writer (**first person**), to the reader (**second person**), or to another person, place, thing, or idea (**third person**). **Number** reveals whether a pronoun is singular or plural. **Case** refers to the form a pronoun takes depending on its function in a sentence. Pronouns can be subjects, objects, or possessives. When they function as subjects (**1b(1)**) they are in the subjective case; when they function as objects (**1c(1)**), they are in the objective case; and when they are possessives, they are in the possessive case (see **5b** for more information on case). Possessives can be divided into two groups based on whether they are followed by nouns. *My, your, his, her, its, our,* and *their* are all followed by nouns; *mine, yours, his, hers, ours,* and *theirs* are not.

Their budget is higher than **ours.**
[*Their* is followed by a noun; *ours* is not.]

CASE:	Subjective		Objective		Possessive	
NUMBER:	Singular	Plural	Singular	Plural	Singular	Plural
First person	I	we	me	us	my mine	our ours
Second person	you	you	you	you	your yours	your yours
Third person	he, she, it	they	him, her, it	them	his, her, hers, its	their theirs

THINKING RHETORICALLY

PRONOUNS

As you write, choose pronouns appropriate for your rhetorical situation. In some situations, you will be expected to use *I*; in others, you will not. In some situations, you will address the reader as *you* (as is done in this handbook), but in others, you will avoid addressing the reader directly. Whatever pronouns you decide to use, be sure to use them consistently.

First, ~~one~~ you must determine **your** priorities.

OR

First, **one** must determine **one's** priorities.

(2) Reflexive pronouns direct the action back to the subject; intensive pronouns are used for emphasis.

Myself, yourself, himself, herself, itself, ourselves, yourselves, and *themselves* are used as either **reflexive pronouns** or **intensive pronouns.** Both types of pronouns are objects and must be accompanied by subjects. Reflexive pronouns are used when the actor and the recipient of the action are the same. Intensive pronouns are used to provide emphasis.

Reflexive pronoun	**He** was always talking to **himself.**
Intensive pronoun	**I, myself,** delivered the letter.

Avoid using a reflexive pronoun as a subject. A common error is using *myself* in a compound subject.

Ms. Palmquist and ~~myself~~ I discussed our concern with the senator.

Hisself, themself, and *theirselves* are inappropriate in college or professional writing. Instead, use *himself* and *themselves.*

The young researchers worked by ~~theirselves~~ themselves.

(3) A relative pronoun introduces a dependent clause functioning as an adjective.

An adjectival clause (or relative clause) ordinarily begins with a relative pronoun: *who, whom, which, that,* or *whose*. To provide a link between this type of dependent clause and the main clause, the relative pronoun corresponds to a word or words in the main clause called the **antecedent.**

The students talked to **a reporter who** had just returned from overseas.

Notice that if you rewrite the dependent clause as a separate independent clause, you use the antecedent in place of the relative pronoun.

A reporter had just returned from overseas.

Who, whose, and *whom* ordinarily refer to people; *which* refers to things; *that* refers to things and, in some contexts, people. The possessive *whose* (used in place of the awkward *of which*) usually refers to people but sometimes refers to things.

The poem, **whose** author is unknown, has recently been set to music.

	Refers to people	Refers to things	Refers to either
Subjective	who	which	that
Objective	whom	which	that
Possessive			whose

Knowing the difference between an essential clause and a nonessential clause will help you decide whether to use *which* or *that*. A clause that a reader needs in order to identify the antecedent correctly is an **essential clause.**

    ant   *ess cl*

The person who presented the award was last year's winner.

If the essential clause were omitted from this sentence, the reader would not know which person was last year's winner.

A **nonessential clause** is *not* needed for correct identification of the antecedent and is thus set off by commas. A nonessential clause often follows a proper noun (a specific name).

     ant   *noness cl*

Andrea Bowen, who presented the award, was last year's winner.

Notice that if the nonessential clause were removed from this sentence, the reader would still know the identity of last year's winner.

According to a traditional grammar rule, *that* is used in essential adjectival clauses, and *which* is used in nonessential adjectival clauses.

I need a job **that** pays well.

I took a job, **which** pays well enough.

However, some professional writers do not follow both parts of this rule. Although they will not use *that* in nonessential clauses, they will use *which* in essential clauses. Nonetheless, if you are following APA guidelines, use *which* only in nonessential clauses.

(4) Interrogative pronouns introduce questions.

The **interrogative pronouns** *what, which, who, whom,* and *whose* are question words. Be careful not to confuse *who* and *whom* (see **5b(5)**). *Who* functions as a subject; *whom* functions as an object.

Who won the award? [COMPARE: **He** won the award.]

Whom did you see? [COMPARE: I saw **him**.]

(5) Demonstrative pronouns provide information about distance in time, space, or thought.
The **demonstrative pronouns** *this* and *these* indicate that someone or something is close by in time, space, or thought. *That* and *those* signal remoteness.

These are important documents; **those** can be thrown away.

Demonstrative pronouns sometimes modify nouns.

These documents should be filed.

(6) Indefinite pronouns are generally nonspecific.
Indefinite pronouns usually do not refer to specific persons, objects, ideas, or events.

anyone	anybody	anything
everyone	everybody	everything
someone	somebody	something
no one	nobody	nothing
each	either	neither

Many indefinite pronouns differ from personal pronouns in that they do not refer to an antecedent. In fact, some indefinite pronouns *serve* as antecedents (see **6b(1)**).

Someone forgot **her** purse.

5b   **Pronoun case**

The term *case* refers to the form a pronoun takes to indicate its relationship to other words in a sentence. There are three cases: subjective, objective, and possessive. The following sentence includes all three.

He [subjective] wants **his** [possessive] legislators to help **him** [objective].

(1) Pronouns in the subject or subject complement position are in the subjective case.

A pronoun that is the subject of a sentence, even when it is part of a compound subject (**1b**), is in the subjective case. To determine which pronoun form is correct in a compound subject, say the sentence using the pronoun alone, omitting the noun. For the following sentence, notice that "*Me* solved the problem" sounds strange, but "*I* solved the problem" sounds fine.

~~Me and~~ Marisa ^*and I* solved the problem.

In addition, remember that when you use the pronoun *I* in a compound subject, you should place it last in the sequence. If the compound subject contains two pronouns, test each one by itself to ensure that you are using the appropriate case.

^*He* ~~Him~~ and I joined the club in July.

A subject complement renames the subject (see **1c**). Pronouns functioning as subject complements should also be in the subjective case.

The first to arrive were Kevin and ^*I* ~~me~~.

NOUN OR PRONOUN AS SUBJECT

In some languages, a noun in the subject position may be followed by a pronoun. In Standardized English, though, such a pronoun should be omitted.

My roommate ~~he~~ works in the library for three hours a week.

(2) Pronouns functioning as objects are in the objective case.
Whenever a pronoun is an object—a direct object (**1c(1)**), an indirect object (**1c(2)**), or the object of a preposition (**1e(4)**)—it takes the **objective case**.

Direct object	The whole staff admired **him**.
Indirect object	The staff sent **him** a card.
Object of a preposition	The staff depended on **him**.

Pronouns in compound objects are also in the objective case.

They will appoint you or _∧I͟. [direct object]
me

They lent Tom and _∧I͟ money for tuition. [indirect object]
me

He gets nowhere by scolding Jane or _∧I͟. [direct object of the gerund]
me

Dad wanted Sheila and _∧I͟ to keep the old car. [direct object of the sentence]
me

Janice sat between my brother and _∧I͟. [object of the preposition]
me

To determine whether to use the subjective or objective case, remember to say the sentence with just the pronoun. Notice that "Dad wanted *I* to keep the old car" does not sound right. Another test is to substitute *we* and *us*. If *we* sounds natural, use the subjective case. If *us* sounds better, use the objective case, as in "Dad wanted *us* to keep the old car."

(3) Possessive forms are easily confused with contractions.

Its, their, and *whose* are possessive forms. Be sure not to confuse them with common contractions: *it's* (*it is*), *they're* (*they are*), and *who's* (*who is*).

(4) Appositive pronouns are in the same case as the nouns they rename.

If the noun that an appositive pronoun renames is in the subjective case, the appositive pronoun should be in the subjective case (**5a(1)**).

> The red team—Rebecca, Leroy, and ~~me~~ I —won by only one point.

Likewise, if the noun is in the objective case, the appositive pronoun should be in the objective case.

> A trophy was presented to the red team—Rebecca, Leroy, and ~~I~~ me.

When the order is reversed and a pronoun is followed by a noun, the pronoun must still be in the same case as the noun.

> ~~Us~~ We students need this policy.

> The director told ~~we~~ us extras to go home.

To test the case of a pronoun that is followed by an appositive, remove the appositive.

We need this policy.

The director told **us** to go home.

Exercise 1

Revise the following paragraph, using appropriate pronouns. Some sentences may not require editing.

> [1]When I was twelve, my family lived in Guatemala for a year. [2]My parents taught English at a university; me and my younger brother went to a local school. [3]Although the Spanish language was new to both Sam and I, we learned to speak it quickly. [4]At first, we couldn't understand much at all, but with the help of a tutor, who we met every day after school, we started learning "survival" Spanish. [5]Sam had better pronunciation than me, but I learned vocabulary and grammar faster than him. [6]After we learned to ask and answer some basic questions, we started making friends, whom eventually introduced us to they're own version of Spanish. [7]They taught us slang words that our tutor didn't even know. [8]However, though Sam and me benefited from all our Spanish lessons, we learned the language so quickly because, unless we were with our parents or by ourself, we listened to it, read it, wrote it, and spoke it all day long.

(5) Who/whoever and whom/whomever are often misused.

To choose between *who* and *whom* or between *whoever* and *whomever,* you must first determine whether the word is functioning as a subject (**1b**) or an object (**1c**). A pronoun functioning as the subject takes the subjective case.

Who won the award? [COMPARE: **She** won the award.]

The teachers know **who** won the award.

The student **who** won the award was quite surprised.

Whoever won the award deserves it.

When the pronoun is an object, use *whom* or *whomever*.

Whom did they hire? [COMPARE: They hired **him**.]

I do not know **whom** they hired.

The student **whom** they hired graduated in May.

Whomever they hired will have to work hard this year.

Whom may be omitted in sentences when no misunderstanding would result.

The friend he relied on moved away.
[*Whom* has been omitted after *friend*.]

Exercise 2

Following the guidelines for college and professional writing, choose the pronouns that appropriately complete the following sentences.

1. Separate the white chess pieces from the black pieces and decide (who/whom) will play with the white pieces.
2. The opening move is made by (whoever/whomever) has received the white game pieces.
3. (Whoever/Whomever) the black pieces were given to makes the next move.
4. The player (who/whom) can put the other player's king in check is close to becoming the winner.
5. (Whoever/Whomever) is unable to free his or her king must concede the game.

(6) Object pronouns precede and follow infinitives; possessive pronouns precede gerunds.

A pronoun grouped with an infinitive, either as its subject or as its object, takes the objective case.

The director wanted **me** to help **him.** [*Me* is the subject of the infinitive; *him* is the object.]

A gerund (*-ing* verb form functioning as a noun) is preceded by a possessive pronoun.

I appreciated **his** helping Denise. [COMPARE: I appreciated **Tom's** helping Denise.]

Notice that a possessive pronoun is used before a gerund but not before a present participle (*-ing* verb form functioning as an adjective).

I saw **him** helping Luke.

(7) The case of a pronoun in an elliptical construction depends on what has been omitted.

The words *as* and *than* frequently introduce **elliptical constructions**—clauses in which the writer has intentionally omitted words. To check whether you have used the correct case in an elliptical construction, read the written sentence aloud, inserting any words that have been omitted from it.

She admires Clarice as much as **I.** [subjective case]
Read aloud: She admires Clarice as much as *I do.*

She admires Clarice more than **I.** [subjective case]
Read aloud: She admires Clarice more than *I do.*

She admires Clarice more than **me.** [objective case]
Read aloud: She admires Clarice more than *she admires me.*

Exercise 3

Correct the pronoun errors in the following sentences. Some sentences may not require editing.

1. The board of directors has asked you and I to conduct a customer survey.
2. They also recommended us hiring someone with extensive experience in statistical analysis.
3. You understand statistics better than me.
4. Although the board asked me to be in charge, I would like you to recruit and interview candidates.
5. The directors recognize your expertise and will surely approve of you taking the lead.

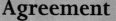

6 Agreement

Hearing the word *agree,* you might think of accord between two people. Perhaps they like the same kinds of movies or support the same political candidates. Grammatical agreement is also about sameness, but in this case, the sameness involves number (singular or plural), person (first, second, or third), or gender (masculine, feminine, or neuter). This chapter will help you ensure that your sentences include agreement

- between subjects and verbs (6a) and
- between pronouns and antecedents (6b).

6a Subject-verb agreement

A verb agrees with its subject in number. That is, when a subject is plural, the verb takes a plural form; when the subject is singular, the verb takes a singular form. The subject and verb also agree in person (5a(1)). First-person subjects require first-person verb forms, second-person subjects require second-person verb forms, and third-person subjects require third-person verb forms. Notice in the following examples that the singular third-person subject takes a singular verb (-*s* form) and that the plural third-person subject takes a plural verb (base form). (To learn more about verb forms, see chapter 7.)

Singular	The **car** in the lot **looks** new. [*Car* and *looks* are both singular.]
Plural	The **cars** in the lot **look** new. [*Cars* and *look* are both plural.]

You can refer to the following subsections for guidance on ensuring subject-verb agreement in particular situations:

- when words come between the subject and the verb (**6a(1)**),
- when two or more subjects are joined by conjunctions (**6a(2)** and **6a(3)**),
- when word order is inverted (**6a(4)**),
- when the subject is a relative pronoun (**6a(5)**), an indefinite pronoun (**6a(6)**), or a collective noun or measurement word (**6a(7)**),
- when the subject is a noun that is plural in form but singular in meaning (**6a(8)**),
- when the subject and its complement differ in number (**6a(9)**), and
- when the subject is a noun clause beginning with *what* (**6a(10)**).

(1) Agreement errors are likely when other words come between the subject and the verb.

The **rhythm** of the pounding waves **is** calming.
[*Waves* is not the subject; it is the object of the preposition *of*.]

Certain phrases commonly occur between the subject and the verb; however, they do not affect the number of the subject or the form of the verb:

accompanied by	in addition to	not to mention
along with	including	together with
as well as	no less than	

Her **salary,** together with tips, **is** just enough to live on.

Tips, together with her salary, **are** just enough to live on.

(2) Subjects joined by *and* usually take a plural verb.

> **Writing on a legal pad** and **writing with a computer are** not the same at all.

A compound subject that refers to a single person or thing takes a singular verb.

> The **founder <u>and</u> president** of the art association **was** elected to the board of the museum.
>
> **Red beans <u>and</u> rice is** the specialty of the house.

(3) Agreement errors are common when subjects are joined by *or* or *nor*.

When singular subjects are linked by *or, either . . . or,* or *neither . . . nor,* the verb is singular as well.

> The **provost <u>or</u> the dean** usually **presides** at the meeting.
>
> **<u>Either</u>** his **accountant <u>or</u>** his **lawyer has** the will.
>
> **<u>Neither</u>** the **car <u>nor</u>** the **motorcycle is** for sale.

If one subject is singular and one is plural, the verb agrees in number with the subject closer to the verb.

> Neither the basket nor the **apples were** expensive. [plural]
>
> Neither the apples nor the **basket was** expensive. [singular]

The verb also agrees in person with the nearer subject.

> Either Frank or **you were** going to make the announcement. [second person]
>
> Either you or **Frank was** going to make the announcement. [third person]

(4) Inverted word order may lead to agreement errors.

In most sentences, the subject precedes the verb.

The large **cities** of the Northeast **were** the hardest hit by the winter storms.

The subject and verb can sometimes be inverted for emphasis; however, they must still agree.

The hardest hit by the winter storms **were** the large **cities** of the Northeast.

When the expletive *there* begins a sentence, the subject and verb are always inverted (**1b(1)**); the verb still agrees with the subject, which follows it.

There **are** several **cities** in need of federal aid.

(5) Clauses with relative pronouns are common sites for agreement errors.

In an adjectival (relative) clause (**1f(2)**), the subject is generally a relative pronoun (*that, who,* or *which*). To determine whether the relative pronoun is singular or plural, you must find its antecedent (the word or words it refers to). When the antecedent is singular, the relative pronoun is singular; when the antecedent is plural, the relative pronoun is plural. In essence, the verb in the adjectival clause agrees with the antecedent.

The person who reviews proposals is out of town this week.

The director met with the **students who are** studying abroad next quarter.

The Starion is one of the new **models that include** a DVD player as standard equipment.

pl ant — models

pl v — include

BEYOND THE RULE

ONE AS A POSSIBLE ANTECEDENT

According to traditional grammar, in sentences containing the pattern *one* + *of* + plural noun + adjectival clause (such as the sentence just before this box), the antecedent for the relative pronoun (*that,* in this case) is the plural noun (*models*). The verb in the adjectival clause is thus plural as well. However, professional writers often consider *one*, instead of the plural noun, to be the antecedent of the relative pronoun and thus make the verb singular:

The Starion is **one** of the new models **that includes** a DVD player as standard equipment.

---

(6) Agreement errors frequently occur with indefinite pronouns.

The indefinite pronouns *each, either, everybody, everyone,* and *anyone* are considered singular and so require singular verb forms (6b(1)).

Each has bought a first-class ticket.

Either of them **is willing** to lead the discussion.

Everybody in our apartment building **has** a parking place.

Other indefinite pronouns, such as *all, any, some, none, half,* and *most,* can be either singular or plural, depending on whether they refer to a unit or quantity (singular) or to individuals (plural).

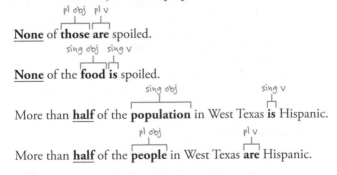

My sister collects comic **books; some are** quite valuable.

My sister collects antique **jewelry; some** of it **is** quite valuable.

Singular subjects that are preceded by *every* or *each* and joined by *and* require a singular verb.

Every cat **and** dog in the county **has** to be vaccinated.

Each fork **and** spoon **has** to be polished.

However, placing *each* after a plural compound subject does not affect the verb form. The verb should agree with the plural subject.

Colleges and vocational schools **each have** their advantages.

When an indefinite pronoun is followed by a prepositional phrase beginning with the preposition *of,* the verb agrees in number with the object of the preposition.

None of **those are** spoiled.

None of the **food is** spoiled.

More than **half** of the **population** in West Texas **is** Hispanic.

More than **half** of the **people** in West Texas **are** Hispanic.

(7) Collective nouns and measurement words often cause agreement difficulties.

Collective nouns (**1a(2)**) and measurement words require singular verbs when they refer to groups or units. They require plural verbs when they refer to individuals or parts.

Singular (regarded as a group or unit)	Plural (regarded as individuals or parts)
The **majority rules.**	The **majority** of us **are** in favor.
Ten million gallons of oil **is** more than enough.	**Ten million gallons** of oil **were spilled.**
The **number is** insignificant.	A **number** of workers **were** absent.

Although using the nouns *data* and *media* as singular has gained currency, treat *data* and *media* as plural in most academic writing. (See the **Glossary of Usage**.)

The data **are** in the appendix.

The media **have** shaped public opinion.

(8) Words ending in -s are sometimes singular.

Titles of works that are plural in form (for example, *Star Wars* and *Dombey and Son*) are treated as singular because they refer to a single book, movie, recording, or other work.

Mr. and Mrs. Smith **is** one of the films she discussed in her paper.

A reference to a word is also considered singular.

Beans **is** slang for "a small amount": I don't know beans about football.

Some nouns ending in -s are actually singular: *linguistics, news,* and *Niagara Falls.*

The **news is** encouraging.

Nouns such as *athletics, politics,* and *electronics* can be either singular or plural, depending on their meanings.

Singular	Plural
Statistics is an interesting subject.	**Statistics are** often misleading.

(9) Verbs agree with subjects, not with subject complements.
Some sentences may have a singular subject (**1b**) and a plural subject complement (**1c**), or vice versa. In either case, the verb agrees with the subject.

Her primary **concern is** rising health-care **costs.**

Croissants are the bakery's **specialty.**

THINKING RHETORICALLY

AGREEMENT OF RELATED SINGULAR AND PLURAL NOUNS

When a sentence has two or more nouns that are related, use either the singular form or the plural form consistently.

The **student** raised her **hand.**

The **students** raised their **hands.**

Occasionally, you may have to use a singular noun to retain an idiomatic expression or to avoid ambiguity.

They kept their **word.**

The **participants** were asked to name their favorite **movie.**

(10) An agreement error may occur when the subject of a sentence is a noun clause beginning with *what*.
In noun clauses (**1f(2)**), *what* may be understood as either "the thing that" or "the things that." If it is understood as "the thing that," the verb in the main clause is singular.

What we need **is** a new policy. [*The thing that* we need is a new policy.]

If *what* is understood as plural (the things that), the verb in the main clause is plural.

What we need **are** new guidelines. [*The things that* we need are new guidelines.]

Note that the main noun following the verb in these examples (*policy, guidelines*) also agrees with the verb: *policy* and *is* are singular; *guidelines* and *are* are plural.

BEYOND THE RULE

WHAT IN NOUN CLAUSES

According to a traditional grammar rule, a singular verb should be used in both the noun clause beginning with *what* and the main clause.

What **is** needed **is** new guidelines.

However, many current writers and editors consider this rule outmoded.

Exercise 1

In each sentence, choose the correct form of the verb in parentheses. Make sure that the verb agrees with its subject according to the conventions for academic and professional writing.

1. There (is/are) at least two good reasons for changing motor oil: risk of contamination and danger of additive depletion.
2. Reasons for not changing the oil (include/includes) the cost to the driver and the inconvenience of the chore.
3. What I want to know (is/are) the number of miles I can drive before changing my oil.
4. My best friend and mechanic (says/say) three thousand miles.
5. But my brother says three thousand miles (is/are) not long enough.
6. Each of the car manuals I consulted (recommends/recommend) five-thousand-mile intervals.
7. Neither the automakers nor the oil station attendants (know/knows) how I drive, however.

Exercise 2

Complete the following sentences, making sure that subjects and verbs agree.

1. Applying for college and enrolling in courses . . .
2. Erik is one of the students who . . .
3. Either of them . . .
4. The list of volunteers . . .
5. Hidden beneath the stairs . . .
6. The teacher, along with her students, . . .
7. What we requested . . .

6b Pronoun-antecedent agreement

A pronoun and its antecedent (the word or word group to which it refers) agree in number (both are singular or both are plural).

The **supervisor** said **he** would help.
[Both antecedent and pronoun are singular.]

My **colleagues** said **they** would help.
[Both antecedent and pronoun are plural.]

A pronoun also agrees with its antecedent in gender (masculine, feminine, or neuter).

Joseph claims **he** can meet the deadline. [masculine antecedent]

Anna claims **she** can meet the deadline. [feminine antecedent]

The **committee** claims **it** can meet the deadline. [neuter antecedent]

MULTILINGUAL WRITERS

POSSESSIVE PRONOUNS

A possessive pronoun (*his, her, its, their, my, our,* or *your*), also called a **possessive determiner,** agrees with its antecedent, not with the noun it precedes.

> Ken Carlson brought ~~her~~ *his* young daughter to the office today.

> [The possessive pronoun *his* agrees with the antecedent, *Ken Carlson,* not with the following noun, *daughter.*]

(1) Indefinite pronouns can serve as antecedents.

Although most antecedents for pronouns are nouns, they can be indefinite pronouns (**5a(6)**). Notice that an indefinite pronoun such as *everyone, someone,* and *anybody* takes a singular verb form.

> Everyone **has** [not *have*] the right to an opinion.

Difficulties arise, however, because words like *everyone* and *everybody* seem to refer to more than one person even though they take a singular verb. Thus, the definition of grammatical number and our everyday notion of number conflict. In conversation and informal writing, a plural pronoun is often used with the singular *everyone.* Nonetheless, when you write for an audience that expects you to follow traditional grammar rules, make sure to use a third-person singular pronoun.

> Each of these companies had ~~their~~ *its* books audited.

> Everyone has the combination to ~~their~~ *his or her* private locker.

You can avoid the awkwardness of using *his or her* by using an article instead, making both the antecedent and the possessive pronoun plural, or rewriting the sentence using the passive voice (**7c**).

Everyone has the combination to **a** private locker. [article]

Students have combinations to **their** private lockers. [plural antecedent and plural possessive pronoun]

The combination to a private locker **is issued** to everyone. [passive voice]

(2) An antecedent sometimes refers to both genders.

When an antecedent can refer to people of either gender, rewrite the sentence to make the antecedent plural or, if not too cumbersome, use *he or she* or *his or her*.

~~A lawyer~~ Lawyers represents ~~his~~ their clients. [plural pronoun and plural antecedent]

A lawyer represents the clients **he or she** has accepted.

A lawyer represents **his or her** clients.

(See **19d** for more information on using inclusive language.)

⚠ CAUTION

Be careful not to introduce errors into your writing when you are trying to avoid sexist language (**19d(1)**).

Whenever ~~a driver lets~~ drivers let their ~~license~~ licenses expire, they have to take a driving test.

(3) The pronoun agrees with the nearer of two antecedents joined by *or* or *nor*.

If a singular and a plural antecedent are joined by *or* or *nor*, place the plural antecedent second and use a plural pronoun.

Either Jennifer **or** her <u>roommates</u> will explain how <u>they</u> chose their majors.

Neither the president **nor** the <u>senators</u> stated that <u>they</u> would support the proposal.

(4) When a collective noun is the antecedent, the number of the pronoun depends on the meaning of the noun.

When an antecedent is a collective noun such as *team, faculty,* or *committee* (1a(2)), determine whether you intend the noun to be understood as singular or plural. Then, make sure that the pronoun agrees in number with the noun.

The choir decided that ~~they~~ _{it} would tour during the winter.
[Because the choir decided as a group, *choir* should be considered singular. The singular form, *it*, replaces the plural, *they*.]

The committee may disagree on methods, but ~~it~~ _{they} must agree on basic aims.
[Because the committee members are behaving as individuals, *committee* is regarded as plural. The plural form, *they*, replaces the singular, *it*.]

Exercise 3

Revise the following sentences so that pronouns and antecedents agree.

1. A researcher relies on a number of principles to help him make ethical decisions.

2. Everyone should have the right to participate in a study only if they feel comfortable doing so.

3. A team of researchers should provide its volunteers with consent forms, in which they describe to the volunteers the procedures and risks involved in participation.

4. Every participant should be guaranteed that the information they provide will remain confidential.

5. Institutions of higher education require that a researcher address ethical issues in their proposal.

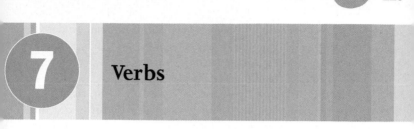

7 Verbs

Choosing verbs to convey your message precisely is the first step toward writing clear sentences. The next step is to ensure that the verbs you choose conform to the conventions your audience expects you to follow.

This chapter will help you

- identify conventional verb forms (**7a**),
- use verb tenses to provide information about time (**7b**),
- distinguish between the active voice and the passive voice (**7c**), and
- use verbs to signal the factuality or likelihood of an action or event (**7d**).

7a Verb forms

Most English verbs have four forms, following the model for *walk.*

walk, walks, walking, walked

However, English also includes irregular verbs, which may have as few as three forms or as many as eight:

let, lets, letting   be, am, is, are, was, were, being, been

(1) Regular verbs have four forms.
A regular verb has a **base form.** This is the form you find in a dictionary. *Talk, act, change,* and *serve* are all base forms.

The second form of a regular verb is the **-s form.** To derive this form, add to the base form either *-s* (*talks, acts, changes, serves*) or, in some cases, *-es* (*marries, carries, tries*). See **18d** for information on changing *y* to *i* before adding *-es*.

The third form of a regular verb is the **-*ing* form,** also called the **present participle.** It consists of the base form and the ending *-ing* (*talking, acting*). Depending on the verb, a spelling change may occur (*changing, chatting*) (**18d**).

The fourth form of a regular verb consists of the base form and the ending *-ed* (*talked, acted*). Again, spelling may vary when the suffix is added (*changed, chatted*) (**18d**). The *-ed* form has two names. When it is used without the auxiliary verb *have* or *be*, it is called the **past form:** We *talked* about the new plan. In contrast, when the *-ed* form is used with one of these auxiliary verbs, it is called the **past participle**: We *have talked* about it several times. A committee *was formed* to investigate the matter.

⚠ CAUTION

When verbs are followed by words with similar sounds, you may find their endings (*-s* or *-ed*) difficult to hear. In addition, these verb endings may seem unfamiliar because your dialect does not have them. Nonetheless, you should use *-s* and *-ed* when you write for an audience that expects you to include these endings.

She seem satisfied with the report.
> *seems*

We were suppose to receive the results yesterday.
> *supposed*

Verb Forms of Regular Verbs			
Base Form	-s Form (Present Tense, Third Person, Singular)	-ing Form (Present Participle)	-ed Form (Past Form or Past Participle)
work	works	working	worked
watch	watches	watching	watched
apply	applies	applying	applied
stop	stops	stopping	stopped

(2) Irregular verbs have from three to eight forms.

Most irregular verbs, such as *write,* have forms similar to some of those for regular verbs: base form (*write*), -s form (*writes*), and -*ing* form (*writing*). However, the past form (*wrote*) and the past participle (*written*) vary from the regular forms. In fact, some irregular verbs have two acceptable past forms and/ or past participles (see *awake, dive, dream,* and *get* in the following chart). Other irregular verbs have only three forms because the same form serves as the base form, the past form, and the past participle (see *set* in the chart). If you are unsure about verb forms not included in the chart, consult a dictionary.

The verb *be* has eight forms:

be	**Be** on time!
am	I **am** going to arrive early tomorrow.
is	Time **is** of the essence.
are	They **are** always punctual.
was	The meeting **was** scheduled for 10 a.m.
were	We **were** only five minutes late.
being	He is **being** delayed by traffic.
been	How long have we **been** here?

Verb Forms of Irregular Verbs

Base Form	-s Form (Present Tense, Third Person, Singular)	-ing Form (Present Participle)	Past Form	Past Participle
arise	arises	arising	arose	arisen
awake	awakes	awaking	awaked, awoke	awaked, awoken
begin	begins	beginning	began	begun
break	breaks	breaking	broke	broken
bring	brings	bringing	brought	brought
buy	buys	buying	bought	bought
choose	chooses	choosing	chose	chosen
come	comes	coming	came	come
dive	dives	diving	dived, dove	dived
do	does	doing	did	done
dream	dreams	dreaming	dreamed, dreamt	dreamed, dreamt
drink	drinks	drinking	drank	drunk
drive	drives	driving	drove	driven
eat	eats	eating	ate	eaten
forget	forgets	forgetting	forgot	forgotten
forgive	forgives	forgiving	forgave	forgiven
get	gets	getting	got	gotten, got
give	gives	giving	gave	given

Base Form	-s Form (Present Tense, Third Person, Singular)	-ing Form (Present Participle)	Past Form	Past Participle
go	goes	going	went	gone
hang (suspend)	hangs	hanging	hung	hung
hang (execute)	hangs	hanging	hanged	hanged
keep	keeps	keeping	kept	kept
know	knows	knowing	knew	known
lay (see the Glossary of Usage)	lays	laying	laid	laid
lead	leads	leading	led	led
lie (see the Glossary of Usage)	lies	lying	lay	lain
lose	loses	losing	lost	lost
pay	pays	paying	paid	paid
rise (see the Glossary of Usage)	rises	rising	rose	risen
say	says	saying	said	said
see	sees	seeing	saw	seen
set (see the Glossary of Usage)	sets	setting	set	set

(Continued on page 118)

(Continued from page 117)

Base Form	-s Form (Present Tense, Third Person, Singular)	-ing Form (Present Participle)	Past Form	Past Participle
sink	sinks	sinking	sank	sunk
sit (see the Glossary of Usage)	sits	sitting	sat	sat
speak	speaks	speaking	spoke	spoken
stand	stands	standing	stood	stood
steal	steals	stealing	stole	stolen
swim	swims	swimming	swam	swum
take	takes	taking	took	taken
tell	tells	telling	told	told
throw	throws	throwing	threw	thrown
wear	wears	wearing	wore	worn
write	writes	writing	wrote	written

MULTILINGUAL WRITERS

OMISSION OF FORMS OF *BE* IN OTHER LANGUAGES

Forms of the verb *be* can be omitted in some languages. In English, however, they are necessary.

Sentence without an auxiliary verb: The population‸growing.
                                                                is

Sentence without a linking verb: It‸quite large.
                                                    is

(3) A phrasal verb consists of a main verb and a particle.

A **phrasal verb** is a combination of a verb and a particle such as *up, out,* or *on.* A **particle** resembles an adverb or a preposition, but it is so closely associated with a verb that together they form a unit of meaning. In fact, a verb + particle unit is often idiomatic, conveying a meaning that differs from the common meanings of the individual words. For example, the definitions that first come to mind for the words *blow* and *up* are not likely to help you understand the phrasal verb *blow up* when it means "to enlarge": She *blew up* the photograph so that she could see the faces better. However, the meanings of other phrasal verbs are similar to common definitions of the verbs themselves; the particles just add a sense of completion or emphasis: They *wrote up* the report by six o'clock. The particle *up* in *wrote up* does not refer to a direction; instead, it emphasizes the completion of the report. Still other phrasal verbs retain the common meanings of the verb and the particle: The protesters *hung up* a banner.

The verb and particle in most phrasal verbs may be separated by a short noun phrase (**1e(1)**) or by a pronoun (**1a(3)**).

She **called** the meeting **off.**

The student **turned** it **in** yesterday.

Some phrasal verbs are not separable, however.

The group **went over** the proposal.

I **came across** an interesting fact.

Particles that add little meaning are often deleted, especially if they seem redundant.

I **sent** ~~out~~ the invitations.

(4) Auxiliary verbs combine with main verbs.

The auxiliary verbs *be, do,* and *have* combine with main verbs, both regular and irregular.

be	*am, is, are, was, were surprised*
	am, is, are, was, were writing
do	*does, do, did call*
	doesn't, don't, didn't spend
have	*has, have, had prepared*
	has, have, had read

When you combine auxiliary verbs with main verbs, you alter the meanings of the main verbs in subtle ways. The resulting verb combinations may provide information about time, emphasis, or action in progress.

Be, do, and *have* are not just auxiliary verbs, though. They may be used as main verbs as well.

be	I **am** from Texas.
do	He **does** his homework early in the morning.
have	They **have** an apartment near a park.

A sentence may even include one of these verbs as both an auxiliary and a main verb.

They **are being** careful.

Did you **do** your taxes by yourself?

She **has** not **had** any free time this week.

Another type of auxiliary verb is called a **modal auxiliary.** There are nine modal auxiliaries: *can, could, may, might, must, shall, should, will,* and *would.* By combining a modal auxiliary with the base form of a main verb, you can make a request (*Could* you help?), give an instruction (You *should* attend), or express certainty (We *shall* overcome), necessity (She *must* sleep), ability (You *can* dream), or probability (It *could* happen).

MULTILINGUAL WRITERS

MODAL AUXILIARIES AND MAIN VERBS

Although English verbs are often followed by the infinitive marker *to* (as in *want to go* and *plan to leave*), modal auxiliaries do not follow this pattern.

We **should to** finish our report by Friday.

Each modal auxiliary has more than one meaning. For example, *may* can indicate permission or probability.

The instructor said we **may** have an extension. [permission]

The weather **may** improve by tomorrow. [probability]

The following box provides examples of common meanings conveyed by modal auxiliaries.

COMMON MEANINGS OF MODAL AUXILIARIES

Meaning	Modal Auxiliary +	Main Verb	Example
Ability	can, could	afford	They *can afford* to buy a small house.
Certainty	will	leave	We *will leave* tomorrow.
Obligation	must	return	You *must return* your books soon.
Advice	should	talk	He *should talk* with his counselor.
Permission	may	use	You *may use* the computers in the library.

⚠️ **CAUTION**

When a modal auxiliary occurs with the auxiliary *have* (*must have forgotten, should have known*), *have* frequently sounds like the word *of*. When you proofread, be sure that modal auxiliaries are not followed by *of*.

        have
They **could ̶o̶f̶ taken** another route.

Writers generally do not combine modal auxiliaries unless they want to portray a regional dialect.

        be able to
We **might ̶c̶o̶u̶l̶d̶** plan the meeting for after the holidays.

MULTILINGUAL WRITERS

PHRASAL MODALS

English also has **phrasal modals**, which consist of more than one word. They have meanings similar to those of one-word modals.

> **be able to** (ability): We **were able to** find the original document.
>
> **have to** (obligation): You **have to** report your test results.

Other common phrasal modals are *be going to, be supposed to, had better, used to,* and *ought to*. Most phrasal modals have more than one form (*am able to, is able to, were able to*). Only *had better, ought to,* and *used to* have a single form.

(5) Participles are accompanied by auxiliary verbs.

Present participles (*-ing* verb forms) are used with the auxiliary verb *be*: We *were waiting* for the next flight. Depending on the intended meaning, past participles can be used with either *be* or *have*: The first flight *was canceled*. We *have waited* for an hour. If a sentence contains only a participle, it is probably a fragment (**2b**).

I sit on the same bench every day. ~~Dreaming~~ , dreaming of far-off places.

When a participle is part of a verbal phrase, it often appears without an auxiliary verb (**7a(4)**).

Swatting at mosquitoes and **cursing** softly, we packed our gear. [COMPARE: We **were swatting** at mosquitoes and **cursing** softly as we packed our gear.]

Exercise 1

Revise the following sentences. Explain any changes you make.

1. Any expedition into the wilderness suffer its share of mishaps.
2. The Lewis and Clark Expedition began in May 1804 and end in September 1806.
3. Fate must of smiled on Meriwether Lewis and William Clark, for there were no fatalities under their leadership.
4. Lewis and Clark lead the expedition from St. Louis to the Pacific Ocean and back.
5. President Thomas Jefferson commission the expedition in 1803 in part because he was interest in finding the Northwest Passage—a hypothetical waterway connecting the Atlantic and Pacific Oceans.
6. By 1805, the Corps of Discovery, as the expedition was call, included thirty-three members.
7. The Corps might of lost all maps and specimens had Sacajawea, a Native American woman, not fish them from the Missouri River.

8. Sacajawea could of went off with her own people in Idaho, but she accompany Lewis and Clark to the Pacific.

9. When the Mandans had finish inspecting York, William Clark's African American servant, they assume he was the expedition's leader.

10. The success of the expedition depend on its members' willingness to help one another.

7b   **Verb tenses**

Verb tenses provide information about time. For example, the tense of a verb may indicate that an action took place in the past or that an action is ongoing. Verb tenses are labeled as present, past, or future; they are also labeled as simple, progressive, perfect, or perfect progressive. The chart shows how these labels apply to the tenses of *walk.*

Verb Tenses			
	Present	**Past**	**Future**
Simple	walk, walks	walked	will walk
Progressive	am, is, are walking	was, were walking	will be walking
Perfect	has, have walked	had walked	will have walked
Perfect progressive	has, have been walking	had been walking	will have been walking

Some of the tenses have more than one form because they depend on the person and number of the subject. **Person** refers to the role of the subject. First person (*I, we*) indicates that the subject of the verb is the writer or writers. Second person (*you*) indicates that the subject is the audience. Third person (*he, she, it, they*) indicates that the subject is someone or something other than the writer or audience. **Number** indicates whether the subject is one or more than one (*I/we, building/buildings*). In the following subsections, conjugation tables show how person and number influence the forms of the regular verb *work*.

(1) Simple tenses have many uses, not all related to specific points in time.

The conjugation for the simple present tense includes two forms of the verb: the base form and the -*s* form. Notice that the third-person singular form is the only form with the -*s* ending.

Simple Present Tense		
	Singular	Plural
First person	I **work**	We **work**
Second person	You **work**	You **work**
Third person	He, she, it **works**	They **work**

Tense is not the same as time. Although the words *present, past,* and *future* may lead you to think that these tenses refer to actions happening now, in the past, and in the future, this strict separation does not always hold. For example, the simple present tense is used to indicate a current state, a habitual action, or a general truth.

We **are** ready. [current state]

Dana **uses** common sense. [habitual action]

The sun **rises** in the east. [general truth]

The simple present tense is also commonly used to add a sense of immediacy to historical actions and to discuss literary and artistic works (see fig. 7.1).

Fig. 7.1. In his painting *Sun Rising through Vapor*, J. M. W. Turner divides the canvas into areas of light and dark. (Notice the use of the simple present tense—"divides"—to describe an artistic work.) © National Gallery Collection. By kind permission of the Trustees of the National Gallery, London/Corbis.

In 1939, Hitler's armies **attack** Poland. [historical present]

Joseph Conrad **writes** about what he sees in the human heart. [literary present]

On occasion, the simple present tense is used to refer to future time.

The festival **begins** next month.

The simple past tense of regular verbs has only one form: the base form with the *-ed* ending. The past tense for irregular verbs varies (7a(2)).

Simple Past Tense
I, you, he, she, it, we, they **worked**

The simple past tense is used to refer to completed past actions or events.

He **traveled** to the Philippines. [past action]

The accident **occurred** several weeks ago. [past event]

The simple future tense also has only one form: the base form accompanied by the auxiliary *will*.

Simple Future Tense
I, you, he, she, it, we, they **will work**

The simple future tense refers to future actions or states.

I **will call** you after work today. [future action]

The video **will be** ready by Friday. [future state]

MULTILINGUAL WRITERS

SIGNALING THE FUTURE WITH *BE GOING TO*

The phrasal modal *be going to* indicates future actions, events, or states.

I **am going to** study in Russia next year.

Be going to is considered less formal than *will*.

(2) Progressive tenses indicate that events have begun but have not been completed.

The present progressive tense of a verb consists of a form of the auxiliary verb *be* and the present participle (*-ing* form) of the main verb.

Present Progressive Tense		
	Singular	Plural
First person	I **am working**	We **are working**
Second person	You **are working**	You **are working**
Third person	He, she, it **is working**	They **are working**

Notice that the present participle remains the same regardless of person and number, but the auxiliary *be* appears in three forms: *am* for first-person singular, *is* for third-person singular, and *are* for the other person-number combinations.

The present progressive tense signals an activity in progress or a temporary situation.

> The doctor **is attending** a conference in Nebraska. [activity in progress]
>
> We **are living** in a yurt right now. [temporary situation]

The present progressive tense can refer to a future event when it occurs with an expression indicating time.

> They **are leaving** for Alaska next week. [*Next week* indicates a time in the future.]

Like the present progressive, the past progressive tense is a combination of the auxiliary verb *be* and the present participle

(-*ing* form) of the main verb. However, the auxiliary verb is in the past tense, rather than in the present tense.

Past Progressive Tense		
	Singular	Plural
First person	I **was working**	We **were working**
Second person	You **were working**	You **were working**
Third person	He, she, it **was working**	They **were working**

The past progressive tense signals an action or event that occurred in the past and was repeated or ongoing.

> The new member **was** constantly **interrupting** the discussion. [repeated past action]

> We **were eating** dinner when we heard the news. [ongoing past action]

The future progressive tense has only one form. Two auxiliaries, *will* and *be*, are used along with the -*ing* form of the main verb.

Future Progressive Tense
I, you, he, she, it, we, they **will be working**

The future progressive tense refers to actions that will occur over some period of time in the future.

> She **will be giving** her report at the end of the meeting. [future action]

MULTILINGUAL WRITERS

VERBS NOT USED IN THE PROGRESSIVE FORM

Some verbs that do not express actions but rather mental states, emotions, conditions, or relationships are not used in the progressive form. These verbs include *believe, belong, contain, cost, know, own, prefer,* and *want.*

              contains
The book ~~is containing~~ many Central American folktales.

       knows
He ~~is knowing~~ many old myths.

(3) Perfect tenses indicate action performed prior to a particular time.

The present perfect tense is formed by combining the auxiliary *have* with the past participle of the main verb.

	Present Perfect Tense	
	Singular	Plural
First person	I **have worked**	We **have worked**
Second person	You **have worked**	You **have worked**
Third person	He, she, it **has worked**	They **have worked**

The participle remains the same regardless of person and number; however, the auxiliary has two forms: *has* for third-person singular and *have* for the other person-number combinations. The present perfect tense signals a time prior to the present. It can refer to a situation originating in the past but continuing into the present. It can also refer to a past action that has current relevance.

They **have lived** in New Zealand for twenty years. [situation originating in the past and still continuing]

I **have read** that book already, but I could certainly read it again. [past action that is completed but currently relevant]

The past perfect tense is also formed by combining the auxiliary *have* with the past participle. However, the auxiliary is in the past tense. There is only one form of the past perfect.

Past Perfect Tense

I, you, he, she, it, we, they **had worked**

The past perfect tense refers to an action completed at a time in the past prior to another past time or past action.

Before 1990, he **had worked** in a shoe factory. [past action prior to a given time in the past]

I **had studied** geology before I transferred to this school. [past action prior to another past action]

The future perfect tense consists of two auxiliaries, *will* and *have*, along with the past participle of the main verb. There is only one form of the future perfect tense.

Future Perfect Tense

I, you, he, she, it, we, they **will have worked**

The future perfect tense refers to an action that is to be completed prior to a future time.

By this time next year, I **will have finished** medical school.

(4) Perfect progressive tenses combine the forms and meanings of the progressive and the perfect tenses.

The present perfect progressive tense consists of two auxiliaries, *have* and *be,* plus the present participle (*-ing* form) of the main verb.

Present Perfect Progressive Tense		
	Singular	Plural
First person	I have been working	We have been working
Second person	You have been working	You have been working
Third person	He, she, it has been working	They have been working

The form of the auxiliary *have* varies with person and number. The auxiliary *be* appears as the past participle, *been.* The present perfect progressive signals that an action, state, or event originating in the past is ongoing or incomplete.

I **have been feeling** tired for a week. [ongoing state]

We **have been organizing** the conference since April. [incomplete action]

The past perfect progressive tense follows the pattern *had* + *been* + present participle (*-ing* form) of the main verb. The auxiliary *have* is in the past tense.

Past Perfect Progressive Tense
I, you, he, she, it, we, they **had been working**

The past perfect progressive tense refers to a situation or an action occurring over a period of time in the past and prior to another past action or time.

> She **had been living** so frugally all year that she saved enough money for a new car. [past situation prior to another action in the past]

The future perfect progressive tense follows the pattern *will* + *have* + *been* + present participle (*-ing* form) of the main verb.

Future Perfect Progressive Tense

I, you, he, she, it, we, they **will have been working**

The future perfect progressive tense refers to an action that is occurring in the present and will continue to occur for a specific amount of time.

> In one more month, I **will have been working** on this project for five years.

(5) The auxiliary verb *do* is used for questioning, negating, or emphasizing.

Unlike *be* and *have*, the auxiliary verb *do* does not occur with other verbs to indicate tense. Instead, it is used in questions, negations, and emphatic sentences.

> **Do** you have any questions? [question]
>
> I **do** not have any questions. [negation]
>
> I **do** have a few questions. [emphatic sentence]

The auxiliary *do* is used only in the simple present (*do, does*) and the simple past (*did*).

Exercise 2

Explain how the meaning of each sentence changes when the verb tense changes.

1. In "Fiji's Rainbow Reef," Les Kaufman (describes/described) the coral reefs of Fiji and (discusses/discussed) the factors affecting their health.
2. Rising water temperatures (damaged/have damaged/did damage) the reefs.
3. The algae that (provide/provided) color (do not survive/did not survive) in the warmer water.
4. The lack of algae (has left/had left) the coral "bleached."
5. Strangely, though, new life (is flourishing/was flourishing/has been flourishing) in some of these areas.
6. Scientists (study/will study) this area to understand its resilience.

(6) Verb tenses help convey the duration or time sequence of actions and events.

When you use more than one tense in a single sentence, you give readers information about how actions or events are related in time and duration.

> Whenever he **calls** on me, I **stutter** nervously. [Both present tense verbs indicate habitual actions.]
>
> When the speaker **had finished,** everyone **applauded.** [The past perfect tense *had finished* indicates a time before the action expressed by *applauded*.]

Infinitives and participles can be used to express time relations within a sentence. The present infinitive (*to* + base form) of a verb expresses action occurring later than the action expressed by the main verb.

> They **want to design** a new museum. [The action of designing will take place in the future.]

The perfect infinitive (*to + have +* past participle) signals that an action, state, or event is potential or hypothetical or that it did not occur.

> She **hopes to have earned** her degree by the end of next year.

> The governor **would like to have postponed** the vote. [The postponement did not occur.]

The present participle (*-ing* form) indicates simultaneous or previous action.

> **Laughing** loudly, the old friends **left** the restaurant arm in arm. [The friends were laughing as they were leaving.]

> **Hearing** that she was ill, I **rushed** right over. [The action of hearing occurred first.]

The perfect participle (*having +* past participle) expresses action completed before the action conveyed by the main verb.

> **Having learned** Spanish at an early age, she **spoke** to the Mexican diplomats in their native language.

The past participle can be used to express either simultaneous action or previous action.

> **Led** by a former Peace Corps worker, the volunteers **provided** medical assistance. [Both actions occurred simultaneously.]

> **Encouraged** by job prospects, he **moved** to Atlanta. [The encouragement preceded the move.]

Exercise 3

Revise the following sentences so that all verbs express logical time sequences.

1. We expected the storm to have bypassed our town, but it didn't.
2. We would like to have prior notice; however, even the police officers were taken by surprise.
3. Not having known much about flooding, the emergency crew was at a disadvantage.
4. Having thrown sandbags all day, the volunteers had been exhausted by 5 p.m.
5. They went home, succeeding in preventing a major disaster.

 Voice

Voice indicates the relationship between a verb and its subject. When a verb is in the **active voice,** the subject is generally a person or thing performing an action. When a verb is in the **passive voice,** the subject is usually the *receiver* of the action.

> Jen Wilson **wrote** the essay. [active voice]

> The essay **was written** by Jen Wilson. [passive voice]

Notice that the actor, Jen Wilson, appears in a prepositional phrase beginning with *by* in the passive sentence. Some sentences, however, do not include a *by* phrase because the actor is unknown or unimportant.

> Jen Wilson's essay **was published** in the student newspaper.

In the preceding sentence, it is not important to know who accepted Jen's essay for publication, only that it was published. The best way to decide whether a sentence is in the passive voice is to examine its verb phrase.

(1) Sentences in the passive voice include a form of the auxiliary verb *be* and a past participle.

The verb phrase in a sentence written in the passive voice consists of a form of the auxiliary verb *be* (*am, is, are, was, were, been*) and a past participle (7a(1)). Depending on the verb tense, other auxiliaries such as *have* and *will* may appear as well. The following sentences include common forms of *call* in the passive voice:

Simple present	The meeting *is called* to order.
Simple past	The recruits *were called* to duty.
Present progressive	The council *is being called* to act on the proposal.
Past perfect	Ms. Jones *had been called* to jury duty twice last year, but she was glad to serve again.

If a verb phrase does not include both a form of the auxiliary verb *be* and a past participle, it is in the active voice.

(2) Sentences in the active voice and the passive voice differ in emphasis.

Sentences in the active voice are generally clearer and more vigorous than their passive counterparts. To use the active voice for emphasizing an actor and an action, first make the actor the subject of the sentence; then choose verbs that will help your readers see what the actor is doing. Notice how the sentence in the active voice emphasizes the role of the students.

Active voice	A group of students planned the graduation ceremony. They invited a well-known columnist to give the graduation address.
Passive voice	The graduation ceremony was planned by a group of students. A well-known columnist was invited to give the graduation address.

For more information on using the active voice to write forceful sentences, see **29e**.

Use the passive voice when you want to stress the recipient of the action, rather than the actor, or when the actor's identity is unimportant or unknown. For example, you may want to emphasize the topic of a discussion.

Tuition increases **will be discussed** at the next board meeting.

Or you may be unable to identify the actor who performed some action.

The lights **were left** on in the building last night.

Writers of scientific prose often use the passive voice to highlight the experiment rather than the experimenter. The following is an excerpt from a lab report by student Heather Jensen:

First, the slides **were placed** on a compound microscope under low power, a 40× magnification level. The end of the root tip **was located**; then the cells immediately behind the root cap **were examined**. These cells appeared as a darker area under low power. This area of cells **was identified** as the apical meristem, an area of rapid growth and division in the onion root tip.

Exercise 4

Identify the voice in each sentence as active or passive.

1. In a *National Geographic* report, Tom O'Neill describes the discovery of ancient art in Guatemala.
2. Archaeologist William Saturno recently discovered the oldest known Maya mural.
3. The mural was found in a tunnel used by looters.
4. The tunnel was actually a small room attached to a pyramid.
5. The small room was covered with debris; its exact dimensions were hard to gauge.
6. The archaeologist found the mural by accident.
7. The mural was dated to about 150 years before the beginning of the Maya Classic period.

7d Mood

The **mood** of a verb expresses the writer's attitude toward the factuality of what is being expressed. The **indicative mood** is used for statements and questions regarding fact or opinion. The **imperative mood** is used to give commands or directions. The **subjunctive mood** is used to state requirements, make requests, and express wishes.

Indicative	We will be on time.
Imperative	Be on time!
Subjunctive	The director insists that we be on time.

The subjunctive mood is also used to signal hypothetical situations (for example, *If I were president, . . .*). By using moods correctly, you can show your readers how you feel about the content of your sentences—certain, confident, doubtful, hesitant, ambivalent, and so on. Verb forms in the indicative mood are presented in **7b**. The form for the imperative mood is simply the base form of the verb. Verb forms used for the subjunctive mood are described in the following subsection.

(1) Verb forms in the subjunctive mood serve a variety of functions.

A verb in the subjunctive mood can be present subjunctive, past subjunctive, or perfect subjunctive. The **present subjunctive** is the base form of the verb. It is used to express necessity.

> The doctor recommended that he **go** on a diet.

> The curator requested that I **be** at the museum by five o'clock.

In the passive voice, the present subjunctive form consists of *be* and the past participle of the main verb.

> We demanded that you **be reimbursed.**

The **past subjunctive** has the same form as the simple past (for example, *had, offered, found,* or *wrote*). However, the past subjunctive form of *be* is *were*, regardless of person or number. This form is used to present hypothetical situations (situations that are not real or not currently true).

> If they **offered** me the job, I would take it.

> She acts as if she **were** the employer rather than the employee.

The past subjunctive form in the passive voice consists of *were* and the past participle.

> Even if he **were promoted,** he would not change his mind.

Although it is called "past," the past subjunctive refers to the present or the future.

The **perfect subjunctive** verb has the same form as the past perfect tense: *had* + past participle. The perfect subjunctive signals that a statement is not factual.

I wish I **had known** about the scholarship competition.

To use a perfect subjunctive form in the passive voice, add the past participle of the main verb to the auxiliaries *had been*.

If she **had been awarded** the scholarship, she would have quit her part-time job.

(2) The subjunctive is used mainly in dependent clauses.

Although you might not use the subjunctive when speaking with your friends, using it in your writing shows readers who may not know you how you feel about your claims. In addition, your audience may expect you to adhere to the conventions for formal writing. The following guidelines should help you avoid pitfalls when using the subjunctive.

TIPS FOR USING THE SUBJUNCTIVE

- In clauses beginning with *as if* and *as though*, use the past subjunctive or the perfect subjunctive:

  He acts as if he ^were^ **was** the owner.

  She looked at me as though she ^had^ **heard** this story before.

- In nonfactual dependent clauses beginning with *if*, use the past subjunctive or the perfect subjunctive. Avoid using *would have* in the *if* clause.

  If I ^were^ **was** rich, I would buy a yacht.

(Continued on page 142)

(Continued from page 141)

>   had
> If the driver ~~would have~~ **checked** his rearview mirror, the accident
> would not have happened.
>
> Note that *if* does not always mark a clause as nonfactual.
>
> If it is sunny tomorrow, I'm going fishing. [indicative mood]
>
> ■ In dependent clauses following verbs that express wishes, re-
>   quirements, or requests, use the past subjunctive or the perfect
>   subjunctive.
>
>   were
> I wish I ~~was~~ taller.
>
>   had
> My brother wishes he ~~studied~~ harder years ago.

Exercise 5

Use subjunctive verb forms to revise the following sentences.

1. The planners of Apollo 13 acted as if the number 13 was a lucky
   number.
2. Superstitious people think that if NASA changed the number of
   the mission, the astronauts would have had a safer journey.
3. They also believe that if the lunar landing would have been
   scheduled for a day other than Friday the Thirteenth, the crew
   would not have encountered any problems.
4. The crew used the lunar module as though it was a lifeboat.
5. If NASA ever plans a space mission on Friday the Thirteenth
   again, the public would object.

M

MECHANICS

Taking the Lead on Technology:

Good for Students, Good for Your School

Did you know that many college stores set the trend for technology on campus? It's true. Many college stores are implementing e-commerce solutions to improve their value, convenience and service to students.

And college stores have unique access to academically discounted software and other computer products for purchase by faculty, students and even administrators.

When college stores take the lead in technology, it generates more sales. Higher store profits create vital financial support for institutional operations and student programs. And that's good for your students and your school.

Get to Know
The Value of Your College Store

A message from the
National Association of College Stores
www.nacs.org

Advertisers frequently use capitalization to highlight important words.

8 Document Design

All of us use visual elements to discern messages every day—even if we are not consciously aware of how we "read" these photos, graphics, and design features. Just as important as understanding how we make sense of visuals is understanding how to compose documents that use visuals in combination with words to communicate information to an intended audience.

In this chapter, you will learn the basic principles of interpreting and composing documents that include both text and images. In other words, you will learn the rhetorical principles of combining visual elements with text, the genres of visual documents, and the conventions of layout—all of which will help you achieve your purpose. More specifically, this chapter will help you

- understand visual documents in terms of the rhetorical situation (**8a**),
- employ the design principles of visual rhetoric (**8b**), and
- use graphics to clarify written material (**8c**).

8a Visual documents and the rhetorical situation

Exigence, sender, audience, purpose, message, context—the rhetorical elements underlying the interpretation and composition of verbal texts—easily apply to visual documents as well. In this chapter, **visual documents** are documents that combine **visual elements** with verbal text to express meaning or deliver a message to an intended audience. In addition to images and

graphics (such as diagrams, tables, and photographs), visual elements also include the design and layout features of documents. Whether their purpose is expressive, expository, or argumentative (**31c**), visual documents, ranging from advertisements, posters, and billboards to brochures, newsletters, and Web sites, must always account for the relationship between purpose and audience.

Consider the advertisement in fig. 8.1, which addresses the topic of global warming. This visual document serves a distinct purpose—and thus employs rhetorical strategies that appeal to a specific audience: it addresses parents, adults with a wide range of interest in and expertise about the topic of global warming. Even parents who are not concerned about

Fig. 8.1. The audience for this ad has a wide range of interest in and expertise regarding the topic.

the future of the planet can be depended on to care about the future of their children. To connect with that concern, the ad's designer (the sender) chose a photo of an infant wrapped in a white blanket to make a powerful emotional appeal to an audience of parents, identifying the cause of the organization (reversing global warming) with the interests of the audience (parents). The text, which reads, "Start college fund. Revise will. Undo global warming," highlights the exigence for the ad and heightens the response of the audience. With this appeal to fear and call to action, the designer hopes to persuade potentially disinterested viewers and impel them to "undo global warming" for the sake of their children.

As the preceding example suggests, the rhetorical situation influences the genre of visual document that is used to deliver a message. The global warming ad contains eight prominent words. Most posters, billboards, and advertisements contain a small amount of text, allowing the audience to absorb the message visually, with only a brief glance. The ease of access helps these predominantly visual documents reach a large, diverse audience. By contrast, the designer of a brochure assumes that the intended audience will take the brochure with them, allowing them time to read the more extensive text. The greater volume of information in a brochure, as well as the specialized focus, makes this genre particularly appropriate for an educated, already interested audience.

Exercise 1

Select a visual document that has caught your attention. Write for five to ten minutes in response to that document. Then, analyze it in terms of its rhetorical situation and the relationship between words and images. Be prepared to share your document and analysis with the rest of the class.

8b The design principles of visual rhetoric

After considering the context of a visual document as a whole, you can analyze how the various elements work together to create a coherent message. Just as writers organize words into sentences and paragraphs, designers structure the visual elements of their documents in order to achieve coherence, develop ideas, and make a point. Presenting complicated material in visual form, however, requires a different set of strategies than those used in writing academic papers. Rather than relying on paragraph breaks and topic sentences, designers of visual documents call on four important principles to organize and develop ideas: alignment, proximity, contrast, and repetition. These four design principles will help you organize complex information, condensing it in a form that is both accessible to your audience and visually appealing. The poster in fig. 8.2, created by an undergraduate student and discussed throughout this section, illustrates how the four design principles can be used to organize detailed information visually.

(1) The principle of alignment involves an invisible grid system.

The principle of alignment involves the use of an invisible grid system that runs vertically and/or horizontally on a page, thereby connecting both visual and verbal elements in different parts of the document. The poster in fig. 8.2 has two primary lines: one down the left side of the page and one through the center. These lines define columns, which organize and unify the poster and give it a sharp, clean look. However, both the title and the statement of objectives in brown are not aligned with the main columns of text. This strategy gives more prominence to these two elements, clarifying the document's topic and purpose for the reader.

The Shipwreck Austria:
by Faith Haney

An Historical and Archaeological Investigation on the Olympic Peninsula Pacific Coast

Introduction

The shipwreck Austria is a mid-nineteenth century wooden ship that foundered on Washington's outer coast during a blustery gale in January of 1887. Located on the tumultuous intertidal zone of Cape Alava in the Olympic Coast National Marine Sanctuary (OCNMS) and on the Makah Reservation, wreckage remains lie scattered in tidepools and beach sand. Though a brief survey was conducted at the site area in 1997, new mapping techniques utilizing GPS technology will fill a data gap of the mapped locations of shipwreck remains in OCNMS and on the Makah Reservation.

The primary objectives of this study are to identify, map, and interpret the remains of the shipwreck *Austria*. Through a comparative analysis of current remains of the *Austria* to those recorded in an earlier study (Terrell, 2000), the aim is to determine the general degradation and movement of materials over time, as well as provide a GIS data layer to the National Oceanic Atmospheric Administration (NOAA) and the Makah Tribe for use in monitoring the shipwreck. Additionally, a field school is proposed at the site location to gather data, educate up-and-coming heritage resource managers, and compile the data for use in an interactive web-page and public presentation geared towards outreach and education. This study will benefit the scientific community by addressing a research data gap of mapped shipwreck remains, contributing to an understanding of site dynamics, and providing a useful source of information for education and public outreach.

> *The primary objectives of this study are to identify, map, and interpret the remains of the shipwreck Austria.*

Methods

The scope of this study includes three main components: 1) *mapping and documentation of shipwreck remains;* 2) *determination of debris movement over time;* and 3) *development of a webpage and presentation for public outreach and education.* These components share many methods, but also incorporate some unique approaches as well.

Mapping and Documentation
The survey area is approximately 360 meters north/south and 300 meters east/west. For the site recordation and mapping constituents, this study will integrate methods utilized by the National Park Service Submerged Resources Unit, which relies heavily on video to fill in details where mapping or illustration alone does not suffice (Lenihan, 1989), and both the National Marine Sanctuary's Maritime Heritage Program (NMSMHP) and Nautical Archaeological Society (NAS), both of which employ triangulation using a baseline grid (Thompson, n.d.). Since this is a foreshore archaeological site that is exposed at low tides, terrestrial site survey techniques will also be incorporated (Green, 2004). Terrestrial and foreshore survey and mapping techniques include:

1) pedestrian survey at five-meter intervals during low-tide
2) locating and flagging artifacts
3) setting up primary and secondary datums
4) using a GPS, compass, tapes, and rangefinder to record artifact, feature, and landmark locations
5) photographing and video-taping site overviews and artifacts

Determination of Debris Movement and Degradation Over Time
This study will also document the movement of shipwreck materials since the initial site survey in 1997 through comparing artifact locations as they were mapped during that study to the current locations of the artifacts, based on the previous datum (Terrell, 2000). Data from both surveys will be incorporated onto GIS data layers and then compared.

Public Outreach and Education
Video and photographic documentation of the site and associated artifacts will be incorporated into a webpage on the OCNMS website and a presentation will be offered to the public. The webpage is planned to be an interactive exploration of the shipwreck *Austria*, where the site visitor can click on various "hot spots" on a map of the wreck and see what the artifacts or features look like (either in a photographic image or small video clip) and view an historical account of the item. Field school participants will be responsible to perform research and documentation in order to contribute slides or video clips to a collaborative presentation.

Expected Results & Conclusion

Through this research, a useful GIS data layer illustrating the precise location of shipwreck remains in the intertidal zone at Cape Alava is expected to be acquired. This locational data combined with information from a previous study at the site will also contribute to an understanding of wreckage movement over space and time.

It is anticipated that many of the heavy metal artifacts will still remain, though locating them may prove difficult, as tidal and current action and human interference has likely caused significant movement. Additionally, the data acquired during the field school phase of the research project — including a site map, data on individual artifacts, and historical information — will be incorporated into an interactive web-page on the Olympic Coast National Marine Sanctuary website and a public presentation. By involving up-and-coming cultural resource managers in site recordation, and including field school participants in the production of an interactive web-page and public presentation of the shipwreck *Austria*, both the academic and public realms will gain a greater understanding of the maritime heritage resources of Washington State and the nation.

References Cited

Green, J. (2004). *Maritime Archaeology: A Technical Handbook.* London, England: Elsevier Academic Press.

Lenihan, D. (ed.) (1989). *Submerged cultural resource study: USS Arizona Memorial and Pearl Harbor National Historic Landmark.* Southwest Cultural Resources Center Professional Papers, Santa Fe, NM: Submerged Cultural Resources Unit, Dept. of the Interior.

Terrell, B. (2000). *Cultural Resource Survey Report The Austria.* Port Angeles, WA: Olympic Coast National Marine Sanctuary.

Thompson, K. (n.d.). *Web Shipwreck: An Exercise in Maritime Archaeology.* National Oceanic and Atmospheric Administration's National Marine Sanctuary Program. Retrieved February 20, 2007, from http://sanctuaries.noaa.gov/education/

Fig. 8.2. The material on this poster is organized according to the four principles of visual rhetoric.

(2) The principle of proximity requires the grouping of related elements.

The principle of **proximity** requires the grouping of related visual or textual elements into chunks. Like elements of text are grouped together visually, whereas unlike elements are separated by significant **white space** (blank areas around blocks of text). In written documents, for example, headings typically appear closer to the section they relate to than to the previous section. Similarly, the audience will perceive each chunk of elements in a visual document as a single unit and interpret it as a whole before moving on to the next group. In other words, the chunks serve a function similar to sections in a written document, organizing the page and reducing clutter. In fig. 8.2, the proximity of the title and subtitle to each other links them and allows them to be read together, despite the fact that they appear in different colors and fonts. Moreover, white space and images distinguish sections and subsections, further clarifying the document's structure.

(3) The principle of contrast helps readers distinguish the most important elements.

The principle of **contrast** allows a reader to distinguish important elements from the rest of the document. The most salient visual or textual elements stand out from the rest of the page, while less important elements are not as noticeable. For example, academic and professional documents usually have headings in bold or italic type or capital letters to distinguish them from the rest of the text. Likewise, visual documents provide the viewer with clear clues as to the relative importance of various elements. Usually, the most significant elements of a document are contrasted with the surrounding elements by differences in size, color, or font. The poster in fig. 8.2 uses several strategies to heighten the contrast between its various components. Because they are so large, the title, images, and statement of objectives attract the most attention, and they convey a sense of the project's purpose. Moreover, lack of contrast also supplies important information about the document's organization. All headings are the same size and typeface, as are all subheadings. With a brief glance, the viewer can determine the hierarchy of information and the basic structure of the poster.

(4) The principle of repetition helps establish coherence.

The principle of **repetition** has to do with the replication of specific visual or textual elements throughout a document. For example, nearly all academic and professional papers use a consistent typeface for large blocks of text, which creates a unified look. Visual documents follow a similar strategy, rarely showing more than three typefaces in a single work. Moreover, other visual elements, such as bullets or colors, also enhance coherence when they are repeated in various parts of a document. In fig. 8.2, the title and statement of objectives appear in one font; the subtitle and the interior headings appear in another. The consistent use of the same two colors, blue and brown, reinforces the sense of unity. In addition, the pale blue waves repeating across the bottom not only give the poster a creative touch but also subtly unify all the elements. Particularly in the title and headings, repetition and contrast work hand in hand to structure the poster.

8c   Using graphics

Many academic and professional documents that are primarily composed of text also include substantial visual displays, or **graphics,** to clarify written material. Graphics can be used to illustrate a concept, present data, provide visual relief, or simply attract readers' attention. Different types of graphics—tables, charts or graphs, and pictures—serve different purposes, and some may serve multiple purposes in a given document. Any of these types of graphics can enable readers to absorb a message more quickly than they would by reading long sections of text. However, if there is any chance that readers might not receive the intended message, it is a good idea to supplement graphics with text discussion.

(1) Tables organize data so that information can be easily accessed and compared.

Tables use a row-and-column arrangement to organize data (numbers or words) spatially; they are especially useful for presenting great amounts of numerical information in a small space, enabling the reader to draw direct comparisons among pieces of data or even to locate specific items. When you design a table, be sure to label all of the columns and rows accurately and to provide both a title and a number for the table. The table number and title traditionally appear above the table body, as table 8.1 demonstrates, and any notes or source information should be placed below it.

Most word-processing programs have settings that let you insert a table wherever you need one. You can determine how many rows and columns the table will have, and you can also size each row and each column appropriately for the information it will hold.

(2) Charts and graphs provide visual representations of data.

Like tables, charts and graphs display relationships among statistical data in visual form; unlike tables, they do so using lines, bars, or other visual elements rather than just letters and numbers. Data can be displayed in several different graphic forms: pie charts, line graphs, and bar charts are the most common examples.

Pie charts are especially useful for showing the relationship of parts to a whole (see fig. 8.3), but they can only be used to display sets of data that add up to 100 percent (a whole).

TABLE 8.1
Modified Monthly Tornado Statistics

Month	2007 Final	2006 Final	2005 Final	2004 Final	4-Year Average
Jan	21	47	33	3	26
Feb	52	12	10	9	21
Mar	171	150	62	50	108
Apr	165	245	132	125	167
May	250	139	123	509	255
Jun	128	120	316	268	208
Jul	69	71	138	124	101
Aug	73	80	123	179	114
Sep	51	84	133	295	141
Oct	87	76	18	79	65
Nov	7	42	150	150	87
Dec	19	40	26	26	28
Total	1093	1106	1264	1817	1321

Source: National Weather Service.

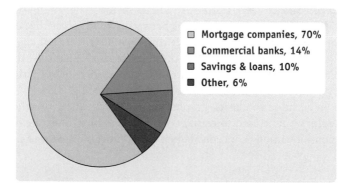

Fig. 8.3. Pie chart showing issuers of mortgage-based securities.

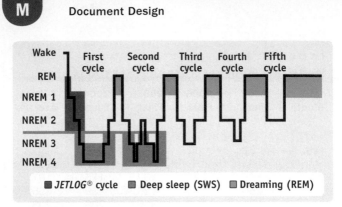

Fig. 8.4. Graph of nightly sleep stages.

Line graphs show the change in the relationship between one variable (indicated as a value on the vertical axis, or y axis) and another variable (indicated as a value on the horizontal axis, or x axis). The most common x-axis variable is time. Line graphs are very good at showing how a variable changes over time. A line graph might be used, for example, to illustrate the progression of sleep stages during one night (see fig. 8.4), increases or decreases in student achievement from semester to semester, or trends in financial markets over a number of years.

Bar charts show correlations between two variables that do not involve smooth changes over time. For instance, a bar chart might illustrate gross national product for several nations, the relative speeds of various computer processors, or statistics about the composition of the U.S. military (see fig. 8.5).

In addition to charts, graphs, and tables, a variety of other graphics can be used to clarify complex ideas or to illustrate relationships among concepts. Figure 8.6 (a process diagram of the

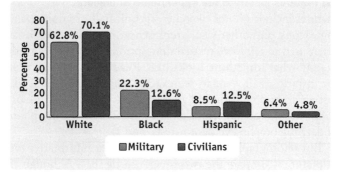

Fig. 8.5. Bar chart illustrating the composition of the U.S. military.

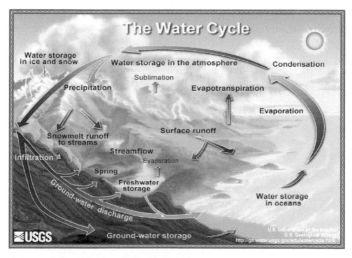

Fig. 8.6. Process diagram of the water cycle.

water cycle, or the movement of water in different forms through the environment) uses a simple graphical convention (superimposing arrows and labels on a semirealistic drawing) to present information that, in textual form, would require a great deal of space.

(3) Pictures illustrate the appearance of objects.

Pictures include photos, sketches, technical illustrations, paintings, icons, and other visual representations. Photographs are often used to reinforce textual descriptions or to show a reader exactly what something looks like. Readers of a used-car ad, for instance, will want to see exactly what the car looks like, not an artistic rendition of its appearance. Likewise, a Costa Rican travel brochure needs to contain lots of full-color photos of dazzling beaches, verdant forests, and azure water.

But photographs are not always the most informative type of picture. Compare the two images in fig. 8.7. Although the photograph is a more realistic image of the actual printer, the illustration more clearly shows the printer's important features: buttons, panels, and so forth. With its simple lines and clear labels, the illustration suits its purpose: to help the viewer set up and use the printer. Line drawings enable the designer of a document, such as a user manual, to highlight specific elements of an object while deemphasizing or eliminating unnecessary information. The addition of arrows, pointers, and labels adds useful detail to such an illustration.

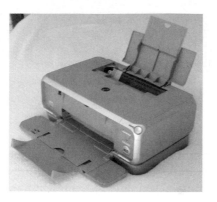

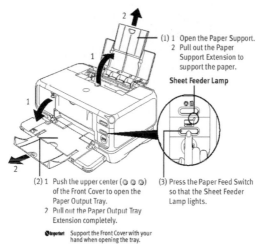

(1) 1 Open the Paper Support.
   2 Pull out the Paper Support Extension to support the paper.

Sheet Feeder Lamp

(2) 1 Push the upper center (○ ○ ○) of the Front Cover to open the Paper Output Tray.
   2 Pull out the Paper Output Tray Extension completely.

   Important Support the Front Cover with your hand when opening the tray.

(3) Press the Paper Feed Switch so that the Sheet Feeder Lamp lights.

Fig. 8.7. A photo and a drawing of the same printer.

9 Capitals

When you look at an advertisement, an e-mail message, or even a paragraph in this book, you can easily pick out capital letters. These beacons draw your attention to significant details—for example, the beginnings of sentences or the names of particular people, places, and products. Although most capitalization conventions apply to any rhetorical situation, others are specific to a discipline or a profession. In this chapter, you will learn the conventions expected in most academic and professional settings. This chapter will help you

- use capitals for proper names (**9a**),
- capitalize words in titles and subtitles of works (**9b**),
- capitalize the first letter of a sentence (**9c**),
- use capitals for computer keys, menu items, and icon names (**9d**), and
- avoid unnecessary capitalization (**9e**).

9a Proper names

When you capitalize a word, you emphasize it. That is why names of people and places are capitalized, even when they are used as modifiers (*Mexico, Mexican government*). Some words,

Advertisers frequently use capitalization to highlight important words.

such as *college, company, park,* and *street,* are capitalized only if they are part of a name (*a university* but *Oregon State University*). The following names and titles should be capitalized.

(1) Names of specific persons or things

Zora Neale Hurston	Flight 224	Honda Accord
John Paul II	Academy Award	USS *Cole*
Skylab	Nike	Microsoft Windows

A word denoting a family relationship is capitalized only when it substitutes for the person's proper name.

I told **Mom** about the event. [I told Catherine about the event.]

I told my **mom** about the event. [NOT I told my Catherine about the event.]

(2) Titles accompanying proper names

A title is capitalized when it precedes the name of a person but not when it follows the name or stands alone.

Governor Peter Dunn	Peter Dunn, the governor
Captain Ray Machado	Ray Machado, our captain
Uncle Rory	Rory, my uncle
President Lincoln	Abraham Lincoln, the president of the United States

(3) Names of ethnic or cultural groups and languages

Asians	African Americans	Latinos/Latinas	Poles
Arabic	English	Korean	Spanish

(4) Names of bridges, buildings, monuments, and geographical features

Golden Gate Bridge	Arctic Circle
Empire State Building	Mississippi River
Lincoln Memorial	Grand Canyon

When referring to two or more geographical features, however, do not capitalize the generic term: *Lincoln and Jefferson memorials, Yellowstone and Olympic national parks.*

(5) Names of organizations, government agencies, institutions, and companies

B'nai B'rith	National Endowment for the Humanities
Phi Beta Kappa	Internal Revenue Service
Howard University	Ford Motor Company

When used as common nouns, *service, company,* and *university* are not capitalized. However, some institutions, such as universities or corporations, capitalize their shortened names.

The policies of Hanson **U**niversity promote the rights of all individuals to equal opportunity in education. The **U**niversity complies with all applicable federal, state, and local laws.

(6) Names of days of the week, months, and holidays

Wednesday	August	Fourth of July

The names of the seasons—spring, summer, fall, winter—are not capitalized.

MULTILINGUAL WRITERS

CAPITALIZING DAYS OF THE WEEK

Capitalization rules vary according to language. For example, in English, the names of days and months are capitalized, but in some other languages, such as Spanish and Italian, they are not.

(7) Designations for historical documents, periods, events, movements, and styles

Declaration of Independence	Renaissance
Industrial Revolution	Impressionism

A historical period that includes a number is not capitalized unless it is considered a proper name.

twentieth century	the Roaring Twenties
the eighteen hundreds	the Gay Nineties

The name of a cultural movement or style is capitalized if it is derived from a proper name (1a(2)) or if capitalization distinguishes the name of the movement or style from the ordinary use of the word or phrase.

Platonism   Reaganomics   New Criticism

Most names of cultural movements and styles are not capitalized.

art deco   impressionism   realism   deconstruction

(8) Names of religions, their adherents, holy days, titles of holy books, and words denoting the Supreme Being

Buddhism, Christianity, Islam, Judaism

Buddhist, Christian, Muslim, Jew

Bodhi Day, Easter, Ramadan, Yom Kippur

Sutras, Bible, Koran, Talmud BUT biblical, talmudic

Buddha, God, Allah, Yahweh

Some writers always capitalize personal pronouns (5a(1)) that refer to the Supreme Being; others capitalize such words only when capitalization is needed to prevent ambiguity:

The Lord commanded the prophet to warn His people.

(9) Words derived from proper names

| Americanize | Orwellian | Marxism |
| [verb] | [adjective] | [noun] |

When a proper name becomes the name of a general class of objects or ideas, it is no longer capitalized. For example, *zipper*, originally a capitalized trademark, now refers to a class of fastening devices and is thus written with a lowercase letter. A word derived from a brand name, such as *Xerox*, *Kodak*, or *Kleenex*, should be capitalized. If possible, avoid using brand names and choose generic terms such as *photocopy, camera,* and *tissue* instead. If you are not sure whether a proper name or derivative has come to stand for a general class, look up the word in a dictionary.

(10) Abbreviations and acronyms

These forms are derived from the initial letters of capitalized word groups:

AMEX AT&T CBS CST NFL OPEC UNESCO YMCA

(See also chapter 11 and 17a(2).)

(11) Military terms

Names of forces and special units are capitalized, as are names of wars, battles, revolutions, and military awards.

United States Army	Eighth Air Force	Green Berets
Russian Revolution	Marine Corps	Purple Heart
Operation Overlord	Gulf War	

Military words such as *army*, *navy,* and *war* are not capitalized when they stand alone.

My sister joined the navy in 2008.

STYLE SHEET FOR CAPITALIZATION

Capitals	No capitals
the West [geographical region]	driving west [compass point]
a Chihuahua [a breed of dog named after a state in Mexico]	a poodle [a breed of dog]
Washington State University [a specific institution]	a state university
Revolutionary War [a specific war]	an eighteenth-century war
U.S. Army [a specific army]	a peacetime army
Declaration of Independence [title of a document]	a declaration of independence
May [specific month]	spring [general season]
Memorial Day [specific day]	a holiday
two Democratic candidates [refers to a political party]	democratic procedures [refers to a form of government]
a Ford tractor [brand name]	a farm tractor
Parkinson's disease [a disease named for a person]	flu, asthma, leukemia
Governor Clay [a person's title]	the governor of our state

9b Titles and subtitles

The first and last words in titles and subtitles are capitalized, as are major words—that is, all words other than articles (*a, an,* and *the*), coordinating conjunctions (*and, but, for, nor, or, so,* and *yet*), prepositions (see the list on page 33), and the infinitive marker *to*. (For more information on titles, see **10a** and **16b**.)

From Here to Eternity

"To Be a Student or Not to Be a Student"

APA guidelines differ slightly from other style guidelines: APA recommends capitalizing any word in a title, including a preposition, that has four or more letters.

Southwestern Pottery from Anasazi to Zuni [MLA]

Southwestern Pottery From Anasazi to Zuni [APA]

MLA and APA advise capitalizing all words in a hyphenated compound, except for articles, coordinating conjunctions, and prepositions.

"The Arab-Israeli Dilemma" [compound proper adjective]

"Stop-and-Go Signals" [lowercase for the coordinating conjunction]

When a hyphenated word containing a prefix appears in a title or subtitle, capitalize both elements if the second element is a proper noun (**1a(2)**) or adjective (*Pre-Columbian*). However, if the word following the prefix is a common noun (as in *anti-independence*), capitalize it only if you are following APA guidelines.

"Pre-Columbian Artifacts in Peruvian Museums" [MLA and APA]

"Anti-Independence Behavior in Adolescents" [APA]

"Anti-independence Behavior in Adolescents" [MLA]

9c Beginning a sentence

It is not difficult to remember that a sentence begins with a capital letter, but there are certain types of sentences that deserve special note.

(1) Capitalizing the first word in a quoted sentence

If a direct quotation is a full sentence, the first word should be capitalized.

> When asked to name the books she found most influential, Nadine Gordimer responded, "**I**n general, the works that mean most to one—change one's thinking and therefore maybe one's life—are those read in youth."

Even if you interrupt the quoted sentence with commentary, just the first letter should be capitalized.

> "**O**ddly," states Ved Mehta, "**l**ike my earliest memories, the books that made the greatest impression on me were the ones I encountered as a small child."

However, if you integrate someone else's sentence into a sentence of your own, the first letter should be lowercase—and placed in brackets if you are following MLA guidelines.

> Nadine Gordimer believes that "**[i]**n general, the works that mean most to one—change one's thinking and therefore maybe one's life—are those read in youth" (102).

(2) Capitalizing the first word in a freestanding parenthetical sentence

If you place a full sentence inside parentheses, and it is not embedded in a sentence of your own, be sure to capitalize the first word.

> Lance Armstrong won the Tour de France a record-breaking seven times. (**P**revious record holders include Jacques Anquetil, Bernard Hinault, Eddy Merckx, and Miguel Indurain.)

If the sentence inside the parentheses occurs within a sentence of your own, the first word should not be capitalized.

> Lance Armstrong won the Tour de France a record-breaking seven times (**p**reviously, he shared the record with four other cyclists).

(3) Lowercasing or capitalizing the first word in an independent clause following a colon

According to one style convention, if there is only one independent clause (1f) following a colon, the first word should be lowercased. However, if two or more independent clauses follow the colon, the first word of each clause is capitalized.

> The ear thermometer is used quite frequently now: this type of thermometer records a temperature more accurately than a glass thermometer.

> Two new thermometers are replacing the old thermometers filled with mercury: The digital thermometer uses a heat sensor to determine body temperature. The ear thermometer is actually an infrared thermometer that detects the temperature of the eardrum.

The APA manual recommends capitalizing the first word of any independent clause following a colon. The MLA manual advises capitalizing the first word only if the independent clause is a rule or principle.

> Think of fever as a symptom, not as an illness: It is the body's response to infection. [APA]

> He has two basic rules for healthy living: Eat sensibly and exercise strenuously at least three times a week. [APA and MLA]

A grammar checker will flag a word at the beginning of a sentence that should be capitalized, but it will not be able to determine whether a word following a colon should be capitalized.

(4) Capitalizing the first word of an abbreviated question

In a series of abbreviated questions, the first words of all the questions are capitalized when the intent is to draw attention to the questions. Otherwise, such questions begin with lowercase letters.

> How do we distinguish the legal codes for families? For individuals? For genetic research?

Did you remember to include your application? your résumé? your recommendations?

(5) Capitalizing a brand name that begins with a lowercase letter
A brand name such as *eBay* or *iPod* that begins with a lower-case letter should be capitalized if it is the first word in a sentence. However, a better choice is to recast the sentence so that the brand name occurs later.

Ebay attracts many shoppers.

Many people like to shop on eBay.

9d Computer keys, menu items, and icon names

When referring to specific computer keys, menu items, and icon names, capitalize the first letter of each.

To find the thesaurus, press Shift and the function key F7.

Instead of choosing Copy from the Edit menu, you can press Ctrl+C.

For additional information, click on Resources.

9e Unnecessary capitals

(1) Unnecessary capitalization of common nouns
The same noun can be either common or proper, depending on the context. A **proper noun** (1a(2)), also called a proper name, identifies a specific entity. A **common noun** (1a(2)), which is usually preceded by a word such as *the, a, an, this,* or *that,* is not capitalized.

a speech course in theater and television [COMPARE: Speech 324: Theater and Television] a university, this high school [COMPARE: University of Michigan, Bolton High School]

(2) Overusing capitalization to signal emphasis

Occasionally, a common noun is capitalized for emphasis.

Some politicians will do anything they can for Power.

If you use capitals for emphasis, do so sparingly; overuse will weaken the effect. For other ways to achieve emphasis, see chapter **29**.

(3) Signaling emphasis online

For online writing in academic and professional contexts, capitalize as you normally do. Be careful not to capitalize whole words for emphasis because your reader may think that you are SHOUTING—the term used to indicate the rudeness of this practice.

Exercise 1

Edit the capitalization errors in the following paragraph. Be prepared to explain any changes that you make.

¹Diana taurasi (Her teammates call her dee) plays basketball for the Phoenix mercury. ²She has all the skills she needs to be a Star Player: She can pass and shoot, as well as rebound, block, and steal. ³While playing for the university of connecticut huskies, she won the Naismith award twice and ranked in the majority of the big east's statistical categories. ⁴Shortly after the huskies won their third straight ncaa title, taurasi was drafted first overall by the Phoenix mercury. ⁵In april of 2004, taurasi played on the u.s. national team against japan, and, in the Summer of 2004, she made her olympic debut in Athens.

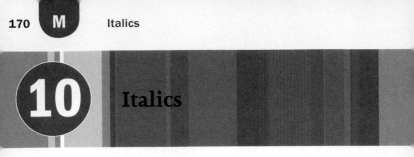

10 Italics

Italics indicate that a word or a group of words is being used in a special way. For example, the use of italics can clear up the ambiguity in the following sentence:

The linguistics students discussed the word stress.

Does this sentence mean that the students discussed a particular word or that they discussed the correct pronunciation of words? By italicizing *stress,* the writer indicates that it was the word, not an accent pattern, that the students discussed.

The linguistics students discussed the word *stress.*

This chapter will help you use italics for

- the titles of separate works (**10a**),
- foreign words (**10b**),
- the names of legal cases (**10c**),
- the names of ships, submarines, aircraft, spacecraft, and satellites (**10d**),
- words, letters, or figures used as such or letters used in mathematical expressions (**10e**), and
- words receiving emphasis (**10f**).

Word-processing programs make it easy to use italics. In handwritten or typewritten documents, you can indicate italics by underlining.

Edward P. Jones's novel <u>The Known World</u> won a Pulitzer Prize.

The use of italics instead of underlining is now widely accepted in business writing and academic writing. Both MLA and APA call for italics.

TECH SAVVY

Remember that in e-mail and on Web pages, an underlined word or phrase often indicates a hyperlink. If you are not able to format your e-mail or other electronic text with italics, use an underscore before and after words you would normally italicize.

Edward P. Jones's novel _The Known World_ won a Pulitzer Prize.

10a Titles of works published or produced separately

Italics indicate the title of a work published or produced as a whole rather than as part of a larger work. A newspaper, for example, is a separate work, but an editorial in a newspaper is not; thus, the title of the newspaper is italicized (or underlined), and the title of the editorial is enclosed in quotation marks (**16b**). These differing conventions help readers recognize the nature of a work and sometimes its relationship to another work.

Helen Keller's "Three Days to See" originally appeared in the *Atlantic Monthly.* [an essay in a magazine]

The titles of the following kinds of separate works are italicized:

Books	*The Hours*	*Unaccustomed Earth*
Magazines	*Wired*	*National Geographic*
Newspapers	*USA Today*	*Wall Street Journal*
Plays, films, videotapes	*Death of a Salesman*	*Akeelah and the Bee*
Television and radio shows	*American Idol*	*A Prairie Home Companion*
Recordings	*Kind of Blue*	*Great Verdi Overtures*
Works of art	*American Gothic*	*David*
Long poems	*Paradise Lost*	*The Divine Comedy*
Pamphlets	*Saving Energy*	*Tips for Gardeners*
Comic strips	*Peanuts*	*Doonesbury*

When an italicized title includes the title of a separate work within it, the embedded title is not italicized.

Modern Interpretations of Paradise Lost

If the italicized title includes the title of a short work within it, both titles are italicized, and the short work is also enclosed in quotation marks.

Willa Cather's "Paul's Case"

Titles should not be placed in italics or between quotation marks when they stand alone on a title page, a book cover, or a newspaper masthead. Likewise, neither italics nor quotation marks are necessary for titles of major historical documents, religious texts, or Web sites.

The Bill of Rights contains the first ten amendments to the U.S. Constitution.

The Bible, a sacred text just as the Koran or the Torah is, begins with the Book of Genesis.

Instructions for making a cane-and-reed basket can be found at Catherine Erdly's Web site, Basket Weaving.

According to MLA guidelines, an initial *the* in a newspaper or periodical title is not italicized. It is not capitalized either, unless it begins a sentence.

The story was published in the *New York Times*.

Also recommended is the omission of an article (*a, an,* or *the*) at the beginning of such a title when it would make a sentence awkward.

The report will appear in Thursday's ~~the~~ *Wall Street Journal*.

10b Foreign words

Use italics to indicate foreign words.

Japan has a rich store of traditional folktales, *mukashibanashi*, "tales of long ago."   —GARY SNYDER, *Back on the Fire*

A foreign word used frequently in a text should be italicized only once—at its first occurrence.

The Latin words used to classify plants and animals according to genus and species are italicized.

Homo sapiens   *Rosa setigera*   *Ixodes scapularis*

Countless words borrowed from other languages have become part of English and are therefore not italicized.

bayou (Choctaw)   karate (Japanese)   arroyo (Spanish)

If you are not sure whether a word has been accepted into English, look for it in a standard dictionary (**19e**).

10c Legal cases

Italics identify the names of legal cases.

Miranda v. Arizona   *Roe v. Wade*

The abbreviation *v.* (for "versus") may appear in either italic or nonitalic type, as long the style is used consistently. Italics are also used for the shortened name of a well-known legal case.

According to the *Miranda* decision, suspects must be informed of their right to remain silent and their right to legal advice.

Italics are not used to refer to a case by other than its official name.

All the major networks covered the O. J. Simpson trial.

10d Names of ships, submarines, aircraft, spacecraft, and satellites

Italicize the names of specific ships, submarines, aircraft, spacecraft, and satellites.

USS *Enterprise*   USS *Hawkbill*   *Enola Gay*   *Atlantis*   *Aqua*

The names of trains, the models of vehicles, and the trade names of aircraft are not italicized.

Orient Express   Ford Mustang   Boeing 747

10e Words, letters, or figures referred to as such and letters used in mathematical expressions

When you refer to a specific word, letter, or figure as itself, you should italicize it.

The word *love* is hard to define. [COMPARE: They were in love.]

The *b* in *bat* is not aspirated. [COMPARE: He earned a B+.]

The *2* on the sign has faded, and the *5* has disappeared. [COMPARE: She sent 250 cards.]

Statistical symbols and variables in algebraic expressions are also italicized.

The Pythagorean theorem is expressed as $a^2 + b^2 = c^2$.

10f Words receiving emphasis

Used sparingly, italics can signal readers to stress certain words.

These *are* the right files. [*Are* receives more stress than it normally would.]

Italics can also emphasize emotional content.

We have to go *now*. [The italicized word signals urgency.]

If overused, italics will lose their impact. Instead of italicizing words, substitute more specific words (chapter 20) or vary sentence structures (chapter 30).

Exercise 1

Identify all words that should be italicized in the following sentences. Explain why italics are necessary in each case.

1. Information about museum collections and exhibits can be found in art books, museum Web sites, and special sections of magazines and newspapers such as Smithsonian Magazine and the New York Times.

2. The Web site for the Metropolitan Museum of Art has pictures of Anthony Caro's sculpture Odalisque and Charles Demuth's painting The Figure 5 in Gold.

3. The title page of William Blake's Songs of Innocence is included in Masterpieces of the Metropolitan Museum of Art.

4. This book includes a photograph of a beautiful script used in the Koran; the script is known as the maghribi, or Western, style.

5. The large Tyrannosaurus rex discovered by Sue Hendrickson in South Dakota is on display at the Field Museum.

6. The International Museum of Cartoon Art provides information about the designers of such comic strips as Blondie, Peanuts, Mutt and Jeff, and Li'l Abner.

7. The Great Train Robbery, It Happened One Night, and Grand Illusion are in the collection at the Celeste Bartos Film Preservation Center.

8. In 1998, the Songwriters Hall of Fame honored John Williams, who has written music for such movies as Jaws, Star Wars, and E.T.

9. The Smithsonian Institution's National Air and Space Museum houses an impressive collection of aircraft and spacecraft, including Spirit of St. Louis and Gemini 4.

10. The digital collection listed on the Web site Experience Music Project includes music from the albums Fresh Cream and Bluesbreakers with Eric Clapton.

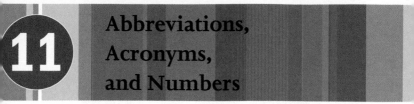

11 Abbreviations, Acronyms, and Numbers

Abbreviations, acronyms, and numbers facilitate easy recognition and effective communication in both academic papers and business documents. An **abbreviation** is a shortened version of a word or phrase: *assn.* (association), *dept.* (department), *et al.* (*et alii,* or "and others"). An **acronym** is formed by combining the initial letters and/or syllables of a series of words: *AIDS* (**a**cquired **i**mmune **d**eficiency **s**yndrome), *sonar* (**so**und **na**vigation **r**anging). This chapter will help you learn

- how and when to abbreviate (**11a**–**11d**),
- when to explain an acronym (**11e**), and
- whether to spell out a number or use numerals (**11f** and **11g**).

11a Abbreviations with names

The abbreviations *Ms., Mr., Mrs.,* and *Dr.* appear before names, whether given as full names or only surnames.

Ms. Gretel Lopez	**Mrs.** Marcus
Mr. Julio Rodriguez	**Dr.** Redshaw

Civil or military titles should not be abbreviated in academic writing.

Senator Larry Johnson   Captain James   Professor Sue Li

Abbreviated brand names create instant recognition for products or services.

Abbreviations such as *Jr., Sr.,* and *MD* appear after names.

Samuel Levy **Jr.**   Deborah Hvidsten, **MD**
Mark Ngo **Sr.**   Erika C. Schuerer, **PhD**

In the past, periods were customarily used in abbreviations for academic degrees, but MLA now recommends omitting periods from abbreviations such as *MA, PhD,* and *MD*. The convention calling for a comma to set off *Jr.* or *Sr.* is also changing; these abbreviations are increasingly considered part of the names they follow and are thus not set off by commas.

Note that when two designations are possible, only one should be used.

Dr. Carol Ballou OR Carol Ballou, **MD** [NOT Dr. Carol Ballou, MD]

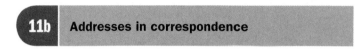

Most abbreviations of plural nouns end in -*s* alone, without an apostrophe: *Drs.* Ballou and Hvidsten. Exceptions are made when adding -*s* would create a different abbreviation, such as for *Mr.* and *Mrs.*

11b Addresses in correspondence

The names of states and words such as *Street, Road, Company,* and *Corporation* are usually written out when they appear in a letter, including in the address at the top of the page. However, they are abbreviated when used in the address on an envelope.

Sentence	Derson Manufacturing Company is located on Madison Street in Watertown, Minnesota.
Address	Derson Manufacturing Co.
	200 Madison St.
	Watertown, MN 55388

When addressing correspondence within the United States, use the two-letter state abbreviations established by the U.S. Postal Service. (No period follows these abbreviations.) If you do not know an appropriate state abbreviation or zip code, you can find it on the Postal Service's Web site.

11c Abbreviations in source documentation

Abbreviations are commonly used when citing research sources in bibliographies, footnotes, and endnotes. Common abbreviations include the following (not all citation styles accept all of these abbreviations).

Bibliographies and Notes

anon., Anon.	anonymous, Anonymous
biog.	biography, biographer, biographical
bull.	bulletin
c. or ca.	circa, about (for example, *c. 1920*)
col., cols.	column, columns
cont.	contents OR continues, continued
et al.	*et alii* ("and others")
fig.	figure
fwd.	foreword, foreword by
illus.	illustrated by, illustrator, illustration
inc., Inc.	including, Incorporated
intl.	international
introd.	introduction, introduction by
ms., mss.	manuscript, manuscripts
natl.	national
n.d.	no date, no date of publication
n.p.	no place of publication, no publisher
n. pag.	no pagination
no., nos.	number, numbers
p., pp.	page, pages
P, Pr.	Press
pref.	preface
pt., pts.	part, parts
trans. or tr.	translation, translated by
U, Univ.	University

Computer Terms

FTP	file transfer protocol
HTML	hypertext markup language
HTTP	hypertext transfer protocol
MOO	multiuser domain, object-oriented
URL	uniform resource locator

Divisions of Government

Cong.	Congress
dept.	department
div.	division
govt.	government
GPO	Government Printing Office
HR	House of Representatives

For abbreviations of Latin terms used in writing, see **11d(6)**.

11d Acceptable abbreviations in academic and professional writing

Abbreviations are usually too informal for use in sentences, but some have become so familiar that they are considered acceptable substitutes for full words.

(1) Abbreviations for special purposes

The names of months, days of the week, and units of measurement are usually written out (not abbreviated) when they are included in sentences, as are words such as *Street* and *Corporation*.

On a Tuesday in September, we drove ninety-nine miles to San Francisco, California, where we stayed in a hotel on Market Street.

Words such as *volume, chapter,* and *page* are abbreviated (*vol., ch.,* and *p.*) in bibliographies and in citations of research sources, but they are written out within sentences.

I read the introductory chapter and the three final pages in the first volume of the committee's report.

(2) Clipped forms

A word shortened by common usage, a **clipped form,** does not end with a period. Some clipped forms—such as *rep* (for representative), *exec* (for executive), and *info* (for information)—are too informal for use in college writing. Others—such as *exam, lab*, and *math*—have become acceptable because they have been used so frequently that they no longer seem like shortened forms.

(3) Abbreviations for time periods and zones

82 BC [OR BCE] for before Christ [OR before the common era]

AD 95 [OR 95 CE] for *anno Domini*, "in the year of our Lord" [OR the common era]

7:40 a.m. for *ante meridiem*, before noon

4:52 EST for Eastern Standard Time

Words designating units of time, such as *minute* and *month,* are written out when they appear in sentences. They can be abbreviated in tables or charts.

sec.   min.   hr.   wk.   mo.   yr.

(4) The abbreviation for the United States (U.S. or US) as an adjective

the U.S. Navy, the US economy

[COMPARE: They moved to the United States in 1990.]

The abbreviation *U.S.* or *US* should be used only as an adjective in academic and professional writing. When using *United States* as a noun, spell it out. The choice of U.S. or US will depend on the discipline in which you are writing: MLA lists US as the preferred form, but APA uses U.S.

(5) Individuals known by their initials

JFK   LBJ   E. B. White   B. B. King

In most cases, however, first and last names should be written out in full.

Oprah Winfrey   Tiger Woods

(6) Some abbreviations for Latin expressions

Certain abbreviations for Latin expressions are common in academic writing.

| cf. [compare] | et al. [and others] | i.e. [that is] |
| e.g. [for example] | etc. [and so forth] | vs. OR v. [versus] |

11e   Acronyms

The ability to identify a particular acronym will vary from one audience to another. Some readers will know that NAFTA stands for the North American Free Trade Agreement; others may not. By spelling out acronyms the first time you use them, you are being courteous and clear. Introduce the acronym by placing it in parentheses after the group of words it stands for.

The Federal Emergency Management Administration (FEMA) was criticized by many after Hurricane Katrina.

MULTILINGUAL WRITERS

USING ARTICLES WITH ABBREVIATIONS, ACRONYMS, OR NUMBERS

When you use an abbreviation, an acronym, or a number, you sometimes need an indefinite article. Choose *a* or *an* based on the pronunciation of the initial sound of the abbreviation, acronym, or number: use *a* before a consonant sound and *an* before a vowel sound.

A picture of **a UN** delegation is on the front page of today's newspaper. [*UN* begins with a consonant sound.]

I have **an IBM** computer. [*IBM* begins with a vowel sound.]

The reporter interviewed **a NASA** engineer. [*NASA* begins with a consonant sound.]

My friend drives **a 1964** Mustang. [*1964* begins with a consonant sound.]

Exercise 1

Place a check mark next to those forms that are appropriate for use in the sentences of a college essay. Correct those that are not.

1. after 8 p.m.
2. 457 *anno Domini*
3. on St. Clair Ave.
4. two blocks from Water Street
5. in Aug.
6. in the second mo. of the yr.
7. in Calif.
8. at the UN
9. Ms. Lydia Snow
10. for a prof.

11f   General uses of numbers

Depending on their uses, numbers are treated in different ways. MLA recommends spelling out numbers that are expressed in one or two words (*nine, ninety-one, nine hundred, nine million*). A numeral is used for any other number (*9½, 9.9, 999*), unless it begins a sentence.

> The register recorded 164 names.

APA advises spelling out only numbers below ten. Both MLA and APA recommend using words rather than numerals at the beginning of a sentence.

> One hundred sixty-four names were recorded in the register. [Notice that *and* is not used in numbers greater than one hundred. NOT One hundred and sixty-four names . . . .]

When numbers or amounts refer to the same entities throughout a passage, use numerals when any of the numbers would be more than two words long if spelled out.

> Only 5 of the 134 delegates attended the final meeting. The remaining 129 delegates will be informed by e-mail.

In scientific or technical writing, numerals are used before abbreviations of measurements (*2 L, 30 cc*).

11g   Special uses of numbers

(1) Expressing specific times of day in either numerals or words
Numerals or words can be used to express times of day. They should be used consistently.

4 p.m. OR four o'clock in the afternoon

9:30 a.m. OR half-past nine in the morning OR nine-thirty in the morning [Notice the use of hyphens.]

(2) Using numerals and words for dates

In a text, months are written as words, years are written as numerals, and days and decades are written as either words or numerals. However, 9/11 is an acceptable alternative to September 11, 2001.

May 20, 1976 OR 20 May 1976 [NOT May 20th, 1976]

the fourth of December OR December 4

the fifties OR the 1950s

from 1999 to 2003 OR 1999–2003 [Use an en dash, not a hyphen, in number ranges.]

TECH SAVVY

To create an en dash, press Option and the hyphen key simultaneously.

MULTILINGUAL WRITERS

DIFFERENT WAYS OF WRITING DATES

Many cultures invert the numerals for the month and the day: *14/2/2009* or *14 February 2009.* In publications from the United States, the month generally precedes the day: *2/14/2009* or *February 14, 2009.*

(3) Using numerals in addresses

Numerals are commonly used in a street address and for a zip code.

25 Arrow Drive, Apartment 1, Columbia, MO 78209

OR, for an envelope, 25 Arrow Dr., Apt. 1, Columbia, MO 78209

(4) Using numerals for identification

A numeral may be used as part of a proper noun (**1a(2)**).

Channel 10   Edward III   Interstate 40   Room 311

(5) Referring to pages and divisions of books and plays

Numerals are used to designate pages and other divisions of books and plays.

page 15   chapter 8   part 2

in act 2, scene 1 OR in Act II, Scene I

(6) Expressing decimals and percentages numerically

Numerals are used to express decimals and percentages.

a 2.5 average   12 percent   0.853 metric ton

(7) Using numerals for large fractional numbers

Numerals with decimal points can be used to express large fractional numbers.

5.2 million inhabitants   1.6 billion years

(8) Different ways of writing monetary amounts

Monetary amounts should be spelled out if they occur infrequently in a piece of writing. Otherwise, numerals and symbols can be used.

two million dollars $2,000,000
ninety-nine cents   99¢ OR $0.99

MULTILINGUAL WRITERS

COMMAS AND PERIODS WITH NUMERALS

Cultures differ in their use of the period and the comma with numerals. In American usage, a decimal point (period) indicates a number or part of a number that is smaller than one, and a comma divides large numbers into units of three digits.

7.65 (seven and sixty-five one-hundredths)

10,000 (ten thousand)

In some other cultures, these usages of the decimal point and the comma are reversed.

7,65 (seven and sixty-five one-hundredths)

10.000 (ten thousand)

Exercise 2

Edit the following sentences to correct the usage of abbreviations and numbers.

1. A Natl. Historic Landmark, Hoover Dam is located about 30 miles s.e. of Las. Vegas, Nev.
2. The dam is named after Herbert Hoover, the 31st pres. of the U.S.
3. It is administered by the U.S. Dept. of the Interior.
4. Built by the fed. gov. between nineteen thirty-three and 1935, this dam is still considered one of the greatest achievements in the history of civ. engineering.
5. Construction of the dam became possible after several states in the Southwest (namely, AZ, CA, CO, NV, NM, UT, and WY) agreed on a plan to share water from the river.

6. The concrete used in the dam would have built a highway 16 ft. wide, stretching all the way from San Francisco to NYC.

7. 3,500 men worked on the dam during an average month of construction; this work translated into a monthly payroll of $500,000.

8. Spanning the Colorado River, Hoover Dam created Lake Mead—a reservoir covering 247 sq. miles.

9. A popular tourist attraction, Hoover Dam was closed to the public after terrorists attacked the U.S. on 9/11/01.

10. Today, certain pts. of the dam remain closed to the public as part of the effort to improve U.S. security.

P

PUNCTUATION

The use of the period, a strong mark of punctuation, with the words "Smart. Tough. Elite." reinforces the strength of the image.

12 The Comma

Punctuation lends to written language the flexibility that pauses and variations in voice pitch give to spoken language. Pauses are often signaled by commas; however, they are not the most reliable guide for comma placement, because commas are often called for where speakers do not pause and pauses can occur where no comma is necessary. A better guide is an understanding of some basic principles of comma usage.

This chapter will help you use commas to

- separate independent clauses joined by coordinating conjunctions (**12a**),
- set off introductory clauses, phrases, and words (**12b**),
- separate items in a series (**12c**),
- set off nonessential (nonrestrictive) elements (**12d**),
- set off geographical names and items in dates and addresses (**12e**), and
- set off direct quotations (**12f**).

12a Before a coordinating conjunction linking independent clauses

Use a comma before a coordinating conjunction (*and, but, for, nor, or, so,* or *yet*) that links two independent clauses. An **independent clause** is a group of words that can stand as a sentence (**1f(1)**).

> INDEPENDENT CLAUSE, **CONJUNCTION**
> INDEPENDENT CLAUSE.
>
> | | **and** | |
> | | **but** | |
> | | **for** | |
> | Subject + predicate, | **nor** | subject + predicate. |
> | | **or** | |
> | | **so** | |
> | | **yet** | |

The Iditarod Trail Sled Dog Race begins in March, **but** training starts much sooner.

In the 1960s, Dorothy Page wanted to spark interest in the role of dog sledding in Alaskan history, **so** she proposed staging a long race.

No matter how many clauses are in a sentence, a comma comes before each coordinating conjunction.

The race takes several days to complete, **and** training is a year-round activity, **but** the mushers do not complain.

When the independent clauses are short, the comma is often omitted before *and, but,* or *or.*

My friend races **but** I don't.

If a coordinating conjunction joins two parts of a compound predicate (which means there is only one subject), a comma is not normally used before the conjunction. (See **1b** and **13c**.)

The race starts in Anchorage and ends in Nome.

A semicolon, instead of a comma, precedes a conjunction joining two independent clauses when at least one of the clauses already contains a comma. (See also **14b**.)

When running long distances, sled dogs burn more than ten thousand calories a day**;** **so** they must be fed well.

Exercise 1

Combine each of the following pairs of sentences by using coordinating conjunctions and inserting commas where appropriate. (Remember that not all coordinating conjunctions link independent clauses and that *but, for, so,* and *yet* do not always function as coordinating conjunctions.) Explain why you used each of the conjunctions you inserted.

1. Dinosaurs lived for 165 million years. Then they became extinct.
2. No one knows why dinosaurs became extinct. Several theories have been proposed.
3. Some theorists believe that a huge meteor hit the earth. The climate may have changed dramatically.
4. Another theory suggests that dinosaurs did not actually become extinct. They simply evolved into lizards and birds.
5. Yet another theory suggests that they just grew too big. Not all of the dinosaurs were huge.

12b | After introductory clauses, phrases, or words

(1) A comma follows an introductory dependent clause.
If you begin a sentence with a dependent (subordinate) clause (**1f(2)**), place a comma after it to set it off from the independent (main) clause (**1f(1)**).

> **INTRODUCTORY CLAUSE,** INDEPENDENT CLAUSE.

Although the safest automobile on the road is expensive, the protection it offers justifies the cost.

(2) A comma follows an introductory phrase.
Place a comma after an introductory phrase to set it off from the independent clause.

> **INTRODUCTORY PHRASE,** INDEPENDENT CLAUSE.

(a) Introductory prepositional phrases

Despite a downturn in the national economy, the number of students enrolled in this university has increased.

If you begin a sentence with a short introductory prepositional phrase (**1e(4)**), you may omit the comma as long as the resulting sentence is not difficult to read.

In 2009 the enrollment at the university increased.
BUT
In 2009, 625 new students enrolled in courses. [A comma separates two numbers.]

A comma is not used after a phrase that begins a sentence in which the subject and predicate (**1b**) are inverted.

With children came responsibilities.
[The subject of the sentence is *responsibilities*: Responsibilities came with children.]

(b) Other types of introductory phrases
If you begin a sentence with a participial phrase (**1e(3)**) or an absolute phrase (**1e(6)**), place a comma after it.

Having traveled nowhere, she believed the rest of the world was like her own small town. [participial phrase]

The language difference aside, life in Germany did not seem much different from life in the United States. [absolute phrase]

(3) A comma often follows an introductory word.

> **INTRODUCTORY WORD**, INDEPENDENT CLAUSE.

Use a comma to set off interjections, **vocatives** (words used to address someone directly), or transitional words.

Oh, I forgot about the board meeting. [interjection]

Bob, I want you to know that your design impressed everyone on the board. [vocative]

Moreover, the design will increase efficiency in the office. [transitional word]

When there is no risk of misunderstanding, some introductory adverbs and transitional words do not need to be set off by a comma (see also **14a**).

Sometimes even a good design is rejected by the board.

Exercise 2

Insert commas wherever necessary in the following paragraph. Explain why each comma is needed. Some sentences may not require editing.

¹If you had to describe sound would you call it a wave? ²Although sound cannot be seen people have described it this

way for a long time. [3]In fact the Greek philosopher Aristotle believed that sound traveling through air was like waves in the sea. [4]Envisioning waves in the air he hypothesized that sound would not be able to pass through a vacuum because there would be no air to transmit it. [5]Aristotle's hypothesis was not tested until nearly two thousand years later. [6]In 1654 Otto von Guericke found that he could not hear a bell ringing inside the vacuum he had created. [7]Thus Guericke established the necessity of air for sound transmission. [8]However although most sound reaches us through the air it travels faster through liquids and solids.

12c   Separating elements in a series

A **series** contains three or more parallel elements. To be parallel, elements must be grammatically equal; for example, all must be phrases, not combinations of phrases and clauses. (See chapter **26**.)

(1) Commas separate words, phrases, or clauses in a series.
A comma appears after each item in a series except the last one.

Ethics are based on **moral, social,** or **cultural values**. [words]

The company's code of ethics encourages **seeking criticism of work, correcting mistakes,** and **acknowledging the contributions of everyone**. [phrases]

Several circumstances can lead to unethical behavior: **people are tempted by a desire to succeed, they are pressured by others into acting inappropriately,** or **they are simply trying to survive**. [clauses in a series]

If elements in a series contain internal commas, you can prevent misreading by separating the items with semicolons.

According to their code of ethics, researchers must disclose all results, without omitting any data; indicate various interpretations of the data; and make the data and methodology available to other researchers, some of whom may choose to replicate the study.

THINKING RHETORICALLY

COMMAS AND CONJUNCTIONS IN A SERIES

How do the following sentences differ?

We discussed them all: life, liberty, **and** the pursuit of happiness.
We discussed them all: life **and** liberty **and** the pursuit of happiness.
We discussed them all: life, liberty, the pursuit of happiness.

The first sentence follows conventional guidelines; that is, a comma and a conjunction precede the last element in the series. The less conventional second and third sentences do more than convey information. Having two conjunctions and no commas, the second sentence slows down the pace of the reading, causing stress to be placed on each of the three elements in the series. In contrast, the third sentence, with commas but no conjunctions, speeds up the reading, as if to suggest that the rights listed do not need to be stressed because they are so familiar. To get a sense of how your sentences will be read and understood, try reading them aloud to yourself.

(2) Commas separate coordinate adjectives.

Two or more adjectives that precede the same noun are called **coordinate adjectives.** To test whether adjectives are coordinate, either interchange them or put *and* between them. If the altered version of the phrase is acceptable, the adjectives are coordinate and should be separated by a comma or commas.

Crossing the **rushing, shallow** creek, I slipped off a rock and
fell into the water.

[COMPARE: a rushing and shallow creek OR a shallow,
rushing creek]

The adjectives in the following sentence are not separated by
a comma. Notice that they cannot be interchanged or joined
by *and*.

Sitting in the water, I saw an **old wooden** bridge.

[NOT a wooden old bridge OR an old and wooden bridge]

12d With nonessential elements

Nonessential (nonrestrictive) elements provide supplemen-
tal information, that is, information a reader does not need
in order to identify who or what is being discussed (see also
1f(2)). Use commas to set off a nonessential word or word
group: one comma separates a nonessential element at the end
of a sentence; two commas set off a nonessential element in
the middle of a sentence.

The Hilltop Folk Festival**, planned for late July,** should
attract many tourists.

In the preceding sentence, the phrase placed between commas, *planned for late July*, conveys nonessential information: the
reader knows which festival will attract tourists without being
told when it will be held. When a phrase follows a proper noun
(1a(2)), such as *The Hilltop Folk Festival*, it is usually nonessential. Note, however, that in the following sentence, the phrase
planned for late July is necessary for the reader to identify the festival as the one scheduled for late July, not for a different time.

The festival **planned for late July** should attract many tourists.

In the preceding sentence, the phrase is an **essential (restrictive) element** because, without it, the reader will not know which festival the writer has in mind. Essential elements are not set off by commas; they are integrated into the sentence (**1f(2)**).

(1) Commas set off nonessential elements used as modifiers.
(a) Adjectival clauses
Nonessential modifiers are often **adjectival (relative) clauses**—those clauses usually introduced by the relative pronoun *who, which,* or *that* (**1f(2)**). In the following sentence, a comma sets off the adjectival clause because the reader does not need the content of that clause in order to identify the mountain.

> We climbed Mt. McKinley**, which is over 15,000 feet high**.

(b) Participial phrases
Nonessential modifiers also include **participial phrases** (phrases introduced by a present or past participle) (**1e(3)**).

> Mt. McKinley**, towering above us,** brought to mind our abandoned plan for climbing it. [participial phrase beginning with a present participle]
>
> My sister**, slowed by a knee injury,** rarely hikes anymore. [participial phrase beginning with a past participle]

(c) Adverbial clauses
An **adverbial clause** (**1f(2)**) begins with a subordinating conjunction signaling cause (*because*), purpose (*so that*), or time (*when, after, before*). This type of clause is usually considered essential and thus is not set off by commas when it appears at the end of a sentence.

> Dinosaurs may have become extinct **because their habitat was destroyed.**

In contrast, an adverbial clause that provides nonessential information, such as an extra comment, should be set off from the main clause.

Dinosaurs are extinct, **though they are alive in many people's imaginations.**

(2) Commas set off nonessential appositives.

Appositives refer to the same person, place, object, idea, or event as a nearby noun or noun phrase but with different words (1e(5)). Nonessential appositives provide extra details about nouns or noun phrases (1e(1)) and are set off by commas; essential appositives are not. In the following sentence, the title of the article is mentioned, so the reader does not need the information provided by the appositive in order to identify the article. The appositive is thus set off by commas.

"Living on the Line," **Joanne Hart's most recent article,** describes the lives of factory workers in China.

In the next sentence, *Joanne Hart's article* is nonspecific, so an essential appositive containing the specific title of the article is integrated into the sentence. It is not set off by commas. Without the appositive, the reader would not know which of Hart's articles describes the lives of factory workers in China.

Joanne Hart's article "Living on the Line" describes the lives of factory workers in China.

If Hart had written only this one article, the title would be set off by commas. The reader would not need the information in the appositive to identify the article.

Abbreviations of titles or degrees after names are treated as nonessential appositives.

Was the letter from Frances Evans, PhD, or from Francis Evans, MD?

Increasingly, however, *Jr., Sr., II,* and *III* are considered part of a name, in which case the comma is omitted.

William Homer Barton**,** Jr.   OR   William Homer Barton Jr.

Exercise 3

Set off nonessential clauses, phrases, and appositives with commas.

1. Maine Coons long-haired cats with bushy tails have adapted to a harsh climate.
2. These animals which are extremely gentle despite their large size often weigh twenty pounds.
3. Most Maine Coons have exceptionally high intelligence for cats which enables them to recognize language and even to open doors.
4. Unlike most cats Maine Coons will play fetch with their owners.
5. According to a legend later proven to be false Maine Coons developed from interbreeding between wildcats and domestic cats.

(3) Commas set off absolute phrases.

An **absolute phrase** (the combination of a noun and a modifying word or phrase; see **1e(6)**) provides nonessential details and so should always be set off by a comma or commas.

The actor**,** **his hair wet and slicked back,** began his audition.

The director stared at him**,** **her mind flipping through the photographs she had viewed earlier.**

(4) Commas set off transitional expressions and other parenthetical elements.

Commas customarily set off transitional words and phrases such as *for example, that is,* and *namely.*

An airline ticket**,** **for example,** can be delivered electronically.

Because they generally indicate little or no pause in reading, transitional words and phrases such as *also, too, at least,* and *thus* need not be set off by commas.

Traveling has **thus** become easier in recent years.

Use commas to set off other parenthetical elements, such as words or phrases that provide commentary you wish to stress.

Over the past year, my flights have**,** **miraculously,** been on time.

(5) Commas set off contrasted elements.

Commas set off sentence elements in which words such as *never* and *unlike* express contrast.

A planet**,** **unlike** a star**,** reflects rather than generates light.

In sentences in which contrasted elements are introduced by *not only . . . but also,* place a comma before *but* if you want to emphasize what follows it. Otherwise, leave the comma out.

Planets **not only** vary in size**,** **but also** travel at different speeds. [Comma added for emphasis.]

12e | **With geographical names and items in dates and addresses**

Use commas to make geographical names, dates, and addresses easy to read.

(1) City and state

Nashville, Tennessee, is the largest country-and-western music center in the United States.

(2) Day and date

Martha left for Peru on **Wednesday, February 12, 2009,** and returned on March 12.

OR

Martha left for Peru on **Wednesday, 12 February 2009,** and returned on 12 March.

In the style used in the second example (which is not as common in the United States as the style in the first example), one comma is omitted because *12* precedes rather than follows *February.*

(3) Addresses

In a sentence containing an address, the name of the person or organization, the street address, and the name of the town or city are all followed by commas, but the abbreviation for the state is not.

I had to write to **Ms. Melanie Hobson, Senior Analyst, Hobson Computing, 2873 Central Avenue, Orange Park, FL 32065.**

12f With direct quotations

Many sentences containing direct quotations also contain attributive tags such as *The author claims* or *According to the author* (**39d(2)**). Use commas to set off these tags whether they occur at the beginning, in the middle, or at the end of a sentence.

(1) Attributive tag at the beginning of a sentence

Place the comma directly after the attributive tag, before the quotation marks.

According to Jacques Barzun, "It is a false analogy with science that makes one think latest is best."

(2) Attributive tag in the middle of a sentence

Place the first comma inside the quotation marks that precede the attibutive tag; place the second comma directly after the tag, before the next set of quotation marks.

"It is a false analogy with science," claims Jacques Barzun, "that makes one think latest is best."

(3) Attributive tag at the end of a sentence

Place the comma inside the quotation marks before the attributive tag.

"It is a false analogy with science that makes one think latest is best," claims Jacques Barzun.

13

Unnecessary or Misplaced Commas

Although a comma may signal a pause, not every pause calls for a comma. As you read the following sentence aloud, you may pause naturally at several places, but no commas are necessary.

Heroic deeds done by ordinary people inspire others to act in ways that are not only moral but courageous.

This chapter will help you recognize unnecessary or misplaced commas that

- separate a subject and its verb or a verb and its object (**13a**),
- follow a coordinating conjunction (**13b**),
- separate elements in a compound predicate (**13c**),
- set off essential words, phrases, or clauses (**13d**), and
- precede the first item of a series or follow the last (**13e**).

13a No comma between a subject and its verb or a verb and its object

Although speakers often pause after the subject (**1b**) or before the object (**1c**) of a sentence, such a pause should not be indicated by a comma.

In this climate, rain at frequent intervals⌢produces mosquitoes. [no separation between the subject (*rain*) and the verb (*produces*)]

The forecaster said⌢that rain was likely. [no separation between the verb (*said*) and the direct object (the noun clause *that rain was likely*)]

13b   No comma following a coordinating conjunction

Avoid using a comma after a coordinating conjunction (*and, but, for, nor, or, so,* or *yet*).

> We worked very hard on her campaign for state representative, but ~~,~~ the incumbent was too strong to defeat in the northern districts.

13c   No comma separating elements in a compound predicate

In general, avoid using a comma between two elements of a compound predicate (**1b**).

> I read the comments carefully ~~,~~ and then started my revision.

However, if you want to place stress on the second element in a compound predicate, you may place a comma after the first element. Use this option sparingly, or it will lose its effect.

> I read the comments word by word**,** and despaired.

13d   No commas setting off essential words, phrases, or clauses

In the following sentences, the elements in boldface are essential and so should not be set off by commas (**12d**).

> Zoe was born ~~,~~ **in Chicago during the Great Depression.**
>
> **Perhaps** ~~,~~ the thermostat is broken.
>
> Everyone ~~,~~ **who has a mortgage** ~~,~~ is required to have fire insurance.
>
> Someone ~~,~~ **wearing an orange wig** ~~,~~ greeted us at the door.

13e No comma preceding the first item of a series or following the last

Make sure that you place commas only between elements in a series, not before or after them.

She was known for her photographs, sketches, and engravings.

The exhibit included her most exuberant, exciting, and expensive photographs.

Exercise 1

Explain the use of each comma in the following paragraph.

[1]Contrails, which are essentially artificial clouds, form when moisture in the air condenses around particles in jet exhaust. [2]Like ordinary clouds, contrails block incoming sunlight and trap heat radiated from Earth's surface. [3]This process reduces daytime highs and increases nighttime lows, narrowing the temperature range. [4]Multiple contrails can cluster together and obscure an area as large as Iowa, Illinois, and Missouri combined, magnifying the effect. [5]Although they may not alter the overall climate, contrails could still have environmental consequences. —LAURA CARSTEN, "Climate on the Wing"

14 The Semicolon

The semicolon indicates that the phrases or clauses on either side of it are closely related. It most frequently connects two independent clauses when the second clause supports or contrasts with the first, but it can be used for other purposes as well. This chapter will help you understand that semicolons

- link closely related independent clauses (**14a**) and
- separate parts of a sentence containing internal commas (**14b**) but
- do not connect independent clauses to phrases or dependent clauses (**14c**).

14a Connecting independent clauses

A semicolon placed between two independent clauses indicates that they are closely related. The second of the two clauses generally supports or contrasts with the first.

For many cooks, basil is a key ingredient; it appears in recipes worldwide. [support]

Sweet basil is used in many Mediterranean dishes; Thai basil is used in Asian and East Indian recipes. [contrast]

Although *and, but*, and similar words can signal these kinds of relationships, consider using an occasional semicolon for variety.

Sometimes, a transitional expression such as *for example* or *however* (3c(5)) accompanies a semicolon and further establishes the exact relationship between the ideas.

Basil is omnipresent in the cuisine of some countries; **for example,** Italians use basil in salads, soups, and many vegetable dishes.

The culinary uses of basil are well known; **however,** this herb also has medicinal uses.

A comma is usually inserted after a transitional word, though it can be omitted if doing so will not lead to a misreading.

Because *basil* comes from a Greek word meaning "king," it suggests royalty; **indeed** some cooks accord basil royal status among herbs and spices.

14b   Separating elements that contain commas

In a series of phrases or clauses (1e–i) that contain commas, semicolons indicate where each phrase or clause ends and the next begins.

To survive, mountain lions need a large area in which to range; a steady supply of deer, skunks, raccoons, foxes, and opossums; and the opportunity to find a mate, establish a den, and raise a litter.

In this sentence, the semicolons help the reader distinguish three separate phrases.

Exercise 1

Revise the following sentences, using semicolons to separate in-dependent clauses or elements that contain internal commas.

1. Soccer is a game played by two opposing teams on a rectangular field, each team tries to knock a round ball, roughly twenty-eight inches in circumference, through the opponent's goal.

2. The game is called *soccer* only in Canada and the United States, elsewhere it is known as *football*.

3. Generally, a team consists of eleven players: defenders (or fullbacks), who defend the goal by trying to win control of the ball, midfielders (or halfbacks), who play both defense and offense, attackers (or forwards), whose primary responsibility is scoring goals; and a goalkeeper (or goalie), who guards the goal.

4. In amateur matches, players can be substituted frequently, however, in professional matches, the number of substitutions is limited.

5. Soccer players depend on five skills: kicking, which entails striking the ball powerfully with the top of the foot, dribbling, which requires tapping or rolling the ball while running, passing, which is similar to kicking but with less power and more control, heading, which involves striking the ball with the forehead, and trapping, which is the momentary stopping of the ball.

14c Revising common semicolon errors

Semicolons do not set off phrases (1e) or dependent clauses (1f(2)) unless they contain commas. Use commas for these purposes.

We consulted Alinka Kibukian;, the local horticulturalist.
                                        ^

Needing summer shade;, we planted two of the largest trees we could afford.
                              ^

We learned that young trees need care; which meant we had to do some extra chores after dinner each night.

Our trees survived; even though we live in a harsh climate.

Exercise 2

Use a comma to replace any semicolon that sets off a phrase or a dependent clause. Do not change properly used semicolons.

1. Every morning I take vitamins; a multivitamin and sometimes extra vitamin C.
2. I used to believe that I could get my vitamins from a balanced diet; then I found out that diet may not provide enough of some vitamins, such as folic acid.
3. By eating a balanced diet, getting plenty of exercise, and keeping stress to a minimum; I thought I would stay healthy.
4. New research suggests that multivitamins are beneficial; when our diets do not provide all the recommended amounts of every vitamin every day; our health can suffer.
5. Although taking one multivitamin tablet a day is a healthy habit; we do not need to buy the most potent or most expensive vitamins available.

Exercise 3

Find or compose one sentence to illustrate each of the following uses of the semicolon.

1. To link two related independent clauses
2. To separate clauses in a sentence containing a transitional expression such as *however* or *for example*
3. To separate phrases or clauses that contain commas

15   The Apostrophe

Apostrophes serve a number of purposes. For example, you can use them to show that someone owns something *(my neighbor's television),* that someone has a specific relationship with someone else *(my neighbor's children),* or that someone has produced or created something *(my neighbor's recipe).* Apostrophes are also used in contractions *(can't, don't)* and in certain plural forms *(x's and y's).* This chapter will help you use apostrophes to

- indicate ownership and other relationships (**15a**),
- mark omissions of letters or numbers (**15b**), and
- form certain plurals (**15c**).

15a   Indicating ownership and other relationships

An apostrophe, often followed by an *s,* signals the possessive case of nouns. (For information on case, see **5b**.) Possessive nouns are used to express a variety of meanings.

Ownership	**Fumi's** computer, the **photographer's** camera
Origin	**Einstein's** ideas, the **student's** decision
Human relationships	**Linda's** sister, the **employee's** supervisor

Possession of physical or psychological traits	**Mona Lisa's** smile, the **team's** spirit
Association between abstractions and attributes	**democracy's** success, **tyranny's** influence
Identification of documents and credentials	**driver's** license, **bachelor's** degree
Identification of things named after people	**St. John's** Cathedral, **Valentine's** Day
Specification of amounts	a **day's** wages, an **hour's** delay

MULTILINGUAL WRITERS

WORD WITH APOSTROPHE AND S OR PHRASE BEGINNING WITH *OF*

In many cases, to indicate ownership, origin, and other meanings discussed in this chapter, you can use either a word with an apostrophe and an *s* or a prepositional phrase beginning with *of*.

Louise Erdrich's novels   OR   the novels **of** Louise Erdrich

the plane's arrival   OR   the arrival **of** the plane

However, the ending -'s is more commonly used with nouns referring to people, and a phrase beginning with *of* is used with most nouns referring to location.

my **uncle's** workshop, **Jan's** car, the **student's** paper [nouns referring to people]

the **end of** the movie, the **middle of** the day, the **front of** the building [nouns referring to location]

(1) Most singular nouns, indefinite pronouns, abbreviations, and acronyms require -'s to form the possessive case.

the dean's office [noun]

Yeats's poems [noun]

anyone's computer [indefinite pronoun]

the NFL's reputation [abbreviation]

OPEC's price increase [acronym]

Walter Bryan Jr.'s letter [To avoid confusion, no comma precedes *Jr.'s* here. *Jr.* is sometimes set off by a comma, however (**12d(2)**).]

To form the possessive of most singular proper nouns, add an apostrophe and an *s: Iowa's governor.* When a singular proper noun ends in *-s*, though, you will have to consult the style guide for the discipline in which you are writing. The *MLA Handbook for Writers of Research Papers* recommends always using *-'s,* as in *Illinois's legislature, Dickens's novels, Ms. Jones's address,* and *Descartes's reasoning.* Other style guides allow some exceptions to this rule. An apostrophe without an *s* may be acceptable in the following circumstances: (1) when a name ends in a syllable pronounced "eez" *(Sophocles' poetry),* (2) when a singular common noun ends in *-s (physics' contribution),* and (3) when the name of a place or an organization ends in *-s* but refers to a single entity *(United States' foreign aid).*

Possessive pronouns *(my, mine, our, ours, your, yours, his, her, hers, its, their, theirs,* and *whose)* are not written with apostrophes (**5b(3)**).

Japanese democracy differs from **ours.**

The committee concluded **its** discussion.

! CAUTION

Be careful not to confuse possessive pronouns with contractions. Whenever you write a contraction, you should be able to substitute the complete words for it without changing the meaning.

Possessive pronoun	Contraction
Its motor is small.	**It's** [It is] a small motor.
Whose turn is it?	**Who's** [Who is] representing us?

---

(2) Plural nouns ending in -s require only an apostrophe for the possessive form.

the boys' game   the babies' toys   the Joneses' house

Plural nouns that do not end in *-s* need both an apostrophe and an *s*.

men's lives   women's health   children's projects

! CAUTION

An apostrophe is not needed to make a noun plural. To make most nouns plural, add *-s* or *-es.* Add an apostrophe only to signal ownership, origin, and other similar relationships.

> protesters
> The ~~protesters'~~ met in front of the conference center.

The protesters' meeting was on Wednesday.

Likewise, to form the plural of a family name, use *-s* or *-es,* not an apostrophe.

> Johnsons
> The ~~Johnson's~~ participated in the study.

[COMPARE: The Johnsons' participation in the study was crucial.]

> Jameses
> The trophy was given to the ~~James's.~~

[COMPARE: The Jameses' trophy is on display in the lobby.]

(3) To show collaboration or joint ownership, add -'s or an apostrophe to the second noun only.

In the examples below, the ending -'s follows the second singular noun (*plumber*). Just an apostrophe follows the second plural noun (*Lopezes*), which already ends in -s.

> the carpenter and the **plumber's** decision [They made the decision collaboratively.]
>
> the Becks and the **Lopezes'** cabin [They own one cabin jointly.]

(4) To show separate ownership or individual contributions, add -'s or an apostrophe to each noun.

In the examples below, each plural noun is followed by an apostrophe, and each singular noun is followed by -'s.

> the **Becks'** and the **Lopezes'** cars [Each family owns a car.]
>
> the **carpenter's** and the **plumber's** proposals [They each made a proposal.]

(5) Add -'s to the last word of a compound noun.

> my brother-in-**law's** friends, the attorney **general's** statements [singular]
>
> my brothers-in-**law's** friends, the attorneys **general's** statements [plural]

To avoid awkward constructions such as the last two, consider using a prepositional phrase beginning with *of* instead: *the statements of the attorneys general.*

(6) Add -'s or just an apostrophe to a noun preceding a gerund.

Depending on its number, a noun that precedes a gerund takes either -'s or just an apostrophe.

> Lucy's **having** to be there seemed unnecessary. [singular noun preceding gerund]
>
> The family appreciated the lawyers' **handling** of the matter. [plural noun preceding gerund]

Sometimes you may find it difficult to distinguish between a gerund and a participle (1e(3)). A good way to tell the difference is to note whether the emphasis is on an action or on a person. In a sentence containing a gerund, the emphasis is on the action; in a sentence containing a participle, the emphasis is on the person.

Our successful completion of the project depends on **Terry's providing** the illustrations. [gerund]

I remember my **brother telling** me the same joke last year. [participle]

(7) Follow an organization's preference for its name or the name of a product; follow local conventions for a geographical location.

Consumers Union	Actors' Equity	Taster's Choice
Devil's Island	Devils Tower	Devil Mountain

Whether an apostrophe is used in a brand name is determined by the organization that owns the name.

Exercise 1

Following the pattern of the examples, change the modifier after each noun to a possessive form that precedes the noun.

EXAMPLES

proposals made by the committee   the committee's proposals

poems written by Keats   Keats's poems

1. the day named after St. Patrick
2. a leave of absence lasting six months
3. the position taken by HMOs
4. the report given by the eyewitness
5. the generosity of the Lees
6. an article coauthored by Gloria and Alan
7. the weights of the children
8. the spying done by the neighbors
9. the restaurants in New Orleans
10. coffee roasted by Starbucks

15b   Marking omissions of letters or numbers

Apostrophes mark omissions in contractions, numbers, and words mimicking speech.

they're [they are]   class of '09 [class of 2009]

y'all [you all]   singin' [singing]

Contractions are not always appropriate for formal contexts. Your audience may expect you to use full words instead (for example, *cannot* instead of *can't* and *will not* instead of *won't*).

15c Forming certain plurals

Although an apostrophe was used in the past to form the plurals of numbers, abbreviations, and words used as words, it is used only rarely for this purpose today. These plurals are generally formed by simply adding -s.

  1990s   fours and fives   YWCAs   two *and*s   the three Rs

Apostrophes are still used, however, with lowercase letters and with abbreviations that include a combination of uppercase and lowercase letters.

  x's and *y*'s   *A*'s and *B*'s   PhD's

Exercise 2

Insert apostrophes where needed in the following sentences. Be prepared to explain why they are necessary.

1. Whose responsibility is it to see whether its working?
2. Hansons book was published in the early 1920s.
3. They hired a rock n roll band for their wedding dance.
4. NPRs fund drive begins this weekend.
5. Youll have to include the ISBNs of the books youre going to purchase.
6. Only three of the proposals are still being considered: yours, ours, and the Wilbers.
7. Few students enrolled during the academic year 06–07.
8. There cant be more *x*s than there are *y*s in the equation.
9. The students formed groups of twos and threes.
10. He is the only person I know who has two PhDs.

16 Quotation Marks

Quotation marks enclose sentences or parts of sentences that play a special role. For example, quotation marks can indicate that the words between them were first written or spoken by someone else or that they are being used in an unconventional way. This chapter will help you use quotation marks

- with direct quotations (**16a**),
- with titles of short works (**16b**),
- for words or phrases used ironically or unconventionally (**16c**), and
- in combination with other punctuation marks (**16d**).

16a | Direct quotations

Double quotation marks set off direct quotations, including those in dialogue. Single quotation marks enclose a quotation within a quotation.

(1) Double quotation marks enclose direct quotations.

Quotation marks enclose only the quotation, not any expression such as *she said* or *he replied*. When a sentence ends with quoted material, place the period inside the quotation marks. For guidelines on comma placement, see **16d(1)**.

> "I believe that we learn by practice," writes Martha Graham. "Whether it means to learn to dance by practicing dancing or to learn to live by practicing living, the principles are the same."

When using direct quotations, reproduce all quoted material exactly as it appears in the original, including capitalization and punctuation. To learn how to set off long quotations as indented blocks, see **40a(2)**.

(2) Quotation marks are not used for indirect quotations or paraphrases.

Indirect quotations and paraphrases (**39d(3)**) are restatements of what someone else has said or written.

> Martha Graham believes that practice is necessary for learning, regardless of what we are trying to learn.

(3) Single quotation marks enclose quotations within quotations.

If the quotation you are using includes another direct quotation, use single quotation marks for the embedded quotation.

> According to Anita Erickson, "when the narrator says, 'I have the right to my own opinion,' he means that he has the right to his own delusion."

However, if the embedded quotation appears in a block quotation, use double quotation marks. (Note that double quotation marks are not used to mark the beginning and end of a block quotation.)

> Anita Erickson claims that the narrator uses the word *opinion* deceptively.

> > Later in the chapter, when the narrator says, "I have the right to my own opinion," he means that he has the right to his own delusion. Although it is tempting to believe that the narrator is making decisions based on a rational belief system, his behavior suggests that he is more interested in deception. With poisonous lies, he has already deceived his business partner, his wife, and his children.

(4) Dialogue is enclosed in quotation marks.

When creating or reporting a dialogue, enclose in quotation marks what each person says, no matter how short. Use a separate paragraph for each speaker, beginning a new paragraph whenever the speaker changes. Narrative details can be included in the same paragraph as a direct quotation.

> Farmer looked up, smiling, and in a chirpy-sounding voice he said, "But that feeling has the disadvantage of being . . ." He paused a beat. "Wrong."
> "Well," I retorted, "it depends on how you look at it."
> —TRACY KIDDER, *Mountains Beyond Mountains*

When quoting more than one paragraph by a single speaker, put quotation marks at the beginning of each paragraph. However, do not place closing quotation marks at the end of each paragraph—only at the end of the last paragraph.

(5) Thoughts are enclosed in quotation marks.

Quotation marks set off thoughts that resemble speech.

> "His silence on this topic has surprised everyone," I noted to myself as I surveyed the faces of the other committee members.

Thoughts are usually marked by such phrases as *I thought, he felt*, and *she believed*. Remember, though, that quotation marks are not used with thoughts that are reported indirectly (**16a(2)**).

> I wondered why he didn't respond.

(6) Short excerpts of poetry included within a sentence are enclosed in quotation marks.

When quoting fewer than four lines of poetry, enclose them in quotation marks and use a slash (**17i**) to indicate the line division.

After watching a whale swim playfully, the speaker in "Visitation" asks, "What did you think, that joy / was some slight thing?"

To learn how to format longer quotations of poetry, see 42e(4).

16b | Titles of short works

Quotation marks enclose the title of a short work, such as a story, an essay, a poem, or a song. The title of a larger work, such as a book, magazine, newspaper, or play, should be italicized.

"The Green Shepherd" first appeared in *The New Yorker*.

Short story	"The Lottery"	"The Fall of the House of Usher"
Essay	"Walden"	"Play-by-Play"
Article	"Small World"	"Arabia's Empty Quarter"
Book chapter	"Rain"	"Cutting a Dash"
Short poem	"Orion"	"Mending Wall"
Song	"Lazy River"	"The Star-Spangled Banner"
TV episode	"Show Down!"	"The Last Time"

Use double quotation marks around the title of a short work embedded in a longer italicized title.

Interpretations of "*Young Goodman Brown*" [book about a short story]

Use single quotation marks for a title within a longer title that is enclosed in double quotation marks.

"Irony in 'The Sick Rose' " [article about a poem]

MULTILINGUAL WRITERS

DIFFERING USES OF QUOTATION MARKS

In works published in Great Britain, you will notice that the use of quotation marks differs in some ways from the style presented here. For example, single quotation marks are used to set off the titles of short works, and a period is placed outside a quotation mark ending a sentence. When writing in the United States, follow the rules for American English.

British usage	In class, we compared Wordsworth's 'Upon Westminster Bridge' with Blake's 'London'.
American usage	In class, we compared Wordsworth's "Upon Westminster Bridge" with Blake's "London."

16c For ironic tone or unusual usage

Writers sometimes use quotation marks to indicate that they are using a word or phrase ironically. The word *gourmet* is used ironically in the following sentence.

His "gourmet" dinner turned out to be processed turkey and instant mashed potatoes.

> ⚠️ **CAUTION**
>
> Avoid using quotation marks around words that may not be appropriate for your rhetorical situation. Instead, take the time to choose suitable words. The revised sentence in the following pair is more effective than the first.
>
> **Ineffective** He is too much of a "wimp" to be a good leader.
>
> **Revised**   He is too indecisive to be a good leader.
>
> Similarly, putting a cliché (20b) in quotation marks may make readers conclude that you do not care enough about conveying your meaning to think of a fresh expression.

16d With other punctuation marks

To decide whether to place some other punctuation mark inside or outside quotation marks, identify the punctuation mark and note whether it is part of the quotation or part of the surrounding context.

(1) With commas and periods

Quoted material is usually accompanied by an attributive tag such as *she said* or *he replied*. When your sentence starts with such an expression, place a comma after it to separate the tag from the quotation.

> She replied, "There's more than one way to slice a pie."

If your sentence starts with the quotation instead, place the comma inside the closing quotation marks.

> "There's more than one way to slice a pie," she replied.

Place a period inside closing quotation marks, whether single or double, if the quotation ends the sentence.

Jeff responded, "I didn't understand 'An Algorithm for Life.' "

When quoting material from a source, provide the relevant page number(s). If you are following MLA guidelines, note the page number(s) in parentheses after the final quotation marks. Place the period that ends the sentence after the final parenthesis, unless the quotation is a block quotation (40a(2)).

According to Diane Ackerman, "Love is a demanding sport involving all the muscle groups, including the brain" (86).

⚠ CAUTION

Do not put a comma after *that* when it precedes a quotation.

Diane Ackerman claims that ⌀ "[l]ove is a demanding sport involving all the muscle groups, including the brain" (86).

---

(2) With semicolons and colons
Place semicolons and colons outside quotation marks.

His favorite song was "Cyprus Avenue"; mine was "Astral Weeks."

Because it is repeated, one line stands out in "The Conductor": "We are never as beautiful as now."

(3) With question marks, exclamation points, and dashes
If the direct quotation includes a question mark, an exclamation point, or a dash, place that punctuation *inside* the closing quotation marks.

Jeremy asked, "What is truth?"

Gordon shouted "Congratulations!"

Laura said, "Let me tell—" Before she could finish her sentence, Dan walked into the room.

Use just one question mark inside the quotation marks when a question you write ends with a quoted question.

Why does the protagonist ask, "Where are we headed?"

If the punctuation is not part of the quoted material, place it *outside* the closing quotation marks.

Who wrote "The Figure a Sentence Makes"?

You have to read "Awareness and Freedom"!

She called me a "toaster head"—perhaps justifiably under the circumstances.

Exercise 1

Revise sentences in which quotation marks are used incorrectly and insert quotation marks where they are needed. Do not alter sentences that are written correctly. (The numbers in parentheses are page numbers, placed according to MLA guidelines.)

1. Have you read Nicholas Negroponte's essay Creating a Culture of Ideas?

2. Negroponte states, Innovation is inefficient (2).

3. However, he also believes that "without innovation we are doomed—by boredom and monotony—to decline" (2).

4. Negroponte suggests that new ideas are fostered by 'providing a good educational system, encouraging different viewpoints, and fostering collaboration' (3).

5. According to the author, "More than ever before, in the new "new economy," research and innovation will need to be housed in those places where there are parallel agendas and multiple means of support."

6. Peter Drucker, in Beyond the Information Revolution, discusses the potential of technological development by using historical references.

7. Drucker maintains, E-commerce is to the Information Revolution what the railroad was to the Industrial Revolution—a totally new, totally unprecedented, totally unexpected development (50).

8. Just as the railroad influenced a person's perception of distance in the nineteenth century, 'distance has been eliminated' through e-commerce in our own times, asserts Drucker (50).

17   The Period and Other Punctuation Marks

To indicate the end of a sentence, you can use one of three punctuation marks: the period, the question mark, or the exclamation point. Your choice depends on whether you want to express a statement, a question, or an exclamation.

Everyone passed the exam.
Everyone passed the exam? [informal usage]
Everyone passed the exam!

Within sentences, you can use colons, dashes, parentheses, square brackets, ellipsis points, and slashes to emphasize, downplay, or clarify the information you want to convey. (For use of the hyphen, see **18f.**)

This chapter will help you use

- end punctuation marks (the period (**17a**), the question mark (**17b**), and the exclamation point (**17c**)),
- the colon (**17d**),
- the dash (**17e**),
- parentheses (**17f**),
- square brackets (**17g**),
- ellipsis points (**17h**), and
- the slash (**17i**).

To accommodate computerized typesetting, APA guidelines call for only one space after a period, a question mark, an exclamation point, a colon, and each of the periods in ellipsis points. According to this manual, there should be no space preceding or following a hyphen or a dash. The MLA style manual recommends using only one space after end punctuation marks but allows two spaces if they are used consistently.

17a The period

(1) A period marks the end of a sentence.
Use a period at the end of a declarative sentence.

> Many adults in the United States are overfed yet undernourished.
> Soft drinks account for 7 percent of their average daily caloric intake.

In addition, place a period at the end of an instruction or recommendation written as an imperative sentence (1i).

> Eat plenty of fruits and vegetables. Drink six to eight glasses of water a day.

Indirect questions are phrased as statements, so be sure to use a period, rather than a question mark, at the end of such a sentence.

> The researcher explained why people eat so much junk food.
> [COMPARE: Why do people eat so much junk food?]

(2) Periods follow some abbreviations.

> Dr. Jr. a.m. p.m. vs. etc. et al.

Only one period follows an abbreviation that ends a sentence.

> The tour begins at 1:00 p.m.

Periods are not used with many common abbreviations (for example, *MVP, mph,* and *FM*). (See 11a–d.) A dictionary lists the conventional form of an abbreviation as well as any alternatives.

17b The question mark

Place a question mark after a direct question.

How does the new atomic clock work? Who invented this clock?

Use a period, instead of a question mark, after an indirect question—that is, a question embedded in a statement.

I asked whether the new atomic clock could be used in cell phones. [COMPARE: Can the new atomic clock be used in cell phones?]

MULTILINGUAL WRITERS

INDIRECT QUESTIONS

In English, indirect questions are written as declarative sentences. The subject and verb are not inverted as they would be in the related direct question.

We do not know when ~~will~~ the meeting _∧end. *(will)*

[COMPARE: When will the meeting end?]

Place a question mark after each question in a series of related questions, even when they are not full sentences.

Will the new atomic clock be used in cell phones? Word processors? Car navigation systems?

If a direct quotation is a question, place the question mark inside the final quotation marks.

Tony asked, "How small is this new clock?"

In contrast, if you include quoted material in a question of your own, place the question mark outside the final quotation marks.

Is the clock really "no larger than a sugar cube"?

If you embed in the middle of a sentence a question not attributable to anyone in particular, place a comma before it and a question mark after it.

When the question, how does the clock work? arose, the researchers described a technique used by manufacturers of computer chips.

The first letter of such a question should not be capitalized unless the question is extremely long or contains internal punctuation.

To indicate uncertainty about a fact such as a date of birth, place a question mark inside parentheses directly after the fact in question.

Chaucer was born in 1340 (?) and died in 1400.

17c   The exclamation point

An exclamation point often marks the end of a sentence, but its primary purpose is rhetorical—to create emphasis.

Whoa! What a game!

When a direct quotation ends with an exclamation point, no comma or period is placed immediately after it.

"Get a new pitcher!" he yelled.
He yelled, "Get a new pitcher!"

Use the exclamation point sparingly so that you do not diminish its value. If you do not intend to signal strong emotion, place a comma after an interjection and a period at the end of the sentence.

Well, no one seriously expected this victory.

17d The colon

A colon calls attention to what follows. It also separates numbers in parts of scriptural references and titles from subtitles.

(1) A colon directs attention to an explanation, a summary, or a quotation.

When a colon appears between two independent clauses, it signals that the second clause will explain or expand on the first.

No one expected the game to end as it did: after seven extra innings, the favored team collapsed.

A colon is also used after an independent clause to introduce a direct quotation.

Marcel Proust explained the importance of mindfulness: "The true journey of discovery consists not in seeking new landscapes but in having fresh eyes."

Although an independent clause should always precede the colon, a phrase may sometimes follow it.

I was finally confronted with what I had dreaded for months: the due date for the final balloon payment on my car loan.

> ⚠ CAUTION
>
> The rules for using an uppercase or a lowercase letter to begin the first word
> of an independent clause that follows a colon vary across style manuals.
>
> **MLA** The first letter should be lowercase unless (1) it begins a word that
> is normally capitalized, (2) the independent clause is a quotation, or
> (3) the clause expresses a rule or principle.
>
> **APA** The first letter should be uppercase.

Both MLA and APA advise using lowercase letters to begin a
phrase following a colon.

(2) A colon may signal that a list follows.

Writers frequently use colons to introduce lists.

> Three students received internships: Asa, Vanna, and Jack.

Avoid placing a colon between a verb and its complement (**1c**)
or after the words *including* and *such as*.

> The winners were Asa, Vanna, and Jack.
> Many vegetarians do not eat dairy products such as butter
> and cheese.

(3) A colon separates a title and a subtitle.

Use a colon between a work's title and its subtitle.

> *Collapse: How Societies Choose to Fail or Succeed*

(4) Colons are used in reference numbers.

Colons are often used between numbers in scriptural references.

> Psalms 3:5   Gen. 1:1

However, MLA requires the use of periods instead of colons.

Psalms 3.5   Gen. 1.1

(5) Colons have specialized uses in business correspondence.
A colon follows the salutation of a business letter and any
notations.

Dear Dr. Horner: Dear Maxine: Enc:

A colon introduces the headings in a memo.

To: From: Subject: Date:

Exercise 1

Insert colons where they are needed in the following sentences.

1. Before we discuss marketing, let's outline the behavior of
   consumers consumer behavior is the process individuals go
   through as they select, buy, or use products or services to satisfy
   their needs and desires.
2. The process consists of six stages recognizing a need or desire,
   finding information, evaluating options, deciding to purchase,
   purchasing, and assessing purchases.
3. Many consumers rely on one popular publication for product
   information *Consumer Reports.*
4. When evaluating alternatives, a consumer uses criteria; for
   example, a house hunter might use some of the following price,
   location, size, age, style, and landscaping design.
5. The postpurchase assessment has one of two results satisfaction
   or dissatisfaction with the product or service.

17e The dash

A dash (or em dash) marks a break in thought, sets off a nonessential element for emphasis or clarity, or follows an introductory list or series. The short dash (or en dash) is used mainly in number ranges (**11g(2)**).

TECH SAVVY

To use your keyboard to create a dash, type two hyphens with no spaces between, before, or after them. Most word-processing programs can be set to convert these hyphens automatically to an em dash.

---

(1) A dash marks a break in the normal flow of a sentence.
Use a dash to indicate a shift in thought or tone.

   I was awed by the almost superhuman effort Stonehenge represents—but who wouldn't be?

(2) A dash or a pair of dashes sets off a nonessential element for emphasis or clarity.

   Dr. Kruger's specialty is mycology—the study of fungi.
   The trail we took into the Grand Canyon—steep, narrow, winding, and lacking guardrails—made me wonder whether we could call a helicopter to fly us out.

(3) A dash follows an introductory list or series.
If you decide to place a list or series at the beginning of a sentence in order to emphasize it, the main part of the sentence (after the dash) should sum up the meaning of the list or series.

   Eager, determined to succeed, and scared to death—all of these describe how I felt on the first day at work.

THINKING RHETORICALLY

COMMAS, DASHES, AND COLONS

Although a comma, a dash, or a colon may be followed by an explanation, an example, or an illustration, is the rhetorical impact the same?

He never failed to mention what was most important to him, the bottom line.

He never failed to mention what was most important to him—the bottom line.

He never failed to mention what was most important to him: the bottom line.

The comma, one of the most common punctuation marks, barely draws attention to what follows it. The dash, in contrast, signals a longer pause and so causes more emphasis to be placed on the information that follows. The colon is more direct and formal than either of the other two punctuation marks.

17f Parentheses

Use parentheses to set off information that is not closely related to the main point of a sentence or paragraph but that provides an interesting detail, an explanation, or an illustration.

We might ask why affairs of state are classified as important and their discussants intelligent, while discussion of family and human interaction (what we disparagingly call "gossip") is dismissed as idle chatter.

—ROBIN LAKOFF, *Language and Woman's Place*

In addition, place parentheses around an acronym or an abbreviation when introducing it after its full form.

The Search for Extraterrestrial Intelligence (SETI) uses the Very Large Array (VLA) outside Sicorro, New Mexico, to scan the sky.

If you use numbers or letters in a list within a sentence, set them off by placing them within parentheses.

Your application should include (1) a current résumé, (2) a statement of purpose, and (3) two letters of recommendation.

For information on the use of parentheses in bibliographies and in-text citations, see chapters 40 and 41.

THINKING RHETORICALLY

DASHES AND PARENTHESES

Dashes and parentheses are both used to set off part of a sentence, but they differ in the amount of emphasis they signal. Whereas dashes call attention to the material that is set off, parentheses usually deemphasize such material.

Her grandfather—born during the Great Depression—was appointed by the president to the Securities and Exchange Commission.

Her grandfather (born in 1930) was appointed by the president to the Securities and Exchange Commission.

17g   Square brackets

Square brackets set off additions or alterations used to clarify direct quotations. In the following example, the bracketed noun specifies what is meant by the pronoun *They*.

"They [hyperlinks] are what turn the Web from a library of pages into a web" (Weinberger 170).

Square brackets also indicate that a letter in a quotation has been changed from uppercase to lowercase, or vice versa.

David Weinberger claims that "[e]ven our notion of self as a continuous body moving through a continuous map of space and time is beginning to seem wrong on the Web" (10).

To avoid the awkwardness of using brackets in this way, you may be able to quote only part of a sentence so that no change in capitalization is needed.

David Weinberger claims that "our notion of self as a continuous body moving through a continuous map of space and time is beginning to seem wrong on the Web" (10).

Within parentheses, square brackets are used to avoid the confusion of having two sets of parentheses.

People frequently provide personal information online. (See, for example, David Weinberger's *Small Pieces Loosely Joined* [Cambridge: Perseus, 2002].)

Angle brackets (< >) are used to enclose any Web address included in an MLA works-cited list (40b) so that the period at the end of an entry is not confused with the dot(s) in the URL: <http://www.mla.org>.

17h Ellipsis points

Ellipsis points indicate an omission from a quoted passage or a reflective pause or hesitation.

(1) Ellipsis points mark an omission within a quoted passage.
Whenever you omit anything from material you quote, replace the omitted material with ellipsis points—three equally spaced periods. Be sure to compare your quoted sentence to the original, checking to see that your omission does not change the meaning of the original. The following examples illustrate how to use ellipsis points in quotations from a passage by Patricia Gadsby.

Original

Cacao doesn't flower, as most plants do, at the tips of its outer and uppermost branches. Instead, its sweet white buds hang from the trunk and along a few fat branches, popping out of patches of bark called cushions, which form where leaves drop off. They're tiny, these flowers. Yet once pollinated by midges, no-see-ums that flit in the leafy detritus below, they'll make pulp-filled pods almost the size of rugby balls.

—PATRICIA GADSBY, "Endangered Chocolate"

(a) Omission within a quoted sentence

Patricia Gadsby notes that cacao flowers "once pollinated by midges . . . make pulp-filled pods almost the size of rugby balls."

(b) Omission at the beginning of a quoted sentence

Do not use ellipsis points to indicate that you have deleted words from the beginning of a quotation, whether it is run into the text or set off in a block. The opening part of the original sentence has been omitted in the following quotation.

According to Patricia Gadsby, cacao flowers will become "pulp-filled pods almost the size of rugby balls."

Note that the first letter of the integrated quotation is not capitalized.

(c) Omission at the end of a quoted sentence

To indicate that you have omitted words from the end of a sentence, put a space between the last word and the set of three spaced ellipsis points. Then add the end punctuation mark (a period, a question mark, or an exclamation point). If the quoted material is followed by a parenthetical source or page reference, the end punctuation comes after the second parenthesis.

Claiming that cacao flowers differ from those of most plants, Patricia Gadsby describes how "the sweet white buds hang from the trunk and along a few fat branches . . . ."

OR ". . . branches . . ." (2).

(d) Omission of a sentence or more

To signal the omission of a sentence or more (even a paragraph or more), place an end punctuation mark (usually a period) before the ellipsis points.

> Patricia Gadsby describes the flowering of the cacao plant: "its sweet white buds hang from the trunk and along a few fat branches, popping out of patches of bark called cushions, which form where leaves drop off. . . . Yet once pollinated by midges, no-see-ums that flit in the leafy detritus below, they'll make pulp-filled pods almost the size of rugby balls."

If, in addition to omitting a full sentence, you omit part of another and that part ends in a comma, colon, or semicolon, place the relevant punctuation mark before the ellipsis points.

> Patricia Gadsby describes the flowering of the cacao plant: "its sweet white buds hang from the trunk and along a few fat branches, . . . Yet once pollinated by midges, no-see-ums that flit in the leafy detritus below, they'll make pulp-filled pods almost the size of rugby balls."

(e) Omission of a line or more of a poem

To signal the omission of a full line or more in quoted poetry, use spaced periods covering the length of either the line above it or the omitted line.

> The yellow fog that rubs its back upon the window-panes,
>
> . . . .
>
> Curled once about the house, and fell asleep.
>
> —T. S. ELIOT, "The Love Song of J. Alfred Prufrock"

To avoid excessive use of ellipses, replace some direct quotations with paraphrases (**39d(3)**).

(2) Ellipsis points show that a sentence has been intentionally left incomplete.

Read aloud the passage that begins "The yellow fog . . ."

(3) Ellipsis points can mark a reflective pause or a hesitation.

Keith saw four menacing youths coming toward him . . . and ran.

A dash can also be used to indicate this type of a pause.

17i The slash

A slash between words, as in *and/or* and *he/she,* indicates that either word is applicable in the given context. There are no spaces before and after a slash used in this way. Because extensive use of the slash can make writing choppy, use it judiciously and sparingly. (If you are following APA or MLA guidelines, avoid using *he/she, him/her,* and so on.)

A slash is also used to mark line divisions in quoted poetry. A slash used in this way is preceded and followed by a space.

Wallace Stevens refers to the listener who, "nothing himself, beholds / Nothing that is not there and the nothing that is."

Exercise 2

Add appropriate dashes, parentheses, square brackets, and slashes to the following sentences. Be ready to explain the reason for each mark you add.

1. Researchers in an exciting field Artificial Intelligence AI are working on devices to assist the elderly.
2. One such device is Pearl a robotic nurse that helps around the house.
3. Another application is cooking software that checks for missing and or incorrect ingredients.
4. Researchers are even investigating Global Positioning Systems GPS as a way to track Alzheimer's patients' daily routines.
5. The actual cost of such devices expensive now but more affordable later is yet to be determined.

Exercise 3

Punctuate the following sentences with appropriate end marks, commas, colons, dashes, and parentheses. Do not use unnecessary punctuation. Give a justification for each mark you add, especially where more than one type of mark (for example, commas, dashes, or parentheses) is acceptable.

1. Many small country towns are very similar a truck stop a gas station a crowded diner and three bars
2. The simple life a nonexistent crime rate and down-home values these are some of the advantages these little towns offer

3. Why do we never see these quaint examples of pure Americana when we travel around the country on the interstates

4. Rolling across America on one of the big interstates I-20 I-40 I-70 I-80 or I-90 you are likely to pass within a few miles of a number of these towns

5. Such towns almost certainly will have a regional or perhaps an ethnic flavor Hispanic in the southwest Scandinavian in the north

6. When I visit one of these out-of-the-way places I always have a sense of well really a feeling of safety

7. There's one thing I can tell you small-town life is not boring

8. My one big question however is what do you do to earn a living in these towns

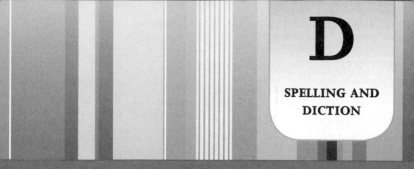

D

SPELLING AND DICTION

Reference books can provide answers to questions about usage.

18 Spelling, the Spell Checker, and Hyphenation

When you first draft a paper, you might not pay close attention to spelling words correctly. After all, the point of drafting is to generate and organize ideas. However, proofreading for spelling mistakes is essential as you near the end of the writing process. Your teachers, employers, or supervisors will expect you to submit polished work.

You can train yourself to be a good proofreader by checking a dictionary every time you question the spelling of a word. If two spellings are listed, such as *fulfill* and *fulfil*, either form is correct, although the first option provided is generally considered more common. Whatever spelling you choose in such cases, use it consistently. You can also learn to be a better speller by studying a few basic strategies. This chapter will help you

- use a spell checker (**18a**),
- spell words according to pronunciation (**18b**),
- spell words that sound alike (**18c**),
- understand how prefixes and suffixes affect spelling (**18d**),
- use *ei* and *ie* correctly (**18e**), and
- use hyphens to link and divide words (**18f**).

18a Spell checker

The spell checker is a wonderful invention, though you must use it with care. A spell checker will usually flag

- misspellings of common words,
- some commonly confused words (such as *affect* and *effect*), and
- obvious typographical errors (such as *tge* for *the*).

However, a spell checker generally will *not* detect

- specialized vocabulary or foreign words not in its dictionary,
- typographical errors that are still correctly spelled words (such as *was* for *saw*), and
- misuses of words that sound alike but are not on the spell checker's list of words commonly confused.

The following strategies can help you use a spell checker effectively.

TIPS FOR USING A SPELL CHECKER

- If a spell checker regularly flags a word that is not in its dictionary but is spelled correctly, add that word to its dictionary by clicking on the Add button. From that point on, the spell checker will accept the word you added.
- Reject any offers the spell checker makes to correct all instances of a particular error.
- Use a dictionary to evaluate the alternative spellings the spell checker provides because some of them may be erroneous.

18b   **Spelling and pronunciation**

Many words in English are not spelled the way they are pronounced, so pronunciation is not a reliable guide to correct spelling. Sometimes, people skip over an unstressed syllable, as when *February* is pronounced "Febwary," or they slide over a sound that is hard to articulate, as when *library* is pronounced "libary." Other times, people add a sound—for instance, when they pronounce *athlete* as "athalete." And people also switch sounds around, as in "irrevelant" for *irrelevant.* Such mispronunciations can lead to misspellings.

You can help yourself remember the spellings of some words by considering the spellings of their root words—for example, the root word for *irrelevant* is *relevant.* You can also teach yourself the correct spellings of words by pronouncing them the way they are spelled, that is, by pronouncing each letter mentally so that you "hear" even silent letters. You are more likely to remember the *b* in *subtle* if you pronounce it when spelling that word. Here are a few words typically misspelled because they include unpronounced letters:

condem*n*   foreign   lab*o*ratory   mus*c*le   solem*n*

Here are a few more that include letters that are often not heard in rapid speech, though they can be heard when carefully pronounced:

can*d*idate   diff*e*rent   gove*rn*ment   sep*a*rate

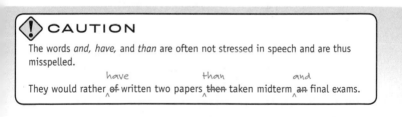

⚠ **CAUTION**

The words *and, have,* and *than* are often not stressed in speech and are thus misspelled.

They would rather ^have^ ~~of~~ written two papers ^than^ ~~then~~ taken midterm ^and^ ~~an~~ final exams.

18c Words that sound alike

Pairs of words such as *forth* and *fourth* or *sole* and *soul* are **homophones:** they sound alike but have different meanings and spellings. Some words that have different meanings sound exactly alike (*break/brake*); others sound alike in certain dialects (*marry/merry*). If you are unsure about the difference in meaning between any two words that sound alike, consult a dictionary. A number of frequently confused words are listed with explanations in this handbook's **Glossary of Usage**.

Also troublesome are two-word sequences that can be written as compound words or as separate words. The following are examples:

Everyday life was grueling.   She attended class **every day.**

They do not fight **anymore.**   They could not find **any more** evidence.

Other examples are *awhile/a while, everyone/every one, maybe/may be,* and *sometime/some time.*

A lot and *all right* are still spelled as two words. *Alot* is always considered incorrect; *alright* is also considered incorrect except in some newspapers and magazines. (See the **Glossary of Usage**.)

Singular nouns ending in *-nce* and plural nouns ending in *-nts* are easily confused.

Assistance is available.   I have two **assistants.**

His **patience** wore thin.   Some **patients** waited for hours.

Contractions and possessive pronouns are also often confused. In contractions, an apostrophe indicates an omitted letter (or letters). In possessive pronouns, there is no apostrophe. (See also **5b** and **15a(1)**.)

Contraction	Possessive
It's my turn next.	Each group waited **its** turn.
You're next.	**Your** turn is next.
There's no difference.	**Theirs** is no different.

TIPS FOR SPELLING WORDS THAT SOUND ALIKE

- Be on the lookout for words that are commonly confused (*accept/ except*).

- Distinguish between two-word sequences and single words that sound similar (*may be/maybe*).

- Use *-nts,* not *-nce,* for plural words (*instants/instance*).

- Mark contractions, but not possessive pronouns, with apostrophes (*who's/whose*).

18d Prefixes and suffixes

When a prefix is added to a base word (often called the **root**), the spelling of the base word is unaffected.

necessary, **un**necessary   moral, **im**moral

However, adding a suffix to the end of a base word often changes the spelling.

beauty, beauti**ful**   describe, descri**ption**

BUT   resist, resist**ance**

Although spellings of words with suffixes are irregular, they follow certain conventions.

(1) Dropping or retaining a final e depends on whether the suffix begins with a vowel.

- If a suffix begins with a vowel, the final *e* of the base word is dropped: bride, brid**al**; come, com**ing**; combine, combina-**tion**; prime, prim**ary**. However, to keep the /s/ sound of *ce* or the /j/ sound of *ge*, retain the final *e* before *-able* or *-ous*: courage**ous,** manage**able,** notice**able**.

- If a suffix begins with a consonant, the final *e* of the base word is retained: entire, enti**rely**; rude, rude**ness**; place, place**ment**; sure, su**rely**. Some exceptions are *argument, awful, ninth, truly,* and *wholly.*

(2) A final consonant is often doubled when a suffix begins with a vowel.

- If a consonant ends a one-syllable word with a single vowel or ends a stressed syllable with a single vowel, double the final consonant: stop, sto**pped**, sto**pping**; omit, omi**tted**, omi**tting**.
- If there are two vowels before the consonant, the consonant is not doubled: seat, seat**ed**, seat**ing**; remain, remain**ed**, remain**ing**.
- If the final syllable is not stressed, the consonant is not doubled: edit, edit**ed**, edit**ing**; picket, picket**ed**, picket**ing**.

(3) A final *y* is changed or retained depending on whether it is preceded by a vowel.

- Change a final *y* following a consonant to *i* when adding a suffix (except *-ing*): lazy, laz**ily**; defy, def**ies**, def**ied**, def**iance** BUT defy**ing**; modify, modif**ies**, modif**ied**, modif**ier** BUT modify**ing**.
- Retain the final *y* when it follows a vowel: gray, gray**ish**; stay, stay**s**, stay**ed**; obey, obey**s**, obey**ed**.
- Some verb forms are irregular and thus can cause difficulties: *lays, laid*; *pays, paid*. For a list of irregular verbs, see pages 116–118.

(4) A final *l* is retained when *-ly* is added.

cool, coo**lly**   formal, forma**lly**   real, rea**lly**   usual, usua**lly**

Exercise 1

Add the specified suffixes to the words that follow. Be prepared to explain the reason for the spelling of each resulting word.

EXAMPLE

-ly: late, casual, psychological
  lately casually psychologically

1. -ing: put, admit, write, use, try, play
2. -ment: manage, commit, require, argue
3. -ous: continue, joy, acrimony, libel
4. -ed: race, tip, permit, carry, pray
5. -able: desire, read, trace, knowledge
6. -ly: true, sincere, normal, general

(5) A noun is made plural by adding -s or -es to the singular form.

- If the sound in the plural form of a noun ending in *f* or *fe* changes from /f/ to /v/, change the ending to *-ve* before adding *-s:* thie**f**, thie**ves**; li**fe**, li**ves** BUT roo**f**, roo**fs**.
- Add *-es* to most nouns ending in *s, z, ch, sh,* or *x:* box, box**es**; peach, peach**es**.
- If a noun ends in a consonant and *y*, change the *y* to *i* and add *-es:* compan**y**, compan**ies**; ninet**y**, ninet**ies**; territor**y**, territor**ies**. (See also **18d(3)**.)
- If a noun ends in a consonant and *o*, add *-es:* hero, hero**es**; potato, potato**es**. However, note that sometimes just *-s* is added (photo, photo**s**; memo, memo**s**) and other times either an *-s* or *-es* suffix can be added (motto**s**, motto**es**; zero**s**, zero**es**).
- Certain nouns have irregular plural forms: woman, wom**en**; child, child**ren**; foot, f**ee**t.
- Add *-s* to most proper nouns: the Lee**s**; the Kennedy**s**. Add *-es* to most proper nouns ending in *s, z, ch, sh,* or *x:* the Rodriguez**es**, the Jones**es** BUT the Bach**s** (in which *ch* is pronounced /k/).

BEYOND THE RULE

WORDS BORROWED FROM OTHER LANGUAGES

Words borrowed from Latin or Greek generally form their plurals as they did in the original language.

Singular

criterion　　alumnus, alumna　　analysis　　datum　　species

Plural

criteria　　alumni, alumnae　　analyses　　data　　species

When a word with such an origin is in the process of changing, two different forms will be listed as acceptable in the dictionary: *syllabus/syllabuses, syllabi.*

Exercise 2

Provide the plural forms for the following words. If you need extra help, check a dictionary.

1. virus	4. copy	7. self	10. portfolio
2. committee	5. delay	8. belief	11. cactus
3. phenomenon	6. embargo	9. foot	12. census

18e　Confusion of *ei* and *ie*

An old rhyme will help you remember the order of letters in most words containing *e* and *i:*

> Put *i* before *e*
> Except after *c*

Or when sounded like *a*
As in *neighbor* and *weigh.*

Words with *i* before *e:* bel**ie**ve, ch**ie**f, pr**ie**st, y**ie**ld

Words with *e* before *i,* after *c:* conc**ei**t, perc**ei**ve, rec**ei**ve

Words with *ei* sounding like *a* in *cake:* **ei**ght, r**ei**n, th**ei**r, h**ei**r

Words that are exceptions to the rules in the rhyme include *either, neither, species, foreign,* and *weird.*

18f Hyphens

Hyphens link two or more words functioning as a single word and separate word parts to clarify meaning. They also have many conventional uses in numbers, fractions, and measurements. (Do not confuse the hyphen with a dash; see **11g(2)** and **17e.**)

(1) Hyphens sometimes link two or more words that form a compound.

Some compounds are listed in the dictionary with hyphens (*eye-opener, cross-examine*), others are written as two words (*eye chart, cross fire*), and still others are written as one word (*eyewitness, crossbreed*). If you have questions about the spelling of a compound word, a dictionary is a good resource. However, it is also helpful to learn a few basic patterns.

- If two or more words serve as a single adjective before a noun, they should be hyphenated. If the words follow the noun, they are not hyphenated.

  You submitted an **up-to-date** report.
  The report was **up to date.**

A **well-known** musician is performing tonight.
The musician is **well known.**

- When the second word in a hyphenated expression is omitted, the first word is still followed by a hyphen.

They discussed both **private-** and **public-sector** partnerships.

- A hyphen is not used after adverbs ending in *-ly* (*poorly planned event*), in names of chemical compounds (*sodium chloride solution*), or in modifiers with a letter or numeral as the second element (*group C homes, type IV virus*).

(2) Hyphens can be used to separate words into parts to clarify meaning.

- To avoid ambiguity or an awkward combination of letters or syllables, place a hyphen between the base word and its prefix: *anti-intellectual, de-emphasize, re-sign the petition* [COMPARE: *resign the position*].
- Place a hyphen between a prefix and a word beginning with a capital letter and between a prefix and a word already containing a hyphen: *anti-American, non-self-promoting.*
- Place a hyphen after the prefix *all-, e-, ex-,* or *self-: all-inclusive, e-commerce, ex-husband, self-esteem.* Otherwise, most words with prefixes are not hyphenated.

(3) Hyphens are frequently used in numbers, fractions, and units of measure.

- Place a hyphen between two numbers when they are spelled out: *thirty-two, ninety-nine.* However, no hyphen is used before or after the words *hundred, thousand,* and *million: five hundred sixty-three, forty-one million.*

- Hyphenate fractions that are spelled out: *three-fourths, one-half*.
- When you form a compound modifier that includes a number and a unit of measurement, place a hyphen between them: *twenty-first-century literature, twelve-year-old boy, ten-year project.*

Exercise 3

Convert the following word groups into hyphenated compounds.

EXAMPLE

a movie lasting two hours   *a two-hour movie*

1. a man who is fifty years old
2. a seminar that lasted all day
3. a street that runs only one way
4. history from the twenty-first century
5. roads that are covered by ice and snow
6. a paper that is well written

19 Good Usage

Using the right words at the right time can make the difference between having your ideas taken seriously and seeing them brushed aside. In academic or professional writing, it is important to sound well informed and respectful. In conversation with friends, it is just as important to sound casual. Whatever the occasion, choosing the right words will help you connect with your audience. This chapter will help you

- understand how word choice is related to the rhetorical situation (**19a**),
- write in a clear, straightforward style (**19b**),
- choose words that are appropriate for your audience, purpose, and context (**19c**),
- use inclusive language (**19d**), and
- realize the benefits of dictionaries (**19e**) and thesauruses (**19f**).

19a Usage and the rhetorical situation

The words you use vary from situation to situation. How you talk to a loan officer differs from how you talk to your best friend. A discussion with a loan officer is likely to be relatively formal; a conversation with a friend will be less so. Understanding such differences in tone and making word choices that reflect those differences are essential in writing because readers cannot see your body language, hear the inflections of your voice, or interrupt to say that they are having trouble following you. Instead, readers respond to the words on the page or the screen. You can help them understand your ideas by choosing words that they know or that you can explain to them. When drafting, use words that come immediately to mind. Some of these words will be good choices. Others you can replace as you revise. Remembering your rhetorical situation will help you use the right word at the right time.

19b Clear style

Although different styles are appropriate for different situations, you should strive to make your writing clear, straightforward, and easy to read. To achieve a clear style, choose words that your audience understands and that are appropriate for the occasion.

Ornate The majority believes that achievement derives primarily from the diligent pursuit of allocated tasks.

Clear Most people believe that success results from hard work.

When you write clearly, you show your readers that you are aware of the time and effort it takes to read closely. If you want readers to take your writing seriously, you must show them respect by not using obscure words when common words will do and by not using more words than necessary. Using words that are precise (**20a**) and sentences that are concise (chapter **21**) can also help you achieve a clear style.

> ### Exercise 1
>
> Revise the following sentences for an audience that prefers a clear, straightforward style.
>
> 1. Expert delineation of character in a job interview is a goal that is not always possible to achieve.
> 2. In an employment situation, social pleasantries may contribute to the successful functioning of job tasks, but such interactions should not distract attention from the need to complete all assignments in a timely manner.
> 3. Commitment to an ongoing and carefully programmed schedule of physical self-management can be a significant resource for stress reduction in the workplace.

19c Appropriate word choice

Unless you are writing for a specialized audience and have good reason to believe that this audience will welcome slang, colloquial expressions, or jargon, the following advice can help you determine which words to use and which to avoid.

(1) Slang is effective in only a few rhetorical situations.

The term **slang** covers a wide range of words or expressions that are considered casual, facetious, or fashionable by people in a particular age group, locality, or profession. Although such words are often used in private conversation or in writing intended to mimic conversation, they are usually out of place in academic or professional writing. If your rhetorical situation does call for the use of slang, be sure that the words or expressions you choose are not so new that your audience will be unable to understand what you mean and not so old that your use of them makes you seem out of touch with popular culture.

(2) Conversational (or colloquial) words are usually too informal for academic and professional writing.

Words labeled *colloquial* in a dictionary are fine for casual conversation and for written dialogues or personal essays on a light topic. Such words are sometimes used for special effect in academic writing, but you should usually replace them with more appropriate words. For example, conversational words such as *dumb* and *kid around* could be replaced by *illogical* and *tease.*

> ⚠ CAUTION
>
> Because contractions (such as *you'll* for "you will" and *she's* for "she is") reflect the sound of conversation, you can use them in some types of writing to create a friendly tone. However, some of your instructors or supervisors may consider them too informal for academic or professional writing.

(3) Regionalisms can make writing vivid.

Regionalisms—such as *tank* for "pond" and *sweeper* for "vacuum cleaner"—can make writing lively and distinctive, but they are effective only when the audience can understand them in a specific context. Furthermore, they are often considered too informal for academic and professional writing.

(4) Technical words are essential when writing for specialists.

When writing for a diverse audience, an effective writer will not refer to the need for bifocals as *presbyopia.* However, technical language is appropriate when the audience can understand it (as when one physician writes to another) or when the audience would benefit by learning the terms in question.

Jargon is technical language tailored specifically for a particular occupation. Jargon can be an efficient shortcut for conveying specialized concepts, but you should use it only when you are sure that you and your readers share an understanding of the terms. *Splash,* for example, does not always refer to water or an effect (as in *making a splash*); the word also signifies a computer screen that can appear after you click on a Web site but before you view its opening page. Terms that originate as jargon sometimes enter mainstream usage because nonspecialists begin to use them. As computer use has grown, for example, technical terms such as *download* and *mouse* have become commonly used and widely understood.

19d   Inclusive language

By making word choices that are inclusive rather than exclusive, you invite readers into your writing. Advertisers follow a similar principle when they choose images that appeal to a diverse audience. Prejudiced or derogatory language has no place in academic or professional writing; using it undermines your authority and credibility as a writer. Even if you are writing for one person you think you know well, do not assume that you know everything about that person. A close colleague at work might have an uncle who is gay, for example, or his sister might be married to someone of a different race or religion. Do not try to justify demeaning language on the grounds that you meant it as a joke. Take responsibility for the words you use.

UNITED COLORS
OF BENETTON.

An inclusive advertisement appeals to a diverse audience. © The Advertising Archives.

(1) Nonsexist language indicates respect for both men and women.

Effective writers show equal respect for men and women. For example, they avoid using *man* to refer to people in general because they understand that the word excludes women.

Achievements [OR Human achievements]

~~Man's achievements~~ in science are impressive.

Sexist language has a variety of sources, such as contempt for the opposite sex and unthinking repetition of words used by others. Stereotyping can also lead to sexist language. Women, like men, can be *firefighters* or *police officers*—words that are increasingly used as gender-neutral alternatives to *firemen* and *policemen*.

Use the following tips to ensure that your writing is respectful.

TIPS FOR AVOIDING SEXIST LANGUAGE

When you review your drafts, revise the following types of sexist language.

- **Generic *he*:** A doctor should listen to *his* patients.

  A doctor should listen to **his or her** patients. [use of the appropriate form of *he or she*]

  Doctors should listen to **their** patients. [use of plural forms]

  By listening to patients, **doctors obtain important diagnostic information.** [elimination of *his* by revising the sentence]

- **Occupational stereotype:** Glenda James, a *female* engineer at Howard Aviation, won the best-employee award.

  Glenda James, an engineer at Howard Aviation, won the best-employee award. [removal of the unnecessary gender reference]

- **Terms such as *man* and *mankind* or those with *-ess* or *-man* endings:** Labor laws benefit the common *man*. *Mankind* benefits from philanthropy. The *stewardess* brought me some orange juice.

  Labor laws benefit **working people.** [replacement of the stereotypical term with a gender-neutral term]

  Everyone benefits from philanthropy. [use of an indefinite pronoun]

  The **flight attendant** brought me some orange juice. [use of a gender-neutral term]

- **Stereotypical gender roles:** I was told that the university offers free tuition to faculty *wives*. The minister pronounced them *man* and *wife*.

  I was told that the university offers free tuition to faculty **spouses.** [replacement of the stereotypical term with a gender-neutral term]

The minister pronounced them **husband** and wife. [use of a term equivalent to *wife*]

- **Inconsistent use of titles:** *Mr.* Holmes and his *wife,* Mary, took a long trip to China.

  Mr. and Mrs. [or Ms.] Holmes took a long trip to China. [consistent use of titles]

  OR **Peter and Mary Holmes** took a long trip to China. [removal of titles]

  OR **Peter Holmes** and **Mary Wolfe** took a long trip to China. [use of full names]

- **Unstated gender assumption:** Have your *mother make your costume* for the school pageant.

  Have your **parents provide you with a costume** for the school pageant. [replacement of the stereotypical words with gender-neutral ones]

Exercise 2

Make the following sentences inclusive by eliminating sexist language.

1. The ladies met to discuss the company's current operating budget.
2. The old boys run the city's government.
3. Mothers should read to their small children.
4. Some fans admired the actress because of her movies; others praised her for her environmental activism.
5. For six years, he worked as a mailman in a small town.

(2) Nonracist language promotes social equity.

Rarely is it necessary to identify anyone's race or ethnicity in academic or professional writing. However, you may need to use appropriate racial or ethnic terms if you are writing a demographic report, an argument against existing racial inequities, or a historical account of a particular event involving ethnic groups. Determining which terms a particular group prefers can be difficult because preferences sometimes vary within a group and change over time. One conventional way to refer to Americans of a specific descent is to include an adjective before the word *American*: *African American, Asian American, European American, Latin American, Mexican American, Native American.* These words are widely used; however, members of a particular group may identify themselves in more than one way. In addition to *African American* and *European American, Black* (or *black*) and *White* (or *white*) have long been used. People of Spanish-speaking descent may prefer *Chicano/Chicana, Hispanic, Latino/Latina, Puerto Rican,* or other terms. Members of cultures that are indigenous to North America may prefer a specific name such as *Cherokee* or *Haida,* though some also accept *American Indians* or *Native People.* An up-to-date dictionary that includes notes on usage can help you choose appropriate terms.

(3) Writing about any type of difference should be respectful.

If a writing assignment requires you to distinguish people based on age, ability, geographical area, religion, or sexual orientation, show respect to the groups or individuals you discuss by using the terms they prefer.

(a) Referring to age

Although some people object to the term *senior citizen,* a better alternative has not been provided. When used respectfully, the term refers to a person who has reached the age of retirement (but may not have decided to retire) and is eligible for certain privileges granted by society. However, if you know your audience would object to this term, find out which alternative is preferred.

(b) Referring to disability or illness

A current recommendation for referring to disabilities and illnesses is "to put the person first." In this way, the focus is placed on the individual rather than on the limitation. Thus, *persons with disabilities* is preferred over *disabled persons.* For your own writing, you can find out whether such person-first expressions are preferred by noting whether they are used in the articles and books (or by the people) you consult.

(c) Referring to geographical areas

Certain geographical terms need to be used with special care. Though most frequently used to refer to people from the United States, the term *American* may also refer to people from Canada, Mexico, and Central or South America. If your audience may be confused by this term, use *people from the United States* or *U.S. citizens* instead.

The term *Arab* refers to people who speak Arabic. If you cannot use specific terms such as *Iraqi* or *Saudi Arabian,* be sure you know that a country's people speak Arabic and not another language. Iranians, for example, are not Arabs because they speak Farsi.

British, rather than *English,* is the preferred term for referring to people from the island of Great Britain or from the United Kingdom.

(d) Referring to religion

Reference to a person's religion should be made only if it is relevant to your rhetorical situation. If you must mention religious affiliation, use only those terms considered respectful. Because religions have both conservative and liberal followers, be careful not to make generalizations about political stances (see **35i(10)**).

(e) Referring to sexual orientation

If your rhetorical situation calls for identifying sexual orientation, choose terms used by the people you are discussing. The words *gay*, *lesbian*, and *bisexual* are generally used as adjectives. Their use as nouns to refer to specific people may be considered offensive.

CHECKLIST for Assessing Usage within a Rhetorical Situation

- Do your words convey the meaning you intend?
- Can your audience understand the words you have used?
- Do you explain any words your audience might not understand?
- Have you used any words that could irritate or offend members of your audience?
- Do any of your words make you sound too casual or too formal?
- Do your words help you to fulfill your rhetorical purpose?
- Are your words appropriate for the context in which you are writing?
- Are your words appropriate for the context in which they will be read?

19e   Dictionaries

A good dictionary is an indispensable tool for writers. Desk dictionaries such as *The American Heritage Dictionary* and *Merriam-Webster's Collegiate Dictionary* do much more than provide the correct spellings of words; they also give meanings, parts of speech, plural forms, and verb tenses, as well as information about pronunciation and origin. In addition, a reliable dictionary also includes labels that can help you decide whether words are appropriate for your purpose, audience, and context. Words labeled *dialect, slang, colloquial, nonstandard,* or *unconventional,* as well as those labeled *archaic* or *obsolete* (meaning that they are no longer in common use), are generally inappropriate for college and professional writing. If a word has no label, you can safely assume that it can be used in writing for school or work. Because language is constantly changing, it is important to choose a desk dictionary with a recent copyright date.

(1) Consulting an unabridged or specialized dictionary can enhance your understanding of a word.

An **unabridged dictionary** provides a comprehensive survey of English words, including detailed information about their origins. A **specialized dictionary** presents words related to a specific discipline or to some aspect of usage.

Unabridged Dictionaries

The Oxford English Dictionary. 2nd ed. 20 vols. 1989– . CD-ROM. 2005.

Webster's Third New International Dictionary of the English Language. CD-ROM. 2002.

Specialized Dictionaries

The American Heritage Dictionary of Idioms. 1997.

The American Heritage Guide to Contemporary Usage and Style. 2005.

The BBI Dictionary of English Word Combinations. 1997.

Merriam-Webster's Dictionary of English Usage. 1994.

The New Fowler's Modern English Usage. 3rd ed. 2000.

MULTILINGUAL WRITERS

DICTIONARIES AND OTHER RESOURCES

The following dictionaries are recommended for nonnative speakers of English.

> *Collins Cobuild New Student's Dictionary.* 2002.
> *Heinle's Newbury House Dictionary of American English.*
> 4th ed. 2003.
> *Longman Advanced American English.* 2000.

Two excellent resources for ESL students are the following:

> *Longman Language Activator.* 2003. (A cross between a
> dictionary and a thesaurus, this book supplies definitions,
> usage guidelines, and sample sentences.)
> Swan, Michael. *Practical English Usage.* 3rd ed. 2005. (This
> is a practical reference guide to problems encountered
> by those who speak English as a second language.)

(2) Dictionary entries provide a range of information.

Figure 19.1 shows sample entries from the tenth edition of *Merriam-Webster's Collegiate Dictionary.* Notice that *move* is listed twice—first as a verb, then as a noun. The types of information these entries provide can be found in almost all desk dictionaries, though sometimes in a different order.

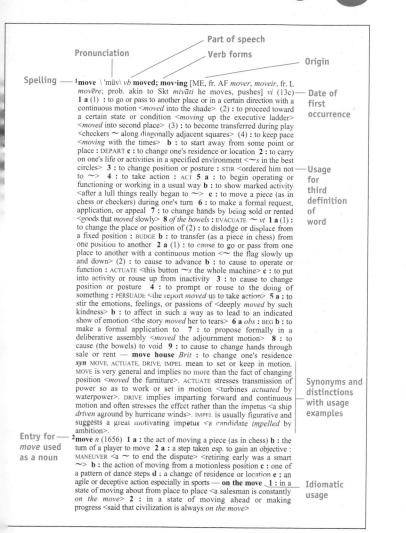

Part of speech

Pronunciation

Verb forms

Origin

Spelling —— ¹**move** \'müv\ *vb* **moved; mov·ing** [ME, fr. AF *mover, moveir*, fr. L *movēre*; prob. akin to Skt *mivāti* he moves, pushes] *vi* (13c) — Date of first occurrence
1 a (1) : to go or pass to another place or in a certain direction with a continuous motion <*moved* into the shade> (2) : to proceed toward a certain state or condition <*moving* up the executive ladder> <*moved* into second place> (3) : to become transferred during play <checkers ~ along diagonally adjacent squares> (4) : to keep pace <*moving* with the times> **b** : to start away from some point or place : DEPART **c** : to change one's residence or location **2** : to carry on one's life or activities in a specified environment <~s in the best circles> **3** : to change position or posture : STIR <ordered him not — Usage for third definition of word
to ~> **4** : to take action : ACT **5 a** : to begin operating or functioning or working in a usual way **b** : to show marked activity <after a lull things really began to ~> **c** : to move a piece (as in chess or checkers) during one's turn **6** : to make a formal request, application, or appeal **7** : to change hands by being sold or rented <goods that *moved* slowly> **8** *of the bowels* : EVACUATE ~ *vt* **1 a** (1) : to change the place or position of (2) : to dislodge or displace from a fixed position : BUDGE **b** : to transfer (as a piece in chess) from one position to another **2 a** (1) : to cause to go or pass from one place to another with a continuous motion <~ the flag slowly up and down> (2) : to cause to advance **b** : to cause to operate or function : ACTUATE <this button ~s the whole machine> **c** : to put into activity or rouse up from inactivity **3** : to cause to change position or posture **4** : to prompt or rouse to the doing of something : PERSUADE <the report *moved* us to take action> **5 a** : to stir the emotions, feelings, or passions of <deeply *moved* by such kindness> **b** : to affect in such a way as to lead to an indicated show of emotion <the story *moved* her to tears> **6 a** *obs* : BEG **b** : to make a formal application to **7** : to propose formally in a deliberative assembly <*moved* the adjournment motion> **8** : to cause (the bowels) to void **9** : to cause to change hands through sale or rent — **move house** *Brit* : to change one's residence
syn MOVE, ACTUATE, DRIVE, IMPEL mean to set or keep in motion. MOVE is very general and implies no more than the fact of changing position <*moved* the furniture>. ACTUATE stresses transmission of power so as to work or set in motion <turbines *actuated* by waterpower>. DRIVE implies imparting forward and continuous motion and often stresses the effect rather than the impetus <a ship *driven* aground by hurricane winds>. IMPEL is usually figurative and suggests a great motivating impetus <a candidate *impelled* by ambition>. — Synonyms and distinctions with usage examples

Entry for —— ²**move** *n* (1656) **1 a** : the act of moving a piece (as in chess) **b** : the turn of a player to move **2 a** : a step taken esp. to gain an objective : MANEUVER <a ~ to end the dispute> <retiring early was a smart ~> **b** : the action of moving from a motionless position **c** : one of a pattern of dance steps **d** : a change of residence or location **e** : an agile or deceptive action especially in sports — **on the move** **1** : in a state of moving about from place to place <a salesman is constantly — Idiomatic usage
on the move> **2** : in a state of moving ahead or making progress <said that civilization is always *on the move*>

Entry for *move* used as a noun

g. 19.1. Examples of dictionary entries.

TYPES OF INFORMATION PROVIDED BY DICTIONARY ENTRIES

- **Spelling, syllabication (word division), and pronunciation.**
- **Parts of speech and word forms.** Dictionaries identify parts of speech—for instance, with *n* for "noun" or *vi* for "intransitive verb." Meanings will vary depending on the part of speech identified. Dictionaries also identify irregular forms of verbs, nouns, and adjectives: *fly, flew, flown, flying, flies; child, children; good, better, best.*
- **Word origin.**
- **Date of first occurrence.**
- **Definition(s).** Generally, the oldest meaning is given first. However, meanings can also be ordered according to the most common usage.
- **Usage.** Quotations show how the word can be used in various contexts. Sometimes a comment on usage problems is placed at the end of the entry.
- **Idioms.** When the word is part of a common idiom (**20c**), the idiom is listed and defined, usually at the end of the entry.
- **Synonyms.** Some dictionaries provide explanations of subtle differences in meaning among a word's synonyms.

Exercise 3

Study the definitions for the pairs of words in parentheses. Then choose the word you think best completes each sentence. Be prepared to explain your answers.

1. Sixteen prisoners on death row were granted (mercy/clemency).
2. The outcome of the election (excited/provoked) a riot.
3. The young couple was (covetous/greedy) of their neighbors' estate.

4. While she was traveling in Muslim countries, she wore (modest/chaste) clothing.
5. The president of the university (authorized/confirmed) the rumor that tuition would be increasing next year.

19f Thesauruses

A **thesaurus** provides alternatives for frequently used words. Unlike a dictionary, which explains what a word means and how it evolved, a thesaurus provides only a list of words that serve as possible synonyms for each term it includes. A thesaurus can be useful, especially when you want to jog your memory about a word you know but cannot recall. You may, however, use a word incorrectly if you simply pick it from a list in a thesaurus. If you find an unfamiliar yet intriguing word, make sure that you are using it correctly by looking it up in a dictionary.

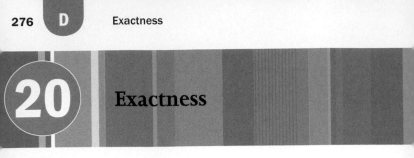

20   Exactness

Make words work for you. By choosing the right word and putting it in the right place, you can communicate exactly what you mean and make your writing memorable to your intended audience. This chapter will help you

- master the denotations and connotations of words (**20a**),
- use fresh, clear expressions (**20b**),
- understand how to use idioms and collocations (**20c**),
- use the first- and second-person pronouns appropriately (**20d**), and
- compose clear definitions (**20e**).

20a   Accurate and precise word choice

(1) A denotation is the literal meaning of a word.

Denotations are definitions of words, such as those that appear in dictionaries. For example, the noun *beach* denotes a sandy or pebbly shore. Select words whose denotations convey your point exactly.

Yosemite National Park ~~is really great.~~ *astounds even an indifferent tourist like me.*

[Because *great* can mean "extremely large" as well as "outstanding" or "powerful," its use in this sentence is imprecise.]

The speaker ~~inferred~~ implied that the team attracted many new fans this year.

[*Imply* means "to suggest," so *implied* is the exact word for this sentence. *Infer* means "to draw a conclusion from evidence": From the figures before me, I *inferred* that the team attracted many new fans this year.]

(2) A connotation is the indirect meaning of a word.

Connotations are the associations evoked by a word. *Beach,* for instance, may connote natural beauty, surf, shells, swimming, tanning, sunburn, and/or crowds. The context in which a word appears affects the associations it evokes. In a treatise on shoreline management, *beach* has scientific and geographic connotations; in a fashion magazine, this word is associated with bathing suits, sunglasses, and sunscreen. The challenge for writers is to choose the words that are most likely to spark the appropriate connotations in their readers' minds.

Mr. Kreuger's ~~relentlessness~~ persistence has earned praise from his supervisors.

[*Relentlessness* has negative connotations, which make it an unlikely quality for which to be praised.]

I love the ~~odor~~ aroma of freshly baked bread.

[Many odors are unpleasant; *aroma* sounds more positive, especially when associated with food.]

MULTILINGUAL WRITERS

CONNOTATIONS

Your ability to recognize connotations will improve as your vocabulary increases. When you learn a new word that seems to mean exactly what another word means, study the context in which each word is used. Then, to help yourself remember the new word, create a phrase or a sentence in which that word is used in the context you studied. If you are confused about the connotations of specific words, consult an ESL dictionary (see page 272).

(3) Specific, concrete words provide readers with helpful details.

A **general word** is all-inclusive, indefinite, and sweeping in scope. A **specific word** is precise, definite, and limited in scope.

General	Specific	More Specific/Concrete
food	fast food	cheeseburger
entertainment	film	*Forgetting Sarah Marshall*
place	city	Atlanta

An **abstract word** refers to a concept or idea, a quality or trait, or anything else that cannot be touched, heard, or seen. A **concrete word** signifies a particular object, a specific action, or anything that can be touched, heard, or seen.

Abstract	democracy, evil, strength, charity
Concrete	mosquito, hammer, plastic, fog

Some writers use too many abstract or general words, making their writing vague and lifeless. As you select words to fit your context, you should be as specific and concrete as you can. For example, instead of the word *bad,* consider using a more precise adjective.

bad neighbors: rowdy, snobby, nosy, fussy, sloppy, threatening

bad meat: tough, tainted, overcooked, undercooked, contaminated

bad wood: rotten, warped, scorched, knotty, termite-ridden

To test whether or not a word is specific, you can ask one or more of these questions about what you want to say: Exactly who? Exactly what? Exactly when? Exactly where? Exactly how? In the following examples, notice what a difference concrete words can make in expressing an idea and how adding details can expand or develop it.

Vague	She has kept no reminders of performing in her youth.
Specific	She has kept no sequined costume, no photographs, no fliers or posters from that part of her youth. —LOUISE ERDRICH, "The Leap"
Vague	I was struck by her makeup.
Specific	What foxed me was her makeup, which was on the heavy side and involved a great deal of peach-colored powder. —DAVID SEDARIS, "This Old House"

As these examples show, sentences with specific details are often longer than sentences without them. But the need to be specific does not necessarily conflict with the need to be concise (chapter 21). Sometimes substituting one word for another can make it far easier for your readers to see, hear, taste, or smell what you are hoping to convey.

(4) Figurative language contributes to exactness.

Figurative language is the use of words in an imaginative rather than a literal sense. Similes and metaphors are the chief **figures of speech.** A **simile** is a comparison of dissimilar things using *like* or *as*. A **metaphor** is an implied comparison of dissimilar things, without *like* or *as*.

Similes

He was **like a piece of rare and delicate china which was always being saved from breaking and finally fell.**
—ALICE WALKER, "To Hell with Dying"

When **her body was hairless as a baby's,** she adjusted the showerhead so that the water burst forth in pelting streams.
—LOIDA MARITZA PÉREZ, *Geographies of Home*

Metaphors

His **money was a sharp pair of scissors** that snipped rapidly through tangles of red tape.   —HISAYE YAMAMOTO, *The Brown House*

Making tacos is a graceful dance.
—DENISE CHÁVEZ, *A Taco Testimony*

Single words can be used metaphorically.

These roses must be **planted** in good soil. [literal]

Keep your life **planted** wherever you can put down the most roots. [metaphorical]

Similes and metaphors are especially valuable when they are concrete and describe or evoke essential relationships that cannot otherwise be communicated. Similes or metaphors can be extended throughout a paragraph of comparison, but be careful not to mix them (**23b**).

Exercise 1

Study the passage below, and prepare to discuss the author's use of exact and figurative language to communicate her ideas.

¹The kitchen where I'm making dinner is a New York kitchen. ²Nice light, way too small, nowhere to put anything unless the stove goes. ³My stove is huge, but it will never go. ⁴My stove is where my head clears, my impressions settle, my reporter's life gets folded into my life, and whatever I've just learned, or think I've learned—whatever it was, out there in the world, that had seemed so different and surprising— bubbles away in the very small pot of what I think I know and, if I'm lucky, produces something like perspective.

—JANE KRAMER, "The Reporter's Kitchen"

Exercise 2

Choose five of the items below, and use them as the bases for five original sentences containing figurative language.

1. the look on someone's face
2. a cold rainy day
3. studying for an exam
4. your favorite food
5. buying textbooks
6. a busy street
7. waiting in a long line for a movie
8. the way someone talks

20b Evocative language

Fresh expressions can capture the attention of readers, but when forced or overused, they lose their impact. Sometimes writers coin expressions as substitutes for words and phrases that have coarse or indelicate connotations. These expressions, called **euphemisms,** occasionally become standardized. To talk about death or dying, for example, you might use words such as *pass away* or *being terminally ill.* Although euphemisms may be pleasant sounding, they have a dark side. They can be used by writers who want to obscure facts or avoid negative reactions by others. Euphemisms such as *revenue enhancement* for *tax hike* and *collateral damage* for *civilian deaths during a war* are considered insincere or deceitful.

The expressions *bite the dust, breath of fresh air,* and *smooth as silk* were once striking and thus effective. Excessive use, though, has drained them of their original force and made them **clichés.** Newer expressions such as *put a spin on something* and *think outside the box* have also lost their vitality because of overuse. Nonetheless, clichés are so much a part of the language that nearly every writer uses them from time to time. But effective writers often give a fresh twist to an old saying.

> I seek a narrative, a fiction, to order days like the one I spent several years ago, on a gray June day in Chicago, when I took a roller-coaster ride on the bell curve of my experience.
> —GAYLE PEMBERTON, "The Zen of Bigger Thomas"

[Notice how much more effective this expression is than frequent references elsewhere to "being on an emotional roller coaster."]

Variations on familiar expressions from literature and history, many of which have become part of everyday language, can often be used to good effect.

We have met the enemy and he is us.

—WALT KELLY, Earth Day poster, 1970

[This statement is a variation on one made by American naval officer Oliver Hazard Perry during the War of 1812: "We have met the enemy and they are ours."]

Good writers, however, do not rely too heavily on the words of others; they choose their own words to communicate their ideas.

Exercise 3

From the following list of overused expressions, select five that you often use or hear and suggest creative replacements. Then, use each replacement in a sentence.

EXAMPLE

beyond the shadow of a doubt
undoubtedly   OR   with total certainty

1. an axe to grind
2. hit the nail on the head
3. see the light
4. business as usual
5. climb the walls

6. eat like a pig
7. beat around the bush
8. bite the bullet
9. breathe down someone's neck
10. strong as an ox

20c   Idioms and collocations

Idioms are fixed expressions whose meanings cannot be entirely determined by knowing the meanings of their parts—*bear in mind, fall in love, in a nutshell, stand a chance.* **Collocations** are combinations of words that frequently occur together. Unlike idioms, they have meanings that *can* be determined by knowing the meanings of their parts—*depend on, fond of, little while, right now*. Regardless of whether you are using an idiom or a collocation, if you make even a small inadvertent change to the expected wording, you may distract or confuse your readers.

She tried to keep a ~~small~~ low profile.

They had ~~an invested~~ a vested interest in the project.

As you edit your writing, keep an eye out for idioms or collocations that might not be worded correctly. Then check a general dictionary, a dictionary of idioms (see page 271), or the **Glossary of Usage** at the end of this book to ensure that your usage is appropriate. Writers sometimes have trouble with the following collocations, all of which contain prepositions.

CHOOSING THE RIGHT PREPOSITION

Instead of	Use
abide **with**	abide **by** the decision
according **with**	according **to** the source
accused **for**	accused **of** the crime
based **off of**	based **on** the novel
bored **of**	bored **by** it
comply **to**	comply **with** rules
conform **of/on**	conform **to/with** standards
differ **to**	differ **with** them
in accordance **to**	in accordance **with** policy
independent **to**	independent **of** his family
happened **on**	happened **by** accident
superior **than**	superior **to** others

MULTILINGUAL WRITERS

UNDERSTANDING AND USING IDIOMS

The context in which an idiom appears can often help you understand the meaning. For example, if you read "When they learned that she had accepted illegal campaign contributions, several political commentators raked her over the coals," you would probably understand that *to rake over the coals* means "to criticize severely." As you learn new idioms from your reading, make a list of those you might want to use in your own writing. If you are confused about the meaning of a particular idiom, check a dictionary of idioms (see page 271).

Exercise 4

Write a sentence using each of the following idioms and collocations correctly.

1. pass muster, pass the time
2. do one's best, do one's part, do one's duty
3. in a pinch, in a rut, in a way
4. cut down, cut back, cut corners
5. make time, make sure, make sense

20d First-person and second-person pronouns

Using *I* is appropriate when you are writing about personal experience. In academic and professional writing, the use of the first-person singular pronoun is also a clear way to distinguish your own views from those of others or to make a direct appeal to readers. However, if you frequently repeat *I feel* or *I think,* your readers may suspect that you do not understand much beyond your own experience or that you are more interested in talking about yourself than about your topic.

We, the first-person plural pronoun, is trickier to use correctly. When you use it, make sure that your audience can tell which individuals are included in this plural reference. For example, if you are writing a paper for a college course, does *we* mean you and the instructor, you and your fellow students, or some other group (such as all Americans)? The use of *we* can blind writers to differences of gender, race, religion, region, class, and sexual orientation. Because you may inadvertently use *we* in an early draft to refer to more than one group of people, as you edit, check to see that you have used the first-person plural pronoun consistently.

If you decide to address readers directly, you will undoubtedly use the second-person pronoun *you* (as has been done frequently in this book). There is some disagreement, though, over whether to permit the use of the indefinite *you* to mean "a person" or "people in general." Check with your instructor about this usage. If you are told to avoid using the indefinite *you*, recast your sentences. For example, use *one* instead of *you*.

Even in huge, anonymous cities, ~~you find~~ ^one finds^ community spirit.

However, owing to the formality of *one*, it might not always be the best choice. Changing the word order is another possibility.

Community spirit can be found even in huge, anonymous cities.

If you are unsatisfied with either of these strategies, use different words.

Community spirit arises even in huge, anonymous cities.

For additional advice on using pronouns, see chapter 5.

Exercise 5

Revise the following paragraph to eliminate the use of the first-
and second-person pronouns.

¹In my opinion, some animals should be as free as we are.
²For example, I think orangutans, African elephants, and Atlantic
bottlenose dolphins should roam freely rather than be held in
captivity. ³We should neither exhibit them in zoos nor use them for
medical research. ⁴If you study animals such as these you will see
that, like us, they show emotions, self-awareness, and intention.
⁵You might even find that some use language to communicate.
⁶It is clear to me that they have the right to freedom.

20e   Clear definitions

Because words often have more than one meaning, you must
clearly establish which meaning you have in mind in a particular piece of writing. By providing a definition, you set the
terms of the discussion.

In this paper, I use the word *communism* **in the Marxist sense
of social organization based on the holding of all property
in common.**

A **formal definition** first states the term to be defined, then
puts it into a class, and finally differentiates it from other
members of that class.

A *phosphene* [term] is **a luminous visual image** [class] that **results from applying pressure to the eyeball** [differentiation].

A short dictionary definition may be adequate when you need to convey a special meaning that may be unfamiliar to readers.

Here, *galvanic* means **"produced as if by electric shock."**

Giving a synonym may also clarify the meaning of a term. Such synonyms are often used as appositives.

Machismo, **confidence with an attitude,** can be a pose rather than a reality.

Writers frequently show—rather than tell—what a word means by giving examples.

Many homophones **(such as *be* and *bee,* *in* and *inn,* or *see* and *sea*)** are not spelling problems.

You can also formulate your own definition of a concept you wish to clarify.

Clichés could be defined as **thoughts that have hardened.**

When writing definitions, do not confuse readers by placing a predicate with a subject that is not logically connected to it (**23c**). Constructions that combine *is* or *are* with *when, where,* or *because* are often illogical because forms of *be* signify identity or equality between the subject and what follows.

Faulty	The Internet is when you look at text and images from across the world.
Revised	The Internet allows you to look at text and images from across the world.

Exercise 6

Using your own words, define any four of the following terms in full sentences.

1. collaboration
2. honesty
3. party
4. style
5. globalization
6. terrorism

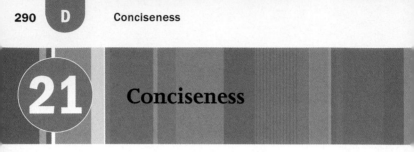

21 Conciseness

To facilitate readers' understanding, effective writers generally convey their thoughts clearly and efficiently, choosing each word wisely. This chapter will help you

- make each word count (**21a**),
- avoid unnecessary repetition (**21b**), and
- use elliptical constructions (**21c**).

21a Eliminating wordiness and other redundancies

After writing a first draft, review your sentences to make sure that they contain only the words necessary to make your point.

(1) Redundancy contributes to wordiness.

Restating a key point in different words can help readers understand it. But if you rephrase readily understood terms, your work will suffer from **redundancy**—repetition for no good reason.

Ballerinas auditioned ~~in the tryouts~~ for *The Nutcracker*.

Each student had a unique talent~~ and ability that he or she~~
for
~~uses in his or her~~ acting.

You should also avoid grammatical redundancy, as in double subjects (*my sister [she] is*), double comparisons (*[more] easier than*), and double negatives (*could[n't] hardly*).

MULTILINGUAL WRITERS

USING RELATIVE PRONOUNS

Review your sentences to make sure that no clause includes both a personal pronoun (**5a(1)**) and a relative pronoun (**5a(3)**) referring to the same antecedent (**6b**).

> The drug **that** we were testing ~~it~~ has not been approved by the Food and Drug Administration.

> The principal investigator, **whom** we depended on ~~her~~ for guidance, had to take a medical leave before the project was completed.

(2) Delete unnecessary words and recast wordy phrases.
One exact word often says as much as several inexact ones.

spoke in a low and hard-to-hear voice	**mumbled**
a person who gives expert advice	**consultant**

Some unscrupulous brokers are ~~taking money and savings~~ cheating ~~from~~ elderly people~~, who need that money because they planned to use it as a retirement pension.~~ out of their pensions.

As you edit a draft, delete words that add no significant meaning to adjacent words, and replace wordy expressions with single words whenever possible.

> ~~In the event that~~ taxes are raised, ~~expect complaints on the part of the voters.~~
>
> *If* ... *voters will complain.*

In addition, watch for empty or vague words such as *area, aspect, element, factor, feature, field, kind, situation, thing,* and *type.* They may signal wordiness.

> ~~In an employment situation, effective~~ communication is essential at work.
>
> *Effective*

REPLACEMENTS FOR WORDY EXPRESSIONS

Instead of	Use
at this moment (point) in time	now, today
due to the fact that	because
in view of the fact that	because
for the purpose of	for
it is clear (obvious) that	clearly (obviously)
there is no question that	unquestionably, certainly
without a doubt	undoubtedly
beyond the shadow of a doubt	certainly, surely
it is my opinion that	I think (believe)
in this day and age	today
in the final analysis	finally

USELESS WORDS IN COMMON PHRASES

yellow [in color]	circular [in shape]
at 9:45 a.m. [in the morning]	return [back]
[basic] essentials	rich [and wealthy] nations
bitter[-tasting] salad	small[-size] potatoes
connect [up together]	[true] facts
because [of the fact that]	was [more or less] hinting
[really and truly] fearless	by [virtue of] his authority

(3) The constructions *there are* and *it is* can often be deleted.
There or *it* followed by a form of *be* is an **expletive**—a word
that signals that the subject of the sentence will follow the verb
(**1b(1)**). Writers use expletives to create a sentence rhythm that
emphasizes words that would not be emphasized in the typical
subject-verb order. Notice the difference in rhythm between
the following two sentences:

> Three children were playing in the yard.

> There were three children playing in the yard.

However, expletives are easily overused. If you find that you
have drafted several sentences that begin with expletives, look
for ways to revise a few of them.

Hundreds   were
~~There were hundreds~~ of fans crowding onto the field.

Joining the crowd
~~It~~ was frightening ~~to join the crowd~~.

OR

I was afraid to join the crowd.

(4) Some relative pronouns can be deleted.

When editing a draft, check whether the relative pronouns *who, which,* and *that* can be deleted from any of your sentences. If a relative pronoun is followed by a form of the verb *be* (*am, is, are, was,* or *were*), you can often omit both the relative pronoun and the verb.

> The change ~~that~~ the young senator proposed yesterday angered most legislators.

> Bromo, ~~which is~~ Java's highest mountain, towers above its neighbors.

When deleting a relative pronoun, you might have to make other changes to a sentence as well.

> The Tsukiji fish market, ~~which handles~~ ^{handling} 2,000 tons of seafood a day, rates as the world's largest.

Exercise 1

Rewrite the sentences below to make them less wordy.

1. He put in an application for every job offered.
2. Prior to the time of the ceremony, he had not received an award.
3. The library is located in the vicinity of the post office.
4. The fans who were watching television made a lot of noise.
5. There was nobody home.
6. The release of certain chemicals, which are called *pheromones*, is a very primitive form of communication.
7. It is important to register early.
8. The road was closed because of the fact that there were so many accidents.

21b Avoiding unnecessary repetition

Repetition is useful only when it contributes to emphasis, clarity, or coherence.

We will not rest until we have pursued **every** lead, inspected **every** piece of evidence, and interviewed **every** suspect. [The repetition of *every* is effective because it emphasizes the writer's determination.]

The following sentences have been revised to remove needless repetition.

~~One week was like the next week.~~ Each week was as boring as the last. She hoped Alex understood that ~~the complaint she made~~ *her complaint did not reflect her feelings about him.*

~~did not mean she was complaining because she disliked him.~~

21c Using elliptical constructions

An **elliptical construction** is one that deliberately omits words that can be understood from the context. In the following sentence, the word group *is the goal* can be taken out of the second and third clauses without affecting the meaning. The revised sentence is more concise than the original.

Speed is the goal for some swimmers, endurance ~~is the goal~~ for others, and relaxation ~~is the goal~~ for still others.

Sometimes, as an aid to clarity, commas mark omissions in elliptical constructions.

My family functioned like a baseball team: my mom was the coach; my brother, the pitcher; and my sister, the shortstop. [Be sure to use semicolons to separate items with internal commas (14b).]

As these examples show, parallelism (chapter 26) reinforces elliptical constructions.

Exercise 2

Revise this paragraph to eliminate wordiness and needless repetition.

[1]When I look back on my high school career, I realize that I was not taught much about international affairs in the world in spite of the fact that improved communications, the media, the Internet, travel, trading with different foreign countries, and immigration have made the world smaller. [2]Nonetheless, because both international affairs and business interest me, I decided to major in political science now that I am in college and to study marketing as my minor. [3]There are advantages to this combination of a major and a minor in my job situation at work as well, for I am now currently working part-time twenty hours a week for a company that imports merchandise into the United States and exports products to other countries. [4]Eventually, at some future time, when I have graduated and received my bachelor's degree, I may go on to law school and pursue my interest in politics, unless, on the other hand, my supervisor makes the recommendation that I develop my skills in marketing by spending time overseas in one of the company's foreign offices. [5]The opportunity to work overseas would provide me with a knowledge, an understanding, and an appreciation of the world economy. [6]Such an understanding is essential for anyone hoping to succeed in business.

22 Clarity and Completeness

Clarity in writing depends on more than grammar. Clarity results as much from critical thinking, logical development, and exact diction (chapter **20**) as it does from correct grammar. However, grammatical slips can mar what would otherwise be clear writing. This chapter will help you

- include all necessary words in a sentence (**22a**),
- complete comparisons (**22b**), and
- complete intensifiers (**22c**).

22a Including necessary words

When we speak or write quickly, we often omit small words. As you revise, be sure to include all necessary articles, prepositions, verbs, and conjunctions. Without the added article, the following sentence is incomplete.

The ceremony took place in ^an^ auditorium.

Even though prepositions are sometimes omitted in speech, they should always be included in writing.

We discussed a couple ^of^ issues at the meeting.

When a sentence has a **compound verb** (two verbs linked by a conjunction), you may need to supply a different preposition for each verb to make your meaning clear.

He neither **believes** ᵢₙ nor **approves of** exercise.

All verbs, both auxiliary and main (**7a(4)**), should be included to make sentences complete.

She ʰᵃˢ seen the movie three times.

Voter turnout has never ᵇᵉᵉⁿ and will never be 100 percent.

In sentences with two short clauses in which the second verb is exactly the same as the first, the second can be omitted.

The wind **was** fierce and the thunder [was] deafening.

Include the word *that* before a clause when it makes the sentence easier to read. Without the added *that* in the following sentence, a reader may stumble over *discovered the fossil* before understanding that *the fossil* is linked to *provided*.

The paleontologists discovered ᵗʰᵃᵗ the fossil provided a link between the dinosaur and the modern bird.

That should always be retained when a sentence has two parallel clauses.

The graph indicated **that the population had increased** but **that the number of homeowners had not.**

 22b   **Completing comparisons**

A comparison has two parts: someone or something is compared to someone or something else. As you revise your writing, make sure that your audience knows who or what is being compared. To revise incomplete comparisons, add necessary words, phrases, or clauses.

Printers today are quite different~~from those sold in the early 1990s~~.

His first novel was better~~than the one just published~~.

After you are sure that your comparisons are complete, check to see that they are also logical.

Her test scores are higher than ~~those of~~ the other students.

In the original sentence, *scores* were being compared to *students*. You could also rewrite this sentence as follows:

Her test scores are higher than the other students'.

Because *test scores* have already been mentioned, it is clear that *students'* (with an apostrophe) is short for *students' test scores*.

22c   Completing intensifiers

In speech, the intensifiers *so, such,* and *too* are used to mean "very," "unusually," or "extremely."

That movie was **so** funny.

In academic and professional writing, however, the intensifiers *so, such,* and *too* require a completing phrase or clause.

That movie was **so** funny **that I watched it twice.**

Julian has **such** a hearty laugh **that it makes everyone else laugh with him.**

The problem is just **too** complex **to solve in one day.**

Exercise 1

Revise the following sentences to make them clear and complete.

1. By studying the villains' faces in the *Star Wars* movies can reveal popular notions about the look of evil.
2. To design the character of Darth Maul for *The Phantom Menace,* Iain McCaig started by illustrating a picture of his worst nightmare.
3. He drew generic male face with metal teeth and long red ribbons of hair falling in front of it.
4. Ralph McQuarrie sketched designs for R2D2 and Darth Vader, including his mask. McCaig wanted to create something scarier.
5. When after arriving at many dead ends, McCaig finally had an idea of what he wanted to do.
6. He designed a face that looked as though it been flayed.
7. The evil visage of Darth Maul was so horrible. To balance the effect, McCaig added elegant black feathers.
8. However, the need to add beauty was not shared by others on the production team, and the feathers eventually became small horns.

S

EFFECTIVE SENTENCES

Let there be justice for all.
Let there be peace for all.
Let there be work, bread, water and salt for all.
　　　—Nelson Mandela, Inaugural Address

At his inauguration in 1994, President Mandela effectively used repetition and parallelism in his call for an end to discrimination in South Africa.

THINKING RHETORICALLY

SENTENCE STYLE

Most professional writers and readers use the following words to describe effective sentences.

- *Exact.* Precise words and word combinations ensure exactness and enable readers to come as close as they can to a full understanding of the writer's message.
- *Conventional.* Sentences are conventional when they conform to the usage expectations of a particular community. For most academic assignments, you will be expected to use Standardized English.
- *Consistent.* A consistent writing style is characterized by the use of the same types of words and grammatical structures throughout a piece of writing. A style that is inconsistent jars the reader's expectations.
- *Parallel.* Related to consistency, parallelism refers to the placement of similar ideas into similar grammatical structures.
- *Concise.* Concise prose is free of redundancies.
- *Coherent.* Coherence refers to clear connections between adjacent sentences and paragraphs.
- *Varied.* To write appealing paragraphs, a writer uses both short and long sentences. When sentences vary in length, they usually also vary in structure, rhythm, and emphasis.

In the following chapters, you will learn to identify the rhetorical options considered effective by most academic and professional writers. Remember, though, that appropriateness varies across rhetorical situations. You may find that it does not make sense to apply a general rule such as "Use the active voice" in all circumstances. For example, you may be expected to write a vigorous description of an event, detailing exactly what happened, but find that you need to use the passive voice when you do not know who was responsible for the event: Several of the campaign signs *were defaced*. Or, as another example, you may need to set aside the rule calling for Standardized English if you are writing dialogue in which the speakers use regional dialects. Analyzing your rhetorical situation, rather than always following general rules, will help you write sentences that are appropriate to you, your audience, and the specific context.

23 Sentence Unity

Effective academic and professional writing is composed of sentences that are consistent, clear, and complete. This chapter can help you

- choose and arrange details (**23a**),
- revise mixed metaphors (**23b**), and
- relate sentence parts (**23c**).

23a Choosing and arranging details

Well-chosen details add interest and credibility to your writing. As you revise, you may occasionally notice a sentence that would be clearer and more believable with the addition of a phrase or two about time, location, or cause.

Missing important detail	An astrophysicist from the Harvard-Smithsonian Center has predicted a galactic storm.
With detail added	An astrophysicist from the Harvard-Smithsonian Center has predicted **that** a galactic storm **will occur within the next 10 million years.**

Without the additional information about time, most readers would wonder when the storm was supposed to occur.

The added detail not only makes the sentence clearer but also helps readers accept the information.

The details you choose will help your readers understand your message. If you provide too many details within a single sentence, though, your readers may lose sight of your main point. When considering how much detail to include, you may sometimes want to write a long and fairly complex sentence. Just be sure that every detail contributes to the central thought, as in the following excerpt.

> A given mental task may involve a complicated web of circuits, which interact in varying degrees with others throughout the brain—not like the parts in a machine, but like the instruments in a symphony orchestra combining their tenor, volume, and resonance to create a particular musical effect.
>
> —JAMES SHREEVE, *Beyond the Brain*

By using parallel structures (see chapter **26**) and careful punctuation, this writer has created a long, yet coherent, sentence—one that indicates a clear connection between the details and the main idea of your sentence.

Exercise 1

Rewrite the following sentences so that the details clearly support the main idea. You may need to combine sentences or add words.

1. Firefighting is a dangerous job, but there are many high-tech devices and fire-resistant materials.
2. Wildfires can trap firefighters. Fire shelters are being developed to withstand temperatures as high as 2,000 degrees.
3. NASA developed Uninhabited Aerial Vehicles. Firefighters need to get accurate information fast.

4. Firefighters have difficulty seeing through smoke. A thermal imaging camera detects differences in heat and distinguishes between humans and surrounding objects.

5. Opticom is a traffic-control system, so firefighters can get to a fire quickly. They can change a red light to green from 2,000 feet away.

23b   Revising mixed metaphors

When you use language that evokes images, make sure that the images are meaningfully related. Unrelated images that appear in the same sentence are called **mixed metaphors.** The following sentence includes incompatible images.

As he climbed the corporate ladder, he ~~sank into a sea of~~ debt.
_{incurred a large}

The combination of two images—climbing a ladder and sinking into a sea—could create a picture in the reader's mind of a man hanging onto a ladder as it disappears into the water. The easiest way to revise such a sentence is to replace the words evoking one of the conflicting images.

23c   Relating sentence parts

(1) Mixed constructions are illogical.

A sentence that begins with one kind of grammatical structure and shifts to another is a **mixed construction.** To untangle a mixed construction, make sure that the sentence includes a conventional subject—a noun, a noun phrase, a gerund phrase, an infinitive phrase, or a noun clause. Prepositional phrases and adverbial clauses are not typical subjects.

Practicing
~~By practicing~~ a new language daily will help you become proficient. [A gerund phrase replaces a prepositional phrase.]

Her scholarship award
~~Although she won a scholarship~~ does not give her the right to skip classes. [A noun phrase replaces an adverbial clause.]

If you find a sentence that has a mixed construction, you can either revise the subject, as in the previous examples, or leave the beginning of the sentence as a modifier and add a new subject after it.

By practicing a new language daily, **you** will become more proficient.

Although she won a scholarship, **she** does not have the right to skip classes.

(2) Sentence parts are linked together logically.

When drafting, writers sometimes compose sentences in which the subject is said to be something or to do something that is not logically possible. This breakdown in meaning is called **faulty predication.** Similarly, mismatches between a verb and its complement can obscure meaning.

(a) Mismatch between subject and verb

The joining of a subject and a verb must create a meaningful idea.

Mismatch The absence of detail screams out at the reader. [An *absence* cannot scream.]

Revision The reader immediately notices the absence of detail.

(b) Illogical equation with *be*

When a form of the verb *be* joins two parts of a sentence (the subject and the subject complement), these two parts should be logically related.

> ^Free speech
> ~~The importance of free speech~~ is essential to a democracy.
> [*Importance* cannot be essential.]

(c) Mismatches in definitions

When you write a sentence that states a formal definition, be sure that the subject and the predicate (**1b**) fit together grammatically. The term being defined should be followed by a noun or a noun phrase, not an adverbial clause (**1f**). Avoid using *is when* or *is where*.

> *Ecology* is ~~when you~~ study^the/of^ the relationships among living organisms and between living organisms and their environment.

> *Exploitative competition* is ~~where~~ ^the contest between^ two or more organisms ^vying^ ~~vie~~ for a limited resource such as food.

(d) Mismatch of *reason* with *is because*

You can see why *reason* and *is because* are a mismatch by looking at the meaning of *because*: "for the reason that." Saying "the reason is for the reason that" is redundant. Thus, revise any sentence containing the construction *the reason is . . . because*.

> The ~~reason the~~ old train station was closed ~~is~~ because it had fallen into disrepair.

(e) Mismatch between verb and complement

A verb and its complement should fit together meaningfully.

Mismatch	Only a few students used the incorrect use of *there.* [To "use an incorrect use" is not logical.]
Revision	Only a few students used *there* incorrectly.

To make sure that a relative pronoun in the object position is connected logically to a verb, replace the pronoun with its antecedent. In the following sentence, *the inspiration* is the antecedent for *that*.

Mismatch	The inspiration that the author created touched young writers. [To "create the inspiration" is not logical.]
Revision	The author inspired young writers.

(3) Verbs used to integrate information are followed by specific types of complements.

Attributive tags are phrases used to identify sources of information (**39d(1)**). Most verbs in attributive tags are followed by a noun clause beginning with *that* or a *wh-* word (**1b(1)**). A few common verbs and their typical complements are listed below. (Some verbs such as *explain* fall into more than one category.)

VERBS FOR ATTRIBUTION AND THEIR COMPLEMENTS

Verb + *that* noun clause

agree	claim	explain	report	suggest
argue	demonstrate	maintain	state	think

Example: The researcher **reported** that the weather patterns had changed.

Verb + noun phrase + *that* noun clause

convince	persuade	remind	tell

Example: He **told** the reporters that he was planning to resign.

(*Continued on page 310*)

(Continued from page 309)
Verb + *wh-* noun clause

| demonstrate | discuss | report | suggest |
| describe | explain | state | wonder |

Example: She **described** what had happened.

Exercise 2

Revise the following sentences so that each verb is followed by a conventional complement.

1. The committee chair discussed that funding requests had specific requirements.
2. He persuaded that mass transit was affordable.
3. The two groups agreed how the problem could be solved.
4. Brown and Edwards described that improvements had been made to the old building.
5. They wondered that such a catastrophe could happen.

24 Subordination and Coordination

Subordination and coordination both refer to the joining of grammatical structures. **Subordination** is the linking of grammatically unequal structures (usually a dependent clause to an independent clause). **Coordination** is the linking of structures that have the same grammatical rank (two independent clauses, for example). By using subordination and coordination, you indicate connections between ideas as well as add variety to your sentences (chapter **30**). This chapter will help you

- use subordination effectively (**24a**),
- use coordination effectively (**24b**), and
- avoid faulty or excessive subordination and coordination (**24c**).

24a Using subordination effectively

Subordinate means "being of lower rank." A subordinate grammatical structure cannot stand alone; it is dependent on the main (independent) clause. The most common subordinate structure is the dependent clause (**1f(2)**), which usually begins with a subordinating conjunction or a relative pronoun.

(1) Subordinating conjunctions

A **subordinating conjunction** specifies the relationship between a dependent clause and an independent clause. For example, it might signal a causal relationship.

The painters finished early **because they work well together.**

Here are a few of the most frequently used subordinating conjunctions:

Cause	*because*
Concession	*although, even though*
Condition	*if, unless*
Effect	*so that*
Sequence	*before, after*
Time	*when*

By using subordinating conjunctions, you can combine short sentences and indicate how they are related.

> After the
> ~~The~~ crew leader picked us up early on Friday. ~~We~~ ate
>   , we
> breakfast together at a local diner.

If the subjects of the two clauses are the same, the dependent clause can often be shortened to a phrase.

> eating
> After ~~we ate~~ our breakfast, we headed back to the
> construction site.

(2) Relative pronouns

A **relative pronoun** (*who, whom, which, that,* or *whose*) introduces a dependent clause that, in most cases, modifies the pronoun's antecedent (**5a(2)**).

The temple has a portico **that faces west.**

By using an **adjectival (relative) clause**—that is, a dependent clause introduced by a relative pronoun—you can embed details into a sentence without sacrificing conciseness.

Japanese automakers have produced a hybrid car *, which has sold well in the United States*.

An adjectival clause can be shortened, as long as the meaning of the sentence remains clear.

The runner ~~who was~~ from Brazil stumbled just before the finish line.

 CAUTION

A relative clause beginning with *which* sometimes refers to an entire independent clause rather than modifying a specific word or phrase. Because this type of reference can be vague, you should avoid it if possible.

As
~~He is~~ a graduate of a top university, ~~which should provide him with~~ *he should have* many opportunities.

24b **Using coordination effectively**

Coordinate means "being of equal rank." Coordinate grammatical elements have the same form. For example, they may be two words that are both adjectives, two phrases that are both prepositional, or two clauses that are both dependent or both independent.

a **stunning** and **satisfying** conclusion [adjectives]

in the attic or **in the basement** [prepositional phrases]

so that everyone would be happy and **so that no one would complain** [dependent adverbial clauses]

The company was losing money, yet **the employees suspected nothing.** [independent clauses]

To indicate the relationship between coordinate words, phrases, or clauses, choose an appropriate coordinating conjunction.

Addition	*and*
Alternative	*or, not*
Cause	*for*
Contrast	*but, yet*
Result	*so*

By using coordination, you can avoid unnecessary repetition and thus make your sentences more concise.

The hike to the top of Angels Landing has countless switchbacks. ~~It also has~~ long drop-offs. _{and}

MULTILINGUAL WRITERS

CHOOSING CONJUNCTIONS

In English, use either a coordinating conjunction or a subordinating conjunction (but not both) to signal a connection between clauses.

Even though I took some aspirin, ~~but~~ I still have a sore shoulder.

Because he had a severe headache, ~~so~~ he went to the health center.

Alternatively, the clauses in these two example sentences can be connected with coordinating conjunctions, rather than subordinating conjunctions.

I took some aspirin, **but** I still have a sore shoulder.

He had a severe headache, **so** he went to the health center.

Exercise 1

Using subordination and coordination, revise the sentences in the following paragraph so that they emphasize the ideas you think are important.

¹The Lummi tribe lives in the Northwest. ²The Lummis have a belief about sorrow and loss. ³They believe that grief is a burden. ⁴According to their culture, this burden shouldn't be carried alone. ⁵After the terrorist attack on the World Trade Center, the Lummis wanted to help shoulder the burden of grief felt by others. ⁶Some of the Lummis carve totem poles. ⁷These carvers crafted a healing totem pole. ⁸They gave this pole to the citizens of New York. ⁹Many of the citizens of New York had family members who were killed in the terrorist attacks. ¹⁰The Lummis escorted the totem pole across the nation. ¹¹They made stops for small ceremonies. ¹²At these ceremonies, they offered blessings. ¹³They also offered songs. ¹⁴The Lummis don't believe that the pole itself heals. ¹⁵Rather, they believe that healing comes from the prayers and songs said over it. ¹⁶For them, healing isn't the responsibility of a single person. ¹⁷They believe that it is the responsibility of the community.

24c Avoiding faulty or excessive subordination and coordination

(1) Precise conjunctions enhance readability.

Effective subordination requires choosing subordinating conjunctions carefully. In the following sentence, the use of *as* is distracting because it can mean either "because" or "while."

Because
~~As~~ time was running out, I randomly filled in the remaining
circles on the exam sheet.

Sometimes you may need to add a subordinating conjunction
to a phrase for clarity. Without the addition of *although* in the
revision of the following sentence, the connection between being a new player and winning games is unclear.

Although   he won
~Chen was a new player, ~~winning~~ more than half of his
games.

Your choice of coordinating conjunction should also convey
your meaning precisely. For example, to indicate a cause-and-
effect relationship, *so* is more precise than *and*.

so
The rain continued to fall, ~~and~~ the concert was canceled.

(2) Excessive subordination and coordination can confuse readers.

As you revise your writing, make sure that you have not overused subordination or coordination. In the following ineffective sentence, two dependent clauses compete for the reader's
focus. The revision is clearer because it eliminates one of the
dependent clauses.

Ineffective

Although researchers used to believe that ancient Egyptians
were the first to domesticate cats, they now think that cats
may have provided company for humans 5,000 years earlier
because the intact skeleton of a cat has been discovered in a
Neolithic village on Cyprus.

Revised

Although researchers used to believe that ancient Egyptians
were the first to domesticate cats, they now think that cats may

have provided company for humans 5,000 years earlier. They base their revised estimate on the discovery of an intact cat skeleton in a Neolithic village on Cyprus.

Overuse of coordination results in a rambling sentence in need of revision.

Ineffective

The lake was surrounded by forest, and it was large and clean, so it looked refreshing.

Revised

Surrounded by forest, the large, clean lake looked refreshing.

Exercise 2

Revise the following sentences to eliminate faulty or excessive coordination and subordination. Be prepared to explain why your sentences are more effective than the originals.

1. The Duct Tape Guys usually describe humorous uses for duct tape, providing serious information about the history of duct tape on their Web site.
2. Duct tape was invented for the U.S. military during World War II to keep the moisture out of ammunition cases because it was strong and waterproof.
3. Duct tape was originally called "duck tape" as it was waterproof and ducks are like that too and because it was made of cotton duck, which is a durable, tightly woven material.
4. Duck tape was also used to repair jeeps and to repair aircraft, its primary use being to protect ammunition cases.
5. When the war was over, house builders used duck tape to connect duct work together, and the builders started to refer to duck tape as "duct tape" and eventually the color of the tape changed from the green that was used during the war to silver, which matched the ducts.

25 Misplaced Modifiers

Modifiers are words, phrases, or clauses that modify; that is, they qualify or limit the meaning of other words. Modifiers enrich your writing with details and enhance its coherence—when they are correctly placed. This chapter will help you

- place modifiers effectively (**25a**) and
- revise dangling modifiers (**25b**).

25a Placement of modifiers

Effective placement of modifiers will improve the clarity and coherence of your sentences. A **misplaced modifier** obscures the meaning of a sentence.

(1) Keep related words together.
Place the modifiers *almost, even, hardly, just,* and *only* before the words or word groups they modify. Altering placement can alter meaning.

The committee can **only** nominate two members for the position. [The committee cannot *appoint* the two members to the position.]

The committee can nominate **only** two members for the position. [The committee cannot nominate more than two members.]

Only the committee can nominate two members for the position. [No person or group other than the committee can nominate members.]

(2) Place phrases and clauses as close as possible to the words or word groups they modify.

Readers expect phrases and clauses to modify the nearest grammatical element. The revision of the following sentence clarifies that the prosecutor, not the witness, was skillful.

    With great skill, the
~~The~~ prosecutor cross-examined the witness ~~with great skill~~.

The following revision makes it clear that the phrase *crouched and ugly* describes the phantom, not the boy.

    The   crouched and ugly
~~Crouched and ugly, the~~ young boy gasped at the phantom moving across the stage.

The next sentence is fine as long as Jesse wrote the proposal, not the review. If he wrote the review, the sentence should be recast.

I have not read the review of the proposal Jesse wrote.

               Jesse's
I have not read ~~the~~ review of the proposal ~~Jesse wrote~~.

(3) Revise squinting modifiers so that they modify only one element.

A **squinting modifier** can be interpreted as modifying either what precedes it or what follows it. To avoid such lack of clarity, you can reposition the modifier and/or add word(s) or punctuation.

Even though Erikson lists some advantages **overall** his vision of a successful business is faulty.

Revisions

Even though Erikson lists some **overall** advantages, his vision of a successful business is faulty. [modifer repositioned; punctuation added]

Erikson lists some advantages**; however, overall,** his vision of a successful business is faulty. [word and punctuation added]

MULTILINGUAL WRITERS

ADVERBS OF FREQUENCY

Adverbs of frequency (such as *always, never, sometimes,* and *often*) appear before one-word verbs.

He **rarely** goes to horror movies.

However, these adverbs appear after a form of *be* when it is the main verb.

Novels written by Stephen King are **always** popular.

When a sentence contains more than one verb in a verb phrase, the adverb of frequency is placed after the first auxiliary verb.

My friends have **never** read *The Shining*.

Exercise 1

Improve the clarity of the following sentences by moving the modifiers. Not all sentences require editing.

1. Alfred Joseph Hitchcock was born the son of a poultry dealer in London.
2. Hitchcock was only identified with thrillers after making his third movie, *The Lodger.*
3. Hitchcock moved to the United States in 1939 and eventually became a naturalized citizen.
4. Hitchcock's most famous movies revolved around psychological improbabilities that are still discussed by movie critics today.
5. Although his movies are known for suspense sometimes moviegoers also remember Hitchcock's droll sense of humor.
6. Hitchcock just did not direct movie thrillers; he also produced two television series.
7. Originally a British citizen, Queen Elizabeth knighted Alfred Hitchcock in 1980.

25b Dangling modifiers

Dangling modifiers are phrases (**1e**) or elliptical clauses (**1f(2)**) that lack an appropriate word to modify. To avoid including dangling modifiers in your essays, first look carefully at any sentence that begins with a phrase or an elliptical clause. If the phrase or clause suggests an action, be sure that what follows the modifier (the subject of the sentence) names the actor. If there is no actor performing the action indicated in the phrase, the modifier is dangling. To revise this type of dangling modifier, name an actor—either in the modifier or in the main clause.

Lying on the beach, time became irrelevant. [Time cannot lie on a beach.]

Revisions

While **we** were lying on the beach, time became irrelevant. [actor in the modifier]

Lying on the beach, **we** found that time became irrelevant. [actor in the main clause]

While eating lunch, the phone rang. [A phone cannot eat lunch.]

Revisions

While **we** were eating lunch, the phone rang. [actor in the modifier]

While eating lunch, **we** heard the phone ring. [actor in the main clause]

The following sentences illustrate revisions of other common types of dangling modifiers:

To avoid getting a sunburn, *you should apply* sunscreen ~~should be applied~~ before going outside.

[Sunscreen cannot avoid getting a sunburn.]

Because they were in ~~In~~ a rush to finish their work, an accident occurred.

[An accident cannot be in a rush.]

Although you will most frequently find a dangling modifier at the beginning of a sentence, you may sometimes find one at the end of a sentence.

Adequate lighting is important *for anyone* ~~when~~ studying.

[Lighting cannot study.]

Sentence modifiers and absolute phrases are not considered to be dangling.

> **The fog finally lifting,** planes were able to depart.
>
> Marcus played well in the final game, **on the whole.**

Exercise 2

Revise the following sentences to eliminate misplaced and dangling modifiers.

1. Climbing a mountain, fitness becomes all-important.
2. In determining an appropriate challenge, considering safety precautions is necessary.
3. Taking care to stay roped together, accidents are less likely to occur.
4. Even when expecting sunny weather, rain gear should be packed.
5. Although adding extra weight, climbers should not leave home without a first-aid kit.
6. By taking pains at the beginning of a trip, agony can be averted at the end of a trip.

25c Noun modifiers

A string of noun modifiers can be cumbersome. The following example shows how a sentence with too many noun modifiers can be revised.

The ~~Friday afternoon~~ Student Affairs Committee meeting ⌃scheduled for Friday afternoon has been postponed.

Exercise 3

Using what you have learned in this chapter and in chapter 4, revise the following sentences to remove modifier errors.

1. As a woman of both the nineteenth and twentieth centuries, the life of Gertrude Bell was unusual.
2. Young, wealthy, and intelligent, many people were impressed by the red-headed Bell.
3. Among the first women to graduate from Oxford, she couldn't hardly be satisfied with domestic life.
4. Instead, Bell traveled to what were considered the most remotest countries in the world, saw the wonders of the Ottoman Empire, and explored the desert of Iraq.
5. Several of the Arab sheiks who knew Bell thought that she acted bold.
6. The war in Iraq did not give Bell no time to pursue her research.
7. She became an Arab rebellion supporter.
8. While traveling in Iraq, meetings with important politicians took place.
9. In 1921, Winston Churchill invited Bell to a conference in the Middle East because the other Great Britain conference participants knew little about Iraq.
10. When the photo of the conference participants was taken, Bell looked elegantly in her feathered hat and silk dress among the thirty-six black-suited males.

26 Parallelism

Parallelism is the use of grammatically equivalent structures to clarify meaning and to emphasize ideas. Parallel structures often occur in a series.

Their goals are **to raise awareness of the natural area, to build a walking path near the creek running through it,** and **to construct a nature center at the east end of the parking lot.**

This chapter will help you

- recognize parallel elements (**26a**),
- create parallelism by repeating words and grammatical forms (**26b**),
- use parallel elements to link sentences (**26c**),
- link parallel elements with correlative conjunctions (**26d**), and
- use parallelism for emphasis in introductions and conclusions (**26e**).

26a Recognizing parallel elements

Two or more elements are considered parallel when they have similar grammatical forms—for example, when they are all nouns or all prepositional phrases. Parallel elements are frequently joined by a coordinating conjunction (*and, but, or, yet, so, nor,* or *for*). In the examples that follow, the elements in boldface have the same grammatical form.

Words

> The dean is both **determined** and
>   **dedicated.**

Phrases

> She emphasized her commitment to **academic freedom,**
>   **professional development,**
>   **cultural diversity,**
>   and **social justice.**

> Her goals include **publicizing student and faculty research,**
>   **increasing the funding for that research,**
>   and **providing adequate research facilities.**

Clauses

> Our instructor explained **what the project had entailed** and
>   **how the results had been used.**

> He said **that we would conduct a similar project** but
>   **that we would likely get different results.**

Sentences

> **When I interviewed for the job, I tried not to sweat.**
> **When I got the job, I managed not to shout.**

26b Repeating words and grammatical forms

(1) The repetition of words often creates parallel elements.
By repeating a preposition, the infinitive marker *to,* or the introductory word of a clause, you can create parallel structures that will help you convey your meaning clearly, succinctly, and emphatically.

Preposition

> For about fifteen minutes, I have been pacing in my office,
>> hands **on** my hips,
>> a scowl **on** my face,
>> and a grudge **on** my mind.

> My embarrassment stemmed not **from** the money lost but
>> **from** the notoriety gained.

Infinitive marker *to*

> She wanted her audience **to remember** the protest song and
>> **to understand** its origin.

Introductory word of a clause

> The team vowed **that** they would support each other,
>> **that** they would play their best, and
>> **that** they would win the tournament.

(2) Parallel structures can be created through the repetition of form only.

Sometimes parallel structures are similar in form even though no words are repeated. The following example includes the *-ing* form (present participle) of three different verbs.

> People all around me are **buying, remodeling,** or **selling** their houses.

The next example includes a compound dependent clause (**1f**), each part of which has a two-word subject and a one-word predicate.

> Whether **mortgage rates rise** or
>> **building codes change,** the real estate market should
>>> remain strong this spring.

26c   Linking two or more sentences

Repeating a pattern emphasizes the relationship of ideas. The following two sentences come from the conclusion of "Letter from Birmingham Jail."

> **If I have said anything** in this letter <u>that overstates the truth and indicates an unreasonable impatience,</u> **I beg you to forgive me. If I have said anything** <u>that understates the truth and indicates my having a patience</u> that allows me to settle for anything less than brotherhood, **I beg God to forgive me.**
>
> —MARTIN LUTHER KING, JR.

Almost every structure in the second sentence is parallel to a structure in the first. To create this parallelism, King repeats words and uses similar grammatical forms. But the second sentence would still be parallel with the first even if more of its words were different. For example, substituting *written* for *said* and *reveals* for *indicates* ("If I have written anything that understates the truth and reveals my having a patience . . . ") would result in a sentence that was still parallel with the first sentence. Such changes, though, would lessen the impact of this particular passage because they would detract from the important substitution of "God" for "you" in the second sentence.

THINKING RHETORICALLY

PARALLELISM

Parallel elements make your writing easy to read. But consider breaking from the parallel pattern on occasion to emphasize a point. For example, to describe a friend, you could start with two adjectives and then switch to a noun phrase.

> My friend Alison is **kind, modest,** and **the smartest mathematician in the state.**

26d Using correlative conjunctions

Correlative conjunctions (or **correlatives**) are pairs of words that link other words, phrases, or clauses (**1a(7)** and **1g(2)**).

> *both . . . and*
> *either . . . or*
> *neither . . . nor*
> *not only . . . but also*
> *whether . . . or*

Notice how the words or phrases following each conjunction in the pair are parallel.

> He will major in **either** <u>biology</u> **or** <u>chemistry</u>.

> **Whether** <u>at home</u> **or** <u>at school</u>, he is always busy.

Be especially careful when using *not only . . . but also*.

> His team practices not only
> ∧ ~~Not only practicing~~ at 6 a.m. during the week, but ~~his team~~ also ~~scrimmages~~ on Sunday afternoons.

OR

> does his team practice   it
> Not only ∧ ~~practicing~~ at 6 a.m. during the week, but ~~his team~~ also scrimmages on Sunday afternoons.

26e Emphasizing key ideas in introductions and conclusions

By expressing key ideas in parallel structures, you emphasize them. However, be careful not to overuse parallel patterns, or they will lose their impact. Parallelism is especially effective in the introduction to a paragraph or an essay. The following passage from the introduction to a chapter of a book on advertising contains three examples of parallel forms.

> While **men are encouraged to fall in love with their cars, women are more often invited to have a romance,** indeed an erotic experience, with **something closer to home, something that truly does pump the valves of our hearts**—the food we eat. And the consequences become even more severe as we enter into the territory of **compulsivity** and **addiction.**
>
> —JEAN KILBOURNE, *Deadly Persuasion*

Parallel structures can also be effective in the conclusion to an essay.

> **Because these men work** with **animals,** not **machines, because they live** outside in landscapes of torrential beauty, **because they are confined** to **a place** and **a routine** embellished with awesome variables, **because calves die** in the arms that pulled others into life, **because they go** to the mountains as if on a pilgrimage to find out what makes a herd of elk tick, **their strength** is also **a softness, their toughness, a rare delicacy.**
>
> —GRETEL EHRLICH, "About Men"

Exercise 1

Make the structures in each sentence parallel. In some sentences, you may have to use different wording.

1. Helen was praised by the vice president, and her assistant admired her.
2. Colleagues found her genial and easy to schedule meetings with.
3. When she hired new employees for her department, she looked for applicants who were intelligent, able to stay focused, and able to speak clearly.
4. At meetings, she was always prepared, participating actively yet politely, and generated innovative responses to department concerns.

5. In her annual report, she wrote that her most important achievements were attracting new clients and revenues were higher.

6. When asked about her leadership style, she said that she preferred collaborating with others rather than to work alone in her office.

7. Although dedicated to her work, Helen also recognized that parenting was important and the necessity of cultivating a life outside of work.

8. She worked hard to save money for the education of her children, for her own music lessons, and investing for her retirement.

9. However, in the coming year, she hoped to reduce the number of weekends she worked in the office and spending more time at home.

10. She would like to plan a piano recital and also have the opportunity to plan a family vacation.

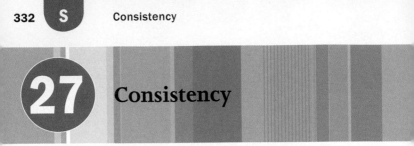

27   Consistency

Consistency in verb tense, point of view, and tone will help your readers to understand your message, your role in creating it, and their role as audience. This chapter will help you maintain consistency

- in verb tense (**27a**),
- in point of view (**27b**), and
- in tone (**27c**).

27a   Verb tense

Every verb tense can be discussed in terms of time frame and aspect. *Time frame* refers to whether the tense is present, past, or future. *Aspect* refers to whether it is simple, progressive, perfect, or perfect progressive. (See the chart on page 124.) Consistency in the time frame of verbs, though not necessarily in their aspect, ensures that sentences reporting a sequence of events link together logically. In the following paragraph, notice that the time frame remains in the past, but the aspect may be either simple, perfect, or progressive.

past perfect

In the summer of 1983, I **had** just **finished** my third year of

simple past

architecture school and **had** to find a six-month internship. I

past perfect (compound predicate)

had grown up and **gone** through my entire education in the Midwest,

past perfect

but I **had been** to New York City once on a class field trip and I

simple past simple past

thought it **seemed** like a pretty good place to live. So, armed with

simple past

little more than an inflated ego and my school portfolio, I **was** off to

Manhattan, oblivious to the bad economy and the fact that the city

past progressive

was overflowing with young architects.

—PAUL K. HUMISTON, "Small World"

If you do need to shift to another time frame, you can use
a time marker:

now, then, today, yesterday
in two years, during the 1920s
after you finish, before we left

For example, in the following paragraph, the time frame shifts
back and forth between present and past—between today,
when Edward O. Wilson is studying ants in the woods around
Walden Pond, and the nineteenth century, when Henry David
Thoreau lived there. The time markers are bracketed.

simple present   simple past

These woods **are** not wild; indeed, they **were** not wild [in Thoreau's

day]. [Today], the beach and trails of Walden Pond State Reservation

simple present   simple present

draw about 500,000 visitors a year. Few of them **hunt** ants, however.

simple present   simple past

Underfoot and under the leaf litter there **is** a world as wild as it **was**

simple past

[before human beings **came** to this part of North America].

—JAMES GORMAN, "Finding a Wild, Fearsome World Beneath Every Fallen Leaf"

On occasion, a shift in time is indicated implicitly—that is, without an explicit time marker. A writer may change tenses, without including time markers, (1) to explain or support a general statement with information about the past, (2) to compare and contrast two different time periods, or (3) to comment on a topic. Why do you think the author of the following paragraph varies verb tenses?

Thomas Jefferson, author of the Declaration of Independence, **is** considered one of our country's most brilliant citizens. His achievements **were** many, as **were** his interests. Some historians **describe** his work as a naturalist, scientist, and inventor; others **focus** on his accomplishments as an educator and politician. Yet Jefferson **is** best known as a spokesman for democracy.

Except for the two uses of *were* in the second sentence, all verbs are in the present tense. The author uses the past tense in the second sentence to provide evidence from the past that supports the opening sentence.

Before you turn in a final draft, check your verb tenses to ensure that they are logical and consistent. Revise any that are not.

The white wedding dress ~~comes~~ *came* into fashion when Queen Victoria

wore a white gown at her wedding to Prince Albert of Saxe.

Soon after, brides who could afford them bought stylish white

dresses for their weddings. Brides of modest means, however,

continued
~~continue~~ to choose dresses they could wear more than once.

Exercise 1

Determine whether the shift in tense in this passage is effective. Be prepared to state your reasoning.

[1]Life at North GRIP [Greenland Ice-Core Project], if not exactly comfortable, **is** at least well supplied. [2]Lunch <u>the day I arrived</u> **was** a fish stew prepared in a delicate tomato base. [The remaining verbs in this paragraph are all in past tense.]

—**ELIZABETH KOLBERT, "Ice Memory"**

Exercise 2

Revise the following paragraph so that it contains no unnecessary shifts in verb tense.

I **had** already **been walking** for a half hour in the semidarkness of Amsterdam's early-morning streets when I **came** to a red light. I **am** in a hurry to get to the train station and no cars **were** out yet, so I **cross** over the cobblestones, passing a man waiting for the light to change. I never **look** back when he **scolds** me for breaking the law. I **had** a train to catch. I **was** going to Widnau, in Switzerland, to see Aunt Marie. I **have** not **seen** her since I **was** in second grade.

27b Point of view

Whenever you write, you must establish your point of view (perspective). Your point of view will be evident in the pronouns you choose. *I* or *we* indicates a first-person point of view, which is appropriate for writing that includes personal views or experiences. If you decide to address the reader as *you*, you are adopting a second-person point of view. However, because a second-person point of view is rare in academic writing, avoid using *you* unless you need to address the reader (**20d**). If you select the pronouns *he, she, it, one,* and *they*, you are writing with a third-person point of view. The third-person point of view is the most common point of view in academic writing.

Although you may find it necessary to use different points of view in a paper, especially if you are comparing or contrasting other people's views with your own, be careful not to confuse readers by shifting perspective unnecessarily. The following paragraph has been revised to ensure consistency of point of view.

> To an observer, a sleeping person appears passive, unresponsive, and essentially isolated from the rest of the world and its barrage of stimuli. While it is true that ~~you are~~ someone asleep is unaware of most surrounding noises ~~when you are asleep,~~ ~~our~~ that person's brain is far from inactive. In fact, it can be as active during sleep as it is ~~when you are awake~~ in a waking state. When ~~our brains are~~ it is asleep, the rate and type of electrical activity change.

For more information on the use of pronouns to indicate point of view, see **20d**.

The tone of a piece of writing conveys a writer's attitude toward a topic (**34a(3)**). The words and sentence forms (**1h**) a writer chooses determine the tone presented. Notice how the tone differs in the following two excerpts, which describe the same scientific experiment. The first paragraph was written for a book intended for the general public; the second was written for a journal article to be read by other researchers.

> Imagine that I asked you to play a very simple gambling game. In front of you, are four decks of cards—two red and two blue. Each card in those four decks either wins you a sum of money or costs you some money, and your job is to turn over cards from any of the decks, one at a time, in such a way that maximizes your winnings. What you don't know at the beginning, however, is that the red decks are a minefield. The rewards are high, but when you lose on red, you lose *a lot*. You can really only win by taking cards from the blue decks, which offer a nice, steady diet of $50 . . . payoffs. The question is: how long will it take you to figure this out? —**MALCOLM GLADWELL**, *Blink*

> In a gambling task that simulates real-life decision-making in the way it factors uncertainty, rewards, and penalties, the players are given four decks of cards, a loan of $2000 facsimile U.S. bills, and asked to play so that they can lose the least amount of money and win the most (1). Turning each card carries an immediate reward ($100 in decks A and B and $50 in decks C and D). Unpredictably, however, the turning of some cards also carries a penalty (which is large in decks A and B and small in decks C and D). Playing mostly from the disadvantageous decks (A and B) leads to an overall loss. Playing from the advantageous decks (C and D) leads to an overall gain. The players have no way of predicting when a penalty will arise in a given deck, no way to calculate with precision the net gain or loss from each deck, and no knowledge

of how many cards they must turn to end the game (the game is stopped after 100 card selections).

—ANTOINE BECHARA, HANNA DAMASIO,
DANIEL TRANEL, AND ANTONIO R. DAMASIO,
"Deciding Advantageously before Knowing the Advantageous Strategy"

In the excerpt from *Blink*, Malcolm Gladwell addresses the readers directly: "Imagine that I asked you to play a very simple gambling game." In the excerpt from the journal article, Antoine Bechara and his co-researchers describe their experiment from a third-person point of view. Gladwell also uses everyday words and expressions. For example, whereas the researchers use words such as "immediate reward" and "penalty," Gladwell conveys the same information informally: "wins you a sum of money or costs you some money." Finally, the researchers include a reference citation (the number one in parentheses) in their description, but Gladwell does not.

Neither of these excerpts is better than the other. The tone of each is appropriate for the given rhetorical situation. However, shifts in tone can be distracting. The following paragraph was revised to ensure consistency of tone:

Scientists at the University of Oslo (Norway), ~~think they~~ *have evidence that*

~~know why~~ the common belief about the birth order of ~~kids~~ *children carries some truth.*

~~has some truth to it.~~ Using as data IQ tests taken from military

records, the scientists found that older children ~~have~~ *score* significantly *higher than their siblings.*

~~more on the ball than kids in second place.~~ According to the

researchers, the average variation in scores is large enough to

account for differences in college admission.

Exercise 3

Revise the following paragraph so that there are no unnecessary shifts in point of view or tone.

[1]Many car owners used to complain about deceptive fuel-economy ratings. [2]They often found, after they had already purchased a car, that their mileage was lower than that on the car's window sticker. [3]The issue remained pretty much ignored until our gas prices started to rise like crazy. [4]Because of increased pressure from consumer organizations, the United States Environmental Protection Agency reviewed and then changed the way it was calculating fuel-economy ratings. [5]The agency now takes into account factors such as quick acceleration, changing road grades, and the use of air conditioning, so the new ratings should reflect your real-world driving conditions. [6]Nonetheless, the ratings can never be right on target given that we all have different driving habits.

28   Pronoun Reference

The meaning of each pronoun in a sentence should be immediately obvious. In the following sentence, the pronouns *them* and *itself* clearly refer to their antecedents, *shells* and *carrier shell,* respectively.

The **carrier shell** gathers small empty **shells** and attaches **them** to **itself.**

A pronoun may refer to two or more antecedents.

Jack and I have collected shells since **we** were eight years old.

Sometimes an antecedent follows a pronoun.

Because of **their** beauty and rarity, **shells** attract collectors worldwide.

The main rhetorical principle to keep in mind regarding pronoun reference is clarity. This chapter will help you maintain clarity by avoiding pronoun references that are

- ambiguous or unclear (**28a**),
- remote or awkward (**28b**), or
- broad, implied (**28c**), or otherwise nonspecific (**28d**).

28a Ambiguous or unclear pronoun references

When a pronoun can refer to either of two antecedents, the ambiguity may confuse readers. To make the antecedent clear, replace the pronoun with a noun or rewrite the sentence. The following revised sentences clarify that Mr. Eggers, not Mr. Anderson, will be in charge of the project.

Mr. Eggers
Mr. Anderson told Mr. Eggers that ∧ ~~he~~ would be in charge of the project.

OR

Mr. Anderson put Mr. Eggers in charge of the project.

28b Remote or awkward pronoun references

To help readers understand your meaning, place pronouns as close to their antecedents as possible. The following sentence needs to be revised so that the relative pronoun *that* is close to its antecedent, *poem*. Otherwise, the reader would wonder how a new book could be written in 1945.

that was originally written in 1945
The **poem** ∧ has been published in a new book ~~that was originally written in 1945~~.

Notice, however, that a relative pronoun does not always have to follow its antecedent directly. In the following example, there is no risk of misunderstanding.

We slowly began to notice **changes** in our lives **that** we had never expected.

28c   Broad or implied pronoun references

Pronouns such as *it, this, that,* and *which* may refer to a specific word or phrase or to the sense of a whole clause, sentence, or paragraph.

The weight of the pack was manageable, once I became used to **it**. [*It* refers specifically to *weight.*]

Large corporations may seem stronger than individuals, but **that** is not true. [*That* refers to the sense of the whole first clause.]

Unless the meaning is clear, avoid reference to the general idea of a preceding clause or sentence. Instead, state clearly what *this* or *that* refers to.

When class attendance is compulsory, some students feel that

education is being forced on them. This∧is unwarranted.

[perception]

[In the original sentence, *this* had no clear antecedent.]

In addition, remember to express an idea explicitly rather than merely implying it.

[Teaching music]

My father is a music teacher. ∧It is a profession that requires

much patience.

[In the original sentence, *it* had no expressed antecedent.]

Be especially careful to provide clear antecedents when you are referring to the work or possessions of others. The following sentence requires revision because *she* can refer to someone other than Jen Norton.

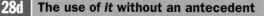

        her   Jen Norton
In ~~Jen Norton's~~ new book, ~~she~~ argues for election reform.

28d   The use of *it* without an antecedent

The expletive *it* does not have a specific antecedent (see **1b(1)**). Instead, it is used to postpone, and thus give emphasis to, the subject of a sentence. A sentence that begins with this expletive can sometimes be wordy or awkward. Revise such a sentence by replacing *it* with the postponed subject.

   Trying to repair the car   useless
   ~~It was~~ ~~no use trying to repair the car~~.

Avoid placing one *it* near another *it* with a different meaning.

  Staying in the old apartment
  ~~It~~ would be simpler ~~to stay in the old apartment~~, but it is

too far from my job.

[The first *it* is an expletive; the second *it* refers to *apartment*.]

Exercise 1

Edit the following sentences to make all references clear. Some sentences may not require editing.

1. It is remarkable to read about Lance Armstrong's victories.

2. A champion cyclist, a cancer survivor, and a humanitarian, it is no wonder that Lance Armstrong is one of the most highly celebrated athletes in the world.

3. Armstrong's mother encouraged his athleticism, which led to his becoming a professional triathlete by age sixteen.

4. Though you might not believe it, Armstrong was only a senior in high school when he started training for the Olympic developmental team.

5. By the time he was twenty-five, Armstrong was ranked as the top cyclist in the world.

6. Not long afterward, because of intense pain, he sought medical attention, and they told him he had testicular cancer.

7. The cancer had spread to his lungs and brain; thus, they said his chances for recovery were slim.

8. Armstrong underwent dramatic surgery and aggressive chemotherapy; this eventually helped him recover.

9. Armstrong started training five months after their diagnosis and went on to win major championships, including the Tour de France.

10. For Lance Armstrong, it hasn't been only about racing bikes; he has become a humanitarian as well, creating the Lance Armstrong Foundation to help cancer patients and to fund cancer research around the world.

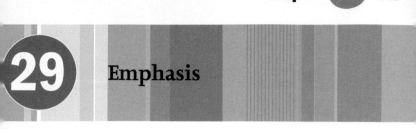

29 Emphasis

In any rhetorical situation, some of your ideas will be more important than others. You can direct the reader's attention to these ideas by emphasizing them. This chapter will help you

- place words where they receive emphasis (**29a**),
- use cumulative and periodic sentences (**29b**),
- arrange ideas in climactic order (**29c**),
- repeat important words (**29d**),
- choose between active voice and passive voice (**29e**),
- invert word order in sentences (**29f**), and
- use an occasional short sentence (**29g**).

You can also emphasize ideas by using subordination and co-ordination (chapter **24**), parallelism (chapter **26**), and exact word choice (chapter **20**).

29a Placing words for emphasis

Words at the beginning or the end of a sentence receive emphasis— especially those at the end. Notice how the revision of the following sentence adds emphasis to the beginning to balance the emphasis at the end.

~~In today's society, most good~~ Good jobs today require a college education.

You can also emphasize an important idea by placing it after a colon (**17d**) or a dash (**17e**).

At a later time [rocks and clay] may again become what they once were: dust.   —**LESLIE MARMON SILKO**, "Interior and Exterior Landscapes"

By 1857, miners had extracted 760 tons of gold from these hills— and left behind more than ten times as much mercury, as well as devastated forests, slopes and streams.
—**REBECCA SOLNIT**, *Storming the Gates of Paradise: Landscapes for Politics*

Exercise 1

Find the most important idea in each set of sentences. Then combine each set into one sentence so that the most important idea is emphasized. Be prepared to explain your changes.

1. Snowboarding is a new sport. It debuted at the Olympics in 1998. The Olympics were held in Nagano, Japan, that year.
2. Snowboarders came from around the world. Some competed in the giant slalom. Others participated in the halfpipe.
3. Snowboarding has increased in popularity. Each year, more and more people go snowboarding. It attracted 50 percent more participants in 2000 than it did in 1999.
4. Snowboarding is a fast-growing sport. The number of snowboards sold each year has increased dramatically.
5. However, the inventor of the snowboard is hard to identify. People have been sliding down hills on sleds for a long time.
6. Some sources credit M. M. "Jack" Burchet. Burchet tied his feet to a piece of plywood in 1929.
7. Sherman Poppen is most frequently cited as the inventor of the snowboard. His Snurfer went into production in 1966. (The name is a combination of the words *snow* and *surfer*.)

8. Poppen created the Snurfer for his daughter. He bound two skis together. He also fixed a rope at the front end.
9. Snowboarding originated as a sport for kids. It eventually became a competitive sport.
10. The United States snowboarding team won two medals in the 1998 Olympic Games. The team won seven medals in the 2006 Olympic Games.

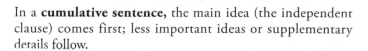

29b | **Using cumulative and periodic sentences**

In a **cumulative sentence,** the main idea (the independent clause) comes first; less important ideas or supplementary details follow.

> **The day was hot for June,** a pale sun burning in a cloudless sky, wilting the last of the irises, the rhododendron blossoms drooping. —ADAM HASLETT, "Devotion"

In a **periodic sentence,** however, the main idea comes last, just before the period.

> In a day when movies seem more and more predictable, when novels tend to be plotless, baggy monsters or minimalist exercises in interior emotion, **it's no surprise that sports has come to occupy an increasingly prominent place in the communal imagination.** —MICHIKO KAKUTANI, "Making Art of Sport"

Both of these types of sentences can be effective. Because cumulative sentences are more common, however, the infrequently encountered periodic sentence tends to provide emphasis.

29c Ordering ideas from least to most important

By arranging your ideas in **climactic order**—from least important to most important—you build up suspense. If you place your most important idea first, the sentence may seem to trail off. If you place it in the middle, readers may not recognize its full significance. If, however, you place it at the end of the sentence, it will not only receive emphasis but also provide a springboard to the next sentence. In the following example, the writer emphasizes a doctor's desire to help the disadvantaged and then implies that this desire has been realized through work with young Haitian doctors.

> While he was in medical school, the soon-to-be doctor discovered his calling: to diagnose infectious diseases, to find ways of curing people with these diseases, and **to bring the lifesaving knowledge of modern medicine to the disadvantaged.** Most recently, he has been working with a small group of young doctors in Haiti.

29d Repeating important words

Although effective writers avoid unnecessary repetition, they also understand that deliberate repetition emphasizes key words or ideas.

> We **forget** all too soon the things we thought we could never **forget.** We **forget** the loves and betrayals alike, **forget** what we whispered and what we screamed, **forget** who we are.
>
> —JOAN DIDION, "On Keeping a Notebook"

In this case, the emphatic repetition of *forget* reinforces the author's point—that we do not remember many things that once seemed impossible to forget. If you decide to repeat a word for emphasis, make sure that the word you choose conveys one of your central ideas.

29e Choosing between the active voice and the passive voice

(1) Sentences in the active and passive voices differ in form.
A sentence in the **active voice** emphasizes an actor and an action by having the actor as the subject. The **passive voice** emphasizes the receiver or the result of the action, with the actor often omitted entirely (7c). If a reference to an actor is included in a passive sentence, this reference appears in a prepositional phrase beginning with *by*. The verb phrase in the passive voice also differs from its active counterpart: it includes the auxiliary verb *be* and the past participle of the main verb.

Active	Bob Dylan wrote that song.
Passive	That song **was written by** Bob Dylan.

(2) Sentences in the active voice highlight actors and actions.
The author of the following excerpt uses the active voice to describe the passage of an airplane and the passengers inside it:

> ¹The tiny red light of an airplane **passes** through the sky. ²It **soars** past a low cloud, the North Star, the bold white W of Cassiopeia—vanishing and reappearing, winking in a long ellipsis. ³Inside, its passengers **read** glossy periodicals, **summon** flight attendants, and **unhitch** the frames of their safety belts. ⁴They **gaze** from the panes of double windows and **float** away in a tight red arc. —KEVIN BROCKMEIER, "Space"

Notice how much less effective the third sentence is when written in the passive voice, with the emphasis on the actors removed.

Inside, glossy periodicals **are read,** flight attendants **are summoned,** and the frames of safety belts **are unhitched.**

(3) Sentences in the passive voice emphasize recipients or objects of actions.

In a paragraph from a government-sponsored Web page that warns against the use of illicit drugs, the passive voice is used to discuss the drug methamphetamine. Paragraphs on users and producers of the drug are written primarily in the active voice, but the paragraph about the drug itself and the various ways in which it is used is written in the passive voice. Drug users and producers are not mentioned in this paragraph because the drug itself is the focus.

Methamphetamine **can be ingested, inhaled,** or **injected.** It **is sold** as a powder or in small chunks which resemble rock candy. It **can be mixed** with water for injection or sprinkled on tobacco or marijuana and smoked. Chunks of clear, high-purity methamphetamine ("ice," "crystal," "glass") **are smoked** in a small pipe, much as "crack" cocaine **is smoked.**

—UTAH ATTORNEY GENERAL'S OFFICE

Because whoever or whatever is responsible for the action is not the subject of a sentence in the passive voice, such a sentence is often imprecise. Politicians sometimes favor the passive voice because it allows them to avoid responsibility by saying, for example, "Taxes will have to be raised" or "A few miscalculations were made."

TECH SAVVY
Grammar checkers flag all uses of the passive voice they find, usually suggesting that they be changed to the active voice. Be sure to determine for yourself whether the active voice or the passive voice is more appropriate for your rhetorical situation.

29f Inverting word order

Most sentences begin with a subject and end with a predicate. When you move words out of their normal order, you draw attention to them.

> **At the back of the crowded room** sat **a newspaper reporter.**
> [COMPARE: **A newspaper reporter** sat **at the back of the crowded room.**]
>
> **Fundamental to life in New York** is **the subway.**
> [COMPARE: **The subway** is **fundamental to life in New York.**]

A sentence with inverted word order will stand out in a paragraph containing other sentences with standard word order. Notice the inverted word order in the second sentence of the following passage.

> [1]The Library Committee met with the City Council on several occasions to persuade them to fund the building of a library annex. [2]So successful were their efforts that a new wing will be added by next year. [3]This wing will contain archival materials that were previously stored in the basement.

The modifier *so successful* appears at the beginning of the sentence, rather than in its normal position, after the verb. Their efforts were *so successful* that . . . . The inverted word order emphasizes the committee's accomplishment.

MULTILINGUAL WRITERS

INVERTING WORD ORDER

English sentences are inverted in various ways. Sometimes the main verb in the form of a participle is placed at the beginning of the sentence. The subject and the auxiliary verb(s) are then inverted.

> part   aux   s
>
> **Carved** into the bench **were someone's initials.**
> [COMPARE: Someone's initials were carved into the bench.]

An adjective may also begin a sentence. In this type of sentence, the subject and the linking verb are inverted.

> adj   link v   s
>
> **Crucial** to our success **was the dedication of our employees.**
> [COMPARE: The dedication of our employees was crucial to our success.]

In other inverted sentences, the auxiliary verb comes before the subject. Sentences beginning with a negative adverb (such as *never, seldom,* or *rarely*) require this type of inversion.

> neg adv aux   s   v
>
> **Rarely have we experienced** such bad weather!

29g   Using an occasional short sentence

In a paragraph of mostly long sentences, try using a short sentence for emphasis. To optimize the effect, lead up to the short sentence with an especially long sentence.

After organizing the kitchen, buying the groceries, slicing the vegetables, mowing the lawn, weeding the garden, hanging the decorations, and setting up the grill, I was ready to have a good time when my guests arrived. **Then the phone rang.**

Exercise 2

Add emphasis to each of the following sentences by using the strategy indicated. You may have to add some words and/or delete others.

1. (climactic order) In the 1960 Olympics, Wilma Rudolph tied the world record in the 100-meter race, she tied the record in the 400-meter relay, she won the hearts of fans from around the world, and she broke the record in the 200-meter race.

2. (periodic sentence) Some sports reporters described Rudolph as a gazelle because of her beautiful stride.

3. (inversion) Rudolph's Olympic achievement is impressive, but her victory over a crippling disease is even more spectacular.

4. (final short sentence) Rudolph was born prematurely, weighing only four and one-half pounds. As a child, she suffered from double pneumonia, scarlet fever, and then polio.

5. (cumulative sentence) She received help from her family. Her brothers and sister massaged her legs. Her mother drove her to a hospital for therapy.

6. (inversion) Her siblings' willingness to help was essential to her recovery, as were her mother's vigilant care and her own determination.

7. (periodic sentence) Her passions became basketball and track after she recovered, built up her strength, and gained self-confidence.

8. (climactic order) Rudolph set a scoring record in basketball, she set the standard for future track and field stars, and she set an Olympic record in track.

9. (active voice) Many female athletes, including Florence Griffith Joyner and Jackie Joyner-Kersee, have been inspired by Wilma Rudolph.

30 Variety

To make your writing lively and distinctive, include a variety of sentence types and lengths. Notice how the sentences in the paragraph below vary in length (short and long), form (simple, compound, and compound-complex), and function (statements, questions, and commands). This assortment of sentences makes this paragraph about pleasure pleasurable to read.

Start with the taste. Imagine a moment when the sensation of honey or sugar on the tongue was an astonishment, a kind of intoxication. The closest I've ever come to recovering such a sense of sweetness was secondhand, though it left a powerful impression on me even so. I'm thinking of my son's first experience with sugar: the icing on the cake at his first birthday. I have only the testimony of Isaac's face to go by (that, and his fierceness to repeat the experience), but it was plain that his first encounter with sugar had intoxicated him—was in fact an ecstasy, in the literal sense of the word. That is, he was beside himself with the pleasure of it, no longer here with me in space and time in quite the same way he had been just a moment before. Between bites Isaac gazed up at me in amazement (he was on my lap, and I was delivering the ambrosial forkfuls to his gaping mouth) as if to exclaim, "Your world contains *this?* From this day forward I shall dedicate my life to it." (Which he basically has done.) And I remember thinking, this is no minor desire, and then wondered: Could it be that sweetness is the prototype of *all* desire?   —**MICHAEL POLLAN,** *The Botany of Desire*

This chapter will help you

- revise sentence length and form (**30a**),
- vary sentence openings (**30b**), and
- use an occasional question, exclamation, or command (**30c**).

If you have difficulty distinguishing between various types of sentence structures, review the fundamentals in chapter **1**.

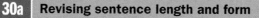

30a Revising sentence length and form

(1) Combine short sentences.
To avoid the choppiness of a series of short sentences, consider using one of the following methods to combine some of the sentences into longer sentences.

(a) Use coordinate or correlative conjunctions.
Try combining ideas using coordinate conjunctions (*and, but, or, for, nor, so,* and *yet*) or correlative conjunctions (*both . . . and, either . . . or, neither . . . nor,* and *not only . . . but also*).

Simple sentences	Minneapolis is one of the Twin Cities. St. Paul is the other. They differ in many ways.
Combined	Minneapolis **and** St. Paul are called the Twin Cities, **but** they differ in many ways.
Simple sentences	The company provides health insurance. It also provides dental insurance.
Combined	The company provides **both** health insurance **and** dental insurance.

(b) Use relative pronouns or subordinating conjunctions.

The relative pronouns *who, which, whose,* and *that* can be used to combine simple sentences.

Simple sentences	Today, lawmakers discussed some new legislation. This legislation would promote the safety of rocket passengers.
Combined	Today, lawmakers discussed some new legislation **that** would promote the safety of rocket passengers.

You can also use subordinating conjunctions such as *because, so that,* and *even though* to join simple sentences. For a full list, see page 43.

Simple sentences	Legislation on space tourism has not been passed. Plans for a commercial rocket service are going forward anyway.
Combined	**Although** legislation on space tourism has not been passed, plans for a commercial rocket service are going forward anyway.

You may also decide to use both a subordinating and a coordinating conjunction.

Simple sentences	Private rockets have been involved in very few accidents. Legislators are discussing safety issues, though. They have not agreed on any regulations yet.
Combined	**Although** private rockets have been involved in very few accidents, legislators are discussing safety issues, **but** they have not agreed on regulations yet.

THINKING RHETORICALLY

SHORT SENTENCES

Occasionally, a series of brief sentences produces an intended effect. For example, a writer may have a rhetorical reason for conveying a sense of abruptness; therefore, what might seem choppy in one situation could be considered dramatic in another. The short sentences in the following passage capture the quick actions taking place as an accident is about to occur.

"There's a truck in your lane!" my friend yelled. I swerved toward the shoulder. "Watch out!" she screamed. I hit the brakes. The wheels locked. The back of the car swerved to the right.

Exercise 1

Convert each set of short sentences into a single longer sentence. Use no more than one coordinating conjunction in the revised sentence.

1. It was the bottom of the ninth inning. The score was tied. The bases were loaded. There were two outs.
2. A young player stepped up to the plate. This was his first season. He had hit a home run yesterday. He had struck out his last time at bat.
3. He knew the next pitch could decide the game. He took a practice swing. The pitcher looked him over.
4. The pitch came in high. The batter swung low. He missed this first pitch. He also missed the second pitch.
5. He had two strikes against him. The young player hit the next ball. It soared over the right-field fence.

(2) Avoid overusing coordinating conjunctions.

In early drafts, some writers overuse the coordinating conjunctions *and* and *but,* so the pattern of long compound sentences becomes tedious. The use of coordinating conjunctions can also be ineffective if the relationship the writer is signaling is vague. The following strategies should help you revise ineffective uses of coordinating conjunctions.

(a) Use a more specific subordinating conjunction or a conjunctive adverb.

You can often replace *and* with a more specific subordinating conjunction or a conjunctive adverb (**1g**).

I worked all summer to earn tuition money, ~~and I didn't~~ so that I wouldn't have to work during the school year.

OR

I worked all summer to earn tuition money, ~~and~~ ; thus I didn't have to work during the school year.

(b) Use a relative clause to embed information.

Seafood ~~is nutritious, and it is low in fat, and it~~ , which is nutritious and low in fat, has become available in greater variety.

(c) Allow two or more verbs to share the same subject.

Marie quickly grabbed a shovel, ~~and then she~~ ran to the edge of the field, and ~~then she~~ put out the fire before it could spread to the trees.

(d) Place some information in an appositive phrase.

Karl Glazebrook ~~is a researcher in astronomy at Johns Hopkins University, and he~~ , a researcher in astronomy at Johns Hopkins University, has questioned the conventional theory of galaxy formations.

(e) Place some information in a prepositional or verbal phrase.

In the thick snow,
~~The snow was thick, and~~ we could not see where we were going.

After pulling
~~The plane pulled~~ away from the gate on time, ~~and then it~~ the plane sat
on the runway for two hours.

OR

The plane, after pulling away from the gate on time, sat on
the runway for two hours.

In the last example, the subject, *plane,* and the verb, *sat,* are
separated. Although it is usually best to keep the subject next
to the verb so that the relationship between them is clear,
breaking this pattern on occasion can add variety without sacrificing clarity.

Exercise 2

Use any of the methods for revising the ineffective use of coordinating conjunctions to improve the following paragraph.

[1]Onions are pungent, they are indispensable, and they are
found in kitchens everywhere. [2]China is the leading producer
of this vegetable. [3]Libya is the leading consumer, and on
average a Libyan eats over sixty-five pounds of onions a year.
[4]One hundred billion pounds of onions are produced each
year, and they make their way into a variety of foods. [5]Raw
onions add zest to salads, but they also add zest to burgers and
salsas. [6]Cooked onions give a sweetness to pasta sauces, and
they can also be added to soups and curries. [7]The onion is a
ubiquitous ingredient, yet its origin remains unknown.

30b Varying sentence openings

Most writers begin more than half of their sentences with the subject. Although this pattern is common, relying on it too heavily can make writing sound dull. Experiment with the following alternatives for beginning your sentences.

(1) Begin with an adverb or an adverbial clause.

Immediately, the dentist stopped drilling and asked me how I was doing. [adverb]

When the procedure was over, he explained that I should not eat or drink anything for an hour. [adverbial clause]

(2) Begin with a prepositional or verbal phrase.

In the auditorium, voters waited in silence before casting their ballots. [prepositional phrase]

To win, candidates need to convey a clear message to voters. [infinitive phrase]

Reflecting on the election, we understood clearly how the incumbent defeated the challenger. [participial phrase]

(3) Begin with a connecting word or phrase.

In each of the following examples, the connecting word or phrase shows the relationship between the ideas in the pair of sentences. (See also **34d**.)

Many restaurants close within a few years of opening. **But** others, which offer good food at reasonable prices, become well established.

Difficulty in finding a place to park keeps some people from going out to lunch downtown. **However,** that problem may be alleviated with the construction of a new underground parking garage.

Independently owned restaurants struggle to get started for a number of reasons. **First of all,** they have to compete against successful restaurant chains.

(4) Begin with an appositive or an absolute phrase.

A town of historic interest, Santa Fe also has many art galleries. [appositive phrase]

History, art, and the color of the sky—these drew her to Santa Fe. [appositive series]

Her face turned to the sky, she absorbed the warmth of the sun. [absolute phrase]

(5) Begin with a direct object or a predicate adjective.

I was an abysmal football player. **Soccer,** though, I could play well. [direct object]

Vital to any success I had were my mother's early lessons. [predicate adjective]

Exercise 3

Rewrite each sentence so that it does not begin with a subject.

1. John Spilsbury was an engraver and mapmaker from London who made the first jigsaw puzzle in about 1760.
2. He pasted a map onto a piece of wood and used a fine-bladed saw to cut around the borders of the countries.
3. The jigsaw puzzle was first an educational toy and has been a mainstay in households all over the world ever since its invention.
4. The original puzzles were quite expensive because the wooden pieces were cut by hand.
5. Most puzzles are made of cardboard today.

30c Using questions, exclamations, and commands

When you have written a long series of declarative statements, you can vary the paragraph by introducing another type of sentence: a question, an exclamation, or a command (1i). The sentence that varies from the others will catch the reader's attention.

(1) Raise a question or two for variety.

If people could realize that immigrant children are better off, and less scarred, by holding on to their first languages as they learn a second one, then perhaps Americans could accept a more drastic change. What if every English-speaking toddler were to start learning a foreign language at an early age, maybe in kindergarten? What if these children were to learn Spanish, for instance, the language already spoken by millions of American citizens, but also by so many neighbors to the South?

—ARIEL DORFMAN, "If Only We All Spoke Two Languages"

You can either answer the question or let readers answer it for themselves, in which case it is called a **rhetorical question** (1i).

(2) Add an exclamatory sentence for variety.

But at other moments, the classroom is so lifeless or painful or confused—and I so powerless to do anything about it—that my claim to be a teacher seems a transparent sham. Then the enemy is everywhere: in those students from some alien planet, in the subject I thought I knew, and in the personal pathology that keeps me earning my living this way. What a fool I was to imagine that I had mastered this occult art—harder to divine than tea leaves and impossible for mortals to do even passably well!

—PARKER PALMER, *The Courage to Teach*

Although you can make your sentences emphatic without resorting to the use of exclamation points (chapter 24), the introduction of an exclamatory sentence can break up a regular pattern of declarative sentences.

(3) Include a command for variety.

> Now I stare and stare at people shamelessly. Stare. It's the way to educate your eye. —**WALKER EVANS**, *Unclassified*

In this case, a one-word command, "Stare," provides variety.

Exercise 4

Explain how questions and commands add variety to the following paragraph. Describe other ways in which this writer varies his sentences.

[1]The gods, they say, give breath, and they take it away. [2]But the same could be said—couldn't it?—of the humble comma. [3]Add it to the present clause, and, of a sudden, the mind is, quite literally, given pause to think; take it out if you wish or forget it and the mind is deprived of a resting place. [4]Yet still the comma gets no respect. [5]It seems just a slip of a thing, a pedant's tick, a blip on the edge of our consciousness, a kind of printer's smudge almost. [6]Small, we claim, is beautiful (especially in the age of the microchip). [7]Yet what is so often used, and so rarely recalled, as the comma—unless it be breath itself?

—**PICO IYER**, "**In Praise of the Humble Comma**"

WRITING

Elements of the rhetorical situation.

31 The Rhetorical Situation

Rhetoric, the purposeful use of language, pervades your daily activities. Every day, you use rhetoric as you read and write—whether you are reading class assignments, course syllabi, e-mails, or directions for your MP3 player or are submitting written assignments, creating a résumé, or text messaging with your friends.

This chapter explains reading and writing rhetorically as processes, each a series of sometimes overlapping steps that help you understand these four elements of the rhetorical situation (**31a**):

- exigence (**31b**),
- purpose (**31c**),
- audience (**31d**), and
- context (**31e**).

Writing rhetorically helps you to fulfill a variety of class assignments, some of which are discussed in this handbook:

- an essay from personal experience (**34h**),
- an argument from personal experience and research (**35j**),
- an argument based on research (chapters **37–39**), and
- a Web page for an organization (**36c, 36d**).

31a Understanding the rhetorical situation

As a communicator, you use visual and verbal language purposefully, every day, in terms of a **rhetorical situation** (fig. 31.1), the

Fig. 31.1. The rhetorical situation.

circumstances in which you are interpreting a reading or composing a piece of writing or even a visual.

The **writer** in a rhetorical situation is the person who identifies the **exigence,** the reason or problem that impels that person to write or speak in the first place. When purposeful language can resolve the exigence, the situation is rhetorical. The writer then prepares a **message** (information delivered through visual or verbal means) with the purpose of resolving that exigence. But to fulfill that purpose, the writer must gauge the message in terms of the intended **audience,** the reader who has the capability of resolving the exigence or problem. Whether or not that audience works to resolve the exigence, the audience reads, hears, or sees the message within a specific **context,** the constraints (obstacles) and resources (positive influences) in the environment of the rhetorical situation. Those constraints and resources include whatever else has already been said on the subject; when, where, and through what medium the transaction between writer and audience takes place; and the writer's relationship with the audience, the writer's credibility (or believability), and the appropriateness of the message in terms of both content and means of delivery (electronic, print, visual, or oral).

Reading and writing rhetorically offer you the opportunity to consider each of these elements separately as well as in combination. You can actively engage a text by establishing the writer's credibility, intended audience, context, purpose, and overall message and by establishing the interdependence of these elements. For instance, a writer's purpose, whether stated or implied, should be appropriate for the intended audience and the context. The writer's choice of audience might change depending on purpose or context; the context affects the audience and the writer's purpose (**31e**).

31b Writing to an exigence

The exigence is the particular problem or situation that calls for words. Words—either spoken or written—can resolve the problem of fining a parking violator, announcing a birth, awarding college admission, or inviting wedding guests. Once you determine the exigence for your writing, you will be better able to gauge all the elements of your writing (from word choice to organizational pattern) in terms of your overall purpose.

Natural disasters provide exigencies for writing and speaking, often with the purpose of stimulating fundraising and relief efforts.

31c Writing with a specific purpose

As soon as you know that words can resolve an exigence or address a particular need or situation, you can concentrate on the general purpose of those words, which depends upon the intended audience or reader. Writers must clarify their purpose, and readers should be influenced according to that purpose—whether the writer wants to express feelings about something, amuse or entertain, report information, explain or evaluate the significance of information, analyze a situation, clarify a point, invite the audience to consider alternative points of view, or argue for or against a course of action.

Depending on the writer's overall purpose, the message (whether composed or received) can be classified as expressive, expository, or argumentative.

(1) Expressive writing emphasizes the writer's feelings and reactions to people, objects, events, or ideas.

Personal letters and journals are often expressive, as are many essays and short stories. The following example (paragraph 1) comes from an essay designed to convey the excitement of a mother-to-be as she imagines telling her husband the happy news. (For ease of reference, each of the sample paragraphs in this chapter is numbered.)

1   I haven't breathed a word to him yet, about having this baby, and I won't until he arrives. I won't blurt out such special news on the telephone. I won't write it in an e-mail. I want to be there standing in front of him—the best seat in the house—to watch the smile break across his face. I want to share the joy of that first moment of knowledge, of all that this baby will mean to our lives. I feel jealously possessive about this moment

to come. He arrives this evening and, impatient as I am, I am hanging on, savouring the scene, playing it out in my head, over and over again. —CAROL DRINKWATER, "The Fruits of Spring"

(2) Expository writing focuses more on objects, events, or ideas than on the writer's feelings about them.

Textbooks, news accounts, scientific reports, and encyclopedia articles are generally expository, as are many of the essays students are expected to write in college. When you report, explain, clarify, or assess, you are practicing exposition. Paragraph 2 is excerpted from a book that explains how paleoanthropologists—specifically, a paleoanthropologist named Mac—discover their prizes.

2   Searching only in the most promising areas isn't the key to [Mac's] success; perseverance is. He walks the same territory over and over again, changing courses around obstacles, and he tells his people to do the same. If you walked to the left around this bush yesterday, then walk to the right today. If you walked into the sun yesterday, then walk with the sun at your back today. And most of all, walk, and walk, and walk, and *look* while you are doing it. Don't daydream; don't scan the horizon for shade; ignore the burning sun even when the temperature reaches 135°F. Keep your eyes on the ground searching for that elusive sliver of bone or gleaming tooth that is not just any old animal, fossilized and turning to rubble, but a hominid. Those are the prizes we seek; those are the messengers from the past.

—ALAN WALKER AND PAT SHIPMAN, *The Wisdom of the Bones*

(3) Argumentative writing is intended to influence the reader's attitudes and actions.

Most writing is to some extent an argument. Through the choice and arrangement of material, even something as apparently straightforward as a résumé can be an argument for an interview. However, writing is usually called argumentative if it clearly supports a specific position (chapter 35). In paragraph 3, note how the writer calls for people to take a winning stance.

3   I warn you, a winning stance is never achieved by *trying.* I hear some say, "I will try as hard as I can." Trying is for losers. Trying implies the possibility of losing. I will *try* to win. I will *try* not to lose. If after trying they have lost, well, they *tried,* did they not? *Losers always try.* Winners never try. Winners only win.

    —GERRY SPENCE, "The Unbeatable Power Argument"

Writers need to identify their overall purpose for each piece of writing, knowing that they can tap various methods of development (such as narration, description, and cause-and-effect analysis; see 33g) to work toward that goal. Whether you are the reader or the writer, you must assess the rhetorical purpose. For instance, when you are the reader, you want to assess the overall purpose of the writing in order to know how best to respond. If you can identify specific words or passages that convey the writer's purpose, you can discern whether the writer wants you to be entertained, informed, or persuaded. When you are the writer, you want to compose a message that responds to an exigence and fulfills a purpose while also alerting your intended audience to that purpose. If you are writing in response to a specific assignment, talk with your instructor or check your assignment sheet to review which elements of the rhetorical situation (exigence, audience, context, purpose) have already been set for you.

CHECKLIST for Assessing Purpose

- Has your instructor provided a purpose for your writing, or are you defining a purpose on your own?

- Are you trying primarily to express how you feel? Are you writing to improve your self-understanding or trying to help others understand you better?

- Are you trying to be entertaining or inspiring? How easily does your topic lend itself to your purpose? What examples or choice of words will help you fulfill that purpose?

- Are you writing primarily to convey information? Are you trying to teach others something they do not know or to demonstrate that you have knowledge in common?

- Are you writing primarily to argue for or against a course of action? Do you want your readers to stop a certain behavior, to undertake a specific action, or to consider alternative points of view?

- Do you have more than one purpose in writing? Which purpose is primary? How can the other purposes help you achieve that primary one? Or are some of your purposes in conflict?

Exercise 1

Select one of the following subjects; write two paragraphs that begin to develop an expressive, expository, or argumentative essay on that subject.

1. your finances
2. your generation
3. your career goals
4. your computer expertise
5. your favorite musical group
6. volunteer work
7. academic pressures
8. music or dance performances
9. student housing
10. your closest relative

31d Considering audience

A clear understanding of the audience—its values, concerns, and knowledge—helps writers tailor their writing in terms of length, quality and quantity of details, the kind of language used, and the examples that will be most effective. Of course, the audience is anyone who reads the text, but that broader audience includes the writer's intended audience, those people whom the writer considers capable of being influenced by the words or who are capable of bringing about change. Therefore, you will need to consider who exactly will be reading what you write and whether your choices are appropriate for that audience.

(1) A specialized audience is predisposed to the message.

A **specialized audience** has a demonstrated interest in the subject. If a relative died as the result of drunk driving, you might become a member of a specialized audience: people whose lives have been affected by alcohol abuse. If you decided to write about the harm done through alcohol abuse, you would probably direct your text to members of an organization such as Alcoholics Anonymous or Mothers Against Drunk Driving, who constitute a specialized audience. Any group of people (such as nutritionists, police officers, or social workers) who have an area of expertise, an agenda, or a specific interest can form a specialized audience, one that you will want to address accordingly.

A general reader might be surprised by the emotional content of the following excerpt, which was created for a specialized audience, one already familiar with the dire consequences of drunk driving.

4   Early on Sunday morning, September 18, 1999, Jacqueline Saburido, 20, and four friends were on their way home from a birthday party. Reggie Stephey, an 18-year-old star football player,

was on his way home from drinking beer with some buddies. On a dark road on the outskirts of Austin, Texas, Reggie's SUV veered into the Oldsmobile carrying Jacqui and the others. Two passengers in the car were killed at the scene and two were rescued. Within minutes, the car caught fire. Jacqui was pinned in the front seat on the passenger side. She was burned over 60% of her body; no one thought she could survive. But Jacqui lived. Her hands were so badly burned that her fingers had to be amputated. She lost her hair, her ears, her nose, her left eyelid and much of her vision. She has had more than 50 operations since the crash and has many more to go.

In June 2001 Reggie Stephey was convicted of two counts of intoxication manslaughter for the deaths of Jacqui's two friends. He was sentenced to seven years in prison and fined $20,000.

—TEXAS DEPARTMENT OF TRANSPORTATION, "Jacqui's Story"

This passage was not written for a general audience. Instead, it is aimed at a specialized audience, most of whose members are educators who are committed to ending drunk driving. These educators can tell Jacqui's story to discourage people from driving while intoxicated.

Many of the essays you will be assigned to write in college—in English, history, economics, psychology, and the sciences, for example—will be aimed at a specialized audience. That audience will often be an instructor, who is already familiar with the subject matter. For example, if you are writing an essay about molecular mapping for your biology instructor, it is not necessary to define *chromosomes*. Instead, your essay needs to communicate your understanding of the overall process and its applications.

Writing for a specialized audience does not mean that you have to know more than the members of that audience, nor does it mean that you have to impress them with your interpretation. Since no one knows everything about a subject, members of a specialized audience will usually appreciate thinking about their subject in a new way, even if they are not learning new information.

(2) A diverse audience represents a range of expertise and interest.

A **diverse audience** consists of readers with differing levels of expertise and varying interest in your subject. For example, if you are writing about upgrading computer software in a report that will be read by all the department heads of a company, you should be aware that some of your readers probably know more about software than others, and some may know more than you. But you can also assume that all of your readers share a willingness to learn about new material if it is presented clearly and respectfully by someone who is establishing common ground with them.

Paragraph 5 helps a diverse audience of readers understand an unusual illness that put a young man in the hospital.

5   I first met Greg in April 1977, when he arrived at Williamsbridge Hospital. Lacking facial hair, and childlike in manner, he seemed younger than his twenty-five years. He was fat, Buddha-like, with a vacant, bland face, his blind eyes roving at random in their orbits, while he sat motionless in his wheelchair. If he lacked spontaneity and initiated no exchanges, he responded promptly and appropriately when I spoke to him, though odd words would sometimes catch his fancy and give rise to associative tangents or snatches of song and rhyme. Between questions, if the time was not filled, there tended to be a deepening silence; though if this lasted for more than a minute, he might fall into Hare Krishna chants or a soft muttering of mantras. He was still, he said, "a total believer," devoted to the group's doctrines and aims.   —OLIVER SACKS, "The Last Hippie"

Oliver Sacks writes for a diverse audience. Although its members share an interest in science writing, and medical stories in particular, they bring varying levels of expertise to Sacks's essay. Therefore, Sacks describes a medical condition in words easily understood by a wide audience. When you are writing for a diverse audience, you too need to establish what the members are likely to have in common in order to make appropriate word choices (chapters **19–22**) and include appropriate details (**33f(1)**).

(3) Multiple audiences read for different reasons.

Writers often need to consider multiple audiences, a task related to—yet different from—addressing a diverse audience. When you address a diverse audience, you try to reach everyone. When you consider multiple audiences, you gauge your choice of words and tone according to your primary audience, knowing that a secondary audience might have access to your text. At work, for instance, you address your research report, employee evaluation, or proposal to your boss. But if you know that she will circulate the text among your colleagues, you adjust your words and tone accordingly. You might not be as frank in writing as you would be speaking in person; you might omit potentially hurtful information or temper your words. When you know that your rhetorical situation includes multiple audiences, you can better select your words.

The use of e-mail for communication (36b) has increased the likelihood of writing for multiple audiences because messages can be forwarded easily—and not always with the writer's permission. Other electronic texts, such as those generated by listserv dialogues or online conversations through a Web site, also reach multiple audiences. When writing for electronic submission, consider whether anyone outside your primary audience might read your work.

While writing essays in college, you may also find yourself addressing multiple audiences. For example, you may use research you have done in your history class as the starting point for developing an essay for a class in literature or economics. You may take a linked or team-taught course in which you submit written work for evaluation by two instructors (your two primary audiences). In each of these cases, you are writing for multiple audiences. This kind of writing requires that you consider a variety of attitudes and positions (35d and 35e).

The following checklist may help you assess your audience.

CHECKLIST for Assessing Audience

- Who is going to be reading what you write?
- What do you know about the members of your audience? What characteristics can you safely assume they have? What do they have in common? How are they different?
- What values do you share with them? How do you differ from them?
- How much do they already know about your topic?
- What kind of language is appropriate or inappropriate for this audience?
- How open are the members of this audience to views that may be different from their own?
- What level of expertise will they expect from you?
- What do you not know about this audience? What assumptions would be risky?
- Are you writing with a primary audience in mind but expecting a secondary audience to also read what you have written? If so, have you clearly identified the primary audience so that you can address that audience specifically, while recognizing the expectations of the secondary audience?

Exercise 2

Examine an introductory and an advanced textbook in a discipline of your choice, and locate a passage in each devoted to the same issue or concept. Photocopy these passages, and prepare a class presentation in which you explain how they reveal differences in audience.

31e Sending and receiving a message within a context

Context includes time and place, writer and audience, and the medium of delivery—the circumstances under which writer and reader communicate. Social, political, religious, and other cultural factors influence context, as do the constraints and resources of the rhetorical situation. Therefore, what you are able to produce in writing is always influenced (positively or negatively) by the context.

Your background and beliefs often shape the stance (or attitude) you take when writing. An essay written shortly before your school's winter break, for example, could be influenced by both your anticipation of a combined religious holiday and family reunion and your uncertainty about whether your audience shares that anticipation. Or an international crisis, such as the war in Iraq or the prolonged disaster in Darfur, might prompt you to reconsider the purpose of an essay you are drafting for your international economics course. Writers who consider the time, the place, and other factors of the context in which they are writing, as well as their audience, are more likely to communicate their ideas effectively.

The medium in which you are writing is also part of the context. Writing material for a Web page or another online medium requires you to think differently about organization, design, and style than does writing a traditional academic essay or business letter. Depending on your familiarity with and aptitude in using the technology, writing in an electronic medium may demand a good deal more time from you, too. Considering the method of delivery for a Web page, for example, requires making different kinds of rhetorical decisions than you would make for a text in a wholly static print medium (chapter 36).

When you read the work of other writers, you will sometimes find that the context is explicitly stated, as in paragraph 6.

6   Katrina tore up lives as well as landscapes. A city below sea level was churned suddenly and convulsively by the hurricane that struck New Orleans in late August 2005. Rich people died along with the indigent. The pricey homes of the professional classes, both black and white, were destroyed, as were rickety cottages owned or rented by the poor. Millionaires and high-flying politicians were undone by Katrina, while other survivors found opportunity in the ruins of the city. That did not make Katrina an "equal opportunity destroyer," as some hastened to call it. Poor blacks did disproportionately more of the dying. And as the engines of recovery creaked into gear, people of means enjoyed advantages that had been theirs all along.
    —JED HORNE, *Breach of Faith: Hurricane Katrina and the*
    Near Death of a Great American City

Often, however, the context must be inferred. Whether the context is announced or not, it is important that writers and readers identify and consider it.

CHECKLIST for Assessing the Context

- Under what circumstances of time and place are you writing?
- Under what circumstances will your writing probably be read? Will it be one among many texts or documents being received, or is your particular message eagerly awaited? In either case, how can you help your reader quickly see the purpose and thrust of your work under these circumstances?
- How has your response to the task been influenced by other events in your life, your country, or the world?
- Have you been asked to write a text of a specific length? If length has not been specified, what seems appropriate for your purpose and audience?
- What document design (chapter 8) is appropriate given the context for your writing?

32   Reading Rhetorically

Reading is more pleasurable and profitable when undertaken as a series of steps. Every time you pick up a newspaper, glance over the headlines, turn to the sports section, skim over the first page, and then go back to read the story that most intrigues you, you are reading rhetorically. For instance, you might find yourself rereading an article about Marion Jones (who agreed to return her five Olympic gold medals after admitting to taking steroids), to make sure that you understand the differences between what the sportswriter is reporting and what Marion Jones is actually admitting.

You are reading rhetorically every time you find yourself previewing a text, reading for content, responding, and rereading. When you follow these steps, you can more easily determine how difficult the text will be to understand, what you are likely to learn from it, and how useful it will be to you. In addition, you can use these steps to consider the features of the rhetorical situation (writer, audience, exigence, context, and meaning).

This chapter explains the process of reading rhetorically and describes ways you can monitor your personal and intellectual responses to a text. Whether **chronological** (in order of occurrence) or **recursive** (alternating between moving forward and looping back), reading rhetorically is a process of

- previewing (**32a**) and
- reading for content (**32b**).

This chapter will not only help you carry out this process but also

- help you distinguish between actual content and your personal response to that content (**32c**) and
- encourage you to write daily about your reading (**32d**).

32a Previewing for an initial impression

You often preview reading material—when you thumb through a newspaper or a magazine looking for articles that stir your interest. A systematic preview, though, gives you more reliable results and makes your reading more efficient. When reading rhetorically, you systematically preview a text by reading the author's name and the title, then skimming the entire text to get a sense of how the information is organized and what you can expect from reading the text.

You will also want to assess what the reading demands of you in terms of time, effort, and previous knowledge. By reading the summary (often located in the preface or introductory chapter) or the abstract (usually preceding a scholarly article), you can decide whether the text will be useful. If the text is difficult, you can preview the major points, often found in headings.

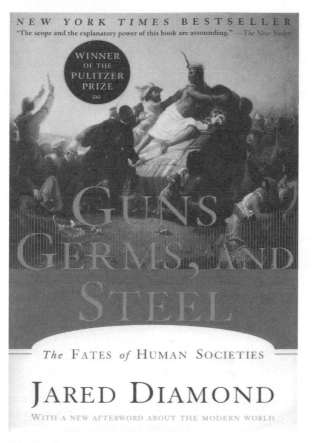

The title of Jared Diamond's book—*Guns, Germs, and Steel: The Fates of Human Societies*—accurately reflects the contents.

FEATURES OF A TEXT FOR PREVIEWING

Title

The title (and subtitle, if any) often reveals the focus of a text and sometimes its thesis (33c). When a title does not provide much information, look at the chapter titles or section headings to get a clearer sense of the work as a whole as well as to gauge how much you may already know about the subject.

Author

If you know anything about the author, you may have an idea about the expertise or tone being brought to the topic. Jared Diamond's science writing is highly respected and widely read, for he has earned a Pulitzer Prize (for *Guns, Germs, and Steel*), a MacArthur Foundation fellowship (otherwise known as a "genius award"), and a National Medal of Science.

Length

Considering a text's length allows you to estimate how much time you should set aside for reading. By checking length, you can also estimate whether a work is long enough to include useful content or so short that it might only skim the surface of the subject it addresses.

Directories

In addition to previewing title and author, you will also want to examine various directories within the text. The **table of contents**, for example, identifies the chapters and main sections within a book, and the **index,** at the back, lists in alphabetical order the specific topics covered. A **bibliography**, or list of research sources and related works, indicates how much research was involved in writing the book and can also direct you to additional sources. Checking these directories can help you determine whether the book has the kind of information you are seeking.

Visual Aids

The extent to which visual aids are useful varies, but a quick check for graphs and other illustrations can help you decide whether the work has the kind of information you need.

Summaries

Reading a summary can help you decide whether the work as a whole will be helpful and also help you follow a difficult text. Summaries can often be found in the preface of a book as well as in introductory and concluding chapters or on the inside cover or the back cover. Scholarly articles often begin with a summary identified as an abstract (37c).

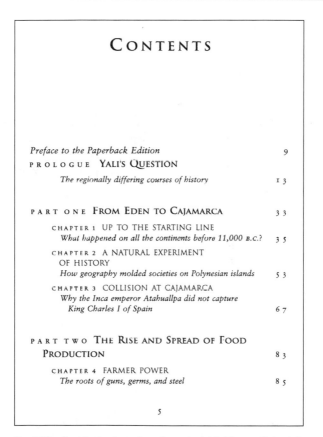

CONTENTS

The table of contents shows how the material in Diamond's book is arranged and indicates how fully that material is developed.

In addition to assessing the title, author, length, directories, visual aids, and summary of a text, assess how much you already know about the subject. If you are unfamiliar with the subject matter, you might want to start with a less demanding treatment of the topic, either in print or online. Finally, if you know that your values or opinions differ greatly from those of the author, you will want to pay close attention to passages in the text that you might be tempted to dismiss without reading carefully.

Previewing helps make your reading easier and helps you select appropriate research materials (chapter 37). But remember that previewing a text is not the same as reading it for understanding.

CHECKLIST for Previewing a Reading Selection

- What do you already know about this subject that you can use to connect with the text?
- What do the title and subtitle reveal about the way the subject is being treated?
- How long is this work, and how is it organized? What do the major divisions indicate to you?
- What information do the table of contents and the index provide about the book?
- Does the article include an abstract, or does the book include a summary?
- What do you know about this author that contributes to his or her credibility? If the author is unfamiliar, what biographical information could help you assess that credibility (35c and 38a)?
- If there are graphs, figures, or other visuals in the text, what do they illustrate?
- Is there a bibliography that indicates how extensive and current the research is?

- Is the text suited to your level of understanding, or should you start with a simpler (or more sophisticated) treatment of the same subject?

- Do you have strong feelings about this subject that could interfere with your ability to understand how it is treated in this text (32c)?

32b Reading for content

Effective readers pay close attention to the words on the page and develop specific strategies for increasing their comprehension as well as for working through misunderstandings. After previewing a text, you should be able to determine what the author wants to communicate, to whom, and for what specific purpose. In other words, you can begin to read for content.

As you read, you will want to note the author's major points, which are often indicated by particular words and key phrases: "There are *three* advantages to this proposal. . . . The *first* is . . . . The *second* is . . . ." The phrase *in other words* signals that the author is about to paraphrase a point—because it is important. And *in this article* (or *chapter*) introduces a statement of the author's focus or purpose, whereas *in summary*, *in conclusion*, and *the point I am making* place a significant emphasis on the information just presented. Thus, transitional words or phrases indicating sequencing (34d) or movement within a text help you grasp content. Transitional expressions—especially those indicating purpose, result, summary, repetition, exemplification, and intensification (see pages 438–439)—alert you to important points. Such phrases identify opportunities for you to talk back to the text itself, as though you were carrying on a conversation with the author.

When reading from a book or periodical (a magazine or professional journal) that you own, you can underline, highlight, or add comments to passages that interest or confuse you. Write in the margins and annotate key passages whenever you have something to say or a question to pose. If you have borrowed a book, use sticky notes to annotate the text. With an electronic text, print out a hard copy and annotate it or use your word-processing program to respond directly on the screen.

Reading for content means making sure you understand the words on the page. When you encounter a word that is new to you, the meaning may be defined in the text itself, or you may be able to infer the meaning from the way the word has been used. Whenever a new term appears in a critically important position such as a thesis statement (**33c**) or a conclusion (**34b(2)**), look it up in a dictionary (**19e**). But even language that is well chosen can sometimes be misleading because words have different specific meanings (**denotations**) as well as strong associations (**connotations**) that vary from reader to reader (**20a**) and culture to culture (chapter **19**)—depending on the rhetorical situation.

Your challenge as a reader is to try to understand what exactly the author wanted the words to mean within the particular rhetorical situation, to understand as much as you can but to keep that understanding flexible enough to accommodate what will come.

HEMISPHERES COLLIDING • 3 5 7

Eurasia's diverse and protein-rich cereals; hand planting of individual seeds, instead of broadcast sowing; tilling by hand instead of plowing by animals, which enables one person to cultivate a much larger area, and which also permits cultivation of some fertile but tough soils and sods that are difficult to till by hand (such as those of the North American Great Plains); lack of animal manuring to increase soil fertility; and just human muscle power, instead of animal power, for agricultural tasks such as threshing, grinding, and irrigation. These differences suggest that Eurasian agriculture as of 1492 may have yielded on the average more calories and protein per person-hour of labor than Native American agriculture did.

[margin note: amazing— all by hand]

[margin note: interesting]

SUCH DIFFERENCES IN food production constituted a major ultimate cause of the disparities between Eurasian and Native American societies. Among the resulting proximate factors behind the conquest, the most important included differences in germs, technology, political organization, and writing. Of these, the one linked most directly to the differences in food production was germs. The infectious diseases that regularly visited crowded Eurasian societies, and to which many Eurasians consequently developed immune or genetic resistance, included all of history's most lethal killers: smallpox, measles, influenza, plague, tuberculosis, typhus, cholera, malaria, and others. Against that grim list, the sole crowd infectious diseases that can be attributed with certainty to pre-Columbian Native American societies were nonsyphilitic treponemas. (As I explained in Chapter 11, it remains uncertain whether syphilis arose in Eurasia or in the Americas, and the claim that human tuberculosis was present in the Americas before Columbus is in my opinion unproven.)

[margin note: oh! I want to hear more]

This continental difference in harmful germs resulted paradoxically from the difference in useful livestock. Most of the microbes responsible for the infectious diseases of crowded human societies evolved from very similar ancestral microbes causing infectious diseases of the domestic animals with which food producers began coming into daily close contact around 10,000 years ago. Eurasia harbored many domestic animal species and hence developed many such microbes, while the Americas had very few of each. Other reasons why Native American societies evolved so few lethal microbes were that villages, which provide ideal breeding grounds for epidemic diseases, arose thousands of years later in the Americas than in Eurasia; and that the three regions of the New World supporting urban

[margin note: So contact w/livestock/animals was a major factor w/ disease]

When you annotate a printed text—that is, talk back to it—you read it actively and rhetorically.

32c Recognizing a personal response

Critical readers consciously work to keep their personal responses from interfering with their ability to understand. So, in addition to reading for content, they also keep track of what they think about or how they are reacting to this content. Reading rhetorically means reading actively, noting where you agree or disagree, become frustrated or intrigued, sympathetic or annoyed—and keeping track of what feature of the writing (or of yourself) triggered each response: was it the writer's tone (34a(3)), an example that evoked a personal memory, a lapse in the organization (33d), the topic itself (33b), or a visual element such as a photo or an illustration?

As you read, try to determine what the author thinks and why he or she holds that opinion. By noting personal responses and recognizing that they are independent of a work's content even if they are inspired by it, you can increase your understanding of the purposeful choices writers make when communicating with readers. Personal responses often serve as the basis for your own writing (32d). Often, good readers and writers use techniques from the following list.

TIPS FOR RECORDING PERSONAL RESPONSES

- Note passages that capture your attention by underlining or highlighting.
- Put a question mark in the margin when you do not understand or trust the accuracy of a passage.
- Put an exclamation point in the margin when a statement or an example surprises you.

- Write *yes* or *no* in the margin when you agree or disagree. When a passage reminds you of another passage (or something else you have read), note that association in the margin. Keep a reading journal (33a(1)). Include at least one question or reservation about something you read each day.

- Correspond by e-mail with other people who are reading the same material (chapter 36).

32d Writing daily about your reading

Effective readers write daily about their reading, often by keeping a personal journal, a writer's notebook, or a reading journal or by participating in an online discussion forum (see 36c). When you respond to a text by listening to it, arguing with it, extending it, and connecting it with your own experience, you are engaging with that text and will be more likely to understand and remember it. Writing regularly about your reading, then, helps you increase your comprehension and identify responses that could be the seeds from which larger pieces of writing subsequently grow. Writing daily about your reading will benefit both your comprehension and your creativity.

33 Planning and Drafting Essays

Experienced writers understand that writing is a process. Think of the writing you do out of school, and you will realize how experienced you already are at the process. Effective writers know they cannot do everything at once, so they generate, organize, develop, and clarify their ideas as well as polish their prose during a series of sometimes separate—but often overlapping—steps.

This chapter will help you understand writing as a process and

- find good topics (**33a**),
- focus your ideas (**33b**),
- write a clear thesis statement (**33c**),
- organize your ideas (**33d**),
- express your ideas in a first draft (**33e**), and
- use various strategies to develop effective paragraphs (**33f**) and essays (**33g**).

The writing process is **recursive,** which means that as you plan and draft an essay, you may need to return to a specific activity several times. For example, drafting may help you see that you need to go back and collect more ideas, modify your thesis, or even start over with a new one. Experienced writers expect the writing process to lead to new ideas as well as uncover passages in need of improvement. Despite the infinite variations of the writing process, writing usually involves four recursive stages (described in the following box).

STAGES OF THE WRITING PROCESS

- **Prewriting** is the initial stage of the writing process. As soon as you begin thinking about a specific writing task, consider what is expected of you in terms of your intended audience, context, and overall purpose. Then start exploring your topic by talking with others working on the same assignment, keeping a journal, free-writing, or questioning. In short, do whatever it takes to energize your thinking and jump-start your writing.

- **Drafting** involves writing down your ideas quickly, writing as much as you can, without worrying about being perfect or staying on topic. The more ideas you get down on paper, the more options you will have as you begin to clarify your thesis and purpose for writing, organizing, and revising. Progress is your goal at this stage, not perfection.

- **Revising** offers you the opportunity to focus your purpose for writing, establish a clear thesis statement (**33c**), and organize your ideas toward those ends (**33d**). This is the time to start stabilizing the overall structure of your essay as well as the structure of the individual paragraphs (**33f** and **34c**) and to reconsider your introduction and conclusion (**34b**). Remember that revising means producing another draft for further revision and editing.

- **Editing** focuses on surface features: punctuation, spelling, word choice, grammar, sentence structure, and all the rest of the details of Standardized English (**34f**). As you prepare your work for final submission, consider reading it aloud to discover which sentence structures and word choices could be improved.

33a Selecting worthwhile subjects for writing

Whether you are assigned a subject or are free to respond to an exigence of your own choosing, you must consider what you already know—or would like to learn about—and what is likely to interest your audience (**31d**). The first step toward engaging an audience is to be interested in the subject yourself, so consider your interests and experience. When subjects are important to you, they usually interest readers, especially when you write with a clear purpose and well-chosen details (**31c** and **33f(1)**).

More often, however, you will be asked to write essays about subjects outside your personal experience but within your academic coursework. In order to find material that interests you, look in your textbook, particularly in the sections listing suggestions for further reading. Go through your lecture notes, your reading journal, or any marginal annotations you have made in your textbook (**32c**). Ask yourself if there is something you feel strongly about and would like to explore further. Writing about a subject is one of the best ways to learn about it, so use a writing assignment not only to impart information to your audience but also to satisfy yourself.

(1) Keeping a journal is one way to explore a subject.

Keeping a journal is a good way to generate subjects for essays. In a **personal journal,** you reflect on your experiences, using writing as a means to explore how you feel about what is happening in your life or in the world around you. Writers who keep personal journals usually write for their own benefit, but in the process of writing a journal—or reading it—they may discover subjects and exigencies they can use for essays.

Other writers prefer to keep a reading journal (**32d**), where they record and explore material for future projects, list quotations and observations that invite development, draft the introduction to an essay, outline an idea for a story, or experiment with writing a poem. You may find it convenient to keep your journal in a word-processing file on your computer. Whichever type of journal you keep, write quickly, without worrying about spelling or grammar.

(2) Freewriting offers a risk-free way to explore a subject.
When **freewriting,** writers record whatever occurs to them, without stopping, for a limited period of time—often no more than ten minutes. Freewriting is another good way to generate ideas for a writing assignment because no matter what you write, it will contain ideas and information you did not realize you had.

In **directed freewriting,** you begin with a general subject and record whatever occurs to you about this subject during the time available. When Richard Petraglia's English instructor asked him to write for five minutes, assessing the reasons for studying a foreign language, Richard produced the following freewriting. (This freewriting represents the first step toward Richard's essay, two different versions of which appear in chapter 34.)

> Why am I taking German? When I'm happiest about my progress, I think I'm taking German so I can travel all around Germany and speak with the natives. Most Americans think that "everyone can speak English," but I know that's not true. At my lowest moments, I think I'm memorizing all this German vocabulary and verb conjugations because I'm fulfilling the foreign language requirement of my major. I read some statistics that show that students who pursue several years of foreign language study in high school tend to score higher on standardized tests. I did. And I did, probably because when I was learning Spanish, I learned so much vocabulary. I also learned a great deal about my native language, English. Maybe that's why I did so well. Or maybe the reason I did so well on those tests was that I've always been a motivated student!

Richard's freewriting generated a number of possibilities for developing an essay about why he is taking German: because it is a requirement, because he is a motivated student, because he wants to speak German and travel to Germany, because he is learning more about English. But perhaps his freewriting is taking him in a completely different direction. Instead of writing about *why* he is taking German, he may write about the positive consequences of taking German. Notice how his freewriting becomes more animated when he refers to his success as a student.

(3) Questioning pushes the boundaries of your subject.

You can also explore a subject by asking yourself some questions. **Journalists' questions**—*Who? What? When? Where? Why?* and *How?*—are easy to use. Using these questions could lead you to think about the reasons for taking a foreign language in a number of ways: *Who* typically has to take a foreign language while in college? *What* foreign language should a college student study? *When* should students fulfill their foreign language requirement? *Where* should students use their foreign language? *Why* is taking a foreign language an important part of the college experience? And *how* might students make the most of what they learn about a foreign language?

33b   Focusing a subject idea into a specific topic

Like photographers, writers need to focus their ideas, moving from a general subject to a more specific topic.

By exploring your subject, you can discover productive strategies for development as well as a specific focus for your topic. As you prewrite, you will decide that some ideas seem worth pursuing, but others seem inappropriate for your purpose, audience, or context. You will find yourself discarding ideas even as you develop new ones and determine your topic.

A simple analogy helps explain focus: When you take a picture of a landscape, you cannot photograph all that your eye can take in. You must focus on just part of it. You can think of your writing the same way—you focus and direct your ideas just as you focus and direct the lens of a camera, moving from a general subject to a more specific topic.

In addition, you can also focus by thinking in terms of how the various rhetorical methods you could use for developing your ideas (33g) might take you in different directions. Responding to the exigence of assessing the reasons for studying a foreign language, Richard needed to focus his subject into a narrow topic. Thus, he considered the subject in terms of the following rhetorical methods of development:

- *Narration.* What kind of story can I tell about learning German?
- *Description.* What kind of German class am I taking? What do we do? What is the teacher like? What are my classmates like?
- *Process analysis.* How have I gone about learning German, from memorizing vocabulary and verb conjugations to actually carrying on conversations?
- *Cause-and-consequence analysis.* What have been the causes of my success in my German class? Concentration? Commitment? My knowledge of Spanish? What are some of the consequences of my learning German? Conversational skill? Less time for other classes? Feeling successful?
- *Comparison and contrast.* How does learning German compare with learning English or Spanish? How does taking German differ from taking history or another course?
- *Classification and division.* How can I classify the types of language courses that college students take? How can I divide up the desirable consequences of those courses?

- *Definition.* How do I define good reasons for taking German? Are those reasons defined by immediate or long-term benefits?

The following sentence suggests a focus on comparison and contrast:

Studying German seems to be mostly memorization whereas studying English seems to be mostly reading and writing.

This sentence focuses on cause and consequence:

Now that I'm taking second-year German, I'll have a chance to talk and write more in German.

A combination of strategies soon led Richard toward a focus:

When I think of how much time I have spent memorizing German vocabulary and verb conjugations, I am really proud of myself. Back in high school I didn't take the time to memorize Spanish the way I should have (and the way other students were), so my Spanish isn't as good as it could be. But, then, neither is my English. Now that I've been concentrating on learning another language, all the grammar and parts of speech, I've found that my English is much better. I write better and with more confidence because I'm making conscious choices about how to use language. I have gained a much better understanding of English grammar while learning German grammar.

Whatever method you use to bring a topic into focus, your choice should be determined not only by your interests but also by your purpose, the needs of your audience, and the time and space available. The following checklist may help you assess your topic.

CHECKLIST for Assessing a Topic

- Are you interested in the topic?
- Is the topic appropriate for your audience?
- Can you interest the audience in your topic?
- What is your purpose in writing about this topic?
- Can you do justice to the topic in the time and space available to you? Or should you narrow it down or expand it?
- Do you know enough about the topic to write a paper of the required length? If not, how will you get additional information?
- Are you willing to learn more about the topic?

Exercise 1

Use the journalists' questions to generate more ideas about a subject that interests you. Then consider how you might focus that general subject into a specific topic appropriate for an essay.

33c   Conveying a clearly stated thesis

Once you have focused your subject into a topic, you have come a long way toward developing the main idea you want to convey. By this point, you have probably also established your purpose for writing (to explain, teach, analyze, argue, or compare). Your subject, purpose, supporting information, and focus all come together in a controlling idea, or **thesis,** which is appropriate for your audience and context (chapter **31**). Initially, your thesis may be tentative. By your final draft, you will have developed a clear thesis statement.

Most pieces of writing have a **thesis statement,** an explicit declaration (usually in one sentence) of the main idea. Your thesis statement, then, will convey a single idea, clearly focused and specifically stated. A thesis can be thought of as a central idea stated in the form of an assertion, or **claim (35d),** which indicates what you believe to be true, interesting, or valuable about your topic.

An explicitly formulated thesis statement helps keep your writing on target. It identifies the topic, the purpose, and, in some cases, the plan of development. Notice how the following thesis statements fulfill their purpose. The first is from a descriptive essay.

> If Lynne Truss were Catholic, I'd nominate her for sainthood.
> —FRANK McCOURT, Foreword, *Eats, Shoots & Leaves*

With this simple statement, McCourt establishes that the topic is Lynne Truss and indicates that he will describe why she should be a saint. He conveys enthusiasm and awe toward Truss's work.

The following thesis statement for a cause-and-consequence essay sets the stage for an analysis of what happened when refugees from Cuba were redefined by the U.S. Government as illegal aliens:

> At 10:30 p.m. on the night of August 18, 1994, Attorney General Janet Reno strode into the White House press room and in her practiced monotone announced new measures to halt the thousands of Cubans who were launching themselves into the Florida Straits aboard flimsy rafts every day that summer.
> —ROBERTO SURO, "Looking North"

The main idea in an argumentative essay usually carries a strong point of view, as in the following, which unmistakably argues for a specific course of action:

> Amnesty International opposes the death penalty in all cases without exception.
>
> —AMNESTY INTERNATIONAL, "The Death Penalty: Questions and Answers"

It is just as important to allow your thesis statement to remain tentative in the early stages of writing as it is to allow your essay to remain flexible through the drafting stage. Rather than starting with a preconceived thesis, let your final thesis statement grow out of your thinking and discovery process as you draft and revise. The following tips might help you develop a thesis statement.

TIPS FOR DEVELOPING A THESIS STATEMENT

- Decide which feature of the topic interests you most.
- Write down your point of view or assertion about that feature.
- Mark the passages in your freewriting, journal, or rough draft that support your position.
- Draft a thesis statement, and consider whether it is too broad or too narrow to be developed sufficiently.
- After your initial drafts, ask yourself whether the scope of your thesis should be adjusted to reflect the direction your essay has taken.
- If you are still unhappy with your thesis, start again with the first tip, and be even more specific.

A clear, precise thesis statement helps unify what you write; it directs your readers to the writing that follows. Therefore, as you write and revise, check your thesis statement frequently to see whether you have drifted away from it. It should inform your decisions about which details to keep, which to toss out, and what additional information will support your assertions. All of your supporting material should pertain to the thesis statement.

The thesis statement, usually stated in a declarative sentence, most often appears in the first paragraph of an essay, although you can put yours anywhere that suits your purpose (occasionally even in the conclusion). The advantage of putting the thesis statement in the first paragraph is that readers know from the beginning what you are writing about and where the essay is going. Especially appropriate in academic writing, this technique helps readers easily locate specific information. If the thesis statement begins the introductory paragraph, the rest of the sentences in the paragraph usually support or clarify it, as is the case in paragraph 1. (For ease of reference, each of the sample paragraphs in this chapter is numbered.)

1　[*Eats, Shoots & Leaves* is] a *book about punctuation.* Punctuation, if you don't mind! (I hesitated over that exclamation mark, and it's all her doing.) The book is so spirited, so scholarly, those English teachers will sweep all other topics aside to get to, you guessed it, punctuation. Parents and children will gather by the fire many an evening to read passages on the history of the semicolon and the terrible things being done to the apostrophe. Once the poor stepchild of grammar (is that comma OK here?), punctuation will emerge as the Cinderella of the English language.
　　　　　　　　—FRANK McCOURT, Foreword, *Eats, Shoots & Leaves*

If the thesis statement is the last sentence of the opening paragraph, the preceding sentences will build toward it, as in paragraph 2.

2　The story of zero is an ancient one. Its roots stretch back to the dawn of mathematics, in the time thousands of years before the first civilization, long before humans could read and write. But as natural as zero seems to us today, for ancient peoples zero was a foreign—and frightening—idea. An Eastern concept, born in the Fertile Crescent a few centuries before the birth of Christ, zero not only evoked images of a primal void, it also had dangerous mathematical properties. *Within zero there is the power to shatter the framework of logic.*

—CHARLES SEIFE, *Zero: The Biography of a Dangerous Idea*

Most of the writing done for college courses contains an obvious thesis statement. The following checklist may help you assess the thesis of your essay.

CHECKLIST for Assessing a Thesis

- Does your thesis make a clear comment about your topic?
- Is your thesis an accurate reflection of what you believe to be true about your topic?
- Does your thesis match your essay in terms of focus and coverage?
- What two assertions can you make to support your thesis?
- What specific examples, illustrations, or experiences support your assertions?
- How does your thesis relate to the interests of your audience? To your purpose? To the context of your essay?
- Where is your thesis located in your essay? Would your readers benefit from having it stated earlier or later?

33d Arranging or outlining ideas

Many writers need a working plan to direct their ideas and keep their writing on course. Some writers quickly compose informal lists. The ideas in these lists can overlap, be discarded, or lead to a tentative thesis statement, conclusions, and the beginning of an overall organizational plan. Other writers rely on outlines. Either method (list or outline) can be helpful when you are writing lengthy papers or writing under pressure. Whatever method you choose for arranging your ideas, remember that you can always alter your arrangement to accommodate any changes your writing undergoes during the process.

Even the simplest outline offers an essay a structure that can quickly become more elaborate and detailed. The main points form the major headings, and the supporting ideas form the subheadings. An outline of Richard's essay might look something like the following:

TENTATIVE THESIS STATEMENT: Studying a foreign language is the best way to learn about English.

I. Many Americans don't think they need to learn another language.

    A. English is the language of global communication.

    B. English speakers always have an advantage in intercultural communication.

II. English-only speakers miss out on benefits of learning another language.

    A. Learning another language is not just about being able to talk to people in different countries.

    B. Studying another language increases a student's knowledge of another culture and so promotes tolerance and understanding.

    C. Knowing the language enriches a student's stay in a foreign country.

III. Students who take a foreign language do better on standardized tests.

    A. Students can compare grammars to better remember the rules of their own language.

    B. Studying a foreign language opens up a student's mind to different ways of speaking and expressing ideas.

    C. Studying a foreign language helps students acquire better reading skills.

IV. Learning a language teaches students to learn in a combination of ways.

   A. Students practice learning intuitively.

   B. Students practice following complex rules.

   C. Learning a language teaches students to be better learners in general.

   D. Studying a language teaches students subtle ways to better express themselves.

V. Learning German grammar improves students' knowledge of English.

   A. Students who learn German grammar also learn English grammar.

   B. Students who study German begin to understand how English really works.

   C. Learning German helps students understand the subtle changes of meaning that can happen with changes in grammar.

   D. Students who study German feel more confident writing in English because they know the grammar better.

   E. Studying German allows a student to see English from a different perspective.

   F. Students learn about how language can be used in different ways to express ideas.

However streamlined or detailed an outline you create, you need enough headings to develop your topic fully within the boundaries stated in your thesis. The important thing to remember, though, is that your final essay does not have to follow your outline. As you write, you may find yourself moving ideas around, deleting some, or adding others. An outline is simply a tool to help you get started.

33e Getting your ideas into a first draft

When writing a first draft, get your ideas down quickly. If you are not sure how to begin, look over some of the journal writing, listing, or outlining you have already done and try to state a tentative thesis. Then write out some main points you would like to develop, along with some of the supporting information for that development. Keep your overall plan in mind as you draft, remembering that experienced writers expect a change in plan as they write and revise.

If you feel stuck, move to another part of your essay and draft paragraphs that might appear later or sections that are easier to write (such as sentences that develop another supporting idea, an introduction, or a conclusion). Do not worry about writing a provocative introduction or a sensible conclusion at this point. Later, when you are revising, you can experiment with ways of polishing those sections of an essay (34b).

Finally, remember that writing is a form of discovering, understanding, and thinking. So, whenever drafting leads you in a direction you did not intend, allow yourself to explore. You can consider whether to integrate or suppress this new material when you prepare to revise.

33f Drafting well-developed paragraphs

You compose a draft by developing the information that will constitute the paragraphs of your essay. If you are working from an informal list (33d), you will have a sense of where you want to take your ideas and will be free to pursue new ideas that occur as you draft. If you are working from an outline (33d), you can anticipate the number of paragraphs you will probably write and can enjoy the security of a clear direction. In both cases, however, you need to develop each paragraph fully.

Paragraphs have no set length. Typically, they range from 50 to 250 words, with paragraphs in books usually longer than those in newspapers and magazines. There are certainly times when a long paragraph makes for rich reading, as well as times when a long paragraph exhausts a single minor point, combines too many points, or becomes repetitive. On the other hand, short, one-sentence paragraphs can be effectively used for emphasis (chapter **29**) or to establish transition (**34d**). Short paragraphs can also, however, indicate inadequate development.

Experienced writers do not worry much about paragraph length; rather, they concentrate on getting words on the paper or on the screen, knowing that all paragraphs can be shortened, lengthened, merged, or otherwise improved later in the writing process. So think of revising and developing your paragraphs as a luxury, an opportunity to articulate exactly what you want to say without anyone interrupting you—or changing the subject.

(1) You can develop a paragraph with details.

A good paragraph developed with details brings your idea to life. Consider the following well-developed paragraph by Alice Walker:

3   I stood in front of the mirror and looked at myself and laughed. *My hair was one of those odd, amazing, unbelievable, stop-you-in-your-tracks creations—not unlike a zebra's stripes, an armadillo's ears, or the feet of the electric-bluefooted boobie—that the Universe makes for no reason other than to express its own limitless imagination.* I realized I had never been given the opportunity to appreciate hair for its true self. That it did, in fact, have one. I remembered years of enduring hairdressers—from my mother onward—doing

missionary work on my hair. They dominated, suppressed, controlled. Now, more or less free, it stood this way and that. I would call up my friends around the country to report on its antics. It never thought of lying down. Flatness, the missionary position, did not interest it. It grew. Being short, cropped off near the root, another missionary "solution," did not interest it either. It sought more and more space, more light, more of itself. It loved to be washed; but that was it.

—ALICE WALKER, "Oppressed Hair Puts a Ceiling on the Brain"

Notice how the series of details in paragraph 3 supports the main idea, or topic sentence (34c), which is italicized. Readers can easily see how one sentence leads into the next, creating a clear picture of the hair being described.

(2) You can develop a paragraph by providing examples.

Like details, examples contribute to paragraph development by making specific what otherwise might seem general and hard to grasp. **Details** describe a person, place, or thing; **examples** illustrate an idea with information that can come from different times and places. Both details and examples support your idea in terms of the rhetorical situation.

The author of paragraph 4 uses several closely related examples (as well as details) to support the main idea with which she begins.

4   *It began with coveting our neighbor's chickens.* Lily would volunteer to collect the eggs, and then she offered to move in with them. Not the neighbors, the chickens. She said if she could have some of her own, she would be the happiest girl on earth. What parent could resist this bait? Our lifestyle could accommodate a laying flock; my husband and I had kept poultry before, so we knew it was a project we could manage, and a responsibility Lily could handle largely by herself. I understood how much that meant to her when I heard her tell her grandmother, "They're going to be just *my* chickens, grandma. Not even one of them will

be my sister's." To be five years old and have some other life form
entirely under your control—not counting goldfish or parents—is
a majestic state of affairs.   —BARBARA KINGSOLVER, "Lily's Chickens"

Exercise 2

Examine some of your own writing—such as an essay you have
recently drafted, e-mail messages still on file, or entries in your
journal—and select one paragraph that holds potential interest.
Write out (by hand) the original paragraph. Then rewrite it,
developing it with additional details or examples.

33g Employing rhetorical methods of development

When drafting essays, you can develop a variety of paragraphs
using **rhetorical methods,** mental operations that help you
think through various types of rhetorical problems—having
to do with establishing boundaries (definition), making sense
of a person, place, or event (description and narration), organizing concepts (classification and division), understanding
or thinking critically about a process (process or cause-and-
consequence analysis), or needing to convince someone
(argumentation). The strategies used for generating ideas,
focusing your topic (33b), developing paragraphs and essays,
and arranging ideas are already second nature to you. Every
day, you use one or more of them to define a concept, narrate a significant incident, supply examples for an assertion,
classify or divide information into specific parts, compare two
or more things, analyze a process, or identify a cause or consequence. When drafting an essay, you may discover that you

need to define a term or explain a process before you can take your readers further into your topic. Writers have the option of tapping one, two, or several rhetorical methods to fulfill their overall purpose, which might be to explain, entertain, argue, or evaluate.

(1) Narrating a series of events tells readers what happened.

A **narrative** discusses a sequence of events, normally in **chronological order** (the order in which they occur), to develop a particular point or set a mood. This rhetorical method, which often includes a setting, characters, dialogue, and description, usually uses transition words or phrases such as *first, then, later, that evening, the following week,* and so forth to guide readers from one incident to the next. Whatever its length, a narrative must remain focused on the main idea. Drawn from an interview with Ben Harper conducted by Austin Scaggs, the narrative in paragraph 5 traces the development of Harper's music.

5   Growing up in the verdant Los Angeles suburb of Claremont, Harper was drawn to the blues and folk—"everything from Woody Guthrie to Son House to Ry Cooder." He also developed an early love for soul music: He remembers sitting on his dad's lap listening to Stevie Wonder's *Talking Book*. At age seven he scored his first acoustic guitar, from the Folk Music Center, a store in Claremont owned by his maternal grandparents, that to this day features a dizzying array of international instruments. In his teens Harper was sidetracked by the rebelliousness of hip-hop—his black friends sneered at his deep knowledge of traditional music, nicknaming him Mr. Ukulele man—but after high school, Harper rekindled his first musical love. "As much as I loved hip-hop, I knew that wasn't going to be my route," he says. "I was just too connected with the music I grew up with."   **—AUSTIN SCAGGS, "Ben Harper's European Vacation"**

(2) Describing how something looks, sounds, smells, or feels adds useful detail.

By describing a person, place, object, or sensation, you can make your material come alive. Often descriptions are predominantly visual, but even visual descriptions can include the details of what you hear, smell, taste, or touch; that is, descriptions appeal to the senses.

Description should suit your purpose and audience. In describing your car, for example, you would emphasize certain features to a potential buyer, others to a mechanic who was going to repair it, and still others to a friend whom you wished to impress. In paragraph 6, Judith Ortiz Cofer employs vivid descriptive details to convey her ideas about cultural influences on adolescent striving and embarrassment.

6   I came to remember Career Day in our high school, when teachers told us to come dressed as if for a job interview. It quickly became obvious that to the barrio girls, "dressing up" sometimes meant wearing ornate jewelry and clothing that would be more appropriate (by mainstream standards) for the company Christmas party than as daily office attire. That morning I had agonized in front of my closet, trying to figure out what a "career girl" would wear because, essentially, except for Marlo Thomas on TV, I had no models on which to base my decision. I knew how to dress for school: at the Catholic school I attended we all wore uniforms; I knew how to dress for Sunday mass, and I knew what dresses to wear for parties at my relatives' homes. Though I do not recall the precise details of my Career Day outfit, it must have been a composite of the above choices. But I remember a comment my friend (an Italian-American) made in later years that coalesced my impressions of that day. She said that at the business school she was attending the Puerto Rican girls always stood out for wearing "everything at once." She meant, of course, too much jewelry, too many accessories. On that day at school, we were simply made the negative models by the nuns who were themselves not credible fashion experts to any of us. But it was painfully obvious to me that to the others, in their tailored skirts and silk blouses, we

must have seemed "hopeless" and "vulgar." Though I now know that most adolescents feel out of step much of the time, I also know that for the Puerto Rican girls of my generation that sense was intensified. The way our teachers and classmates looked at us that day in school was just a taste of the culture clash that awaited us in the real world, where prospective employers and men on the street would often misinterpret our tight skirts and jingling bracelets as a come-on.

—JUDITH ORTIZ COFER, "The Myth of the Latin Woman:
I Just Met a Girl Named María"

(3) Explaining a process shows readers how something happens.

Process paragraphs, in explaining how something is done or made, often use both description and narration. You might describe the items used in a process and then narrate the steps of the process chronologically. By adding an explanation of a process to a draft, you could illustrate a concept that might otherwise be hard for your audience to grasp. In paragraph 7, Sam Swope explains the process by which an elementary school assistant principal tried (unsuccessfully) to intimidate students into "ratting on" a fellow student who stole report cards.

Explanations of a process, such as learning sign language, often combine description and narration.

7   Later that day, a frowning assistant principal appeared in the doorway, and the room went hush. Everyone knew why he was there. I'd known Mr. Ziegler only as a friendly, mild-mannered fellow with a comb-over, so I was shocked to see him play the heavy. His performance began calmly, reasonably, solemnly. He told the class that the administration was deeply disappointed, that this theft betrayed the

trust of family, teachers, school, and country. Then he told the children it was their duty to report anything they'd seen or heard. When no one responded, he added a touch of anger to his voice, told the kids no stone would go unturned, the truth would come out; he vowed he'd find the culprit—it was only a question of time! When this brought no one forward, he pumped up the volume. His face turned red, the veins on his neck bulged, and he wagged a finger in the air and shouted, "I'm not through with this investigation, not by a long shot! And if any of you know anything, you better come tell me, privately, in private, because they're going to be in a lot of trouble, *a lot of trouble!*"

—SAM SWOPE, "The Case of the Missing Report Cards"

(4) Analyzing cause or consequence establishes why something happens or predicts results.

Writers who analyze cause or consequence raise the question *Why?* and must answer it to the satisfaction of their audience, differentiating the **primary cause** (the most important one) from **contributory causes** (which add to but do not directly cause a situation) or the **primary consequence** (the most important one) from **secondary consequences** (which occur because of an event but are less important than the primary consequence). Writers who analyze cause or consequence usually link events along a time line,

Although companies market credit cards on many campuses, some students do not realize that a possible consequence of card use is debt.

just as you would if you were describing a traffic accident to a police officer. Always keep in mind, though, that just because one event occurs before—or after—another event does not necessarily make it a cause—or a consequence—of that event. In paragraph 8, undergraduate Robyn Sylves analyzes some causes of credit card debt among college students.

8   Experts point to several factors for excessive credit card debt among college students. High on the list is students' lack of financial literacy. The credit card representatives on campus, the preapproved applications that arrive in the mail several times a week, and the incessant phone offers for credit cards tempt students into opening accounts before they really can understand what they are getting themselves into. The people marketing these cards depend on the fact that many students don't know what an annual percentage rate is. Credit card companies count on applicants' failing to read the fine print, which tells them how after an "introductory" period, the interest rate on a given card can increase two to three times. The companies also don't want students to know that every year people send money (in the form of interest charges) to these companies that there is no need to send. That annual fee that credit card companies love to charge can be waived. I think that many people, students and nonstudents alike, might be surprised how often and easily it can disappear if people call the company to say they don't want to pay it.

—ROBYN SYLVES, "Credit Card Debt among College Students: Just What Does It Cost?"

Writers also catalogue consequences, as Jonathan Franzen does in paragraph 9, listing the effects of Alzheimer's disease on its victims.

9   For [award-winning science writer] David Shenk, one of the most illuminating aspects of Alzheimer's is its slowing down of death. Shenk likens the disease to a prism that refracts death into a spectrum of its otherwise tightly conjoined parts—death of autonomy, death of memory, death of self-consciousness, death of personality, death of body—and he subscribes to the

most common trope of Alzheimer's: that its particular sadness and horror stem from the sufferer's loss of his or her "self" long before the body dies.   —JONATHAN FRANZEN, "My Father's Brain"

(5) Comparing or contrasting helps readers see similarities or differences.

A **comparison** points out similarities, and a **contrast** points out differences—to reveal information. When drafting, consider whether a comparison might help your readers see a relationship they might otherwise miss or whether a contrast might help them establish useful distinctions. In paragraph 10, Trudier Harris uses descriptive details in a revealing comparison of singing and performing.

10   I think of Zora Neale Hurston, folklorist and anthropologist, who complained about singer-actor Paul Robeson turning the spirituals into concerts. To her, he had taken the spirit out of the songs by performing them instead of singing them; he had transformed feeling that emerges from the heart, which cannot be duplicated, into feeling that can be constructed through art, which means that it can be duplicated on demand. One is genuine; the other is genuinely constructed. Hurston preferred the sounds emitted by the folks who couldn't compete and sing in the gospel choir or any other choir, but whose sincerity and relationship with God were apparent in their singing. These included those little old ladies who usually occupy what we refer to as the "amen corners." They are better at lining-out hymns, using the "long meter" that folks untrained in music historically make when they sing their joyful noises in African American churches.

—TRUDIER HARRIS, "Make a Joyful Noise"

Two valuable kinds of comparisons are metaphors and analogies. A **metaphor** is a figure of speech that makes an indirect comparison of one thing to another, as in "He was a lion in uniform" (20a(4)). An **analogy,** on the other hand, makes a direct comparison of the similarities between two things, as in "His hair was as thick and tawny as a lion's mane." In paragraph 11,

Nelson Mandela uses a metaphor to compare leadership and gardening.

11   In some ways, I saw the garden as a metaphor for certain aspects of my life. A leader must also tend his garden; he, too, plants seed, and then watches, cultivates, and harvests the result. Like the gardener, a leader must take responsibility for what he cultivates; he must mind his work, try to repel enemies, preserve what can be preserved, and eliminate what cannot succeed.

—NELSON MANDELA, "Raising Tomatoes and Leading People"

(6) Classifying and dividing can give order to material.

To classify is to place things into groups based on shared characteristics. **Classification** is a way to understand or explain something by establishing how it fits within a category or group. For example, a book reviewer might classify a new novel as a mystery—leading readers to expect a plot based on suspense. **Division,** in contrast, separates an object or group into smaller parts and examines the relationships among them.

KINGDOM	Animalia
PHYLUM	Arthropoda
CLASS	Insecta
ORDER	Hymenoptera
FAMILY	Apidae
GENUS	*Apis*
SPECIES	*mellifera*

The scientific identification of the honeybee (*Apis mellifera*) requires a classification in the genus *Apis* and a division within that genus, the species *mellifera*.

A novel can also be discussed according to components such as plot, setting, and theme (chapter 42).

Classification and division represent two different perspectives: ideas can be put into groups (classification) or split into subclasses (division). As a strategy for organizing (or developing) an idea, classification and division often work together. In paragraph 12, for example, classification and division work together to clarify the differences between the two versions of the cowboy icon. Like most paragraphs, this one mixes rhetorical methods; the writer uses description, comparison and contrast, and classification to make her point.

12   First, and perhaps most fundamentally, the cowboy icon has two basic incarnations: the cowboy hero and the cowboy villain. Cowboy heroes often appear in roles such as sheriff, leader of a cattle drive, or what I'll call a "wandering hero," such as the Lone Ranger, who appears much like a frontier Superman wherever and whenever help is needed. Writers and producers most commonly place cowboy heroes in conflict either with "Indians" or with the cowboy villain. In contrast to the other classic bad guys of the Western genre, cowboy villains pose a special challenge because they are essentially the alter ego of the cowboy hero; the cowboy villain shares the hero's skill with a gun, his horse-riding maneuvers, and his knowledge of the land. What distinguishes the two, of course, is character: the cowboy hero is essentially good, while the cowboy villain is essentially evil.

—JODY M. ROY, "The Case of the Cowboy"

(7) Defining an important concept or term clarifies meaning.
By defining a concept or a term, you efficiently clarify your meaning and develop your ideas. Your readers will know exactly what you are and are not talking about. Definitions are usually constructed in a two-step process: the first step locates a term by placing it in a class; the second step differentiates this particular term from other terms in the same class. For instance, "A concerto [the term] is a symphonic piece [the

class] consisting of three movements performed by one or more solo instruments accompanied at times by an orchestra [the difference]." A symphony belongs to the same basic class as a concerto; it too is a symphonic piece. However, a symphony is differentiated from a concerto in two specific ways: a symphony consists of four movements, and its performance involves the entire orchestra.

Paragraph 13 defines volcanos by putting them into a class ("landforms") and by distinguishing them ("built of molten material") from other members of that class. The definition is then clarified by examples.

13   Volcanos are landforms built of molten material that has spewed out onto the earth's surface. Such molten rock is called lava. Volcanos may be no larger than small hills, or thousands of feet high. All have a characteristic cone shape. Some well-known mountains are actually volcanos. Examples are Mt. Fuji (Japan), Mt. Lassen (California), Mt. Hood (Oregon), Mt. Etna and Mt. Vesuvius (Italy), and Paricutín (Mexico). The Hawaiian Islands are all immense volcanos whose summits rise above the ocean, and these volcanos are still quite active.

—JOEL AREM, "Rocks and Minerals"

Use the rhetorical methods just described to make your essay as a whole more understandable to your audience. Make sure, however, that you are using these methods to support your thesis and fulfill your overall purpose. If a paragraph developed with one of the methods is contributing to the main idea of your essay, then it is contributing to your purpose. If the development of a paragraph does not support the thesis, then you need to revise or delete that paragraph (**34c** and **34f**).

Revising and Editing Essays

Revising, which literally means "seeing again," lies at the heart of all successful writing. When you see again, you see with a different set of eyes—those of the reader instead of the writer. **Revising** entails rethinking what you have already written in terms of your overall purpose: how successfully you have addressed your audience, how clearly you have stated your thesis, how effectively you have arranged your information, and how thoroughly you have developed your assertions. **Editing,** on the other hand, focuses on issues that are smaller in scale. When you are editing, you are polishing your writing: you choose words more precisely (chapter **20**), shape prose more distinctly (chapter **21**), and structure sentences more effectively (chapters **23–30**). While you are editing, you are also **proofreading,** focusing even more sharply to eliminate surface errors in grammar, punctuation, and mechanics. Revising and editing often overlap (just as drafting and revising do), but they are distinct activities that concentrate on large-scale and small-scale issues, respectively.

As you revise and edit your essays, this chapter will help you

- consider your work as a whole (**34a(1)** and **34a(2)**),
- evaluate your tone (**34a(3)**),
- compose an effective introduction and conclusion (**34b**),
- strengthen the unity and coherence of paragraphs (**34c**),
- improve transitions (**34d**),
- benefit from a reviewer's comments (**34e**),
- edit to improve style (**34f**),
- proofread to eliminate surface errors (**34g**), and
- submit a final draft (**34h**).

34a The essentials of revision

In truth, you are revising throughout the planning and drafting stages of the writing process, whether at the word, phrase, sentence, example, or paragraph level. A few writers prefer to start revising immediately after drafting, while their minds are still fully engaged by their topic. But most writers like to let a draft "cool off," so that when they return to it, they can assess it more objectively, with fresh eyes. Even an overnight cooling-off period will give you more objectivity as a reader and will reveal more options to you as a writer the following morning.

TECH SAVVY

Most newer word-processing programs enable you to track your revisions easily, a feature that is especially useful if your instructor requires you to submit all drafts or if a peer group is reviewing your drafts. On the toolbar, click on Tools in order to see the pulldown menu. Track Changes will be listed on that menu. If your word-processing program does not have this feature, you can save each new version of your work in a separate file and date each one. By opening two or more of those files on your computer screen, you can easily compare the different versions.

(1) Anything and everything on the page can be revised.

As you reread your essay as a whole, you will want to recall your purpose, restate your thesis, and reconsider your audience. Does your main point come through clearly in every paragraph, or do some paragraphs digress, repeat information, or contradict what has come before (33c)?

In addition to sharpening your main idea, you will also want to revise in terms of audience expectations. Revising demands that you gauge what you have written to the audience you are addressing (31d). How will your audience respond to your thesis statement? Which of your assertions will your audience immediately understand or accept? Which examples or details will interest your audience? Which of your language choices are aimed expressly at this audience? In other words, revising successfully requires that you examine your work both as a writer and as a reader.

(2) What is *not* on the page can be more important than what is on the page.

Writers are always aware of what they have put on the page—but they seldom spend enough time considering what they may have left out. What information might your audience be expecting? What information might strengthen your thesis? Your best ideas will not always surface in your first draft; you will sometimes come up with an important idea only after you have finished that draft and taken another look at it.

(3) Your tone helps you fulfill your purpose.

Tone reflects a writer's attitude toward a subject, so you will want to make sure that your tone is appropriate to your purpose, audience, and context (31a). Because you want to present yourself as confident, well informed, and fair minded, all of your words as well as your sentence structures should convey that tone. Your challenge is to make sure that your tone contributes to eliciting from your readers the desired response—to you as well as to the information you are presenting.

Consider the tone in paragraph 1, which describes the wonders and terrors of growing up a poor young girl in South Carolina. (For ease of reference, each of the sample paragraphs in this chapter is numbered.)

The expressive tone of Dorothea Lange's photograph of a poor mother and children added depth and richness to a photodocumentary of the Great Depression.

1   Where I was born—Greenville, South Carolina—smelled like nowhere else I've ever been. Cut wet grass, split green apples, baby shit and beer bottles, cheap makeup and motor oil. Everything was ripe, everything was rotting. Hound dogs butted my calves. People shouted in the distance; crickets boomed in my ears. That country was beautiful, I swear to you, the most beautiful place I've ever been. Beautiful and terrible. It is the country of my dreams and the country of my nightmares: a pure pink and blue sky, red dirt, white clay, and all that endless green—willows and dogwood and firs going on for miles.

—DOROTHY ALLISON, *Two or Three Things I Know for Sure*

Exercise 1

Establishing your own tone, create a paragraph about the place where you were born (or grew up). Identify specific words and phrases from paragraph 1 that helped you with your version. Be prepared to read your paragraph aloud and share your list of words and phrases with the rest of the class.

TECH SAVVY
The thesaurus and grammar checker in your word-processing program may give you advice that can affect the tone of your writing. When you click on Tools on the toolbar, the pulldown menu will reveal the spelling and grammar checkers and usually a dictionary and a thesaurus as well. These tools are easy to find and use; however, only you can make the choices that will enhance the tone that is appropriate to your rhetorical situation. For example, a thesaurus may suggest a synonym for a word that you have been intentionally repeating in order to establish a rhythm. A grammar checker may flag a short fragment that you have deliberately inserted among some long sentences in order to highlight a point. If you are using these features of your word-processing program as you revise, give careful consideration to the suggestions they make, weighing those suggestions in terms of your rhetorical situation.

34b Guiding readers with your introduction and conclusion

Your introduction and conclusion play a special role in helping readers understand your essay as a whole. In fact, readers look for these parts of an essay and read them carefully, expecting guidance and clarification from them.

(1) An effective introduction arouses your reader's interest and establishes your topic and tone.

Experienced writers know that the opening paragraph is important; it is their best chance to arouse the reader's interest with provocative information, establish the topic and the writer as worthy of consideration, and set the tone. Effective introductions make readers want to read on. In paragraph 2, Nancy

Mairs speaks directly to her readers—shocking them—in order to get their attention.

2   The other day I was thinking of writing an essay on being a cripple. I was thinking hard in one of the stalls of the women's room in my office building, as I was shoving my shirt into my jeans and tugging up my zipper. Preoccupied, I flushed, picked up my book bag, took my cane down from the hook, and unlatched the door. So many movements unbalanced me, and as I pulled the door open I fell over backward, landing fully clothed on the toilet seat with my legs splayed in front [of] me: the old beetle-on-its-back routine. Saturday afternoon, the building deserted, I was free to laugh aloud as I wriggled back to my feet, my voice bouncing off the yellowish tiles from all directions. Had anyone been there with me, I'd have been still and faint and hot with chagrin. I decided that it was high time to write the essay.   —NANCY MAIRS, "On Being a Cripple"

Mairs's unsettling introduction takes her readers off guard: they are in the bathroom with a cripple—and a witty one at that. Her especially strong introduction orients readers to the direction her essay will take: she will candidly reveal her daily humanity in order to remind her readers that "cripples" are people, too.

Introductions have no set length; they can be as brief as a couple of sentences or as long as two or more paragraphs. Although introductions always appear first, they are often drafted and revised much later in the writing process—for introductions, as well as the thesis statements they often contain (**33c**), evolve naturally as writers revise their material, sharpening its focus and developing it to fulfill the overall purpose. You may wish to try several different introductions as you revise, to determine which is most effective.

You can arouse the interest of your audience by writing introductions in a number of ways.

(a) Opening with an unusual fact or statistic

3   Americans aren't just reading fewer books, but are reading less and less of everything, in any medium. That's the doleful conclusion of "To Read or Not to Read," a report released last week by the National Endowment for the Arts.

      —JENNIFER HOWARD,
Americans Are Closing the Book on Reading, Study Finds"

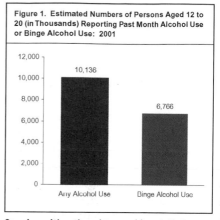

Figure 1. Estimated Numbers of Persons Aged 12 to 20 (in Thousands) Reporting Past Month Alcohol Use or Binge Alcohol Use: 2001

Opening with a thought-provoking statistic can be an effective introduction.

(b) Opening with an anecdote or example

4   When I used to ask my mother which we were, rich or poor, she refused to tell me. I was then nine years old and of course what I was dying to hear was that we were poor. I was reading a book called *Five Little Peppers* and my heart was set on baking a cake for my mother in a stove with a hole in it. Some version of rich, crusty old Mr. King—up till that time not living on our street—was sure to come down the hill in his wheelchair and rescue me if anything went wrong. But before I could start a cake at all I had to find out if we were rich or poor, and poor *enough*; and my mother wouldn't tell me, she said she was too busy. I couldn't wait too long; I had to go on reading and soon Polly Pepper got into more trouble, some that was a little harder on her and easier on me.

      —EUDORA WELTY, "A Sweet Devouring"

(c) Opening with a question your essay will answer

5   Fellow-Citizens—pardon me, and allow me to ask, why am I called upon to speak here today? What have I, or those I represent, to do with your national independence? Are the great

principles of political freedom and of natural justice, embodied in that Declaration of Independence, extended to us? and am I, therefore, called upon to bring our humble offering to the national altar, and to confess the benefits, and express devout gratitude for the blessings, resulting from your independence to us?

—FREDERICK DOUGLASS, "What to the Slave Is the Fourth of July?"

(d) Opening with an appropriate quotation

6   NO TRESPASSING, it says. "*This railroad, all sidings, yards, buildings, and lands connected therewith, are the private property of Consolidated Rail Corporation. . . .*" Conrail. The company that took over the failing offspring of the Pennsylvania Railroad. Someone has scrawled [an expletive] across it. And someone, in neat, blue script, has written along the margin: *Gotta be prudent.* My mother and I used to stand on the landing of the fire escape behind my parents' restaurant, holding tight onto the iron grille, looking at the furious vast expanse of shop yards below: the engines crisscrossing in slow force, the screech of metal on metal, the fire in the smoke. . . . Now I'm leaning into the fence and looking at suspension springs and running gear, rusted and covered with the delicate cream of Queen Anne's lace.

—MIKE ROSE, *The Mind at Work*

(e) Opening with general information or background about the topic

7   Scientists have long touted the benefits of the Mediterranean diet for heart health. But now researchers are finding more and more evidence that the diet can keep you healthy in other ways, too, including lowering the risk of certain cancers and easing the pain and stiffness of arthritis.

—MELISSA GOTTHARDT, "The Miracle Diet"

(f) Opening with a thesis, simply stated

8   My grandmother was American.

—ELENA PONIATOWSKA, "Yellow Magazine"

Whatever type of introduction you choose to write, use your opening paragraph to indicate your topic, engage your readers' attention, set your tone, and establish your credibility (35f(1)).

(2) An effective conclusion helps readers understand the most important points of your essay and why they are significant.

Just as a good introduction tantalizes readers, a good conclusion satisfies them. It helps readers recognize the important points of your essay and the significance of those points while, at the same time, wrapping up the essay in a meaningful, often thought-provoking way. As you draft and revise, you may want to keep a list of ideas for your conclusion, especially ones that go beyond a simple restatement of the thesis (33c). Some suggestions for writing effective conclusions follow, beginning with the technique of restating the thesis and main points.

(a) Rephrasing the thesis and summarizing the main points

9   The Endangered Species Act should not take into account economic considerations. Economics doesn't know how to value a species or a forest. Its logic drives people to exploit resources to the point of extinction. The Endangered Species Act tells us that extinction is morally unacceptable. It was enacted by a Congress and president in a wise mood, to express a higher value than a bottom line.

—**DONELLA MEADOWS**, "Not Seeing the Forest for the Dollar Bills"

(b) Calling attention to larger issues

10   Well, yes. But I'm imagining myself with five children under the age of 7, all alone after Dad goes off to work. And they're bouncing off the walls in that way little boys do, except for the baby, who needs to be fed. And fed. And fed again. And changed. The milk gets spilled. The phone rings. Mommy, can I have juice? Mommy, can I have lunch? Mommy, can I go out back? Mommy,

can I come in? And I add to all that depression, mental illness, whatever was happening in that house. I'm not making excuses for Andrea Yates [who systematically drowned her five young children]. I love my children more than life itself. But just because you love people doesn't mean that taking care of them day in and day out isn't often hard, and sometimes even horrible. If God made mothers because he couldn't be everywhere, maybe he could have met us halfway and eradicated vomiting, and colic too, and the hideous sugarcoating of what we are and what we do that leads to false cheer, easy lies and maybe sometimes much, much worse, almost unimaginable.   —ANNA QUINDLEN, "Playing God on No Sleep"

(c) Calling for a change in action or attitude

11   As anyone who takes care of herself knows, the body is always trying to find and maintain a balance. Run on a treadmill and your body will sweat to bring your core temperature back to normal. Eat a meal and your insulin levels rise to metabolize the glucose produced. But often the balance is delicate, and losing it can have a domino effect on all kinds of other bodily processes. Sleep is one of those delicate functions—so vital that the body will actively force it on you if you fight it too long. Our message to you? Be as vigilant about sleep as you are about your time in the gym. It's just as important to your health.

—JORDANA BROWN, "The Science of Sleep"

(d) Concluding with a vivid image

12   At just past 10 a.m., farm workers and scrap-yard laborers in Somerset County looked up to see a large commercial airliner dipping and lunging as it swooped low over the hill country of southern Pennsylvania, near the town of Shanksville. A man driving a coal truck on Route 30 said he saw the jet tilt violently from side to side, then suddenly plummet "straight down." It hit nose first on the grassy face of a reclaimed strip mine at approximately 10:05 Eastern Daylight Time and exploded into a fireball, shattering windowpanes a half-mile away. The seventy-two-year-

old man who was closest to the point of impact saw what looked to him like the yellow mushroom cloud of an atomic blast. Twenty-eight-year-old Eric Peterson was one of the first on the scene. He arrived to discover a flaming crater fifty feet deep. Shredded clothing hung from the trees, and smoldering airplane parts littered the ground. It did not look much like the site of a great American victory, but it was. —RANDALL SULLIVAN, "Flight 93"

Whatever technique you choose for your conclusion, provide readers with a sense of closure. Bear in mind that they may be wondering, "So what? Why have you told me all this?" Your conclusion gives you an opportunity to address that concern.

Exercise 2

Thumb through a magazine you enjoy, skimming the introductions of all the articles. Select two introductions that catch your attention. Copy them, word for word, and then consider the reasons *why* they interest you. What specific techniques for an introduction did the authors use? Next, look through the same or another magazine for two effective conclusions. Copy these, and analyze their effectiveness as well. Be prepared to share your findings with the rest of the class.

34c Revising for unified and coherent paragraphs

When revising the body of an essay, writers are likely to find opportunities for further development within each paragraph (33f and 33g) and to discover ways to make each paragraph more **unified** by relating every sentence within the paragraph to a single main idea (**34c(2)**), which might appear in a topic sentence. After weeding out unrelated sentences, writers concentrate on **coherence,** ordering the sentences so that ideas progress logically and smoothly from one sentence to the next. A successful paragraph is well developed, unified, and coherent.

(1) The topic sentence expresses the main idea.

Much like the thesis statement of an essay, a **topic sentence** states the main idea of a paragraph and comments on that main idea. Although the topic sentence is usually the first sentence in a paragraph, it can appear in any position within the paragraph. If you need to work at improving the unity and coherence of your paragraphs, you might want to keep your topic sentences at the beginning. Not only will they serve to remind you of your focus, but they will also be obvious to your readers, who will grasp your main ideas immediately.

When you announce your general topic and then provide specific support for it, you are writing **deductively.** Your topic sentence appears first, like the one in italics in paragraph 13, which announces that the author will offer evidence as to why we are suspicious of rapid cognition.

13   *I think we are innately suspicious of . . . rapid cognition.* We live in a world that assumes that the quality of a decision is directly related to the time and effort that went into making it. When doctors are faced with a difficult diagnosis, they order more tests, and when we are uncertain about what we hear, we ask for a second opinion. And what do we tell our children? Haste makes waste. Look before you leap. Stop and *think.* Don't judge a book by its cover. We believe that we are always better off gathering as much information as possible and spending as much time as possible in deliberation. We really only trust conscious decision making. But there are moments, particularly in times of stress, when haste does not make waste, when our snap judgments and

first impressions can offer a much better means of making sense of the world. —MALCOLM GLADWELL, *Blink*

As you prepare to revise a draft, try underlining the topic sentences you can identify. If you cannot find a topic sentence, add a sentence stating the main idea of that paragraph. If you find that you open every paragraph with a topic sentence, you might try experimenting with another pattern, revising a paragraph so that the topic sentence appears at the end, as in paragraph 14.

14   The first time I visited Texas, I wore a beige polyester-blend lab coat with reinforced slits for pocket access and mechanical-pencil storage. I was attending a local booksellers' convention, having just co-written a pseudo-scientific book . . . , and my publicist suggested that the doctor getup would attract attention. It did. Everyone thought I was the janitor. Lesson No. 1: When in Texas, do not dress down.   —PATRICIA MARX, "Dressin' Texan"

Placing the topic sentence toward or at the end of the paragraph works well when you are moving from specific supporting details to a generalization about those ideas—that is, when you are writing **inductively.** Effective writers try to meet the expectations of their readers, which often include the anticipation that the first sentence will be the topic sentence; however, writers and readers alike enjoy an occasional departure from the expected.

(2) In a unified paragraph, every sentence relates to the main idea.

Paragraphs are **unified** when every sentence relates to the main idea; unity is violated when something unrelated to the rest of the material appears. Consider the obvious violation in paragraph 15.

15   The Marion, Ohio of my childhood offered activities to suit any child's taste. In the summer, I could walk to the library and spend the afternoon browsing or reading, either in the children's

library in the dark cool basement or in the adult library, which was sunnier and warmer. On the way home, I could stop by Isaly's Dairy and buy a skyscraper ice cream cone for twenty-five cents. I could swim every afternoon in our neighborhood swimming pool, Fair Park pool, where kids played freely and safely, often without any parents around. If I wanted, I could make plans to meet up with my cousin Babs and walk downtown for a movie matinée or a grilled-cheese sandwich at Woolworth's lunch counter. *We used to be so close, but I haven't seen Babs since her mother's funeral five years ago.* If we didn't want to stay downtown, we could take a city bus out to the roller rink or, if something big was going on, out to the fairgrounds.

Easy to delete, the italicized sentence about not seeing Babs since her mother's funeral violates the unity of a paragraph devoted to childhood activities in a small town.

As you revise your paragraphs for unity, the following tips may help you.

TIPS FOR IMPROVING PARAGRAPH UNITY

Identify	Identify the topic sentence for each paragraph. Where is each located?
Relate	Read each sentence in a paragraph, and decide if and how it relates to the topic sentence.
Eliminate	Any sentence that violates the unity of a paragraph should be cut (or saved for use elsewhere).
Clarify	Any sentence that "almost" relates to the topic sentence should be revised until it does relate. You may need to clarify details or add information or a transitional word or phrase to make the relationship clear.
Rewrite	If more than one idea is being conveyed in a single paragraph, either split the paragraph in two or rewrite the topic sentence so that it includes both ideas and establishes a relationship between them.

(3) Clearly arranged ideas contribute to coherence.

Some paragraphs are unified (34c(2)) but not coherent. In a unified paragraph, every sentence relates to the main idea of the paragraph. In a **coherent** paragraph, the relationship among the ideas is clear and meaningful, and the progression from one sentence to the next is easy for readers to follow. Paragraph 16 has unity but lacks coherence.

Lacks coherence

16   The inside of the refrigerator was covered with black mold, and it smelled as if something had been rotting in there for years. I put new paper down on all the shelves, and my roommate took care of lining the drawers. The stove was as dirty as the refrigerator. *When we moved into our new apartment, we found that the kitchen was in horrible shape.* We had to scrub the walls with a brush and plenty of Lysol to get rid of the grease. The previous tenant had left behind lots of junk (from dented canisters and broken can openers to dirty dish towels and towel rack parts) that we had to get rid of. All the drawers and cabinets had to be washed.

Although every sentence in this paragraph concerns cleaning the kitchen after moving into an apartment, the sentences are not arranged coherently. This paragraph can easily be revised so that the italicized topic sentence controls the meaningful flow of ideas—from what the roommates saw to what they did.

Revised for coherence

17   *When we moved into our new apartment, we found that the kitchen was in horrible shape.* The previous tenant had left behind lots of junk that we had to get rid of, from dented canisters and broken can openers to dirty dish towels and towel rack parts. The inside of the refrigerator was covered with black mold, and it smelled as if something had been rotting in there for years. The stove was as dirty as the refrigerator. [New sentence:] So we set to work. All the drawers and cabinets had to be washed. I put new paper down on all the shelves, and my roommate took care

of lining the drawers. We had to scrub the walls with a brush and plenty of Lysol to get rid of the grease.

Paragraph 17 is coherent as well as unified.

To achieve coherence and unity in your paragraphs, study the following patterns of organization (chronological, spatial, emphatic, and logical), and consider which ones you might use.

(a) Using chronological order, according to time

When you use **chronological order,** you arrange ideas according to the order in which things happened. This organizational pattern is particularly useful in narrations.

18   When everyone was finished, we were given the signal to put our silverware on our plates. Each piece of silverware had its place—the knife at the top of the plate, sharp edge toward us; then the fork, perfectly lined up next to the knife; then the spoon—and any student who didn't put the silverware in the right place couldn't leave the table. Lastly, our napkins were refolded and put in their original spot. When we stood, we pushed our chair under the table and waited for the signal to turn right. Then we marched outside, single file, while the kitchen staff started to clean the dining room.   —ANNE E. BOLANDER AND ADAIR N. RENNING, *I Was #87*

(b) Using spatial order, according to the movement of the eyes

When you arrange ideas according to **spatial order,** you orient the reader's focus from right to left, near to far, top to bottom, and so on. This organizational pattern is particularly effective in descriptions, often allowing the writer to forgo a topic sentence, as in paragraph 19.

19   The stores on Tremont Avenue seemed to be extensions of my domestic space. Each one had sensory memories that I associate with my mother. On the corner was the delicatessen. From its counter, which was like a bar complete with a brass footrest, came the deeply dark smell of cured meats, the tang of

frankfurters, with the steaming background scent of hot knishes on the griddle. —LENNARD J. DAVIS, *My Sense of Silence*

(c) Using emphatic order, according to importance

When you use **emphatic order,** you arrange information in order of importance, usually from least to most important. Emphatic order is especially useful in expository and persuasive writing, both of which involve helping readers understand logical relationships. In paragraph 20, the writer emphasizes the future as the most important arena for change.

20   Among the first things Goldsmith had taught the executive was to look only to the future, because, whatever he had done to make people angry, he couldn't fix it now. "Don't ask for feedback about the past," he says. Goldsmith has turned against the notion of feedback lately. He has written an article on a more positive methodology, which he calls "feedforward." "How many of us have wasted much of our lives impressing our spouse, partner, or significant other with our near-photographic memory of their previous sins, which we document and share to help them improve?" he says. "Dysfunctional! Say, 'I can't change the past—all I can say is I'm sorry for what I did wrong.' Ask for suggestions for the future. Don't promise to do everything they suggest—leadership is not a popularity contest. But follow up on a regular basis, and you know what's going to happen? You will get better." —LARISSA MacFARQUHAR, "The Better Boss"

(d) Using logical order, moving from specific to general or from general to specific

Sometimes the movement within a paragraph follows a **logical order,** from specific to general (see paragraphs 14 and 21) or from general to specific (see paragraphs 17 and 22).

21   This winter, I took a vacation from our unfinished mess. Getting back to it was tough, and one morning, I found myself on my knees before the dishwasher, as if in prayer, though

actually busting a water-pipe weld. To my right were the unfinished cabinets, to my left the knobless backdoor, behind me a
hole I'd torn in the wall. There in the kitchen, a realization hit me
like a 2-by-4: for two years I'd been working on this house, and
there was still no end in sight. It had become my Vietnam.

—**ROBERT SULLIVAN, "Home Wrecked"**

22   It was not the only disappointment my mother felt in me. In
the years that followed, I failed her so many times, each time as-
serting my own will, my right to fall short of expectations. I didn't
get straight As. I didn't become class president. I didn't get into
Stanford. I dropped out of college.   —**AMY TAN, "Two Kinds"**

34d   Transitions within and between paragraphs

Even if the sentences are arranged in a seemingly clear sequence,
a single paragraph may lack internal coherence and a series of
paragraphs may lack overall coherence if transitions are abrupt
or nonexistent. When revising your writing, you can improve
the coherence by using pronouns, repetition, conjunctions,
and transitional words or phrases (3c(5)).

(1) Pronouns help establish links between sentences.

In paragraph 23, the writer enumerates the similarities of identical twins raised separately. She mentions their names only
once, but uses the pronouns *both, their,* and *they* to keep the
references to the twins always clear.

23   Jim Springer and Jim Lewis were adopted as infants into
working-class Ohio families. **Both** liked math and did not like
spelling in school. **Both** had law enforcement training and worked
part-time as deputy sheriffs. **Both** vacationed in Florida, **both**

drove Chevrolets. Much has been made of the fact that **their** lives are marked by a trail of similar names. **Both** married and divorced women named Linda and had second marriages with women named Betty. **They** named **their** sons James Allan and James Alan, respectively. **Both** like mechanical drawing and carpentry. **They** have almost identical drinking and smoking patterns. **Both** chew **their** fingernails down to the nubs.

—CONSTANCE HOLDEN, "Identical Twins Reared Apart"

(2) Repetition of words, phrases, structures, or ideas can link a sentence to those that precede it.

In paragraph 24, the repetition of the key word *never* links sentences to preceding sentences and also provides emphasis (**29d**).

24   *Never* is the most powerful word in the English language, or perhaps any language. It's magic. Every time I have made an emphatic pronouncement invoking the word *never,* whatever follows that I don't want to happen happens. *Never* has made a fool of me many times. The first time I remember noticing the powerful effect of this word I was a student at Indian school. My best friend, Belinda Gonzalez, and I were filling out our schedules for spring semester. She was Blackfeet, a voice major from Yakima, Washington. I was a painting major and checking out times for painting and drawing courses. She suggested I sign up for drama class with her. I said, no I will *never* go on stage. Despite my initial protest I did sign up for drama and dance troupes in the country, and now I make my living performing. *Never* is that powerful.   —JOY HARJO, "The Power of Never"

In this case, the author wished to stress the expectations many people hold when they declare "never." By repeating the word five times in one paragraph, Harjo emphasizes its power.

Parallelism, another kind of repetition, is a key principle in writing coherent sentences and paragraphs (chapter **26**).

(3) Using conjunctions and other transitional words or phrases also contributes to coherence.

Conjunctions and other transitional words or phrases demonstrate the logical relationship between ideas. In the following sentences, in which two clauses are linked by different conjunctions, notice the subtle changes in the relationship between the two ideas:

> The dog ran, **and** she threw the Frisbee.
>
> The dog ran **while** she threw the Frisbee.
>
> The dog ran **because** she threw the Frisbee.
>
> The dog ran, **so** she threw the Frisbee.
>
> The dog ran; **later** she threw the Frisbee.

The following list of frequently used transitional connections can help you with your critical reading as well as your writing.

TYPES OF TRANSITIONAL CONNECTIONS

Addition	and, and then, further, furthermore, also, too, again, in addition, besides
Alternative	or, nor, either, neither, on the other hand, conversely, otherwise
Comparison	similarly, likewise, in like manner
Concession	although this may be true, even so, still, nevertheless, at the same time, notwithstanding, nonetheless, in any event, that said
Contrast	but, yet, or, and yet, however, on the contrary, in contrast
Exemplification	for example, for instance, in the case of
Intensification	in fact, indeed, moreover, even more important, to be sure

Place	here, beyond, nearby, opposite to, adjacent to, on the opposite side
Purpose	to this end, for this purpose, with this objective, in order to, so that
Repetition	as I have said, in other words, that is, as has been noted, as previously stated
Result or cause	so, for, therefore, accordingly, consequently, thus, thereby, as a result, then, because, hence
Sequence	next, first, second, third, in the first place, in the second place, finally, last, then, afterward, later
Summary	to sum up, in brief, on the whole, in sum, in short
Time	meanwhile, soon, after a few days, in the meantime, now, in the past, while, during, since

The following checklist can guide you in revising your paragraphs.

CHECKLIST for Revising Paragraphs

- Does the paragraph have a clear (or clearly implied) topic sentence (34c(1))?
- Do all the ideas in the paragraph belong together (34c(2))? Do sentences link to previous and later ones? Are the sentences arranged in chronological, spatial, emphatic, or logical order (34c(3))?
- How does the paragraph link to the preceding and following ones (34d)?
- Are sentences connected to each other with effective transitions (34d(2))?
- What evidence do you have that the paragraph is adequately developed (33f)? What idea or detail might be missing (34a(2))? What rhetorical methods have been used to develop each of the paragraphs (33g)?

Some writers like to revise at the paragraph level before addressing larger concerns; other writers cannot work on the individual paragraphs until they have grappled with larger issues related to the rhetorical situation (overall purpose, attention to audience, and context; 31c–e) or have finalized their thesis (33c). Since there is no universal, predetermined order to the writing process, you can follow whichever steps work best for you each time you are revising. Be guided by the principles and strategies discussed in this chapter, but trust also in your own good sense.

34e   The benefits of peer review

Because writing is a form of communication, good writers check to see whether they are communicating their ideas effectively to their readers. Instructors are one set of readers, but they are often the last people to see your writing. Before you submit your work to an instructor, take advantage of other opportunities for getting responses to it. Consult with readers—at the writing center, in your dorm, in your classes, or from online writing groups—asking them for honest responses to your concerns.

(1) Clearly defined evaluation standards help both writers and reviewers.

Although you will always write within a rhetorical situation (31a), you will often address that situation in terms of an assigned task with specific evaluation standards. For example, if your instructor has told you that your essay will be evaluated primarily in terms of whether you have a clear thesis (33c) and adequate support for it (33f and 33g), then those features should be your primary focus. Your secondary concerns may be the overall effectiveness of your introduction (34b(1)) and sentence length and variety (chapter 30).

Evaluation guidelines do not guarantee useful feedback every time, but they help you focus on the advice you want to ask for, and they help your reviewers focus on what kinds of specific advice to give as they read your draft.

If a reviewer sees a problem that the writer did not identify, the reviewer should ask the writer if she or he wants to discuss it and should abide by the writer's decision. A reviewer's comments should point out what the writer has done well and suggest how to improve particular passages. Ultimately, however, the success of the essay is the responsibility of the writer, who will evaluate the reviewer's advice, rejecting any comments that would take the essay in a different direction and applying any suggestions that help fulfill the rhetorical purpose (31c).

If you are developing your own criteria for evaluation, the following checklist can help you get started. It can be easily adjusted so that it meets your specific needs for a particular assignment.

CHECKLIST for Evaluating a Draft
of an Essay

- Does the essay fulfill the assignment?
- Does the essay address a specific audience, one appropriate for the assignment (31d)?
- What is the tone of the essay (34a(3))? How does the tone align with the overall purpose, the intended audience, and the context for the writing (31c–e)?
- Is the topic sufficiently focused (33b)? What is the thesis statement (33c)?
- What assertions support the thesis statement? What specific evidence supports these assertions?
- Are paragraphs arranged in an effective sequence (33d and 34c(3))? What is the pattern of organization? Is each paragraph thoroughly developed (33f and 33g)?
- Is the introduction effective (34b(1))? How does it engage the reader's attention?
- Is the conclusion appropriate for the essay's purpose (34b(2))? How exactly does it draw the essay together?

(2) You can help your reviewers by telling them about your purpose and your concerns.

When submitting a draft for review, you can increase your chances of getting the kind of help you want by introducing your work and indicating what your concerns are. You can provide such an orientation orally or in writing. In either case, adopting the following model can help ensure that reviewers will give you useful responses.

SUBMITTING A DRAFT FOR REVIEW

Topic and Purpose

State your topic and your exigence for writing (31b). Indicate your thesis (33c) and purpose (31c). Providing this information gives reviewers useful direction.

Strengths

Mark the passages of the draft you are confident about. Doing so directs attention away from areas you do not want to discuss and saves time for all concerned.

Concerns

Put question marks by the passages you find troublesome, and ask for specific advice wherever possible. For example, if you are worried about your conclusion, say so. Or if you suspect that one of your paragraphs may not fit the overall purpose, direct attention to that particular paragraph. You are most likely to get the kind of help you want and need when you ask for it specifically.

Richard submitted the draft on pages 443–449 for peer review in a first-year writing course. He worked with a class-mate, who was working on the same assignment, and gave this reviewer a set of criteria that he had prepared. Because the reviewer was learning how to conduct peer evaluations, her comments are representative of responses you might receive in a similar situation. As members of writing groups gain experience and learn to employ the strategies outlined in this section, their advice usually becomes more helpful.

As you read the assignment and then Richard's draft, remember that it is only a first draft—not a model of perfect writing—and also that this is the first time the peer reviewer, Alyssa Gaebel, responded to it. Richard sent his draft to Alyssa electronically, and she used the Track Changes function of her word-processing program to add suggested changes and comments throughout the essay.

The assignment. Draft a three- to four-page, double-spaced essay in which you analyze the causes or consequences of a choice you have had to make in the last year or two. Moreover, consider the expectations of your audience and whether the topic you have chosen will help you communicate something meaningful to your readers. As you draft, establish an audience for your essay, a group that might benefit from or be interested in any recommendation that grows out of your analysis.

First Draft

Why Take a Foreign Language?

Richard Petraglia

> Alyssa Gaebel 10/15/08 9:11 AM
> **Comment:** What a great topic! We're all wondering why we have to take a foreign language.

It is commonly acknowledged that as native English speakers we have an advantage when it comes to intercultural communication. Our language is, after all, the language of business, diplomacy, and global communication in general. It is therefore tempting to think that knowing English is enough because we are

> Alyssa Gaebel 10/15/08 9:12 AM
> **Comment:** Yes, I agree—that's why we shouldn't have to take a foreign language. I like your opening.

likely to find English speakers wherever we go

and don't need to learn any other languages.

Ironically, this potential advantage of ours then

becomes a disadvantage, because it makes us

less motivated to study other languages. We end

up missing out on the other benefits—beyond

communicating with others—that come with

studying a language other than our own.

> Alyssa Gaebel 10/15/08 9:12 AM
>
> **Comment:** I think your tone in the last two sentences sounds too formal. Maybe it would help to get rid of the "we" and talk about English speakers in general?

The primary reason we often give for

studying a foreign language has to do with

communication. The straight-forward, common

sense answer you'll hear on the first day of

elementary German when the instructor asks

the students why they want to learn German

will inevitably be along the lines of "because I

want to be able to communicate with people in

their own language" or "because I want to learn

more about German culture." And these are, of

course, wonderful reasons for studying German

or French or Spanish. Becoming familiar with

other cultures is crucial to opening our minds

and increasing our tolerance and understanding.

Studying the language of a country you will visit

will undoubtedly enrich your stay, and in my

personal experience I've also found that we tend

to overestimate how many people speak English

> Alyssa Gaebel 10/15/08 9:13 AM
>
> **Comment:** This is an interesting point! However, it's not clear if this is your thesis.

> Alyssa Gaebel 10/15/08 9:15 AM
>
> **Comment:** Richard, you need a better transition between talking about communication and then culture. It might be worthwhile to consider putting these ideas into two separate paragraphs.

abroad. Learning a foreign language for these reasons makes good sense.

There is, however, another answer to that question, and one that I would argue is just as important, but that you'll probably never hear on that first day of German class. On that first day you won't hear a student saying that they want to learn German in order to learn more about English. And that, for me, has been the most rewarding part of studying foreign languages continuously since middle school. I think that we need to look beyond the idea that all we will learn is how to speak someone else's language. Learning another language has the fortunate side-effect of teaching us more about our own.

> Alyssa Gaebel 10/15/08 9:34 AM
> **Comment:** If this last sentence is your thesis statement (and I think it is), it needs to appear earlier in your essay.

There are statistics that show that students who pursue several years of foreign languages in high school tend to score higher on standardized tests. I am mostly interested in the reason for this, what produces these results. You could say that in general, more highly motivated students will be the ones who pursue an elective like Spanish or French all four years; that language study is just a characteristic of the more motivated students who will score higher on standardized tests any way. But it really has

> Alyssa Gaebel 10/15/08 9:34 AM
> **Comment:** This change in topic from learning more about English to doing better on standardized tests sounds abrupt. Will you consider composing a sentence here that explains how learning more about English (and other languages) leads to better scores on standardized tests?

> Alyssa Gaebel 10/15/08 9:34 AM
> **Comment:** These two sentences seem repetitive. Maybe combine them?

to do with the way studying a foreign language builds awareness of our own language. Studying a foreign language can improve reading comprehension because it gets students to think about how ideas are expressed, and therefore more easily get a better grasp of the idea a writer is trying to convey.

Learning languages also teaches us to learn in a combination of ways. First, learning a different language can be done intuitively, using the knowledge of your own language as a base and making educated guesses about the way the foreign language will work to express ideas. In conjunction with this method, foreign language learning develops the student's ability to follow complex rules. Expressing yourself in a different language is done differently than in English. Instead of being able to simply remember how ideas are expressed because you've been hearing it since you were a child, expressing yourself in the foreign language requires following complex rules of grammar that must be learned. Because learning a foreign language teaches us to learn in a combination of ways, it makes us better learners in general. A student can carry this knowledge of being able to apply complex rules as well as learn intuitively to any other discipline.

Learning German grammar improves writing in English because it improves knowledge of grammar. Confidence in grammar is the key to clear writing because knowing the structure of a language allows the student to express his or her ideas more clearly and precisely. There is an on-going debate about just how useful teaching grammar in our schools is in improving student writing. This is unclear. Because we intuitively know how to conjugate our verbs and generally make ourselves understood, it can seem pointless and frustrating to students to be taught the minute details of the language we already speak. The effects aren't immediately apparent or rewarding. But when learning about a foreign language, each time you learn to say something new, there is a sense of having produced a tangible result. As we learn how to express ourselves in a foreign language, we are also indirectly learning those things about our own language's structure.

> Alyssa Gaebel 10/15/08 9:36 AM
> **Comment:** Do you mean teaching English grammar to English speakers? It's not clear what exactly you mean here.

Moving beyond grammar, the way foreign languages express elements of time and patterns of description open up new ways of expressing ideas through language.

> Alyssa Gaebel 10/15/08 9:38 AM
> **Comment:** I think you'll want to reorganize this paragraph so that it has a clear topic sentence in the beginning. Otherwise, a reader won't know where this paragraph is going and what point you want to make.

Studying a foreign language also gives the student a basis for comparison because languages express the same ideas in different ways. This leads to a more creative use of our own language because the student is aware of the different ways the structures of language can be used to express ideas. |

Alyssa Gaebel 10/15/08 9:39 AM

Comment: You're making some really good points. You will want those points to be clearer so that you can show how they relate to the rest of your essay. This paragraph needs to have those connections made clearer.

Overall, studying a foreign language has many benefits, but among the most rewarding is learning more about English and becoming a better writer. Learning a foreign language allows us to see English from a different perspective and enables us to understand the grammatical structures of language we take for granted. Gaining a better understanding of our own language through studying the language of another country helps us to understand the subtle changes of meaning that happen with changes of grammar, which allows for a more varied, precise, and effective use of our own language in both speaking and in writing.

Richard,

You make some really great points! However, I think you need to organize your essay, and especially your conclusion, to better reflect your thesis.

It seems like you're arguing that learning a foreign language makes you a better student, but the conclusion only talks about how it makes you a better writer. The point about becoming a better writer sounds like it belongs after the third paragraph, which ends with the sentence "Learning another language has the fortunate side effect of teaching us more about our own." I say that because your essay's argument focuses on more than just making the student a better writer. It makes more sense to have the paragraphs about doing better on standardized tests and learning in a combination of ways closer to the end of your essay.

Also, make sure your thesis clearly states your position in the argument. If your thesis is "We end up missing out on the other benefits— beyond communicating with others—that come with studying a language other than our own," your essay might have more focus if you can name some of those benefits in your thesis.

Great first draft! Thanks for letting me read it and respond.

Alyssa

Before revising, Richard considered the comments he received from Alyssa. Since he had asked her to respond to his introduction, conclusion, and organization, he had to weigh all of her comments—relevant and irrelevant—and use the ones that seemed to be most useful as he prepared his next draft.

After Richard had time to reconsider his first draft and to think about Alyssa's response, he made a number of large-scale changes, especially with regard to focus. He also strengthened his thesis statement. In addition, he dealt with the issues of organization that Alyssa had pointed out by rearranging some information. After several more revisions, more peer review, and some careful editing and proofreading, Richard was ready to submit his essay to his instructor. His final draft is on pages 453–457.

34f Editing for clearer ideas, sentences, and paragraphs

If you are satisfied with the revised structure of your essay and the content of your paragraphs, you can begin editing individual sentences for clarity, effectiveness, and variety (chapters 22–30). The following checklist for editing contains cross-references to chapters or sections where you can find more specific information.

CHECKLIST for Editing

1 Sentences

- What is the unifying idea of each sentence (23)?
- Are the sentences varied in length? How many words are in your longest sentence? Your shortest sentence?
- How many of your sentences use subordination? Coordination? If you overuse any one sentence structure, revise for variation (30).

- Which sentences have or should have parallel structure (26)?
- Do any sentences contain misplaced or dangling modifiers (25)?
- Does each verb agree with its subject (6a)? Does every pronoun agree with its antecedent (6b)?

2 Diction

- Have you repeated any words? Is your repetition intentional?
- Are your word choices exact, or are some words vague or too general (20)?
- Is the vocabulary you have chosen appropriate for your audience, purpose, and context (19, 31c, 31d, and 31e)?
- Have you defined any technical or unfamiliar words for your audience (19c(4))?

34g Proofreading for an error-free essay

Once you have revised and edited your essay, it is your responsibility to format it properly (chapter 8) and proofread it. Proofreading means making a special search to ensure that the final product you submit is free from error, or nearly so. An error-free essay allows your reader to read for meaning, without encountering incorrect spelling or punctuation that can interfere with meaning. As you proofread, you may discover problems that call for further revision or editing, but proofreading is usually the last step in the writing process.

The proofreading checklist that follows refers to chapters and sections in this handbook where you will find detailed information to help you. Also, keep your dictionary (19e) at hand to look up any words whose meaning or spelling you aren't sure of.

CHECKLIST for Proofreading

1 Spelling (18)

- Have you double-checked the words you frequently misspell and any the spell checker may have missed (for example, misspellings that still form words, such as *form* for *from*)?

- If you used a spell checker, did it overlook homophones (such as *there/their, who's/whose,* and *it's/its*) (18c)?

- Have you double-checked the spelling of all foreign words and all proper names?

2 Punctuation (12–17) and Capitalization (9)

- Does each sentence have appropriate closing punctuation, and have you used only one space after each end punctuation mark (17)?

- Is all punctuation within sentences—commas (12–13), semicolons (14), apostrophes (15), hyphens (18f), and dashes (17e)—used appropriately and placed correctly?

- Are direct quotations carefully and correctly punctuated (16a)? Where have you placed end punctuation with a quotation (16d)? Are quotations capitalized properly (16a and 9c(1))?

- Are all proper names, people's titles, and titles of published works correctly capitalized (9a and 9b)?

- Are titles of works identified with quotation marks (16b), underlining (40b), or italics (10a)?

34h The final draft

Richard continued to edit and polish his essay. In the process, each draft was improved. The essay that Richard ultimately submitted to his teacher follows.

Richard Petraglia

Professor Glenn

English 15

20 October 2008

Why Take a Foreign Language?

Native English speakers have an advantage when it comes to intercultural communication: English is the language of business, diplomacy, and global communication in general. It is therefore tempting to think that as English speakers we don't need to learn a foreign language because we are likely to find someone who speaks English in any foreign country we visit. This potential advantage of already knowing the language of intercultural communication, however, can prove to be a disadvantage because it makes English speakers less motivated to study other languages. There are many benefits of studying a foreign language that have nothing to do with being able to communicate with people in foreign countries. Students who study a foreign language in school often have better writing skills, reading comprehension, and scores on standardized tests.

Still, the primary reason people often give for wanting to study a foreign language has to do with communicating with people in foreign countries. The straightforward, commonsense answer you'll hear on the first day of elementary German when the instructor asks the students why they want to learn German will inevitably be along the lines of "because I want to be able to communicate with people in their own language" or "because I want to learn more about German culture." And these are, of course, wonderful reasons for studying German (or French or Spanish). Communicating with people in their own language and becoming familiar with other cultures is crucial to opening our minds and increasing our tolerance and understanding, and studying the language of a country you visit will undoubtedly enrich your stay. I have also found that English speakers tend to overestimate how many people actually speak English abroad.

There is, however, another reason for studying a foreign language that I would argue is just as important, but that you'll probably never hear about on the first day of German class. And that is that learning German helps us learn more about English. For me, learning about English has been the most rewarding part of studying foreign languages continuously since middle school. I think that we need to look beyond the idea that all we will learn in a foreign language class is how to speak someone else's language and realize that learning another language has the fortunate side effect of teaching us more about our own.

For example, there is an ongoing debate about just how useful teaching grammar in our schools is in improving student writing. Because students intuitively know how to conjugate English verbs and generally make themselves understood, it can seem pointless and frustrating for them to be taught the minutiae of the language they already speak. The effects aren't immediately apparent or rewarding. But when learning about a foreign language, each time a student learns to say something new, there is a sense of having produced a tangible result. As students learn how to express themselves in a foreign language, they are also indirectly learning those things about their own language's structure. Therefore, learning German grammar improves writing as a side effect because it improves the student's knowledge of similar grammatical structures in English.

While studying a foreign language has many benefits, among the most fundamental is learning more about English and becoming a better writer. Learning a foreign language allows students to see English from a different perspective and enables them to understand the grammatical structures of their language that they often take for granted. Gaining a better understanding of their own language through studying the language of another country helps them to understand the subtle changes of meaning that happen with changes of grammar. This understanding of the subtleties of grammar allows the student to have a more varied, precise, and effective use of his or her own language in both speaking and writing.

There are also statistics that show that students who pursue several years of foreign languages in high school tend to score higher on standardized tests. I think it will be interesting to examine what produces these results. You could say that in general, more highly motivated students will be the ones who pursue an elective like Spanish or French all four years and that language study is just a characteristic of the more motivated students who will score higher on standardized tests anyway. But it really has to do with the way studying a foreign language builds awareness of our own language. Studying a foreign language improves reading comprehension because it gets students to think about how ideas are expressed through language and allows students to understand the complex use of language in any text more precisely. Once a student has more awareness of how ideas are expressed through language, he or she can more easily grasp the idea a writer is trying to convey.

Studying a foreign language also makes students better learners because it teaches them to learn in a combination of ways. First, students practice learning intuitively, using the knowledge of their native language to make educated guesses about the way the foreign language will work. In conjunction with this intuitive method, foreign language learning develops the students' ability to follow complex rules. A different language often expresses ideas in a different way than in English, using unfamiliar grammatical rules and structures. The students are therefore forced to rely on their knowledge of complex grammatical rules to express ideas in a foreign language. Because learning a foreign language teaches students to learn in a combination of both the intuitive and rule-based methods, it makes them better learners in general. A student can carry this knowledge of being able to apply complex rules as well as the ability to learn intuitively to any other discipline.

35 Writing Arguments

You write arguments on a regular basis. When you send your business partner a memo to tell her that a client needs to sign a contract, when you e-mail your parents to ask them for a loan, when you petition your academic advisor for a late drop, or when you demand that a mail-order company refund your money, you are writing an argument. You are expressing a point of view and then using logical reasoning to invite a specific audience to accept that point of view or adopt a course of action. *Argument* and *persuasion* are often used interchangeably, but they differ in two basic ways. Traditionally, **persuasion** has referred to winning or conquering with the use of emotional reasoning, whereas **argument** has been reserved for the use of logical reasoning to convince listeners or readers. But because writing often involves some measure of "winning" (even if it is only gaining the ear of a particular audience) and uses both emotion and reason, this book uses *argument* to cover the meanings of both terms.

Argumentative writing is distinct from other kinds of writing in its emphasis on the inseparability of audience and purpose. Recognizing and respecting the beliefs, values, and expertise of a specific audience is the only way to achieve the rhetorical purpose of an argument, which goes beyond victory over an opponent. Argument can be an important way to invite exchange, understanding, cooperation, consideration, joint decision making, agreement, or negotiation of differences. Thus, argument serves three basic and sometimes overlapping purposes: to analyze a complicated issue or question an established belief, to express or defend a point of view, and to invite or convince an audience to change a position or adopt a course of action. This chapter will help you

- determine the purpose of an argument (**35a**),
- consider different viewpoints (**35b**),
- distinguish fact from opinion (**35c**),
- take a position or make a claim (**35d**),
- provide evidence to support a claim (**35e**),
- use the rhetorical appeals to ground an argument (**35f**),
- arrange ideas (**35g**),
- use logical reasoning (**35h**),
- avoid rhetorical fallacies (**35i**), and
- analyze an argument (**35j**).

As you proceed, you will understand the importance of determining your purpose, identifying your audience, marshaling your arguments, arguing ethically, and treating your audience with respect.

35a Determining the purpose of your argument

What is your topic? What is at stake? What is likely to happen as a result of making this argument? Who is in a position to act or react in response to your argument?

When writing an argument, you need to establish the relationships among your topic, purpose, and audience. The relationship between audience and purpose is particularly significant because the audience often shapes the purpose.

- If there is little likelihood that you can convince members of your audience to change a strongly held opinion, you might achieve a great deal by inviting them to understand your position.
- If the members of your audience are not firmly committed to a position, you might be able to convince them to agree with the opinion you are expressing or defending.
- If the members of your audience agree with you in principle, you might invite them to undertake a specific action—such as voting for the candidate you are supporting.

No matter how you imagine those in your audience responding to your argument, you must establish **common ground** with them, stating a goal toward which you both want to work or identifying a belief, assumption, or value that you both share. In other words, common ground is a necessary starting point, regardless of your ultimate purpose.

35b Considering differing viewpoints

If everyone agreed on everything, there would be no need for argument, for taking a position or questioning a position held by someone else. But people do not always agree. For that reason, a good deal of the writing you will do in school or at work will require you to take an arguable position on a topic.

Behind any effective argument is a question that can generate more than one reasonable answer. If you ask "Is there racism in the United States?" almost anyone will agree that there is. But if you ask "Why is there still racism in the United States?" or "What can Americans do to eliminate racism?" you will hear different answers. Answers differ because people approach questions with various backgrounds, experiences, and assumptions. As a consequence, are often tempted to use reasoning that supports what they already believe. As a writer, you will be tempted to employ such reasoning, and doing so is a good place to start. But as you expand and shape your argument, you will want to demonstrate not only that you are knowledgeable about your topic but also that you are aware of and have given fair consideration to other views about it.

When you write an argument, you are trying to solve a problem or answer a question—with or for an audience. When you choose a topic for argumentation, you will want to take a stance that allows you to question, that provides you an exigence (or reason) for writing. First, you focus on a topic, on the part of some general subject that you will address in your essay (33b), and then you pose a question about it. As you craft your question, consider the following: (1) your own values and beliefs with respect to the question, (2) how your assumptions might differ from those of your intended audience, and (3) how you might establish common ground with members of your audience, while at the same time respecting any differences between your opinion and theirs. The question you raise will evolve into your **thesis,** an arguable statement.

The most important criterion for choosing an arguable statement for an essay is knowledge of the topic, so that you will be an informed writer, responsive to the expectations of your audience. When you are in a position to choose your own topic, you can draw on your knowledge of current events, politics, sports, fashion, or a specific academic subject.

To determine whether a topic might be suitable, make a statement about the topic ("I believe strongly that . . . " or "My view is that . . . ") and then check to see if that statement can be argued.

TIPS FOR ASSESSING AN ARGUABLE STATEMENT ABOUT A TOPIC

- What reasons can you think of to support your belief about the topic? List those reasons.

- Who or what groups might disagree with your statement? Why? List those groups.

(Continued on page 462)

(Continued from page 461)

- Do you know enough about this topic to discuss other points of view? Can you find out what you need to know?
- What are other viewpoints on the topic and reasons supporting those viewpoints? List them.
- What is your purpose in writing about this topic?
- What do you want your audience to do in response to your argument? In other words, what do you expect from your audience? Write out your expectation.

As you move further into the writing process, researching and exploring your topic in the library or on the Web (chapter 37), you may be able to clarify your purpose and improve your thesis statement.

35c   Distinguishing between fact and opinion

When you develop your thesis statement into an argument, you use both facts and opinions. It is important to distinguish between these two kinds of information so that you can use both to your advantage, especially in terms of establishing your credibility (35f(1)), an essential feature of successful argumentation. **Facts** are reliable pieces of information that can be verified through independent sources or procedures. **Opinions,** on the other hand, are assertions or inferences that may or may not be based on facts. Opinions that are widely accepted, however, may seem to be factual when they are not.

Facts are significant only when they are used responsibly to support a claim; otherwise, a thoughtful and well-informed opinion might have more impact. To determine whether a statement you have read is fact or opinion, ask yourself questions like these: Can it be proved? Can it be challenged? How often is the same result achieved? If a statement can consistently be proved true, then it is a fact. If it can be disputed, then it is an opinion.

The line between fact and opinion is not always clear. Therefore, writers and readers of arguments should always be prepared to interpret and assess the reliability of the information before them, evaluating the beliefs supporting the argument's stance, the kinds of sources used, and the objections that could be made to the argument.

Exercise 1

Determine which of the following statements are fact and which are opinion. In each case, what kind of verification would you require in order to accept the statement as reliable?

1. Toni Morrison won the Nobel Prize in literature in 1993.
2. Women often earn less money than men who hold the same positions.
3. *Monsters, Inc.* is the most financially successful of all the Disney movies.
4. Writing well is a gift, like musical genius.
5. A college degree guarantees a good job.
6. The United States won World War II.

35d Taking a position or making a claim

When making an argument, a writer takes a position on a particular topic. Whether the argument analyzes, questions, expresses, defends, invites, or convinces, the writer needs to make clear his or her position. That position, which is called the **claim,** or **proposition,** clearly states what the writer wants the audience to do with the information being provided. The claim is the thesis of the argument and usually appears in the introduction and sometimes again in the conclusion.

(1) Effective writers claim no more than they can responsibly support.

Claims vary in extent; they can be absolute or moderate, large or limited. Absolute claims assert that something is always true or false, completely good or bad; moderate claims make less sweeping assertions.

Absolute claim	College athletes are never good students.
Moderate claim	Most colleges have low graduation rates for their athletes.
Absolute claim	Harry Truman was the best president we have ever had.
Moderate claim	Truman's domestic policies helped advance civil rights.

Moderate claims are not necessarily superior to absolute claims. After all, writers frequently need to take a strong position in favor of or against something. But the stronger the claim, the stronger the evidence needed to support it. Be sure to consider the quality and the significance of the evidence you use—not just its quantity.

(2) Types of claims vary in terms of how much they encompass.

(a) Substantiation claims assert that something exists or is evident. Without making a value judgment, a **substantiation claim** makes a point that can be supported by evidence.

> The job market for those who just received a PhD in English is limited.

> The post office is raising rates again.

(b) Evaluation claims assert that something has a specific quality. According to an **evaluation claim,** something is good or bad, effective or ineffective, attractive or unattractive, successful or unsuccessful.

> The graduation rate for athletes at Penn State is very high compared with that at the other Big Ten universities.

> The public transportation system in Washington DC is reliable and safe.

(c) Policy claims call for a specific action. When making **policy claims,** writers call for something to be done.

> We must find the funds to hire better qualified high school teachers.

> We need to build a light-rail system linking downtown with the airport and the western suburbs.

Much writing involves substantiation, evaluation, and policy claims. When writing about the job market for engineers with newly minted degrees, you might tap your ability to substantiate a claim; when writing about literature (chapter 42), you might need to evaluate a character. Policy claims are commonly found in arguments about social issues such as health

Policy claims, such as the one made by this famous Army recruiting poster, call for a specific action.

care, social security, and affirmative action. These claims often grow out of substantiation or evaluation claims: first, you demonstrate that a problem exists; then, you establish the best solution for that problem.

TIPS FOR MAKING A CLAIM ARGUABLE

- Write down your opinion.
- Describe the situation that produced your opinion.
- Decide who constitutes the audience for your opinion and what you want that audience to do about your opinion.
- Write down the verifiable and reliable facts that support your opinion.
- Using those facts, transform your initial opinion into a thoughtful claim that considers at least two sides to the issue under discussion.
- Ask yourself, "So what?" If the answer to this question shows that your claim leads nowhere, start over, beginning with the first tip.

35e Providing evidence for an effective argument

Effective arguments are well developed and supported. You should explore your topic in enough depth to have the evidence to support your position intelligently and ethically, whether that evidence is based on personal experience or research (chapters 33 and 37). You will want to consider the reasons others might disagree with you and be prepared to respond to those reasons.

(1) An effective argument clearly establishes the thinking that leads to the claim.

If you want readers to take your ideas seriously, you must communicate the reasons that have led to your position as well as the values and assumptions that underlie your thinking. When you are exploring your topic, make a list of the reasons that have led to your belief (33d and 33f). For example, when Anna Seitz was working on her argumentative essay (at the end of this chapter; see pages 483–490), she listed the following reasons for her belief that universities should not allow individuals or corporations to buy naming rights to campus buildings:

1. By purchasing naming rights, donors gain influence over educational policy decisions, even though they are not qualified to make such decisions.

2. Significant donations can adversely affect overall university finances by replacing existing funding sources.

3. Donors who purchase naming rights are associated with the university, in spite of the fact that they or their corporations may subscribe to a different set of values.

Although it is possible to base an argument on one good reason (such as "The selling of naming rights distracts from the educational purposes of universities"), doing so can be risky. If your audience does not find this reason convincing, you have no other support for your position. When you show that you have more than one reason for believing as you do, you increase the likelihood that your audience will find merit in your argument. Sometimes, however, one reason is stronger—and more appropriate for your audience—than several others you could advance. To develop an argument for which you have only one good reason, explore the bases underlying your reason: the values and assumptions that led you to take your stand.

Whether you have one reason or several, be sure to provide sufficient evidence from credible sources to support your claim:

- facts,
- statistics,
- examples, and
- testimony from personal experience or professional expertise.

This evidence must be accurate, representative, and sufficient. Accurate information should be verifiable by others (**35c**). Recognize, however, that even if the information a writer provides is accurate, it may not be representative or sufficient if it was drawn from an exceptional case, a biased sample, or a one-time occurrence. If, for example, you are writing an argument about the advantages of using Standardized English but draw all of your supporting evidence from a proponent of the English-Only movement, your evidence represents only the views of that movement. If you draw all of your evidence from just one person, your evidence is neither representative of all the support for the use of Standardized English nor sufficient to support a thoughtful argument. In order to better represent your viewpoint, you should gather supporting evidence from sociolinguists, speakers of other dialects and languages, education specialists, professors, and other experts. In other words, consult more than a single source (chapter **37**).

When gathering evidence, be sure to think critically about the information you find. If you are using the results of polls or other statistics or statements by authorities, determine how recent and representative the information is and how it was gathered. Consider, too, whether the authority you plan to quote is qualified to address the topic under consideration and is likely to be respected by your readers. Whatever form of evidence you use—facts, statistics, examples, or testimony—you need to make clear to your audience exactly *why* and *how* the evidence supports your claim.

(2) Effective arguments respond to diverse views.

Issues are controversial because good arguments can be made on all sides. Therefore, effective arguments consider and respond to other points of view, fairly and respectfully. The most common strategy for addressing opposing points of view is referred to as **refutation:** you introduce diverse views and then respectfully demonstrate why you disagree with each of them. As you consider opposing points of view, you are likely to discover some you cannot refute and some that have real merit. If you understand the reasons behind opposing viewpoints but remain unconvinced, you will need to demonstrate why.

When you find yourself agreeing with a point that supports another side of the issue, you can benefit from offering a **concession.** By openly admitting that you agree with opponents on one or more specific points, you demonstrate that you are fair-minded and at the same time increase your credibility (35f(1)). Concessions also increase the likelihood that opponents will be inclined to find merit in your argument.

Whether you agree or disagree with other positions, work to recognize and assess them. If you admit that others are partially right, they are more likely to admit that you could be partially right as well. Argument involves working with an audience as much as getting them to work with you.

35f Using the rhetorical appeals to ground your argument

Effective arguments always incorporate several appeals to the audience simply because logical reasoning—providing good reasons—is rarely enough (35e and 35h). Aristotle, a Greek philosopher who lived over two thousand years ago, was the first to help speakers shape effective arguments through a combination of three persuasive strategies: the **rhetorical appeals** of ethos, logos, and pathos. **Ethos** (an ethical appeal) establishes the speaker's or writer's credibility and trustworthiness. An ethical appeal demonstrates goodwill toward the audience, good sense or knowledge of the subject at hand, and good character. Establishing common ground with the audience is another feature of ethos. But ethos alone rarely carries an argument; therefore, you also need to use **logos** (a logical appeal). Logos demonstrates an effective use of reason and judicious use of evidence, whether that evidence consists of facts, statistics, comparisons, anecdotes, expert opinions, personal experiences, or observations. You employ logos in the process of supporting claims, drawing reasonable conclusions, and avoiding rhetorical fallacies (35i). Aristotle also taught that persuasion comes about only when the audience feels emotionally stirred by the topic under discussion. Therefore, **pathos** (an emotional appeal) involves using language that will stir the feelings of the audience. If you misuse pathos in an attempt to manipulate your audience, your effort can backfire. But pathos can be used successfully when it establishes empathy and authentic understanding. Thus, the most effective arguments combine these three persuasive appeals responsibly and knowledgeably.

As a writer and a speaker, Dr. Martin Luther King, Jr., successfully used the rhetorical appeals of ethos, logos, and pathos.

In the next three subsections, excerpts from Martin Luther King, Jr.'s "Letter from Birmingham Jail" illustrate how a writer can use all three of the classical rhetorical appeals.

(1) Ethical appeals establish a writer's credibility.

In his opening paragraph, King notes that his professional life is very demanding but that his critics' views are worthy of response. He thus demonstrates respect for his audience. He also indicates that he wishes to engage in "constructive work," thereby establishing common ground with his audience, whom he characterizes as being well-intentioned and sincere. He also establishes that he will argue in good faith.

1   My Dear Fellow Clergymen:
    While confined here in the Birmingham city jail, I came across your recent statement calling my present activities "unwise and untimely." Seldom do I pause to answer criticism of my work and ideas. If I sought to answer all the criticisms that cross my desk, my secretaries would have little time for anything other than such correspondence in the course of the day, and I would have no time for constructive work. But since I feel that you are men of genuine good will and that your criticisms are sincerely set forth, I want to try to answer your statement in what I hope will be patient and reasonable terms.

(2) Logical appeals help an audience clearly understand the writer's ideas.

To help his audience understand why segregation is wrong, King defines key terms:

2   Let us consider a more concrete example of just and unjust laws. An unjust law is a code that a numerical or power majority group compels a minority group to obey but does not make binding on itself. This is difference made legal. By the same token, a just law is a code that a majority compels a minority to follow and that it is willing to follow itself. This is sameness made legal.

(3) Emotional appeals can move the audience to a new way of thinking or acting.

As he moves toward his conclusion, King evokes feelings of idealism as well as guilt:

3   I have travelled the length and breadth of Alabama, Mississippi, and all the other southern states. On sweltering summer days and crisp autumn mornings I have looked at the South's beautiful churches with their lofty spires pointing heavenward. I have beheld the impressive outlines of her massive religious-education buildings. Over and over I have found myself asking: "What kind of people worship here? Who is their God? . . . Where were their voices of support when bruised and weary Negro men and women decided to rise from the dark dungeons of complacency to the bright hills of creative protest?"   —MARTIN LUTHER KING, JR., "Letter from Birmingham Jail"

The full text of King's argument includes other examples of ethos, logos, and pathos.

Although ethos is often developed in the introduction, logos in the body, and pathos in the conclusion, these classical rhetorical appeals often overlap and appear throughout an argument.

35g Purposefully arranging an effective argument

No single arrangement is right for every written argument. Unless your instructor asks you to demonstrate a particular type of arrangement, the decisions you make about arrangement should be based on several factors: your topic, your audience, and your purpose. You can develop a good plan by simply listing the major points you want to make, deciding what order to put them in (33d), and then determining where to include refutation or concession (35g(2)). You must also decide whether to place your thesis statement or claim at the beginning or the end of your argument. Once you sort out the reasons supporting your claim, you need to develop each reason with a separate paragraph (unless, of course, you are summarizing your reasons in the conclusion).

No matter which arrangement you use, your conclusion should move beyond a mere summary of what has already been stated and instead emphasize your emotional connection with your audience, a connection that reinforces your rhetorical purpose: presenting the course of action you want your audience to take, an invitation to further understanding, or the implications of your claim (35h). In deciding how to arrange an argumentative essay, you may find the following basic principles useful.

(1) Classical arrangement works well if your audience has not yet taken a position on your issue.

One way to organize your argument is to follow the plan recommended by classical rhetoric, which assumes that an audience is prepared to follow a well-reasoned argument.

FEATURES OF THE CLASSICAL ARRANGEMENT

Introduction	Introduce your issue, and capture the attention of your audience. Try using a short narrative or a strong example (33f(2) and 33g). Begin establishing your credibility (using ethos) and common ground.
Background information	Provide your audience with a history of the situation and state how things currently stand. Define any key terms. Even if you think the facts speak for themselves, draw the attention of your audience to those points that are especially important and explain why they are meaningful.
Proposition	Introduce the position you are taking: present the argument itself and provide the basic reasons for your belief. Frame your position as a thesis statement or a claim (33c and 35d).

(Continued on page 474)

(Continued from page 473)

Proof or confirmation	Discuss the reasons that have led you to take your position. Each reason must be clear, relevant, and representative. Provide facts, expert testimony, and any other evidence that supports your claim.
Refutation	Recognize and disprove the arguments of people who hold a different position and with whom you continue to disagree.
Concession	Concede any point with which you agree or that has merit; show why this concession does not damage your own case.
Conclusion	Summarize your most important points and appeal to your audience's feelings, making a personal connection. Describe the consequences of your argument in a final attempt to encourage your audience to consider (if not commit to) a particular course of action.

(2) Refutation and concession are most effective when placed where readers will accept them.

Classical arrangement places refutation after the proof or confirmation of the argument, an arrangement that works well for an audience familiar with this organizational model. Sometimes, however, that refutation can come too late. Readers unfamiliar with classical arrangement may have decided that you are too one-sided—and may even have stopped reading. Therefore, when you are taking a highly controversial stand on an emotionally loaded subject, strive to establish common ground and then acknowledge opposing viewpoints and respond to them. This variation on classical arrangement assumes that readers will be unwilling to hear a new proposition unless they are first shown what is weak or incomplete about their current thinking.

However, sometimes readers may react negatively to a writer who responds to opposing views before offering any reasons to support his or her own view. These readers want to know from the start where an argument is headed. For this reason, writers often choose to state their position at the beginning of the argument and offer at least one strong reason to support it before turning to opposing views. They sometimes keep at least one other reason in reserve (often one responsibly laden with emotion, or pathos), so that they can present it after responding to opposing views, thereby ending with an emphasis on their confirmation.

Unless you are required to follow a specific arrangement, you should respond to opposing views wherever your audience is most likely either to expect this discussion or to be willing to hear it. If your audience is receptive, you can place refutation and concession after your confirmation. If your audience adheres to a different position, you should respond to their views toward the beginning of your argument. You might also want to keep in mind that if you open a paragraph with an opposing view, you will want to move quickly to your response to that view so that your readers make only one shift between differing views. Your goal is to keep your readers focused on your line of thinking.

Exercise 2

Read the editorial pages of several consecutive issues of your community or college newspaper. Look for editorials that analyze or question an established belief, express or defend an opinion, invite consideration, or try to convince. Choose an editorial that strikes you as well argued, well developed, and well organized—even if it does not change your belief or action (it may only have changed your level of understanding). Bring several copies of the editorial to class, and be prepared to discuss its purpose, audience, use of appeals, and conclusion.

35h Using logic to argue effectively and ethically

Because writers cannot argue on the basis of ethos alone, they need to understand the ways in which **logic**—the reasoning behind an argument—enhances or detracts from the argument. Logic is a means through which you can develop your ideas, realize new ones, and determine whether your thinking is clear enough to persuade readers to agree with you. By arguing logically, you increase the likelihood that your arguments will be taken seriously.

(1) Inductive reasoning is the process of using a number of specific facts or observations to draw a logical conclusion.

You use inductive reasoning every day. For example, if you get a stomachache within fifteen minutes of eating ice cream, you might conclude that there is a connection. Perhaps you are lactose intolerant. This use of evidence to form a generalization is called an **inductive leap,** and the leap should be in proportion to the amount of evidence gathered.

Inductive reasoning involves moving (or leaping) from discovering evidence to interpreting it, and it can help you arrive at probable, believable conclusions (but not absolute truth). Making a small leap from evidence (a stomachache) to a probable conclusion (lactose intolerance) is more effective and ethical than using the same evidence to make a sweeping claim that could easily be challenged (ice cream is bad for everyone) (**35d(1)**). Generally, the greater the weight of the evidence, the more reliable the conclusion.

When used in argument, inductive reasoning often employs facts (**35c**) and examples (**33f(2)** and **33g**). When writers cannot cite all the information that supports their conclusions, they choose the evidence that is most reliable and most closely related to the point they are making.

(2) Deductive reasoning is the process of applying a generalization (or generalized belief) to a series of specific cases.

At the heart of a deductive argument is a **major premise** (a generalized belief that is assumed to be true), which the writer applies to a specific case (the **minor premise**), thereby yielding a conclusion, or claim. For example, if you know that all doctors must complete a residency and that Imogen is in medical school, then you can conclude that Imogen must complete a residency. This argument can be expressed in a three-part structure called a **syllogism.**

Major premise	All doctors must complete a residency. [generalized belief]
Minor premise	Imogen is studying to become a doctor. [specific case]
Conclusion	Imogen must complete a residency. [claim]

Sometimes premises are not stated, for the simple reason that the writer assumes a shared belief with the audience. A syllogism with an unstated premise—or even an unstated conclusion—is called an **enthymeme.** Frequently found in written arguments, enthymemes can be very effective because they presume shared beliefs or knowledge.

35i   Avoiding rhetorical fallacies

Logical reasoning not only enhances the overall effectiveness of an argument, it also enhances the ethos of the speaker or writer. Almost as important as constructing an argument effectively is avoiding errors in argument, or **rhetorical fallacies.** Rhetorical fallacies signal to your audience that your thinking is not entirely trustworthy and that your argument is not well reasoned.

Therefore, you need to recognize and avoid several kinds of fallacies. As you read the arguments of others (**38a**) and revise the arguments you draft (chapter 34), try to keep the following common rhetorical fallacies in mind:

(1) *Non sequitur*, Latin for "it does not follow," means that just because the first part of a statement is true doesn't mean the second part will necessarily happen or become true.

Non sequitur is the basis for most of the other rhetorical fallacies.

Faulty   Eddie is smart; therefore, he will do well in college.
[This assertion is based on the faulty premise that *all* smart people do well in college (35h(2)).]

(2) *Ad hominem* refers to a personal attack on an opponent that draws attention away from the issues under consideration.

Faulty   She is unfit to be a minister because she is divorced.
[The fact that a woman is divorced may reveal the condition of a previous marriage, but a divorce has little if anything to do with her spiritual beliefs and principles that could benefit a congregation.]

(3) *Appeal to tradition* is an argument that says something should be done a certain way simply because it has been done that way in the past.

Faulty   Because they are a memorable part of the pledge process, fraternity hazings should not be banned.
[Times change; what was considered good practice in the past is not necessarily considered acceptable now.]

(4) *Bandwagon* is an argument saying, in effect, "Everyone's doing or saying or thinking this, so you should, too."

Faulty   Everyone drives over the speed limit, so why shouldn't we raise the limit?
[The majority is not always right.]

(5) *Begging the question* **is an argument that assumes what in fact needs to be proved.**

Faulty   We need to fire corrupt officials in order to reduce the city's crime rate.
[If there are corrupt officials in city government, this point needs to be established.]

This cartoon begs the question "Are children brain damaged?" It also oversimplifies the potential causes of that damage.

(6) *False analogy* **is the assumption that because two things are alike in some ways, they must be alike in others.**

Faulty   The United States lost credibility with other nations during the war in Vietnam, so we should not get involved in the Middle East, or we will lose credibility again.
[The differences between the war in Southeast Asia in the 1960s and 1970s and the current conflict in the Middle East may well be greater than their similarities.]

(7) *False authority* **is the assumption that an expert in one field can be credible in another.**

Faulty   We must stop sending military troops into Afghanistan, as Bruce Springsteen has argued.
[Springsteen's expertise in music does not automatically qualify him as an expert in foreign policy.]

(8) *False cause* (sometimes called *post hoc, ergo propter hoc*, meaning "after this, so because of this") is the assumption that because one event follows another, the first is the cause of the second.

Faulty   When Penn State football coach Joe Paterno turned 81, he was finally inducted into the College Football Hall of Fame.
[The assumption is that Paterno's age is solely responsible for his Hall of Fame honor.]

(9) *False dilemma* (sometimes called the *either/or fallacy*) is a statement that only two alternatives exist, when in fact there are more than two.

Faulty   We must either build more nuclear power plants or be completely dependent on foreign oil.
[Other possibilities exist.]

(10) *Hasty generalization* is a conclusion based on too little evidence or on exceptional or biased evidence.

Faulty   Ellen is a poor student because she failed her first history test.
[Her performance may improve in the weeks ahead or be good in all her other subjects.]

Without careful thinking, we often make hasty judgments about the people who are not like us.

(11) *Oversimplification* **is a statement or argument that leaves out relevant considerations in order to imply that there is a single cause or solution for a complex problem.**

Faulty   We can eliminate unwanted pregnancies by teaching birth control and abstinence.
[Teaching people about birth control and abstinence does not guarantee the elimination of unwanted pregnancies.]

(12) *Slippery slope* **is the assumption that if one thing is allowed, it will be the first step in a downward spiral.**

Faulty   Handgun control will lead to a police state.
[Handgun control has not led to a police state in England.]

"It started out with lactose, but now he's intolerant of everything."

Applying a slippery slope argument, this cartoon suggests that lactose intolerance leads to general intolerance.

Be alert for rhetorical fallacies in your writing. When you find such a fallacy, be sure to moderate your claim, clarify your thinking, or, if necessary, eliminate the fallacious statement. Even if your argument as a whole is convincing, rhetorical fallacies can damage your credibility (**35d** and **38a**).

 35j   **Sample argument**

As you read the following essay, by Anna Seitz, consider how she argued her case and whether she argued it effectively. Note her use of classical rhetorical appeals (ethos, logos, and pathos) and arrangement and her inductive reasoning. Also, identify the kinds of evidence she uses (facts, examples, testimony, or authority).

Anna Seitz

Professor Byerly

Library Science 313

30 November 2007

Naming Opportunities: Opportunities for Whom?

> Chevy Chase Bank and the University of Maryland
> have expanded their long-term relationship in an
> agreement that will mean the Terrapins' football and
> lacrosse teams will play on Chevy Chase Bank Field
> at Byrd Stadium. . . . The agreement will provide the
> university with $20 million. . . . ("Chevy Chase")

All over the nation, football stadiums, business schools,
law schools, dining halls, and even coaching positions have
become naming opportunities (also known as "naming rights" and
"legacy opportunities"). Since the first college deal in 1979, when
Syracuse University signed a deal with the Carrier Corporation
for lifetime naming rights to their sports stadium—the Carrier
Dome—naming has become a common practice with an alleged
two-fold payoff: universities raise money and donors get their
names writ large. Universities use the money from naming
opportunities to hire more faculty, raise salaries, support faculty
research, provide travel opportunities for students, and build

Introduction

Seitz 2

stadium suites and boxes for game watching. Reser Stadium
(Oregon State), The Donald Bren School of Law (University
of California-Irvine), or the Malloy Paterno Head Football
Coach Endowment (Penn State University)—all these naming
opportunities seem like a good solution for raising money,
especially at a time when state legislatures have cut back on

Introduction university funding and when wealthy alumni are being besieged
for donations from every college they have ever attended. Naming
opportunities seem like a good solution for donors, too, because their
donations will be broadly recognized. While naming opportunities
may seem like a perfect solution for improving colleges and
universities and simplifying funding, in reality they are not. In this
paper, I argue against naming opportunities on college and university
campuses because they create more problems than they solve.

The naming of sports stadiums is a familiar occurrence; after
all, universities commonly highlight the sponsors of their athletic
programs. But naming opportunities in other spheres of academic

Background
information life are unfamiliar to most people, even though such naming is an
established practice. A quick search of the Web pages of university
libraries reveals that many of them, especially those in the midst
of major development campaigns, have created a price list just for
naming opportunities. Entire buildings are available, of course. For

example, a $5 million donation earns the right to name the music
library at Northwestern University (Northwestern). But parts of
buildings are also available these days. North Carolina State University
will name an atlas stand according to the donor's wishes for only
$7,500 or put a specific name on a lectern for $3,500 (North Carolina).

Naming opportunities can clearly bring in a good deal of
money. It has become commonplace for schools to offer naming
opportunities on planned construction in exchange for 51 percent
of the cost of the building! That's a big head start to a building
project, and naming opportunities may be what allow some schools
to provide their students with better facilities than their unnamed
counterparts. In fact, donors are often recruited for the opportunity
to pay for named faculty chairs, reading rooms, or major library or
art collections—all of which enhance student life.

Background
information

Clearly the more opportunities and resources any university
can offer current and potential students and even alumni, the
more that university enhances its own growth and that of its
faculty. Library donors and recipients say that if it is possible
for a library to pay for a new computer lab just by adding a sign
with someone's name over the door, the advantages often
seem to outweigh the disadvantages. Proponents of naming
opportunities point out that small donors are often hailed as library

Seitz 4

supporters, even when big donors are maligned as corporate flag-wavers.

Few would argue that these donations necessarily detract from the educational mission of the institution. However, selling off parts of a university library, for example, does not always please people, especially those whose responsibility includes managing that donation. The curator of rare books and manuscripts at a prominent state

Background information university told me that one of the most frustrating parts of her job is dealing with "strings-attached" gifts, which is what too many library donations turn out to be. Some major donors like to make surprise visits, during which they monitor the prominence of their "legacy opportunity." Others like to create rules which limit the use of their funds to the purchase of certain collections or subjects; still others just need constant personal maintenance, including lunches, coffees, and regular invitations to events. But meddling in their donation after the fact is just a minor inconvenience compared to some donors' actions.

Donors who fund an ongoing educational program and who give money on a regular basis often expect to have regular

Proposition input. Because major donors want major prestige, they try to align themselves with successful programs. Doing that can result in damage to university budgets. First of all, high-profile programs can become increasingly well funded, while less prominent, less

Seitz 5

glamorous ones are continually ignored. Second, when corporate
or private funds are regularly available, it can have the result of
eroding existing funding sources. Simply put, if budgeted programs
become funded by donation, those funds will, for better or worse,
be redirected, and the next time the program needs funding, the
department or unit will likely be told that finding a donor is their
only option. Essentially, once donor-funded, always donor-funded.

Additionally, many academics feel that selling off naming
rights can create an image problem for a university. While
buildings, schools, endowed chairs, even football stadiums were
once named for past professors, university presidents, or others
with strong ties to the university, those same facilities are now
named for virtually anyone who can afford to donate, especially
corporations. Regular input from a corporation creates the
appearance of a conflict of interest in a university, which is exactly
the reason such arrangements are so often vehemently opposed by
the university community. Boise State University in Idaho received
such negative press for negotiating a deal with labor-unfriendly
Taco Bell that it was finally pressured to terminate the $4 million
contract (Langrill 1).

Given these drawbacks, many universities are establishing
guidelines for the selection of appropriate donors for named gifts.

Proposition

Proof

Seitz 6

To that end, fundraising professional and managing director of Changing Our World, Inc. Robert Hoak suggests that naming opportunities should be mutually beneficial for the donor (whether a corporation or an individual) and the organization (university, for instance) and that these opportunities should be viewed as the start of a long-term relationship between the two, not the final gift. Additionally, he cautions that even if the donor seems the right fit for the organization, it is in the best interest of both parties to add an escape clause to the contract in order to protect either side from potential embarrassment or scandal. He provides the example of Seton Hall University, which regrettably had both an academic building and the library rotunda named for Tyco CEO Dennis Kozlowski. When Kozlowski was convicted of grand larceny, the university pulled the names (Hoak).

Although many people prefer that naming be an honor given to recognize an accomplished faculty member or administrator, most realize that recruiting named gift donors is good business. Whether it is "good education" is another question. While signing contracts with donors has become a sales transaction, naming university property for major donors is not. New College in Cambridge, Massachusetts was just that—until local clergyman John Harvard died and left half

Seitz 7

his estate and his entire library to what would soon become
Harvard College. Modern naming opportunities, however,
are rarely so simple. They do not necessarily recognize and
remember individuals who had significant influence on
university life; rather, they create obligations for the university
to operate in such a way as to please living donors or their
descendants. Pleasing wealthy donors should not replace
educating students as a university's primary goal.

Refutation

Seitz 8

Works Cited

"Chevy Chase Bank Signs Naming Rights Agreement for Byrd
Stadium Field." *UM News*. U of Maryland, 24 Aug. 2006.
Web. 17 Nov. 2007.

Hoak, Robert. "Making the Most of Naming Opportunities."
onPhilanthropy. Changing Our World, 28 Mar. 2003. Web.
5 Nov. 2007.

Langrill, Chereen. "BSU Faculty Says 'No Quiero' to Taco Bell."
Idaho Statesman [Boise] 27 Oct. 2004: 1+. Print.

North Carolina State University Libraries. "NCSU Libraries East
Wing Renovation: Naming Opportunities." *NCSU Libraries*.
North Carolina State U, n.d. Web. 5 Nov. 2007.
<http://www.lib.ncsu.edu/renovation/namingOp/>.

Northwestern University Library. "Making a Gift: Naming
Opportunities." *Naming Opportunities: Library Development
Office*. Northwestern U, 2007. Web. 20 Nov. 2007.

Exercise 3

Reread Anna Seitz's essay and identify her claim and proof. What values does she reveal as she argues against naming opportunities?

36 Online Writing

In addition to word-processing capabilities, computers offer you the opportunity to communicate with a wider, often global, audience. Online writing is often **interactive** (that is, a writer is linked to other writers, and a document is linked to other documents), dramatically expanding your work's audience and context. Because composing in this medium differs somewhat from writing essays or research papers delivered in hard copy, it calls for different skills—many of which you already have. This chapter will help you

- assess the rhetorical situation for online writing (**36a**),
- understand conventions for electronic communication (**36b**),
- compose effective Web documents (**36c**), and
- manage the visual elements of a Web site (**36d**).

36a Assessing the online rhetorical situation

Whenever you compose material for a Web page, engage in online communication, or post updates on a blog, you are using rhetoric, or purposeful language, to influence the outcome of your interaction (chapter **31**). You are responding to a rhetorical situation, but your response can differ markedly from one you offer in a static, print medium.

Because the Web gives you access to so many different audiences, the unique nature of the online rhetorical situation becomes instantly evident when you begin composing for a Web site or a newsgroup posting. If you are constructing a Web page for a course assignment, your primary audience is probably your instructor and classmates. But as soon as you put your composition online, you open up your work to a variety of secondary audiences (**31d(3)**), whose responses you will also want to consider as you compose.

Keep in mind that primary or secondary audiences for online writing may be specialized, diverse, or multiple (**31d**). When writing an e-mail to an individual recipient, you have a very narrow audience. When writing a message for a listserv (an e-mail–based discussion forum organized around a particular subject), you are addressing a broader but specialized audience and can assume that its members share an interest in your topic. However, when creating a Web page about an important event or a current controversy, such as the devastation caused by the May 2008 earthquake in China or the debate over genetically modified food, you will write for a diverse audience, whose members have varying levels of knowledge, understanding of specialized terms, and interest in your subject matter.

In response to an online rhetorical situation, specify your purpose clearly, whether you wish to express your point of view, create a mood, or amuse or motivate your audience. For example, the purpose of a Web site such as the one developed by The Green Belt Movement (shown in fig. 36.1 on page 496) is to inform and then motivate the audience to become involved. Because readers may encounter your composition in a number of different ways—by having an e-mail message forwarded to them, by finding your Web page through a search engine, or by entering an online discussion forum—you need to take extra care to clarify your purpose and make it readily apparent.

Composing online also requires a greater responsiveness to context than you may be used to, given your experience in composing conventional academic writing projects (31e). Within the rhetorical situation of online composition, the boundary between writer and audience is often blurred, because participants are writing and responding simultaneously. In addition, the accessibility of online discussion communities encourages many people to add to or comment on compositions. This flow of new material contributes to an always evolving rhetorical situation, requiring you to be familiar with the preceding discussion and to understand the conventions of the forum in order to compose effectively.

In addition, many Internet users have come to expect online compositions to be especially timely, given the relative ease of updating an electronic document compared to a print-based publication. For example, a Web page about the effects of earthquakes produced just after the one in China in May 2008 would surely differ from one produced before that date. In order for such a document to be current, it would have to include continuous updates of the death count, the numbers of displaced people, and the effects of the aftershock, which included disastrous flooding.

36b Netiquette and online writing

Netiquette (from the phrase *Internet etiquette*) is a set of social practices that was developed by Internet users in order to regulate online language and manners. The most fundamental requirement of online etiquette is to convey respect.

TIPS FOR NETIQUETTE IN ONLINE DISCUSSION FORUMS

Audience

- Keep in mind the potential audience(s) for your message: those for whom it is intended and others who may read it.
- Make the subject line of your message as descriptive as possible so that your reader(s) will immediately recognize the topic.
- Keep your message focused and limit it to one screen, if possible. The reader's time and bandwidth may be limited, so delete anything that is not essential when posting or replying.
- Give people adequate time to respond.
- Consider the content of your posting, making sure that it pertains to the interests of a specific forum's audience.
- Respect copyright. Never post something written by someone else or pass it off as your own.

Style and Presentation

- Take care to establish a tone appropriate for your message and your audience.
- Be sure of your facts.
- Present ideas clearly and logically.
- Pay attention to spelling and grammar.
- Use emoticons (such as :>)) and abbreviations (such as IMHO for "in my humble opinion") only when you are sure your audience will understand them and find them appropriate.
- Use all capital letters only when you want to be perceived as SHOUTING.
- Abusive or profane language is never appropriate.

Context

- Observe what others say and how they say it before you engage in an online discussion; note what kind of information participants find appropriate to exchange.

- If someone is abusive, ignore that person or change the subject. Do not participate in **flaming** (online personal attacks).
- Understand that sarcasm and irony may appear to be personal attacks.
- Do not use your school's or employer's network for personal business.

Credibility

- Use either your real name or an appropriate online pseudonym to identify yourself to readers. Avoid suggestive or inflammatory pseudonyms.
- Be respectful of others even when you disagree, and be kind to new members of an online community.

36c Composing Web documents

The Web offers you the chance to communicate to many different audiences for a variety of purposes. More than an electronic library for information and research, the Web is also a kind of global marketplace, allowing people all over the world to exchange ideas. For example, the home page of The Green Belt Movement (fig 36.1) presents to an international audience themes that are conveyed throughout the Web site, emphasizing the group's values and mission. The text on the page is designed to appeal to a diverse audience, from environmental activists to people interested in international development to conservationists planning to start their own grass-roots organizations. Even though the group is based in Kenya, its Web site strives for international appeal by highlighting the founder's Nobel Peace Prize, offering multiple ways of contacting the organization, and providing the option of making an online donation in various currencies.

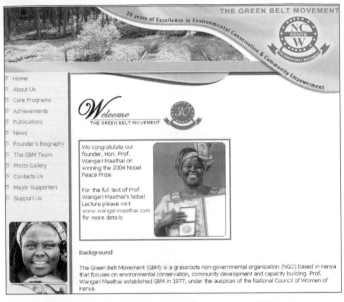

Fig. 36.1. The home page for The Green Belt Movement highlights the activities of the founder, Wangari Maathai, and emphasizes the group's values and focus: volunteerism, environmental conservation, accountability, and empowerment.

The home page of The Green Belt Movement introduces eleven main topics—from "About Us" to "Support Us"—each of which is the subject of a separate Web page. The **arrangement** (the pattern of organization of the ideas, text, and visual elements in a composition) of the site is clear. The site is thus easy to use: every page maintains the list of main topics in a navigation bar on the left. Arrangement also involves the balance of visual elements and text. The home page is unified by the use of several shades of green for the background, links, and headings, and the entire site is given coherence by the appearance of the organization's logo in the upper-right corner of every page. Finally, the trees shown in the bar that runs across the top of the home page create a visual link to one of The Green Belt Movement's key activities: planting trees as a means of fostering environmental consciousness and concern for the local environment. That visual link combines arrangement and **delivery** (the presentation and interaction of visual elements with content). Your intentions for your Web documents may well be more modest than those of The Green Belt Movement. Nevertheless, you will want to remember that Web sites (and other online compositions) are available to diverse audiences, and so their composition should be given as much forethought as possible in terms of context, purpose, and message (31a). Because of the flexible nature of electronic composition, you can have fun planning, drafting, and revising your Web documents.

(1) Effective Web documents take advantage of the unique features of electronic composition.

When you plan and compose a Web page or site, you can create consistency as well as help orient users by placing design elements (such as logos and color) carefully and by including links to the home page on all other pages of the Web site.

The visual elements included on a Web page or site create important associations among the concepts and ideas that underlie your online composition. For instance, the central image on The Green Belt Movement's home page (fig. 36.1) is a photo of the organization's founder, which immediately creates an association for users who already know about Maathai as well as connecting the organization to African women more generally.

A true electronic document contains **hypertext,** which includes links to other online text, graphics, and animations, as an integral part of its arrangement and content. You are probably accustomed to navigating Web sites by clicking on hyperlinks, one of the distinguishing features of online documents.

However, you may not have thought about how valuable hyperlinks can be as tools for Web site development. Of course, print documents converted for use on the Web often have hyperlinks (as well as text and images; see chapter **8**), but because they were not originally created with online capabilities in mind, these documents are not truly hypertextual.

Hypertext is rhetorically important because it allows users to customize their approach to a Web document. The inclusion of hyperlinks transfers control over the sequence of information from you (the writer) to your audience (the user). In other words, Web documents offer unlimited options for ordering the content, as users may click on links in any order they choose. Because the individual interests and personalities of those who read your Web document will lead them to navigate it in different ways, you will want to consider how different approaches may affect the intended purpose of your document and try to arrange your document accordingly.

Some basic principles can help you use hyperlinks effectively in your Web documents.

(a) Hyperlinks enhance the coherence of a Web document.

The choice and placement of hyperlinks should be a vital part of your organizational plan. Considering the ways in which users can exploit these links is an important part of your rhetorical strategy, leading you to use the links purposefully to connect related ideas and to provide additional information. A site map is essential for a large site and helpful for a compact one. Notice that the main sections of The Green Belt Movement Web site (fig. 36.1) are featured as a list of links in the navigation bar that appears along the left side of the home page. A link to a relevant external site—Wangari Maathai's professional Web site—appears within the text. Hyperlinks to the individual pages of a Web site provide transitions based on key words or ideas or logical divisions of the document. Because these links provide coherence and help users navigate your site, they are powerful rhetorical tools that aid you in creating an effective arrangement.

(b) Hyperlinks can be textual or graphical, linking to internal or external material.

You can use individual words, phrases, or even sentences as textual hyperlinks. Hyperlinks can also be icons, pictures, or logos. If you do use graphical links, be sure that their appearance is appropriate for the transitions you are indicating and that you obtain permission for any text, graphics, or multimedia elements you draw from other sources. Even though such material is often free, its source must be acknowledged (39e).

Internal hyperlinks are those that take the user between pages or sections of the Web site in which they appear. When choosing hyperlinks that take the user to content *external* to your Web site (such as a hyperlink in a Web page about hurricanes that links to a meteorologist's Web site), be sure to select sites containing relevant, accurate, and well-presented information. You should also use any contact information provided on a site to request permission to link to it, and you should check your links periodically to be sure that they are still active.

(c) Hyperlinks have rhetorical impact.

Textual and graphical links establish persuasive rhetorical associations for the user. Compare the rhetorical impact of linking an image of the World Trade Center towers to a page about public memorials or to a page about global terrorism. Because hyperlinks serve various rhetorical purposes, evaluate the impact of those you include as you plan, compose, and revise your Web document.

TECH SAVVY

To create a Web page, you do not have to understand the computer code (HTML) that allows a browser to display text. Programs such as FrontPage and Netscape Composer, referred to generally as WYSIWYG (What You See Is What You Get) HTML editors, will do such coding for you automatically. But some writers find that knowledge of the basic HTML commands can be useful for troubleshooting and editing a Web page. A number of tutorials on the use of HTML are available on the Web.

(2) Planning a Web site involves working out an arrangement for presenting ideas.

As you develop a Web document, you need to keep all the elements of the rhetorical situation in mind. Depending on your audience and purpose, you must decide which ideas or information to emphasize and then work out how best to arrange your Web document to achieve that emphasis. While you are generating the textual content, you need to consider the supplementary links that will help you achieve your overall purpose. But you do not have to do everything at once; fine-tuning the visual design can wait until the content is in place.

When you are planning a Web site, you may find it helpful to create a storyboard or other visual representation of the site's organization. You can sketch a plan on a sheet of paper or in a word-processing file if your site is fairly simple, or you can use index cards tacked to a bulletin board if it is more complex. If you have some time to devote to the planning process, you may want to learn how to use software such as Web Studio or FrontPage to help you map out your site (such Web site design programs are often available on computers in school labs).

You can consider three basic arrangement patterns: linear, radial, and hierarchical. A linear site (fig. 36.2) is easy to set up. Hierarchical and radial arrangements are more complex

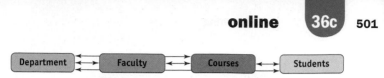

Fig. 36.2. Linear pattern for organizing a Web site.

to develop and may be better suited to group projects. The hierarchical arrangement (fig. 36.3) branches out at each level, and the radial arrangement (fig. 36.4), in which individual pages can be linked in a variety of sequences, allows the user to determine the sequence in which pages are viewed.

The possibilities for organizing a Web site are endless. The most important consideration is how the arrangement of your site will affect a user's experience in navigating it. However you decide to organize your site, be sure to represent each main element in your plan. A good plan will be invaluable to you as you draft text, incorporate visual and multimedia elements, and refine your arrangement.

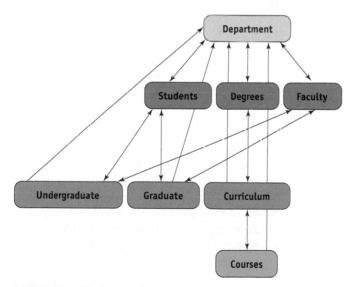

Fig. 36.3. Hierarchical pattern for organizing a Web site.

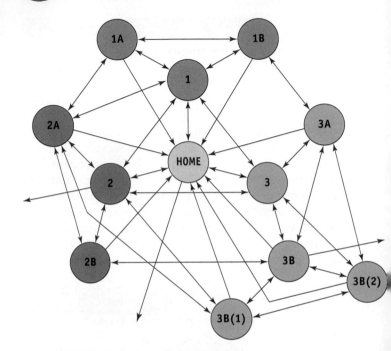

Fig. 36.4. Radial pattern for organizing a Web site.

(3) Drafting Web documents can transform your composing process.

When drafting a Web document, you will undoubtedly consider various ways to organize your material. You may draft text for a linear arrangement and then later break the text into separate sections for different pages, which you link in sequence. At times, however, the arrangement and means of delivery required for an online document will force you to draft in unfamiliar ways. For example, you may find that you need to write the text for a Web site in chunks, drafting the text for a single page, including hyperlinks, and then moving on to the next page. Or you might wait until you revise your site to add hyperlinks or to replace some of your initial text links with graphical ones.

Once you have drafted and revised your site, get feedback from your classmates or colleagues, just as you would for an essay or a report. Since a Web site can include many pages with multiple links and images, you may want to ask for feedback not only about the content of your site but also about layout, graphics, and navigation.

Professional Web developers often put a site that is still in a draft stage on the Web and solicit reactions from users, a process called **usability testing**. The developers then use those reactions to refine the site. Because Web sites are more interactive than printed texts, it is a good idea to seek input from users during site development. To solicit feedback, specify on your home page how users can contact you. Be careful, though, to consider your own security—you may want to use a free e-mail account through Yahoo! or Hotmail or allow users to post comments directly on your site. Usability testing can help you make your Web document accessible to a wide variety of potential users, including those who do not have a fast Internet connection or who have physical limitations affecting seeing, hearing, or keyboarding.

The following checklist will help you plan a Web site and develop ideas for each page.

CHECKLIST for Planning and Developing a Web Site

- What information or ideas should a user take away from your site?

- How does the arrangement of your site reflect your purpose? How does it assist your intended users in understanding your purpose?

- How would you like a user to navigate your Web site? How might different users navigate within your site?

- Should you devote each page to a single main idea or combine several ideas on one page?

- How will you help users return to the home page and find key information quickly?

- What key connections between ideas or pieces of information might be emphasized through the use of hyperlinks?

- Will a user who follows external links be able to get back to your site?

- To ensure that your Web site has more impact than a paper document, have you used Web-specific resources—such as hyperlinks, sound and video clips, and animations—in creating it? How do those multimedia elements help you achieve your purpose?

- Do you need graphics—charts, photos, cartoons, clip art, logos, and so on—to enhance the site so that it will accomplish your purpose? Where should key visual elements be placed to be most effective?

- How often will you update your site?

- How will you solicit feedback for revisions to your site?

- Will your site be accessible to users with slow Internet access and those with physical limitations?

Exercise 1

Plan and compile information for a Web page that supports a paper you are writing for one of your classes. If you have access to software that converts documents to Web pages, start by converting your document. Make adjustments to it based on the criteria in the preceding checklist. Then, critique your Web page.

36d Visual elements and rhetorical purpose

Visual design sends messages to users: an effective design not only invites them to explore a Web site but also conveys the designer's rhetorical purpose (chapter 8). All the design elements of an online document, like the tone and style of a printed one, are rhetorical tools that help you achieve your purpose and reach your intended audience.

(1) Adhering to basic design principles makes an online document visually pleasing and easy to navigate.
A number of basic principles apply to the visual design of writing presented on the Web.

- **Balance** involves the way in which design elements used in a document are spatially related to one another. Web pages with a symmetrical arrangement of elements convey a formal, static impression, whereas asymmetrical arrangements are informal and dynamic.
- **Proportion** has to do with the relative sizes of design elements. Large elements attract more attention than small ones and will be perceived as more important.

- **Movement** concerns the way in which our eyes scan a page for information. Most of us look at the upper-left corner of a page first and the lower-right corner last. Therefore, the most important information on a Web page should appear in those locations. Vertical or horizontal arrangement of elements on a page implies stability; diagonal and zigzagging arrangements suggest movement.

- **Contrast** between elements can be achieved by varying their focus or size. For instance, a Web page about the Siberian Husky might show a photo of one of these dogs in sharp focus against a blurred background. In text, you can emphasize an idea by presenting it in a contrasting font—for example, a playful display font such as Marker Felt Thin or an elegant script font such as Edwardian Script. An easy-to-read font such as Arial or Helvetica, however, should be used for most of the text on a Web page.

- **Unity** refers to the way all the elements (and pages) of a site combine to give the impression that they are parts of a complete whole. For instance, choose a few colors and fonts to reflect the tone you want to convey, and use them consistently throughout your site.

(2) Color and background play an important rhetorical role in online composition.

Like the other elements of a Web document, color and background are rhetorical tools that can be used to achieve various visual effects. Designers recommend using no more than three main colors for a document, although you may use varying intensities, or shades, of a color (for example, light blue, dark blue, and medium blue) to connect related materials. Besides helping to organize your site, color can have other specific effects. Bright colors, such as red and yellow, are more noticeable and can be used on a Web page to emphasize a point or idea. In addition, some colors have associations you may wish to consider. For instance, reds can indicate danger or an emergency, whereas brown shades such as beige and tan suggest a formal atmosphere. Textual hyperlinks usually appear in a color different from that of the surrounding text on a Web page so that they are more visible to users. Select colors for textual hyperlinks that fit in with the overall color scheme of your document and help readers navigate between pages on your site.

Background, too, contributes to a successful Web site. If you do use a dark or patterned background, be sure that the text is bright enough to be readable on screen and will print clearly. You may need to change the color of the text or adjust the pattern of the background to make the page easier to read.

R

RESEARCH and DOCUMENTATION

The Internet gives students and scholars instant access to information from worldwide sources.

37 Finding Sources in Print, Online, and in the Field

Too often, the word *research* brings to mind laboratory experiments, archaeological digs, or hours spent in the library and not the ordinary research you yourself do every day as you decide which computer to buy (and then how to use that computer), how to prepare your taxes, which books to read for your courses, and even where to spend your vacation. To conduct useful research efficiently, you must first develop skills in accessing information. This chapter will help you

- use the rhetorical situation to frame your research (37a),
- find books (37b),
- find articles (37c),
- find Web-based sources (37d), and
- conduct field research (37e).

37a Research and the rhetorical situation

To make the most of the time you spend doing research, determine your rhetorical situation early in the research process. By understanding your exigence, audience, and purpose, you can gather relevant sources efficiently.

(1) Identifying an exigence can help you form a research question.

The starting point for any writing project is your exigence—the issue or problem that has prompted you to write (31b).

For research assignments, the exigence also prompts you to find more information before you write. Once you are sure of the exigence, craft a question to guide your research.

Research questions often arise when you try to relate what you are studying to your own experience. For instance, you may start wondering about voting regulations and procedures while reading about past elections for a history class and at the same time noticing the number of news stories about the role technology plays in elections or the unfair practices reported in some states. Such observations may prompt you to find more information. Each observation, however, may give rise to a different question. Focusing on the influence of technology may prompt you to ask, "What are the possible consequences of having electronic ballots only?" If you focus on unfair voting practices instead, you may ask, "How do voting procedures differ from state to state?" Because you can ask a variety of research questions about any topic, choose the one that interests you the most and that allows you to fulfill your assignment.

To generate research questions, you may find it helpful to ask yourself about causes, consequences, processes, definitions, or values, as in the following examples.

Questions about causes

What are the causes of low achievement in our schools?

What causes power outages in large areas of the country?

Questions about consequences

What are the consequences of taking antidepressants for a long period of time?

How might stronger gun control laws affect the frequency of public shootings?

Questions about processes

How can music lovers prevent corporations from controlling the development of new music?

How are presidential campaigns funded?

Questions about definitions

How do you know if you are addicted to something?

What is the opportunity gap in the American educational system?

Questions about values

Should the Makah tribe be allowed to hunt gray whales?

Would the construction of wind farms be detrimental to the environment?

If you have trouble coming up with a research question, you may need a jump start. The following tips can help you.

TIPS FOR FINDING A RESEARCH QUESTION

- Can you remember an experience that you did not understand fully? What was it that you did not understand?
- What have you observed recently (on television, in the newspaper, on campus, or online) that piqued your curiosity? What were you curious about?
- What widely discussed local or national problem would you like to help solve?
- Is there anything (lifestyles, political views, fashion preferences) that you find unusual or intriguing and would like to explore?

Exercise 1

Each of the following subjects would need to be narrowed down for a research paper. To experiment with framing a research question, compose two questions about each subject that could be answered in a ten-page paper (refer to the list on pages 512–513 for examples of questions).

1. literacy
2. the job market
3. gender differences
4. globalization
5. No Child Left Behind Act
6. health care

(2) Research can help you address your audience and achieve a specific purpose.

Your audience and your purpose are interconnected. In general terms, your purpose is to have an impact on your audience; in more specific terms, your purpose may be to entertain your readers, to inform them, to explain something to them, or to persuade them to do or think something. Research can help you achieve any of these goals.

A research paper often has one of the following rhetorical purposes.

- *To inform an audience.* The researcher reports current thinking on a specific topic, including opposing views, without analyzing them or siding with a particular position.
- *To analyze and synthesize information and then offer possible solutions.* The researcher analyzes a topic and synthesizes the available information about it, looking for points of agreement and disagreement and for gaps in coverage. After presenting the analysis and synthesis, the researcher sometimes offers possible ways to address any problems found.
- *To convince or issue an invitation to an audience.* The researcher states a position and backs it up with data, statistics, testimony, corroborating texts or events, or supporting arguments. The researcher's purpose is to persuade or invite readers to take the same position.

A researcher presenting results from an original experiment or study must often achieve all of these purposes. In the introduction of a lab report, for example, the researcher analyzes and synthesizes previous work done on the same topic and locates a research niche—an area needing further study. The researcher then attempts to convince the readers that his or her current study will help address the need for more research. The body of the report is informative, describing the materials used, explaining the procedures followed, and presenting the results. In the conclusion, the researcher may try, based on the results of the experiment or study, to persuade the audience to take some action (for example, give up smoking, eat fewer carbohydrates, or fund future research).

(3) The sources you use may be primary, secondary, or both.

Experienced researchers usually consult both primary and secondary sources. **Primary sources** for researching topics in the humanities are generally documents such as archived letters, records, and papers, as well as literary, autobiographical, and philosophical texts. In the social sciences, primary sources can be field observations, case histories, and

Primary sources, such as a report from an archeological dig, are useful for many research projects.

survey data. In the natural sciences, primary sources are generally empirical, including field observations, measurements, or discoveries and experimental results.

Secondary sources are commentaries on primary sources. For example, a review of a new novel is a secondary source, as is a discussion of adolescence based on survey data. Thinking about the rhetorical situations that underlie the sources you consider will help you locate those most useful to you, read them with a critical eye, and incorporate them into your paper appropriately.

37b Finding books

Three types of books are commonly used in the research process. **Scholarly books** are written by experts to advance knowledge of a certain subject. Most include original research. Before being published, these books are reviewed by scholars in the same field as the author(s). **Trade books** may also be written by experts or scholars, though they may be authored by journalists or freelance writers instead. But the audience and purpose of trade books differ from those of scholarly books. Rather than addressing other scholars, authors of trade books write to inform a general audience of research that has been done by others. **Reference books** such as encyclopedias and dictionaries provide factual information. These secondary sources contain short articles or entries written and reviewed by experts in the field. Their audience includes both veteran scholars and those new to a field of study.

(1) An online catalog helps you locate books.

The easiest way to find books related to your research question is to consult your library's online catalog, doing either keyword searches or subject searches. To perform a **keyword search,** choose a word or phrase that you think might be found in the title of a book or in notes in the catalog's records. The keyword search page in fig. 37.1 provides options for specifying a language, a location in the library, a type of book (or type of material other than a book, such as a brochure or government document), the way the results should be organized, the publisher, and the date of publication. The keyword search page in fig. 37.1 also provides some recommendations for entering words. By using a word or part of a word followed by asterisks, you can find all sources that include that root, even when suffixes have been added. For example, if you entered *environment***, you would find not only sources with *environment* in the title, subject headings, and content notes, but also sources with *environments, environmental,* or *environmentalist* in those locations. This search technique is called **truncation.**

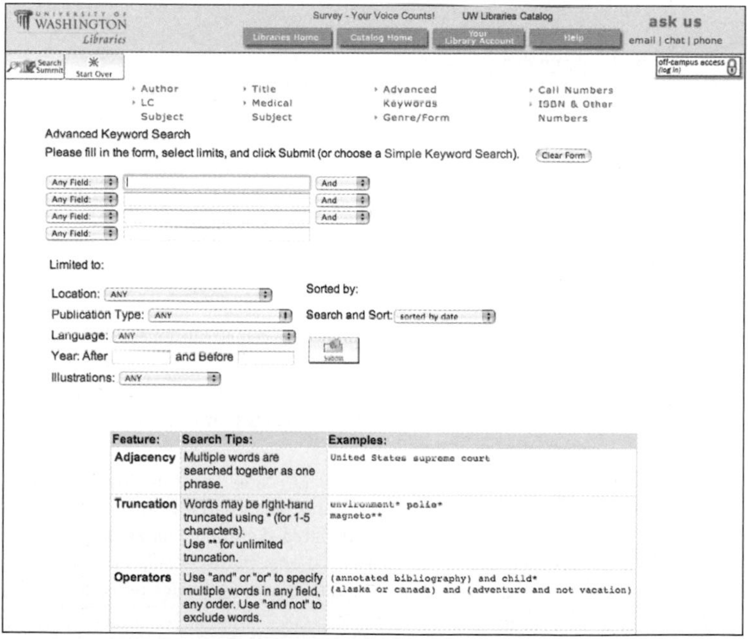

Fig. 37.1. Keyword search page from a university library's Web site.

You can also enter multiple keywords in search boxes by using **logical,** or **Boolean, operators** such as *and, or, not,* and *near,* words that narrow or broaden a search. They are used in electronic searches for books and for other documents such as articles and government brochures.

Although you will probably begin your research by using keyword searches, you may employ **subject searches** as well. To perform a successful subject search, you will have to enter words that correspond to the subject categories established by the Library of Congress. The best strategy for performing this type of search is to enter words familiar to you. Author searches and title searches can also be useful when you already have a particular author or title in mind.

LOGICAL OPERATORS

The words *and, or, not,* and *near* are the most common logical operators. However, online catalogs and periodical databases have various instructions for using them. If you have trouble following the guidelines presented here, check the instructions for the particular search box you are using.

and   narrows a search (Entering "genetically modified **and** food" returns only those records that contain both keywords.)

or   broadens a search (Entering "genetically modified **or** food" finds all records that contain information about either keyword.)

not   excludes specific items (Entering "genetically modified **and** food **not** humans" excludes any records that mention genetic modification of human beings.)

near   finds records in which the two keywords occur in close proximity, within a preset number of words, and excludes those in which the keywords are widely separated (Entering "genetically modified **near** vegetables" lists only those records in which references to *genetically modified* and *vegetables* occur in close proximity.)

Once you find the online catalog record for a book you would like to use, write down its **call number.** This number appears on the book itself and indicates where the book is shelved. The online record will reveal the status of the book, letting you know whether it is currently checked out or has been moved to a special collection.

(2) Specialized reference books are listed in your library's online catalog.

A specialized encyclopedia or dictionary can often provide background information on people, events, and concepts related to the topic you are researching. To find such sources using an online search page, enter the type of reference book and one or two keywords identifying your topic. For example, entering "encyclopedia of alcoholism" resulted in the following list of titles:

Encyclopedia of Drugs, Alcohol, and Addictive Behavior
Encyclopedia of Drugs and Alcohol
The Encyclopedia of Alcoholism

USEFUL REFERENCE BOOKS

For a detailed list of reference books and a short description of each, consult *Guide to Reference Books* by Robert Balay and *American Reference Books Annual* (*ARBA*). A few widely used reference books are listed here.

Specialized Dictionaries and Encyclopedias

- *Dictionary of American History*
- *Dictionary of Art*
- *Encyclopedia of Bioethics*
- *Encyclopedia of Higher Education*
- *Encyclopedia of Psychology*

(Continued on page 520)

(*Continued from page 519*)

Collections of Biographies

- *American National Biography*
- *Dictionary of Scientific Biography*
- *Notable American Women*
- *Who's Who in America*

(3) You may need to consult books not listed in your library's online catalog.

If you cannot find a particular book in your library, you have several options. Frequently, libraries have links to the catalogs of other libraries, which you can use to order the book you need through your library's interlibrary loan service. In addition, your library may have the database WorldCat, which locates books as well as images, sound recordings, and other materials. You may also access reference, fiction, and nonfiction books at **www.Bartleby.com**.

Exercise 2

Choose a research question, perhaps one you composed in exercise 1. Find the titles of a scholarly book, a trade book, and a reference book related to your choice.

37c Finding articles

Articles can be found in various **periodicals** (publications that appear at regular intervals), which offer information that is often more recent than that found in books. **Scholarly journals** contain reports of original research written by experts for an

academic audience. **Professional,** or **trade, magazines** feature
articles written by staff writers or industry specialists. Written for members of a particular trade, these articles address
on-the-job concerns. **Popular magazines** and **newspapers**
are generally written by staff writers. These periodicals carry a
combination of news stories that attempt to be objective and
essays that reflect the opinions of editors or guest contributors.
The following are examples of the various types of periodicals:

Scholarly journals: *The Journal of Developmental Psychology,
The Journal of Business Communication*

Trade magazines: *Farm Journal, Automotive Weekly*

Magazines (news): *Time, Newsweek*

Magazines (public affairs): *The New Yorker, National Review*

Magazines (special interest): *National Geographic, Discover*

Newspapers: *The New York Times, The Washington Post*

(1) An electronic database can help you find articles.
Your library's online catalog lists the titles of periodicals; however, it does not provide the titles of individual articles within
these periodicals. The best strategy for finding print articles is
to use an **electronic database,** which is a collection of articles
compiled by a company that indexes them according to author, title, date, keywords, and other features. The electronic
databases available in libraries are sometimes called **subscription databases, licensed databases,** or **aggregated databases.**
Similar to an online catalog, an electronic database allows
you to search for sources by author, title, keyword, and so on.
However, such databases focus on specific subject areas.

A database search will generally yield an **abstract,** a short
summary of an article. By scanning the abstract, you can
determine whether to locate the complete text of the article,
which can often be downloaded and printed. You can access
your library's databases by using its computers or, if you have a
password, by using an Internet link from a remote computer.

College libraries subscribe to a wide variety of database services, but the following are the most common:

ERIC: Articles related to education

JSTOR: Articles from journals in the arts, humanities, ecology, and social sciences

PsycINFO: Articles related to psychology

You may be able to access the search boxes for databases directly, or you may have to access databases through the search boxes of a vendor such as OCLC, InfoTrac, LexisNexis, or EBSCO. Your library's Web site probably offers a lengthy list of databases accessible by name, by subject, and so on (see the Databases link near the top of the screen in fig. 37.2). To use the list, you can choose a database according to name, description, category, type, or database vendor (see the box at the left of the screen in fig. 37.2).

If you were using this list of databases to research the relationship between alumni contributions and campus naming opportunities, as Anna Seitz did for her paper (35j), you could start with one of the following databases: ProQuest (Multiple

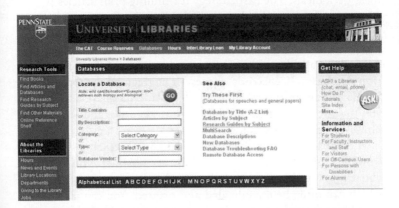

Fig. 37.2. Example of an online database access page from a university library.

Databases), Penn State University Libraries Web site, or Standard & Poor's NetAdvantage. To research the status of genetically modified foods in the United States, as Marianna Suslin did for her paper (**40c**), you could select Agropedia (agriculture encyclopedias), Consumer Health, or Engineered Materials. To research tattooing trends, as Rachel L. Pinter and Sarah M. Cronin did for their paper (**41c**), you could select PsycARTICLES or Social Sciences Citation Index.

TIPS FOR CONDUCTING A SEARCH FOR PERIODICAL LITERATURE

- Identify keywords that clearly represent the topic.
- Determine the databases you want to search.
- Perform your search, using logical operators (**37b(1)**).
- Refine your search strategy if the first search returns too many, too few, or (worse) irrelevant citations.
- Download and print the relevant articles.

(2) Print indexes provide essential information not found in electronic databases.

Before computers were widely used, researchers relied on **print indexes.** These bound volumes still provide essential backup when computers are out of service as well as access to older articles that may not be included in electronic databases. Some of the most useful print indexes, with their dates of beginning publication, are as follows:

Applied Science and Technology Index. 1958– .

Art Index. 1929– .

Biological and Agricultural Index. 1946– .

Business Periodicals Index. 1958– .

Cumulative Index to Nursing and Allied Health Literature (CINAHL). 1982– .

General Science Index. 1978– .

Humanities Index. 1974– .

Index to Legal Periodicals. 1908– .

Music Index. 1949– .

Philosopher's Index. 1967– .

Public Affairs Information Service (PAIS) Bulletin. 1915– .

Social Sciences Index. 1974– .

When they publish electronic versions of their indexes, some publishers change the title: *Current Index to Journals in Education* (*CIJE*) and *Resources in Education* (*RIE*) are the bound volumes for research in education, and ERIC is the electronic version. Consult the front of any bound volume for a key to the abbreviations used in individual entries.

(3) InfoTrac College Edition provides easy access to articles.
With InfoTrac College Edition and a passcode, you can conveniently search for articles with the Web browser on your own computer. You do not have to be networked to your library's Web site. InfoTrac College Edition indexes articles in over 3,800 journals and magazines and provides the full text of these articles. The InfoTrac screens in figs. 37.3 and 37.4 illustrate part of the research Marianna Suslin conducted for her paper (40c). Clicking in the box labeled "Mark" next to the article about labeling genetically modified foods, shown in fig. 37.3, and then clicking on "text and full content retrieval choices" (not shown in fig. 37.3) brought up the complete article, whose first page appears in fig. 37.4.

Exercise 3

Choose a research question, perhaps one from exercise 1. Find the titles of a scholarly article, a magazine article, and a newspaper article related to your choice.

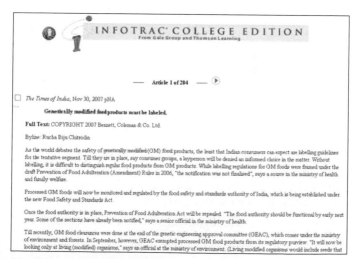

INFOTRAC° COLLEGE EDITION
From Gale Group and Thomson Learning

Keyword search (in title, citation, abstract): genetically modified food

——————— Citations 1 to 20 (of 284) ——————— ▶ ▶|

☐ Mark all items on this page

☐ 📄 **Genetically modified food products must be labeled.**
   The Times of India Nov 30, 2007 pNA (438 words)

☐ 📄 **Fourteen Global Experts Comment on the Safety and Use of Genetically Modified Food Crops; Online Video Captures Support for Contributions to the Environment and Third-World Farmers.**
   Internet Wire Nov 5, 2007 pNA (817 words)

☐ 📄 **Fourteen Global Experts Comment on the Safety and Use of Genetically Modified Food Crops.**
   PR Newswire Nov 5, 2007 pNA (827 words)

☐ 📄 **EU set to approve GM potato.(regulatory)(genetically modified food)(Brief article)** Kara Sissell.
   Chemical Week July 25, 2007 v169 i25 p35(1) (147 words)

Fig. 37.3. Example of an InfoTrac screen.

INFOTRAC° COLLEGE EDITION
From Gale Group and Thomson Learning

——— Article 1 of 284 ——— ▶

☐ *The Times of India, Nov 30, 2007 pNA*

   Genetically modified food products must be labeled.

   Full Text: COPYRIGHT 2007 Bennett, Coleman & Co. Ltd.

   Byline: Rucha Biju Chitrodia

   As the world debates the safety of genetically modified (GM) food products, the least that Indian consumers can expect are labelling guidelines for the tentative segment. Till they are in place, say consumer groups, a layperson will be denied an informed choice in the matter. Without labelling, it is difficult to distinguish regular food products from GM products. While labelling regulations for GM foods were framed under the draft Prevention of Food Adulteration (Amendment) Rules in 2006, "the notification was not finalised," says a source in the ministry of health and family welfare.

   Processed GM foods will now be monitored and regulated by the food safety and standards authority of India, which is being established under the new Food Safety and Standards Act.

   Once the food authority is in place, Prevention of Food Adulteration Act will be repealed. "The food authority should be functional by early next year. Some of the sections have already been notified," says a senior official in the ministry of health.

   Till recently, GM food clearances were done at the end of the genetic engineering approval committee (GEAC), which comes under the ministry of environment and forests. In September, however, GEAC exempted processed GM food products from its regulatory purview. "It will now be looking only at living (modified) organisms," says an official at the ministry of environment. (Living modified organisms would include seeds that

Fig. 37.4. First page of an article found through InfoTrac.

37d   Finding online sources

On the Internet, you can find not only text files but also audio and video files. Most researchers start their online research by using search engines, meta-search engines, or subject directories. **Search engines** are electronic indexes of words and terms from Web pages. To use them effectively, you should understand their features; consult the Help feature to learn how to perform both ordinary and advanced searches. As you do with online and database searches, you can specify which words or phrases to use, how close words should be, which words should be excluded, and whether any word should be truncated (**37b(1)**). The following are the addresses for some commonly used search engines:

Google	**www.google.com**
Infoseek	**infoseek.go.com**
Lycos	**www.lycos.com**
MSN Search	**search.msn.com**
WebCrawler	**www.webcrawler.com**

If you are looking solely for news stories, consider using the following:

Google News	**www.google.com/news**
TotalNEWS	**www.totalnews.com**

Meta-search engines are also useful research tools. *Meta-* means "transcending" or "more comprehensive." Meta-search engines check a number of search engines, including those previously listed. Try the following for starters:

Dogpile	**www.dogpile.com**
MetaCrawler	**www.metacrawler.com**

Unlike search engines, **subject directories** are collections of Web sources arranged topically. Yahoo! (**www.yahoo.com**) offers a subject directory under Web Directory on its home page; it includes categories such as "Arts," "Health," and "Education." Some researchers find subject directories easier to use because most of the irrelevant Web sites have been weeded out. The following are some other useful subject directories for academic and professional research:

Academic Info	**www.academicinfo.net**
The Internet Public Library	**www.ipl.org/ref**
Librarians' Index to the Internet	**lii.org**
The WWW Virtual Library	**vlib.org**

Although searching the Web is a popular research technique, it is not the only technique you should use. Search engines cover only the portion of the Internet that allows free access. You will not find library books or database materials through a Web search because library and database services are available only to paid subscribers (students fall into this category). When you search the Web, use more than one search engine because surprisingly little overlap occurs when different search engines are used to find information on the same topic.

(1) Knowing your location on the Web will help you keep track of your sources.

It is easy to get lost on the Web as you click from link to link. You can keep track of your location by looking at the Web address, or **URL (uniform resource locator),** at the top of the screen. Web addresses generally include the following information: server name, domain name, directory (and perhaps subdirectory) name, file name, and file type.

Because sites change and even disappear, scholarly organizations such as the Modern Language Association (MLA; see chapter **40**) require that bibliographic entries for Web sites include both the **access date** (the date on which the site was visited) and the **publication date** (the date when the site was published or last modified). When you print out material from the Web, the access date usually appears at the top or bottom of the printout. The publication date often appears on the site itself. Some sites do not show such a date, however, and printouts sometimes will not have an access date. Keeping a separate record of this information can help you when you need to verify information on a site or list it in a bibliography. If a site does not have a publication date, note that it is undated; doing so will establish that you did not accidentally omit a piece of information.

(2) The U.S. Government provides vast amounts of public information.

If you need information on particular federal laws, court cases, or population statistics, U.S. Government documents may be your best sources. You can find these documents by using online databases such as Congressional Universe, MARCIVE, LexisNexis Academic Universe, Census 2000, and STAT-USA. In addition, the following Web sites are helpful:

FirstGov	**www.firstgov.gov**
U.S. Government Printing Office	**www.gpoaccess.gov**
U.S. Courts	**www.uscourts.gov**
FedWorld	**www.fedworld.gov**

(3) Your rhetorical situation may call for the use of images.

If your rhetorical situation calls for the use of images, as did Marianna Suslin's (**40c**), the Internet offers you billions from which to choose. However, if an image you choose is copy-righted, you will need to contact the author, artist, or designer for permission to use it. Figure 37.5 is an example of an image with a caption and a credit line, which signifies that the image is used with permission. You do not need to obtain permis-sion to use public domain images or those that are cleared for reuse.

Fig. 37.5. **Genetically modified foods look like naturally produced foods.** (Photo courtesy of Alix/ Phanie/First Light, Canada.)

Many search engines allow you to search for im-ages. On the search pages for Google and AltaVista, you must first click on the Image button. For MetaCrawler, you must choose Images from the pull-down menu. Collections of specific images are available at the following Web sites:

Advertisements

Ad*Access	**scriptorium.lib.duke.edu/adaccess**
Adflip	**www.adflip.com**
Advertising World	**advertising.utexas.edu/world**

Art

The Artchive	**www.artchive.com**
The Web Gallery of Art	**www.wga.hu**

Clip art

The Icon Browser   **www.ibiblio.org/gio/
                                    iconbrowser**

Webclipz   **www.webclipz.com**

Photography

The New York Public Library   **digital.nypl.org/mmpco**
Picture Collection Online

Smithsonian Images   **smithsonianimages.com**

37e   Field research

Although much of your research will consist of reading, view-
ing, or listening to sources, you may also find it helpful to conduct **field research**—to gather information in a natural setting.
Interviews, discussions, questionnaires, and observations are
the most common methods for such research.

(1) Consider interviewing an expert.

After you have consulted some sources on your topic, you
may find that you still have questions that might best be answered by someone who has firsthand experience in the area
you are researching. Consider contacting a teacher, government official, business owner, or other person with the relevant
background to see whether it would be possible to schedule
an interview. Most people welcome the opportunity to discuss
their work, especially with a student who shows genuine interest. Because you will have done some reading on your topic
before your meeting, you will be prepared to conduct a well-
informed interview.

To arrange an interview, introduce yourself, briefly describe your project, and then explain your reasons for requesting the interview. Try to accommodate the person you hope to interview by asking him or her to suggest an interview date. If you intend to tape your interview, ask for permission ahead of time.

Start preparing your list of questions before the day of the interview, using a blend of open (or broad) questions and focused (or narrow) questions. Rather than posing a question that elicits just "yes" or "no," reformulate the question so that it begins with *why, when, what, who, where,* or *how.* By doing so, you give your interviewee a chance to elaborate. If the person you are speaking with says something you did not expect but would like to know more about, do not be afraid to ask questions that come to mind during the interview. Along with your list of questions, be sure to bring pen and paper so that you can take notes and a voice recorder if you will be recording the interview.

After the interview, review and expand your notes. If you recorded the interview, transcribe the relevant parts of the recording. The next step is to write extensively about the interview. Ask yourself what you found most important, most surprising, and most puzzling. You will find this writing especially worthwhile when you are able to use portions of it in your final paper.

(2) Consider participating in an online discussion group.

Less formal than an interview, a discussion with other people interested in your topic can also be useful. Online discussion groups, or forums, allow you to read messages posted to all the members of a group interested in a specific topic and to post messages or questions yourself. For instance, a writing teacher may belong to a specialized e-mail list, or **listserv,** that is operated by the Alliance for Computers and Writing and called ACW-L. Participants in this online forum discuss issues related to using computers to teach writing. Someone on the ACW-L list can send an e-mail message to the **listserv address,** which redistributes it to hundreds of other writing teachers around the world, and then receive replies from any of those teachers. You can find addresses of online discussion groups at **www.forumone.com** or **groups.google.com**.

(3) Consider using a questionnaire to gather information from a large number of people.

Whereas an interview elicits information from one person whose name you know, a questionnaire provides information from a number of anonymous people. To be effective, a questionnaire should be short and focused. If the list of questions is too long, people may not be willing to take the time to answer them all. If the questions are not focused on your research topic, you will find it difficult to integrate the results into your paper.

The first four types of questions in the following box are the easiest for respondents to answer. Open questions, which require much more time to answer, should be asked only when the other types of questions cannot elicit the information you want.

EXAMPLES OF TYPES OF SURVEY QUESTIONS

Questions that require a simple yes-or-no answer:

Do you commute to work in a car? (Circle one.)

Yes   No

Multiple-choice questions:

How many people do you commute with? (Circle one.)

0 1 2 3 4

Questions with answers on a checklist:

How long does it take you to commute to work? (Check one.)

___ 0–30 minutes ___ 60–90 minutes
___ 30–60 minutes ___ 90–120 minutes

Questions with a ranking scale:

If the car you drive or ride in is not working, which of the following types of transportation do you rely on? (Rank the choices from 1 for most frequently used to 4 for least frequently used.)

___ bus ___ shuttle van ___ subway ___ taxi

Open questions:

What feature of commuting do you find most irritating?

Begin your questionnaire with an introduction stating the purpose of the questionnaire, how the results will be used, and how many questions it contains or approximately how long it should take to complete. In the introduction, assure participants that their answers will remain confidential. To protect survey participants' privacy, colleges and universities have **institutional review boards (IRBs)** set up to review questionnaires. Before you distribute your questionnaire, check with the institutional review board on your campus to make certain that you have followed its guidelines.

Administering a questionnaire can sometimes be problematic. If you do decide to mail out a questionnaire, provide a self-addressed envelope and directions for returning it. It is a good idea to send out twice as many copies as you would like returned because the proportion of responses is generally low. Questionnaires can sometimes be distributed in college dormitories or in classes, but this procedure must be approved by school officials. Listservs can also be used to conduct surveys, especially if you remember that a survey limited to people who have a strong interest in a topic will not yield results representative of larger, more diverse groups.

Once the questionnaires have been completed and returned, tally the results for all but the open questions. To find patterns in the responses to the open questions, first read through them all, and try to create categories for the responses. For example, the open question "What feature of commuting do you find most irritating?" might elicit answers that fall into such categories as "length of time," "amount of traffic," or "bad weather conditions." By first creating categories, you will find it easier to tally the answers to the open questions.

CHECKLIST for Creating a Questionnaire

- Does each question relate directly to the purpose of the survey?
- Are the questions easy to understand?
- Are they designed to elicit short, specific responses?
- Are they designed to collect concrete data that can be analyzed easily?
- Have respondents been given enough space to write their answers to open questions?
- Do you have access to the group you want to survey?
- Have you asked a few classmates to "test-drive" your questionnaire?

38

Evaluating Print and Online Sources

As you find sources that seem to address your research question, you have to evaluate them to determine whether the information they contain is credible, relevant, and timely. This chapter will help you

- assess an author's credibility (**38a**),
- evaluate a publisher's credibility (**38b**),
- evaluate online sources (**38c**), and
- determine the relevance and timeliness of a source (**38d**).

38a Credibility of authors

Credible (or trustworthy) authors present facts accurately, support their opinions with evidence, connect their ideas reasonably, and demonstrate respect for any opposing views. To evaluate the credibility of the authors of your sources, find out what their credentials are, consider what world view informs their ideas, and note how other readers respond to their work.

(1) Credentials help establish an author's credibility.

When evaluating sources, consider whether the authors have credentials that are relevant to the topics they address. Although many works have only one author, some are composed collaboratively, so be sure to take into account the credentials of all of the authors responsible for the material in the sources you use.

Credentials include academic or professional training, publications, and experience. A college biology professor who specializes in genetics is likely to be credible when writing about genes, for example, but would not necessarily be considered a credible source of information on the foraging habits of black bears.

To find information about the credentials of an author whose work you want to use, look

- on the jacket of a book,
- on a separate page near the front or back of the book,
- in the preface of the book,
- in a note at the bottom of the first or last page of an article in print, or
- on a separate page of a periodical or a Web page devoted to providing background on contributors.

CHECKLIST for Assessing an Author's Credentials

- Does the author's education or profession relate to the subject of the work?
- With what institutions, organizations, or companies has the author been affiliated (38b)?
- What awards has the author won?
- What other works has the author produced?
- Do other experts speak of the author as an authority (38a(3))?

(2) An author's work reflects a specific world view.

An author's values and beliefs about the world constitute his or her **world view,** which underpins his or her research and publications. To determine what these values and beliefs are, consider the author's purpose and intended audience. For example, each of the following excerpts about malpractice lawsuits was written for a specific audience, with a specific purpose.

Published on a Web site for doctors, excerpt 1 focuses on the frivolous nature of some malpractice suits.

1   Just as quickly as medical knowledge and disease treatment options increase, so too do advances in the strategies lawyers use to bring medical malpractice suits.

Last year, an Ohio jury awarded $3.5 million to the family of a man who died of a heart attack.

His family claimed that the physician didn't do enough to help the man lose weight and stop smoking, given that physicians now know how smoking and excess weight contribute to heart disease and given the significant advances in treatment.

—TANYA ALBERT, "Lawyers Try New Tacks in Malpractice Suits"

Taken from an article in a university newspaper (in which no author was identified), excerpt 2 highlights the research of a professor at that university, whose findings downplay medical negligence and instead highlight poor doctor-patient rapport as the cause of malpractice suits.

2   A new study led by Wendy Levinson, Professor in Medicine, suggests that the most important reason a patient with a bad outcome decides to sue his or her doctor for malpractice is not medical negligence but how the doctor talks with the patient.

—"Bad Rapport with Patients to Blame for Most Malpractice Suits,"
University of Chicago Chronicle

In contrast to the first two excerpts, the next two are sympathetic toward patients. Appearing in a magazine for retired people, excerpt 3 stresses an action patients can take to protect themselves.

3   The more doctors you see, the more medical files you have. And the more scattered your medical records are, the higher your risk of drug errors, missed diagnoses, and other dangerous glitches.

　　　　The solution: Keep a set of your own records at home. It's easier than it sounds. And along with avoiding errors, you might even make yourself healthier.

> —KRISTEN STEWART, "The Paper Chase: Why You Need to
> Keep Your Own Medical Records"

In excerpt 4, taken from a news bulletin for retired people, the reporter questions whether doctors have the right to pass along the high costs of malpractice insurance to their patients.

4   A growing number of doctors fed up with skyrocketing malpractice insurance premiums are calling on their patients to bear part of the burden.

　　　　Some physicians are requiring patients to sign waivers promising not to sue for "frivolous" reasons or, in some cases, for any reason at all. Others are billing for telephone consultations, paperwork and other services that once were free.

　　　　Perhaps the most controversial—and possibly illegal—approach is charging user, or administrative, fees. Patients increasingly are protesting paying more—on top of their copayments, deductibles and premiums—for medical services already covered by their health plans.

> —CAROLE FLECK, "Doctors' Fees Try Their Patients"

As you read and use sources, keep in mind that they reflect the world views of the authors and often of the audience for whom they were written. By identifying these various values and beliefs, you can responsibly represent and report the information in your sources. When you find yourself referring to information that reveals economic, political, religious, or social biases, you should feel free to question or argue with the author.

CHECKLIST for Determining an Author's World View

- What is the author's educational and professional background?

- What are the author's and publisher's affiliations; that is, with what types of organizations do they align themselves?

- What is the editorial slant of the organization publishing the author's work? Where does it lie on the political spectrum from conservative to liberal?

- Can you detect any signs of bias on the part of the author or the publisher?

- Is the information purported to be factual? Objective? Personal?

- Who advertises in the source?

- To what types of Web sites do any links lead?

- How can you use the source? As fact? Opinion? Support? Authoritative testimony? Material to be refuted?

(3) Online sources, book reviews, and texts written by other authors can provide additional information about an author.

You can learn more about authors by searching the Internet for information about them. To locate information about authors on the Internet, use a general search engine such as Google or AltaVista or a specialized search engine such as the People search option offered by Lycos (**www.whowhere.lycos.com**). Either type of engine will locate sites containing background information on the author or bibliographical information about his or her other works.

Book reviews, both in print and online, often include information for determining whether an author is credible, even if not perfect. A work by a credible author may get some negative responses. Look for the main point of a review, and decide whether that main point amounts to a positive or negative response to the book as a whole. Dismiss from further consideration any writer whom more than one reviewer characterizes as ill-informed, careless with facts, biased, or dishonest in any way. Keep in mind, though, that few writers please all reviewers all the time, so you need to read reviews critically.

As you research a topic, you will find that writers often refer to the work of other writers. To gain insight into how an author influences the work of others, keep track of who is being discussed or cited by whom. If several well-known writers offer negative evaluations of an author's work or do not mention the work at all, that author's contribution is likely considered insignificant or unreliable. If, on the other hand, several writers praise or build on the work of the author you are evaluating, you can be confident in the credibility of your source.

Exercise 1

Choose a book you plan to use for your research paper. Locate at least two reviews of this book. Then, write a one-page report of what the reviews have in common and how they differ.

38b Credibility of publishers

When you are doing research, consider not only the credibility of authors but also the credibility of the media through which their work is made available to you. Some publishers hold authors accountable to higher standards than others do.

(1) Book publishers are either commercial or academic.

When evaluating books, you can usually assume that publishers associated with universities demand a high standard of scholarship. Although some university presses have better reputations than others, the works such publishers produce are generally considered trustworthy, having been reviewed by experts before publication. Books published by commercial (or trade) presses, in contrast, typically do not undergo the same type of review. Thus, to determine how a trade book has been received by others writing in the same area, you have to rely on book reviews (38a(3)).

(2) Periodicals are written for an academic audience or for the general public.

Periodicals are published daily, weekly, or monthly (37c). They include scholarly journals, magazines (trade, news, public affairs, and special interest), and newspapers. An article published in a scholarly journal is generally considered more credible than one published in a magazine because it has usually been both written and reviewed by an expert. Authors of these journal articles are expected to include both in-text citations and bibliographies so that other researchers can consult the sources used (chapters **40** and **41**).

Articles that appear in magazines and newspapers may be reliable but are usually written quickly and chosen for publication by someone on the periodical's staff—not by an expert in the field. Because magazines and newspapers often report research results that were initially published elsewhere, you should try to find the original source to ensure the accuracy of their reports. Locating that source is not always an easy task, especially since in-text citations and bibliographies are rarely provided in these periodicals. Your best bet for finding the original source is to search online using a search engine (**37d**).

When evaluating an article in a magazine or newspaper, also take into account the reputation of the publication itself, examining several issues in terms of the space devoted to various stories, the tone of the commentary on the editorial pages, and the extent to which staff members (as opposed to wire services) are responsible for stories.

38c Online sources

If you are evaluating a periodical source that you obtained online, you can follow the guidelines for print-based sources (**38a** and **38b**). But if you are evaluating a Web site, you also need to consider the nature of the site and its sponsor. Although many sites are created by individuals working on their own, many others are sponsored by colleges or universities, professional or nonprofit organizations, and commercial enterprises. The type of sponsor is typically indicated in the site's address (URL) by a suffix that represents the domain. Colleges and universities are indicated by the suffix **.edu**, government departments and agencies by **.gov**, professional and nonprofit organizations by **.org**, network sites by **.net**, and businesses by **.com**. As you access the various types of sites to evaluate their content, remember that every site is shaped to achieve a specific purpose and to address a specific audience.

Suppose, for example, you wanted to write a paper about how a corporate bankruptcy revealed serious irregularities in the practices of a major communications company. An education site could provide a scholarly analysis of the practices in question; a government site could contain data compiled by the Securities and Exchange Commission (SEC); an organization site could give you the viewpoint of an association of accountants; and a business site could convey information from the communications company in question. Each of these sites would offer different content, which would be shaped by the rhetorical situation as envisioned by each site's sponsor.

Exercise 2

Find Web sites that have three different kinds of sponsors but contain material relevant to a specific subject, such as global warming, saving energy, or disaster relief efforts. Explain the differences and similarities among the three sites you choose.

38d   Relevance and timeliness

A source is useful only when it is relevant to your research question. Given the ever-growing amount of information available on most topics, you should be prepared to put aside a source that will not help you answer your research question or achieve your rhetorical purpose.

As you conduct research, draft, and revise, you may reject some sources altogether and use only parts of others. Seldom will an entire book, article, or Web site be useful for a specific research paper. A book may have just a chapter or a section or two on your topic. The table of contents can lead you to these relevant chapters or sections, and the index can lead you to relevant pages. Web sites have hyperlinks or buttons that you can click on to locate relevant information. Once you find potentially useful material, read it with your research question and rhetorical purpose in mind.

Useful sources are also timely. You should always seek up-to-date information. However, if you are writing about a specific era in the past, you should also consult sources written during that period. To determine when a source was published, look for the date of publication. In books, it appears with other copyright information on the page following the title page (see page 592). Dates of periodicals appear on their covers and frequently on the top or bottom of pages throughout each issue (see page 588). The date on which a Web site was established or last updated frequently appears on the site, and the date on which you access it will usually appear on any hard copy you print out (see page 604). Do not confuse the access date with the publication date.

CHECKLIST for Establishing Relevancy and Timeliness

- Does the table of contents, index, or directory of the work include key words related to your research question?

- Does the abstract of a journal article contain information on your topic?

- If an abstract is not available, are any of the article's topic sentences relevant to your research question?

- Do the section heads of the source include words connected to your topic?

- On a Web site, are there hyperlinks or buttons that can lead you to relevant information?

- Is the work recent enough to provide up-to-date information?

- If you need a source from another time period, is the work from the right period?

39 Using Sources Effectively and Responsibly

To use sources effectively, you need to remember that you are a *writer,* not just a compiler of data. To use sources responsibly, you acknowledge others' ideas and words as you incorporate them into your paper. But even when you use sources responsibly, your voice remains the most important voice in the paper. This chapter will help you

- consider your rhetorical situation (**39a**),
- organize notes effectively (**39b**),
- compose a working bibliography or an annotated bibliography (**39c**),
- integrate sources (**39d**),
- avoid plagiarism (**39e**), and
- respond to sources (**39f**).

39a The rhetorical situation and the research paper

Like any other paper, a research paper should respond to an exigence with a purpose appropriate for a particular audience and context. It should not be a mere compilation of research findings or a list of works consulted. Rather, in a research paper, you discuss what others have discovered, creating a conversation in which you play an essential role: you orchestrate how your sources interact with one another and at the same time talk back to them.

By studying the following introductory paragraphs of a research article, you can see how the author, Timothy Quinn, chooses words, sentence types, organization strategies, and citation conventions according to his rhetorical situation. In the first paragraph, he alludes to his exigence: the increasing presence of coyotes in areas inhabited by people and the lack of a clear explanation for this presence. Because he states a problem with no easy solution, Quinn finds his own research niche. At the end of the second paragraph, Quinn states his purpose: to document coyotes' typical diet and assess changes in that diet caused by human population density and land use. Quinn shows his understanding of audience and context by citing other researchers' work according to the appropriate convention of providing the name(s) of author(s) and the year of publication.

Coyotes (*Canis latrans*) are becoming increasingly common in human-modified habitats throughout North America (Atkinson and Shackleton 1991, MacCracken 1982). One possible explanation for this trend is that human-dominated areas produce abundant food sources for coyotes. Coyotes living in urban habitats have relatively small home ranges (Atkinson and Shackleton 1991, Shargo 1988), which may indicate abundant food resources. However, little is known about the diet of coyotes in these areas. MacCracken's (1982) description of the annual diet of coyotes in residential habitats was based on a small number of scats ($n = 97$) collected during a single month. Atkinson and Shackleton (1991) described the diet of coyotes in an area that was mostly agricultural (>50% of the study area) and Shargo's (1988) description of urban coyote diet was based on 22 scats. Additionally, none of these studies looked at diet as a function of human density.

Coyotes may play an important role in human-modified landscapes. Soulé et al. (1988) suggested that coyotes may reduce the abundance of house cats (*Felis catus*) and other small mammalian carnivores that prey on songbirds and thus indirectly contribute to the maintenance of native avifauna. My objectives were to document the annual diet of coyotes in three types of urban habitat of western Washington and to qualitatively assess how coyote diets changed as a function of land use patterns and human density.

—TIMOTHY QUINN, "Coyote (*Canis latrans*) Food Habits and Three Urban Habitat Types of Western Washington"

As you work toward providing an appropriate response to your rhetorical situation, be sure to present yourself as thoughtful and informed. Whether your audience consists of a single instructor or some larger group, you must establish that you are a credible author (**38a**). By conducting research and citing sources, you demonstrate that you have

- educated yourself about your topic,
- drawn accurately on the work of others (including diverse points of view),
- understood what you have discovered,
- integrated research data into a paper that is clearly your own, and
- provided all the information readers will need to consult the sources you have used.

The rest of this chapter and chapters **40** and **41** will help you fulfill these responsibilities.

39b Organizing notes

Taking thorough and organized notes is critical when you are preparing to write a research paper in which you attribute specific words and ideas to others while taking credit for your own ideas. Some researchers are most comfortable taking notes in notebooks. Others like to write notes directly on pages they have photocopied or printed out from an online source. Still others write notes on index cards (also known as three-by-five cards) or type them into computer files—two methods that allow notes to be rearranged easily. Each method has advantages and disadvantages, and your choice should be guided by the requirements of your project and your own working style.

(1) Taking notes on photocopies and printouts

An easy way to take notes is to use photocopies of articles and excerpts from books or printouts of sources from the Web. On a printout or photocopy, you can mark quotable material while also jotting down your own ideas in the margins. The example in fig. 39.1 comes from the work Marianna Suslin did for her research paper on genetically modified foods (40c). This method reduces the risk of including inaccurate quotations in your paper, because you have eliminated the step of copying quotes exactly as they appear in the original source. Make sure to record the source on a photocopy if this information is not shown on the original page(s). Printouts from the Web almost always indicate the source and the date of access, but you should also note the date on which the site was posted or last updated (37d(1)).

(2) Organizing notes in computer files

You may find it efficient to use a computer for taking notes—recording them quickly and storing them safely. Then, later, you can easily copy and paste information into various files and ultimately into a draft of your paper. Given the ease of computer use, though, it is important to remember to identify which records are direct quotations (39d(2)), which are paraphrases (39d(3)), and which are your own thoughts. Always provide complete bibliographic information so that you will not have trouble finding the source later. The tips on page 551 can help you use your computer efficiently when taking and filing notes for a research paper.

Genetic tinkering is the process of adding a gene or genes (the transgene) to plant or animal DNA (the recipient genome) to confer a desirable trait, for example, inserting the genes of an arctic flounder into a tomato to give antifreeze properties, or inserting human genes into fish to increase growth rates.

Author defines "genetic engineering"; his use of the word "tinkering" reveals how he feels about the technology.

examples of genetic modification

But, as we are about to discover, this is a technology that no one wants, that no one asked for, and that no one but the biotech companies will benefit from. This is why the biotech lobby has such a vast, ruthless, and well-funded propaganda machine. If they can reinvent our food and slap a patent on it all, they have just created an unimaginably vast new market for themselves.

Author believes no one but big corporations will benefit from this technology.

And to try to convince a suspicious public, they have given us dozens of laudable reasons why the world will benefit from this tinkering. The companies who so enthusiastically produce millions of tons of pesticides every year are now telling us that GMOs will help reduce pesticide use. The companies who have so expertly polluted the world with millions of tons of toxic chemicals are now telling us that GM will help the environment. The companies who have so nonchalantly used child labor in developing countries, and exported dangerous pesticides that are banned in the developed countries to the developing countries, are now telling us that they really do care about people and that we must have GM to feed the world.

Author seeks to discredit biotech companies.

Rees, Andy. Genetically Modified Food: A Short Guide for the Confused. Ann Arbor: Pluto, 2006. 8.

Fig. 39.1. Photocopied source with notes.

TIPS ON USING A COMPUTER TO ORGANIZE NOTES

- Create a separate master folder (or directory) for the paper.
- Create folders within the master folder for your bibliography, notes, and portions of drafts.
- Keep all the notes for each source in a separate file.
- Use a distinctive font or a different color to distinguish your own thoughts from the ideas of others.
- Place direct quotations in quotation marks.
- When taking notes, record exactly where the information came from.
- When you discover new sources, add them to your working bibliography (39c).
- Consider using the Annotation or Comment feature of your word-processing program to make notes on documents you have downloaded.

(3) Arranging notes on note cards

Taking notes on index cards can be useful if you are working in a library without a laptop or if you prefer handwritten notes that you can rearrange as your research proceeds. Each index card should show the author's name (and a short title if the bibliography contains more than one work by that author), the exact page number(s) from which the information is drawn, and a brief comment on how you intend to use the information or a reflection on what you think about it. By putting a heading of two or three key words at the top of each card, you can easily arrange your cards as you prepare to draft your paper.

Whatever method you use to create your notes, consider the points in the following list.

TIPS FOR TAKING NOTES

- Identify the source for every note.
- Put the full bibliographic citation on the first page of every photocopy.
- Copy verbatim any useful passage you think you may quote. Put quotation marks around quoted words. In computer files, you can also use different fonts or different colors to identify quoted text.
- When a source has stimulated your thinking, identify both the source and your own idea based on that source.

39c Working bibliography and annotated bibliography

A **working bibliography,** or preliminary bibliography, contains information (titles, authors' names, publication dates, and so on) about the materials you think you might use. Creating a working bibliography can help you evaluate the quality of your research. If you find that your most recent source is five years old, for example, or that you have relied exclusively on information from magazines or Web sites, you may need to find some other sources.

Some researchers find it convenient to put each bibliographic entry on a separate index card; this practice makes it easy to add or drop a card and to arrange the list alphabetically without recopying it. Others prefer to use a computer, which can sort and alphabetize automatically, making it easier to move material directly to the final draft.

It is also a good idea to follow the bibliographical format you have been instructed to use in your paper right from the start, such as that of the Modern Language Association (MLA;

see chapter **40**) or that of the American Psychological Association (APA; see chapter **41**). The examples given in the rest of this chapter follow the MLA's bibliographical and documentation style.

If you are asked to prepare an **annotated bibliography,** you should list all your sources alphabetically according to the last name of the author. Then, at the end of each entry, summarize the content of the source in one or two sentences.

Zimmer, Carl. *Soul Made Flesh: The Discovery of the Brain—and How It*

Changed the World. New York: Free, 2004. Print. This book is a historical

account of how knowledge of the brain developed and influenced

ideas about the soul. It covers a span of time and place, beginning four

thousand years ago in ancient Egypt and ending in Oxford, England, in the

seventeenth century.

39d Integrating sources

You can integrate sources into your own writing in a number of ways: quoting exact words, paraphrasing sentences, and summarizing longer pieces of text or even entire texts. Whenever you borrow others' ideas in these ways, be careful to integrate the material—properly cited—into your own sentences and paragraphs. Once you have represented source material accurately and responsibly, you will be ready to respond to it.

(1) Writers introduce the sources they use.
When you borrow textual material, introduce it to readers by establishing the source, usually an author's name. You may also need to include additional information about the author, especially if the author's name is unfamiliar to your audience.

For example, in a paper on medications given to children, the following statement becomes more credible if the audience is given the added information about Jerome Groopman's background.

professor of medicine at Harvard University,

According to Jerome Groopman, ^ "Pediatricians sometimes adopt extraordinary measures to insure that their patients are not harmed by treatments that have not been adequately studied in children" (33).

Phrases such as *According to Jerome Groopman* and *from the author's perspective* are called **attributive tags** because they attribute, or ascribe, information to a source. Most attributive tags in academic writing consist of the name of an author (or a related noun or pronoun) and a verb in order to report what that author has said, written, thought, or felt. Verbs commonly found in attributive tags are listed below. For a list of the types of complements that follow such verbs, see **23c(3)**.

VERBS USED IN ATTRIBUTIVE TAGS

admit	disagree	observe
advise	discuss	point out
argue	emphasize	reject
believe	explain	reply
claim	find	state
concede	imply	suggest
conclude	insist	think
deny	note	

If you decide to integrate graphics as source material, you must label them as figures and assign them arabic numbers. You can then refer to them within the text of your paper in a parenthetical

Fig. 39.2. Western coral snake.

comment, as in this example: "The red and black bands of the Western coral snake are bordered by narrower bands of yellow or white (fig. 39.2)." You may also want to include a title or caption with the figure number.

(2) Direct quotations draw attention to key passages.

Include a direct quotation in a paper only if

- you want to retain the beauty or clarity of someone's words,
- you need to reveal how the reasoning in a specific passage is flawed or insightful, or
- you plan to discuss the implications of the quoted material.

Keep quotations as short as possible, and make them an integral part of your text.

Quote *accurately.* Any quotation of another person's words should be placed in quotation marks or, if longer than four lines, set off as an indented block (**40a(2)**). If you need to clarify a quotation by changing it in any way, place square brackets around the added or changed words.

"In this role, he [Robin Williams] successfully conveys a diverse range of emotion."

If you want to omit part of a quotation, replace the deleted words with ellipsis points (**17h**).

"Overseas markets . . . are critical to the financial success of Hollywood films."

When modifying a quotation, be sure not to alter its essential meaning.

CHECKLIST for Using Direct Quotations

- Have you copied all the words and punctuation accurately?
- Have you attributed the quotation to a specific source?
- Have you used square brackets around anything you added to or changed in a direct quotation (**17g**)?
- Have you used ellipsis points to indicate anything you omitted (**17h**)?
- Have you used quotations sparingly? If not, consider paraphrasing or summarizing the information instead.

---

(3) Paraphrases convey another person's ideas in different words.

A **paraphrase** is a restatement of someone else's ideas in approximately the same number of words. Paraphrasing allows you to demonstrate that you have understood what you have read; it also enables you to help your audience understand it. Paraphrase when you want to

- clarify difficult material by using simpler language,
- use another writer's idea but not his or her exact words,
- create a consistent tone (**34a(3)**) for your paper as a whole, or
- interact with a point that your source has made.

Your paraphrase should be almost entirely in your own words and should accurately convey the content of the original passage.

(a) Use your own words and sentence structure when paraphrasing.

As you compare the source below with the paraphrases that follow, note the similarities and differences in both sentence structure and word choice.

Source

Zimmer, Carl. *Soul Made Flesh: The Discovery of the Brain—and How It Changed the World*. New York: Free, 2004. 7. Print.

> The maps that neuroscientists make today are like the early charts of the New World with grotesque coastlines and blank interiors. And what little we do know about how the brain works raises disturbing questions about the nature of our selves.

Inadequate paraphrase

The maps used by neuroscientists today resemble the rough maps of the New World. Because we know so little about how the brain works, we must ask questions about the nature of our selves (Zimmer 7).

If you simply change a few words in a passage, you have not adequately restated it. You may be committing plagiarism (39e) if the wording of your version follows the original too closely, even if you provide a page reference for the source.

Adequate paraphrase

Carl Zimmer compares today's maps of the brain to the rough maps made of the New World. He believes that the lack of knowledge about the workings of the brain makes us ask serious questions about our nature (7).

In the second paraphrase, both vocabulary and sentence structure differ from those in the original. This paraphrase also includes an attributive tag ("Carl Zimmer compares").

(b) Maintain accuracy.

Any paraphrase must accurately maintain the sense of the original. If you unintentionally misrepresent the original because you did not understand it, you are being *inaccurate.* If you deliberately change the gist of what a source says, you are being *unethical.* Compare the original statement below with the paraphrases.

Source

Hanlon, Michael. "Climate Apocalypse When?" *New Scientist*
17 Nov. 2007: 20. Print.

> Disastrous images of climate change are everywhere. An alarming graphic recently appeared in the UK media showing the British Isles reduced to a scattered archipelago by a 60-metre rise in sea level. Evocative scenes of melting glaciers, all-at-sea polar bears and forest fires are routinely attributed to global warming. And of course Al Gore has just won a Nobel prize for his doomsday flick *An Inconvenient Truth,* starring hurricane Katrina.
> . . . There is a big problem here, though it isn't with the science. The evidence that human activities are dramatically modifying the planet's climate is now overwhelming—even to a former paid-up sceptic like me. The consensus is established, the fear real and justified. The problem is that the effects of climate change mostly haven't happened yet, and for journalists and their editors that presents a dilemma. Talking about what the weather may be like in the 2100s, never mind the 3100s, doesn't sell.

Inaccurate or unethical paraphrase

Evocative scenes of melting glaciers, landless polar bears, and forest fires are attributed to global warming in Al Gore's *An Inconvenient Truth.* The trouble is that Gore cannot predict what will happen (Hanlon 20).

Accurate paraphrase

According to Michael Hanlon, the disastrous images of climate change that permeate the media are distorting our understanding of what is actually happening now globally and what might happen in the future (20).

Although both paraphrases include a reference to an author and a page number, the first focuses misleadingly on Al Gore, whereas the second paraphrase notes the much broader problem, which can be blamed on the media's focus on selling a story.

(4) Summaries convey ideas efficiently.

When you summarize, you condense the main point(s) of your source. Although a summary omits much of the detail used by the writer of the original source, it accurately reflects the essence of that work. In most cases, then, a **summary** reports a writer's main idea (33c) and the most important support given for it.

Whereas the length of a paraphrase (39d(3)) is usually close to that of the original material, a summary conveys the gist of the author's ideas, in fewer words. Summaries can include short quotations of key phrases or ideas, but you must always enclose another writer's exact words in quotation marks when you blend them with your own.

Source

Marshall, Joseph M., III. "Tasunke Witko (His Crazy Horse)." *Native Peoples* Jan.-Feb. 2007: 76-79. Print.

The world knows him as Crazy Horse, which is not a precise translation of his name from Lakota to English. *Tasunke Witko* means "his crazy horse," or "his horse is crazy." This slight mistranslation of his name seems to reflect the fact that Crazy

Horse the man is obscured by Crazy Horse the legendary warrior. He was both, but the fascination with the legendary warrior hides the reality of the man. And it was as the man, shaped by his family, community and culture—as well as the events in his life—that he became legend.

Summary

The Lakota warrior English speakers refer to as "Crazy Horse" was actually called "his crazy horse." That mistranslation may distort what Crazy Horse was like as a man.

This example reduces five sentences to two, retaining the key idea but eliminating the source author's analysis and speculation. A writer who believes that the audience needs to read such analysis might decide to paraphrase the passage instead.

Exercise 1

Find a well-developed paragraph in one of your recent reading assignments. Rewrite it in your own words, varying the sentence structure of the original. Make your paraphrase approximately the same length as the original. Next, write a one-sentence summary of the same paragraph.

39e Avoiding plagiarism

To use the work of other writers responsibly, you need to ensure that your audience can distinguish between those writers' ideas and your own contributions and that you give credit for all information you gather through research. It is not necessary, however, to credit information that is **common knowledge,** which includes well-known facts such as the following: "The *Titanic* hit an iceberg and sank on its maiden voyage." This event has been the subject of many books and movies, so some information about it has become common knowledge.

If, however, you are writing a research paper about the *Titanic* and wish to include the ship's specifications, such as its overall length and gross tonnage, you will be providing *un*-common knowledge, which must be documented. After you have read a good deal about a given subject, you will be able to distinguish between common knowledge and the distinctive ideas or interpretations of specific writers. If you have been scrupulous about recording your own thoughts as you took notes, you should have little difficulty distinguishing between what you knew to begin with and what you learned through your research.

Taking even part of someone else's work and presenting it as your own leaves you open to criminal charges. In the film, video, music, and software businesses, this sort of theft is called **piracy.** In publishing and education, it is called **plagiarism.** Whatever it is called, it is illegal, and penalties range from failing a paper or course to being expelled from school. Never compromise your integrity or risk your future by submitting someone else's work as your own.

TECH SAVVY

Although it is fairly easy to copy material from a Web site or even to purchase a paper on the Web, it is just as easy for a teacher or employer to locate that same material and determine that it has been plagiarized. Many teachers routinely use Internet search tools such as Google or special services such as Turnitin (available from Wadsworth, the publisher of this handbook) if they suspect that a student has submitted a paper that was plagiarized.

To review how to draw responsibly on the words and ideas of others, consider the following examples.

Source

McConnell, Patricia B. *The Other End of the Leash*. New York: Ballantine, 2002. 142. Print.

> Status in male chimpanzees is particularly interesting because it is based on the formation of coalitions, in which no single male can achieve and maintain power without a cadre of supporting males.

Paraphrase with documentation

Patricia B. McConnell, an authority on animal training, notes that by forming alliances with other male chimpanzees, a specific male can enjoy status and power (142).

This example includes not only the original author's name but also a parenthetical citation, which marks the end of the paraphrase and provides the page number where the source can be found.

Quotation with documentation

Patricia B. McConnell, an authority on animal training, argues that male chimpanzees achieve status "based on the formation of coalitions, in which no single male can achieve and maintain power without a cadre of supporting males" (142).

Quotation marks show where the copied words begin and end; the number in parentheses indicates the exact page on which those words appear. Again, the author is identified in the sentence, although her name could have been omitted at the beginning of the sentence and noted within the parenthetical reference instead:

An authority on animal training argues that male chimpanzees achieve status "based on the formation of coalitions, in which no single male can achieve and maintain power without a cadre of supporting males" (McConnell 142).

If, after referring to the following checklist, you cannot decide whether you need to cite a source, the safest policy is to cite it.

CHECKLIST of Sources That Should Be Cited

- Writings, both published and unpublished
- Opinions and judgments that are not your own
- Statistics and other facts that are not widely known
- Images and graphics, such as works of art, drawings, charts and graphs, tables, photographs, maps, and advertisements
- Personal communications, such as interviews, letters, and e-mail messages
- Public electronic communication, including television and radio broadcasts, motion pictures and videos, sound recordings, Web sites, and online discussion groups or forums

---

39f Responding to sources

When incorporating sources, not only will you summarize, paraphrase, quote, and document them, you will often respond to them as well. To prepare for interacting with your sources, you may find it useful to make notes in the margins of whatever you are reading. Next to relevant passages, jot down your agreement, disagreement, surprise, questions, and so on (32c).

As you read and work with published research, you will want to know whether facts are accurate or erroneous, whether logic is strong or weak, whether the organization is well planned or ill conceived, and whether conclusions are valid or doubtful. You will also evaluate the strengths and weaknesses of sources in order to motivate your own line of research. For example, you may try to show that previous research is insufficient in some way so that you can establish an exigence for your own research. Overall, consider responding to your sources by examining their timeliness, coverage, reliability, and reasoning.

(1) Considering the currency of sources

Using up-to-date sources is crucial when researching most topics. When you consider the currency of a source, start by looking for the date of its publication. Then, examine any data reported. Even a source published in the same year that you are doing research may include data that are several years old and thus possibly irrelevant. In the following example, the writer questions the usefulness of an out-of-date statistic mentioned in a source:

According to Jenkins, only 50% of all public schools have Web pages (23); however, this statistic is taken from a report published in 1997. A more recent count would likely yield a much higher percentage.

(2) Noting the thoroughness of research

Coverage refers to the comprehensiveness of research. The more comprehensive a study is, the more convincing are its findings. Similarly, the more examples an author provides, the more compelling are his or her conclusions. Claims that are based on only one instance are often criticized for being merely anecdotal or otherwise unsubstantiated. The writer of the following response suggests that the author of the source in question may have based his conclusion on too little information:

Johnson concludes that middle-school students are expected to complete an inordinate amount of homework given their age, but he bases his conclusion on research conducted in only three schools. To be more convincing, Johnson needs to conduct research in more schools, preferably located in different parts of the country.

(3) Checking the reliability of findings

Research, especially when derived from experiments or surveys, must be reliable. Experimental results are considered **reliable** if they can be reproduced by researchers using a similar methodology. Results that cannot be replicated in this way are not reliable because they are supported by only one experiment.

Reliability is also a requirement for reported data. Researchers are expected to report their findings accurately and honestly, not distorting them to support their own beliefs or claiming others' ideas as their own. To ensure the reliability of their work, researchers must also report all relevant information, not intentionally excluding any that weakens their conclusions. When studies of the same phenomenon give rise to disputes, researchers should discuss conflicting results or interpretations. The writer of the following response focuses on the problematic nature of her source's methodology:

Jamieson concludes from her experiment that a low-carbohydrate diet can be dangerous for athletes, but her methodology suffers from lack of detail. No one would be able to confirm her experimental findings without knowing exactly what and how much the athletes consumed.

(4) Examining the author's reasoning

When a source is logical, its reasoning is sound. Lapses in logic may be the result of using evidence that does not directly support a claim, appealing to the reader's emotions, or encouraging belief in false authority. Faulty reasoning is often discussed in terms of rhetorical fallacies. A list of these fallacies, along with examples, can be found on pages 478–481.

40 MLA Documentation

The Modern Language Association (MLA) provides guidelines
for documenting research in literature, languages, linguistics,
and composition studies. The *MLA Handbook for Writers of
Research Papers* is published specifically for undergraduates.
This chapter includes

- guidelines for citing sources within the text of a paper (40a),
- guidelines for documenting sources in the works-cited list
  (40b), and
- a sample student paper (40c).

40a MLA-style in-text citations

(1) In-text citations indicate that a writer has drawn material from other sources.

The citations you use within the text of a research paper refer
your readers to the list of works cited at the end of the paper,
tell them where to find the borrowed material in the original
source, and indicate the boundaries between your ideas and
those you have borrowed. In the following example, the parenthetical citation guides the reader to page 88 of the book by
Pollan in the works-cited list.

In-text citation

Since the 1980s virtually all the sodas and most of the fruit drinks sold in the supermarkets have been sweetened with high-fructose corn syrup (HFCS)—after water, corn sweetener is their principal ingredient (Pollan 88).

Works-cited entry

Pollan, Michael. *The Omnivore's Dilemma: A Natural History of Four Meals.*
   New York: Penguin, 2006. Print.

The MLA suggests reserving numbered notes for supplementary comments—for example, when you wish to explain a point further but the subject matter is tangential to your topic. When numbered notes are used, superscript numbers are inserted in the appropriate places in the text, and the notes are gathered at the end of the paper on a separate page titled "Notes." Each note begins with an indent. You can create a superscript number in Microsoft Word by typing the number, highlighting it, pulling down the menu for Format, clicking on Font, and then clicking in the box next to Superscript.

In-text note number

Most food found in American supermarkets is ultimately derived from corn.[1]

Notes entry

   1. Nearly all farm animals—from cows and chickens to various kinds of farmed fish—are fed a diet of corn.

An in-text citation usually provides two pieces of information about borrowed material: (1) information that directs the reader to the relevant source on the works-cited list and (2) information that directs the reader to a specific page or section within that source. An author's last name and a page number generally suffice. To create an in-text citation, either place both the author's last name and the page number in parentheses or introduce the author's name in the sentence and supply just the page number in parentheses.

A "remarkably narrow biological foundation" supports the variety of America's supermarkets (Pollan 18).

Pollan explains the way corn products "feed" the familiar meats, beverages, and dairy products that we find on our supermarket shelves (18).

When referring to information from a range of pages, separate the first and last pages with a hyphen: (34-42). If the page numbers have the same hundreds or thousands digit, do not repeat it when listing the final page in the range: (234-42) or (1350-55) but (290-301) or (1395-1402). If you refer to an entire work or a work with only one page, no page numbers are necessary.

The following examples are representative of the types of in-text citations you might be expected to use. For more details on the placement and punctuation of citations, including those following long quotations, see pages 575–578.

Directory of MLA Parenthetical Citations

1. Work by one author

Set on the frontier and focused on characters who use language sparingly, Westerns often reveal a "pattern of linguistic regression" (Rosowski 170).

OR

Susan J. Rosowski argues that Westerns often reveal a "pattern of linguistic regression" (170).

2. More than one work by the same author(s)

When your works-cited list includes more than one work by the same author(s), provide a shortened title in your in-text citation that identifies the relevant work. Use a comma to separate the name (or names) from the shortened title when both are in parentheses. For example, if you listed two works by Antonio Damasio on your works-cited page, then you would cite one of those within your text as follows:

According to one neurological hypothesis, "feelings are the expression of human flourishing or human distress" (Damasio, *Looking for Spinoza* 6).

OR

Antonio Damasio believes that "feelings are the expression of human flourishing or human distress" (*Looking for Spinoza* 6).

3. Work by two or three authors

Some environmentalists seek to protect wilderness areas from further development so that they can both preserve the past and learn from it (Katcher and Wilkins 174).

Use commas to separate the names of three authors: (Bellamy, O'Brien, and Nichols 59).

4. Work by more than three authors

Use either the first author's last name followed by the abbreviation *et al.* (from the Latin *et alii*, meaning "and others") or all the last names. (Do not italicize the abbreviated Latin phrase, which ends with a period.)

In one important study, women graduates complained more frequently about "excessive control than about lack of structure" (Belenky et al. 205).

OR

In one important study, women graduates complained more frequently about "excessive control than about lack of structure" (Belenky, Clinchy, Goldberger, and Tarule 205).

5. Works by different authors with the same last name

When your works-cited list includes works by different authors with the same last name, provide a first initial, along with the last name, in parenthetical citations, or use the author's first and last name in the text. For example, if your works-cited list included entries for works by both Richard Enos and Theresa Enos, you would cite the work of Theresa Enos as follows.

Pre-Aristotelian rhetoric still has an impact today (T. Enos 331-43).

OR

Theresa Enos mentions the considerable contemporary reliance on pre-Aristotelian rhetoric (331-43).

If two authors have the same last name and first initial, spell out each author's first name in a parenthetical citation.

6. Work by a corporate author

A work has a corporate author when individual members of the group that created it are not identified. If the corporate author's name is long, you may use common abbreviations for parts of it—for example, *Assn.* for "Association" and *Natl.* for "National." Do not italicize the abbreviations.

Strawbale constructions are now popular across the nation (Natl. Ecobuilders Group 2).

7. Two or more works in the same citation

When two sources provide similar information or when you combine information from two sources in the same sentence, cite both sources, separating them with a semicolon.

Agricultural scientists believe that crop productivity will be adversely affected by solar dimming (Beck and Watts 90; Harris-Green 153-54).

8. Multivolume work

When you cite material from more than one volume of a multivolume work, include the volume number (followed by a colon and a space) before the page number.

Katherine Raine claims that "true poetry begins where human personality ends" (2: 247).

You do not need to include the volume number in a parenthetical citation if your list of works cited includes only one volume of a multivolume work.

9. Anonymous work

The Tehuelche people left their handprints on the walls of a cave, now called Cave of the Hands ("Hands of Time" 124).

Use the title of an anonymous work in place of an author's name. If the title is long, provide a shortened version. For example, the shortened title for "Chasing Down the Phrasal Verb in the Discourse of Adolescents" is "Chasing Down."

10. Indirect source

If you need to include material that one of your sources quoted from another work because you cannot obtain the original source, use the following format (*qtd.* is the abbreviation for "quoted").

The critic Susan Hardy Aikens has argued on behalf of what she calls "canonical multiplicity" (qtd. in Mayers 677).

A reader turning to the list of works cited should find a bibliographic entry for Mayers, the source consulted, but not for Aikens.

11. Poetry, drama, and sacred texts

When you refer to poetry, drama, or sacred texts, you should give the numbers of lines, acts and scenes, or chapters and verses, rather than page numbers. This practice enables readers to consult an edition other than the one you have used. Act, scene, and line numbers (all arabic numerals) are separated by periods with no space before or after them. The MLA suggests that biblical chapters and verses be treated similarly, although some writers prefer to use colons instead of periods in such citations. In all cases, the progression is from larger to smaller units.

The following example illustrates a citation referring to lines of poetry.

Emily Dickinson alludes to her dislike of public appearance in "I'm Nobody! Who Are You?" (5-8).

The following citation shows that the famous "To be, or not to be" soliloquy appears in act 3, scene 1, lines 56-89 of *Hamlet*.

In *Hamlet*, Shakespeare presents the most famous soliloquy in the history of the English theater: "To be, or not to be . . ." (3.1.56-89).

Citations of biblical material identify the book of the Bible, the chapter, and the pertinent verses. In the following example, the writer refers to the creation story in Genesis, which begins in chapter 1 with verse 1 and ends in chapter 2 with verse 22.

The Old Testament creation story, told with remarkable economy, culminates in the arrival of Eve (*New American Standard Bible*, Gen. 1.1-2.22).

Mention in your first citation which version of the Bible you are using; list only book, chapter, and verse in subsequent citations. Note that the names of biblical books are neither italicized nor enclosed in quotation marks.

The MLA provides standard abbreviations for the parts of the Bible, as well as for the works of Shakespeare and Chaucer and certain other literary works.

12. Constitution

When referring to the U.S. Constitution, use in-text citations only. You do not need to include a works-cited entry. The following are common abbreviations for in-text citations:

United States Constitution   US Const.

article   art.

section   sec.

The testimony of two witnesses is needed to convict someone of treason (US Const., art. 3, sec. 3).

13. Works with numbered paragraphs or sections

If paragraphs in an electronic source are numbered, cite the number(s) of the paragraph(s) after the abbreviation *par.* (for one paragraph) or *pars.* (for more than one). If a section number is provided, cite that number after the abbreviation *sec.* (or *secs.* for more than one).

Alston describes three types of rubrics for evaluating customer service (pars. 2-15).

Hilton and Merrill provide examples of effective hyperlinks (sec. 1).

If an electronic source includes no numbers distinguishing one part from another, you should cite the entire source. In this case, to establish that you have not accidentally omitted a number, avoid using a parenthetical citation by providing what information you have within the sentence that introduces the material.

Raymond Lucero's *Shopping Online* offers useful advice for consumers who are concerned about transmitting credit card information over the Internet.

(2) The MLA offers guidelines for placing and punctuating in-text citations and quotations.

(a) Placement of in-text citations

When you acknowledge your use of a source by placing the author's name and a relevant page number in parentheses, insert this parenthetical citation directly after the information you used, generally at the end of a sentence but *before* the final punctuation mark (a period, question mark, or exclamation point).

Oceans store almost half the carbon dioxide released by humans into the atmosphere (Wall 28).

However, you may need to place a parenthetical citation earlier in a sentence to indicate that only the first part of the sentence contains borrowed material. Place the citation after the clause containing the material but before a punctuation mark (a comma, semicolon, or colon).

Oceans store almost half the carbon dioxide released by humans into the atmosphere (Wall 28), a fact that provides hope for scientists studying global warming but alarms scientists studying organisms living in the oceans.

If you cite the same source more than once in a paragraph, with no intervening citations of another source, you can place one parenthetical citation at the end of the last sentence in which the source is used: (Wall 28, 32).

(b) Lengthy quotations

When a quotation is more than four lines long, set it off from the surrounding text by indenting all lines one inch from the left margin. The first line should not be indented further than the others. The right margin should remain the same. Double-space the entire quotation and do not begin and end it with quotation marks.

In *Nickel and Dimed*, Barbara Ehrenreich describes the dire living conditions of the working poor:

> The lunch that consists of Doritos or hot dog rolls, leading to faintness before the end of the shift. The "home" that is also a car or a van. The illness or injury that must be "worked through," with gritted teeth, because there's no sick pay or health insurance and the loss of one day's pay will mean no groceries for the next. These experiences are not part of a sustainable lifestyle, even a lifestyle of chronic deprivation and relentless low-level punishment. They are, by almost any standard of subsistence, emergency situations. And that is how we should see the poverty of millions of low-wage Americans—as a state of emergency. (214)

A problem of this magnitude cannot be fixed simply by raising the minimum wage.

Note that the period precedes the parenthetical citation at the end of an indented (block) quotation. Note, too, how the writer introduces and then comments on the block quotation from Ehrenreich, explaining the signficance of the quotation to the larger essay.

Rarely will you need to quote more than a paragraph, but if you do, indent the first line of each paragraph an extra quarter of an inch.

(c) Punctuation within citations and quotations

Punctuation marks clarify meaning in quotations and citations. The following list summarizes their common uses.

- A colon separates volume numbers from page numbers in a parenthetical citation.

  (Raine 2: 247)

- A comma separates the author's name from the title when it is necessary to list both in a parenthetical citation.

  (Kingsolver, *Animal Dreams*)

  A comma also indicates that page or line numbers are not sequential.

  (44, 47)

- Ellipsis points indicate an omission within a quotation.

  "They lived in an age of increasing complexity and great hope; we in an age of . . . growing despair" (Krutch 2).

- A hyphen indicates a continuous sequence of pages or lines.

  (44-47)

- A period separates acts, scenes, and lines of dramatic works.

  (3.1.56)

  A period also distinguishes chapters from verses in biblical citations.

  (Gen. 1.1)

- A question mark placed inside the final quotation marks indicates that the quotation is a question. Notice that the period after the parenthetical citation marks the end of the sentence.

  Peter Elbow asks, "What could be more wonderful than the pleasure of creating or appreciating forms that are different, amazing, outlandish, useless—the opposite of ordinary, everyday, pragmatic?" (542).

  When placed outside the final quotation marks, a question mark indicates that the quotation has been incorporated into a question posed by the writer of the paper.

  What does Kabat-Zinn mean when he advises people to practice mindfulness "as if their lives depended on it" (305)?

■ Square brackets enclose words that have been added to
the quotation as clarification and are not part of the
original material.

"The publication of this novel [*Beloved*] establishes Morrison as one of

the most important writers of our time" (Boyle 17).

40b   MLA list of works cited

All of the works you cite should be listed at the end of your
paper, beginning on a separate page with the heading "Works
Cited." Use the following tips as you prepare your list.

TIPS FOR PREPARING A LIST OF WORKS CITED

■ Center the heading "Works Cited" (not enclosed in quotation
marks) one inch from the top of the page.

■ Arrange the list of works alphabetically by the author's last name.

■ If a source has more than one author, alphabetize the entry
according to the last name of the first author.

■ If you use more than one work by the same author, alphabetize
the works by the first major word in each title. For the first entry,
provide the author's complete name (last name given first), but
substitute three hyphens (---) for the author's name in subsequent
entries. If that author is also the first author in a collaboration,
write out the author's name in full.

■ For a work without an author or editor, alphabetize the entry
according to the first important word in the title.

■ Type the first line of each entry flush with the left margin and
indent subsequent lines one-half inch (a hanging indent).

■ Double-space equally throughout—between lines of an entry and
between entries.

Directory of MLA-Style Entries for a Works-Cited List

PRINT PUBLICATIONS

Online Communications and Web Sites

Other Online Documents

Online Recordings and Images

OTHER COMMON SOURCES

Live and Recorded Performances

When writing down source information for your bibliography, be sure to copy the information directly from the source (e.g., the first page of a journal article or the title page of a book). (See fig. 40.1 on page 588 for an example of the first page from a journal article and fig. 40.2 on page 592 for an example of a book title page.)

General Documentation Guidelines for Print-Based Sources

Author or Editor

One author. Place the last name before the first, separating them with a comma. Add any middle name or initial after the first name. Use another comma before any abbreviation or number that follows the first name. Indicate the end of this unit of the entry with a period.

Halberstam, David.

Johnston, Mary K.

King, Martin Luther, Jr.

Two or three authors. List names in the same order used in the original source. The first person's name is inverted (that is, the last name appears first); the others are not. Separate all names with commas, placing the word *and* before the final name.	West, Nigel, and Oleg Tsarev. Green, Bill, Maria Lopez, and Jenny T. Graf.
Four or more authors. List the names of all the authors or provide just the first person's name (inverted) and the abbreviation *et al.* (for *et alii,* meaning "and others").	Quirk, Randolph, Sidney Greenbaum, Geoffrey Leech, and Jan Svartvik. OR Quirk, Randolph, et al.
Corporate or group author. Omit any initial article (*a, an,* or *the*) from the name.	Institute of Medicine. Department of Natural Resources.
Editor. If an editor or editors are listed instead of an author or authors, include the abbreviation *ed.* for "editor" or *eds.* for "editors."	Espinoza, Toni, ed. Gibb, Susan, and Karen Enochs, eds.

Title

Italicized titles. Italicize the titles of books, magazines, journals, newspapers, plays, and screenplays. Capitalize all major words (nouns, pronouns, verbs, adjectives, adverbs, and subordinating conjunctions).	*Newsweek* *Hamlet.* *Weird English.* *The Aviator.*

(Continued on page 584)

Title *(Continued from page 583)*

Do not use a period after the
title of a periodical.

Titles in quotation marks.
Use quotation marks to enclose
the titles of short works such
as journal or magazine articles,
short stories, poems, and songs
(**16b**).

"Three Days to See."

"Selling the Super Bowl."

"Generations."

Subtitles. Always include a
subtitle if the work has one. Use
a colon to separate a main title
and a subtitle.

*Lost in Translation: Life in a
New Language.*

"Silence: Learning to Listen."

Titles within titles. When
an italicized title includes the
title of another work normally
italicized, do not italicize the
embedded title.

Essays on Death of a Salesman.

BUT

Death of a Salesman.

If the embedded title normally
requires quotation marks, it
should be italicized as well as
enclosed in quotation marks.

*Understanding "The Philosophy
of Composition" and the Aesthetic
of Edgar Allan Poe.*

BUT

"The Philosophy of
Composition."

When a title in quotation marks includes the title of another work normally italicized, retain the italics.	"A Salesman's Reading of *Death of a Salesman*."
If the embedded title is normally enclosed in quotation marks, use single quotation marks.	"The European Roots of 'The Philosophy of Composition.'"

Publication Data

City of publication. If more than one city is listed on the title page, mention only the first. Place a colon after the name of the city.	Boston: New York:
Publisher's name. Provide a shortened form of the publisher's name, and place a comma after it. To shorten the name of the publisher, use the principal name. For books published by university presses, abbreviate *University* and *Press* without periods or italics.	Knopf (for Alfred A. Knopf) Random (for Random House) Harvard UP (for Harvard University Press)
If two publishers are listed, provide the city of publication and the name of the publisher for each. Use a semicolon to separate the two.	Manchester: Manchester UP; New York: St. Martin's

(Continued on page 586)

Publisher's imprint. You will sometimes need to list both a publisher's name and an imprint. The imprint is usually listed above the publisher's name on the title page. In a works-cited entry, use a hyphen to separate the two names: imprint-publisher.

Quill-Harper

Vintage-Random

Copyright date. Although the copyright date may be found on the title page, it is usually found on the next page—the copyright page (see fig. 40.3 on page 593). Place a period after the date.

Medium of publication. Entries for all print publications—books, newspapers, magazines, journals, maps, articles, reviews, editorials, letters to the editor, pamphlets, published dissertations, and so on—must include the medium of publication: *Print.* Do not italicize the medium of publication. End with a period.

PRINT PUBLICATIONS

Print Articles

A **journal** is a publication written for a specific discipline or profession. **Magazines** and **newspapers** are written for the general public. You can find most of the information required for a works-cited entry for a journal article on the first page of the journal (fig. 40.1) or at the bottom of the first page of the article you are citing.

Title of article and name of periodical

Put the article title in quotation marks with a period inside the closing quotation marks. Italicize the name of the periodical, but do not add any punctuation following the name. Capitalize all major words (nouns, pronouns, verbs, adjectives, adverbs, and subordinating conjunctions). Omit the word *A*, *An*, or *The* from the beginning of the name of a periodical.

"Into the Void." *New Scientist*

Volume and issue numbers

In an entry for an article from a journal, provide the volume number. If the issue number is available, put a period after the volume number and add the issue number.

Contemporary Review 194   *Studies in the Literary Imagination* 26.3

Date

For journals, place the year of publication in parentheses after the volume or issue number. For magazines and newspapers, provide the date of issue after the name of the periodical. Note the day first (if provided), followed by the month (abbreviated except for May, June, and July) and year.

Date of publication
Volume number
Issue number

Spring/Summer 2008
Volume 20
Number 1–2

American
Literary
History — Name of journal

Twenty Years of American Literary History: The Anniversary Volume

Title of article
Author

Fig. 40.1. First page of a journal.

Journal	*American Literary History* 20.1-2 (2008)
Magazine	*Economist* 13 Aug. 2005
Newspaper	*Chicago Tribune* 24 July 2002

Page numbers

Use a colon to separate the date from the page number(s). Note all the pages on which the article appears, separating the first and last page with a hyphen: 21-39. If the page numbers have the same hundreds or thousands digit, do not repeat it when listing the final page in the range: 131-42 or 1680-99. Magazine and newspaper articles are often interrupted by advertisements or other articles. If the first part of an article appears on pages 45 through 47 and the rest on pages 92 through 94, give only the first page number followed by a plus sign: 45+.

Medium of publication

Be sure to include the medium of publication (*Print*) at the end of the entry. Do not italicize the medium of publication.

1. Article in a journal

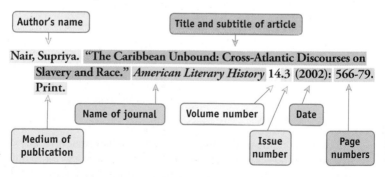

2. Article in a monthly magazine

Keizer, Garret. "How the Devil Falls in Love." *Harper's* Aug. 2002: 43-51. Print.

3. Article in a weekly magazine or newspaper

Chown, Marcus. "Into the Void." *New Scientist* 24 Nov. 2007: 34-37. Print.

4. Article in a daily newspaper

Moberg, David. "The Accidental Environmentalist." *Chicago Tribune*
24 Sept. 2002, final ed., sec. 2: 1+. Print.

When the name of the city is not part of a locally published newspaper's name, it should be given in brackets after the title: *Star Telegram* [Fort Worth]. If a specific edition is not identifed on the masthead, put a colon after the date and then provide the page reference. Specify the section by inserting the section letter as it appears in the newspaper (A7 or 7A, for example).

5. Unsigned article or wire service article

"View from the Top." *National Geographic* July 2001: 140. Print.

6. Editorial in a newspaper or magazine

Beefs, Anne. "Ending Bias in the Human Rights System." Editorial.
New York Times 22 May 2002, natl. ed.: A27. Print.

7. Book or film review in a magazine

Denby, David. "Horse Power." Rev. of *Seabiscuit*, dir. Gary Ross.
New Yorker 4 Aug. 2003: 84-85. Print.

Include the name of the reviewer, the title of the review (if any), the phrase *Rev. of* (for "Review of"), the title of the work being reviewed, and the name of the editor, author, or director.

8. Book or film review in a journal

Graham, Catherine. Rev. of *Questionable Activities: The Best*, ed. Judith

Rudakoff. *Canadian Theatre Review* 113 (2003): 74-76. Print.

Print Books

9. Book by one author

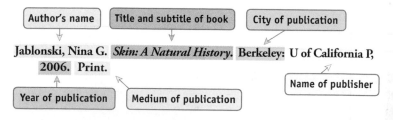

The title page and copyright page of a book (see figs. 40.2 and 40.3) provide the information needed to create a bibliographic entry. Be sure to include the medium of publication at the end of the entry.

10. Book by two authors

West, Nigel, and Oleg Tsarev. *The Crown Jewels: The British Secrets at the

Heart of the KGB Archives*. New Haven: Yale UP, 1999. Print.

11. Book by three authors

Spinosa, Charles, Ferdinand Flores, and Hubert L. Dreyfus. *Disclosing New

Worlds: Entrepreneurship, Democratic Action, and the Cultivation of

Solidarity*. Cambridge: MIT P, 1997. Print.

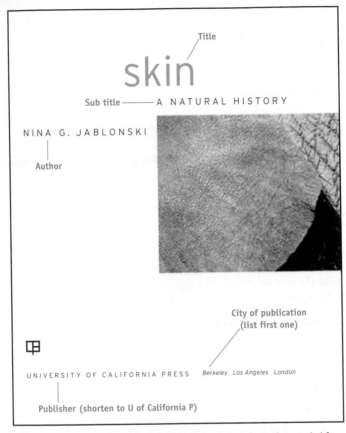

Fig. 40.2. A title page includes most, if not all, of the information needed for a bibliographic entry. In this case, the title page omits the publication date.

University of California Press, one of the most distinguished
university presses in the United States, enriches lives around the
world by advancing scholarship in the humanities, social sciences,
and natural sciences. Its activities are supported by the UC Press
Foundation and by philanthropic contributions from individuals
and institutions. For more information, visit www.ucpress.edu.

University of California Press
Berkeley and Los Angeles, California

University of California Press, Ltd.
London, England

Copyright year

©2006 by Nina G. Jablonski

Fig. 40.3. If the title page does not give the book's date of publication, turn to the copyright page, which is usually the page following the title page.

12. Book by more than three authors

Bullock, Jane A., George D. Haddow, Damon Cappola, Erdem Ergin, Lissa
    Westerman, and Sarp Yeletaysi. *Introduction to Homeland Security*.
    Boston: Elsevier, 2005. Print.

OR

Bullock, Jane A., et al. *Introduction to Homeland Security*. Boston: Elsevier,
    2005. Print.

13. Book by a corporate author

Institute of Medicine. *Blood Banking and Regulation: Procedures, Problems,
    and Alternatives*. Washington: Natl. Acad., 1996. Print.

14. Book by an anonymous author

Primary Colors: A Novel of Politics. New York: Warner, 1996. Print.

Begin the entry with the title. Do not use *Anonymous* or *Anon.*

15. Book with an author and an editor

Stoker, Bram. *Dracula*. Ed. Glennis Byron. Peterborough: Broadview,

1998. Print.

Include both the name of the author and the name of the editor
(preceded by *Ed.*).

16. Book with an editor instead of an author

Kachuba, John B., ed. *How to Write Funny*. Cincinnati: Writer's Digest, 2000. Print.

17. Edition after the first

Murray, Donald. *The Craft of Revision*. 4th ed. Boston: Heinle, 2001. Print.

18. Introduction, preface, foreword, or afterword to a book

Olmos, Edward James. Foreword. *Vietnam Veteranos: Chicanos Recall the*

War. By Lea Ybarra. Austin: U of Texas P, 2004. ix-x. Print.

The name that begins the entry is that of the author of the section of the book, not of the entire book. That person's name
is followed by the title of the section (Introduction, Preface,
Foreword, or Afterword).

19. Anthology (a collection of works by different authors)

Buranen, Lisa, and Alice M. Roy, eds. *Perspectives on Plagiarism and*

Intellectual Property in a Postmodern World. New York: State U of

New York P, 1999. Print.

Include the name(s) of the editor(s), followed by the abbreviation *ed.* (or *eds.*). For individual works within an anthology, consult the following two models.

20. A work originally published in an anthology

Rowe, David. "No Gain, No Game? Media and Sport." *Mass Media and*

Society. Ed. James Curran and Michael Gurevitch. 3rd ed. New York:

Oxford UP, 2000. 346-61. Print.

Use this form for an article, essay, story, poem, or play that was published for the first time in the anthology you are using. Place the title of the anthology after the title of the individual work. Provide the name(s) of the editor(s) after the abbreviation *Ed.* for "edited by," and note the edition if it is not the first. List the publication data for the anthology and the range of pages on which the work appears. (See pages 569 and 589 for information on noting inclusive page numbers.)

If you cite more than one work from an anthology, provide only the name(s) of the author(s), the title of the work, the name(s) of the editor(s), and the inclusive page numbers in an entry for each work. Then, also provide an entry for the entire anthology, in which you include the relevant publication data (see the sample entry for an anthology in item 19).

Clark, Irene L. "Writing Centers and Plagiarism." Buranen and Roy 155-67.

Howard, Rebecca Moore. "The New Abolitionism Comes to Plagiarism."

Buranen and Roy 87-95.

21. A work from a journal reprinted in a textbook or an anthology

Selfe, Cynthia L. "Technology and Literacy: A Story about the Perils of Not

Paying Attention." *College Composition and Communication* 50.3

(1999): 411-37. Rpt. in *Views from the Center: The CCCC Chairs'*

Addresses 1977-2005. Ed. Duane Roen. Boston: Bedford; Urbana:

NCTE, 2006. 323-51. Print.

Use the abbreviation *Rpt.* (not italicized) for "Reprinted." Two cities and publishers are listed in the sample entry because the collection was copublished.

22. A work from an edited collection reprinted in a textbook or an anthology

Brownmiller, Susan. "Let's Put Pornography Back in the Closet." *Take Back
the Night: Women on Pornography*. Ed. Laura Lederer. New York:
Morrow, 1980. 252-55. Rpt. in *Conversations: Readings for Writing*.
By Jack Selzer. 4th ed. New York: Allyn, 2000. 578-81. Print.

See item 20 for information on citing more than one work from the same anthology.

23. Translated book

Garrigues, Eduardo. *West of Babylon*. Trans. Nasario Garcia. Albuquerque:
U of New Mexico P, 2002. Print.

Place the abbreviation *Trans.* (not italicized) for "Translated by" before the translator's name.

24. Republished book

Alcott, Louisa May. *Work: A Story of Experience*. 1873. Harmondsworth: Penguin,
1995. Print.

After the title of the book, provide the original publication date, followed by a period.

25. Multivolume work

Young, Ralph F., ed. *Dissent in America*. 2 vols. New York: Longman-
Pearson, 2005. Print.

Cite the total number of volumes in a work when you have used material from more than one volume. Include the year the volumes were published. If the volumes were published over a span of time, provide inclusive dates: 1997-99 or 1998-2004.

If you have used only one volume, include that volume's number (preceded by the abbreviation *Vol.*) in place of the total number of volumes.

Young, Ralph F., ed. *Dissent in America*. Vol. 1. New York: Longman-
    Pearson, 2005. Print.

Note that the publisher's name in this entry is hyphenated: the first name is the imprint; the second is the publisher.

26. Article in a multivolume work

To indicate a specific article in a multivolume work, provide the author's name and the title of the article in quotation marks. Note the page numbers for the article after the date of publication.

Baxby, Derrick. "Jenner, Edward." *Oxford Dictionary of National Biography*.
    Ed. H. C. G. Matthew and Brian Harrison. Vol. 30. Oxford: Oxford UP,
    2004. 4-8. Print.

If required by your instructor, include the number of volumes and the inclusive publication dates after the medium of publication: 382-89. Print. 23 vols. 1962-97.

27. Book in a series

Sumner, Colin, ed. *Blackwell Companion to Criminology*. Malden: Blackwell,
    2004. Print. Blackwell Companions to Sociology 8.

When citing a book that is part of a series, add the name of the series and, if one is listed, the number designating the work's place in it. The series name is not italicized. Abbreviate words in the series name according to the MLA guidelines; for example, the word *Series* is abbreviated *Ser.* (not italicized).

Other Print Texts

28. Encyclopedia entry

Robertson, James I., Jr. "Jackson, Thomas Jonathan." *Encyclopedia of the*

    American Civil War: A Political, Social, and Military History.

    Ed. David S. Heidler and Jeanne T. Heidler. Santa Barbara: ABC-CLIO,

    2000. 1058-66. Print.

When the author of an encyclopedia article is indicated only by initials, check the table of contents for a list of contributors. If an article is anonymous, begin the entry with the article title.

Full publication information is not necessary for a well-known reference work that is organized alphabetically. Along with the author's name, the title of the article, and the name of the encyclopedia, list the edition and year of publication in one of two ways: 5th ed. 2004 or 2002 ed. Conclude with the publication medium.

Petersen, William J. "Riverboats and Rivermen." *The Encyclopedia*

    Americana. 1999 ed. Print.

29. Dictionary entry

When citing a specific dictionary definition for a word, use the abbreviation *Def.* (for "Definition"), and indicate which one you used if the entry has two or more.

"Reactive." Def. 2a. *Merriam-Webster's Collegiate Dictionary.* 10th ed. 2001. Print.

30. Sacred text

Begin your works-cited entry for a sacred text with the title of the work, rather than information about editors or translators.

New American Standard Bible. Anaheim: Foundation, 1997. Print.

The Qur'an. Trans. Muhammad A. S. Abdel Haleem. Oxford: Oxford UP,

    2004. Print.

31. Government publication

United States. Office of Management and Budget. *A Citizen's Guide to the*
  Federal Budget. Washington: GPO, 1999. Print.

When citing a government publication, list the name of the
government (e.g., United States or Minnesota) and the agency
that issued the work. Italicize the title of a book or pamphlet.
Indicate the city of publication. Federal publications are usually printed by the Government Printing Office (GPO) in
Washington, DC, but be alert for exceptions.

When the name of an author, editor, or compiler appears
on a government publication, you can begin the entry with
that name, followed by the abbreviation *ed.* or *comp.* if the
person is not the author. Alternatively, insert that name
after the publication's title and introduce it with the word
By or the abbreviation *Ed.* or *Comp.* to indicate the person's
contribution.

32. Law case

Chavez v. Martinez. 538 US 760. Supreme Court of the US. 2003. *United*
  States Reports. Washington: GPO, 2004. Print.

Include the last name of the first plaintiff, the abbreviation *v.*
for "versus," the last name of the first defendant, data on the law
report (volume, abbreviated name, and page or reference number), the name of the deciding court, and the year of the decision.
Although law cases are italicized in the text of a paper, they are *not*
italicized in works-cited entries.

33. Public law

No Child Left Behind Act of 2001. Pub. L. 107-10. 115 Stat. 1425-2094. 8 Jan.
  2002. Print.

Include the name of the act, its public law number, its Stat-
utes at Large cataloging number and page numbers, the date

it was enacted, and the medium of publication. Notice the use of abbreviations in the example.

Although no works-cited entry is needed for familiar sources such as the U.S. Constitution, an in-text citation should still be included (see page 574).

34. Pamphlet or bulletin

Stucco in Residential Construction. St. Paul: Lath & Plaster Bureau, 2000. Print.

If the pamphlet has an author, begin with the author's name, as you would for a book.

35. Published dissertation

Fukuda, Kay Louise. *Differing Perceptions and Constructions of the Meaning
    of Assessment in Education*. Diss. Ohio State U, 2001. Ann Arbor: UMI,
    2002. Print.

After the title of the dissertation, include the abbreviation *Diss.,* the name of the university granting the degree, the date of completion, and the publication information. In the example, *UMI* stands for "University Microfilms International," which publishes many dissertations.

36. Published letter

In general, treat a published letter like a work in an anthology, adding the date of the letter and the number (if the editor assigned one).

Jackson, Helen Hunt. "To Thomas Bailey Aldrich." 4 May 1883. *The Indian
    Reform Letters of Helen Hunt Jackson, 1879-1885*. Ed. Valerie Sherer
    Mathes. Norman: U of Oklahoma P, 1998. 258-59. Print.

Print Cartoons, Maps, and Other Visuals

37. Cartoon or comic strip

Cheney, Tom. Cartoon. *New Yorker* 9 June 2003: 93. Print.

Trudeau, Garry. "Doonesbury." Comic strip. *Daily Record* [Ellensburg]

21 Apr. 2005: A4. Print.

After the creator's name, place the title of the work (if given) in quotation marks and include the descriptor *Cartoon* or *Comic strip*.

38. Map or chart

Cincinnati and Vicinity. Map. Chicago: Rand, 2008. Print.

Include the title and the appropriate descriptor, *Map* or *Chart*.

39. Advertisement

Nu by Yves Saint Laurent. Advertisement. *Allure* June 2003: 40. Print.

The name of the product and/or that of the company being advertised is followed by the designation *Advertisement*.

ONLINE PUBLICATIONS

Many of the guidelines for documenting online sources are similar to those for print sources. For sources found online, provide electronic publication information and access information.

Electronic publication information

Indicate the author's name, the title of the work, the title of the Web site, the site's sponsoring organization (usually found at the bottom of the site's home page; see fig. 40.4), the date of publication, and the medium of publication (*Web*). All of this information precedes the access information.

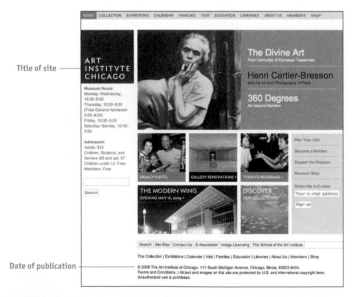

Fig. 40.4. The home page for the Art Institute of Chicago indicates the title of the site (which is also the name of the sponsoring organization) and the date of publication.

Access information

When you document an online source, you must include the date of access: the day, month, and year on which you consulted the source. Either keep track of the date of access or print out the source so that you have a record (see fig. 40.5).

You are not required to include the URL if your readers can easily locate the online source by searching for the author's name and the title of the work. For cases in which your readers cannot easily locate a source, you should provide the complete URL (between angle brackets), including the protocol (http, ftp, telnet, or news). When a URL does not fit on a single line, break it only after a slash. Make sure that the URL is accurate. Take care to distinguish between uppercase and lowercase letters and to include hyphens and underscores. The URL follows the date of access, appearing after a period and a space. The closing angle bracket should also be followed by a period.

BEYOND THE RULE

THE COLUMBIA GUIDE TO ONLINE STYLE

Recognizing that increasing numbers of writers conduct most of their research online, Columbia University Press publishes *The Columbia Guide to Online Style*, 2nd edition (COS), which offers formatting guidelines, sample in-text citations, and sample bibliographic entries.

Fig. 40.5. When you print a page from a Web site, the URL and the date of access usually appear at the top or bottom of the page.

Online Articles

The following formats apply to articles available only online. For articles available through online databases, see pages 607–609. If you need to include a URL, follow the instructions on page 603.

40. Scholarly journal article

Harnack, Andrea, and Gene Kleppinger. "Beyond the MLA Handbook:

Documenting Sources on the Internet." *Kairos* 1.2 (1996): n. pag. Web.

14 Aug. 1997.

Page numbers may not be provided for online journals; if this is the case, write *n. pag.* (for "no pagination"). If they are provided, place them after the year and a colon. The first date is the publication date; the second is the date of access.

41. Popular magazine article

Plotz, David. "The Cure for Sinophobia." *Slate.com.* Newsweek Interactive,

4 June 1999. Web. 15 June 1999.

42. Newspaper article

"Tornadoes Touch Down in S. Illinois." *New York Times.* New York Times,

16 Apr. 1998. Web. 20 May 1998.

When no author is identified, begin with the title of the article. If the article is an editorial, include *Editorial* (not italicized) after the title: "America's Promises." Editorial. (In the sample entry, the first mention of *New York Times* is the title of the Web site, and the second, which is not italicized, is the name of the site's sponsor.)

Online Books

43. Book available only online

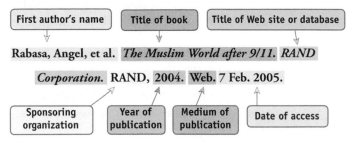

Rabasa, Angel, et al. *The Muslim World after 9/11. RAND Corporation.* RAND, 2004. Web. 7 Feb. 2005.

Because there are more than three authors, the abbreviation *et al.* has been used in the example, but listing all names is also acceptable: Rabasa, Angel, Cheryl Benard, Peter Chalk, C. Christine Fair, Theodore W. Karasik, Rollie Lal, Ian O. Lesser, and David E. Thaler. Note that in this example the name of the sponsoring organization is in the title of the Web site.

44. Book available online and in print

Rohrbough, Malcolm J. *Days of Gold: The California Gold Rush and the American Nation.* Berkeley: U of California P, 1997. *History E-book Project.* Web. 17 Feb. 2005.

Begin the citation with print citation information: the author's name, the title of the work, city of publication, publisher, and date. Follow this information with the title of the database or Web site (italicized), the medium of publication (*Web*), and the date of access.

45. Part of an online book

Strunk, William, Jr. "Elementary Rules of Usage." *The Elements of Style.* Ithaca: Humphrey, 1918. N. pag. *Bartleby.com.* Web. 6 June 2003.

Online Databases

Many print materials are available online through databases such as JSTOR, Project MUSE, ERIC, PsycINFO, Academic Universe, LexisNexis, ProQuest, InfoTrac, Silver Platter, or EBSCO. To cite material from an online database, begin with the author, the title of the article (in quotation marks), the title of the publication (in italics), the volume and issue numbers, the year of publication, and the page numbers (or the abbreviation *n. pag.*). Then add the name of the database (in italics), the medium of publication consulted (*Web*), and the date of access. You can find most of the information you need for a works-cited entry on the abstract page of the article you select (see fig. 40.6).

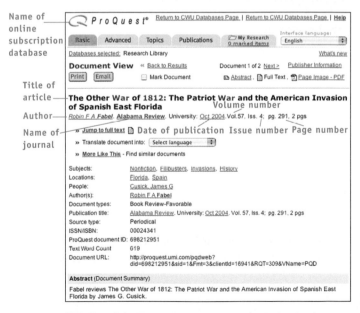

Fig. 40.6. Abstract page from an online subscription database.

46. ERIC

Taylor, Steven J. "Caught in the Continuum: A Critical Analysis of the
        Principle of the Least Restrictive Environment." *Research and Practice
        for Persons with Severe Disabilities* 29.4 (2004): 218-30. *ERIC*. Web.
        3 Mar. 2009.

47. EBSCO

Folks, Jeffrey J. "Crowd and Self: William Faulkner's Sources of Agency in
        The Sound and the Fury." *Southern Literary Journal* 34.2 (2002): 30+.
        EBSCO. Web. 6 June 2003.

For sources that list only the page number on which a work
begins, include that number and a plus sign.

48. LexisNexis

Suggs, Welch. "A Hard Year in College Sports." *Chronicle of Higher
        Education* 19 Dec. 2003: 37. *LexisNexis*. Web. 17 July 2004.

49. ProQuest

Fabel, Robin F. A. "The Other War of 1812: The Patriot War and the
        American Invasion of Spanish East Florida." *Alabama Review* 57.4
        (2004): 291-92. *ProQuest*. Web. 8 Mar. 2005.

50. InfoTrac

Priest, Ann-Marie. "Between Being and Nothingness: The 'Astonishing
        Precipice' of Virginia Woolf's *Night and Day*." *Journal of Modern
        Literature* 26.2 (2002-03): 66-80. *InfoTrac*. Web. 12 Jan. 2004.

51. JSTOR

Blum, Susan D. "Five Approaches to Explaining 'Truth' and 'Deception' in
Human Communication." *Journal of Anthropological Research* 61.3
(2005): 289-315. *JSTOR*. Web. 3 Mar. 2009.

52. Project MUSE

Muñoz, Alejandro Anaya. "Transnational and Domestic Processes in the
Definition of Human Rights Policies in Mexico." *Human Rights
Quarterly* 31.1 (2009): 35-58. *Project MUSE*. Web. 3 Mar. 2009.

53. Online encyclopedia entry from a subscription database

Turk, Austin T. "Terrorism." *Encyclopedia of Crime and Justice*. Ed. Joshua
Dressler. 2nd ed. Vol. 4. New York: Macmillan Reference USA, 2002.
Gale Virtual Reference Library. Web. 7 Feb. 2005.

54. Abstract from a subscription database

Landers, Susan J. "FDA Panel Findings Intensify Struggles with Prescribing
of Antidepressants." *American Medical News* 47.37 (2004): 1-2.
ProQuest Direct. Web. 7 Feb. 2005.

Online Communications and Web Sites

55. Web site

McGann, Jerome, ed. *The Complete Writings and Pictures of Dante Gabriel
Rossetti*. Inst. for Advanced Technology in the Humanities, U of
Virginia, n.d. Web. 16 Mar. 2009.

Include the name of the author, editor, compiler, director, or translator, followed by the title of the site (italicized), the version or edition (if given), the publisher or sponsor (if not available, use *N.p.*), the date of publication (if not available, use *n.d.*), the medium of publication (*Web*), and the date of access.

56. Web site with incomplete information

Breastcancer.org. N.p., 2 Feb. 2008. Web. 5 Feb. 2008.

If a Web site does not provide all the information usually included in a works-cited entry, list as much as is available.

57. Section of a Web site

Altman, Andrew. "Civil Rights." *Stanford Encyclopedia of Philosophy.* Ed.
Edward N. Zalta. Center for the Study of Lang. and Information, Stanford
U, 3 Feb. 2003. Web. 12 June 2003.

Mozart, Wolfgang Amadeus. "Concerto No. 3 for Horn, K. 447." *Essentials of
Music.* Sony Music Entertainment, 2001. Web. 3 Mar. 2009.

58. Personal home page

Gladwell, Malcolm. Home page. N.p., 8 Mar. 2005. Web. 2 Mar. 2009.

After the name of the site's creator, provide the title or include the words *Home page* (not italicized).

59. E-mail

Peters, Barbara. "Scholarships for Women." Message to Rita Martinez.
10 Mar. 2003. E-mail.

The entry begins with the name of the person who created the e-mail. Put the subject line of the e-mail message in quotation marks. The recipient of the message is identified after the words *Message to.* If the message was sent to you, use *the author* rather than your name. The date of the message and the medium complete the citation.

60. Discussion group or forum

Schipper, William. "Re: Quirk and Wrenn Grammar." *Ansaxnet*. N.p., 5 Jan.

1995. Web. 12 Sept. 1996.

Provide the name of the forum (in this case, *Ansaxnet*) between the title of the work and the sponsor. If the posting is untitled, put the genre (e.g., *Online posting*) in place of the title.

61. Newsgroup

May, Michaela. "Questions about RYAs." *Generation X.* N.p., 19 June 1996.

Web. 29 June 1996.

The name of a newsgroup (*Generation X*) takes the place of the title of the Web site.

62. Web log (blog)

Cuthbertson, Peter. "Are Left and Right Still Alright?" *Conservative*

Commentary. N.p., 7 Feb. 2005. Web. 18 Feb. 2005.

Other Online Documents

63. Online encyclopedia entry

"Iran." *Encyclopaedia Britannica Online*. Encyclopaedia Britannica, 2002.

Web. 6 Mar. 2004.

64. Online congressional document

United States. Cong. Senate. Special Committee on Aging. *Global Aging:*

Opportunity or Threat for the U.S. Economy? 108th Cong., 1st sess. S.

Hrg. 108-30. Washington: GPO, 2003. *GPO Access.* Web. 7 Jan. 2005.

Provide the number and session of Congress and the type and number of publication. (*S* stands for "Senate"; *H* or *HR* stands for "House of Representatives.")

Bills	S 41, HR 82
Reports	S. Rept. 14, H. Rept. 18
Hearings	S. Hrg. 23, H. Hrg. 25
Resolutions	S. Res. 32, H. Res. 52
Documents	S. Doc. 213, H. Doc. 123

65. Online document from a government office

United States. Dept. of State. Bur. of Democracy, Human Rights, and Labor.

Guatemala Country Report on Human Rights Practices for 1998. Feb.

1999. Web. 1 May 1999.

Begin with the name of the country, state, or city whose government is responsible for the document and the department or agency that issued it. If a subdivision of the larger organization is responsible, name the subdivision. If an author is identified, provide the name, preceded by the word *By*, between the title and the date of issue of the document.

66. Online law case

Tennessee v. Lane. 541 US 509. Supreme Court of the US. 2004. *Supreme*

Court Collection. Legal Information Inst., Cornell U Law School, n.d.

Web. 28 Jan. 2005.

67. Online public law

Individuals with Disabilities Education Act. Pub. L. 105-17. 104 Stat. 587-

698. *Thomas*. Lib. of Cong., 4 June 1997. Web. 29 Jan. 2005.

68. Online sacred text

Sama Veda. Trans. Ralph T. H. Griffith. 1895. *Sacred-Texts.com*. Ed. John B.

Hare. N.p., 2008. Web. 6 Mar. 2008.

Online Recordings and Images

69. Online music

Moran, Jason. "Jump Up." *Same Mother.* Blue Note, 2005. *Blue Note.* Blue

Note Records. Web. 7 Mar. 2005.

In this entry, "Blue Note" is the manufacturer of the CD, Blue Note is the title of the Web site where the song was accessed, and "Blue Note Records" is the sponsor of that site.

70. Online speech

Malcolm X. "The Ballot or the Bullet." Detroit. 12 Apr. 1964. *American*

Rhetoric: Top One Hundred Speeches. Ed. Michael E. Eidenmuller.

N.p., 2005. Web. 14 Jan. 2005.

"12 Apr. 1964" is the date the speech was delivered, "2005" is the year of the speech's electronic publication, and "14 Jan. 2005" is the date of access.

71. Online video

Riefenstahl, Leni, dir. *Triumph of the Will.* Reichsparteitag-Film, 1935.

Movieflix.com. MovieFlix, 2005. Web. 17 Feb. 2005.

"1935" is the year in which the movie was originally released, "2005" is the year in which it was made available online, and "17 Feb. 2005" is the date of access.

72. Online television or radio program

"Religion and the American Election." Narr. Tony Hassan. *The Religion*

Report. ABC Radio National, 3 Nov. 2004. Web. 18 Feb. 2005.

73. Online interview

McLaughlin, John. Interview by Wolf Blitzer. *CNN.com.* Cable News

Network, 14 July 2004. Web. 21 Dec. 2004.

74. Online work of art

Vermeer, Johannes. *Young Woman with a Water Pitcher*. c. 1660.
Metropolitan Museum of Art, New York. *The Metropolitan Museum of Art*. Web. 2 Oct. 2002.

75. Online photograph

Marmon, Lee. *Engine Rock*. 1985. *Lee Marmon Gallery*. Web. 9 Feb. 2009.

76. Online map or chart

"Virginia 1624." Map. *Map Collections 1544-1996*. Lib. of Cong. Web.
26 Apr. 1999.

United States. Dept. of Health and Human Services. Centers for Disease
Control and Prevention. "Daily Cigarette Smoking among High School
Seniors." Chart. 27 Jan. 2005. *National Center for Health Statistics*.
Web. 25 Feb. 2005.

77. Online advertisement

Milk Processor Education Program. "Got Milk?" Advertisement. *MilkPEP*.
MilkPEP, n.d. Web. 16 Feb. 2005.

78. Online cartoon or comic strip

Cagle, Daryl. "Social Security Pays 3 to 2." Cartoon. *Slate.com*. Newsweek
Interactive, 4 Feb. 2005. Web. 5 Feb. 2005.

OTHER COMMON SOURCES

Live and Recorded Performances

79. Play performance

Proof. By David Auburn. Dir. Daniel Sullivan. Walter Kerr Theater, New York.

8 Oct. 2002. Performance.

Cite the date of the performance you attended.

80. Lecture or presentation

Guinier, Lani. Barbara Jordan Lecture Ser. Schwab Auditorium, Pennsylvania

State U, University Park. 4 Oct. 2004. Address.

Scharnhorst, Gary. English 296.003. Dane Smith Hall, U of New Mexico,

Albuquerque. 30 Apr. 2008. Class lecture.

Identify the site and the date of the lecture or presentation. Use the title if available; otherwise, provide only a descriptive label.

81. Interview

Furstenheim, Ursula. Personal interview. 16 Jan. 2003.

Sugo, Misuzu. Telephone interview. 20 Feb. 2003.

For an interview you conducted, give only the name of the person you interviewed, the type of interview, and the date of the interview. If the interview was conducted by someone else, add the name of the interviewer, a title or a descriptive label, and the name of the source.

Harryhausen, Ray. Interview by Terry Gross. *Fresh Air.* Natl. Public Radio.

WHYY, Philadelphia, 6 Jan. 2003. Radio.

82. Film

My Big Fat Greek Wedding. Dir. Joel Zwick. IFC, 2002. Film.

The name of the company that produced or distributed the film (IFC, in this case) appears before the year of release. It is not necessary to cite the city in which the production or distribution company is based.

When you want to highlight the contribution of a specific person, list the contributor's name first. Other supplementary information may be included after the title.

Gomez, Ian, perf. *My Big Fat Greek Wedding*. Screenplay by Nia Vardalos.

Dir. Joel Zwick. IFC, 2002. Film.

83. Radio or television program

When referring to a specific episode, place quotation marks around its title. Italicize the title of the program.

"'Barbarian' Forces." *Ancient Warriors*. Narr. Colgate Salsbury. Dir. Phil

Grabsky. Learning Channel. 1 Jan. 1996. Television.

To highlight a specific contributor or contributors, begin the entry with the name or names and note the nature of the contribution.

Abumrad, Jad, and Robert Kulwich, narrs. "Choice." *Radiolab*. New York

Public Radio. WNYC, New York, 14 Nov. 2008. Radio.

Works of Visual Art

84. Painting

Gauguin, Paul. *Ancestors of Tehamana*. 1893. Oil on canvas. Art Inst. of

Chicago, Chicago.

Identify the artist's name, the title of the work (italicized), the date of composition (if known; otherwise, write *N.d.*), the medium of composition, the organization or individual holding the work, and the city in which the work is located. For a photograph or reproduction of a work of art, provide the preceding information followed by complete publication information for the source, including medium of publication.

85. Photograph

Marmon, Lee. *White Man's Moccasins*. 1954. Photograph. Native American
     Cultural Center, Albuquerque.

Digital Sources

86. CD-ROM

"About *Richard III*." *Cinemania 96*. Redmond: Microsoft, 1996. CD-ROM.

Indicate which part of the CD-ROM you are using, and then
provide the title of the CD-ROM. Begin the entry with the
name of the author if one has been provided.

Jordan, June. "Moving towards Home." *Database of Twentieth-Century
     African American Poetry on CD-ROM*. Alexandria: Chadwyck-Healey,
     1999. CD-ROM.

87. Work from a periodically published database on CD-ROM

Parachini, John V. *Combating Terrorism: The 9/11 Commission
     Recommendations and the National Strategies*. CD-ROM. *RAND
     Electronically Distributed Documents*. RAND. 2004. Disc 8.

88. DVD

A River Runs through It. Screenplay by Richard Friedenberg. Dir. Robert
     Redford. 1992. Columbia, 1999. DVD.

Cite relevant information about the title and director as you
would for a film. Note the original release date of the film and
the release date for the DVD. If the original company producing the film did not release the DVD, list the company that
released the DVD instead.

89. Sound recording on CD

Franklin, Aretha. *Amazing Grace: The Complete Recordings*. Atlantic, 1999. CD.

For a sound recording on another medium, identify the type (*Audiocassette* or *LP*).

Raitt, Bonnie. *Nick of Time*. Capitol, 1989. Audiocassette.

When citing a recording of a specific song, begin with the name of the performer, and place the song title in quotation marks. Identify the author(s) after the song title. If the performance is a reissue from an earlier recording, provide the original date of recording (preceded by *Rec.* for "Recorded").

Horne, Lena. "The Man I Love." By George Gershwin and Ira Gershwin.

Rec. 15 Dec. 1941. *Stormy Weather*. BMG, 1990. CD.

40c | Sample MLA-style paper

(1) Submit a title page if your instructor requires one.

The MLA recommends omitting a title page and instead providing the identification on the first page of the paper (see page 621). Some instructors require a final outline with a paper; this serves as a table of contents. If you are asked to include an outline, prepare a title page as well. A title page usually provides the title of the paper, the author's name, the instructor's name, the name of the course with its section number, and the date—all centered on the page. A sample title page is shown in fig. 40.7. (If your instructor requires a title page, you may omit the heading on the first page of your paper.)

Genetically Modified Foods and Developing Countries

Marianna Suslin

Professor Squier

Sociology 299, Section 1

November 27, 2007

Fig. 40.7. Sample title page for an MLA-style paper.

(2) Studying a sample MLA-style paper prepares you to write your own.

Interested in the controversy surrounding genetically modified foods, Marianna Suslin explores both sides of the debate as she comes to her conclusion. As you study her paper, notice how she develops her thesis statement, considers more than one point of view, and observes the conventions for an MLA-style paper.

TIPS FOR PREPARING AN MLA-STYLE PAPER

- Number all pages (including the first one) with an arabic numeral in the upper-right corner, one-half inch from the top. Put your last name before the page number.

- On the left side of the first page, one inch from the top, type a heading that includes your name, the name of your professor, the course number, and the date of submission.

- Double-space between the heading and the title of your paper, which should be centered on the page. If your title consists of two or more lines, double-space them and center each.

- Double-space between your title and the first line of text.

- Indent the first paragraph, and every subsequent paragraph, one-half inch.

- Double-space throughout.

1 inch

1/2 inch

The writer's last name and the page number

Marianna Suslin

Professor Squier

Sociology 299, Section 1

27 November 2007

Heading

Genetically Modified Foods and Developing Countries

Center the title.

Genetic engineering first appeared in the 1960s. Since then, thousands of genetically modified plants, also referred to as "genetically modified organisms" (GMOs) and "transgenic crops," have been introduced to global markets. Those who argue for continued support of genetic modification claim that the crops have higher yield, grow in harsher conditions, and benefit the ecology. Some experts even argue that genetic engineering holds great potential for benefiting poor farmers in developing countries, given that genetically modified plants increase the production of food, thereby alleviating world hunger. Despite these claims, the practice of genetic engineering—of inserting genetic material into the DNA of a plant—continues to be controversial, with no clear answers as to whether genetically engineered foods can be the answer for developing countries, as proponents insist.

Double-space throughout.

Use one-inch margins on both sides of the page.

Thesis

One of the most important potential benefits of the technology to both proponents and opponents of genetic engineering is its potential to improve the economies of developing countries.

1 inch

Suslin 2

Background
information
According to Sakiko Fukuda-Parr, "Investing in agricultural technology increasingly turns up these days on the lists of the top ten practical actions the rich world could take to contribute to reducing global poverty." Agriculture is the source of income for the world's poorest—70 percent of those living on less than a dollar a day support themselves through agriculture. These farmers could benefit greatly from higher yield crops that could grow in nutrient poor soil. Genetic modification "has shown how high-yielding varieties developed at international centers can be adapted to local conditions, dramatically increasing yields and farm incomes" (Fukuda-Parr 3).

Indent
each
paragraph
one-half
inch.
Theoretically, genetic engineering can bring about an increase in farm productivity that would give people in developing countries the chance to enter the global market on better terms. Developing countries are often resource poor and thus have little more than labor to contribute to the world economy. Farming tends to be subsistence level as farmers can grow only enough on the land—which tends to be nutrient poor—to feed themselves. But the higher yield of genetically modified crops along with the resistance to pests and ability to thrive in nutrient poor soil can enable the farmers to produce more crops, improve the economy, and give their countries something more to contribute globally by exporting extra crops not needed for

The writer
describes
some
advantages
of growing
genetically
modified
crops.

Suslin 3

subsistence (Fukuda-Parr 1). Genetic modification can also help poor

farmers by using genetics to delay the ripening process. If fruits and

vegetables don't ripen as quickly, the farmer is able to store the crops

longer and thus have more time in which to sell the crops without fear

of spoilage. Small-scale farmers often "suffer heavy losses because

of uncontrolled ripening and spoiling of fruits and vegetables" (Royal

Society et al. 238).

Today, eighteen percent of people living in developing

countries do not have enough food to meet their needs (Royal

Society et al. 235). "Malnutrition plays a significant role in half

of the nearly 12 million deaths each year of children under five

in developing countries" (UNICEF, qtd. in Royal Society et al.

235). Genetically modified foods that produce large yields even

in nutrient poor soils could potentially help to feed the world's

increasing population. Moreover, scientists are working on ways

to make the genetically modified foods more nutritious than

unmodified crops, which would not only feed large numbers of

people, but help to combat malnutrition. The modification of the

composition of food crops has already been achieved in some

species to increase the amount of protein, starch, fats, or vitamins.

Genetically modified rice, for example, has already been created

that "exhibits an increased production of beta-carotene," which is a

Citation of a
work by an
organization

Suslin 4

precursor to vitamin A (Royal Society et al. 240). Because vitamin A deficiencies are common in developing countries and contribute to half a million children becoming partially or totally blind each year, advances in genetic engineering offer hope for millions of people who live with nutrient deficiencies (Royal Society et al. 239).

Proponents of genetic engineering have also argued that genetically modified crops have the potential to decrease the amount of damage modern farming technologies have on ecology, thereby improving the economy of developing countries without the ecological damage many developed countries have suffered. For example, genetically modified plants with resistance to certain insects would decrease the amount of pesticides that farmers have to use. Genes for insect resistance have already been introduced into cotton, making possible a huge decrease in insecticide use (Royal Society et al. 238). A decrease in the amount of pesticides used is good from an ecological perspective.[1] Pesticides not only can be washed into streams and be harmful to wildlife but have also been known to appear in groundwater, thus potentially causing harm to humans.

Scientists have argued that genetic engineering is only the latest step in the human involvement in plant modification that has been going on for thousands of years.[2] Since the dawn

A superscript number indicates an endnote.

Suslin 5

of the agricultural revolution, people have been breeding plants for desirable traits and thus altering the genetic makeup of plant populations. The key advantage of genetic engineering over traditional plant breeding is that genetic engineering produces plants with the desirable trait much faster (Fukuda-Parr 5).

While there are many potential benefits that can come from genetic engineering for farmers in developing countries and even in the United States, many people remain skeptical about this new technology. Research shows that many Americans are uneasy about consuming foods that have been genetically enhanced. That same research points out potential risks of consuming GMOs, which some believe outweigh the benefits of this new technology (Brossard, Shanahan, and Nesbitt 10). Considering the risks of genetically modified foods, people in developing countries are likely to feel the same way: that the risks outweigh the benefits. No matter how many potential benefits genetically modified crops may bring, if they are not safe for consumption, they will not help but hurt the economies of developing countries.

The writer describes disadvantages of eating genetically modified foods.

In "Genetically Modified Food Threatens Human Health," Jeffrey Smith argues that inserting foreign genetic material into food is extremely dangerous because it may create unknown toxins or allergens. Smith argues that soy allergies increased significantly after genetically modified soybean plants were introduced in the United Kingdom (103). Smith also points to the fact that gene insertion could damage a plant's DNA in unpredictable ways. For example, when scientists were working with the soybean plant, the process of inserting the foreign gene damaged a section of the plant's own DNA, "scrambling its genetic code" (105). The sequence of the gene that was inserted had inexplicably rearranged itself over time. The protein the gene creates as a result of this rearrangement is likely to be different, and since this new protein has not been evaluated for safety, it could be harmful or toxic (105).

In *Genetically Modified Food: A Short Guide for the Confused*, Andy Rees argues a similar point: genetically modified foods carry unpredictable health risks. As an example, he cites the 1989 incident in which bacteria genetically modified to produce large amounts of the food supplement L-tryptophan "yielded impressively toxic contaminants that killed 37 people, partially paralyzed 1,500 and temporarily disabled 5,000 in the US" (75). Rees also argues that genetically modified foods can have possible carcinogenic effects. He states that "given the huge complexity of genetic coding, even in very simple organisms such as bacteria, no one can possibly predict the overall,

Direct quotation of a phrase from a cited work

Suslin 7

long-term effects of GM [genetically modified] foods on the
health of those who eat them" (78). Rees cites the 1999 study
on male rats fed genetically modified potatoes to illustrate
the possible carcinogenic effect. The study found that the
genetically modified potatoes had "a powerful effect on the
lining of the gut (stomach, small bowel, and colon)" leading to
a proliferation of cells. According to histopathologist Stanley
Ewen, this proliferation of cells caused by genetically modified
foods is then likely to "act on any polyp present in the colon . . .
and drastically accelerate the development of cancer in
susceptible persons" (qtd. in Rees 78).

Three
ellipsis
points
mark an
omission
in quoted
material.

   In addition to the health risks involved in consuming
genetically modified foods, some experts also argue that such foods
will not benefit farmers in developing countries but will aid big
corporations here in the United States. Brian Halweil, author of
"The Emperor's New Crops," brings up the fact that global sales for
genetically modified crops grew from seventy-five million dollars
in 1995 to one and a half billion dollars in 1998, which is a twenty-
fold increase. Genetically modified crops are obviously lucrative
for large companies. In addition, of the fifty-six transgenic products
approved for commercial planting in 1998, thirty-three belonged to
just four corporations (Halweil 256).

Suslin 8

The spread of genetic engineering can change power relations between nations (Cook 3). The big American corporations that sell genetically modified seeds can hold power over the governments of developing countries, hindering their further economic development. For example, all transgenic seeds are patented. Because the seeds are patented, it is illegal for farmers to practice "seed saving"—reserving a certain amount of seeds from the harvest to plant in the next growing season. Farmers thus have to depend entirely on the big corporations for their seeds. Since these corporations have a monopoly on genetically modified seeds, the prices for these seeds are likely to remain high, and poor farmers are unlikely to be able to afford them. Genetically altered seeds can then become just one more way that rich countries and their corporations exploit the people of developing countries. Genetic engineering could then become one more way of hindering the development of poor countries, and not the opportunity for economic improvement and increased social equality that its proponents claim it is. Thus, unscrupulous companies could use the economic vulnerability of developing countries to develop and test genetically modified products that have been rejected in the United States or Europe (Newell 68). People in developing countries would be the ones to suffer if the genetically modified products turned out to be hazardous.

Suslin 9

With many concerned about the health risks associated with
GMOs, there has been a push to institute the practice of labeling
genetically modified foods. International organizations such as
Greenpeace and Friends of the Earth have advocated food labeling
for GMOs because they believe that consumers should have the
right to choose whether or not to buy genetically modified foods
and expose themselves to the risks associated with consuming
GMOs (Huffman 3). The FDA, however, contends that scientific
studies "detect no substantial difference between food from
traditional crops and GM crops" (*Federal Register*) and regards
genetic modification as not altering the product enough to require
labeling (see fig. 1). Interestingly, one of the reasons for not labeling
genetically modified food is the concern that consumers will shun
the products with the GMO label, and thus the industry producing
genetic modifications will suffer (Weirich 17). The interests of
corporate giants, therefore, appear to be able to influence decision
making in the United States, where the government and economy
are comparatively strong. The impact of corporations on the
governments of poorer countries, then, is likely to be much more
pronounced, and poorer countries are likely to be victimized by big
corporations.

The writer continues to explore both sides of the controversy.

Fig. 1. Not all genetically modified foods are labeled. Photograph © Susan Van Etten/PhotoEdit, Inc.

Moreover, there is some evidence that genetically modified foods do not live up to their promise and, therefore, lack the benefits that could help farmers in poor countries. For example, Rees argues against the assertion that genetically modified crops will be able to ameliorate world hunger. Rather, he believes that more than enough food is produced to feed everyone in the world without these crops and that people go hungry because they cannot afford to buy from the plenty around them for socioeconomic reasons (49). Rees also argues that genetically modified crops have not increased farmers' incomes, regardless of what proponents of genetic engineering may claim. He points to a 2003 study by Professor Caroline Saunders at Lincoln

University, New Zealand, which found that "GM food releases have not benefited producers anywhere in the world" and that "the soil association's 2002 'Seeds of Doubt' report, created with feedback from farmers and data from six years of commercial farming in North America, shows that GM soy and maize crops deliver less income to farmers (on average) than non-GM crops" (50-51). The potential benefit of genetically modified crops thus remains uncertain.

While proponents of genetic engineering insist that genetically modified crops can increase yield and help feed the hungry, opponents point to health risks and challenge the research that appears to prove that genetically modified foods are beneficial. However, even if genetically modified crops do prove to be as beneficial as proponents claim, there is nothing to ensure that this technology would benefit poor farmers in developing countries. Since large corporations hold patents on all genetically modified seeds, there is nothing to guarantee that poor farmers would have access to these seeds, no matter how advanced or beneficial the technology turns out to be. As of now, developing countries continue to be at a disadvantage despite the creation and wide distribution of genetically modified crops. Therefore, it is far from certain whether this new technology will benefit developing nations in the dramatic way that proponents of genetic engineering assert.

The writer's conclusion is drawn from research reported on the previous pages.

1 inch

Notes

Center the heading.

Numbers on notes match the superscript numbers in the body of the paper.

1. There is some concern, however, about the long-term effects of crops genetically engineered for pest resistance. Since these plants are engineered to continually produce a form of the pesticide used to combat the pest problem, insects are constantly exposed to the chemical used to kill them. Such exposure increases the likelihood that the insects will develop a tolerance for this chemical, making the pesticide ineffective.

The writer continues to explore both sides of the controversy.

2. The main difference between genetic engineering and the breeding of plants for desired traits that people have practiced for thousands of years is that genetic engineering actually alters the DNA of a particular plant. Traditional breeding cannot alter the DNA of an individual plant but instead seeks to increase the number of plants that have a trait that occurs naturally. While the end product of both genetic engineering and selective breeding is similar in that both produce plants with desirable traits, the actual processes are radically different.

Suslin 13

Works Cited

Brossard, Dominique, James Shanahan, and T. Clint Nesbitt, eds. *The Public, the Media, and Agricultural Biotechnology*. Cambridge: CABI, 2007. Print.

Cook, Guy. *Genetically Modified Language: The Discourse of Arguments for GM Crops and Food*. New York: Routledge, 2005. Print.

Easton, Thomas A., ed. *Taking Sides: Clashing Views on Controversial Environmental Issues*. 11th ed. Dubuque: McGraw, 2005. Print.

Federal Register 54.104 (1992): 22991. Print.

Fukuda-Parr, Sakiko, ed. *The Gene Revolution: GM Crops and Unequal Development*. Sterling: Earthscan, 2007. Print.

Halweil, Brian. "The Emperor's New Crops." Easton 249-59.

Huffman, W. E. "Production, Identity Preservation, and Labeling in a Marketplace with Genetically Modified and Non-Genetically Modified Foods." *Plant Physiology* 134 (2004): 3-10. Web. 5 Nov. 2007.

Newell, Peter. "Corporate Power and 'Bounded Autonomy' in the Global Politics of Biotechnology." *The International Politics of Genetically Modified Food: Diplomacy, Trade, and Law*. Ed. Robert Falkner. Hampshire: Palgrave, 2007. 67-84. Print.

1 inch

Center the heading.

Alphabetize the entries according to the authors' last names.

Indent second and subsequent lines of each entry one-half inch.

Rees, Andy. *Genetically Modified Food: A Short Guide for the Confused*. Ann Arbor: Pluto, 2006. Print.

Royal Society et al. "Transgenic Plants and World Agriculture." Easton 234-45.

Smith, Jeffrey M. "Genetically Modified Food Threatens Human Health." *Humanity's Future*. Ed. Louise I. Gerdes. Detroit: Gale, 2006. 103-08. Print.

Weirich, Paul, ed. *Labeling Genetically Modified Food: The Philosophical and Legal Debate*. New York: Oxford UP, 2007. Print.

41 APA Documentation

The American Psychological Association (APA) publishes a style guide entitled *Publication Manual of the American Psychological Association.* Its documentation system (called an *author-date system*) is used for work in psychology and many other disciplines, including education, economics, and sociology. Updates to the style guide are provided at **www.apastyle.org**. This chapter includes

- guidelines for citing sources within the text of a paper (**41a**),
- guidelines for documenting sources in a reference list (**41b**), and
- a sample student paper (**41c**).

41a APA-style in-text citations

APA-style in-text citations usually include just the last name(s) of the author(s) of the work and the year of publication. However, be sure to specify the page number(s) for any quotations you use in your paper. The abbreviation *p.* (for "page") or *pp.* (for "pages") should precede the number(s). If you do not know the author's name, use a shortened version of the source's title instead. If your readers want to find more information about your source, they will look for the author's name, or in its absence, the title of the work, in the bibliography at the end of your paper.

You will likely consult a variety of sources for your research paper. The following examples are representative of the types of in-text citations you can expect to use.

Directory of APA-Style Parenthetical Citations

1. Work by one author

Yang (2006) admits that speech, when examined closely, is a "remarkably messy means of communication" (p. 13).

OR

When examined closely, speech is "a remarkably messy means of communication (Yang, 2006, p. 13).

Use commas within a parenthetical citation to separate the author's name from the date and the date from the page number. Include a page number or numbers only when you are quoting directly from the source.

2. Work by two authors

Darvas and Walsh (2002) claim that, regardless of whether children spend time in day care, their development in early childhood is

determined primarily by the nature of the care they receive from
parents.

OR

Regardless of whether children spend time in day care, their development in
early childhood is determined primarily by the nature of the care they receive
from parents (Darvas & Walsh, 2002).

When the authors' names are in parentheses, use an ampersand (&) to separate them.

3. Work by more than two authors

The speech of Pittsburgh, Pennsylvania, is called *Pittsburghese* (Johnstone,
Bhasin, & Wittkofski, 2002).

For works with three to five authors, cite all the authors the
first time the work is referred to, but in subsequent references
give only the last name of the first author followed by *et al.*
(meaning "and others").

According to Johnstone et al. (2002), newspapers and magazines published in
Pittsburgh frequently use nonstandard spelling to represent the pronunciation
of /aw/.

For works with six or more authors, provide only the last name
of the first author followed by *et al.* in both the first and subsequent citations.

4. Anonymous work

Use a shortened version of the title to identify an anonymous work.

Chronic insomnia often requires medical intervention ("Sleep," 2009).

This citation refers to an article identified in the bibliography
as "Sleep disorders: Standard methods of treatment."

   If the word *Anonymous* is used in the source itself to designate the author, it appears in place of an author's name.

The documents could damage the governor's reputation (Anonymous, 2009).

5. Two or more works by different authors in the same parenthetical citation

Smokers frequently underestimate the long-term effects of smoking

(O'Conner, 2005; Polson & Truss, 2007).

Arrange the citations in alphabetical order, using a semicolon to separate them.

6. Two or more works by the same author in the same parenthetical citation

The amygdala is active when a person experiences fear or anger (Carey,

2001, 2002).

Jameson (2007a, 2007b) has proposed an anxiety index for use by counselors.

Order the publication dates of works by the same author from earliest to most recent; however, if the works have the same publication date, distinguish the dates with lowercase letters (a, b, c, and so on) assigned according to the order in which the entries for the works are listed in your bibliography (see page 639).

7. Personal communication

State educational outcomes are often interpreted differently by teachers in the

same school (J. K. Jurgensen, personal communication, May 4, 2009).

Personal communications include letters, memos, e-mail messages, interviews, and telephone conversations. These sources are cited in the text only; they do not appear in the reference list.

8. Indirect source

Korovessis (2002, p. 63) points out Toqueville's description of the "strange

melancholy" exhibited by citizens living amid abundance.

Toqueville (as cited in Korovessis, 2002, p. 63) observed the "strange melancholy" exhibited by citizens living amid abundance.

In the reference list, include a bibliographic entry for the source read, not for the original source. Use an indirect source only when you are unable to obtain the original.

41b   APA-style reference list

All of the works you cite should be listed at the end of your paper, beginning on a separate page with the heading "References." The following tips will help you prepare your list.

TIPS FOR PREPARING A REFERENCE LIST

- Center the heading "References" one inch from the top of the page.

- Include in your reference list only those sources you explicitly cited in your paper. Do not, however, include entries for personal communications or for original works cited in indirect sources.

- Arrange the list of works alphabetically by the author's last name. If a source has more than one author, alphabetize by the last name of the first author.

- If you use more than one work by the same author(s), arrange the entries according to the date of publication, placing the entry with the earliest date first. If two or more works by the same author(s) have the same publication date, the entries are arranged so that the titles of the works are in alphabetical order, according to the first important word in each title; lowercase letters are then added to the date (e.g., 2008a, 2008b) to distinguish the works.

- When an author's name appears both in a single-author entry and as the first name in a multiple-author entry, place the single-author entry first.

(Continued on page 640)

(*Continued from page 639*)

- For a work without an author, alphabetize the entry according to the first important word in the title.
- Type the first line of each entry flush with the left margin and indent subsequent lines one-half inch or five spaces (a hanging indent).
- Double-space throughout—between lines of each entry and between entries.

Whether you are submitting an APA-style paper in a college course or preparing a manuscript for publication, you can be guided by the format of the following sample entries.

Directory of APA-Style Entries for the Reference List

BOOKS

ARTICLES IN PRINT

SOURCES PRODUCED FOR ACCESS BY COMPUTER

OTHER SOURCES

The following guidelines are for books, articles, and most electronic sources. For additional guidelines for documenting electronic sources, see pages 654–659.

When preparing entries for your reference list, be sure to copy the bibliographic information directly from the sources (e.g., the title page of a book). (See fig. 41.1, on page 648.)

General Documentation Guidelines for Print-Based Sources

Author or Editor

One author. Use the author's first initial and middle initial (if given) and his or her last name. Invert the initials and the last name; place a comma after the name. Include a space between the first and middle initials. Any abbreviation or number that is part of a name, such as *Jr.* or *II*, is placed after a comma following the initials. Indicate the end of this information unit with a single period.

Walters, D. M.

Thayer-Smith, M. S.

Villa, R. P., Jr.

Two to six authors. Invert the last names and initials of all authors. Use a comma to separate names from initials and use an ampersand (&) (in addition to the comma) before the last name of the last author.

Vifian, I. R., & Kikuchi, K.

Kempf, A. R., Cusack, R., & Evans, T. G.

Seven or more authors. List the names of the first six authors, but substitute *et al.* for the remaining names.	Bauer, S. E., Berry, L., Hacket, N. P., Bach, R., Price, T. M., Brown, J. B., et al.
Corporate or group author. Provide the author's full name.	Hutton Arts Foundation. Center for Neuroscience.
Editor. If a work has an editor or editors instead of an author or authors, include the abbreviation *Ed.* for "editor" or *Eds.* for "editors" in parentheses after the name(s).	Harris, B. E. (Ed.). Stroud, D. F., & Holst, L. F. (Eds.).

Publication Date

Books and journals. Provide the year of publication in parentheses, placing a period after the closing parenthesis. For books, this date can be found on the copyright page, which is the page following the title page (see fig. 41.2, on page 649). The publication date of a journal article can be found at the bottom of the first page of the article (see fig. 41.3, on page 652). For a work that has been accepted for publication but has not yet been published, place *in press* in parentheses. For a work without a date of publication, use *n.d.* in parentheses.	(2008). (in press). (n.d.).

(Continued on page 644)

Publication Date *(Continued from page 643)*

Magazines and newspapers. For monthly publications, provide both the year and the month, separated by a comma. For daily publications, provide the year, month, and day. Use a comma between the year and the month.	(2007, January). (2008, June 22).

Conferences and meetings. If a paper presented at a conference, symposium, or professional meeting is published, the publication date is given as the year only, in parentheses. For unpublished papers, provide the year and the month in which the gathering occurred, separated by a comma.	(2008). (2009, September).

Title

Books. Capitalize only the first word and any proper nouns in a book title. Italicize the entire title and place a period at the end of this information unit.	*Language and the mind.* *Avoiding work-related stress.*

Journals, magazines, or newspapers. In the name of a journal, magazine, or newspaper, capitalize all major words, as well as any other words consisting of four or more letters. Italicize the entire name and place a comma after it.	*Journal of Child Psychology,* *Psychology Today,* *Los Angeles Times,*

Articles and chapters. Do not italicize the titles of short works such as journal articles or book chapters. In a bibliographic entry, titles of articles and chapters appear before book titles and the names of journals, magazines, or newspapers. Capitalize only the first word of the title and any proper nouns.

Treating posttraumatic stress disorder.

Subtitles. Always include any subtitle provided for a source. Use a colon to separate a main title and a subtitle. Capitalize only the first word of the subtitle and any proper nouns.

Reading images: The grammar of visual design.

Living in Baghdad: Realities and restrictions.

Volume, Issue, Chapter, and Page Numbers

Journal volume and issue numbers. A journal paginated *continuously* designates only the first page of the first issue in a volume as page 1. The first page of a subsequent issue in the same volume is given the page number that follows the last page number of the previous issue. In contrast, each issue of a journal paginated *separately* begins with page 1. When you use an article from a journal paginated continuously, provide only the volume number (italicized). When you use an article from a journal paginated separately, provide the

Journal of Applied Social Psychology, 32,

Behavior Therapy, 33(2),

(Continued on page 646)

Volume, Issue, Chapter, and Page Numbers
(Continued from page 645)

issue number (placed in parentheses) directly after the volume number. Do not insert a space between the volume and issue numbers. Italicize only the volume number. Place a comma after this unit of information.

Book chapters. Provide the numbers of the first and last pages of the relevant chapter preceded by the abbreviation *pp.* (for "pages"). Place this information in parentheses. Use an en dash (a short dash; see **11g(2)**) between the page numbers.

New communitarian thinking (pp. 126–140).

Articles. List the page numbers after the comma that follows the volume or issue number.

TESOL Quarterly, 34(2), 213–238.

Publication Data

City and state. Identify the city in which the publisher of the work is located. If two or more cities are given on the title page, use the first one listed.

Boston:

Add the two-letter U.S. Postal Service abbreviation for the state unless the city is one of the following: Baltimore, Boston, Chicago, Los Angeles, New York, Philadelphia, or San Francisco.

Lancaster, PA:

If the publisher is a university press whose name mentions a state, do not include the state abbreviation. When a work has been published in a city outside the United States, add the name of the country unless the city is Amsterdam, Jerusalem, London, Milan, Moscow, Paris, Rome, Stockholm, Tokyo, or Vienna—in these cases, the name of the city alone is sufficient.	University Park: Pennsylvania State University Press. Oxford, England:
Publisher's name. Provide only enough of the publisher's name so that it can be identified clearly. Omit words such as *Publishers* and abbreviations such as *Inc.* However, include *Books* and *Press* when they are part of the publisher's name. The publisher's name follows the city and state or country, after a colon. A period ends this unit of information.	New Haven, CT: Yale University Press. New York: Harcourt. Cambridge, England: Cambridge University Press.

BOOKS

1. Book by one author

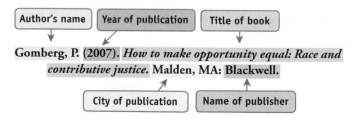

Gomberg, P. (2007). *How to make opportunity equal: Race and contributive justice.* Malden, MA: Blackwell.

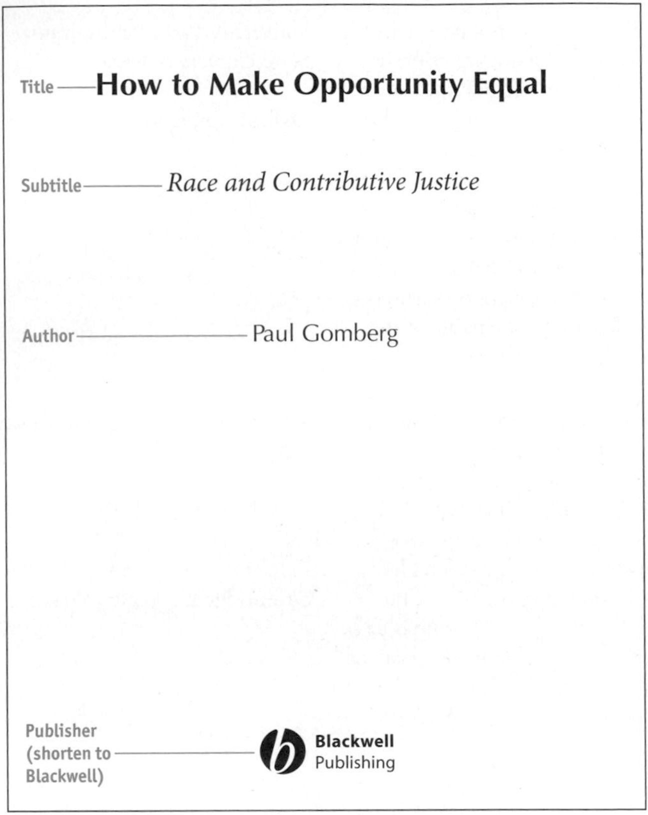

Title —**How to Make Opportunity Equal**

Subtitle——— *Race and Contributive Justice*

Author——————— Paul Gomberg

Publisher
(shorten to —————— **Blackwell**
Blackwell) Publishing

Fig. 41.1. The title page of a book provides most of the information necessary for creating a bibliographic entry for a research paper.

2. Book by two or more authors

Thomas, D., & Woods, H. (2003). *Working with people with disabilities:*
    Theory and practice. London: Jessica Kingsley.

If there are more than six authors, list the first six names and use the abbreviation *et al.* in place of the remaining names (see page 643).

3. Book with editor(s)

Wolfe, D. A., & Mash, E. J. (Eds.). (2005). *Behavioral and emotional*

disorders in adolescents: Nature, assessment, and treatment. New York:

Guilford Press.

Year of —— © 2007 by Paul Gomberg
publication

               BLACKWELL PUBLISHING
Cities of   ┌350 Main Street, Malden, MA 02148-5020, USA
publication ──┤9600 Garsington Road, Oxford OX4 2DQ, UK
(use Malden, └550 Swanston Street, Carlton, Victoria 3053, Australia
MA)

The right of Paul Gomberg to to identified as the Author of this Work has been asserted in accordance with the UK Copyright, Designs, and Patents Act 1988.

All rights reserved. No part of this publication may be reproduced, stored in a retrieval system, or transmitted, in any form or by any means, electronic, mechanical, photocopying, recording or otherwise, except as permitted by the UK Copyright, Designs, and Patents Act 1988, without the prior permission of the publisher.

First published 2007 by Blackwell Publishing Ltd.

Fig. 41.2. The year in which a book was published and the city where it was published can be found on the copyright page, which follows the title page.

4. Book with a corporate or group author

U.S. War Department. (2003). *Official military atlas of the Civil War*.

New York: Barnes & Noble.

When the author and the publisher of a book are the same, use the publisher's name at the beginning of the entry and *Author* at the end.

American Psychiatric Association. (1995). *American Psychiatric Association*

capitation handbook. Washington, DC: Author.

5. Edition after the first

Lycan, W., & Prinz, J. (Eds.). (2008). *Mind and cognition* (3rd ed.). Malden,

MA: Blackwell.

Identify the edition in parentheses immediately after the title. Use abbreviations: *2nd, 3rd,* and so on for the edition number and *ed.* for "edition."

6. Translation

Rank, O. (2002). *Psychology and the soul: A study of the origin, conceptual*

evolution, and nature of the soul (G. C. Richter & E. J. Lieberman,

Trans.). Baltimore: Johns Hopkins University Press. (Original work

published 1930)

A period follows the name of the publisher but not the parenthetical note about the original publication date.

7. Multivolume work

Doyle, A. C. (2003). *The complete Sherlock Holmes* (Vols. 1–2). New York:

Barnes & Noble.

If the multivolume work was published over a period of more than one year, use the range of years for the publication date.

Hawthorne, N. (1962–1997). *The centenary edition of the works of Nathaniel Hawthorne* (Vols. 1–23). Columbus: Ohio University Press.

8. Government report

Executive Office of the President. (2003). *Economic report of the President, 2003* (GPO Publication No. 040-000-0760-1). Washington, DC: U.S. Government Printing Office.

9. Selection from an edited book

Empson, R. (2007). Enlivened memories: Recalling absence and loss in Mongolia. In J. Carsten (Ed.), *Ghosts of memory: Essays on remembrance and relatedness* (pp. 58–82). Malden, MA: Blackwell.

Italicize the book title but not the title of the selection.

10. Selection from a reference book

Wickens, D. (2001). Classical conditioning. In *The Corsini encyclopedia of psychology and behavioral science* (Vol. 1, pp. 293–298). New York: John Wiley.

ARTICLES IN PRINT

11. Article with one author in a journal with continuous pagination

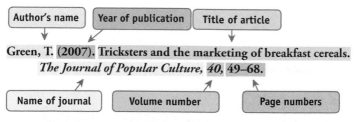

Green, T. (2007). Tricksters and the marketing of breakfast cereals. *The Journal of Popular Culture, 40,* 49–68.

Figure 41.3 shows where the information for this type of entry is found on the first page of an article.

Title —— Tricksters and the Marketing of
Breakfast Cereals

Author —— THOMAS GREEN

REAKFAST CEREALS ARE SOLD BY TRICKSTERS. FROM LUCKY THE
Leprechaun to the Cookie Crook to the mischievous live-action
squirrels who vend General Mills Honey Nut Clusters, an astounding number of Saturday morning television commercials feature 30-second dramatizations of trickster tales that are designed to promote breakfast cereals. True, breakfast cereals are not the only products sold by tricksters, and not all cereals are sold by tricksters—especially in the last decade. But the association is common enough to persist as an unexamined assumption that seems obvious to most Americans once it is pointed out. Naturally, breakfast cereals are often sold by animated tricksterish mascot characters, and naturally such commercials feature motifs and narrative patterns that are common in trickster tales. But the perception of an inherent internal logic in this scheme overlooks a couple of key questions. Why, for example, are tricksters considered a particularly appropriate or effective means of marketing breakfast cereals? And why breakfast cereals in particular (and a few other breakfast products), almost to the exclusion of tricksters in other types of marketing campaigns? The answers to these questions, it turns out, may lie back in the semi-mystical, pseudoreligious origins of prepared breakfast foods and the mating of the mythology of those foods with the imperatives of the competitive, prepared-foods marketplace.

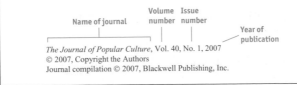

Name of journal | Volume number | Issue number | Year of publication

The Journal of Popular Culture, Vol. 40, No. 1, 2007
© 2007, Copyright the Authors
Journal compilation © 2007, Blackwell Publishing, Inc.

Fig. 41.3. The first page of a journal article provides the information needed to complete a bibliographic entry for that source.

12. Article with two authors in a journal with each issue paginated separately

Rudisill, J. R., & Edwards, J. M. (2002). Coping with job transitions. *Consulting Psychology Journal, 54*(1), 55–62.

13. Article with three to six authors

Frost, R. O., Steketee, G., & Williams, L. (2002). Compulsive buying, compulsive hoarding, and obsessive-compulsive disorder. *Behavior Therapy, 33*(2), 201–213.

14. Article with more than six authors

Reddy, S. K., Arora, M., Perry, C. L., Nair, B., Kohli, A., Lytle, L. A., et al. (2002). Tobacco and alcohol use outcomes of a school-based intervention in New Delhi. *American Journal of Health Behavior, 26,* 173–181.

15. Article in a monthly, biweekly, or weekly magazine

Winson, J. (2002, June). The meaning of dreams. *Scientific American, 12,* 54–61.

For magazines published weekly or biweekly, add the day of the issue: (2003, May 8).

16. Article in a newspaper

Simon, S. (2007, October 14). Winning hearts, minds, homes. *Los Angeles Times,* p. A1.

Include the letter indicating the section with the page number.

17. Letter to the editor

Mancall, M. (2002, June 17). Answer to cynicism [Letter to the editor]. *The New York Times,* p. A20.

After the title, indicate within brackets that the work is a letter to the editor.

18. Book review

Orford, J. (2007). Drug addiction and families [Review of the book *Drug*

   addiction and families]. *Addiction, 102,* 1841–1842.

If the review has its own title, use that instead of the title of the book. Retain the bracketed information.

SOURCES PRODUCED FOR ACCESS BY COMPUTER

The APA guidelines for electronic sources are similar to those for print sources. Exceptions are explained after the sample entries that follow. Information about when and/or how a source was retrieved appears at the end of the entry. The period that normally ends an entry is omitted after a URL because it could cause difficulty in retrieving a file. If a URL has to continue on a new line, break it before a punctuation mark or other special character. Note that many scholarly journals now use a Digital Object Identifier (DOI) to simplify searching for an article. Whenever possible, use a DOI (without a period following it) instead of a URL at the end of a reference list entry. The DOI will be listed on the first page of the article, which usually contains the abstract. Figure 41.4 shows the location of a DOI and other pertinent bibliographic information on the first page of an online journal article.

Journal of Experimental Psychology: Applied — Name of journal
2001, Vol. 7, No. 1, 27–50

Copyright 2001 by the American Psychological Association, Inc.
1076-898X/01/S5.00 DOI: 10.1037//1076-898X.7.1.27

Volume and issue number
Page numbers
DOI
Year of publication

Children's Eyewitness Reports After Exposure to Misinformation From Parents

Title of article

Debra Ann Poole
Central Michigan University

Authors of article

D. Stephen Lindsay
University of Victoria

This study examined how misleading suggestions from parents influenced children's eyewitness reports. Children (3 to 8 years old) participated in science demonstrations, listened to their parents read a story that described experienced and nonexperienced events, and subsequently discussed the science experience in two follow-up interviews. Many children described fictitious events in response to open-ended prompts, and there were no age differences in suggestibility during this phase of the interview. Accuracy declined markedly in response to direct questions, especially for the younger children. Although the older children retracted many of their false reports after receiving source-monitoring instructions, the younger children did not. Path analyses indicated that acquiescence, free recall, and source monitoring all contribute to mediating patterns of suggestibility across age. Results indicate that judgments about the accuracy of children's testimony must consider the possibility of exposure to misinformation prior to formal interviews.

During the past decade, there has been keen interest in young children's performance when interviewed about autobiographical events. This interest was sharpened by broad social changes that led the public to be more concerned about crimes to which child victims are often the sole witnesses (e.g., child sexual abuse), but it also reflected a movement in psychology away from relatively artificial research paradigms (e.g., studies of memory for word lists) and toward more naturalistic and multifaceted approaches to research. Although the field of eyewitness testimony receives considerable attention for its forensic implications, researchers increasingly view eyewitness paradigms as tools for studying basic issues in memory and cognition.

There have been several recent reviews of the literature on interviewing children for forensic purposes

Debra Ann Poole, Department of Psychology, Central Michigan University; D. Stephen Lindsay, Department of Psychology, University of Victoria.

This material is based on work supported by National Science Foundation Grant SBR-9409231. Any opinions, findings, and conclusions or recommendations expressed in this material are those of the authors and do not necessarily reflect the views of the National Science Foundation. We thank the members of our research team for assistance in data collection and coding (Sonya Lucke, Scott Kuligoski, Lisa Wolf, Carolyn Miska, Chad Stabler, Rachel Johnson, Erin Henderson, Doug Haseley, Rachel Franceschina, Laura Whitlock, and Susan Williams), and Dan and Linda King (National Center for PTSD, Boston VA Medical Center) for consultations regarding data analyses. We also extend special thanks to the parents and children in Michigan who have volunteered their time to support our work.

Correspondence concerning this article should be addressed to Debra Ann Poole, Department of Psychology, 231 Sloan Hall, Central Michigan University, Mt. Pleasant, Michigan 48859.

(e.g., Ceci & Bruck, 1995; Poole & Lamb, 1998), and we do not offer an exhaustive recapitulation here. In its broadest outlines, the literature can be crudely summarized by saying that even very young children (i.e., 3- to 4-year-olds) can provide quite detailed and accurate accounts of past autobiographical events under some conditions but that even older children and adults often provide impoverished and inaccurate accounts under others. The aim of the current research was to provide additional insight into factors that compromise or enhance the amount and accuracy of the information interviewers gain from young children. Borrowing terms from Wells's (1993) analysis of eyewitness suspect identification, our research examined both "system variables" (i.e., factors that are under the control of investigators in forensic cases, such as the way questions are phrased) and "estimator variables" (i.e., factors that may affect the amount or accuracy of information children report but that cannot be controlled by investigators, such as the age of the child or the nature of the alleged event).

Numerous studies have documented that the accuracy of children's testimonies can be degraded when interviewers ask misleading questions or provide social feedback that favors particular answers (Ceci & Bruck, 1995). Rather than emphasizing suggestive interviewing techniques, the central focus of the current study was on the effects of misleading information presented to young children by their parents prior to and outside of an interviewing situation. It is likely that many children who are involved in forensic investigations were exposed to misinformation from trusted adults, ranging from overheard conversations to deliberate coaching before participating in a formal forensic interview. This worrisome possibility that false reports based on prior exposure to suggestions may intrude into forensic interview responses even when those interviews are conducted in an optimally nonsuggestive manner.

Fig. 41.4. First page of an online journal article.

19. Online journal article with a Digital Object Identifier (DOI)

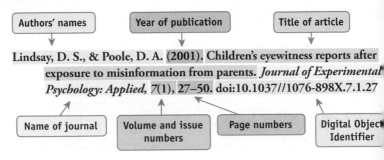

Authors' names → Year of publication → Title of article

Lindsay, D. S., & Poole, D. A. (2001). Children's eyewitness reports after exposure to misinformation from parents. *Journal of Experimental Psychology: Applied, 7*(1), 27–50. doi:10.1037//1076-898X.7.1.27

Name of journal — Volume and issue numbers — Page numbers — Digital Object Identifier

20. Online journal article without a DOI

Tuladhar-Douglas, W. (2007). Leaf blowers and antibiotics: A Buddhist stance for science and technology. *Journal of Buddhist Ethics, 14,* 200–238. Retrieved from http://www.buddhistethics.org/14 /tuladhar-article.html

If the article is available only by subscription, use the URL for the journal's home page instead of the URL for the article.

21. Online magazine article based on a print source

Acocella, J. (2008, May 26). A few too many. *The New Yorker, 84*(15), 32–37. Retrieved from http://www.newyorker.com/reporting/2008/05/26/080526fa _fact_acocella?currentPage=1

22. Online magazine article not found in print

Saletan, W. (2008, August 27). Unfinished race: Race, genes, and the future of medicine. *Slate.* Retrieved August 29, 2008, from http://www.slate.com /id/2198731/

23. Article in an online newspaper

McGrath, C. (2002, June 15). Father time. *The New York Times.* Retrieved
  from http://nytimes.com/pages/science/index.html

24. Online book

Stevens, K. (n.d.). *The dreamer and the beast.* Available from http://www
  .onlineoriginals.com/showitem.asp?itemID=321&action=setvar&vartype
  =history&varname=bookmark&v1=1&v2=46&v3=1

If access to the book is not free, use "Available from" instead of
"Retrieved from."

25. Online book chapter

Wallner, F., & Durnwalder, K. (1994). Sciences, psychology and realism. In
  V. Shen, R. Knowles, & T. Van Doan (Eds.), *Psychology, phenomenology
  and Chinese philosophy: Vol. 6. Chinese philosophical studies.* Retrieved
  from http://www.crvp.org/book/Series03/III-6/chapter_i
  __science.htm

26. Message posted to a newsgroup, forum, or discussion group

Vellenzer, G. (2004, January 24). Synonyms of entreaty [Msg 2]. Message
  posted to http://groups.google.com/groups?selm=MPG
  .1a7cacccd54e9c27989b95%40news.CIS.DFN.DE&output=gplain

If the message has been archived at another address, a comma
should be placed after the first URL, followed by "archived at"
and the URL for the archived version.

27. Weblog posting

Chatham, C. (2008, August 29). Action without intention: Parietal damage
    alters attention awareness. Message posted to http://scienceblogs.com
    /developingintelligence/2008/08/action_without_intention_parie.php

28. Lecture notes posted online

Wolfe, J. (2004). *Lecture 8: Freud and fairy tales.* Retrieved from
    Massachusetts Institute of Technology OpenCourseWare Web site:
    http://ocw.mit.edu/OcwWeb/Brain-and-Cognitive-Sciences/9-00Fall
    -2004/LectureNotes/index.htm

29. Authored document from a Web site

Ennis, R. H. (2002, July 20). *An outline of goals for a critical thinking
    curriculum and its assessment.* Retrieved August 6, 2007, from
    http://faculty.ed.uiuc.edu/rhennis/outlinegoalsctcurassess3.html

When the document is from a large Web site, such as one
sponsored by a university or government body, provide the
name of the host organization before the URL.

Darling, C. (2002). *Guide to grammar and writing.* Retrieved September 12,
    2003, from Capital Community College Web site: http://cctc2.commnet
    .edu/grammar/modifiers.htm

30. Online document with no identified author

American School Counselor Association. (2006). *Position statement:
    Equity for all students.* Retrieved October 17, 2007, from http://asca2
    .timberlakepublishing.com/content.asp?contentid=503

Use the name of the organization hosting the Web site as the
author of the document. If a date for the document is provided, place it in parentheses. If no date is listed, use the abbreviation *n.d.* The date of retrieval and the URL are located
at either the top or the bottom of a printout.

31. Personal communication

Personal communications such as e-mail messages, letters, interviews, and telephone conversations are not included in the reference list but should be cited in the text as follows: (S. L. Johnson, personal communication, September 3, 2003).

32. Online encyclopedia

Dowe, P. (2007). Causal processes. In E. N. Zalta (Ed.), *The Stanford encyclopedia of philosophy*. Retrieved August 29, 2008, from http://plato.stanford.edu/archives/sum2007/entries/cognitive-science/

33. Online dictionary

Paranormal. (2000). In *The American Heritage dictionary of the English language: Fourth edition*. Retrieved September 2, 2008, from http://www.bartleby.com/61/35/P0063500.html

34. Online consumer brochure

American Psychological Association. (2008). Elder abuse and neglect: In search of solutions [Brochure]. Retrieved from http://www.apa.org/pi/aging/eldabuse.html

35. Online white paper

Yones, M. (n.d.). Psychology of happiness and unhappiness [White paper]. Retrieved from International Institute of Management: http://www.iim-edu.org/executivejournal/index.htm

OTHER SOURCES

36. Motion picture

Smith, M. (Producer/Writer), & Gaviria, M. (Producer/Director). (2001). *Medicating kids* [Motion picture]. (Available from the Public Broadcasting Service, 1320 Braddock Place, Alexandria, VA 22314)

Begin with the primary contributor(s), identifying the nature of the contribution. Then provide the release date, the title, and the descriptive label in square brackets. For a film with limited distribution, provide, within parentheses, information about how it can be obtained. For a widely distributed film, indicate the country where it was produced and the name of the studio, after the descriptive label: [Motion picture]. United States: Paramount Pictures.

37. Television program

Holt, S. (Producer). (2002, October 1). *The mysterious lives of caves*

[Television broadcast]. Alexandria, VA: Public Broadcasting Service.

Give the title of the program in italics. If citing an entire series (e.g., *Nova* or *The West Wing*), cite the producer for the series as a whole. Use the descriptive label *Television series* in the square brackets.

41c Sample APA-style paper

The APA recognizes that a paper may have to be modified so that it adheres to an instructor's requirements. The following boxes offer tips for preparing a title page, an abstract page, and the body of a typical student paper. For tips on preparing a reference list, see **41b**.

TIPS FOR PREPARING THE TITLE PAGE OF AN APA-STYLE PAPER

- Place the number 1 (to indicate that this is the first page) an inch from the right side of the paper and a half inch from the top.

- Place a **manuscript page header** (the first two or three words of the title) in the upper-right corner, five spaces before the page number. The manuscript page header should appear on all subsequent pages along with the appropriate page number.

- Below the page header but on the left side of the page, list the **running head**, a shortened version of the title (no more than fifty characters). Use *all* uppercase letters for the running head.

- Place the title in the center of the page, with your name below it. You may include your affiliation or a course name or number if your instructor requests one. Double-space these lines.

TIPS FOR PREPARING THE ABSTRACT AND THE BODY OF AN APA-STYLE PAPER

- Place the number 2 an inch from the right side of the paper and a half inch from the top on the abstract page.

- Place a manuscript page header five spaces to the left of the page number.

- Center the word *Abstract* (neither italicized nor underlined) one inch from the top of the paper.

- Be sure that the abstract (a short summary) is no more than 120 words. For advice on summarizing, see **39d(4)**.

- Double-space throughout the body of the abstract. Do not indent the first line of the abstract.

- Place the number 3 on the first page of the body of the paper, along with the manuscript page header.

- Center the title of the paper one inch from the top of the page.

- Use one-inch margins on both the left and right sides of your paper.

- Double-space throughout the body of the paper, indenting each paragraph one-half inch or five to seven spaces.

Place the page header in the top right corner, five spaces to the left of the page number.

Running Head: THE SCIENCE BEHIND AN ART

The running head should consist of no more than 50 characters.

Use 1-inch margins on both sides of the page.

If required by the instructor, the course name and number replace the affiliation.

The Science Behind an Art:

Historical and Current Trends in Tattooing

Rachel L. Pinter and Sarah M. Cronin

Central Washington University

1 inch · The Science Behind · 2 · 1/2 inch

Center the heading.

Abstract

Current research demonstrates that the social practice of tattooing has changed greatly over the years. Not only have the images chosen for tattoos and the demographic of people getting tattoos changed, but the ideology behind tattooing itself has evolved. This paper first briefly describes the cross-cultural history of the practice. It then examines current social trends in the United States and related ideological issues.

The maximum length for an abstract is 120 words.

1 inch

The Science Behind an Art: Historical and Current Trends in Tattooing

Center the title.

Tattoos, defined as marks made by inserting pigment into

the skin, have existed throughout history in countless cultures.

Currently, tattoos are considered popular art forms. They can

be seen on men and women from all walks of life in the United

Use 1-inch margins on both sides of the page.

States, ranging from a trainer at the local gym to a character on a

television show or even a sociology professor. Due to an increase

in the popularity of tattooing, studies of tattooing behavior have

The writers' thesis statement forecasts the content of the essay.

proliferated as researchers attempt to identify trends. This paper

seeks to explore both the history of tattooing and its current practice

in the United States.

Tattooing can be found in the histories of people worldwide,

The writers provide historical and cultural information about tattooing.

though its origin is currently unknown. Krcmarik (2003) provides

a helpful geographical overview. In Asia, tattooing has existed

for thousands of years in Chinese, Japanese, Middle Eastern, and

Indian cultures. Evidence of its existence can be seen on artifacts

such as 7,000-year-old engravings. In Europe, tattooing flourished

during the 19th century, most notably in England. Many of the

sailors traveling with Captain James Cook returned with tales of

exotic tattooing practices and sometimes with tattoos themselves.

The Samoans in the South Pacific are famous for their centuries old

tattooing practice, known as *tatau*—the word from which *tattoo* is

The Science Behind 4

said to have originated. The Maori of New Zealand are also well known for their hand-carved facial tattoos, known as *Moko* (see Figure 1).

Figure 1. A Maori man with a facial tattoo. *Note.* Photo © Tim Graham/ Getty Images.

In Africa, tattoos can be found on Egyptian and Nubian mummies, which date back to approximately 2000 BCE. The tattooing history of South America is noted in the written accounts of Spanish explorers' encounters with tattooed Mayans. Finally, in North America, tattooing became popular during the 1900s and has experienced advances and retreats in social acceptance since then. Starting in the 1960s, its popularity rose dramatically and continues to rise.

Clearly, the history of tattooing spans generations and cultures. The practice has gained and lost popularity, often as a result of rather extreme changes in the ideologies supporting or discouraging it. This rollercoaster pattern of acceptance is well

The writers discuss changing perspectives on the appropriateness of tattoos. demonstrated in the United States. Since the 19th century, the wearing of tattoos has allowed for subculture identification by such persons as sailors, bikers, circus "freak" performers, and prison inmates (DeMello, 1995). As a collective group behavior indicating deviant subculture membership, tattooing flourished during this time but remained plagued by negative stereotypes and associations. In the last 10 years, however, the practice has represented a more individualistic yet mainstream means of body adornment, gaining popularity in unprecedented numbers. Now, tattooing can be seen among both teenagers and older adults, men and women, urbanites and suburbanites, the college-educated and the uneducated, and the rich as well as the poor (Kosut, 2006).

Citation of a work by one author   The trend toward acceptance of tattoos may be a result of how American society views the people who wear them. Earlier, tattoos were depicted in mainstream print and visual media as worn by people with low socioeconomic or marginal status; now, they are considered to be an artful expression among celebrities as well as educated middle and upper classes, as Figure 2 illustrates (Kosut, 2006). This shift in the symbolic status of tattoos—self-expression among the social elite rather than deviant expression among the working class—has allowed tattoos to be obtained in greater numbers, owing in great part to the importance placed on self-expression in the United States.

The Science Behind   6

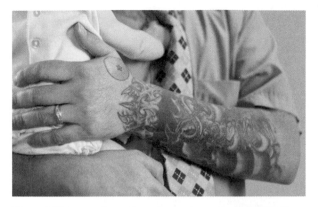

Figure 2. Tattoos are becoming more common among middle-class professionals. *Note.* Photo © Eric Anthony Photography/Monsoon Images/PhotoLibrary.

Even in the workplace, where employees were often forbidden to display tattoos, employers now "take advantage of the open-mindedness and innovation that younger [tattooed] employees bring into the workplace" (Org, 2003, p. D1).

To clarify a direct quotation from a source, the writers insert a word in square brackets.

As the popularity and acceptability of tattoos have increased, tattooing has become part of the greater consumer culture and has thus undergone the process of commercialization that frequently occurs in American society. Tattoos are now acquired as embodied status symbols and are used to sell tattoo maintenance products, clothing lines, skateboards, décor, and other fashion items (Kosut, 2006). This introduction into the consumer culture allows tattoos to gain even more

popularity; they are now intertwined with mainstream enterprises.

Researchers have been tracking the popularity of tattoos,

though no one seems able to agree on a number (Libbon, 2000).

In 2000, MSNBC aired a documentary called "Skin Deep," which

cited the tattooing rate at 20% of the population (Rosenbaum, 2000).

In 2003, citing a lower number, Harris Interactive reported that 16%

of all adults in the United States have at least one tattoo (Sever,

2003). The actual number of individuals with tattoos is unknown,

but most researchers believe the trend has been consistently gaining

ground since the 1960s. Within the context of the larger population,

statistics on the frequency of tattooing among specific age groups

show a similar increase (Armstrong, Owen, Roberts, & Koch, 2002;

Mayers, Judelson, Moriarty, & Rundell, 2002). However, due to

the limitations of the various research designs, more research on a

national level is needed to obtain truly representative figures.

Significantly, the increase in acquisition of tattoos has

resulted in trends concerning the images and locations of tattoos,

which appear to be divided down lines of gender. Many of the tattoo

images commonly found on men include, but are not limited to,

death themes, various wildlife, military insignia, tribal armbands,

and family crests or last names. During the 1980s, cartoon images

The writers list statistics to support a claim.

Two citations of articles, both written by four authors, are separated by a semicolon.

The Science Behind 8

such as Bugs Bunny and the Tasmanian Devil were also popular for males. Males choose various locations for tattoos, but the most popular male sites are the upper back, back of the calves, and the upper arm, according to tattoo artist Ben Reames (personal communication, July 12, 2007). Conversely, females often obtain tattoos that symbolize traditional femininity, such as flowers, stars, hearts, and butterflies. A noticeable trend for females in the 1980s was the rose tattoo, which was often located on the breast or ankle. Stars and butterflies now rival the rose in popularity. The ankle continues to be a popular location for females today. Other popular spots for tattoos include the hip, the foot (see Figure 3), and the lower back. In fact, the lower back experienced a huge surge in popularity during the 1990s (B. Reames, personal communication, July 12, 2007).

The art of tattooing has existed in many culturally determined

Figure 3. Many females who get a tattoo choose to have it on the foot. *Note.* Photo © Color-Blind Images/ Blend Images/Corbis.

Citation of an interview with a tattoo artist

The writers include a photograph to support a point.

Conclusion forms throughout human history, and its current manifestations
are as varied as the cultures themselves. However, based on the
current literature, the social behavior of tattooing is experiencing
unparalled growth in the United States. In fact, Kosut (2006) argues,
"New generations of American children are growing up in a cultural
landscape that is more tattoo-friendly and tattoo-flooded than any
other time in history" (p. 1037). Because today's children see
tattoos and tattoo-related products everywhere, usually in neutral or
positive situations, they will likely be more accepting of tattoos than
earlier generations were. Certainly, the tattooing trend shows no
signs of leveling off.

1/2 inch

1 inch The Science Behind 10

References

Armstrong, M. L., Owen, D. C., Roberts, A. E., & Koch, J. R. (2002). College students and tattoos: Influence of image, identity, and family. *Journal of Psychosocial Nursing*, *40*(10), 20–30.

DeMello, M. (1995). Not just for bikers anymore: Popular representations of American tattooing. *Journal of Popular Culture*, *29*(3), 37–53.

Kosut, M. (2006). An ironic fad: The commodification and consumption of tattoos. *Journal of Popular Culture*, *39*(6), 1035–1049.

Krcmarik, K. L. (2003). *History of tattooing*. Retrieved April 7, 2007, from Michigan State University: http://www.msu.edu/~krcmari1/individual/history.html

Libbon, R. P. (2000). Dear data dog: Why do so many kids sport tattoos? *American Demographics*, *22*(9), 26. Retrieved from http://amiga.adage.com/de

Mayers, L. B., Judelson, D. A., Moriarty, B. W., & Rundell, K. W. (2002). Prevalence of body art (body piercing and tattooing) in university undergraduates and incidence of medical complications. *Mayo Clinic Proceedings, 77,* 29–34.

Org, M. (2003, August 28). The tattooed executive. *The Wall Street Journal*. Retrieved from http://online.wsj.com/public/us

Center the heading.

Alphabetize the entries according to the first or only author's last name.

Indent second and subsequent lines of each entry one-half inch or five spaces.

Rosenbaum, S. (Executive Producer). (2000, August 20). *MSNBC investigates: Tattoos—skin deep* [Television broadcast]. New York and Englewood Cliffs, NJ: MSNBC.

Sever, J. (2003, October 8). *A third of Americans with tattoos say they make them feel more sexy*. Retrieved July 20, 2007, from http://www.harrisinteractive.com/harris_poll/index .asp?PID=868

Identification of the type of medium is placed in square brackets.

No period follows a URL at the end of an entry.

42 Writing about Literature

You have been interpreting and writing about literature ever since you wrote your first book report. When you write about literature in college, you will still discuss plot, characters, and setting, but you will also respond to an exigence, explore and focus your subject, formulate a thesis statement that can be supported by reference to the literary work itself, address an audience, and arrange your thoughts in the most effective way. In short, you will respond to the rhetorical situation.

Figure 42.1 shows how the elements of the rhetorical situation apply to a specific piece of writing about literature: a student essay on Alice Walker's short story "Everyday Use." In response to a disagreement among the characters in the story, Kaitlyn Andrews-Rice argues that embracing one's heritage every day is the best way to honor it.

This chapter will help you

- recognize the various genres of literature (42a),
- realize the value of a careful reading (42b),
- use the specialized vocabulary for discussing literature (42c),
- employ various critical approaches for interpreting literature (42d), and
- apply the special conventions for writing about literature (42e and 42f).

Exigence: Responding to the characters' disagreement about the best way to honor one's heritage

Writer: Kaitlyn Andrews-Rice

Audience: Kaitlyn's professor and her classmates

Message: Embracing one's heritage every day is the most authentic way to honor it.

Context: Classroom discussion about the disagreement among the characters in the story "Everyday Use" by Alice Walker

Fig. 42.1. Sample rhetorical situation for writing about literature.

42a Literature and its genres

Like all specialized fields, literature can be divided into categories, which are referred to as **genres.** A genre can be identified by its particular features or conventions. Even when genres overlap (some poems are referred to as prose poems, whereas some plays are written in verse), the identifiable features of each genre are still evident.

Some of the most widely studied literary genres are fiction, drama, and poetry, though many forms of nonfiction (including personal essays and memoirs, literacy narratives, and manifestos) are being studied in college courses on literature. All imaginative literature can be characterized as fictional, but the term **fiction** is applied specifically to novels and short stories. Drama differs from all other imaginative literature in one specific way: it is meant to be performed. In a novel, you often find extensive descriptions of characters and setting as well as passages revealing what characters are thinking. In a play, you learn what a character is thinking when he or she shares thoughts with another character in dialogue or presents a **dramatic soliloquy** (a speech delivered to the audience by an actor alone on the stage). Poetry shares the components of fiction and drama. But poetry is primarily characterized by its extensive use of connotative language, imagery, allusions, figures of speech, symbols, sound, meter, and rhythm.

42b Active reading and literary interpretation

The most successful writing about literature starts with active reading. Were you amused, moved, or confused? Which characters interested you? Were you able to follow the plot? Did the work remind you of any experience of your own or other works you have read? Did it introduce you to a different historical or geographical setting, or did you encounter a familiar setting and cast of characters? These first impressions can provide the seeds from which strong essays will grow.

(1) You can understand your response by considering how it may be shaped by your identity.

When reflecting on your response to some element in a work of literature, consider how your reading might be shaped by the factors that define who you are. For example, if you find yourself responding positively or negatively to a character in a novel or play, you might ask yourself whether this response has anything to do with your

- psychological makeup,
- political beliefs,
- gender or sexual orientation,
- race,
- social class,
- religion, or
- geographic location.

Thinking about what you bring to a work of literature can help you decide how to focus your essay and prepare you for using one or more theoretical approaches as the basis for your interpretation (42d).

(2) After choosing a topic, develop it, using evidence in the text.

If you are choosing your own topic, your first step is to reflect on your personal response, focusing on that response as you formulate a tentative thesis statement. Next, consider what specific evidence from the text will best explain and support your interpretation and thesis statement.

Because most readers will be interested in what *you* think, you need to discover a way to demonstrate your originality by focusing on a topic you can develop adequately and applying one or more rhetorical methods (33g). You might define why you consider a character heroic or describe a setting that anchors a work's meaning. Or you might show how the description of a family's house in a novel defines that family's values or reveals the effects of an underlying conflict.

(3) Research can reveal the ways other readers have responded to a literary work.

You will undoubtedly anchor your essay in your own interpretation. But if you read works of literary criticism, visit online discussion groups or forums (**36b**), participate in class discussions, or become active in a book club or reading group, you can engage in a dialogue that can enrich your own ideas. Although it is tempting to lean heavily on the interpretations of scholarly experts, remember that your readers are mainly interested in your interpretation and in your use of the sometimes conflicting interpretations of others (including the other members of your class) to support your own points.

To locate material on a specific writer or work, consult your library's catalog (see **37b** and **37c**) and *The MLA International Bibliography,* an index of books and articles about literature that is an essential resource for literary studies and is available in print and online. Works such as *Contemporary Authors, The Oxford Companion to English Literature,* and *The New Princeton Handbook of Poetic Terms* can be useful when you are beginning your research or when you have encountered terms you need to clarify.

(4) Consider the types of literary interpretation you may be asked to write.

Writing a paper about a literary work usually requires you to focus on the work itself and to demonstrate that you have read it carefully—a process known as **close reading.** (Compare close reading with reading rhetorically, discussed in chapter **32**.) Through close reading, you can offer an **interpretation,** an explanation of what you see in a work. An interpretation that attempts to explain the meaning of one feature (a character, scene, symbol, or theme) of a literary work is called an **analysis.** A common form of analysis is **character analysis,** in which a writer interprets one or more features of a single character.

An interpretation that attempts to explain every element in a literary work is called an **explication** and is usually used only with poetry. When explicating William Wordsworth's "A Slumber Did My Spirit Seal," a writer might note that the *s* sound reinforces the hushed feeling of sleep and death in the poem. But it would also be necessary to consider the meanings of *slumber, spirit,* and *seal.*

An **evaluation** of a work gauges how successful the author is in communicating meaning to readers. The most common types of evaluation are book, theater, and film reviews. Like any other interpretation, an evaluation is a type of argument in which a writer cites evidence to persuade readers to accept a clearly formulated thesis. (See chapters 33 and 35.) An evaluation of a literary work should provide evidence from the text of its strengths as well as its weaknesses, if any.

42c   Vocabulary for discussing literature

Like all specialized fields, literature has a unique vocabulary, which describes the various features of literary texts and concepts of literary analysis. As you learn this vocabulary, you will learn how to understand, interpret, and write about literature.

(1) Characters carry the plot forward.

The **characters** are the humans or humanlike personalities (aliens, robots, animals, and other creatures) who carry the plot forward; they usually include a main character, called a **protagonist,** who is in external conflict with another character or an institution or in internal

Understanding how a particular character moves the plot forward will help you interpret the work as a whole.

conflict with himself or herself. This conflict usually reveals the **theme,** or the central idea of the work (**42c(7)**).

Because you need to understand the characters in any work you read, pay close attention to their appearance, their language, and their actions. You also need to pay attention to what the narrator or other characters say about them.

(2) Imagery is conveyed by descriptive language.

The imagery in a piece of literature is conveyed by **descriptive language,** or words that describe a sensory experience. Notice the images in "Portrait," a prose poem by Pinkie Gordon Lane that focuses on the death—and life—of a mother.

> My mother died walking along a dusty road on a Sunday morning in New Jersey. The road came up to meet her sinking body in one quick embrace. She spread out like an umbrella and dropped into oblivion before she hit the ground. In that one swift moment all light went out at the age of forty-nine. Her legacy: the blackened knees of the scrub-woman who ransomed her soul so that I might live, who bled like a tomato whenever she fought to survive, who laughed fully when amused—her laughter rising in one huge crescendo—and whose wings soared in dark despair. . . .
> —**PINKIE GORDON LANE,** *Girl at the Window*

The dusty road, the sinking body, the quick embrace—these images convey the loneliness and swiftness of death. The blackened knees, tomato-like bleeding, and rising laughter are, in contrast, images of a life's work, struggle, and joy.

(3) The narrator tells the story.

The **narrator** of a literary work tells the story, and this speaking voice can be that of a specific character (or of characters taking turns), can seem to be that of the work's author (referred to as the **persona,** which should not be confused with the author), or can be that of an all-knowing presence (referred to as an **omniscient narrator**) that transcends both characters and author.

The narrator's tone reveals his or her attitude toward events and characters and even, in some circumstances, toward readers.

(4) Plot is the sequence of events and more.

The plot is what happens in the story, the sequence of events (the narrative)—and more. The plot establishes how events are patterned or related in terms of conflict and resolution. Narrative answers "What comes next?" and plot answers "Why?" Consider this example:

Narrative	The sister returned home to visit her family and left again.
Plot	The city sister visited her country family, for whom she had no respect, and they were relieved when she left again.

Plot usually begins with a conflict, an unstable situation that sets events in motion. In what is called the **exposition,** the author introduces the characters, setting, and background—the elements that not only constitute the unstable situation but also relate to the events that follow. The subsequent series of events leads to the **climax** (or **turning point**). What follows is **falling action** (or **dénouement**) that leads to a resolution of the conflict and a stable situation.

In Alice Walker's "Everyday Use," Dee and her boyfriend come to the country to visit her mother and sister.

(5) Setting involves place and time.

Setting involves place—not just the physical setting, but also the social setting (the morals, manners, and customs of the characters). Setting also involves time—not only historical time, but also the length of time covered by the narrative. Setting includes atmosphere, or the emotional response to the situation, often shared by the reader with the characters. Being aware of the features of the setting will help you better understand the story, whether it is written as fiction, drama, or poetry.

(6) Symbols resonate with broader meaning.
Frequently used by writers of literature, a **symbol** is an object, usually concrete, that stands for something else, usually abstract. For example, at the beginning of *A Streetcar Named Desire,* a play by Tennessee Williams, one of the main characters buys a paper lantern to cover a naked light bulb. During the scenes that follow, she frequently talks about light, emphasizing her preference for soft lighting. Anyone seeing this play performed or reading it carefully would note that the paper lantern is a symbol. It is an object that is part of the setting and the plot, but it also stands for something more—a character's avoidance of harsh truths.

When you write about a particular symbol, first note where it appears in the literary work and then consider why it appears in those places and to what effect. Once you have an idea about the meaning, trace the incidents in the literary work that reinforce that interpretation.

(7) The theme is the main idea of a literary work.
The main idea of a literary work is its **theme.** Depending on how they interpret a work, different readers may identify different themes. To test whether the idea you have identified is central to the work in question, check to see if it is supported by the setting, plot, characters, and symbols. If it is, then that idea can be considered the work's theme. The most prominent literary themes arise out of conflict: person versus person, person versus self, person versus nature, or person versus society.

When you believe you have identified the theme, state it as a sentence—and be precise. A theme conveys a specific idea; it should not be confused with a topic.

Topic	family heritage
Vague theme	Alice Walker's "Everyday Use" is about family heritage.
Specific theme	"Everyday Use" reveals a conflict between a sister who puts her heritage on display and a sister who puts her heritage to use, every day.

CHECKLIST for Interpreting a Literary Work

- From whose point of view is the story told?
- Who is the protagonist? How is his or her character developed?
- With whom or what is the protagonist in conflict?
- How are the other characters depicted and distinguished through dialogue?
- What symbols, images, or figures of speech does the author use? To what effect?
- What is the theme of the work? How does the author use setting, plot, characters, and symbols to establish that theme?

42d Approaches to interpreting literature

An interpretation of a literary work can be shaped by your personal response to what you have read, by the views of other readers, whom you wish to support or challenge, or by a specific type of literary theory.

Literary theory, the scholarly discussion of how the nature and function of literature can be determined, ranges from approaches that focus almost exclusively on the text itself (its language and structure) to approaches that show how the text relates to author, reader, language, society, culture, economics, or history. Familiarity with literary theory enriches your reading of literature as well as your understanding of the books and essays about literature that you will discover when you do research (chapter 37).

(1) Reader-response theory focuses on the reader.

According to **reader-response theory,** readers construct meaning as they read and interact with the elements within a text. Thus, meaning is not fixed *on* the page but rather depends on what each reader brings *to* the page. Furthermore, the same reader can have different responses to the same literary work when rereading it after a number of years: a father of teenagers might find Gwendolyn Brooks's "we real cool" more disturbing than it had seemed when he first read it in high school. Although a reader-response approach to literature encourages diverse interpretations, you cannot simply say, "Well, that's what this work means to me" or "That's my interpretation." You must demonstrate to your audience how each element of the work supports your interpretation.

(2) Both feminist and gender-based literary theories focus on issues related to gender and sexuality.

Feminist and **gender-based literary theories** enable a reader to analyze the ways in which a work (through its characters, theme, or plot) promotes or challenges the prevailing intellectual or cultural assumptions of its day regarding issues related to gender and sexuality, such as patriarchy and compulsory heterosexuality. When writing about Edith Wharton's *The Age of Innocence,* a feminist critic might emphasize the oppression of nineteenth-century women and the repression of their sexuality. On reading Henry James's *The Bostonians,* another critic, using a gender-based approach, might focus on the positive features of the domestic relationship between the financially independent Olive and Verena. That same critic might also try to explain why Jake Barnes in Ernest Hemingway's *The Sun Also Rises* bonds with some men and is contemptuous of others.

Like the early suffragists, many feminist literary critics focus on prevailing social and cultural constraints affecting women.

(3) Race-based literary theory focuses on issues related to race relations.

Critical race theory focuses on the significance of race relations within a specific historical and social setting in order to explain the experience and literary production of any people whose history is characterized by political, social, and psychological oppression. Previously neglected works such as Zora Neale Hurston's *Their Eyes Were Watching God,* Rudolfo

Beloved, written by Nobel prize winner Toni Morrison, details the horrors of institutionalized racism, otherwise known as slavery.

Anaya's *Bless Me, Ultima,* and Frederick Douglass's *Narrative,* which demonstrate how racism affects the characters' lives, have taken on considerable cultural value in the last twenty years. **African American literary criticism,** for example, has been particularly successful in invigorating the study of great African American writers. Closely associated with critical race theory is **postcolonial theory,** which takes into account the relationship between those formerly colonized and their colonizer. Joseph Conrad's *Heart of Darkness,* Jean Rhys's *Wide Sargasso Sea,* Daniel Defoe's *Robinson Crusoe,* and E. M. Forster's *A Passage to India* can all be read productively through the lens of postcolonial theory.

(4) Class-based literary theory focuses on socioeconomic issues.
Class-based literary theory draws on the work of Karl Marx, Terry Eagleton, and others who have addressed the implications of social hierarchies and the accompanying economic tensions, which divide people in profoundly significant ways. Thus, a class-based approach can be used to explain why Emma Bovary is unhappy, despite her "good" (that is, financially advantageous) marriage, in Gustave Flaubert's *Madame Bovary,* why Bigger Thomas gets thrown into such a confused mental state in Richard Wright's *Native Son,* or why a family loses its land in John Steinbeck's *The Grapes of Wrath.*

(5) Text-based literary theory focuses on the work itself.
Text-based literary theory demands concentration on the piece of literature itself; with this approach, only the use of concrete, specific examples from the text validates an interpretation. Nothing more than what is contained within the text itself—not information about the author's life or about his or her culture or society—is needed to understand and appreciate the text's unchanging meaning. Readers may change, but the meaning of the text does not.

(6) Context-based literary theory focuses on the time and place in which a work was created.

Context-based literary theory considers the historical period during which a work was written and the cultural and economic patterns that prevailed during that period. For example, understanding that Arthur Miller wrote *The Crucible* in response to the accusations of the House Un-American Activities Committee in the 1950s helps explain why that play generated so much excitement when it was first produced. Critics who use a context-based and class-based approach known as **cultural studies** consider how a literary work interacts with economic conditions, socioeconomic classes, and other cultural artifacts (such as songs or fashion) from the period in which it was written.

(7) Psychoanalytic theories focus on psychological factors affecting the writing and the reading of literature.

Psychoanalytic theories seek to explain human experience and behavior in terms of sexual impulses and unconscious motivations (drives, desires, fears, needs, and conflicts). When applied to literature, these theories (based on the work of Nancy Chodorow, Sigmund Freud, and others) help readers discern the motivations of characters, envision the psychological state of the author as implied by the text, and evaluate the psychological reasons for their own interpretations. Readers may

The powerful Hindu goddess Durga represents an archetype known as the warrior.

apply the psychoanalytic approach to explain why Hamlet is deeply disturbed by his mother's remarriage, why Holden Caulfield rebels at school (in J. D. Salinger's *The Catcher in the Rye*), or why Rochester is blinded (in Charlotte Brontë's *Jane Eyre*).

Theorists who use the work of psychiatrist Carl Jung to explore **archetypes** (meaningful images that arise from the human unconscious and that appear as recurring figures or patterns in literature) are also using a psychoanalytic approach to interpret literature. Archetypal figures include the hero, the earth mother, the warrior, the outcast, and the cruel stepmother; archetypal patterns include the quest, the initiation, the test, and the return.

Exercise 1

Attend a film, a play, or a poetry reading at your school or in your community. Write a two- to three-page essay evaluating the work, using one of the theoretical approaches discussed in this chapter.

42e Conventions for writing about literature

Writing about literature involves adhering to several conventions.

(1) The first person is typically used.

When writing an analysis of a piece of literature, you usually use the first-person singular pronoun, *I*.

Although some critics believe Rudolfo Anaya's novel to be about witchcraft, I think it is about the power of belief.

By using *I,* you indicate that you are presenting your opinion about a work. To propose (or argue or offer) an opinion, belief, or interpretation, you must support it with specific evidence from the text itself.

(2) The present tense is used in discussions of literary works.

Use the present tense when discussing a literary work, since the author of the work is communicating to the reader at the present time (7b(1)).

In "A Good Man Is Hard to Find," the grandmother reaches out to touch her killer just before he pulls the trigger.

Similarly, use the present tense when reporting how other writers have interpreted the work you are discussing.

As Toni Morrison demonstrates in her analysis of the American literary tradition, black Americans continue to play a vital role.

(3) Documentation of sources follows certain formats.

When writing about a work assigned by your instructor, you may not need to give the source and publication information. However, if you are using an edition or translation that is different from the one your audience will use, you should indicate this. You can cite the version of the work you are discussing by using the MLA format for listing works cited (40b), although your bibliography in this case will consist of only a single work. An alternative way of providing documentation for a single source is by acknowledging the first quotation from the work in an explanatory note on a separate page at the end of your paper and then giving parenthetical page numbers in the body of the paper for all subsequent references to the work.

1. Toni Morrison, *Playing in the Dark: Whiteness and the Literary Imagination* (New York: Vintage, 1992). All subsequent references to this work will be identified with page numbers within the text.

If you use this note form, you may not need to repeat the bibliographical information in a separate entry, nor will you need to include the author's name in subsequent parenthetical references. Check with your instructor about the format he or she prefers.

When you use a bibliography to provide publication data, you must indicate specific references whenever you quote a line or passage. According to MLA style, such bibliographic information should be placed in the text in parentheses directly after the quotation, and a period, a semicolon, or a comma should follow the parentheses (**16d(1)** and **40a(1)**). Quotations from short stories and novels are identified by the author's name and page number.

"A man planning to spend money on me was an experience rare enough to feel odd" (Gordon 19).

Quotations from poems are referred to by line number.

"O Rose, thou are sick!" (Blake 1).

And quotations from plays require act, scene, and line numbers.

"How much better it is to weep at joy than to joy at weeping" (*Ado* 1.1.28).

This reference indicates that the line quoted is from act I, scene I, line 28 of Shakespeare's play *Much Ado about Nothing*.

(4) Quoting poetry involves several conventions.

For poems and verse plays, type quotations involving three or fewer lines in the text and insert a slash (**17i**) with a space on each side to separate the lines.

"Does the road wind uphill all the way? / Yes, to the very end" (Rossetti 1-2).

Christina Rossetti opens her poem "Uphill" with this two-line question and answer.

Quotations of more than three lines should be indented one inch from the left-hand margin and double-spaced. Do not use slashes at the ends of lines, and make sure to follow the original text for line breaks, special indenting, or spacing. For this type of block quotation, place your citation outside the final punctuation mark.

(5) Authors' names are referred to in standard ways.

Use the full name of the author of a work in your first reference and only the last name in all subsequent references. For instance, refer to "Charles Dickens" or "Willa Cather" the first time, and after that, use "Dickens" or "Cather." Never refer to a female author differently than you do a male author.

42f   Sample literary interpretation

In the following essay, undergraduate English major Kaitlyn Andrews-Rice analyzes Alice Walker's short story "Everyday Use." In addition to reading the story, she watched a dramatization of it on DVD. Andrews-Rice had the opportunity to choose her own topic, and she focused (**33b**) on the ways two sisters use their heritage, showing that everyday use is the best way.

Kaitlyn Andrews-Rice

Professor Glenn

English 100

7 March 2008

Honoring Heritage with Everyday Use

"Everyday Use," one of the short stories in Alice Walker's

In Love & Trouble: Stories of Black Women, vividly demonstrates

how three women, Mrs. Johnson and her two daughters, regard their

heritage.[1] Through the eyes of Mrs. Johnson, the story unfolds when

her older daughter returns to her country home, mother, and sister.

Throughout the story, Walker emphasizes the shared heritage of

these three women and the different ways they use it. In "Everyday

Use," an authentic appreciation of heritage does not come from

showcasing fashionable artifacts or practices; rather, it comes from

embracing that heritage every day.

Walker's physical description of the sisters illustrates

the different ways each puts her heritage to use. The beautiful,

sophisticated Dee embraces her heritage by showcasing the

fashionable Afrocentric sentiment of the time. Her mother describes

her as wearing "a dress so loud it hurts my eyes. There are yellows

and oranges enough to throw back the light of the sun," and her hair

"stands straight up like the wool on a sheep" (52). But in addition to her African style, Dee also has "neat-looking" feet, "as if God himself had shaped them with a certain style" (52). That she's stylish comes as no surprise, for even before she appears in the story, the reader is told that "at sixteen, she had a style of her own, and knew what style was" (50). Dee is a book-smart city woman, who uses her knowledge of fashion and style to enhance her physical attributes: she is "lighter than [her sister] Maggie, with nicer hair and a fuller figure" (49). Maggie, on the other hand, replicates her Southern black heritage every day, by helping her mother clean up the dirt yard (raking, lifting, sweeping), in preparation for Dee's homecoming. In addition, Maggie works hard churning butter, cooking over a wood-burning stove, and using the outhouse. She's darker skinned, "homely and ashamed of the burn scars down her arms and legs" (47), and her simple country clothes, "pink skirt and red blouse" (49), are in sharp contrast with Dee's fancy garb.

The filmed version of the story allows the viewer to see Dee arrive home with her boyfriend, Hakim-a-barber, both in their African clothes, exchanging glances of amusement as they take Polaroid snapshots of the unsophisticated mother and sister and their shabby house, as though Dee was completely separated from such living conditions, that heritage, her family (see fig. 1).

Andrews-Rice 3

Fig. 1. Dee wants to capture the living conditions of her mother and sister. Photograph © Denna Bendell/Worn Path Productions.

Another way that Walker illustrates the divide between Dee's understanding of her heritage and her family's is through the use of names. When Dee arrives, she announces that she is "Not 'Dee,' Wangero Leewanika Kemanjo!" (53). According to the interview with Walker that accompanies the Wadsworth Original Film Series in Literature's filmed version of "Everyday Use," the changing of one's name to a more Afrocentric name was common during this time (*Everyday Use*). In Dee's mind, this fashionable African name is yet another way she is honoring her roots, embracing her heritage, and she tells her family that she "couldn't bear it any longer, being named after the people who oppress [her]" (53). Ironically, her given name carried with it a rich inheritance, that of a long line of Dees or Dicies. Yet Dee is the daughter who denies her Southern heritage and is embarrassed by her Southern family, especially by Maggie, who has taken no steps to "make something of [herself]" (59) other than a wife to local John Thomas Dee. At this point in the story, though, Mrs. Johnson and Maggie agree to go along with Dee's ways and continue to try to please her, even if they do not understand her. It is not until later in Dee's visit that they come to realize the way Dee has embraced a heritage she does not fully understand or appreciate.

To further emphasize the differences among the ways these women understand their heritage, Walker focuses on their educations. Mrs. Johnson describes the way Dee would read to them before she left for college: "She washed us in a river of make-believe, burned us with a lot of knowledge we didn't necessarily need to know" (50). Even though she's somewhat puzzled by Dee's knowledge, she maintains pride in her daughter, especially since Mrs. Johnson never had an education, and Maggie "knows she is not bright" and can read only by "stumbling along good-naturedly" (50). But when Dee accuses Maggie of being "backward," Mrs. Johnson realizes how little Dee's education has taught her about appreciating her heritage.

The focus on family-made quilts at the end of the story shines light on Walker's final take on how heritage is used differently by these women. Mrs. Johnson explains that Dee was offered these quilts before she left for college but refused them because they were "old-fashioned, out of style" (57). Now that the quilts are stylish, Dee wants them in her life. She wants to hang them on her walls, displaying them alongside the butter churn top that she plans to use as a "centerpiece on the alcove table" and dasher that she will do "something artistic" (56) with. For Dee, these artifacts should be on display, not used. But for Maggie and her mother, the quilts represent not only a direct link with their ancestors but a distinct form of African American expression. These particular quilts are made from scraps of Grandma Dee's dresses and from a scrap of fabric from Great Grandpa Ezra's uniform "that he wore in the Civil War" (56). The piecing together of these scraps to form a quilt is a testament to their importance in the heritage of this family. As Dee holds the quilts, she repeats "Imagine!" (57), as if it is so difficult to think of a time when all the stitching was done by hand, something that Maggie is capable of doing every day because "it was Grandma Dee and Big Dee who taught her how to quilt" (58). When Dee asks to take some quilts back to the city to hang on the wall, her mother resists, saying that Maggie planned to use them. Only then does Dee reveal her prejudices, accusing her sister of being "backward enough to put them [the quilts] to everyday use" (57), right before she storms out of the house.

At this point, when she's been denied the quilts, Dee accuses her family of not understanding their true heritage, saying "It's really a new day for us. But from the way you and Mama still live you'd never know it" (59). She considers herself to be forward looking, because of her African style and name, her education, her cultural displays. In Dee's eyes, her "backward" family does not understand their heritage because they do not display the quilts or the butter churn, they *use* them every day. As Dee drives away, Maggie smiles, and it is "a real smile, not scared" (59), because she knows she embraces, lives, and understands her heritage in a very intimate way.

Andrews-Rice 7

Notes

1. All subsequent quotations from this work by Alice Walker will be identified by page numbers.

Andrews-Rice 8

Works Cited

Everyday Use. Dir. Bruce Schwartz. Perf. Karen ffolkes, Rachel Luttrell, and Lyne Odums. 2003. Thomson Wadsworth, 2005. DVD.

Walker, Alice. *In Love & Trouble: Stories of Black Women*. New York: Harcourt, 1973. 47-59. Print.

Exercise 2

Based on your reading of Kaitlyn Andrews-Rice's paper on "Everyday Use," what personal or political values do you think she brought to her interpretation of that text? Which of the theoretical approaches to literature did she use as the basis for her interpretation (42d)? Write a one- to two-page paper analyzing her interpretation of the story.

43   Writing in Business

Writing in business requires the same attention to audience, purpose, and context as writing in any other situation or discipline. However, the nature of authorship differs: although you are the writer, you must project both your own image and that of your employer as credible and reliable. To do so, you need to follow the conventions and formats expected by the business community.

If you take business courses, you will receive a variety of writing assignments: letters, memos and e-mails, business plans, PowerPoint presentations, oral reports, and business reports are some of the more common. To complete such assignments successfully, you must start by analyzing the rhetorical situation. This chapter will help you

- recognize the stylistic conventions of standard business writing (43a),
- draft a business letter (43b),
- produce business memos and e-mails (43c),
- compose a résumé (43d) and a letter of application (43e),
- develop a business plan (43f),
- prepare an oral report including a PowerPoint presentation (43g), and
- research and write a formal business report (43h).

43a Conventions of language and organization

Whether you are writing on a screen or on paper, preparing a memo or a business plan, you will need to meet deadlines—both anticipated and unexpected ones. The strategies presented in the following box will help you produce comprehensive, concise, and well-organized documents on time, by introducing you to some of the stylistic characteristics of effective business communication.

STRATEGIES FOR EFFECTIVE BUSINESS COMMUNICATION

Be direct.

- Know who your audience members are and consider their needs.
- State the purpose of your document in your opening sentence or paragraph.
- Write straightforward sentences, beginning with a subject and an active verb (7c(2)).
- Use technical language sparingly, unless the document is intended for a specialized audience (19c(4)).

Be concise.

- Compose direct sentences that are neither too long nor too complicated.
- Include only necessary details.
- Use numbers, bullets, or descriptive headings that help readers locate information easily.
- Use graphs, tables, and other visual elements that convey information succinctly.

Use conventional formatting.

- Follow the standard formats developed for your type of business or company, or use those outlined in this chapter (43b–h).

(Continued on page 700)

(Continued from page 699)

- Avoid using informal language, unless you know that a casual tone is acceptable.

- Edit carefully for errors; typos, grammatical mistakes, sentence fragments, and missing words detract significantly from your ethos as a businessperson and as a representative of your employer.

43b   Business letters

Business letters serve a variety of purposes—to inquire, to inform, to complain, to respond. (For letters of application, see 43e.) Regardless of its purpose, a business letter usually fits on a single sheet of paper, single-spaced. It also follows a standard block format: each element is typed flush with the left margin, with double spacing between paragraphs.

ELEMENTS OF A STANDARD BUSINESS LETTER

- **Return address.** Your employer may require you to use letterhead stationery. If not, type your mailing address one inch from the top of the paper, flush left on a one-inch margin, and single-spaced.

- **Date.** Type the date beneath your return address. If you are using letterhead stationery, type the date one or two lines below the letterhead's last line.

- **Recipient's name and address.** Provide the full name and address of the recipient. Single-space these lines, and allow an extra line space above them. If you do not know the person's name, try to find it by checking the company's Web site or phoning the company. If you cannot find the recipient's name, use an appropriate title such as *Personnel Director* or *Customer Service Manager* (not italicized).

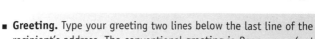

- **Greeting.** Type your greeting two lines below the last line of the recipient's address. The conventional greeting is *Dear* _____ (not italicized) followed by a colon. If you and the recipient use first names to address each other, use the person's first name. Otherwise, use *Mr., Ms., Mrs., or Miss* and the last name. (Choose *Ms.* when you do not know a woman's preference.)

- **Body of the letter.** Begin the first paragraph two lines below the greeting. Single-space lines within a paragraph; double-space between paragraphs. If your letter must continue on a second page, include the recipient's last name, the date, and the page number in three single-spaced lines at the top left on the second page.

- **Closing.** Close your letter two lines after the end of the body with an expression such as *Sincerely* or *Cordially* (not italicized) followed by a comma.

- **Signature.** Type your full name four lines below the closing. Then, in the space above your typed name, sign your full name, using blue or black ink. If you have addressed the recipient by his or her first name, sign just your first name.

- **Additional information.** If you are enclosing extra material such as a résumé, type the word *Enclosure* or the abbreviation *Encl.* (not italicized) two lines below your name. You may also note the number of enclosures or the identity of the document(s): for example, *Enclosures (3)* or *Encl.: 2002 Annual Year-End Report*. If you would like the recipient to know the names of people receiving copies of the letter, use the abbreviation *cc* (for "carbon copy") and a colon followed by the other recipients' names. Place this element on the line directly below the enclosure line or, if there is no enclosure, two lines below your name.

The sample **letter of inquiry** (a letter intended to elicit information) on the next page illustrates the parts of a typical business letter.

Letter of inquiry

<table>
<tr>
<td>Return
address
and
date</td>
<td>550 First Avenue
Ellensburg, WA 98926
February 4, 2008</td>
</tr>
<tr>
<td>Name and
address of
recipient</td>
<td>Mr. Mark Russell
Bilingual Publications
5400 Sage Avenue
Yakima, WA 98907</td>
</tr>
<tr>
<td>Greeting</td>
<td>Dear Mr. Russell:</td>
</tr>
<tr>
<td>Body of
letter</td>
<td>I am a junior in the Bilingual Education Program at Central Washington University. For my coursework, I am investigating positions in publishing that include the use of two languages. Your name and address were given to me by my instructor, Marta Cole, who worked for you from 2002 through 2006.

I have learned something about your publications on your Web site. I am most interested in dual documents—one in English and one in Spanish. Could you please send me samples of such documents so that I can have a better idea of the types of publications you produce?

I am also interested in finding out what qualifications I would need to work for a business like yours. I am fluent in both Spanish and English and have taken a course in translation. If possible, I would like to ask you a few questions about your training and experience. Would you have time for an interview some day next week?</td>
</tr>
<tr>
<td>Closing</td>
<td>Sincerely,</td>
</tr>
<tr>
<td>Signature</td>
<td>Chris Humphrey

Chris Humphrey</td>
</tr>
</table>

A **memo** (short for *memorandum*) is a brief document sent within a business to announce a meeting, set a schedule, or request information or action. E-mail is also used for these purposes as well as for external communication with clients, prospective employees, or other companies. The basic guidelines for writing memos also apply to e-mail messages.

Because it is circulated internally, a memo or e-mail is usually less formal than a letter, but it should still be direct and concise—a memo should be no longer than a page, and an e-mail no longer than a screen. The following guidelines for formatting these kinds of documents are fairly standard, but note that a particular company or organization may establish its own format.

ELEMENTS OF A STANDARD BUSINESS MEMO OR E-MAIL

- **Heading.** On four consecutive lines, type *To* (not italicized) followed by a colon and the name(s) of the recipient(s), *From* followed by a colon and your name and title (if appropriate), *Date* followed by a colon and the date, and *Subject* followed by a colon and a few words identifying the memo's subject. (The abbreviation *Re*, for "regarding," is sometimes used instead of *Subject*.) This information should be single-spaced. If you are sending copies to individuals whose names are not included in the *To* line, place those names on a new line beginning with *cc* ("carbon copy") and a colon. Most e-mail software supplies these header lines on any new message.

- **Body.** Use the block format (43b), single-spacing lines within each paragraph and double-spacing between paragraphs. Double-space between the heading and the body of the memo.

Business memo

Heading

To: Intellectual Properties Committee
From: Leo Renfrow, Chair of Intellectual Properties Committee
Date: March 15, 2008
Subject: Review of Policy Statement

Body of
memo

At the end of our last meeting, we decided to have our policy statement reviewed by someone outside our university. Clark Beech, chair of the Intellectual Properties Committee at Lincoln College, agreed to help us. Overall, as his review shows, the format of our policy statement is sound. Dr. Beech believes that some of the content should be further developed, however. It appears that we have used some ambiguous terms and included some conditions that would not hold up in court.

Early next week, my assistant will deliver a copy of Dr. Beech's review to each of you. Please look it over by our next meeting, on March 29. If you have any questions or comments before then, please call me at ext. 1540.

The effectiveness of memos and e-mails depends on several characteristics, especially tone, length, and directness. A conversational tone may be acceptable for a message to a co-worker asking about a deadline, but a professional tone is required for a memo or an e-mail to a supervisor or a group. To enhance your ethos as a professional, create a signature line for your e-mails that identifies yourself and your institution or company. Consider the content of a message, especially anything that the sender might prefer to keep private, before forwarding it to others. Also keep in mind that anything you send in an e-mail can easily be forwarded. (For information on writing to multiple audiences, see 31d(3)).

Lengthiness can detract from the effectiveness of your memos and e-mails. Keep such messages to one rhetorical unit: one page for a memo, one screen (or twenty lines) for an e-mail. Because people tend to read only one rhetorical unit, you will want to compose a message that fits on a single screen or page yet has the white space necessary for easy reading.

Because most regular users of e-mail receive a large volume of messages, they have become used to scanning the messages and quickly responding to or deleting them. Announcing your topic in the subject line and then arranging and presenting it in concise, readable chunks help ensure that recipients do not overlook important information. Short paragraphs also provide more white space, which helps readers to maintain attention and absorb the key points.

TIPS FOR SENDING ATTACHMENTS WITH E-MAIL MESSAGES

- Before you send any attachment, consider the size of the file—many inboxes have limited space and cannot accept or store large files that contain streaming video, photographs, or sound clips. If you want to send a large file or multiple files, call or e-mail your recipient first to ask permission.

- If you do not know the type of operating system or software installed on your recipient's computer, send text-only documents in rich text format (**.rtf**), which preserves most formatting and is recognized by many word-processing programs.

(Continued on page 706)

(Continued from page 705)

- Because attachments are notorious for transmitting computer viruses, never open an attachment sent by someone you do not know. Before opening an attachment, make sure that you are working on a computer with antivirus software that scans all incoming files for viruses.

43d Résumés

A **résumé** is essentially an argument (chapter 35) designed to emphasize a person's job qualifications by highlighting his or her experience and abilities. If you create and save your résumé as a word-processing file, you can easily tailor it for each position you seek.

The first step in writing a résumé is listing your current and past employment as well as your relevant educational background and extracurricular activities. Be sure to include dates, job titles, and responsibilities, emphasizing specific information according to what the job advertisement says about desired experience and traits.

The next step is to decide how to organize your résumé. A **chronological résumé** lists positions and activities in *reverse* chronological order; that is, your most recent experience comes first. This format works well if you have a steady job history and want to emphasize your most recent experience because it is closely related to the position for which you are applying. An alternative way to organize a résumé is to list experience in terms of job skills rather than jobs held. This format, called a **functional résumé**, is especially useful when you have the required skills but your work history in the particular field is modest or you are just starting your career.

Remember that your résumé is, in effect, going to someone's office for a job interview. Make sure that it is dressed for success. Whenever possible, design the résumé to fit on a single page. Use good-quality paper (preferably white or off-white) and a laser printer. Choose a format and make sure to apply it consistently throughout. Use boldface or italic type for headings. Resist the impulse to make the design unnecessarily complicated, however. When in doubt, opt for simplicity.

Joe Delaney's résumé incorporates features of both the chronological and the functional formats. He starts with his education, then proceeds to a description of his computer skills, clubs, and activities because those skills and experiences relate directly to the position he is applying for, much more so than his library job, which he lists later.

Sample résumé

Joseph F. Delaney III
138 Main Street, Apt 10D
Cityville, PA 16800
(555) 544-9988
JoeDel4@psu.edu

Objective
To obtain a position specializing in project and risk management

Education
Pennsylvania State University, University Park, PA, 2003–2007
Majors: IST B.S. (Information Context Option),
 Psychology B.S. (Quantitative Option)
Dean's List: Summer 2006, Fall 2006, and Spring 2007
Cumulative G.P.A.: 3.60
Relevant Classes:
- Project Management in Technology — dealt with the application of basic concepts, methodologies, and tools of project management in the field of information sciences and technology
- Database Management — managed a project team that applied MySql, PHP, and HTML in completing Rabble Mosaic Creator, which is described at www.schoolproject.psu.edu/~100

Computer and Technical Skills
- MySql, PHP, GD Library, C++ (2 years experience), Java (1 year experience)
- TCP/IP, network security, LANs and WANs
- HTML, XML, and project and risk management

Clubs/Activities
IST Student Government:
- Active and voting member of my college's student government

- Regular participation in the student government's Academic Committee
- Student resource for the IST Student Executive Board

IST Academic Committee:

- Participated in regularly scheduled meetings with the dean, Henry C. Foley, and the professor in charge, John Yen
- Worked with the administration to address students' problems

Work Experience

Penn State Pollock Library, University Park, PA, May–July 2006

- Assisted patrons of the library in using computers, printers, and the Internet via a wireless network using VPN
- Coordinated computers in my designated area and assisted with defragmenting, rebooting, reformatting, charging, and normal maintenance of laptops

Honors

- 2005 scholarship student in the College of IST; recipient of the Cingular Wireless Trustee Scholarship
- Pollock Library 2004 student employee of the year

TIPS FOR RÉSUMÉ WRITING

- Include your name, address, telephone number, and an e-mail address or fax number, if available.

- Identify your career or job objective simply. If you do not feel that you have such an objective, do not mention one in the résumé. You can provide details about your future plans when you are asked about them during an interview.

- Whenever possible, establish a clear relationship between jobs you have had and the job you are seeking. Offer detailed explanations of the tasks and responsibilities in each of your jobs that most closely correspond with the position you seek.

- List your college or university degree and any pertinent areas in which you have had special training. Decide what details about your education best show your qualifications for the job at hand. Consider including your GPA (your overall GPA or your GPA in your major, whichever is more impressive), particular coursework (list specific classes or note areas of specialization, such as twenty hours of coursework in accounting), and relevant class projects.

- Do not include personal data such as age, marital status, race, religion, or ethnicity.

- Even if an advertisement or posting asks you to state a salary requirement, any mention of salary is usually deferred until an interview.

- The names and addresses of **references** (people who have agreed to speak or write on your behalf) are not usually listed on a résumé, though you may want to mention that references are available on request. Instead, job candidates are advised to take a list of references to interviews. Make sure that the individuals on your list understand the nature of the position you are seeking. The list should include their names and addresses as well as their telephone numbers and/or e-mail addresses.

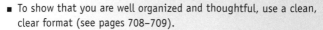

- To show that you are well organized and thoughtful, use a clean, clear format (see pages 708–709).
- Meticulously proofread your résumé before sending it and have others read it carefully as well. Errors in business writing always detract from your credibility, but errors in a résumé or letter of application (43e) can ruin your chances of getting an interview.

43e Letters of application

Writing a letter of application is an essential step in applying for a job: it gives you the opportunity to present yourself as articulate, interesting, and professional (rather than as someone who merely repeats information that can be found on the résumé).

Address your letter to a specific person; if necessary, call the company to find out who will be screening the application letters and how to spell that person's name. You can assume that the recipient will be reviewing many letters, so try to keep yours to one page.

In your opening paragraph, identify the position you are applying for, explain how you learned about it, and—in a single sentence—state why you believe you are qualified to fill it. This statement serves as the thesis for the rest of the letter. In the paragraphs that follow, describe the experience and abilities that qualify you for the job. Generally, two body paragraphs follow the introductory paragraph, paragraphs that describe relevant education, relevant work experience, and/or particular course projects. In your closing paragraph, offer any additional useful information and make a direct request for an interview; be specific about how you can be reached.

Model letter of application

Return address and date	Joseph F. Delaney III 138 Main Street, Apt 10D Cityville, PA 16800 June 4, 2007
Name and address of recipient	Mr. Jim Konigs, Human Resource Director E. G. Hickey Technical Enterprise 333 Cumberville State Road, Suite 110 West Cumberville, PA 19428-2949
Greeting	Dear Mr. Konigs:
Body of letter	I am applying for the position of project manager advertised on Monster.com. I graduated on May 15 with a B.S. degree in information sciences and technology from Pennsylvania State University. I believe that my in-depth research and education in information technology make me an ideal candidate for this position. I have completed the required coursework and an internship in information technology, consulting, and security, working under such distinguished professors as James Wendle and David Markison. I am currently a teaching instructor with Dr. Markison, responsible for student evaluation and advising. I have served as a project team leader in database management; my team created Rabble Mosaic Creator, a Web site that allows users to create mosaics out of images. In addition to my studies, I have applicable experience as a member of the student government's Academic Committee, which manages students' problems through policy and hands-on work before presenting the issues to the dean and professor in charge. I would appreciate the opportunity to talk with you about the position. I can be reached at the phone number or e-mail address at the top of my résumé.
Closing	Sincerely,
Signature	*Joseph F. Delaney* Joseph F. Delaney III
Enclosure line	Encl.: résumé

43f Business plans

Business plans have three main purposes: (1) to ensure that the writer of the plan has considered all the potential risks as well as benefits of the business venture, (2) to persuade lenders and potential investors that their money will be safely invested because the writer has planned realistically and has sufficient expertise, and (3) to help the new business stay on track during its early development. To fulfill these purposes adequately, a business plan should be well researched, clearly written, and complete—that is, it should provide all the information a loan officer or investor might need.

ELEMENTS OF A BUSINESS PLAN

- **Cover page.** Include the name and address of the business.
- **Table of contents.**
- **Executive summary.** State briefly the objectives of the business and describe the business. Indicate who will own the business and under what form of ownership (partnership, corporation, or sole proprietorship). Finally, explain why the business will be successful. Write the summary *after* you have completed the following sections.
- **Business overview.** Identify the kind of business you are planning to start up (service or retail), explain why the business is distinctive, and briefly describe its market.
- **Market.** Characterize the market—its size and potential for growth and the typical customers. Describe how the business will attract customers—through advertising, pricing, product quality, and/or services.
- **Business location.** Discuss lease or sale terms, the need for and costs of renovation, and features of the neighborhood.

(Continued on page 714)

(Continued from page 713)

- **Licenses and permits.** Explain what kinds of licenses and permits must be obtained and whether the business name is registered.

- **Management.** Include information about managers' experience and education, the organizational structure, proposed salaries and wages, and any other pertinent management resources (accountant, attorney, and so on).

- **Personnel.** List the personnel needed—full-time or part-time, skilled or unskilled—and explain whether training will be required and how it will be provided.

- **Insurance.** Describe insurance needs and potential risks.

- **Competition.** Analyze competitors, and describe how the business addresses a market need.

- **Financial data.** Include a current balance sheet and income statement and projected (or actual) income statements by month and quarter for two years as well as cash flow and balance sheet projections.

- **Supporting documents.** Include résumés, financial statements, and letters of reference for the owner(s) as well as letters of intent from suppliers, leases, contracts, deeds, and other legal documents.

For an assignment requiring them to design and start their own business, Emily Cohen and her group started a business called Posters Ink, through which college students in the Boston area could create their own posters from a collage of existing pictures and documents. Three brief excerpts from the group's business plan follow, providing examples of a market analysis, description of management responsibilities, and projected financial plan for the first six weeks.

5

III. Market

In the company's short selling period, the target market must be
made aware of the product and the promotions that Posters Ink will
offer. Posters Ink's target market consists mainly of college students
who attend Babson College, Boston University, Boston College,
Northeastern University, and Wellesley College. Posters Ink will
attempt to reach friends and family members of these college
students as well as Wellesley high school students. This provides
the company with a target market of about 64,000. The plan is to
reach 1 percent of this target market.

There is no direct competition that offers the same one-of-
a-kind collage option that Posters Ink offers its customers. Similar
products can be produced by several online photo programs such
as Webshots, PhotoMix, and 111 Print. They offer options such as
enlarging pictures, lining the pictures up on a poster, and online
scrapbooking, all of which are different from Posters Ink's main
collage option. Our product is also convenient because people with
enough computer skills to create their own digital picture collage
will no longer need to lay out their own photos or take them to a
print shop.

The
introduction
to the Market
section of the
Posters Ink
business plan

7

VI. Management

The first
portion
of the
Management
section
of the
Posters Ink
business
plan

Company Job Descriptions for Posters Ink

Division/Department: CEO

Reports to: Board of Directors

Summary: As the leader of the business, the CEO will coordinate and motivate staff, manage the business, and troubleshoot.

Primary Responsibilities:

1. Ensure that the needs of employees are in accord with the needs of the organization as a whole

2. Act as a spokesperson to inform others of the progress of the business

3. Find both problems and opportunities and come up with the ways to deal with them

4. Approve all major actions of the business

5. Oversee the day-to-day functions of the business

6. Develop an interpersonal relationship with employees through motivation and definition of achievable goals

7. Preside at board meetings

8. Sign all contracts relating to the business

9. Be available to important clients

10. Be present at any negotiations involving an agreement or contract with another organization

10

Posters Ink Cash Budget (Weeks 1–6)

	Week 1 1/29/2007	Week 2 2/5/2007	Week 3 2/12/2007	Week 4 2/19/2007	Week 5 2/26/2007	Week 6 3/5/2007
Beginning Cash Balance	193.75	0.00	361.87	530.21	499.17	348.33
Receipts						
Sales— Small Posters	494.09	411.75	219.60	137.25	109.80	164.70
Sales— Large Posters	469.39	391.16	208.62	130.39	104.31	156.46
Sales— Foam Posters	271.75	226.46	120.78	75.49	60.39	90.58
Total Receipts	$1235.24	$1029.36	$548.99	$343.12	$274.50	$411.75
Cash Available	1428.99	1029.36	910.87	873.33	773.66	760.80
Disbursements						
Inventory Purchases						
Small	313.71	261.43	139.43	87.14	69.71	104.57
Large	223.52	186.27	99.34	62.09	49.67	74.51
Foam	161.76	134.80	71.89	44.93	35.95	53.92
Rent	0.00	0.00	0.00	0.00	100.00	0.00
Website Expense	380.00	30.00	15.00	15.00	15.00	15.00
Advertising	125.00	30.00	30.00	30.00	30.00	30.00
Phone	0.00	0.00	0.00	10.00	0.00	0.00
Supplies	200.00	0.00	0.00	100.00	0.00	0.00
Entertainment	0.00	0.00	0.00	0.00	100.00	0.00
Sales Tax	0.00	0.00	0.00	0.00	0.00	0.00
Miscellaneous	25.00	25.00	25.00	25.00	25.00	25.00
Total Disbursed	$1428.99	$667.49	$380.66	$374.16	$425.33	$303.00

Outline for the first six weeks' income and expenses, from the Finances section of the business plan

43g   Oral presentations with PowerPoint

Oral reports accompanied by PowerPoint presentations are commonplace in business, whether used internally or externally. They may take the form of project status reports, demonstrations of new equipment or software, research reports, or recommendations.

ELEMENTS OF A STANDARD ORAL PRESENTATION

- **Introduction.** Taking no more than one-tenth of your overall presentation time (for example, one minute of a ten-minute presentation), your introduction should indicate who you are, your qualifications, your topic, and the relevance of that topic to your audience. The introduction provides an outline of your main points so that listeners can easily follow your presentation.

- **Body.** Make sure the organization of your presentation is clear through your use of transitions. You can number each point (first, second, third, and so on) and use cause-and-consequence transitions (*therefore, since, due to*) and chronological transitions (*before, following, next, then*). Provide internal summaries to remind your listeners where you have been and where you are going as well as comments to help your audience sense the weight of various points (for example, "Not many people realize that . . ." or "The most important thing I have to share is . . .").

- **Conclusion.** Anyone can simply restate the main ideas in the conclusion to an oral presentation; you will want to consider ways to make your conclusion memorable. To do so, you may want to end with a proposal for action, a final statistic, recommendations, or a description of the benefits of a certain course of action. In general, conclusions should be even shorter than introductions.

Keep in mind the following guidelines as you create PowerPoint slides to accompany an oral report.

TIPS FOR INCORPORATING POWERPOINT INTO
AN ORAL PRESENTATION

- Design your slides for your audience, not for yourself. If you need speaking notes for your talk, write them on notecards or type them into the notes section provided below each slide in the PowerPoint program.

- Use text and visuals on the PowerPoint slides that complement— not repeat—the oral part of your presentation. If your listeners realize that everything you are saying is on the slide, they will quickly become bored.

- Be aware of the limitations of PowerPoint. Because PowerPoint slides do not accommodate large amounts of text, use no more than five lines of text per slide, with a text font of 14 to 16 points. PowerPoint tends to encourage oversimplification of information, so be sure to tell your audience whenever you had to simplify the information presented on a slide and let them know where they can find more details.

- In general, keep text and visuals separate. Alternating predominantly visual slides with slides of text will keep your audience's attention. Let visuals (charts, pictures, or graphs) stand alone with just a heading or a title. Use text slides to define terms, to present block quotes that might be difficult to follow orally, and to list the main points you will be making.

- Time your speaking with your presentation of the slides so that the two components are synchronized. Make sure to give your audience enough time to absorb complex visuals.

For their Posters Ink business plan, Emily Cohen and her group members created PowerPoint slides to accompany an oral presentation requesting funding. Figures 43.1 through 43.4 show a few of those slides.

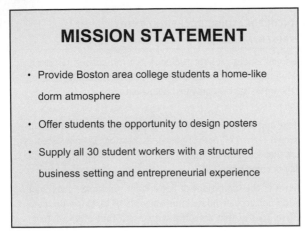

Fig. 43.1. This mission statement uses the maximum amount of text recommended for a PowerPoint slide, but the bulleted list effectively presents the main goals of the company.

Fig. 43.2. This slide uses visuals to complement the spoken part of the presentation.

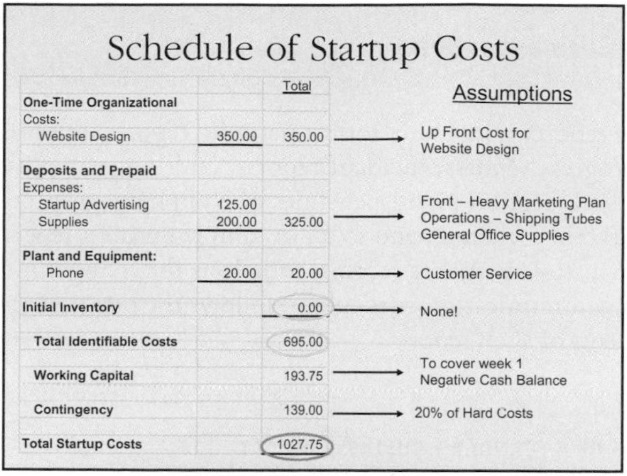

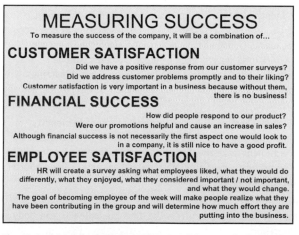

Fig. 43.3. This slide illustrates the versatility of PowerPoint, which allows a user to display a chart and add highlighting and comments on key parts.

Fig. 43.4. This slide uses too much text and does not incorporate bullets or numbers to organize the text.

43h Business reports

Business reports take many forms: periodic reports, sales reports, progress reports, incident reports, and longer reports that assess relocation plans, new lines of equipment or products, marketing schemes, and so on. A sample business report, in which a student makes recommendations for changes in a business communication curriculum, follows the box describing elements of such reports.

ELEMENTS OF A STANDARD BUSINESS REPORT

- **Front matter.** Depending on the audience, purpose, and length of a given report, the front matter materials may include a letter of transmittal, a title page, a table of contents, a list of illustrations, and/or an abstract.

- **Introduction.** This section should include background information, identification of the problem addressed by the report (the exigence), a purpose statement, and a description of the scope of the report (a list of the limits that framed the investigation). In a long report, each of these elements may be several paragraphs long, and some may have their own subheadings. An introduction should not take up more than ten to fifteen percent of a report.

- **Body or discussion.** This, the longest section of the report, presents the research findings. It often incorporates charts and graphs to help make the data user-friendly. This section should be subdivided into clear subsections by subheadings or, for a shorter report, paragraph breaks.

- **Conclusion(s).** This section summarizes any conclusions and generalizations deduced from the data presented in the body of the report.

- **Recommendation(s).** While not always necessary, a section that outlines for readers what should be done about the findings is included in many business reports.
- **Back matter.** Like the front matter, the back matter of a report depends on the audience, purpose, and length of the report. Back matter may include a glossary, references cited, and/or one or more appendixes.

Changing Forms of Business Communication:

Implications for Business Communication Curricula

Joseph F. Delaney III

Penn State University

June 11, 2007

2

Table of Contents

3

Abstract

American businesses gain a competitive advantage in today's global economy by properly and effectively using various means of business communication. The use of different communication strategies in the workplace is essential to the success of businesses ranging from large corporations to on-campus student technology centers. Thus, any successful business education program must also prepare students to use and choose between the diverse media used for business communication today. This report discusses the strengths and weaknesses of different communication modes such as telephone, e-mail, and face-to-face communication, relying largely on an in-depth study of the Computer Store at Penn State University. Based on research and observations of staff, managers, and executives of the organization, the research team developed some strategies for successful business communication, in particular a critique of the overuse of e-mail in business settings. Finally, this report proposes changes to the business communication curriculum at Penn State University, in light of the team's research into real-world business communication practices.

Introduction

Background

Business communication is constantly evolving as technology provides new and better methods for communication. In the past two decades, e-mail, instant messaging, video conferencing, and cell phone technology have allowed business colleagues to cooperate with unparalleled efficiency. The number of e-mails sent daily in 2006 is estimated at around 62 billion. The International Data Corporation also reports 600 billion minutes of usage by mobile phone users (Berkeley School of Information Management and Systems, 2003, p. 10). However, these new methods have not replaced more traditional forms of communication. The average office worker uses about 12,000 sheets of paper per year. With so many options available, it is sometimes difficult to choose the best option for the situation at hand. Furthermore, the range of options for business communication necessitates changes to business communication curricula.

Problem

In the world of modern business, it can be difficult to choose between memos, telephone calls, voice mails, e-mails, meetings, and other modes of communication. All too often employees choose a form of communication that may not be properly suited to their purpose. More specifically, e-mail is easy to use, but at the same time it leads to impersonal interactions between the sender and the receiver. Many employees use e-mail when contacting individuals they are not closely acquainted with, such as new clients. The problem with this strategy is that, in business, building relationships and networking are valuable activities and can increase productivity and quality throughout an organization.

Jeremy Burton, Vice-President of VERITAS Software Corporation in Silicon Valley, like many other executives, has taken this issue to heart. Burton banned e-mails on Fridays, imposing a small fine for each e-mail sent. Though his 240 employees initially resisted the change, they began to think more critically about their communication with others, and productivity increased (Walker, 2004). The real problem, however, is that this kind of critical thinking should be encouraged before employees reach the workforce. Business communication skills like those that innovative employers like Burton are teaching their employees should be addressed in college coursework, not just on the job. The research team believes that the Penn State College of Business is not currently addressing this need.

Purpose

The object of this report is to encourage the College of Business at Penn State to consider changes to the business communication curriculum. Specifically, this report examines a few major forms of communication, evaluates their strengths and weaknesses, and gives suggestions for when and how to use them

6

effectively. This analysis shows that such topics need to be more thoroughly addressed in business classes at Penn State. The analysis is followed by a set of recommendations for the college.

Scope

This report includes a general analysis of various types of communication and their uses. A case study of communication practices at Penn State's Computer Store examines, in particular, e-mail overuse and some factors that may contribute to it. The report shows the value of employees who can properly identify appropriate communication strategies and media. The recommendations suggest the relevance and consequences of the findings for the business curriculum at Penn State.

Discussion

Successful Business Communication

Like those at many other contemporary businesses, the employees of the Computer Store at Penn State University use many forms of communication. As Robin Becker, the Director of Sales and Marketing, said, "There is no one ideal form of communication" (personal communication, June 5, 2007). The Computer Store uses three effective forms of communication for communicating with clients, besides e-mail. During in-house technical consulting, employees assist students and parents in person as they purchase and learn to use a laptop. Second, consultants use telephones to advise individuals about purchasing laptops and accessories. The last medium, which has taken off recently, is the store's Web site. The Computer Store Web site has become a very useful tool for assisting people in their decision making and preparing them for computer ownership, and it complements the first two methods for communicating with clients. The site helps the meeting with a consultant run more smoothly, whether it takes place face to face or over the phone.

As for communication between the workers at the Computer Store, no one form is ideal. Figure 1 shows the different modes of communication and ranks them on their appropriateness for different day-to-day events. Generally, e-mail is used for follow-ups or quick notes. For other tasks, such as negotiating an agreement with a corporation to make its software available to all Penn State students, a face-to-face conference or a conference call is preferred. For passing quick notes and bits of information through the office in the Computer Store, Becker explains, e-mail or instant messaging works best (personal communication, June 5, 2007). James Murphy, the team leader for consultants, advised, "Use a mix [of communication], try not to limit yourself to one style, and try to cater to other people. If I need to get a lot of information across, I'll write a memo and send it via e-mail, but if I just need to get across one thing to one person, I will walk over there and tell that person face to face" (personal communication, June 5, 2007).

8

How Well Medium Is Suited to:	Hard Copy	Phone Call	Voice Mail	E-mail	Meeting	Web Site
Assessing commitment	3	2	3	3	1	3
Building consensus	3	2	3	3	1	3
Mediating a conflict	3	2	3	3	1	3
Resolving a misunderstanding	3	1	3	3	2	3
Addressing negative behavior	3	2	3	2	1	3
Expressing support/ appreciation	1	2	2	1	2	3
Encouraging creative thinking	2	3	3	1	3	3
Making an ironic statement	3	2	2	3	1	3
Conveying a reference document	1	3	3	3	3	2
Reinforcing one's authority	1	2	3	3	1	1
Providing a permanent record	1	3	3	1	3	3
Maintaining confidentiality	2	1	2	3	1	3
Conveying simple information	3	1	1	1	2	3
Asking an informational question	3	1	1	1	3	3
Making a simple request	3	1	1	1	3	3
Giving complex instructions	3	3	2	2	1	2
Addressing many people	2	2	2	2	3	1
Key: 1 = Excellent 2 = Adequate 3 = Inappropriate						

Figure 1. Effective business communication.
Note. From *Email Composition and Communication (EmC2)* by
T. Galati. Practical Communications, Inc. (www.praccom.com), 2001.

9

Research into business communication confirms the necessity of the Computer Store's reliance on modes of communication other than e-mail. When working with a large number of people, businesses need to be able to get a message across accurately and in a timely manner. If a message is misinterpreted by just one individual, a large-scale problem might result. When an e-mail message requires immediate attention, some businesses, like the Computer Store at Penn State, address the problem of delayed response by using instant messaging.

Though instant messaging may alleviate in-house communication lapses, other forms of media, like Web sites, are more suited to growing foreign audiences. Foreign investment by U.S. companies was approximately 9 trillion dollars in 1966 but had grown to 300 trillion dollars in 2002 (Blalock, 2005). This rising foreign investment by U.S. companies has increased the need for better communication among companies that are now communicating globally. Though the Penn State Computer Store is, for the most part, not communicating on a global scale, its practices demonstrate the same sense of a need for a variety of communication media, without an uncritical overreliance on e-mail.

E-mail Overuse

Many factors go into choosing the proper medium for a given rhetorical situation, such as privacy concerns, the size of the group, the type of information, and the desired level of immediacy. People tend to overuse e-mail because it is an easy, inexpensive way to send information to several people. When asked why sending an e-mail to a team of 100 people is not as effective as sending to a team of five, Carol Hildenbrand, a CIO, answered:

> As a group increases in size, you have a whole slew of management challenges. Communicating badly exponentially increases the possibility of making fatal mistakes. A large-scale project has a lot of moving parts, which makes it that much easier to break down. Communication is the oil that keeps everything working properly. It's much easier to address an atmosphere of distrust among a group of five team members than it is with a team of 500 members. (Schwalbe, 2006, p. 399)

Information distribution, therefore, involves more than creating and sending status reports, and different media are suited to different contexts, purposes, and audiences. Figure 1 shows some findings about the suitability of forms of communication to particular business goals, but each situation should be assessed individually.

11

Implementation of Communication Strategies

One of the most important functions of business communication is to transfer information from one level in a hierarchy to another: from employee to manager, for example, or vice versa. After examining the functioning of the Penn State Computer Store, the research team found that it had a very effective communication structure. Employees shared their insights as to how different kinds of information are conveyed through different media. Ideas, proposals, and other important information are generally communicated in person or over the phone. E-mail is relied on for notifications and follow-ups, but not for complex tasks where interactivity and collaboration are desired.

Personal Relationships

It is vital for a business to network and build successful relationships that might prove beneficial in the future. Yet in today's workplace, it is becoming harder to develop relationships because of the overuse of e-mail. The Penn State Computer Store avoids this problem by having employees within the office interact face to face. The store also maintains good relationships with customers at other campuses by sending out consultants to meet clients. Face-to-face communication creates

12

a perceived added value to the services and products the store offers. When a consumer buys a product or a warranty from the Computer Store on campus, he or she reaps the benefits of a strong network of co-workers who have good communication skills that they use among themselves as well as with clients.

Conclusion

Over the past few decades, modes of communication have changed rapidly. When we have something to say, we have the option of sending an instant message or an e-mail, making a phone call, sending a text message, posting information on a Web site or blog, or even creating a podcast. The rise of these new methods of communication has posed some problems for businesses that are not operating with a high level of efficiency. Without employees who can both use the technologies and, more importantly, choose the most fitting technology for a given situation, businesses will not be able to communicate efficiently either internally or externally, with clients and other businesses.

Research at the Penn State Computer Store showed that each form of communication has its own benefits and drawbacks. If an important message needs to be conveyed, a face-to-face meeting is recommended. However, if an employee wants to check with a supervisor before leaving the office for an hour, an instant message

13

is sufficient. However, there is an overuse of e-mail, which has become a mode used between people who are unfamiliar with each other and are likely, if using this medium, to remain that way. This impersonality may hurt businesses because networking and building relationships are crucial to business success.

Recommendation

Overview of the Problem

Business curricula are not spending enough time teaching potential new employees strategies and procedures for communicating properly through different media. This issue needs to be addressed immediately by the College of Business at Penn State.

Possible Solutions

The way to correct this problem is to increase the amount of business communication courses offered in the College of Business. The inclusion of more communication-oriented material will increase graduates' abilities to begin and maintain careers in the business world. The curriculum should cover facets of contact such as the use and misuse of e-mail and the advantages and disadvantages thereof. Courses should cover networking within businesses and explore how this networking can create successful relationships among employees. The curriculum should also present students with multiple opportunities to work in groups using various media as well as

14

the opportunity to develop these skills before entering the business community.

Benefits

Implementation of this new curriculum will put Penn State business students in an enviable position for future employment with successful companies. Businesses need employees well versed in communication techniques crucial to a global market. Penn State students will be well placed with these revisions to the business communication curriculum. Ultimately, as Penn State students achieve more success in business, the prestige and reputation of the College of Business will continue to grow.

15

References

Berkeley School of Information Management and Systems. (2003). *Executive summary: How much information?* Retrieved June 10, 2007, from http://www2.sims.berkeley .edu/research/projects/how-much-info-2003/execsum.htm

Blalock, M. (2005, December 23). *Why good communication is good business.* Retrieved June 5, 2007, from http://www .bus.wisc.edu/update/winter05/business_communication.asp

Schwalbe, K. (2006). *Information technology project management* (4th ed.). Waterloo, Ontario, Canada: Thomson Course Technology.

Walker, M. (2004, August 26). The day the e-mail dies. *The Wall Street Journal Online*. Retrieved June 4, 2007, from http://www.lucid-minds.com/public/p66.htm

Glossary of Usage

The term *usage* refers to the ways words are used in specific contexts. As you know from speaking and writing every day, the words you choose depend on your audience and your purpose. For example, you might use *guys* when you are at lunch with your friends but choose *people, classmates, employees,* or another more formal or precise word when you are writing a report. By learning about usage in this glossary, you will increase your ability to use words effectively. Many of the entries are context-specific; others distinguish between words that sound or look similar.

The definitions and guidelines in this glossary will help you write clear and precise prose. Nonetheless, you should be aware that the idea of standard usage potentially carries with it the assumption that words not considered standard are inferior. Words labeled "nonstandard" are commonly condemned, even though they may be words some people have grown up hearing and using. A better way to discuss usage is to label what is conventional, or accepted practice, for a specific context. Thus, words commonly used in one context may not be appropriate in another. The following labels will help you choose appropriate words for your rhetorical situation.

Conventional   Words or phrases listed in dictionaries without special usage labels; generally considered appropriate in academic and professional writing.

Conversational   Words or phrases that dictionaries label *informal, slang,* or *colloquial;* although often used in informal speech and writing, not generally appropriate for formal writing assignments.

Unconventional   Words or phrases not generally considered appropriate in academic or professional writing and often labeled *nonstandard* in dictionaries; best avoided in formal contexts.

Agreement on usage occurs slowly, often after a period of debate. In this glossary, entries are marked with an asterisk (*) when new usages have been reported by dictionary editors but may not yet be accepted by everyone.

a lot of   *A lot of* is conversational for *many, much,* or *a great deal of:* They do not have ~~a lot of~~ **much** time. *A lot* is sometimes misspelled as *alot.*

a while, awhile   *A while* means "a period of time." It is often used with the prepositions *after, for,* and *in:* We rested for **a while.** *Awhile* means "a short time." It is not preceded by a preposition: We rested **awhile.**

accept, except   The verb *accept* means "to receive": I **accept** your apology. The verb *except* means "to exclude": The policy was to have everyone wait in line, but mothers and small children were **excepted.** The preposition *except* means "other than": All **except** Joe will attend the conference.

advice, advise   *Advice* is a noun: They asked their attorney for **advice.** *Advise* is a verb: The attorney **advised** us to save all relevant documents.

affect, effect   *Affect* is a verb that means "to influence": The lobbyist's pleas did not **affect** the politician's decision. The noun *effect* means "a result": The **effect** of his decision on the staff's morale was positive and long lasting. When used as a verb, *effect* means "to produce" or "to cause": The activists believed that they could **effect** real political change.

all ready, already *All ready* means "completely prepared": The rooms are **all ready** for the conference. *Already* means "by or before the time specified": She has **already** taken her final exams.

* **all right** *All right* means "acceptable": The students asked whether it was **all right** to use dictionaries during the exam. *Alright* is not yet a generally accepted spelling of *all right,* although it is becoming more common in journalistic writing.

all together, altogether *All together* means "as a group": The cast reviewed the script **all together.** *Altogether* means "wholly, thoroughly": That game is **altogether** too difficult.

allude, elude *Allude* means "to refer to indirectly": The professor **alluded** to a medieval text. *Elude* means "to evade" or "to escape from": For the moment, his name **eludes** me.

allusion, illusion An *allusion* is a casual or indirect reference: The **allusion** was to Shakespeare's *Twelfth Night.* An *illusion* is a false idea or an unreal image: His idea of college is an **illusion.**

alot See **a lot of.**

already See **all ready, already.**

alright See **all right.**

altogether See **all together, altogether.**

* **among, between** To follow traditional usage, use *among* with three or more entities (a group): The snorklers swam **among** the fish. Use *between* when referring to only two entities: The rivalry **between** the two teams is intense. Current dictionaries also note the possibility of using *between* to refer to more than two entities, especially when these entities are considered distinct: We have strengthened the lines of communication **between** the various departments.

amount of, number of Use *amount of* before nouns that cannot be counted: The **amount of** rain that fell last year was insufficient. Use *number of* with nouns that can be counted: The **number of** students attending college has increased.

and/or This combination denotes three options: one, the other, or both: The student's application should be signed by a parent **and/or** a teacher. These options can also be presented separately with *or:* The student's application should be signed by a parent, a teacher, **or** both.

* **angry at, angry with**   Both *at* and *with* are commonly used after *angry,* although according to traditional guidelines, *with* should be used when a person is the cause of the anger: She was **angry with** me because I was late.

another, other, the other   *Another* is followed by a singular noun: **another** book. *Other* is followed by a plural noun: **other** books. *The other* is followed by either a singular or a plural noun: **the other book, the other books.**

anymore, any more   *Anymore* meaning "any longer" or "now" most frequently occurs in negative sentences: Sarah doesn't work here **anymore.** Its use in positive sentences is considered conversational; *now* is generally used instead: All he ever does ~~anymore~~ now is watch television. As two words, *any more* appears with *not* to mean "no more": We do not have **any more** time.

anyone, any one   *Anyone* means "any person at all": We did not know **anyone.** *Any one* refers to one of a group: **Any one** of the options is better than the current situation.

* **anyplace, everyplace, someplace**   These words are becoming increasingly common in academic writing. However, according to traditional usage rules, they should be replaced by *anywhere, everywhere,* and *somewhere.*

as   Conversational when used after such verbs as *know, say,* and *see.* Use *that, if,* or *whether* instead: I do not know ~~as~~ whether my application is complete. Also considered conversational is the use of *as* instead of *who, which,* or *that:* Many of the performers ~~as~~ who have appeared on our program will be giving a concert this evening.

as, because   The use of *as* to signal a cause may be vague; if it is, use *because* instead: ~~As~~ Because we were running out of gas, we turned around.

* **as, like**   According to traditional usage, *as* begins either a phrase or a clause; *like* begins only a phrase: My brother drives too fast, just ~~like~~ as my father did. Current dictionaries note the informal use of *like* to begin clauses, especially after verbs such as *look, feel,* and *sound.*

assure, ensure, insure *Assure* means "to state with confidence, alleviating any doubt": The flight attendant **assured** us that our flight would arrive on time. *Ensure* and *insure* are usually interchangeable to mean "make certain," but only *insure* means "to protect against loss": The editor **ensured** [OR **insured**] that the reporter's facts were accurate. Physicians must **insure** themselves against malpractice suits.

awhile See **a while, awhile.**

bad Unconventional as an adverb; use *badly* instead. The team played **badly.** However, the adjective *bad* is used after sensory verbs such as *feel, look,* and *smell:* I feel **bad** that I forgot to return your book yesterday.

because See **as, because.**

being as, being that Unconventional; use *because* instead. ~~Being as~~ Because the road was closed, traffic was diverted to another route.

* **beside, besides** According to traditional usage, these two words have different meanings. *Beside* means "next to": The president sat **beside** the prime minister. *Besides* means "in addition to" or "other than": She has written many articles **besides** those on political reform. Current dictionaries report that professional writers regularly use *beside* to convey this meaning, as long as there is no risk of ambiguity.

better, had better *Better* is conversational. Use *had better* instead: We ~~better~~ had better finish the report by five o'clock.

between See **among, between.**

* **bring, take** Both words describe the same action but from different standpoints. *Bring* indicates movement toward the writer: She **brought** me some flowers. *Take* implies movement away from the writer: He **took** my overdue books to the library. Dictionaries report that this distinction is often blurred when the writer's position is ambiguous or irrelevant: He **brought** [OR **took**] her some flowers.

* **can, may** *Can* refers to ability, and *may* refers to permission: You **can** [are able to] drive seventy miles an hour, but you **may** not [are not permitted to] exceed the speed limit. Current dictionaries report that in contemporary usage *can* and *may* are used interchangeably

to denote possibility or permission, although *may* is used more
frequently in formal contexts.

can't hardly, can't scarcely   Unconventional. Use *can hardly* or *can
scarcely:* The students **can't hardly** wait for summer vacation.

capital, capitol   *Capital* means either "a governing city" or "funds":
The **capital** of Minnesota is St. Paul. An anonymous donor
provided the **capital** for the project. As a modifier, *capital* means
"chief" or "principal": This year's election is of **capital** importance.
It may also refer to the death penalty: **Capital** punishment is legal
in some states. A *capitol* is a statehouse; the *Capitol* is the U.S.
congressional building in Washington, DC.

censor, censure, sensor   As a verb, *censor* means "to remove or
suppress because of immoral or otherwise objectionable ideas":
Do you think a ratings board should **censor** films? As a noun,
censor refers to a person who is authorized to remove material
considered objectionable: The **censor** recommended that the
book be banned. The verb *censure* means "to blame or criticize";
the noun *censure* is an expression of disapproval or blame. The
Senate **censured** Joseph McCarthy. He received a **censure** from
the Senate. A *sensor* is a device that responds to a stimulus: The
sensor detects changes in light.

cite, site, sight   *Cite* means "to mention": Be sure to **cite** your
sources. *Site* is a location: The president visited the **site** for the
new library. As a verb, *site* also means "to situate": The builder
sited the factory near the freeway. *Sight* means "to see": The crew
sighted land. *Sight* also refers to a view: What an incredible **sight!**

climactic, climatic   *Climactic* refers to a climax, or high point:
The actors rehearsed the **climactic** scene. *Climatic* refers to the
climate: Many environmentalists are worried about the recent
climatic changes.

coarse, course   *Coarse* refers to roughness: The jacket was made of
coarse linen. *Course* refers to a route: Our **course** to the island
was indirect. *Course* may also refer to a plan of study: I want to
take a **course** in nutrition.

compare to, compare with   *Compare to* means "to regard as similar," and *compare with* means "to examine for similarities and/or

differences": She **compared** her mind **to** a dusty attic. The student **compared** the first draft **with** the second.

complement, complementary, compliment, complimentary
Complement means "to complete" or "to balance": Their personalities **complement** each other. They have **complementary** personalities. *Compliment* means "to express praise": The professor **complimented** the students on their first drafts. Her remarks were **complimentary.** *Complimentary* may also mean "provided free of charge": We received **complimentary** tickets.

* **compose, comprise**   *Compose* means "to make up": That collection **is composed** of medieval manuscripts. *Comprise* means "to consist of": The anthology **comprises** many famous essays. Dictionary editors have noted the increasing use of *comprise* in the passive voice to mean "to be composed of."

conscience, conscious, consciousness   *Conscience* means "the sense of right and wrong": He examined his **conscience** before deciding whether to join the protest. *Conscious* means "awake": After an hour, the patient was fully **conscious.** After an hour, the patient regained **consciousness.** *Conscious* may also mean "aware": We were **conscious** of the possible consequences.

continual, continually, continuous, continuously   *Continual* means "constantly recurring": **Continual** interruptions kept us from completing the project. Telephone calls **continually** interrupted us. *Continuous* means "uninterrupted": The job applicant had a record of ten years' **continuous** employment. The job applicant worked **continuously** from 2000 to 2009.

* **convince, persuade**   *Convince* means "to make someone believe something": His passionate speech **convinced** us that school reform was necessary. *Persuade* means "to motivate someone to act": She **persuaded** us to stop smoking. Dictionary editors note that many speakers now use *convince* as a synonym for *persuade.*

could of   *Of* is often mistaken for the sound of the unstressed *have:* They **could of have** [OR might **have,** should **have,** would **have**] gone home.

couldn't care less   *Couldn't care less* expresses complete lack of concern: She **couldn't care less** about her reputation. *Could care less* is considered unconventional in academic writing.

council, counsel   A *council* is an advisory or decision-making group: The student **council** supported the new regulations. A *counsel* is a legal adviser: The defense **counsel** conferred with the judge. As a verb, *counsel* means "to give advice": She **counsels** people with eating disorders.

criteria, criterion   *Criteria* is a plural noun meaning "a set of standards for judgment": The teachers explained the **criteria** for the assignment. The singular form is *criterion:* Their judgment was based on only one **criterion.**

* **data**   *Data* is the plural form of *datum,* which means "piece of information" or "fact": When the **data are** complete, we will know the true cost. However, current dictionaries also note that *data* is frequently used as a mass entity (like the word *furniture*), appearing with a singular verb.

desert, dessert   *Desert* can mean "a barren land": Gila monsters live in the **deserts** of the Southwest. As a verb, *desert* means "to leave": I thought my friends had **deserted** me. *Dessert* refers to something sweet eaten at the end of a meal: They ordered apple pie for **dessert.**

device, devise   *Device* is a noun: She invented a **device** that measures extremely small quantities of liquid. *Devise* is a verb: We **devised** a plan for work distribution.

differ from, differ with   *Differ from* means "to be different": A bull snake **differs from** a rattlesnake in a number of ways. *Differ with* means "to disagree": Senator Brown has **differed with** Senator Owen on several issues.

different from, different than   *Different from* is generally used with nouns, pronouns, noun phrases, and noun clauses: This school was **different from** most others. The school was **different from** what we had expected. *Different than* is used with adverbial clauses; *than* is the conjunction: We are no **different than** they are.

discreet, discrete   *Discreet* means "showing good judgment or self-restraint": His friends complained openly, but his comments were quite **discreet.** *Discrete* means "distinct": The participants in the study came from three **discrete** groups.

disinterested, uninterested   *Disinterested* means "impartial":
A **disinterested** observer will give a fair opinion. *Uninterested*
means "lacking interest": She was **uninterested** in the outcome
of the game.

distinct, distinctive   *Distinct* means "easily distinguishable or
perceived": Each proposal has **distinct** advantages. *Distinctive*
means "characteristic" or "serving to distinguish": We studied
the **distinctive** features of hawks.

* **due to**   Traditionally, *due to* was not synonymous with *because
of:* ~~Due to~~ Because of holiday traffic, we arrived an hour late.
However, dictionary editors now consider this usage of *due to*
acceptable.

dyeing, dying   *Dyeing* comes from *dye,* meaning "to color something,
usually by soaking it": As a sign of solidarity, the students are **dyeing**
their shirts the same color. *Dying* refers to the loss of life: Because of
the drought, the plants are **dying.**

effect   See **affect, effect.**

elicit, illicit   *Elicit* means "to draw forth": He is **eliciting**
contributions for a new playground. *Illicit* means "unlawful":
The newspaper reported their **illicit** mishandling of public funds.

elude   See **allude, elude.**

emigrate from, immigrate to   *Emigrate* means "to leave one's
own country": My ancestors **emigrated from** Ireland. *Immigrate*
means "to arrive in a different country to settle": The Ulster Scots
immigrated to the southern United States.

eminent, imminent   *Eminent* means "distinguished": An **eminent**
scholar in physics will be giving a public lecture tomorrow.
Imminent means "about to happen": The merger of the two
companies is **imminent.**

ensure   See **assure, ensure, insure.**

especially, specially   *Especially* emphasizes a characteristic or
quality: Some people are **especially** sensitive to the sun. *Especially*
also means "particularly": Wildflowers are abundant in this area,
especially during May. *Specially* means "for a particular purpose":
The classroom was **specially** designed for music students.

etc.   Abbreviation of *et cetera,* meaning "and others of the same kind." Use only within parentheses: Be sure to bring appropriate camping gear (tent, sleeping bag, mess kit, **etc.**). Because *and* is part of the meaning of *etc.,* avoid using the combination *and etc.*

eventually, ultimately   *Eventually* refers to some future time: She has made so many valuable contributions that I am sure she will **eventually** become the store supervisor. *Ultimately* refers to the final outcome after a series of events: The course was difficult but **ultimately** worthwhile.

everyday, every day   *Everyday* means "routine" or "ordinary": These are **everyday** problems. *Every day* means "each day": I read the newspaper **every day.**

everyone, every one   *Everyone* means "all": **Everyone** should attend. *Every one* refers to each person or item in a group: **Every one** of you should attend.

everyplace   See **anyplace, everyplace, someplace.**

except   See **accept, except.**

explicit, implicit   *Explicit* means "expressed clearly and directly": Given his **explicit** directions, we knew how to proceed. *Implicit* means "implied or expressed indirectly": I mistakenly understood his silence to be his **implicit** approval of the project.

farther, further   Generally, *farther* refers to geographic distance: We will have to drive **farther** tomorrow. *Further* means "more": If you need **further** assistance, please let me know.

* **feel**   Traditionally, *feel* was not synonymous with "think" or "believe": I ~~feel~~ think that more should be done to protect local habitat. Dictionary editors now consider this use of *feel* to be a standard alternative.

fewer, less   *Fewer* occurs before nouns that can be counted: **fewer** technicians, **fewer** pencils. *Less* occurs before nouns that cannot be counted: **less** milk, **less** support. *Less than* may be used with measurements of time or distance: **less than** three months, **less than** twenty miles.

* **first, firstly; second, secondly**   Many college instructors prefer the use of *first* and *second.* However, dictionary editors state that *firstly* and *secondly* are also well-established forms.

foreword, forward   A *foreword* is an introduction: The **foreword** to the book provided useful background information. *Forward* refers to a frontward direction: To get a closer look, we moved **forward** slowly.

former, latter   Used together, *former* refers to the first of two; *latter* to the second of two. John and Ian are both English. The **former** is from Manchester; the **latter** is from Birmingham.

further   See **farther, further.**

get   Considered conversational in many common expressions: The weather ~~got better~~ improved overnight. I did not know what he ~~was getting at~~ meant.

go, goes   Unconventional for *say(s), respond(s),* and other similar words: My friends say I'm strange, and I ~~go,~~ reply, "You're right!"

good, well   *Good* is an adjective, not an adverb: He pitched ~~good~~ well last night. *Good* in the sense of "in good health" may be used interchangeably with *well:* I feel **good** [OR **well**] this morning.

had better   See **better, had better.**

half   A *half a* or *a half an* is unconventional; use *half a/an* or *a half:* You should be able to complete the questionnaire in **a half** ~~an~~ hour.

hanged, hung   *Hanged* means "put to death by hanging": The prisoner was **hanged** at dawn. For all other meanings, use *hung:* He **hung** the picture above his desk.

hardly   See **can't hardly, can't scarcely.**

has got, have got   Conversational; omit *got:* I **have** ~~got~~ a meeting tomorrow.

he/she, his/her   As a solution to the problem of sexist language, these combinations are not universally accepted. Consider using *he or she* and *his or her.* See **19d.**

herself, himself, myself, yourself   Unconventional as subjects in a sentence. Joe and ~~myself~~ I will lead the discussion. See **5a(2).**

hopefully   Conversational to mean "I hope": ~~Hopefully,~~ I hope the game will not be canceled.

hung   See **hanged, hung.**

i.e.   Abbreviation of *id est,* meaning "that is." Use only within parentheses: All participants in the study ran the same distance (**i.e.,** six kilometers). Otherwise, replace *i.e.* with the English equivalent, *that is:* Assistance was offered to those who would have difficulty boarding, ~~i.e.,~~ **that is,** the elderly, the disabled, and parents with small children. Do not confuse *i.e.* with *e.g.,* meaning "for example."

illicit   See **elicit, illicit.**

illusion   See **allusion, illusion.**

immigrate   See **emigrate from, immigrate to.**

imminent   See **eminent, imminent.**

* **impact**   Though *impact* is commonly used as a verb in business writing, many college teachers still use it as a noun only: The new tax ~~impacts~~ affects everyone.

implicit   See **explicit, implicit.**

imply, infer   *Imply* means "suggest without actually stating": Though he never mentioned the statistics, he **implied** that they were questionable. *Infer* means "draw a conclusion based on evidence": Given the tone of his voice, I **inferred** that he found the work substandard.

in regards to   Unconventional; see **regard, regarding, regards.**

inside of, outside of   Drop *of* when unnecessary: Security guards stood **outside** ~~of~~ the front door.

insure   See **assure, ensure, insure.**

irregardless   Unconventional; use *regardless* instead.

its, it's   *Its* is a possessive form: The committee forwarded **its** recommendation. *It's* is a contraction of *it is:* **It's** a beautiful day.

kind of a, sort of a   The word *a* is unnecessary: This **kind of** ~~a~~ book sells well. *Kind of* and *sort of* are not conventionally used to mean "somewhat": The report was ~~kind of~~ somewhat difficult to read.

later, latter   *Later* means "after a specific time" or "a time after now": The concert ended **later** than we had expected. *Latter* refers to the second of two items: Of the two versions described, I prefer the **latter.**

lay, lie   *Lay* (*laid, laying*) means "put" or "place": He **laid** the book aside. *Lie* (*lay, lain, lying*) means "rest" or "recline": I had just **lain** down when the alarm went off. *Lay* takes an object (to **lay**

something), while *lie* does not. These verbs may be confused because the present tense of *lay* and the past tense of *lie* are spelled the same way.

lead, led As a noun, *lead* means "a kind of metal": The paint had **lead** in it. As a verb, *lead* means "to conduct": A guide will **lead** a tour of the ruins. *Led* is the past tense of the verb *lead:* He **led** the country from 1949 to 1960.

less, less than See **fewer, less.**

lie See **lay, lie.**

like See **as, like.**

literally Conversational when used to emphasize the meaning of another word: I was ~~literally~~ nearly frozen after I finished shoveling the sidewalk. *Literally* is conventionally used to indicate that an expression is not being used figuratively: My friend **literally** climbs the walls after work; his fellow rock climbers join him at the local gym.

lose, loose *Lose* is a verb: She does not **lose** her patience often. *Loose* is chiefly used as an adjective: A few of the tiles are **loose.**

lots, lots of Conversational for *many* or *much:* He has ~~lots of~~ many friends. We have ~~lots~~ much to do before the end of the quarter.

mankind Considered sexist because it excludes women: All ~~mankind~~ humanity will benefit from this new discovery.

many, much *Many* is used with nouns that can be counted: **many** stores, too **many** assignments. *Much* is used with nouns that cannot be counted: **much** courage, not **much** time.

may See **can, may.**

may of, might of See **could of.**

maybe, may be *Maybe* is an adverb: **Maybe** the negotiators will succeed this time. *May* and *be* are verbs: The rumor **may be** true.

* **media, medium** According to traditional definitions, *media* is a plural word: The **media** have sometimes created the news in addition to reporting it. The singular form is *medium:* The newspaper is one **medium** that people seem to trust. Dictionary editors note the frequent use of *media* as a collective noun taking a singular verb, but this usage is still considered conversational.

might could   Conversational for "might be able to": The director **might** ~~could~~ **be able to** review your application next week.

most   Unconventional to mean "almost": We watch the news ~~most~~ **almost** every day.

much   See **many, much**.

myself   See **herself, himself, myself, yourself**.

neither . . . or   *Nor*, not *or*, follows *neither*: The book is **neither** as funny ~~or~~ **nor** as original as critics have reported.

nothing like, nowhere near   Unconventional; use *not nearly* instead: Her new book is ~~nowhere near~~ **not nearly** as mysterious as her previous novel.

number of   When the expression *a number of* is used, the reference is plural: **A number of** positions **are** open. When *the number of* is used, the reference is singular: **The number of** possibilities **is** limited. See also **amount of, number of**.

off of   Conversational; omit *of*: He walked **off** ~~of~~ the field.

on account of   Conversational; use *because of*: The singer canceled her engagement ~~on account of~~ **because of** a sore throat.

on the other hand   Use *however* instead or make sure that the sentence or independent clause beginning with this transitional phrase is preceded by one starting with *on the one hand*.

other   See **another, other, the other**.

passed, past   *Passed* is the past tense of the verb *pass*: Deb **passed** the other runners right before the finish line. *Past* means "beyond a time or location": We walked **past** the high school.

per   In ordinary contexts, use *a* or *an*: You should drink at least six glasses of water ~~per~~ **a** day.

percent, percentage   *Percent* (also spelled *per cent*) is used with a specific number: **Sixty percent** of the students attended the ceremony. *Percentage* refers to an unspecified portion: The **percentage** of high school graduates attending college has increased in recent years.

perspective, prospective   *Perspective* means "point of view": We discussed the issue from various **perspectives**. *Prospective* means "likely to become": **Prospective** journalists interviewed the editor in chief.

persuade   See **convince, persuade.**

phenomena, phenomenon   *Phenomena* is the plural form of *phenomenon*: Natural **phenomena** were given scientific explanations.

plus   *Plus* joins nouns or noun phrases to make a sentence seem like an equation: Her endless curiosity **plus** her boundless energy makes her the perfect camp counselor. Note that a singular form of the verb is required (e.g., *makes*). *Plus* is not used to join clauses: I telephoned ~~plus~~ **and** I sent flowers.

precede, proceed   To *precede* is to "go ahead of": A moment of silence **preceded** the applause. To *proceed* is to "go forward": After stopping for a short rest, we **proceeded** to our destination.

prejudice, prejudiced   *Prejudice* is a noun: They were unaware of their **prejudice**. *Prejudiced* is an adjective: She accused me of being **prejudiced**.

pretty   *Pretty* means "attractive," not "rather" or "fairly": We were ~~pretty~~ **fairly** tired after cooking all day.

principal, principle   As a noun, *principal* means "chief official": The **principal** greeted the students every day. It also means "capital": The loan's **principal** was still quite high. As an adjective, *principal* means "main": Tourism is the country's **principal** source of income. The noun *principle* refers to a rule, standard, or belief: She explained the three **principles** supporting the theory.

proceed   See **precede, proceed.**

prospective   See **perspective, prospective.**

quotation, quote   In academic writing, *quotation,* rather than *quote,* refers to a repeated or copied sentence or passage: She began her speech with a ~~quote~~ **quotation** from *Othello*. *Quote* expresses an action: My friend sometimes **quotes** lines from television commercials.

raise, rise   *Raise* (*raised, raising*) means "to lift or cause to move upward, to bring up or increase": Retailers **raised** prices. *Rise* (*rose, risen, rising*) means "to get up" or "to ascend": The cost of living **rose** sharply. *Raise* takes an object (to **raise** something); *rise* does not.

real, really   *Really* rather than *real* is used to mean "very": He is from a ~~real~~ **really** small town. To ensure this word's effectiveness, use it sparingly.

* **reason why**   Traditionally, this combination was considered redundant: No one explained **the reason ~~why~~** the negotiations failed. [OR No one explained ~~the reason~~ **why** the negotiations failed.] However, dictionary editors report its use by highly regarded writers.

regard, regarding, regards   These forms are used in the following expressions: *in regard to, with regard to, as regards,* and *regarding* [NOT *in regards to, with regards to,* or *as regarding*].

* **relation, relationship**   According to traditional definitions, *relation* is used to link abstractions: We studied the **relation** between language and social change. *Relationship* is used to link people: The **relationship** between the two friends grew strong. However, dictionary editors now label as standard the use of *relationship* to connect abstractions.

respectfully, respectively   *Respectfully* means "showing respect": The children learned to treat one another **respectfully.** *Respectively* means "in the order designated": We discussed the issue with the chair, the dean, and the provost, **respectively.**

rise   See **raise, rise.**

sensor   See **censor, censure, sensor.**

sensual, sensuous   *Sensual* refers to gratification of the physical senses, often those associated with sexual pleasure: Frequently found in this music are **sensual** dance rhythms. *Sensuous* refers to gratification of the senses in response to art, music, nature, and so on: **Sensuous** landscape paintings lined the walls of the gallery.

shall, will   Traditionally, *shall* was used with *I* or *we* to express future tense, and *will* was used with the other personal pronouns, but *shall* has almost disappeared in contemporary American English. *Shall* is still used in legal writing to indicate an obligation.

should of   See **could of.**

sight   See **cite, site, sight.**

sit, set   *Sit* means "to be seated": Jonathan **sat** in the front row. *Set* means "to place something": The research assistant **set** the chemicals on the counter. *Set* takes an object (to **set** something); *sit* does not.

site   See **cite, site, sight.**

so   *So* intensifies another word when it is used with *that:* He was **so** nervous **that** he had trouble sleeping. Instead of using *so* alone, find a precise modifier: She was ~~so~~ **intensely** focused on her career. See **22c.**

someplace   See **anyplace, everyplace, someplace.**

sometime, sometimes, some time   *Sometime* means "at an unspecified time": They will meet **sometime** next month. *Sometimes* means "at times": **Sometimes** laws are unfair. *Some time* means "a span of time": They agreed to allow **some time** to pass before voting on the measure.

sort of a   See **kind of a, sort of a.**

specially   See **especially, specially.**

stationary, stationery   *Stationary* means "in a fixed position": Traffic was **stationary** for an hour. *Stationery* means "writing paper and envelopes": The director ordered new department **stationery.**

supposed to, used to   Be sure to include the frequently unsounded *d* at the end of the verb form: We are **supposed** to leave at 9:30 a.m. We **used** to leave earlier.

take   See **bring, take.**

than, then   *Than* is used in comparisons: The tape recorder is smaller **than** the radio. *Then* refers to a time sequence: Go straight ahead for three blocks; **then** turn left.

* **that, which**   *Which* occurs in nonessential (nonrestrictive) clauses: Myanmar, **which** borders Thailand, was formerly called Burma. Both *that* and *which* occur in essential (restrictive) clauses, although traditionally only *that* was considered acceptable: I am looking for an atlas **that** [OR **which**] includes demographic information. (For more information on essential and nonessential clauses, see **1f(2)** and **12d.**)

* **that, which, who**   In essential (restrictive) clauses, *who* and *that* refer to people. We want to hire someone **who** [OR **that**] has had experience programming. Traditionally, only *who* was used to refer to people. *That,* as well as *which,* refers to things: He proposed a design **that** [OR **which**] will take advantage of solar energy.

their, there, they're   *Their* is the possessive form of *they:* They will give **their** presentation tomorrow. *There* refers to location: I lived **there** for six years. *There* is also used as an expletive (see **21a(3)**): **There** is no explanation for the phenomenon. *They're* is a contraction of *they are:* **They're** leaving in the morning.

theirself, theirselves   Unconventional; use *themselves.* The students finished the project by ~~theirself~~ **themselves.**

then   See **than, then.**

thru   *Through* is preferred in academic and professional writing: We drove ~~thru~~ **through** the whole state of South Dakota in one day.

thusly   Unconventional; use *thus, in this way,* or *as follows* instead: He accompanied his father on archeological digs and ~~thusly~~ discovered his interest in ancient cultures.

to, too, two   *To* is an infinitive marker: She wanted **to** become an actress. *To* is also used as a preposition, usually indicating direction: They walked **to** the memorial. *Too* means either "also" or "excessively": I voted for her **too.** They are **too** busy this year. *Two* is a number: She studied abroad for **two** years.

toward, towards   Although both are acceptable, *toward* is preferred in American English.

try and   Conversational for *try to:* The staff will **try ~~and~~ to** finish the project by Friday.

ultimately   See **eventually, ultimately.**

uninterested   See **disinterested, uninterested.**

* **unique**   Traditionally, *unique* meant "one of a kind" and thus was not preceded by a qualifier such as *more, most, quite,* or *very:* Her prose style is ~~quite~~ **unique.** However, dictionary editors note that *unique* is also widely used to mean "extraordinary."

use, utilize   In most contexts, *use* is preferred to *utilize:* We ~~utilized~~ **used** a special dye in the experiment. However, *utilize* may suggest an effort to employ something for a purpose: We discussed how to **utilize** the resources we had been given.

used to   See **supposed to, used to.**

very   To ensure this word's effectiveness, use it sparingly. Whenever possible, choose a stronger word: She was ~~very satisfied~~ **delighted** with her new digital camera.

ways   Conversational when referring to distance; use *way* instead: It's a long ~~ways~~ way from home.

well   See **good, well.**

where   Conversational for *that:* I noticed ~~where~~ that she had been elected.

where . . . at, where . . . to   Conversational; omit *at* and *to:* **Where** is the library ~~at?~~ **Where** are you moving ~~to?~~

which   See **that, which** and **that, which, who.**

* **who, whom**   *Who* is used as the subject or subject complement in a clause: We have decided to hire Marian Wright, ~~whom~~ who I believe is currently finishing her degree in business administration. [*Who* is the subject in *who is currently finishing her degree in business administration.*] See also **that, which, who.** *Whom* is used as an object: Jeff Kruger, ~~who~~ whom we hired in 2007, is now our top sales representative. [*Whom* is the object in *whom we hired.*] Dictionary editors note that in conversation *who* is commonly used as an object as long as it does not follow a preposition. See **5b(5).**

whose, who's   *Whose* is a possessive form: **Whose** book is this? The book was written by a young Mexican-American woman **whose** family still lives in Chiapas. *Who's* is the contraction of *who is:* **Who's** going to run in the election? See **5b(3).**

will   See **shall, will.**

with regards to   Unconventional; see **regard, regarding, regards.**

would of   See **could of.**

your, you're   *Your* is a possessive form: Let's meet in **your** office. *You're* is a contraction of *you are:* **You're** gaining strength.

yourself   See **herself, himself, myself, yourself.**

Glossary of Terms

This glossary provides brief definitions of frequently used terms. Consult the index for references to terms not listed here.

absolute phrase A sentencelike structure containing a subject and its modifiers. Unlike a sentence, an absolute phrase has no verb marked for person, number, or tense: *The ceremony finally over,* the graduates tossed their mortarboards in the air. See **1e(6)**.

acronym A word formed by combining the initial letters or syllables of a series of words and pronounced as a word rather than as a series of letters: *NATO* for North Atlantic Treaty Organization. See **11e**.

active voice See **voice.**

adjectival clause A dependent clause, also called a **relative clause,** that modifies a noun or a pronoun. See **1f(2)**.

adjective A word that modifies a noun or a pronoun. Adjectives typically end in suffixes such as *-al, -able, -ant, -ative, -ic, -ish, -less, -ous,* and *-y.* See **1a(4)** and **4a**. **Coordinate adjectives** are two or more adjectives modifying the same noun and separated by a comma: a *brisk, cold* walk. See **12c(2)**.

adverb A word that modifies a verb, a verbal, an adjective, or another adverb. Adverbs commonly end in *-ly.* Some adverbs modify entire sentences: *Perhaps* the meeting could be postponed. See **1a(5)** and **4a**.

adverbial clause A dependent clause that modifies a verb, an adjective, or an adverb. See **1f(2)**.

antecedent A word or group of words referred to by a pronoun. See **1a(3)** and **6b**.

appositive A pronoun, noun, or noun phrase that identifies, describes, or explains an adjacent pronoun, noun, or noun phrase. See **1e(5)** and **5b(4)**.

article   A word used to signal a noun. *The* is a definite article; *a* and *an* are indefinite articles. See **1a(4)**.

attributive tag   Short phrase that identifies the source of a quotation: *according to Jones, Jones claims.* See **39d**.

auxiliary verb, auxiliary   A verb that combines with a main verb. *Be, do,* and *have* are auxiliary verbs when they are used with main verbs. Also called **helping verbs. Modal auxiliaries** include *could, should,* and *may* and are used for such purposes as expressing doubt or obligation and making a request. See **1a(1)** and **7a(4)**.

Boolean operators   See **logical operators.**

case   The form of a noun or pronoun that indicates the relationship of the noun or pronoun to other words in a sentence. Nouns and pronouns can be subjects or subject complements (**subjective case**), objects (**objective case**), or markers of possession and other relations (**possessive case**). See **5b**.

claim   A statement that a writer wants readers to accept; also called a **proposition.** See **35d**.

clause   A sequence of related words forming an independent unit (**independent clause,** or **main clause**) or an embedded unit (**dependent clause** used as an adverb, adjective, or noun). A clause has both a subject and a predicate. See **1f**.

cliché   An expression that has lost its power to interest readers because of overuse. See **20b**.

clipped form   A word that is a shortened form of another word: *bike* for *bicycle.* See **11d(2)**.

collective noun   A noun that refers to a group: *team, faculty, committee.* See **1a(2)**.

collocation   Common word combination such as *add to, adept at,* or *admiration for.* See **20c**.

colloquial   A label for any word or phrase that is characteristic of informal speech. *Kid* is colloquial; *child* is used in formal contexts. See **19c(2)**.

common noun   A noun referring to any or all members of a class or group (*woman, city, holiday*) rather than to specific members (*Susan, Reno, New Year's Day*). COMPARE: **proper noun.** See **1a(2)**.

complement A word or words used to complete the meaning of a verb. A **subject complement** is a word or phrase that follows a linking verb and categorizes or describes the subject. An **object complement** is a word or phrase that categorizes or describes a direct object when it follows such verbs as *make, paint, elect,* and *consider.* See **1c**.

complete predicate See **predicate.**

complete subject See **subject.**

complex sentence A sentence containing one independent clause and at least one dependent clause. See **1h(3)**.

compound-complex sentence A sentence containing at least two independent clauses and one or more dependent clauses. See **1h(4)**.

compound predicate A predicate that has two parts joined by a connecting word such as *and, or,* or *but;* each part contains a verb: Clara Barton *nursed the injured during the Civil War* and *later founded the American Red Cross.* See **1b**.

compound sentence A sentence containing at least two independent clauses and no dependent clauses. See **1h(2)**.

compound subject Two subjects joined by a connecting word such as *and, or,* or *but: Students* and *faculty* are discussing the issue of grade inflation. See **1b**.

compound word Two or more words functioning as a single word: *ice cream, double-check.* See **18f(1)**.

conditional clause An adverbial clause (**1f(2)**), usually beginning with *if,* that expresses a condition: *If it rains,* the outdoor concert will be postponed.

conjunction A word used to connect other words, phrases, clauses, or sentences. **Coordinating conjunctions** (*and, but, or, nor, for, so,* and *yet*) connect and relate words and word groups of equal grammatical rank. See **1a(7)** and **1g(1)**. A **subordinating conjunction** such as *although, if,* or *when* begins a dependent clause and connects it to an independent clause. See **1a(7)** and **1g(3)**. COMPARE: **conjunctive adverb.**

conjunctive adverb A word such as *however* or *thus* that joins one independent clause to another. See **1g(4)**. COMPARE: **conjunction.**

convention, conventional Refers to language or behavior that follows the customs of a community such as the academic, medical, or business community.

coordinate adjective　See **adjective.**

coordinating conjunction　See **conjunction.**

coordination　The use of grammatically equivalent constructions to link or balance ideas. See chapter **24.**

correlative conjunctions, correlatives　Two-part connecting words such as *either . . . or* and *not only . . . but also.* See **1a(7)** and **1g(2).**

count nouns　Nouns naming things that can be counted (*word, student, remark*). See **1a(2).** COMPARE: **noncount nouns.**

dangling modifier　A word or phrase that does not clearly modify another word or word group. See **25b.** COMPARE: **misplaced modifier.**

dangling participial phrase　A verbal phrase that does not clearly modify another word or word group.

deductive reasoning　A form of logical reasoning in which a conclusion is formed after relating a specific fact (minor premise) to a generalization (major premise). See **35h(2).** COMPARE: **inductive reasoning.**

demonstratives　Four words (*this, that, these,* and *those*) that distinguish one individual, thing, event, or idea from another. Demonstratives may occur with or without nouns: *This law* will go into effect in two years. *This* will go into effect in two years.

dependent clause　See **clause.**

determiner　A word that signals the approach of a noun. A determiner may be an article, a demonstrative, a possessive, or a quantifier: *a reason, this reason, his reason, three reasons.*

direct address　See **vocative.**

direct object　See **object.**

direct quotation　See **quotation.**

elliptical clause　A clause missing one or more words that are assumed to be understood. See **1f(2).**

essential element　A word or word group that modifies another word or word group, providing information that is essential for identification. Essential elements are not set off by commas, parentheses, or dashes: The woman *who witnessed the accident* was called to testify. Also called a **restrictive element.** COMPARE: **nonessential element.** See **1f(2)** and **12d.**

ethos   One of the three classical appeals; the use of language to demonstrate the writer's trustworthy character, good intentions, and substantial knowledge of a subject. Also called an **ethical appeal.** See **35f(1).** See also **logos** and **pathos.**

exigence   The circumstance compelling one to write. See **31b.**

expletive   A word signaling a structural change in a sentence, usually used so that new or important information is given at the end of the sentence: *There were over four thousand runners in the marathon.* See **1b(1).**

faulty predication   A sentence error in which the predicate does not logically belong with the given subject. See **23c(2).**

figurative language   The use of words in an imaginative rather than in a literal sense. See **20a(4).**

first person   See **person.**

flaming   Heated, confrontational exchanges via e-mail. See **36b.**

gender   The grammatical label that distinguishes nouns or pronouns as masculine, feminine, or neuter. In English, grammatical gender usually corresponds to natural gender. Gender also describes how people see themselves, or are seen by others, as either male or female. See **6b(2)** and **19d(1).**

genre   A literary category, such as drama or poetry, identified by its own conventions. See **42a.**

gerund   A verbal that ends in *-ing* and functions as a noun: *Snowboarding* is a popular winter sport. See **1e(3).**

gerund phrase   A verbal phrase that employs the *-ing* form of a verb and functions as a noun: Some students prefer *studying in the library.* See **1e(3).**

helping verb   See **auxiliary verb.**

homophones   Words that have the same sound and sometimes the same spelling but differ in meaning: *their, there,* and *they're* or *capital* meaning "funds" and *capital* meaning "the top of a pillar." See **18c.**

idiom   An expression whose meaning often cannot be derived from its elements. *Burning the midnight oil* means "staying up late studying." See **20c.**

imperative mood   See **mood.**

indefinite article   See **article.**

indefinite pronoun   A pronoun such as *everyone* or *anything* that does not refer to a specific individual, object, event, and so on. See **6b(1)**.

independent clause   See **clause.**

indicative mood   See **mood.**

indirect object   See **object.**

indirect question   A sentence that includes an embedded question, punctuated with a period instead of a question mark: My friends asked me *why I left the party early.* See **17a(1)**.

indirect quotation   See **quotation.**

inductive reasoning   The reasoning process that begins with facts or observations and moves to general principles that account for those facts or observations. See **35h(1)**. COMPARE: **deductive reasoning.**

infinitive   A verbal that consists of the base form of the verb, usually preceded by the infinitive marker *to.* An infinitive is used chiefly as a noun, less frequently as an adjective or adverb: My father likes *to golf.* See **1e(3)** and **7b(6)**.

infinitive phrase   A verbal phrase that contains the infinitive form of a verb: They volunteered *to work at the local hospital.* See **1e(3)**.

intensifier   See **qualifier.**

intensive pronoun   See **reflexive pronoun.**

interjection   A word expressing a simple exclamation: *Hey! Oops!* When used in sentences, mild interjections are set off by commas. See **1a(8)**.

intransitive verb   A verb that does not take an object: Everyone *laughed.* See **1d**. COMPARE: **transitive verb.**

invention   Using strategies to generate ideas for writing.

inversion   A change in the usual subject-verb order of a sentence: *Are you* ready? See **1d**.

keywords   Specific words used with a search tool (such as Google) to find information. See **37b(1)**.

linking verb   A verb that relates a subject to a subject complement. Examples of linking verbs are *be, become, seem, appear, feel, look, taste, smell,* and *sound.* See **1a(1)**.

logical operators   Words used to broaden or narrow electronic database searches. These include *or, and, not,* and *near.* Also called **Boolean operators.** See **37b(1)**.

logos   One of the three classical appeals; the use of language to show clear reasoning. Also called a **logical appeal.** See **35f(1).** See also **ethos** and **pathos.**

major premise.   See **premise.**

main clause   Also called **independent clause.** See **clause.**

minor premise.   See **premise.**

misplaced modifier   A descriptive or qualifying word or phrase placed in a position that confuses the reader: I read about a wildfire that was out of control *in yesterday's paper.* [The modifier belongs after *read.*] See chapter **25.**

mixed construction   A confusing sentence that is the result of an unintentional shift from one grammatical pattern to another: When police appeared who were supposed to calm the crowds showed up, most people had already gone home. [The sentence should be recast with either *appeared* or *showed up,* not with both.] See **23c(1).**

mixed metaphor   A construction that includes parts of two or more unrelated metaphors: Her *fiery* personality *dampened* our hopes of a compromise. See **23b.**

modal auxiliary   See **auxiliary verb.**

modifier   A word or word group that describes, limits, or qualifies another word or word group. See chapters **24** and **25.**

mood   A set of verb forms or inflections used to indicate how a speaker or writer regards an assertion: as a fact or opinion **(indicative mood)**; as a command or instruction **(imperative mood)**; or as a wish, hypothesis, request, or condition contrary to fact **(subjunctive mood).** See **7d.**

netiquette   Word formed from *Internet* and *etiquette* to name a set of guidelines for writing e-mail messages and listserv postings and for online behavior in general. See **36b.**

nominalization   Formation of a noun by adding a suffix to a verb or an adjective: *require, requirement; sad, sadness.*

nominative case   Also called **subjective case.** See **case.**

noncount nouns   Nouns naming things that cannot be counted (*architecture, water*). See **1a(2).** COMPARE: **count nouns.**

nonessential element   A word or word group that modifies another word or word group but does not provide information essential for identification. Nonessential elements are set off by commas, parentheses, or dashes: Carol Murphy, *president of the university,* plans to meet with alumni representatives. Also called a **nonrestrictive element.** See **1f(2)** and **12d.** COMPARE: **essential element.**

nonrestrictive element   See **nonessential element.**

nonstandard, nonstandardized   Refers to speech forms that are not considered conventional in many academic and professional settings. See the **Glossary of Usage.**

noun   A word that names a person, place, thing, idea, animal, quality, event, and so on: *Alanis, America, desk, justice, dog, strength, departure.* See also **collective noun, common noun, count noun, noncount noun,** and **proper noun.** See **1a(2).**

noun clause   A dependent clause used as a noun. See **1f(2).**

noun phrase   A noun and its modifiers. See **1e(1).**

number   The property of a word that indicates whether it refers to one **(singular)** or to more than one **(plural).** Number is reflected in the word's form: *river/rivers, this/those, he sees/they see.* See **6a** and **6b(4).**

object   A noun, pronoun, noun phrase, or noun clause that follows a preposition or a transitive verb or verbal. A **direct object** names the person or thing that receives the action of the verb: I sent the *package.* See **1c(1).** An **indirect object** usually indicates to whom the action was directed or for whom the action was performed: I sent *you* the package. See **1c(2).** The **object of a preposition** follows a preposition: I sent the package to *you.* See **1e(4).**

object complement   See **complement.**

object of a preposition   See **object.**

objective case   See **case.**

parenthetical element   Any word, phrase, or clause that adds detail to a sentence or any sentence that adds detail to a paragraph but is not essential for understanding the core meaning. Commas, dashes, or parentheses separate these elements from the rest of the sentence or paragraph. See **12d, 17e,** and **17f.**

participial phrase   A verbal phrase that includes a participle: The stagehand *carrying the trunk* fell over the threshold. See **1e(3).** See also **participle** and **phrase.**

participle A verb form that may function as part of a verb phrase (had *determined,* was *thinking*) or as a modifier (a *determined* effort; the couple, *thinking* about their past). A **present participle** is formed by adding *-ing* to the base form of a verb. A **past participle** is usually formed by adding *-ed* to the base form of a verb (*walked, passed*); however, many verbs have irregular past-participle forms (*written, bought, gone*). See 7a(1) and 7a(5).

particle A word such as *across, away, down, for, in, off, out, up, on,* or *with* that combines with a main verb to form a phrasal verb: *write down, look up.* See 7a(3).

parts of speech The classes into which words may be grouped according to their forms and grammatical relationships. The traditional parts of speech are verbs, nouns, pronouns, adjectives, adverbs, prepositions, conjunctions, and interjections.

passive voice See **voice.**

past participle See **participle.**

pathos One of the three classical appeals; the use of language to stir the feelings of an audience. Also called an **emotional appeal** or a **pathetic appeal.** See 35f(1). See also **ethos** and **logos.**

person The property of nouns, pronouns, and their corresponding verbs that distinguishes the speaker or writer **(first person)**, the individuals addressed **(second person)**, and the individuals or things referred to **(third person).** See 7b.

personal pronoun A pronoun that refers to a specific person, place, thing, and so on. Pronoun forms correspond to three cases: subjective, objective, and possessive. See 5a(1).

phrasal verb A grammatical unit consisting of a verb and a particle such as *after, in, up, off,* or *out: fill in, sort out.* See 7a(3).

phrase A sequence of grammatically related words that functions as a unit in a sentence but lacks a subject, a predicate, or both: *in front of the stage.* See 1e.

point of view The vantage point from which a topic is viewed; also, the stance a writer takes: objective or impartial (third person), directive (second person), or personal (first person). See 7b.

possessive case See **case.**

predicate   The part of a sentence that expresses what a subject is, does, or experiences. It consists of the main verb, its auxiliaries, and any complements and modifiers. The **simple predicate** consists of only the main verb and any accompanying auxiliaries. See **1b** and **1c**. COMPARE: **subject.**

premise   An assumption or a proposition on which an argument or explanation is based. In logic, premises are either **major** (general) or **minor** (specific); when combined correctly, they lead to a conclusion. See **35h(2)**. See also **syllogism.**

preposition   A word such as *at, in, by,* or *of* that relates a pronoun, noun, noun phrase, or noun clause to other words in the sentence. See **1a(6)**.

prepositional phrase   A preposition with its object and any modifiers: *at the nearby airport, by the sea.* See **1e(4)**.

present participle   See **participle.**

primary source   A source that provides firsthand information. See **37a(3)**. COMPARE: **secondary source.**

pronoun   A word that takes the position of a noun, noun phrase, or noun clause and functions as that word or word group does: *it, that, he, them.* See **1a(3)** and chapter **5**.

proper adjective   An adjective that is derived from the name of a person or place: *Marxist* theories. See **9a(9)**.

proper noun   The name of a specific person, place, organization, and so on: *Dr. Pimomo, Fargo, National Education Association.* Proper nouns are capitalized. See **1a(2)**. COMPARE: **common noun.**

proposition   See **claim.**

qualifier   A word that intensifies or moderates the meaning of an adverb or adjective: *quite* pleased, *somewhat* reluctant. Words that intensify are sometimes called **intensifiers.**

quotation   A **direct quotation** (also called **direct discourse**) is the exact repetition of someone's spoken or written words. An **indirect quotation** is a report of someone's written or spoken words not stated in the exact words of the writer or speaker. See chapter **16** and **39d(2)**.

reflexive pronoun   A pronoun that ends in *-self* or *-selves* (*myself* or *themselves*) and refers to a preceding noun or pronoun in the sentence: *He* added a picture of *himself* to his Web page. When used to provide emphasis, such a pronoun is called an **intensive pronoun:** The president *herself* awarded the scholarships. See **5a(2)**.

refutation A strategy for addressing opposing points of view by discussing those views and explaining why they are unsatisfactory. See **35e(2)** and **35g(2)**.

relative clause See **adjectival clause.**

relative pronoun A word (*who, whom, that, which,* or *whose*) used to introduce an adjectival clause, also called a **relative clause.** An antecedent for the relative pronoun can be found in the main clause. See **1f(2)**.

restrictive element See **essential element.**

rhetorical appeal The means of persuasion in argumentative writing, relying on reason, authority, or emotion. See **35f**.

search engine A Web-based program that enables users to search the Internet for documents containing certain words or phrases. Sometimes called a **search tool.** See **37d**.

secondary source A source that analyzes or interprets firsthand information. See **37a(3)**. COMPARE: **primary source.**

sentence modifier A modifier related to a whole sentence, not to a specific word or word group within it: *All things considered,* the committee acted appropriately when it approved the amendment to the bylaws.

simple predicate See **predicate.**

simple subject See **subject.**

split infinitive The separation of the two parts of an infinitive form by at least one word: *to completely cover.* See **1e(3)**.

squinting modifier A modifier that is unclear because it can refer to words either preceding it or following it: Proofreading *quickly* results in missed spelling errors. See **25a(3)**.

Standardized English The usage expected in most academic and business settings. See the **Glossary of Usage.**

subject The general area addressed in a piece of writing. See **33a**. COMPARE: **topic.** Also, the pronoun, noun, or noun phrase that carries out the action or assumes the state described in the predicate of a sentence. Usually preceding the predicate, the subject includes the main noun or pronoun and all modifiers. A **simple subject** consists of only the main noun or pronoun. See **1b** and **1d**. COMPARE: **predicate.**

subject complement   See **complement.**

subjective case   See **case.**

subjunctive mood   See **mood.**

subordinating conjunction   See **conjunction.**

subordination   The connection of a grammatical structure to another, usually a dependent clause to an independent clause: *Even though customers were satisfied with the product,* the company wanted to improve it. See chapter **24**.

syllogism   Method for deductive reasoning consisting of two premises and a conclusion. See **35h(2)**. See also **premise.**

tense   The form of a verb that indicates when and for how long an action or state occurs. See **7b**.

theme   The main idea of a literary work. See **42c(7)**.

thesis   The central point or main idea of an essay. See **33c**.

tone   The writer's attitude toward the subject and the audience, usually conveyed through word choice and sentence structure. See **34a(3)**.

topic   The specific, narrowed main idea of an essay. See **33b**. COMPARE: **subject.**

topic sentence   A statement of the main idea of a paragraph. See **34c(1)**.

transitions   Words, phrases, sentences, or paragraphs that relate ideas by linking sentences, paragraphs, or larger segments of writing. See **3c(5)** and **34d**.

transitive verb   A verb that takes an object. The researchers *reported* their findings. See **1d**. COMPARE: **intransitive verb.**

usability testing   The process of soliciting reactions from potential users of a Web site or other complex electronic document in order to improve the content or design of the document. See **36c(3)**.

verb   A word denoting action, occurrence, or existence (state of being). See **1a(1)** and chapter **7**.

verb phrase A main verb and any auxiliaries. See **1e(2)** and **7a(4).**

verbal A verb form functioning as a noun, an adjective, or an adverb. See **1e(3).** See also **gerund, infinitive,** and **participle.**

vocative Set off by commas, the name of or the descriptive term for the person or persons being addressed. See **12b(3).**

voice A property of a verb that indicates the relationship between the verb and its subject. The **active voice** is used to show that the subject performs the action expressed by the verb; the **passive voice** is used to show that the subject receives the action. See **7c** and **29e.**

Credits

These pages constitute an extension of the copyright page. We have made every effort to trace the ownership of all copyrighted material and to secure permission from copyright holders. In the event of any question arising as to the use of any material, we will be pleased to make the necessary corrections in future printings. Thanks are due to the following authors, publishers, and agents for permission to use the material indicated.

Text

p. 1: © The New Yorker Collection 1987 Michael Maslin from cartoonbank.com. All Rights Reserved.

p. 154 (Fig. 8.4): Reprinted by permission of JETLOG Corporation, www.jetlog24x7.com.

p. 273 (Fig. 19.1): By permission. From *Merriam-Webster's Collegiate Dictionary,* Eleventh Edition © 2008 by Merriam-Webster, Incorporated (www.Merriam-Webster.com).

pp. 337–338: Excerpt from "Deciding Advantageously before Knowing the Advantageous Strategy" from *Science, 275,* p. 1293. Reprinted by permission.

pp. 374–375: "Jaqui's Story" by David Hafetz from AUSTIN AMERICAN-STATESMAN, May 12, 2002. Copyright 2002 by Austin American-Statesman. Reproduced with permission of Austin American Statesman in the format Textbook via Copyright Clearance Center.

pp. 385, 389: From GUNS, GERMS, AND STEEL: THE FATES OF HUMAN SOCIETIES by Jared Diamond. Copyright © 1997 by Jared Diamond. Used by permission of W. W. Norton & Company, Inc., and The Random House Group Ltd.

p. 410: Austin Scaggs, "Ben Harper's European Vacation." ROLLING STONE (6 Sept. 2007); 83–84. © Rolling Stone LLC 2007. All Rights Reserved. Reprinted by permission.

p. 414: Excerpt from "Credit Card Debt among College Students: Just What Does It Cost?" by Robyn Sylves. Reprinted by permission of the author.

pp. 414–415: "My Father's Brain." Originally published in *The New Yorker.* Copyright © 2001 by

American Psychological Association. Reproduced with permission.

p. 679: "Prose Poems: Portrait" from GIRL AT THE WINDOW by Pinkie Gordon Lane. Reprinted by permission of Louisiana State University Press.

Photos and Illustrations

p. 5: Courtesy of Sunset House, Grand Cayman; (top photo) Keith E. Sahm (bottom photo) Cathy Church.

p. 50: Courtesy of United Airlines.

p. 77: © Random House.

p. 126 (Fig. 7.1): *Sun Rising through Vapor: Fishermen Cleaning and Selling Fish* by Joseph Mailor William Turner, c. 1808 © National Gallery Collection. By kind permission of the Trustees of the National Gallery, London/Corbis.

p. 143: Reprinted courtesy of the National Association of College Stores.

p. 146 (Fig. 8.1): (advertisement) Green Team Advertising for Environmental Defense Fund; (photo of baby) © Stockbyte/Getty Images.

p. 149 (Fig. 8.2): Poster courtesy of Faith Haney; (inset photos) University of Washington Libraries, Special Collections NA 815 and NA 134OF.

p. 157: (Fig. 8.7) Courtesy of Canon USA, Inc. © 2005 Canon USA, Inc.

p. 159: Reprinted courtesy of the National Association of College Stores.

p. 178: Courtesy of UPS Worldwide.

p. 191: Courtesy, United States Marine Corps.

p. 219 (left): © Nigel Reed/Alamy; **(right):** © Joe Skipper/Reuters/ Landov.

p. 247: © Erv Schowengerdt.

p. 265: © The Advertising Archives.

p. 301: © Associated Press.

p. 369: © AFP/Getty Images.

p. 383: From GUNS, GERMS, AND STEEL: THE FATES OF HUMAN SOCIETIES by Jared Diamond. Copyright © 1997 by Jared Diamond. Used by permission of W. W. Norton & Company, Inc., and The Random House Group Ltd.

p. 396: © Jeremy Woodhouse/ Photodisc/Getty Images.

p. 412: © Mary Kate Denny/ PhotoEdit.

p. 413: © Amy Etra/PhotoEdit, Inc.

p. 416: © Scott T. Smith/Corbis.

p. 422: *Migrant Mother* by Dorothea Lange, 1936 Library of Congress, Farm Security Administration Office of War Information Collection.

p. 470: © Bettmann/Corbis.

p. 496 (Fig. 36.1): Copyright © 2005 The Green Belt Movement.

p. 509: © David R. Frazier/ Photo Researchers, Inc.

p. 515: © Danny Daniels/ PhotoLibrary.

p. 517 (Fig. 37.1): University of Washington Libraries.

p. 522 (Fig. 37.2): Courtesy University Libraries, Pennsylvania State University.

p. 525 (Figs. 37.3 and 37.4): Screenshots from InfoTrac © Gale, a part of Cengage Learning, Inc. Reproduced by permission. www .cengage.com/permissions.

p. 529: Courtesy of Alix/Phanie/First Light, Canada.

Index

Numbers and letters in color refer to chapters and sections in the handbook; other numbers refer to pages.

(cont.)

UNDERSTANDING PLAGIARISM

A Student Guide to Writing Your Own Work

Rosemarie Menager-Beeley, Ed.d
Foothill College

Lyn Paulos
Santa Barbara City College

CENGAGE
Learning

Australia • Brazil • Japan • Korea • Mexico • Singapore • Spain • United Kingdom • United States

CONTENTS

CHAPTER

Introduction

What is in this guide?

This booklet is designed to help students avoid the pitfalls of plagiarism. Chapters cover the correct way to credit sources, quote, cite, paraphrase, summarize, create a list of references, and more. Knowledge checks are provided at the end of each section for review.

Why is this guide important to you as a student?

What do you want from college? You probably want to succeed in your classes. The last thing you want is to fail a class for cheating or plagiarizing by mistake. If you are unfamiliar with the practices and rules of incorporating work from other sources, then you will find this guide a useful resource.

You can use the knowledge checks in each chapter or the quiz at the end of the booklet to practice all the skills necessary to use resources correctly. We've tried to make it as clear and simple as possible. Citing correctly can be confusing. Most colleges have very specific requirements about giving references, depending on the subject or instructor. Citing correctly is more involved than inserting footnotes or listing references at the end of a paper. This guide provides information and samples of the kinds of citations that are necessary to correctly reference different types of academic work.

What is plagiarism?

Plagiarism is using someone else's work and passing it off as one's own. The term comes from the Latin word *plagiarius*, which means *kidnapper*.

This means that if a student uses another writer's work without giving credit, it may be considered deceptive even if it is an honest mistake. Knowing the definition of plagiarism and when to cite sources is the best way to avoid problems.

When should you credit another author's work?

Because many things such as information, pictures, and music are now so easy to copy from the Internet, it's more tempting than ever to find and use those materials for free. How can you tell when it is appropriate to use something without a citation and when it isn't?

Generally any time you use someone else's work as a source of ideas or inspiration, credit is required. There are a few exceptions, such as when the information is common knowledge. An example of common knowledge is the fact that Christopher Columbus crossed the Atlantic Ocean in 1492. To be safe, if you consult a source and that source's ideas become part of your work, then you need to cite that source. If you use a direct quotation, then you need to reproduce it accurately and to cite it correctly. These practices will prevent inadvertent plagiarizing, and this guide will provide the basics to get you started.

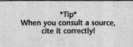

Tip
When you consult a source,
cite it correctly!

There are also limitations to how much of someone else's work can be used as part of an assignment. Exclusively, excessively, or inappropriately using another author's work by copying, paraphrasing, summarizing, or directly quoting is plagiarizing. It is important to use your own words and ideas in a paper. One suggested rule of thumb for acceptable use of content in a submitted assignment is up to 10 percent, provided it is properly cited (Zaharoff). Make sure to check your instructor's preferences.

Many students worry that their own words do not sound as professional as those used by the original author. But that fear ignores the point of using a source in the first place. Instructors do not give assignments so students can give them back another author's work. Instructors do not expect the same quality of work from a novice as from an expert. College is a place of learning. If instructors wanted to read only the professional author's words and ideas, they could go directly to the original source and skip the student's work.

The whole point of having you use sources is to enable you to learn from those sources and to develop your own writing and analytical skills. It's important for you to work with ideas and to express them in writing so you can develop your own writing style, perspective, and voice. This is a big investment of time and effort. Often when students risk plagiarizing, they haven't allowed themselves sufficient time to complete an assignment. These types of miscalculations can lead to trouble.

Know the rules.

Because academic honesty and the validity of a college degree are vitally important to institutions of higher learning, schools create codes or policies governing instances of

Tip
Know the rules about plagiarism;
ignorance is no excuse.

dishonesty. Many of these policies are listed as Academic Integrity, Academic Honesty, Honor Code, Cheating, Student Conduct Code, or Plagiarism. The codes may consist of a list of rules, definitions, specific behaviors, procedures, and consequences of academic dishonesty. It is your responsibility to know the rules of your institution and to follow them. Rules are usually published in school catalogs and considered a part of the enrollment agreement for the college. If you have any questions about academic policies, then check with your instructor or the dean's office to get the facts.

When instructors suspect plagiarism, they will follow steps prescribed by the institution to address the problem. These steps include contacting the student and forwarding a report to the dean or a disciplinary committee, which will probably conduct a hearing.

Consequences to the student can include failing the assignment or the course, as well as being given community service or some other restitution to the campus community. Some students have been unhappily surprised to learn that the consequences for a first-time offense of plagiarism can be as severe as expulsion from the institution. Being caught as a plagiarizer is humiliating, can directly affect a student's progress toward a degree, is costly, and is entirely avoidable.

Knowledge Check: True or False?

1. Most students who plagiarize do so inadvertently.
2. Students cannot be accused of plagiarizing if they don't know the citation style expected by the instructor.
3. Using sources for educational purposes means that those sources are exempt from citation rules.

Answers

1. (True) Don't be one of them. This can be a costly mistake!
2. (False) It is your job to find out.
3. (False) All sources should be cited.

CHAPTER 2

How to Avoid Plagiarism

12 Tips to Avoid Plagiarizing

1. Do your own work, and use your own words.
2. Allow yourself enough time to research the assignment.
3. Keep careful track of your sources.
4. Take careful notes.
5. Assemble your thoughts, and make clear who is speaking.
6. If you use an idea, a quotation, paraphrase, or summary, then credit the source.
7. Learn how to cite sources correctly both in the body of your paper and in your List of Works Cited.
8. Quote accurately and sparingly.
9. Paraphrase carefully.
10. Do not patchwrite.
11. Summarize, don't auto-summarize.
12. Do not rework another student's paper or buy paper-mill papers.

Do your own work, and use your own words.

College gives you the opportunity to be exposed to new ideas, to formulate ideas of your own, and to develop skills to communicate your ideas. Strengthening your writing skills requires hard work and practice, but you will learn thinking and communicating skills that will benefit both your studies in college and your career.

Expressing a thought in your own words may seem overwhelming. The difficulty may stem from not understanding the language, not understanding the research material, or a lack of confidence in expressing ideas and concepts. Don't be discouraged that your paper may not sound as professional as you would like. By creating and practicing your own personal style, you will improve your ability to state ideas clearly and support arguments, and your vocabulary will increase.

These skills are not built by using another researcher's or student's words or by paying a service to write a paper for your class. Attempting to cheat on your paper cheats you the most because you are depriving yourself of the thinking, learning, and writing practice that would have benefited all of your classwork and beyond. But cheating also creates the risk of humiliation and punishment. Most professors are so familiar with the work in their field that they can spot a fake quickly. New plagiarism detection methods are also making it easier for professors to catch cheaters electronically. And as discussed in Chapter 1, all institutions will punish students who plagiarize. Doing honest work is the way to avoid the humiliation of being accused of cheating.

Allow yourself enough time to research the assignment.

Often students who are caught plagiarizing claim that they didn't have time to do the work. This excuse rarely works. Allow sufficient time to do all the steps necessary in an assignment. The best way is to plan for each part: selecting the topic, doing the research, then writing and refining your ideas. Minimizing the time it will take to do the work, or procrastinating because you feel that you do better work when you are anxious, will easily create trouble.

The most productive strategy is to begin the assignment as soon as it is given and try to complete it early. This allows you to adjust the schedule if you encounter any research difficulties, provides time for questions or clarification, and offsets other events that can interfere or cut into study time. If you are unsure about how to plot out your time for each step, then ask your instructor to help you plan your schedule.

Keep careful track of your sources.

As you look through books, articles, and electronic materials, you will be able to identify which content is relevant to your paper. The sources that you decide to take notes from are the ones you will need to keep careful records of.

Create a master list of all your sources that contains detailed bibliographic information for each item. (You will need to record the author; title of article or book; publisher, periodical title, electronic medium, or URL; date, and page number. See Chapter 6 for a detailed list of the information you will need and the format you will need to provide it in.) As you conduct your research, you will likely add or delete sources from this list, but keeping it current and complete will make your work much easier when it comes time to format the list into your formal List of Works Cited (for MLA papers) or Reference List (for APA papers). This list of references will enable the readers of your paper to locate the exact content you discuss in your paper-as well as to assist you to find it again, should you need to.

Take careful notes.

Some students find they take more complete notes (and can easily refer back to their sources) if they make photocopies of the relevant pages from their sources. If you decide to use this method, for print sources, such as articles and books, copy the copyright page and relevant content pages of each source. Make sure the page numbers or other identifiers are visible on each page. For electronic sources, such as the websites, databases, CDs, or even web logs, print out both the home or copyright page and the relevant content pages, making sure that identifiers such as the URL and the date, or page numbers, are visible.

If you take notes on note cards or in computer files, then make sure to keep a detailed record of where each note came from and take down the information carefully and accurately.

Next scrutinize your resources, thinking about the ideas expressed, noting and recording the relevant points, and adding to the notes your reactions, questions, and thoughts. If you find a particular phrasing that you want to quote, then highlight it to separate it from the regular notes.

Assemble your thoughts, and make clear who is speaking.

As you write the first draft of your paper, make sure you are expressing your thoughts and ideas in your own voice. Use the thoughts or words of others only to support your own thoughts, *not to make your point for you.* Your writing should make clear at all times who is speaking.

Decide from your notes whether you need to quote, summarize, or paraphrase the source. (See Chapters 3, 4, and 5 for a discussion of each method.) Then make sure to introduce the guest voice (the source) and explain why the source's information is relevant to your topic.

If you use an idea, a quotation, paraphrase, or summary, then credit the source.

When you draft your paper, if you are stating another person's thought, then make clear where that thought came from. Identify the source of all borrowed content in your paper, even if it's from a blog on the Internet. Your readers need to know where to find the original source if they want to explore the idea further.

Identify your source by inserting a brief parenthetical citation in the paper where the source's content appears, and then list the complete source information at the end of the paper. Follow the documentation style directed by your instructor (usually MLA or APA; see Chapter 6 for examples.)

Cite sources correctly, both in the body of your paper and in your list of Works Cited.

A **citation**—that is, stating the source of an idea, a conclusion, or a specific collection of information—of another person's work is the highest form of respect that a serious writer can make. It is also the single best way to avoid accusations of plagiarism and cheating. Properly citing sources involves acknowledging them both in the body of your work (when and where your writing borrows from a given source) and in a list of all the sources at the end of your paper.

Citation styles differ by subject or discipline. There are styles for English, the Social Sciences, the Humanities, and the Sciences. Check with your instructor or writing center for the proper format style of your writing project.

See Chapter 3, Quotations; Chapter 4, Paraphrases; Chapter 5, Summaries; and Chapter 6, Citations, for basic models of citations. Guidebooks such as MLA, APA, and Chicago, which are available in most bookstores, provide models for all common types of sources. Online citation generators (see Chapter 8) can also help you with listing references in the correct format.

Quote accurately and sparingly.

Quotations should be used *only to emphasize your own point,* which you have already stated in your own words. A good quotation from an original source can underscore a theme and introduce thoughts or direction, but quotations should be relevant, necessary, accurate, and limited.

Using too many direct quotations (more than ten percent) is a sign both that you have not developed your own idea enough and that you are relying on others to make your point for you. Over-quoting is also an opportunity for plagiarism to creep in. If you are using several sources, then limit how much those sources contribute, and give correct citation and credit every time you use them.

Paraphrase carefully.

The practice of taking another writer's sentence and then looking up words and replacing them with synonyms is a common way for students to think they are paraphrasing from a source. (See Chapter 4.) Merely changing some of another writer's words, or reversing the order of the clauses in the sentences, is still copying. This is another way students can inadvertently plagiarize. Use paraphrase to state in your own words what another writer believes or argues.

Do not patchwrite.

Patchwriting consists of mixing several references together and arranging paraphrases and quotations to constitute much of a paper. In essence, the student has assembled others' works with a bit of embroidery here and there but with very little original thinking or expression. Turning in work that has been woven into a quilt with patches arranged together constitutes plagiarism. Instead, work on developing a position and bringing in sources to support the viewpoint or argument that you are presenting.

A way to avoid patchwriting is good preparation. Read the material several times to make sure you understand what the source is saying; then put it aside and think about it. Analyze the readings and what they mean, and then try to organize the main points. Create an outline of what you want to say, and then go back and pull in the supporting information from the sources. Good writers think of the reader as listening to what is being said; this process will help you create and organize your own, original work.

Summarize, don't auto-summarize.

Most word processors have an automatic summarize function that can take fifty pages and turn them into ten. The problem with this feature is that it condenses material by selecting key sentences. Therefore a summarized version is still in the exact words of the original source, only shorter and not necessarily making the same point as the original. The auto-summary feature is intended for writers to summarize their *own* work, *not* the work of others. If a student uses any portion of the auto-summary from another writer's work, then it is plagiarism.

If you wish to summarize another writer's work, then describe briefly in your own words the writer's idea (identifying who that writer is and providing a citation to the work) and state how it relates to your own ideas. (See Chapter 5.)

Do not rework another student's paper or buy papermill papers.

Don't cross the line from looking at someone else's paper as an example of how to do the assignment, to the action of using it as original work. Reworking someone else's paper is plagiarism. It also shows that the student is unwilling to think for him- or herself.

Similarly, buying papers from paper mills, or paying for someone else to write a paper, is obviously dishonest and is a clear example of plagiarizing and cheating. Databases of written papers are often kept by colleges and by plagiarism detection services, so instructors who have a question about the authenticity of a student's paper can easily verify its source.

Knowledge Check: True or False?

1. One way to avoid plagiarizing is to give yourself enough time to do a good job on the assignment.
2. As long as you put everything in quotation marks, you are not plagiarizing.
3. Getting a paper from a friend or the Internet is a good way to get a head start on your assignment.

Answers

1. (True) Most people who plagiarize use poor time management and even worse judgment.
2. (False) If you quote more than 10 percent of your paper, you may be graded down for over-quoting.
3. (False) Using a friend's paper or an Internet paper is plagiarizing and considered to be academic cheating.

CHAPTER 3

Using Quotations

Using quotations is an effective way to support your arguments and add credibility to your research paper. Quotations are most useful when they highlight or help to refine a point you are making. Inserting too many quotations in your paper distracts your readers from the argument you are trying to construct, and makes your paper sound as if you are letting others speak for you, so use quotations selectively and sparingly.

You can use a **direct quotation** (a word-for-word repetition from another source) or an **indirect quotation** (a recasting in your own words of the ideas of another person—see Chapters 4 and 5). Each time you insert a direct or indirect quotation into your paper, you must add a citation to the source at the quotation. This in-text citation follows an abbreviated, parenthetical format that points your reader to the full citation in a Works Cited or References list at the end of your paper (see Chapter 6).

Quotations can be used in various ways within a research paper. This chapter will cover some of those uses and the proper citation styles needed for each.

Follow these basic rules for using quotations:

- Use quotations sparingly.
- Make sure the quotation exactly fits the idea of your paragraph.
- Make sure direct quotations stay identical to the original passage. Do not change the wording, the spelling, or the punctuation of the original passage.
- Cite the source! Include a parenthetical citation for all quotations.
- If a direct quotation is longer than four lines, use a block quotation.

Using direct quotations

A direct quotation is an exact copy of the original author's work. Make your point first, and then enclose the quote in quotation marks (or if it is long set it apart as a block quotation) and provide a parenthetical citation directly after.

Example: parenthetical citation, MLA

The MLA style of citing a quotation includes the author's last name followed by the page number directly after the quotation. Note that no comma separates the name from the page number.

> Personal growth is a painful process, and part of that process is taking personal responsibility for your actions. This includes remembering that "you can't talk your way out of problems you behaved yourself into" (Covey 186).

Example: parenthetical citation, APA

The APA style of citing the same quotation includes the publication year as well as the author's last name and page number. Note that no comma separates the name from the date, but that a comma does follow the date and that the abbreviation *p.* precedes the page number.

> Personal growth is a painful process, and part of that process is taking personal responsibility for your actions. This includes remembering that "you can't talk your way out of problems you behaved yourself into" (Covey 1989, p. 186).

Notice that in both cases the citation is included in the sentence, with the period after the citation.

Example: author's name in text, MLA

You can introduce the name of the author in the text and then cite the page number for reference.

> Noted author Stephen Covey suggests that to be effective, one must "begin with the end in mind" (97).

Example: author's name in text, APA

Note that the APA style includes the year of publication directly after the author's name and the page number at the end for easy reference.

> Weeks (1994) believes that "we need to celebrate diversity, not fear it or perceive it as a threat" (33).

Quoting a secondary source

When using research sources it is common to find that the original author has quoted a **secondary source**, another author, in his or her work. The following example shows such a quotation and the proper citation for it.

Example: secondary source, MLA

The addition of *qtd. in* (for "quoted in") shows that this quote by Jung was found in a second-ary resource, written by Byrne.

> Psychology has had its masters of theory and quite a bit of humor as well. C. G. Jung, a noted psychologist, once claimed, "Show me a sane man and I will cure him for you" (qtd. in Byrne 453).

Using ellipses to show omissions and brackets to show insertions

An **ellipsis** (shown by three evenly spaced periods: ...) is a break or omission of words within a direct quote. Using only part of a quotation is common practice, especially if the entire quota-tion is too long or cumbersome. But make sure to use ellipses cautiously so you don't present the author's words out of intended context.

Example: ellipses to show omitted words from the middle of a quote

> We can now plainly and painfully see that "components of human interaction ... often lead to conflict" (Weeks 33).

Example: bracketed insertion to make a sentence correct

Sometimes a quote will be worded in a way that could read awkwardly or make an incomplete sentence when inserted in a paper. If you need to add a word or phrase within a quotation to make your sentence grammatically correct or clearer, then put brackets around your insertion.

> There are many examples of how "components of human interaction...[can] often lead to conflict" (Weeks 33).

In this instance the word *can* was added to clarify the thought for the reader.

Block quotations

A quotation from poetry, plays, or any text longer than four lines should be set apart in a block quotation format. A block quotation is indented about one inch (ten spaces) from the left margin and double-spaced. A block quotation needs no quotation marks and is introduced by a complete sentence. Often a colon, rather than a period, follows the introductory words.

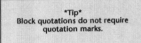

Tip
Block quotations do not require quotation marks.

Example: block quotation, MLA

The block quotation is introduced by a sentence that contains the author's name, ends with a colon, and uses ellipsis to show that it is not complete. Note that the page number is in parentheses after the period.

> As Jess Tavares explains, older students face different challenges when returning to school:
>
> As an older student, returning to the academic world was quite a shock. I hadn't seen a classroom in
>
> twenty-five years. But with a new backpack, pens, and a bill from the bookstore that equaled my rent,
>
> I sat in my very first college class, ... scared to death I could not pass the tests I had just set for myself.
> (2)

Knowledge Check: True or False?

1. Quotations must be used in original form.
2. Quotation marks are required for all direct quotations.
3. Brackets indicate that a word has been added that is not in the original text.

Answers

1. (True) Quotations should be identical to the original passage.
2. (False) Block quotations do not require quotation marks.
3. (True) Brackets show that text was added to the original passage.

CHAPTER 4

Paraphrasing

What is a paraphrase?

A **paraphrase** is a restatement of an author's writing by using your own words and accurately conveying the original information. You would paraphrase an author when you want to explain the content of his or her passage while maintaining your own voice and rhythm. You might also paraphrase after you have introduced a source earlier in your paper and wish to continue to discuss that source's ideas without needing to quote the source verbatim.

The length of a paraphrase should be about equal to the length of the original work. (By contrast, a summary - as explained in Chapter 5 - describes in just a few words the ideas or points made in another author's long passage or large work.)

It is vital that the paraphrase not alter the original meaning of the source. Adding words that distort the intention of the author or leaving out significant parts of what the author was intending misstates that author.

A paraphrase, because it's an indirect quotation, always requires a parenthetical citation. See the MLA and APA examples below.

To restate an author's ideas accurately but in your own words and writing style can be difficult. You might be tempted to shift some words around from the original, but doing so would be plagiarizing because those words and the idea still belong to the author. Remember that improving your writing skills is part of the goal of using others' works. Instructors want you to learn to write and think, not just to hand back what someone else has created.

Tips

DO
1. Use your own words.
2. Present the author's ideas without changing, adding to, or deleting from the original meaning.
3. Make the paraphrase about equal in length to the original.
4. Give credit to the source.

DON'T
1. Keep the author's sentences and just replace the words with synonyms.
2. Flip-flop clause and leave the words the same.
3. Lose track of original sources.

Accuracy is vital.

One way to develop paraphrasing skills is to read the material several times to make sure that you understand completely what the writer is saying. Next, put aside the author's work and try to explain the passage in your own words. This will help you to develop a personal voice and style. Compare the explanation with the original and decide whether it is accurate and conveys the original ideas. Consider whether something is missing that a person who didn't read the first passage would need to know in order to understand it. Make sure to explain for your reader how the paraphrased content relates to your idea. Once you have worked the paraphrase into your draft, be sure to cite the original.

Always give credit to the source of an idea.

It may be confusing when and how to add a citation to the original source. A good practice to follow is if a sentence or idea came from an outside source, then it should be acknowledged with a parenthetical citation.

Sample paraphrases

Example 1: paraphrase with citation, MLA

Original work

Poll after poll indicates that one of the primary concerns of contemporary U.S. citizens is violence. Terrorism is obviously one part of this concern, but there is also considerable concern about nonterrorist forms of violence. Violence among the nation's youth is especially troubling and difficult to explain. This difficulty is frequently the reason that social psychologists are often asked to make sense of seemingly senseless acts of violence. Why are there so many shootings in the U.S. high schools? Why are there so many gangs, and why are they growing at such alarming rates? (Potter 1999)

Incorrect paraphrase

<u>Survey</u> after <u>survey show</u> that one of the <u>big things</u> that <u>people</u> in the <u>U.S. worry</u> about <u>today</u> is **violence. Terrorism is** <u>clearly</u> a <u>reason</u> **but there is also** <u>a lot of worry</u> about <u>other</u> **forms of violence. Violence** <u>from the young people in this country</u> **is** <u>very confusing</u> **and** <u>hard to understand.</u> **This** <u>problem</u> **is** <u>often</u> **the** <u>issue</u> **that** <u>researchers</u> **are** <u>frequently required to</u> <u>explain incomprehensible violent crimes. What is the reason for the number of gun related crimes in schools in America? Is it because the number of gangs are going up?</u>

In the above example the writing style of the original piece was copied. It was plagiarized, not paraphrased. Sentence by sentence, the information is exactly restated using different words. The substituted words in exact sequence are <u>underlined</u>. The sequence of each idea and structure of each sentence is the same, and words have been replaced with synonyms. In some cases original phrases have been kept in order (shown in **bold**). This patchwork paraphrasing merely uses a thesaurus to find synonyms for words in the original text, but everything is essentially identical. Finally, there was no indication of the source of this paraphrase.

Correct paraphrase

Many recent **polls** have suggested that people in the United States are very concerned about **terrorism** and other acts of **violence.** Increasing violence, including **shootings,** among **high-school-aged** children is one of these concerns. People in the community want to understand why this is happening. **Social psychologists** have been asked to explain this troubling trend. It is difficult to understand why young people may be joining **gangs** and committing acts of violence in greater numbers. (Potter 306)

This example maintains the ideas of the original piece, but the style of writing is different. Instead of following an identical sequence to the original work, the correctly paraphrased paragraph conveys the information but does not pull out words and substitute them with synonyms. It uses some of the words from the original to accurately present the author's ideas and is complete in presenting the original author's ideas, but it uses the student's own original sentences. It also cites the author of the original work.

Example 2: paraphrase with citation, MLA

Original work

At first glance, there appears to be little justification for telling the story of California's early Indian wars. Aside from the brief Modoc conflict of 1873, and possibly the Mariposa war of 1851, few people are aware that California had any Indian troubles during the Gold Rush days of the 1850's. Certainly the Far West never had a Custer's Last Stand or a grand retreat such as that made by Chief Joseph of the Nez Perce. Here there have no Sitting Bull or Geronimo, no spectacular uprisings, like Adobe Walls or Beecher's Islands. On the contrary, many California tribes were generally peaceful by nature, few having even a war club or a tomahawk as part of their culture. Yet in California, the bloodiest drama in the settlement of the West took place, a brutal disruption and destruction so devastating that by the 1870's many native groups were extinct. (Secrest xi)

Incorrect paraphrase

Unless you know about the events, you would think there isn't much reason to write about what happened in the Indian wars in early California. There were two conflicts, one in 1873 with the Modoc and another in Mariposa in 1851. But most people don't know anything about California having trouble with Indians during the 1850's Gold Rush. The Far West didn't have any famous Indian conflicts like Custer's Last Stand or any other Indians that were well known like Chief Joseph of the Nez Perce, Sitting Bull, or Geronimo. It didn't have Indian revolts like Adobe Walls or Beecher's Islands. In California the Indians were peaceful and didn't carry weapons. But California had the bloodiest wars in the West. It was harsh and destructive and annihilated the Indians to the point where by the 1870's many of the groups were dead and gone.

This paragraph is plagiarized. Notice that the writing style of the original piece was copied. Sentence by sentence the information is restated using different words, and the sequence of each idea and sentence is the same. In most cases, words have been substituted for synonyms (see underlined). In some cases words have been kept (see **bold**). This is another example of patchwork paraphrasing. In addition, no indication of the source of this paraphrase is provided in the text.

Correct paraphrase

If history books are to be believed, there is little to say about the California Indian conflicts. Indeed it would seem that all of the great battles such as Custer's Last Stand and the great chiefs took place far away. While history shows us the Gold Rush and its effect on California, it also leaves us with the false impression that California Indians were peaceful, with no weapons or conflicts with the intruding whites. This type of historical omission negates the devastation and annihilation that the California Indians suffered; annihilation so complete "that by the 1870's many native groups were extinct". (Secrest, xi)

In this example the ideas of the original piece are maintained, but the style of writing is different and belongs to the writer of the paper. Instead of following an identical sequence to the original work, the correctly paraphrased paragraph conveys the information but does not pull out words and substitute them with synonyms. It still uses some of the phrasing from the original, but this instance is identified by quotation marks and is used to accurately convey and emphasize the ideas of the original author. It also cites the author of the original work.

To avoid the errors of adding information that wasn't in the original work or omitting something important to the original meaning, carefully track your sources and acknowledge them in your writing. You need to correctly present the meaning, and you need to cite the source accurately. Sometimes it is difficult to try to work with many different ideas, but remember that your professor is very familiar with many of the ideas and sources you'll use and can help you work out how best to present them.

Style of citation for paraphrases

Like direct quotations, the only difference between APA and MLA styles is the citation at the end.

Example: parenthetical citation, MLA

MLA style includes the name of the author and the page number. This example shows a block quotation.

> ...Yet in California, the bloodiest drama in the settlement of the West took place, a brutal disruption and destruction so devastating that by the 1870's many native groups were extinct. (Secrest xi)

Example: parenthetical citation, APA

APA style includes the name of the author and the date of publication. This example shows a block quotation.

> ...Yet in California, the bloodiest drama in the settlement of the West took place, a brutal disruption and destruction so devastating that by the 1870's many native groups were extinct. (Secrest, 2003)

Provide the complete information in your Works Cited or References list at the conclusion of your paper.

Knowledge Check: True or False?

1. Keeping the writing style of the original passage when you paraphrase is appropriate as long as you change most of the words.
2. Correct paraphrasing includes a citation for the original source after the paraphrased passage.
3. A paraphrase should be roughly the same length as the original.

Answers

1. (False) This is a common mistake students make because they don't know the rules and they lack confidence in their own writing ability. You should restate the writer's idea in your own words.
2. (True) Always acknowledge when you've used ideas from someone else, no matter whether it's a clause, sentence, or paragraph.
3. (True) The paraphrase restates another person's idea in your own words.

CHAPTER 5

Summarizing

What is a summary?

A **summary** condenses the idea of the original author while retaining the message of the original passage. A summary enables you to comment briefly on another writer's ideas and to express how they relate to your own ideas. Summarizing shortens the length of the original passage, whereas paraphrasing nearly matches the original in length.

Tips

DO
1. Be accurate to the original meaning.
2. Cite the original source.
3. Make your summary significantly shorter than the original.
4. Use your own words and explain how the writer's ideas relates to yours.

DON'T
1. Copy the original writing style; use your own.
2. Replace the original words with synonyms.
3. Change the meaning of a passage.

To summarize another writer's passage, read it several times-taking notes if necessary-to make sure you understand what the writer is saying. It might help to read the passage aloud so you can hear the words. Then say to yourself, "In other words, ..." and complete the thought. If you find that you are using almost as many words to explain or express the thought, then you need to revise it and make it simpler and briefer. Reduce the original passage to its basic idea. And make sure to explain for your reader how the writer's idea relates to the point you are making in your paper.

Sample summary

Original work

Polls show that large majorities of Americans believe that anyone who works hard can succeed, and even higher percentages of Americans say they admire people who get rich by their own efforts. Those who fall behind, meanwhile, are often blamed for their misery. In a typical recent survey finding, three quarters of Americans agreed with the statement that if a person is poor, their own "lack of effort" is to blame. In other words, Americans tend to make moral judgments about people based upon their level of economic success. Everybody loves a winner, the saying goes, and nowhere is that more true than in America. Winners are seen as virtuous, as people to admire and emulate. Losers get the opposite treatment for their own good, mind you. As Marvin Olasky, ... has said: "An emphasis on freedom should also include a willingness to step away for a time and let those who have dug their own hole 'suffer the consequences of their misconduct.'" The prevalence of a sink-or-swim mentality in the United States is unique among Western democracies, as is the belief that individuals have so much control over their destiny. Elsewhere people are more apt to believe that success or failure is determined by circumstances beyond individual control. Scholars attribute the difference in outlook to the "exceptionalism" of American and, especially to the American Dream ethos that dominates U.S. culture - an ethos at once intensely optimistic and brutally unforgiving. (Callahan 124-25)

Incorrect Summary

Polls show that large majorities of Americans believe that anyone who works hard can succeed, and even higher percentages of Americans say they admire people who get rich by their own efforts. Winners are seen as virtuous, as people to admire and emulate. Elsewhere people are more apt to believe that success or failure is determined by circumstances beyond individual control.

The above summary was created using the autosummarize feature of Word set for 25 percent. It selects key sentences from the original document and puts those sentences together to form an abbreviated copy. (Note that the auto-summarize feature is intended for writers to provide summaries of their *own* work, not the work of others.) This is *not* an acceptable summary because it is entirely copied, word for word. It is plagiarism. It does not change the writing style of the original author, nor does it give credit with a correct citation to indicate the source. Additional problems with this method of summary may be the altering of the original meaning of the piece. Note that the original piece was about the difference between how Americans view winners and losers, but the summary does not mention how losers are viewed. That thesis has not been mentioned in the summary. It is important to connect a summary to the point you fire making in your paper and the reason why you referred to the source you are summarizing.

Correct summary

According to Callahan, American culture, unlike other Western democracies, takes the moral perspective that success is the result of individual effort. According to polls, a person's success is considered to be a product of his or her labor and thus deserved. Conversely, a person's poverty or failure is viewed as the outcome of his or her lack of sufficient effort and therefore also deserved. (124-25)

In the correct summary, the ideas of the original passage are maintained, but the style of writing is different from the original passage. The summary is shorter than the original. The summary conveys the main points of the original, but it does not copy full sentences or pull out words and substitute them with synonyms. It still uses some of the words from the original to accurately present the author's ideas. When you use a summary is a paper, make sure it clearly addresses your thesis or argument and that you cite it correctly.

Knowledge Check: True or False?

1. You can keep the writing style of the original passage when you summarize as long as you significantly shorten the length and leave out some of the original.
2. Correct summarizing includes a citation for the original source next to the summarized passage.
3. A summary should convey the same meaning as the original.

Answers

1. (False) A summary should be in your own words and writing style but convey the message of the original. Do not use auto-summarize for someone else's work because it is just an abridged copy.
2. (True) Always acknowledge when you've used ideas from someone else, no matter whether it's a clause, sentence or paragraph, paraphrase or summary.
3. (True) Do not alter the meaning, just express it concisely and in your own words.

CHAPTER 6

Listing the Works Cited

As you draft your paper and decide how to use your final sources, you will assemble a complete list of the references that you use in your paper (as discussed in Chapters 3-5), and you will need to format that list of Works Cited and present that list at the end of your paper. This chapter presents the basics of how to format your reference list items in the MLA and APA styles, which your general coursework will likely require. You can find more detailed examples in your textbook, from your school's library or writing center, and from electronic resources such as those listed in Chapter 8.

> *Tip*
> Always check with your
> instructor for the documentation
> style that he or she requires.

Content of citations

While the information presented in all styles is the same, the order of the information and how it is shown can be quite different. The basic information contained by all citation styles includes the following:

- Author name
- Title of article, essay, book, or Web site
- Publisher information
- Year of publication
- Place or form of publication

Basic format of citations

All documentation styles place the list of references at the end of the paper. Follow these basic formatting rules for all citation styles:

- Arrange all citations in alphabetical order by the author's last name.
- Arrange authors' names in a multiple-author work exactly as they appear in the source.
- Reverse the first author's name so that the last name appears first.
- Double-space your list of references, the way you double-space your paper.
- Indent the second and subsequent lines of a citation by 1/2 inch or 5 spaces, so the author's name always appears by itself at the left margin.
- Include in your list of references only the works that your paper refers to.

Always check with your course instructor for the preferred citation style. (See Chapter 8 for sources of citation styles for specific subject areas such as mathematics, biology, physics, and so on.) This guide does not discuss footnotes, as parenthetical citations are emphasized.

MLA citations: Books

The basic MLA style of citation for a book is as follows:

- Author last name first, first name followed by a period.
- <u>Book Title</u> underlined, followed by a period.
- City of publication followed by a colon.
- Publisher's name followed by a comma. Use only the first name of the publisher, and abbreviate University Press to UP.
- Year of publication followed by a period.

Example: single-author book

Maguire, Gregory. <u>Wicked: The Life and Times of the Wicked Witch of the West</u>. New York: Harper, 1995.

Examples: multiple authors of a book

When you are citing a book that has two or three authors, list them in the order that they appear on the title page. Invert the first author's name but not the names of the second or third author. Separate all the authors by commas.

For a book by four or more authors, MLA allows the listing to include all authors listed in order *or* just the first author followed by the Latin words **et al.** (which is short for *et alii,* meaning "and others"). Check with your instructor about the form that he or she prefers.

A book by two authors

Norman, Michael, and Beth Scott. <u>Historic Haunted America</u>. New York: Tor, 1995.

A book by four or more authors

Kauffman, James, Mark Mostert, Stanley Trent, and Daniel Hallahan. <u>Managing Classroom Behavior</u>. Boston: Allyn, 2002.

or

Kauffman, James, et al. <u>Managing Classroom Behavior</u>. Boston: Allyn, 2002.

MLA citations: Articles or essays

You might use an article from a periodical or an essay from an anthology. While the basic structure of citations for articles is the same as for books, there are some significant differences. You need to list both the title of the article or essay and the journal or book that it was published in.

Example: essay in an anthology

The information in a citation of a source from an anthology follows this order:

- Author of the article or essay (last name first) followed by a period.
- "Title of the article or essay" in quotation marks, followed by a period.
- <u>Title of the Book</u> underlined, followed by a period.
- Comp. (for Compiled by) or Ed. (for Edited by).
- Author of the book (first name first), followed by a period.
- City followed by a colon.
- Publisher followed by a comma.
- Year followed by a period.
- Page range (hyphenated) followed by a period.

> Anson, Chris. "Taking Off." <u>Finding Our Way: A Writing Teacher's Sourcebook.</u> Ed. Wendy Bishop and Deborah Coxwell Teague. Boston: Houghton, 2005. 44-51.

For citations from an anthology or magazine, always include the page numbers.

Example: article from a magazine

Magazine or journal articles include the month of publication in the citation. Note the abbreviated month and the colon following the year.

> Myers, Michaela. "Pole Results." <u>Horse Illustrated</u> Feb. 2005: 68-74.

Example: article from a journal

Note the volume number following the journal title, the year in parentheses, the colon following the year, and the inclusive page numbers.

> Paulos, Lyn. "Sexuality in Women: Feminism in Conflict." <u>Women's Studies Weekly</u> 1 (2000): 15-20.

APA citations: Books

The APA style contains the same information as MLA, but it formats the content differently, putting more emphasis on the date of publication. The basic APA style of citation for a book is as follows:

- Author, last name first, then first initial, followed by a period. For a work by more than one author, invert all names, use initials instead of first names, and insert an ampersand (&) before the last author.
- Year of publication in parentheses, followed by a period.
- Book title *italicized* (capitalize the first word of the title, the first word of the subtitle, and any proper nouns), followed by a period.
- City and full publisher's name, separated by a colon and followed by a period.

Example: book

> Maguire, G. (1995). *Wicked: The life and times of the Wicked Witch of the West.* New York: HarperCollins.

APA citations: Articles

The basic APA style of citation for a journal article by a single author is as follows:

- Author last name, and first initial followed by a period. For a work by more than one author, invert all names, use initials instead of first names, and insert an ampersand (&) before the last author.
- Year (in parentheses) with a period.
- Title of article (capitalize only first word and first word after a colon, no quotation marks), followed by a period.
- *Title of journal in italics* followed by a comma.
- *Volume number in italics* followed by a comma.
- Full page range of article, followed by a period.

Example: journal article by a single author

> Paulos, L. (2000). Sexuality in women: Feminism in conflict. *Women's Studies Weekly, 1,* 15-20.

Example: journal article by two to five authors

Paulos, L., & Walker. K. (2005). Understanding twin rivalry: A case study. *Sibling Circular, 10,* 70-72.

Menager, R., Herch, S., Lewis, G., & Walker, K. (2005). Friends and family. *Relations, 5,* 21-24.

MLA and APA citations: Online sources

Provide the following information for online sources:

- Author (if available).
- Title of Web page.
- Title of full work (if available).
- Date of work (if available).
- File number (if available).
- Date that you accessed it.
- URL or Web address.

Example: MLA online citation

The MLA citation shows the author's full name and the date after the title. Note that the year of publication is followed by a period, that the date of access is inverted and abbreviated and that no punctuation follows it, that the URL is put in angle brackets, that the line break of the URL falls after a slash, and that a period follows the URL.

Warlick, David. "Landmarks Citation Machine: <u>The Landmark Project</u>. 2000. 19 Mar. 2005
<http:// www.landmarkproject.com/citationmachineindex.php>.

Example: APA online citation, no print source

APA electronic citations likewise follow the rules of normal APA style of formatting such as capitalization, first initial, year placement, and italics. Note that the retrieval date is spelled out, that a comma follows it, and that no punctuation follows the URL. If the URL extends to more than one line, then break it only after a slash or a period.

Lee. I. (1998). *A research guide for students: Research, writing, and style guides.* Retrieved
March 19, 2005, from http://www.aresearchguide.com/styleguides.html

Example: APA online citation, print source

McCabe, D. L., Trevino, L. K., & Butterfield, K. D. (1999). Academic integrity in honor code and non-
honor code environments: A qualitative investigation. *Journal of Higher Education, 70,* 211-
234. Retrieved May 19, 2003, from http://www.questia.com/SM.qst

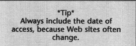

Tip
Always include the date of
access, because Web sites often
change.

Example: online citation, no author, MLA style

If the Web site does not have an author or organization listed, then list the title of the Web site.
Include the date of publication if available and the date of access.

Some Web sites are sponsored or maintained by universities or companies and do not list
authors for their Web materials. If that is the case, list the university or company name in the
author space of the citation.

DSPS Policies and Procedures. 2003. Santa Barbara City College. 3 Jan. 2004
    <http://www.sbcc.edu/dsps/>.

Example: online citation, no author, APA style

DSPS policies and procedures. (2003). Santa Barbara City College. Retrieved January 3, 2004, from
    http://www.sbcc.edu/dsps/

List of cited works

At the end of your paper, make sure to provide the complete list of works that you have cited
in the body of the paper.

Example: MLA Works Cited

Works Cited

Anson, Chris. "Taking Off." Finding Our Way: A Writing Teacher's Sourcebook. Ed. Wendy Bishop and
    Deborah Coxwell Teague. Boston: Houghton, 2005. 44-51.

DSPS Policies and Procedures. 2003. Santa Barbara City College. 3 Jan. 2004
    <http://www.sbcc.edu/dsps l>.

Kauffman, James, Mark Mostert, Stanley Trent, and Daniel Hallahan. Managing Classroom Behavior.
    Boston: Allyn, 2002.

Maguire, Gregory. Wicked: The Life and Times of the Wicked Witch of the West. New York:
    Harper, 1995.

Myers, Michaela. "Pole Results." Horse Illustrated Feb. 2005: 68-74.

Norman, Michael, and Beth Scott. Historic Haunted America. New York: Tor, 1995.

Paulos, Lyn. "Sexuality in Women: Feminism in Conflict." Women's Studies Weekly 1 (2000): 15-20.

Warlick, David. "Landmarks Citation Machine." The Landmark Project. 2000. 19 Mar. 2005
    <http:" www.landmarkproject.com\citationmachine/index.php> .

Example: APA References

References

DSPS policies and procedures. (2003). Santa Barbara City College. Retrieved January 3, 2004, from
    http://www.sbcc.edu/dsps/

Lee, I. (1998). *A research guide for students: Research, writing, and style guides.* Retrieved March 19,
    2005, from http://www.aresearchguide.com\styleguides.html

Maguire, G. (1995). *Wicked: The life and times of the Wicked Witch of the West.* New York: HarperCollins.

McCabe, D. L., Trevino, L. K., & Butterfield, K. D. (1999). Academic integrity in honor code and non-
    honor code environments: A qualitative investigation. *Journal of Higher Education, 70,* 211-
    234. Retrieved May 19, 2003, from http://www.questia.com\ISM.qst

Menager, R., Herch, S., Lewis, G., & Walker, K. (2005). Friends and family. *Relations, 5,* 21-24.

Paulos, L. (2000). Sexuality in women: Feminism in conflict. *Women's Studies Weekly, 1,* 15-20.

Paulos, L., & Walker, K. (2005). Understanding twin rivalry: A case study. *Sibling Circular, 10,* 70-72.

Knowledge Check: True or False?

1. Works Cited or References should be single-spaced.
2. Only works actually cited in the body of the paper should be listed in the Works Cited or Reference pages.
3. References or Works Cited should be listed in alphabetical order by author's last name.
4. Each reference item can be provided in any style (MLA, APA, etc.) as long as it's complete.

Answers

1. (False) All references should be double-spaced.
2. (True)
3. (True)
4. (False) All of the references should follow the style used in the body of the paper. The choice of style is determined by the academic subject (unless instructed otherwise by your professor).

CHAPTER 7

Practice Quiz

1. Cheating may include
a. plagiarizing or copying without attribution.
b. using an essay or paper from someone who has previously taken the course.
c. using answers to an exam from someone who has previously taken the course.
d. all of the above.

2. Plagiarism is
a. quoting someone else's work and giving credit to them.
b. using someone else's ideas, work, sentences, research, or information and presenting it as your own.
c. using original ideas in your written work.
d. using Web sources.

3. Citation of sources is required
a. whenever paraphrasing or summarizing another author's idea.
b. only in the works cited section of your paper.
c. when using your own ideas in an original paragraph.
d. a and b.

4. The word *paraphrase* means
a. to replace original words with synonyms.
b. to maintain the writing style of the original author.
c. to give an exact idea of the original author's meaning in your own writing style.
d. to give a general, but not exact, idea of the original author's meaning.

5. A paragraph is not properly paraphrased when
a. only a few words are different.
b. you express in your own words the general idea of what the author is saying.
c. the sentences have been rearranged but not changed much.
d. a and b.
e. a and c.

6. Correct summarizing includes
a. a copy of the original writing style.
b. replacing the original work with synonyms.
c. the accurate meaning of the original work but significantly shorter than the original.
d. using the autosummarize feature of your word processing program.

7. Citation of sources is required

a. when quoting a source in your paper that you use word for word.

b. when browsing the internet.

c. when describing another writer's idea in your paper.

d. a and c.

8. Over-quoting in your work

a. shows you have not synthesized or analyzed the material from your resources.

b. is acceptable because it shows the amount of work and research you have done.

c. means using too many direct quotes from your sources.

d. a and c.

e. a and b.

9. John's paper is based on several different sources,

including a research paper from a friend who took the same class last summer. Seeing that his friend's research closely matches his own, does John need to cite his friend in his final draft?

a. No, he just needs to cite the other sources.

b. Yes, anything John consults and incorporates needs to be cited.

10. Look at the original and choose which paraphrase is correct.

Original

> Because there are many ways to cheat, and there is temptation to do so, students may assume that this is something that everyone is doing. Surveys of college students show that cheating is a common occurrence, and some students consider it an accomplishment to get away with this type of behavior. These kinds of attitudes and behaviors are unethical and have consequences. (Menager-Beeley 2003)

a. Students can be tempted to cheat by the many resources available to them that make it easy. They may believe that a majority of students cheat in some form or another. Surveys done in colleges suggest that cheating is more rampant than once thought and that students see it as a triumph to cheat and not get caught. This shows a serious lack of ethics in behavior and can lead to repercussions from the academic institution. (Menager-Beeley, 2003)

b. Because there are so many different ways to cheat, and temptations for students are great, a lot of students think everyone is doing it. Students surveyed say that cheating is a common occurrence and it is an accomplishment to get away with it. This kind of attitude is unethical and can have some consequences.

Answers:

1. d   2. b   3. a   4. c   5. e   6. c   7. d   8. d   9. b   10. a

CHAPTER 8

Additional Sources of Information

The following links are subject to change. They were accessed March 25-26, 2005.

Web site with information on documentation styles, general

University of California, Berkeley
<http://www.lib.berkeley.edu/TeachingLib/Guides/Internet/Style.html>

Web sites with information on documentation styles, by discipline

Anthropology
<http://www.aaanet.org/pubs/style_guide.htm>

Biology
<http://www.wisc.edu/writing/Handbook/DocCBE.html>

Chemistry
<http://pubs.acs.org/books/references.shtml>

Legal
<http://www.law.cornell.edu/citation/>

Math
<http://www.longwood.edu/mathematics/stylesheet.html>

Physics
<http://www.aip.org/pubservs/style.html>

Sociology
<http://www.calstatela.edu/library/bi/rsalina/asa.styleguide.html>

Free Citation Generators

Landmark's Citation Machine
<http://www.citationmachine.net/>

Style Wizard
<http://www.stylewizard.com/>

Reference Tracking, Subscriptions, and Free Trials

Easy Bib
<http://easybib.com/>

RefWorks
<http://www.refworks.com>

Links for Articles on Plagiarism

Center for Academic Integrity
<http://www.academicintegrity.org/links.asp>

Plagiarism.org
<http://www.plagiarism.org/articles.html>

Samford University Library
<http://library.samford.edu/topics/plagiarism.html>

University of Indiana
<http://www.indiana.edu/~istd/definition.html>

Print Resources, Style Guides

American Psychological Association. *Concise Rules of APA Style.* Washington: APA, 2005.
<http://www.apa.org/books/>.

Gibaldi, Joseph. *The MLA Style Guide for Writers of Research Papers.* 6th ed. New York: MLA,
2003. <http://www.mla.org/store/>.

Huth, Edward J. *Scientific Style and Format: The CBE Manual for Authors, Editors and Publishers.*
6th ed. New York: Cambridge UP, 1994.
http://www.councilscienceeditors.org/publications/style.cfm>.

University of Chicago Press Staff. *The Chicago Manual of Style.* 15th ed. Chicago: U of
Chicago P, 2003. <http://www.chicagomanualofstyle.org/about.html>.

CHAPTER 9

Works Cited

Byrne, Robert. *The 2,548 Best Things Anybody Ever Said.* New York: Galahad, 1996. Sec. 453.

Covey, Stephen. *The Seven Habits of Highly Effective People.* New York: Simon, 1989. 97, 186.

Melville, Herman. Quotation 4797 in *Cole's Quotables.* 30 Mar. 2005 <http://www.quotationspage.com/ quotes/Herman _Melville/>.

Potter, W. James. "Is Media Violence Harmful to Children?" *Taking Sides: Clashing on Controversial Psychological Issue.* 13th ed. Ed. Brent Slife. New York: McGraw, 2004. 306.

Secrest, William B. *When the Great Spirit Died: Destruction of the California Indians, 1850-1860.* Sanger: Word Dancer, 2003.

Tavares, Jess. "Returning Students." Scholarship essay. May 2002.

Weeks, Dudley. *The Eight Essential Steps to Conflict Resolution.* 2002. New York: Tarcher-Penguin, 1994. 33.

Zaharoff, Howard. "A Writer's Guide to Fair Use in Copyright Law." *Writers Digest* Jan. 2001. 3 Mar. 2005 <http://www.writersdigest.com/articles/zaharoff_fair_copyright_law .asp>.

REVISION SYMBOLS

ab	9a(10), 11a–d	Abbreviation	**n**	11f–g, 15b, 17d(4)	Number
ac	9a(10), 11e	Acronym	**^**		Omission
adj	1a(4), 4a–b, 25a	Adjective	**¶**		Paragraph
adv	1a(5), 1g, 25a	Adverb	**//**	26	Parallelism
agr		Agreement	**( )**	17f	Parentheses
	6b, 28d	pronoun-antecedent	**.**	16d(1), 17a	Period
	6a	subject-verb	**pl**		Plural
apa	41a–c	APA documentation	**pred**	1b(2), 23c(2)	Predication
ᵛ	15	Apostrophe	**pro**	5, 6b, 24a(2), 28	Pronoun
arg	31c(3), 35	Argument	**?**	16d(3), 17b	Question mark
awk		Awkward	**" "**	16	Quotation marks
cap	9	Capital	**red**	21a(1)	Redundant
coh		Coherence	**ref**	28	Reference
	25a–b	modifiers	**rep**	8b(4), 21b, 26b, 29d	Repetition
	34c–d	paragraphs	**rev**	34a–g	Revision
:	16d(2), 17d	Colon	**;**	14, 16d(2)	Semicolon
,	12, 13, 16d(1)	Comma	**sg**		Singular
cs	3	Comma splice	**/**	17i	Slash
con	21	Conciseness	**sp**	18a–e	Spelling
coor	13b, 24b–c	Coordination	**sub**	24a, 24c	Subordination
—	16d(3), 17e	Dash	**[ ]**	17g	Square brackets
ℐ		Delete	**t**	7b	Tense
dev		Development	**trans**	34d	Transition
	33g	essays	**∪**		Transpose
	33f	paragraphs	**u**		Unity
ed	34a–g	Editing		34c	paragraph
. . .	17h	Ellipsis points		22, 23	sentence
emp	29	Emphasis	**ℐ**	13	Unnecessary
ex	20	Exactness	**usg**	16c, 19, Glossary of Usage	Usage
!	16d(3), 17c	Exclamation point	**var**	30	Variety
frag	2	Fragment	**vb**	6a, 7, 27a	Verb
fs	3	Fused sentence	**wc**	19c–d, 20a–d, 22a–c	Word choice
hy	18f	Hyphenation			
id	20c	Idiom	**w**	21a–b	Wordiness
ital	10	Italics	**ww**		Wrong word
log	35h–i	Logic			
lc		Lowercase			
mm	4c, 25a–c	Misplaced modifier			
mla	40a–c	MLA documentation			